Kaplan Publishing are constantly finding new difference to your studies and our exciting o offer something different to students looking

C000225157

This book comes with free MyKaplan online study anytime, anywhere. **This free online resource is not sold separately and is included in the price of the book.**

Having purchased this book, you have access to the following online study materials:

CONTENT	ACCA (including FBT, FMA, FFA)		FIA (excluding FBT, FMA, FFA)	
	Text	Kit	Text	Kit
Electronic version of the book	✓	✓	✓	✓
Check Your Understanding Test with instant answers	✓			
Material updates	✓	✓	✓	✓
Latest official ACCA exam questions*		✓		
Extra question assistance using the signpost icon**		✓		
Timed questions with an online tutor debrief using clock icon***		✓		
Interim assessment including questions and answers	✓		✓	
Technical answers	✓	✓	✓	✓

* Excludes BT, MA, FA, FBT, FMA, FFA; for all other papers includes a selection of questions, as released by ACCA
** For ACCA SBL, SBR, AFM, APM, ATX, AAA only
*** Excludes BT, MA, FA, LW, FBT, FMA and FFA

How to access your online resources

Kaplan Financial students will already have a MyKaplan account and these extra resources will be available to you online. You do not need to register again, as this process was completed when you enrolled. If you are having problems accessing online materials, please ask your course administrator.

If you are not studying with Kaplan and did not purchase your book via a Kaplan website, to unlock your extra online resources please go to www.mykaplan.co.uk/addabook (even if you have set up an account and registered books previously). You will then need to enter the ISBN number (on the title page and back cover) and the unique pass key number contained in the scratch panel below to gain access. You will also be required to enter additional information during this process to set up or confirm your account details.

If you purchased through the Kaplan Publishing website you will automatically receive an e-mail invitation to MyKaplan. Please register your details using this email to gain access to your content. If you do not receive the e-mail or book content, please contact Kaplan Publishing.

Your Code and Information

This code can only be used once for the registration of one book online. This registration and your online content will expire when the final sittings for the examinations covered by this book have taken place. Please allow one hour from the time you submit your book details for us to process your request.

Please scratch the film to access your unique code.

nVHY-kWvd-bUtU-93C6

Please be aware that this code is case-sensitive and you will need to include the dashes within the passcode, but not when entering the ISBN.

KAPLAN

PUBLISHING

ACCA

Strategic Professional

Strategic Business Leader (SBL)

EXAM KIT

British Library Cataloguing-in-Publication Data

A catalogue record for this book is available from the British Library.

Published by:

Kaplan Publishing UK
Unit 2 The Business Centre
Molly Millar's Lane
Wokingham
Berkshire
RG41 2QZ

ISBN: 978-1-78740-892-0

© Kaplan Financial Limited, 2021

Printed and bound in Great Britain

Acknowledgements

These materials are reviewed by the ACCA examining team. The objective of the review is to ensure that the material properly covers the syllabus and study guide outcomes, used by the examining team in setting the exams, in the appropriate breadth and depth. The review does not ensure that every eventuality, combination or application of examinable topics is addressed by the ACCA Approved Content. Nor does the review comprise a detailed technical check of the content as the Approved Content Provider has its own quality assurance processes in place in this respect.

The past ACCA examination questions are the copyright of the Association of Chartered Certified Accountants. The original answers to the questions from June 1994 onwards were produced by the examiners themselves and have been adapted by Kaplan Publishing.

We are grateful to the Chartered Institute of Management Accountants and the Institute of Chartered Accountants in England and Wales for permission to reproduce past examination questions. The answers have been prepared by Kaplan Publishing.

CONTENTS

Section

Versions of some questions in this Exam Kit may also be available on the ACCA Practice Platform on the ACCA website. They are a very useful reference, in particular to attempt using ACCA's exam software. However, you should be aware that ACCA will decide when those questions will be amended for syllabus changes or replaced, so they may differ slightly from the versions in this Exam Kit

> **Key features in this edition**
>
> In addition to providing a wide ranging bank of adapted real past exam questions and new case studies, we have also included in this edition:
>
> - Paper specific information and advice on exam technique.
>
> - Our recommended approach to make your revision for this particular subject as effective as possible.
>
>   This includes step by step guidance on how best to use our Kaplan material (Study text, pocket notes and exam kit) at this stage in your studies.
>
> - Enhanced tutorial answers packed with specific key answer tips, technical tutorial notes and exam technique tips from our experienced tutors.
>
> - Complementary online resources including full tutor debriefs and question assistance to point you in the right direction when you get stuck.

You will find a wealth of other resources to help you with your studies on the following sites:

www.mykaplan.co.uk

www.accaglobal.com/SBL/

Quality and accuracy are of the utmost importance to us so if you spot an error in any of our products, please send an email to mykaplanreporting@kaplan.com with full details, or follow the link to the feedback form in MyKaplan.

Our Quality Co-ordinator will work with our technical team to verify the error and take action to ensure it is corrected in future editions.

INDEX TO QUESTIONS AND ANSWERS

INTRODUCTION

The SBL exam is a 4-hour integrated case study with a single compulsory section with a range of tasks and requirements related to one scenario. The aim of the exam is to demonstrate and test organisational leadership and senior consultancy or advisory capabilities and relevant professional skills, through the context of a 'real world' scenario. The basic structure of each exam will require the candidate to take the role of an organisational leader or as a consultant or adviser to senior management.

The exam thus requires candidates to demonstrate both technical ability but also a range of professional skills demanded by effective leaders in advising or supporting senior management in directing organisations.

This examination kit contains both full exam-style case studies and shorter questions focussed on individual syllabus areas.

KEY TO THE INDEX

PAPER ENHANCEMENTS

We have added the following enhancements to the answers in this exam kit:

Key answer tips

Most answers include key answer tips to help your understanding of each question.

Tutorial note

Most answers include more tutorial notes to explain some of the technical points in detail.

Tutor top tips

For selected questions, we 'walk through the answer' giving guidance on how to approach the questions with helpful 'tips from a top tutor', together with technical tutor notes.

These answers are indicated with the 'footsteps' icon in the index.

TECHNICAL PRACTICE QUESTIONS

PAPER SPECIFIC INFORMATION

THE EXAM

FORMAT OF THE EXAM

	Number of marks
A range of compulsory questions	100

Total time allowed: 4 hours.

Note that:

- The examination is based on an integrated case study containing a number of assignments which will vary at each examination.

- These assignments or tasks may require you to take on different roles, depending on the situation. The number of marks allocated to all these assignments or the sub-parts of these will add up to 100 in total.

- Within the total marks available, there are 20 Professional Skills marks. Usually each task will contain some professional skills marks which may vary by examination, depending on the requirements.

- All tasks must be completed.

- The examination is of 4 hours duration, but this includes **Reading, Planning and Reflection time (RPRT)**. This time can be used flexibly at any time during the exam.

PASS MARK

The pass mark for all ACCA Qualification examination papers is 50%.

DETAILED SYLLABUS

The detailed syllabus and study guide written by the ACCA can be found at:

www.**acca**global.com/students/

PROFESSIONAL SKILLS

Within the total marks available, there are 20 marks relating to five professional skills:

COMMUNICATION	To express yourself clearly and convincingly through the appropriate medium while being sensitive to the needs of the intended audience.
COMMERCIAL ACUMEN	To show awareness of the wider business and external factors affecting business, using commercially sound judgement and insight to resolve issues and exploit opportunities.
ANALYSIS	To thoroughly investigate and research information from a variety of sources and logically process it with a view to considering it for recommending appropriate action.
SCEPTICISM	To probe deeply into underlying reasons for issues and problems, to question facts, opinions and assertions and to challenge information presented or decisions made.
EVALUATION	To carefully assess situations, proposals and arguments in a balanced way, using professional and ethical judgement to predict future outcomes and consequences as a basis for sound decision-making

Question tasks will detail which skills are being tested in which requirements. Advice on how to earn professional skills marks is given in the next section on exam technique.

EXAM TECHNIQUE

GENERAL GUIDANCE

The SBL exam is different from any other exams that you have sat before and good exam technique is vital for success.

- **Time management** is critical

  - You will have four hours (240 minutes) to read and analyse the case study and requirements, plan your approach to answering each of the tasks, and produce full answers to them all.

  - The examiners' recommended approach is that you allocate <u>at least</u> **40 minutes to RPRT** – reading, annotating and planning your answers to the requirements, leaving <u>approximately</u> **200** minutes for writing up your answers.

  - Given the 20 professional marks are earned how you write your answers (rather than writing anything extra), this means 200 minutes for 80 technical marks, or 2.5 minutes per technical mark.

- Using the **reading time (RPRT)** effectively

  - Your objective here is to read and understand the scenario and requirements fully within 40 minutes. This may take longer than you first think so be prepared to spend a maximum of 60 minutes

  - Start by reading the requirements, so that when you read through 12 or more pages of exhibits, you can evaluate the information and link all pieces of relevant information to the requirements. As you do this, start thinking about the implications of what you are reading, and mentally compile a big picture of the organisation and the issues it is currently facing.

  - More detail is noted below on the specific examination technique for CBE papers and you should use the technology at the earliest opportunity to practise examination technique in this environment, highlighting and annotating those areas that you consider to be useful to answering the questions and linking them to the different requirements.

  - Weaker candidates annotate far too much, so try to be selective <u>and prioritise</u> issues as you go along.

- **Planning** answers – start by analysing the **requirement** itself:

  - What role are you adopting?

  - Who is the report for and what do they want?

  - What verbs have been used to express the requirement?

  - Are there any limitations of scope highlighted?

  - Are there any key issues mentioned that need addressing?

  - Are any calculations, ratios or other quantitative analysis required?

  - Does the question lend itself to the use of a specific theoretical model?

  - Which professional skill is being explicitly tested?

- Writing up a plan:

  - Set up key headings – these should now be obvious from the wording of the requirement and the choice of model (if any).

  - Fill in key issues under the headings, firstly from what you remember and then by looking again at your annotations on the exam paper.

- **Earning professional skills marks as you write up your answers**

  To demonstrate professionalism and earn skills marks you need to do the following:

  - Address the requirements as written, taking particular notice (again!) of the verbs used

  - Make sure you include the most important, relevant and crucial points relating to the requirement.

  - Only make relevant points and try not to include superfluous information or make unsupported points.

  - Show deep/clear understanding of underlying or causal issues and integrate or link different sources of information from various parts of the scenario or different exhibits to make points

  - Avoid repeating points already made.

  - Show your ability to prioritise and make points in a logical and progressive way, building arguments rather than using a random or 'scattergun' approach to answering the question.

  - Structure and present your answers in a professional manner through faithfully simulating the task as would be expected of the person being asked to carry it out and always have a clear stakeholder focus in mind when constructing the answer.

  - Demonstrate evidence of your knowledge from previous learning or wider reading and apply this knowledge appropriately to strengthen arguments and make points more convincing.

  - In addition to being clear, factual and concise, you should express yourself convincingly, persuasively and with credibility.

Always keep your eye on the clock and do not over run on any part of any question!

KAPLAN'S RECOMMENDED REVISION APPROACH

QUESTION PRACTICE IS THE KEY TO SUCCESS

Success in professional examinations relies upon you acquiring a firm grasp of the required knowledge at the tuition phase. In order to be able to do the questions, knowledge is essential.

However, the difference between success and failure often hinges on your exam technique on the day and making the most of the revision phase of your studies.

The **Kaplan study text** is the starting point, designed to provide the underpinning knowledge to tackle all questions. However, in the revision phase, pouring over text books is not the answer.

Kaplan Online fixed tests help you consolidate your knowledge and understanding and are a useful tool to check whether you can remember key topic areas.

Kaplan pocket notes are designed to help you quickly revise a topic area, however you then need to practice questions. There is a need to progress to full exam standard questions as soon as possible, and to tie your exam technique and technical knowledge together.

The importance of question practice cannot be over-emphasised.

The recommended approach below is designed by expert tutors in the field, in conjunction with their knowledge of the examiner and their recent real exams.

The approach taken for the fundamental papers is to revise by topic area. However, with the professional stage papers, a multi topic approach is required to answer the scenario based questions.

You need to practice as many questions as possible in the time you have left.

OUR AIM

Our aim is to get you to the stage where you can attempt exam standard questions confidently, to time, in a closed book environment, with no supplementary help (i.e. to simulate the real examination experience).

Practising your exam technique on real past examination questions, in timed conditions, is also vitally important for you to assess your progress and identify areas of weakness that may need more attention in the final run up to the examination.

In order to achieve this we recognise that initially you may feel the need to practice some questions with open book help and exceed the required time.

The approach below shows you which questions you should use to build up to coping with exam standard question practice, and references to the sources of information available should you need to revisit a topic area in more detail.

EXAMINER COMMENTS

The SBL examination represents a different challenge.

However, there are <u>general points</u> from other high-level discursive papers that can be applied to SBL.

In such papers, the examiners have often commented that students had been unsuccessful due to:

- "not answering the question"

- "not pitching their answers at the verb level set"

- "a poor understanding of why something is done, not just how it is done"

- "simply writing out numbers from the question. Candidates must understand what the numbers tell them about business performance"

- "a lack of common business sense" and

- "ignoring clues in the question".

For SBL the following additional guidance is worthy of note:

- SBL is not about linguistic prowess and/or extensive vocabulary, be sure however to express points clearly, factually and concisely

- Demonstrate your ability to prioritise points in a logical and progressive way

- Write in a persuasive and convincing style, be sure to include the most important, relevant and crucial points

- Integrate/link different sources of information from various parts of the scenario exhibits to illustrate your points

- Prepare your answer in a logical and progressive way, selecting and writing about the prioritised points in the first instance. Do not present your answer in a random or 'scatter gun' approach

- Do not simply restate information included in the case, always <u>support and justify</u> the points that you include in your answer – follow the simple guidance i.e. "what and why" for each point that you make

- Do not repeat points already made. You can however reinforce a previous point in order to develop it

- Have a clear stakeholder focus in mind when constructing your answer i.e. address the answer to the recipient, referencing all those affected by your response

- <u>Stay on topic</u> – do not make more points than required for the marks available. As a general guide, it is possible to earn up to two marks for a well-made and justified point. For a 10 mark allocation therefore at least five well-made and justified points should be made.

Based on the above it is clear that good exam technique is crucial to success.

It is recommended therefore that you complete <u>at least</u> two full exams, <u>to time</u> as a key part of your revision.

EXAMINATION TIPS – COMPUTER BASED EXAM (CBE)

Strategic Professional CBE will be extended to all locations from September 2021 onwards and the paper-based exam will no longer be available. The exam format may impact upon your approach to revision.

Some overview guidance for CBE:

In addition to reading the tips contained here, we recommend that you review the resources available on the ACCA Global Website before sitting the CBE. Here you will find guidance documents, videos and a link to the CBE question practice platform.

https://www.accaglobal.com/gb/en/student/exam-support-resources/professional-exams-study-resources/strategic-business-leader/cbe-exam-technique.html

The exam is 240 minutes (4 hours) – You should allocate between 40 and 60 minutes reading and planning your answer. This is referred to as **RPRT** (reading, planning and reflection time)

Plan your strategy before you go in allocating up to 60 minutes for RPRT and (assuming you have used the full 60 minutes) allocate 2.25 minutes for each technical mark allocated. This is calculated as follows (240 – 60)/80 = 2.25 minutes per mark.

If possible factor in 10 – 15 minutes to skim through the questions at the start and as a buffer to review your answers at the end. Be warned however that achieving "buffer" time is a very tough ask for SBL given the significant time pressures.

Planning your answers:

1   When the exam starts spend a few minutes skimming through the whole exam to get a feel for what is included.

- ACCA recommend that you **Copy and Paste** each of the requirements into the word document – this is the bold lettering.

- **Copy and Paste** the professional skills detail also to ensure that you focus on this key aspect when compiling your plan and writing your answer.

2   Planning process. Using your rough paper OR the word document/scratch pad to make notes:

- Read the first exhibit – an overview of the company

- Read the tasks – and summarise the detail briefly

- Read the exhibits – and summarise the detail briefly

- Reflect on how the exhibits relate to the tasks

- Note down key words onto the word doc for each task – i.e. prepare an outline plan

NB:

- Be prepared to 'park' some of the latter exhibits if they solely relate to a latter task

You can move around and resize the windows that you open to lay the screen out in a format that suits you. These steps will help with your planning and structure but will also enable you to minimise the number of windows you have open.

NB: Steps 1 and 2 should take about 40 – 60 minutes. It is <u>essential</u> that you leave sufficient time to complete the examination requirements in full.

Now that you have completed your RPRT:

3   Establish your "time per task" deadlines based on the actual time you have remaining.

   For example:

   - Minutes per technical mark = Time left/80 marks (For example – if you have used 60 minutes so far you have (240 – 60)/80 = 2.25 minutes per mark)

   - Note down the time per Task = technical marks x minutes per mark

   - Note down on the answer plan your "minutes per task"

You are now ready to write your answer.

For each task:

- Pay close attention to:
   - Format of Answer

   - Your Role

   - Your Audience

   - Professional Skill

   - The Verb used

   - The actual task requirement!

- Before you start your answer, note down headings and key words – your answer will need a clear STRUCTURE and a LOGICAL FLOW particularly to achieve the professional marks

- Linking and applying the relevant part of the syllabus may help you generate ideas but <u>do not</u> waste anytime defining or explaining theory. The key message from the examining team is to APPLY the theory.

Completing your answers – Start by revisiting the relevant exhibits for each requirement. Decide on the use of a word processing format, a spreadsheet format or both.

For calculations, use a logical and well laid out structure. It is unlikely that there will be detailed calculations in the SBL exam but if prepared they should be labelled and referenced in to any relevant discussion.

For discursive answers use bold headings and sub-headings and professional language. Ensure all aspects of the requirement are covered in a sensible and balanced way. It is vital that you relate your answer to the specific circumstances given.

If you get completely stuck with a question return to it later.

If you do not understand what a question is asking, state your assumptions. Even if you do not answer in precisely the way the examiner hoped, you should be given some credit, if your assumptions are reasonable.

Finally, use your buffer time to read through the answers, ensuring they are clear and organised, and to make any necessary changes.

Remember that in the real examination, all you have to do is:

- attempt all questions required by the exam
- only spend the allotted time on each question, and
- get them at least 50% right!

Try and practice this approach on every question you attempt from now to the real exam.

For additional support with your studies please also refer to the ACCA Global website.

FURTHER GUIDANCE FROM THE ACCA

The use of theories or models in the Strategic Business Leader exam

The Strategic Business Leader exam set by the ACCA Examining Team is a practical exam and unlike other exams will not test individual theories or models in isolation or require for the these theories or models to be quoted in answers to exam questions. However, understanding the technical theories, models and knowledge is essential as these provide a framework for students to help them approach the practical tasks that they will need to complete in the Strategic Business Leader exam.

The use of models in the exam will be a judgement made by students and is part of the ACCA Professional Skills for analysis and evaluation. Students are advised to use models which they judge to be relevant to structure their answers for a particular task or scenario to generate the scope of their answer. It is not required that students define models as part of their answer unless they judge that doing so will aid the understanding of the recipient answer content.

There is not a prescriptive list of theories and models, however, the textbook and kit focuses on the most relevant models which it considers to be most relevant to the syllabus and to aid students in being successful in Strategic Business Leader.

THE KAPLAN PAPER SBL REVISION PLAN

Stage 1: Assess areas of strengths and weaknesses

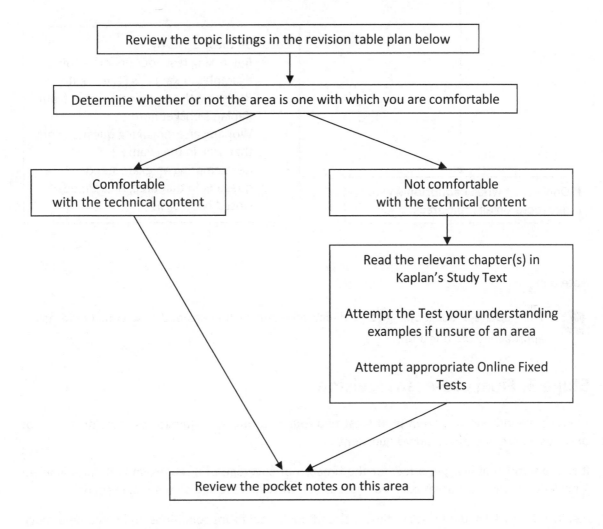

Stage 2: Practice questions

Follow the order of revision of topics as recommended in the revision table plan below and attempt the questions in the order suggested.

Try to avoid referring to text books and notes and the model answer until you have completed your attempt.

Try to answer the question in the allotted time.

Review your attempt with the model answer and assess how much of the answer you achieved in the allocated exam time.

Make sure you revise both technical aspects but also how to achieve professional marks. Towards this you are advised to attempt all of the full length case style questions in this kit, even if you don't feel you have sufficient time to work all the shorter questions.

Fill in the self-assessment box below and decide on your best course of action.

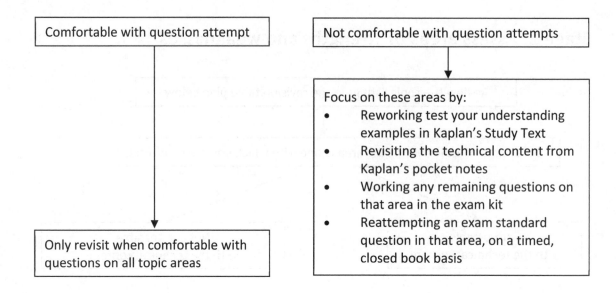

Comfortable with question attempt

Not comfortable with question attempts

Focus on these areas by:
- Reworking test your understanding examples in Kaplan's Study Text
- Revisiting the technical content from Kaplan's pocket notes
- Working any remaining questions on that area in the exam kit
- Reattempting an exam standard question in that area, on a timed, closed book basis

Only revisit when comfortable with questions on all topic areas

Note that:

 The 'footsteps questions' give guidance on exam techniques and how you should have approached the question.

Stage 3: Final pre-exam revision

We recommend that you **attempt at least two four hour mock examinations** containing a set of previously unseen exam standard questions.

It is important that you get a feel for the breadth of coverage of a real exam without advanced knowledge of the topic areas covered – just as you will expect to see on the real exam day.

Ideally this mock should be sat in timed, closed book, real exam conditions and could be a mock examination offered by your tuition provider.

KAPLAN'S DETAILED REVISION PLAN

Syllabus area / topic	Study Text Chapter	Pocket note Chapter	Questions to attempt	Guidance	Date attempted	Self-assessment
A: Leadership						
– Qualities of leadership	1, 10	1, 10	1	You need to be able to apply excellent leadership and ethical skills to set the 'tone from the top' and promote a positive culture within the organisation, adopting a whole organisation perspective in managing performance and value creation.		
– Leadership and organisational culture	10, 24	10, 24	2, 3			
– Professionalism, ethical codes and the public interest	17	17	4, 5			

Syllabus area / topic	Study Text Chapter	Pocket note Chapter	Questions to attempt	Guidance	Date attempted	Self-assessment
B: Governance						
– Agency	7	7	9	You need to be able to evaluate the effectiveness of the governance and agency system of an organisation and recognise the responsibility of the board or other agents towards their stakeholders, including the organisation's social responsibilities and the reporting implications.		
– Stakeholder analysis and organisational social responsibility	9	9	10, 12			
– Governance scope and approaches	7	7	14			
– Reporting to stakeholders	12	12	13, 16			
– The board of directors	11	11	18, 19			
– Public sector governance	8	8	11			

Syllabus area / topic	Study Text Chapter	Pocket note Chapter	Questions to attempt	Guidance	Date attempted	Self-assessment
C: Strategy						
– Concepts of strategy	2	2	24	You need to be able to evaluate the strategic position of the organisation against the external environment and the availability of internal resources, to identify feasible strategic options		
– Environmental issues	3	3	28. 33			
– Competitive forces	3	3	32, 35			
– The internal resources, capabilities and competences of an organisation	3, 4	3,4	26, 29			
– Strategic choices	5	5	31, 34			

Syllabus area / topic	Study Text Chapter	Pocket note Chapter	Questions to attempt	Guidance	Date attempted	Self-assessment
D: Risk						
– Identification, assessment and measurement of risk	15	15	39, 43	You need to be able to analyse the risk profile of the organisation and of any strategic options identified, within a culture of responsible risk management.		
– Managing, monitoring and mitigating risk	16	16	42, 46			

KAPLAN PUBLISHING

Syllabus area / topic	Study Text Chapter	Pocket note Chapter	Questions to attempt	Guidance	Date attempted	Self-assessment
E: Technology and data analytics						
– Cloud, mobile and smart technology	20	20	Note, 85	You need to be able to select and apply appropriate information technologies and data analytics, to analyse factors affecting the organisation's value chain to identify strategic opportunities and implement strategic options within a framework of robust IT security controls.		
– Big data and data analytics	20	20	Note			
– Machine learning, AI and robotics	20	20	84,85			
– E- business: value chain	19, 21	19, 21	48, 52			
– IT systems security and control	20	20	50			

Note: These syllabus areas are covered in case studies 2, 4 and in the first specimen exam.

Syllabus area / topic	Study Text Chapter	Pocket note Chapter	Questions to attempt	Guidance	Date attempted	Self-assessment
F: Organisational control and audit						
– Management and internal control systems	13	13	54, 56	You need to be able to evaluate management reporting and internal control and audit systems to ensure compliance and the achievement of organisation's objectives and the safeguarding of organisational assets.		
– Audit and compliance	14	14	58, 60			
– Internal control and management reporting	13	13	55, 61			

Syllabus area / topic	Study Text Chapter	Pocket note Chapter	Questions to attempt	Guidance	Date attempted	Self-assessment
G: Finance in planning and decision-making						
– Finance transformation	23	23	63	You need to be able to apply high level financial techniques from Applied Skills exams in the planning, implementation and evaluation of strategic options and actions.		
– Financial analysis and decision-making techniques	23	23	65			
– Cost and management accounting	23	23	66			

Syllabus area / topic	Study Text Chapter	Pocket note Chapter	Questions to attempt	Guidance	Date attempted	Self-assessment
H: Innovation, performance excellence and change management						
– Enabling success - organising	18	18	71	You need to be able to enable success through innovative thinking, applying best in class strategies and disruptive technologies in the management of change; initiating, leading and organising projects, while effectively managing talent and other business resources		
– Enabling success – disruptive technologies	20	20	82,83			
– Enabling success – talent management	24	24	68, 70			
– Enabling success – performance excellence	4, 5	4, 5	68, 70			
– Managing strategic change	24	24	77, 79			
– Leading and managing projects	22	22	73,74			

Note that not all of the questions in the kit are referred to in the programme above. We have recommended a large number of exam standard questions and successful completion of these should reassure you that you have a good grounding of all of the key topics and are well prepared for the exam. The remaining questions are available in the kit for extra practice for those who require more questions on some areas.

KAPLAN PUBLISHING

CASE STYLE QUESTIONS

As well as the shorter questions referred to above, it is vital that you work through the case style questions in this kit with a focus on exam technique, time management and demonstrating professional skills.

Be professional and record your attempts and self- assessment as follows, for example. Make a note of areas on which you need to improve.

Case study question	Date attempted	Self-assessment: Technical aspects	Self-assessment: Professional skills
Dixon Smith Burrell			
Foodmart			
Swann Hill Company (SHC)			
Fishnet			
Cofold Construction – September 2018			
HiLite – December 2018			
Smartwear – March/June 2020			
Dulce Co – Sept/Dec 2019			
Techthere4U – March 2020			

Section 1

TECHNICAL PRACTICE QUESTIONS

NOTE: THE MAIN PURPOSE OF THE QUESTIONS IN THIS SECTION IS TO HELP YOU FOCUS ON SPECIFIC SYLLABUS AREAS TO ENSURE YOU HAVE THE LEVEL OF TECHNICAL ABILITY REQUIRED FOR SUCCESS IN SBL. MANY OF THESE QUESTIONS ALSO HAVE PROFESSIONAL SKILLS ASPECTS AS WELL.

A: LEADERSHIP

1 ACADEMIC RECYCLING COMPANY (ARC)

Ten years ago Sully Truin formed the Academic Recycling Company (ARC) to offer a specialised waste recycling service to schools and colleges. The company has been very successful and has expanded rapidly. To cope with this expansion, Sully has implemented a tight administrative process for operating and monitoring contracts. This administrative procedure is undertaken by the Contracts Office, who track that collections have been made by the field recycling teams. Sully has sole responsibility for obtaining and establishing recycling contracts, but he leaves the day-to-day responsibility for administering and monitoring the contracts to the Contracts Office. He has closely defined what needs to be done for each contract and how this should be monitored. 'I needed to do this', he said, 'because workers in this country are naturally lazy and lack initiative. I have found that if you don't tell them exactly what to do and how to do it, then it won't get done properly.' Most of the employees working in the Contracts Office like and respect Sully for his business success and ability to take instant decisions when they refer a problem to him. Some of ARC's employees have complained about his autocratic style of leadership, but most of these have now left the company to work for other organisations.

A few months ago, ARC was acquired by an international company Scat. Scat intend to leave the management of ARC completely in Sully Truin's hands but want to integrate its activities into complementary activities carried out by the Scat group.

As part of Scat's human resource strategy every manager must attend one of Scat's internal leadership programmes. Scat's programmes actively advocate and promote a democratic style of management. Sully Truin attended once such course programme as part of the conditions for him retaining his managing directorship of ARC.

The course caused Sully to question his previous approach to leadership. It was also the first time, for three years, that Sully had been out of the office during working hours for a prolonged period of time. However, each night, while he was attending the course, he had to deal with emails from the Contracts Office listing problems with contracts and asking him what action they should take. He became exasperated by his employees' inability to take actions to resolve these issues.

He discussed this problem with the leaders of Scat's training programme. They suggested that his employees would be more effective and motivated if their jobs were enriched and that they were empowered to make decisions themselves.

On his return from the course, Sully called a staff meeting with the Contracts Office where he announced that, from now on, employees would have responsibility for taking control actions themselves, rather than referring the problem to him. Sully, in turn, was to focus on gaining more contracts and setting them up.

However, problems with the new arrangements arose very quickly. Fearful of making mistakes and unsure about what they were doing led to employees discussing issues amongst themselves at length before coming to a tentative decision. The operational (field) recycling teams were particularly critical of the new approach. One commented that 'before, we got a clear decision very quickly. Now decisions can take several days and appear to lack authority.' The new approach also caused tensions and stress within the Contracts Office and absenteeism increased.

At the next staff meeting, employees in the Contracts Office asked Sully to return to his old management style and job responsibilities. 'We prefer the old Sully Truin', they said, 'problems are again referred up to him. However, he is unhappy with this return to the previous way of working as he feels that this may upset the new company owners. He is also working long hours and is concerned about his health. On top of this, he realises that he has little time for obtaining and planning contracts and this is severely restricting the capacity of the company to expand in order to integrate activities with other parts of the Scat group.

Scat performs a 100 day review of all newly acquired businesses. This 100 day review examines the impact of the acquisition after the first 100 days of Scat ownership. A review of ARC has determined that ARC has yet to achieve integration targets that were set as objectives for the first 100 days post acquisition.

The Scat human resource director is concerned that this may be caused by a poor management style employed by Sully Truin or that perhaps Scat's own internal training programmes are not as effective as hoped. She believes that the management training course promotes the best approach to leadership, one that she herself employs across all of Scat's business units.

Required:

You work as a member of the 100 day review team at Scat.

Prepare a brief report for the Scat HR director to explain why the change of leadership style at ARC was unsuccessful and whether this reflects a poor approach to Scat's management training programme. **(15 marks)**

Professional skills marks will be awarded for demonstrating commercial acumen in demonstrating awareness of the wider external factors that may have affected the success of Sully Truin's new management style. **(3 marks)**

(Total: 18 marks)

2   ICOMPUTE

iCompute was founded twenty years ago by the technology entrepreneur, Ron Yeates. It initially specialised in building bespoke computer software for the financial services industry. However, it has expanded into other specialised areas and it is currently the third largest software house in the country, employing 400 people.

It still specialises in bespoke software, although 20% of its income now comes from the sales of a software package designed specifically for car insurance.

The company has grown based on a 'work hard, play hard work ethic' and this still remains. Employees are expected to work long hours and to take part in social activities after work. Revenues have continued to increase over the last few years, but the firm has had difficulty in recruiting and retaining staff. Approximately one-third of all employees leave within their first year of employment at the company. The company appears to experience particular difficulty in recruiting and retaining female staff, with 50% of female staff leaving within 12 months of joining the company. Only about 20% of the employees are female and they work mainly in marketing and human resources.

The company is currently in dispute with two of its customers who claim that its bespoke software did not fit the agreed requirements. iCompute currently outsources all its legal advice problems to a law firm that specialises in computer contracts and legislation. However, the importance of legal advice has led to iCompute considering the establishment of an internal legal team, responsible for advising on contracts, disputes and employment legislation.

The support of bespoke solutions and the car insurance software package was also outsourced a year ago to a third party. Although support had been traditionally handled in-house, it was unpopular with staff. One of the senior managers responsible for the outsourcing decision claimed that support calls were 'increasingly varied and complex, reflecting incompetent end users, too lazy to read user guides.' However, the outsourcing of support has not proved popular with iCompute's customers and a number of significant complaints have been made about the service given to end users. The company is currently reviewing whether the software support process should be brought back in-house.

The company is still regarded as a technology leader in the market place, although the presence of so many technically gifted employees within the company often creates uncertainty about the most appropriate technology to adopt for a solution. One manager commented that 'we have often adopted, or are about to adopt, a technology or solution when one of our software developers will ask if we have considered some newly released technology. We usually admit we haven't and so we re-open the adoption process. We seem to be in a state of constant technical paralysis.'

Although Ron Yeates retired five years ago, many of the software developers recruited by him are still with the company. Some of these have become operational managers, employed to manage teams of software developers on internal and external projects. Subba Kendo is one of the managers who originally joined the company as a trainee programmer. 'I moved into management because I needed to earn more money. There is a limit to what you can earn here as a software developer. However, I still keep up to date with programming though, and I am a goalkeeper for one of the company's five-a-side football teams. I am still one of the boys.'

However, many of the software developers are sceptical about their managers. One commented that 'they are technologically years out of date. Some will insist on writing programs and producing code, but we take it out again as soon as we can and replace it with something we have written. Not only are they poor programmers, they are poor managers and don't really know how to motivate us.' Although revenues have increased, profits have fallen. This is also blamed on the managers. 'There is always an element of ambiguity in specifying customers' requirements. In the past, Ron Yeates would debate responsibility for requirements changes with the customer. However, we now seem to do all amendments for free. The customer is right even when we know he isn't. No wonder margins are falling. The managers are not firm enough with customers.'

The software developers are also angry that an in-house project has been initiated to produce a system for recording time spent on tasks and projects. Some of the justification for this is that a few of the projects are on a 'time and materials' basis and a time recording system would permit accurate and prompt invoicing. However, the other justification for the project is that it will improve the estimation of 'fixed-price' contracts. It will provide statistical information derived from previous projects to assist account managers preparing estimates to produce quotes for bidding for new bespoke development contracts.

Vikram Soleski, one of the current software developers, commented that 'managers do not even have up-to-date mobile phones, probably because they don't know how to use them. We (software developers) always have the latest gadgets long before they are acquired by managers. But I like working here, we have a good social scene and after working long hours we socialise together, often playing computer games well into the early hours of the morning. It's a great life if you don't weaken!'

Required:

In order to understand the failures within iCompute, analyse the company's culture, and assess the implications of your analysis for the company's future performance. (13 marks)

Professional skills marks will be awarded for demonstrating analytical skills in considering the implications of the issues raised. **(2 marks)**

(Total: 15 marks)

3   THE NATIONAL MUSEUM (NM)   *Walk in the footsteps of a top tutor*

Introduction

The National Museum (NM) was established in 1857 to house collections of art, textiles and metal ware for the nation. It remains in its original building which is itself of architectural importance. Unfortunately, the passage of time has meant that the condition of the building has deteriorated and so it requires continual repair and maintenance. Alterations have also been made to ensure that the building complies with the disability access and health and safety laws of the country. However, these alterations have been criticised as being unsympathetic and out of character with the rest of the building. The building is in a previously affluent area of the capital city. However, what were once large middle-class family houses have now become multi-occupied apartments and the socio-economic structure of the area has radically changed. The area also suffers from an increasing crime rate. A visitor to the museum was recently assaulted whilst waiting for a bus to take her home. The assault was reported in both local and national newspapers.

Thirty years ago, the government identified museums that held significant Heritage Collections. These are collections that are deemed to be very significant to the country. Three Heritage Collections were identified at the NM, a figure that has risen to seven in the intervening years as the museum has acquired new items.

Government change

One year ago, a new national government was elected. The newly appointed Minister for Culture implemented the government's election manifesto commitment to make museums more self-funding. The minister has declared that in five years' time the museum must cover 60% of its own costs and only 40% will be directly funded by government. This change in funding will gradually be phased in over the next five years.

The 40% government grant will be linked to the museum achieving specified targets for disability access, social inclusion and electronic commerce and access. The government is committed to increasing museum attendance by lower socio-economic classes and younger people so that they are more aware of their heritage. Furthermore, it also wishes to give increasing access to museum exhibits to disabled people who cannot physically visit the museum site. The government have asked all museums to produce a strategy document showing how they intend to meet these financial, accessibility and technological objectives. The government's opposition has, since the election, also agreed that the reliance of museums on government funding should be reduced.

Required:

(a)   Analyse the macro-environment of the National Museum.   (20 marks)

(b)   The failure of the Director General's strategy has been explained by one of the trustees as 'a failure to understand our organisational culture; the way we do things around here'.

       Assess the underlying organisational cultural issues that would explain the failure of the Director General's strategy at the National Museum.   (20 marks)

       Professional skills marks will be awarded for demonstrating commercial acumen in applying judgement and insight into the cultural issues of the organisation which have led to its failure.   (2 marks)

                                                                (Total: 42 marks)

Exhibit 1 – Funding and structure

The NM is currently 90% funded by direct grants from government. The rest of its income comes from a nominal admission charge and from private sponsorship of exhibitions. The direct funding from the government is based on a number of factors, but the number of Heritage Collections held by the museum is a significant funding influence. The Board of Trustees of the NM divide the museum's income between departments roughly on the basis of the previous year's budget plus an inflation percentage. The division of money between departments is heavily influenced by the Heritage Collections. Departments with Heritage Collections tend to be allocated a larger budget.

The budgets for 20X8 and 20X9 are shown in Figure 1.

Collection Sections	Number of Heritage Collections	Budget ($000s) 20X8	Budget ($000s) 20X9
Architecture	2	120.00	125.00
Art	2	135.00	140.00
Metalwork	1	37.50	39.00
Glass		23.00	24.00
Textiles	1	45.00	47.50
Ceramics		35.00	36.00
Furniture		30.00	31.50
Print and books		35.00	36.50
Photography		15.00	15.50
Fashion		10.00	10.50
Jewellery	1	50.00	52.50
Sculpture		25.00	26.00
Administration		60.50	63.00
Total		621.00	647.00

Exhibit 2 – Organisational structure

The head of each collection section is an important position and enjoys many privileges, including a large office, a special section heads' dining room and a dedicated personal assistant (PA). The heads of sections which have 'Heritage Collections' also hold the title of professor from the National University.

The departmental structure of the NM (see Figure 2) is largely built around the twelve main sections of the collection. These sections are grouped into three departments, each of which has a Director. The Board of Directors is made up of the three directors of these departments, together with the Director of Administration and the Director General. The museum is a charity run by a Board of Trustees. There are currently eight trustees, two of whom have been recently appointed by the government. The other six trustees are people well-known and respected in academic fields relevant to the museum's collections.

The organisational structure is illustrated in the following organisational chart:

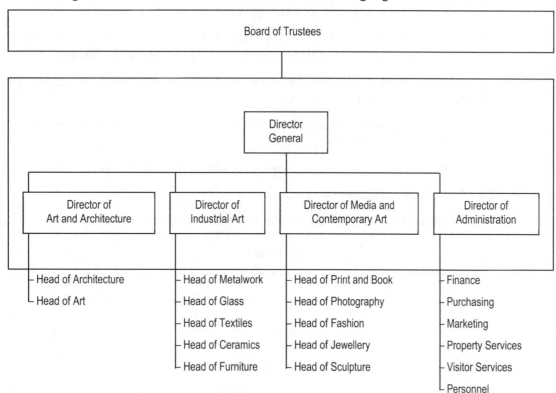

Exhibit 3 – Director General's proposal

Traditionally, the NM has provided administrative support for sections and departments, grouped together beneath a Director of Administration. The role of the Director General has been a part-time post. However, the funding changes introduced by the government and the need to produce a strategy document, has spurred the Board of Trustees to appoint a full-time Director General from the private sector. The trustees felt they needed private industry expertise to develop and implement a strategy to achieve the government's objectives. The new Director General was previously the CEO of a major chain of supermarkets.

The new Director General has produced a strategic planning document showing how the NM intends to meet the government's objectives. Proposals in this document include:

1   Allocating budgets (from 20Y0) to sections based on visitor popularity. The most visited collections will receive the most money. The idea is to stimulate sections to come up with innovative ideas that will attract more visitors to the museum. Visitor numbers have been declining since 20X4.

Visitor numbers 20X4–20X7

Visitor numbers (000s)	20X7	20X6	20X5	20X4
Age 17 or less	10	12	15	15
Age 18–22	5	8	12	10
Age 23–30	10	15	20	20
Age 31–45	20	20	18	25
Age 46–59	35	35	30	30
Age 60 or more	40	35	35	30
Total	120	125	130	130

2   Increasing entrance charges to increase income, but to make entry free to pensioners, students, children and people receiving government benefit payments.

3   Removing the head of sections' dining room and turning this into a restaurant for visitors. An increase in income from catering is also proposed in the document.

4   Removing the head of sections' personal assistants and introducing a support staff pool to reduce administrative costs.

5   Increasing the display of exhibits. Only 10% of the museum's collection is open to the public. The rest is held in storage.

6   Increasing commercial income from selling posters, postcards and other souvenirs.

Exhibit 4 – Proposed organisational structure

The Director General has also suggested a major re-structuring of the organisation as:

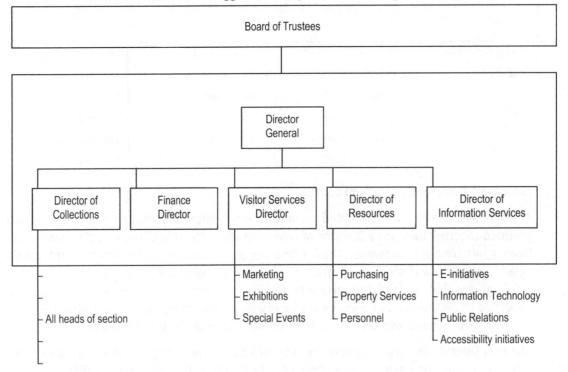

Exhibit 5 – Reaction to the proposals

Employees have reacted furiously to the Director General's suggestions. The idea of linking budgets to visitor numbers has been greeted with dismay by the Director of Art and Architecture. 'This is a dreadful idea and confuses popularity with historical significance. As previous governments have realised, what is important is the value of the collection. Heritage Collections recognise this significance by putting the nation's interests before those of an undiscerning public. As far as I am concerned, if they want to see fashion, they can look in the high street shops. Unlike fashion, great art and architecture remains.' The Director of Art and Architecture and the two professors who hold the Head of Architecture and Head of Art posts have also lobbied individual members of the Board of Trustees with their concerns about the Director General's proposals.

The Director of Industrial Arts and the Director of Media and Contemporary Art have contacted powerful figures in both television and the press and as a result a number of articles and letters critical of the Director General's proposals have appeared. A recent television programme called 'Strife at the NM' also featured interviews with various heads of collections criticising the proposed changes. They were particularly critical of the lack of consultation; 'these proposals have been produced with no input from museum staff. They have been handed down from on high by an ex-grocer', said one anonymous contributor.

Eventually, the criticism of staff and their lack of cooperation prompted the Director General to ask the Board of Trustees to publicly back him. However, only the two trustees appointed by the government were prepared to do so. Consequently, the Director General resigned. This has prompted an angry response from the government which has now threatened to cut the museum's funding dramatically next year and to change the composition of the Board of Trustees so that the majority of trustees are appointed directly by the government. The Minister of Culture has asked the museum to develop and recommend a new strategy within one month.

4 PHARMA

Pharma is a global pharmaceutical company producing many of the world's leading over-the-counter and prescription drugs. Many of these brands are household names sold through major retail chains in over 100 countries or direct to governments for use through public sector health services. Recently, the company has funded a research project into the effectiveness of one of its new products designed to combat a particular childhood disease. The project is designed to evaluate effectiveness in comparison with a competitor brand as a foundation for a future marketing campaign. The drug was released into markets around the world two years ago.

All trials of the new drug have been carried out by Professor Zac Jones at the Massachusetts State University who receive a multi-million dollar support grant for their assistance in projects of this nature. The contract with Pharma insists on no publicity being given to projects and that all findings are kept strictly confidential.

Professor Jones has just returned from a meeting with Chief Executive and Chief Finance Officer (CFO) of Pharma. He has told them that, in his view, although the new product is effective, its side effects can be damaging to children in some cases and possibly even fatal. Although the probability of loss of life is small he is recommending removing the product from the shelves immediately. Professor Jones also states that he is ethically bound to publish his findings so that governments and health services around the world may take appropriate action.

The CFO has reminded him of the considerable revenue loss involved in such a move and of the size of the grant given to the University. He insists the findings remain confidential, pointing out a clause in the contract between Pharma and the University that forbids the disclosure of 'trade secrets' to third parties. Professor Jones is appalled and has openly questioned the CFO's integrity as a member of an esteemed profession.

Professor Jones has approached you, an external consultant, for advice on what to do in this situation. In particular he is anxious over some of the CFO's comments; whether being part of an esteemed profession should influence the CFO's behaviour, whether publishing his concerns would be a breach of the Professor's confidentiality, and how best to act ethically in this case. The professor recognises that some of these issues are not clear cut, so wants you to discuss different perspectives rather than simply telling him what to do.

Required:

Draft a letter to Professor Jones addressing his concerns. **(13 marks)**

Professional skills marks will be awarded for demonstrating communication skills in clarifying the different factors involved, thus ensuring that the statement meets the needs of Professor Jones. **(2 marks)**

(Total: 15 marks)

5 JOHN MATHERS

John Mathers, a qualified accountant and the finance director of the international construction company Parkstone, was recently jailed for 18 months as a result of being convicted of insider trading. Mathers profited from dealing in his company's shares around the time that a $50m government contract was awarded for the construction of 2,000 new social houses, which sent Parkstone's share price soaring in value.

Using a false name to avoid being detected, Mathers bought 100,000 Parkstone shares in small batches regularly during the three-month period before the lucrative deal was finalised, when the price was settled at around $5·40. He sold all of the shares the day after the government-financed building contract was announced when the share price had risen by 22%, thereby making a clear profit of around $120,000.

Mathers was jailed because he used his inside knowledge at Parkstone to personally profit, abusing his senior position in the company because he was privy to all the negotiations leading up the deal. The judge at his trial acknowledged that Mathers had shown genuine remorse for his crime, but the offence was so serious that it warranted a custodial sentence. He said that Mathers used his position as finance director to unlawfully profit from information about the forthcoming contract, and had shown a clear breach of the trust placed in him. He had been motivated by personal greed and knew at the time that his actions were illegal. The judge told him that insider trading was not a victimless crime, and his actions had had a very negative impact on overall public confidence in the integrity of the market.

Since the trial a number of Directors at Parkstone has been approached by journalists asking questions about the case. Some Directors have felt very exposed by this and admit that they do not know enough about insider trading and don't feel confident discussing how John Mathers' actions breached ethical codes. You have been asked, as Chairman of Parkstone, to draft some briefing notes to be sent to all Directors immediately, making a clear distinction between general principles or definitions and Mather's behaviour.

Required:

Prepare a set of briefing notes that addresses the following issues

- **What is meant by 'insider trading' and how it can compromise directors' corporate responsibilities.**

- **How John Mathers' behaviour was a clear breach of the IESBA [IFAC] code of ethics which, as a professional accountant, he should have strictly followed.** **(14 marks)**

Professional skills marks will be awarded for demonstrating communication skills in producing briefing notes that inform concisely and unambiguously. **(2 marks)**

(Total: 16 marks)

6   HAPPY AND HEALTHY

'Happy and Healthy' is a traditional independent health food business that has been run as a family company for 40 years by Ken and Steffi Potter. As a couple they have always been passionate campaigners for healthy foods and are more concerned about the quality of the foods they sell than the financial detail of their business.

Since the company started in 1970, it has been audited by Watson Shreeves, a local audit firm. Mr Shreeves has overseen the Potters' audit for all of the 40 year history (rotating the engagement partner) and has always taken the opportunity to meet with Ken and Steffi informally at the end of each audit to sign off the financial statements and to offer a briefing and some free financial advice in his role as what he calls, 'auditor and friend'. In these briefings, Mr Shreeves, who has become a close family friend of the Potters over the years, always points out that the business is profitable (which the Potters already knew without knowing the actual figures) and how they might increase their margins. But the Potters have never been too concerned about financial performance as long as they can provide a good service to their customers, make enough to keep the business going and provide continued employment for themselves and their son, Ivan.

Whilst Ken and Steffi still retain a majority shareholding in 'Happy and healthy' they have gradually increased Ivan's proportion over the years. They currently own 60% to Ivan's 40%. Ivan was appointed a director, alongside Ken and Steffi, in 2008.

Ivan grew up in the business and has helped his parents out since he was a young boy. As he grew up, Ken and Steffi gave him more and more responsibility in the hope that he would one day take the business over. By the end of 2009, Ken made sure that Ivan drew more salary than Ken and Steffi combined as they sought to ensure that Ivan was happy to continue in the business after they retired.

During the audit for the year ended 31 March 2010, a member of Watson Shreeves was performing the audit as usual when he noticed a dramatic drop in the profitability of the business as a whole. He noticed that whilst food sales continued to be profitable, a large amount of inventory had been sold below cost to Barong Company with no further explanation and it was this that had caused the reduction in the company's operating margin. Each transaction with Barong Company had, the invoices showed, been authorised by Ivan.

Mr Shreeves was certain Ken and Steffi would not know anything about this and he prepared to tell them about it as a part of his annual end of audit meeting. Before the meeting, however, he carried out some checks on Barong Company and found that it was a separate business owned by Ivan and his wife.

Mr Shreeves's conclusion was that Ivan was effectively stealing from 'Happy and healthy' to provide inventory for Barong Company at a highly discounted cost price. Although Mr Shreeves now had to recommend certain disclosures to the financial statements in this meeting, his main fear was that Ken and Steffi would be devastated if they found out that Ivan was stealing and that it would have long-term implications for their family relationships and the future of 'Happy and healthy'.

Required:

Discuss the professional and ethical dilemma facing Mr Shreeves in deciding whether or not to tell Ken and Steffi about Ivan's activity. Advise Mr Shreeves of the most appropriate course of action. **(10 marks)**

7   AEI

You are the audit manager in charge of the field work of the AEI Co; it is the first year you have been involved with this client, although your audit firm has carried out the audit for the last eight years.

AEI is a general manufacturing company which is listed on the stock exchange of the country it is based in. The company manufactures and distributes household products including kitchen equipment, chairs, tables, and bedroom furniture.

The audit work for the year to 30 June has been in progress for the last three weeks, and there is one week to go before it is completed. The audit team of five staff comprises two juniors, two seniors and yourself.

Ethical issues

P, one of the audit juniors, has been working exclusively on checking the existence and valuation of the inventory in the kitchen equipment division of AEI. The work is not particularly difficult, but it is quite time-consuming and means checking many items of inventory in a large warehouse. A lot of the inventory is old and dirty and P normally brings old clothes each day to wear around the warehouse. The warehouse manager recently approached P and offered a free re-fitting of P's kitchen as a 'thank you' for carrying out the inventory work. The warehouse manager stated this was a normal activity each year, in recognition of P's difficult working conditions. During the audit P has identified that the inventory is over-valued, particularly in respect of many old kitchen units being maintained at full cost price, even though those units have had no sales in the last 18 months. The extent of the over-valuation appears to be material to the financial statements.

Q, an audit senior, has been working on the disclosure elements of directors' remuneration for the financial statements and the directors' remuneration regulations disclosure for that jurisdiction. Q has discovered that disclosure in the financial statements and remuneration regulations is different from the information provided by and checked by the audit committee. When queried, the newly appointed chair of the audit committee stated that share options were not considered part of disclosable remuneration as the value was uncertain, being based on future share price, which could not be determined. This element of remuneration was therefore omitted from the financial statements and remuneration regulations disclosure. The chair informed Q that due to the confidential nature of directors' remuneration, no further disclosure of this situation was to be made. The chair also noted that recent review of shareholdings indicated that Q had a 2.5% share of the company and again this would not be disclosed due to the confidential nature of the information.

Finally, the chair noted that the facts that the chair of the remuneration committee was also a director of IEA and that the chair of the remuneration committee of IEA was also a director of AEI should not be disclosed in the financial statements; again citing confidentiality issues.

R, the second audit junior, has been auditing the bank reconciliations on AEI's 26 different bank accounts. The work is considered suitable for a junior member as it mainly entails checking that cheques issued prior to the year-end were presented to the bank for payment after the end of the year. R has completed work on the reconciliations, and stated correctly that all cheques were presented to AEI's bank for payment after the end of the year. However, R failed to state that a number of cheques, material in amount, were only presented two months after the year end. In other words the financial statements were 'window dressed' to show a lower creditors' amount than was actually the case at the year end.

When queried about this omission during final review of the audit files, R correctly stated that he was never informed that timing of presentation of cheques was part of the audit procedures.

Required:

From the information above, explain any ethical threats and recommend appropriate ethical safeguards explaining why that safeguard is appropriate. (20 marks)

8 MRA

MRA is a weapons manufacturer based in a Northern European country.

When MRA was shortlisted for a valuable contract for the development of a coastal defence system for another country, it was contingent on the payment of a facilitation fee to an official in the defence ministry. Clearly this was an unusual request but it was also made very clear that MRA would not be awarded the contract, worth $2 billion over 10 years, unless the relatively modest sum of $1 million was paid immediately.

Recently, business activity in the defence sector had been very slow, and MRA was about to announce around 500 staff redundancies. Therefore news that this contract was about to be awarded came as a great relief to the board of MRA, as the jobs would now be secured. However, only the chief executive officer (CEO) and operations director knew about the facilitation fee, so an emergency meeting of the board was convened with only one item on the agenda.

Due to the very sensitive nature of the matter at hand, it was decided not to make a formal record of the discussions at the board meeting. This was more likely to result in a frank exchange of views and encourage all directors to express their opinions openly.

The CEO, Charlie Desborough, explained the dilemma to the board, making it very clear that without this contract there would be no way to protect jobs. The finance director, Jake Neilson, said that he was personally very uncomfortable with the idea of paying a facilitation fee, which was in effect a 'bribe'. As a professional accountant he was bound by a code of ethics which strictly prohibited making such payments, therefore he could not sanction the payment under any circumstances.

The HR director, Sarah Shue, took a far more pragmatic stance. She acknowledged that any form of corruption was utterly deplorable; however, it was a fact of life in many countries. She asserted that if the board of MRA decided not to make the payment and forego the contract, then it could be assured that a competitor would not adopt such a high-minded position.

The net effect was that by avoiding a relatively small payment, the firm would be doing a disservice to both its employees and its shareholders, who would undoubtedly suffer a reduction in their shareholder value. She maintained that sometimes it is necessary to take difficult decisions in business that are for the greater good, and so suggested that the payment to the official should be made.

The marketing director added that as far as she was aware, facilitation payments were considered bribes under some jurisdictions (such as the UK Bribery Act 2010) but not others, so 'can't be that bad'.

At the end of the meeting, the Board voted in favour of authorising the facilitation payment and proceeding with the contract.

While respecting the views of the Board, Charlie Desborough wants a better understanding of how bribery could affect MRA, firstly in terms of corporate governance and, secondly, in terms of best practice MRA could adopt. As a result he has contacted you, a non-executive director of MRA with particular expertise in corporate governance.

Required:

Prepare an email to Charlie Desborough that:

(a) **Assesses how bribery and corruption could undermine confidence and trust in MRA, with reference to the principles of corporate governance.** **(8 marks)**

(b) **Describes best practice measures which could be employed by MRA to combat bribery and corruption.** **(6 marks)**

(Total: 14 marks)

B: GOVERNANCE

9   ROSH AND COMPANY

Mary Hobbes joined the board of Rosh and Company, a large retailer, as finance director earlier this year. Whilst she was glad to have finally been given the chance to become finance director after several years as a financial accountant, she also quickly realised that the new appointment would offer her a lot of challenges. In the first board meeting, she realised that not only was she the only woman but she was also the youngest by many years.

Rosh was established almost 100 years ago. Members of the Rosh family have occupied senior board positions since the outset and even after the company's flotation 20 years ago a member of the Rosh family has either been executive chairman or chief executive. The current longstanding chairman, Timothy Rosh, has already prepared his slightly younger brother, Geoffrey (also a longstanding member of the board) to succeed him in two years' time when he plans to retire. The Rosh family, who still own 40% of the shares, consider it their right to occupy the most senior positions in the company so have never been very active in external recruitment. They only appointed Mary because they felt they needed a qualified accountant on the board to deal with changes in international financial reporting standards.

Several former executive members have been recruited as non-executives immediately after they retired from full-time service. A recent death, however, has reduced the number of non-executive directors to two. These sit alongside an executive board of seven that, apart from Mary, have all been in post for over ten years.

Mary noted that board meetings very rarely contain any significant discussion of strategy and never involve any debate or disagreement. When she asked why this was, she was told that the directors had all known each other for so long that they knew how each other thought. All of the other directors came from similar backgrounds, she was told, and had worked for the company for so long that they all knew what was 'best' for the company in any given situation. Mary observed that notes on strategy were not presented at board meetings and she asked Timothy Rosh whether the existing board was fully equipped to formulate strategy in the changing world of retailing and whether a nominations committee would help address weaknesses. She did not receive a reply.

Timothy Rosh has subsequently approached you, an external consultant, to see if there are any weaknesses in the current governance structures of Rosh and Company. He also wanted your views on the role and usefulness of a nominations committee.

Required:

Write a report to Timothy Rosh criticising the governance arrangements of Rosh and Company and assessing the usefulness of a nominations committee to the company.

(18 marks)

Professional skills marks will be awarded for demonstrating scepticism skills in probing into the governance structure at Rosh and Company.

(3 marks)

(Total: 21 marks)

10 ROWLANDS & MEDELEEV (R&M)

Rowlands & Medeleev (R&M), a major listed European civil engineering company, was successful in its bid to become principal (lead) contractor to build the Giant Dam Project in an East Asian country. The board of R&M prided itself in observing the highest standards of corporate governance. R&M's client, the government of the East Asian country, had taken into account several factors in appointing the principal contractor including each bidder's track record in large civil engineering projects, the value of the bid and a statement, required from each bidder, on how it would deal with the 'sensitive issues' and publicity that might arise as a result of the project.

The Giant Dam Project was seen as vital to the East Asian country's economic development as it would provide a large amount of hydroelectric power. This was seen as a 'clean energy' driver of future economic growth. The government was keen to point out that because hydroelectric power did not involve the burning of fossil fuels, the power would be environmentally clean and would contribute to the East Asian country's ability to meet its internationally agreed carbon emission targets. This, in turn, would contribute to the reduction of greenhouse gases in the environment. Critics, such as the environmental pressure group 'Stop-the-dam', however, argued that the project was far too large and the cost to the local environment would be unacceptable. Stop-the-dam was highly organised and, according to press reports in Europe, was capable of disrupting progress on the dam by measures such as creating 'human barriers' to the site and hiding people in tunnels who would have to be physically removed before proceeding. A spokesman for Stop-the-dam said it would definitely be attempting to resist the Giant Dam Project when construction started.

The project was intended to dam one of the region's largest rivers, thus creating a massive lake behind it. The lake would, the critics claimed, not only displace an estimated 100,000 people from their homes, but would also flood productive farmland and destroy several rare plant and animal habitats.

A number of important archaeological sites would also be lost. The largest community to be relocated was the indigenous First Nation people who had lived on and farmed the land for an estimated thousand years. A spokesman for the First Nation community said that the 'true price' of hydroelectric power was 'misery and cruelty'. A press report said that whilst the First Nation would be unlikely to disrupt the building of the dam, it was highly likely that they would protest and also attempt to mobilise opinion in other parts of the world against the Giant Dam Project.

When it was announced that R&M had won the contract to build the Giant Dam Project, some of its institutional shareholders contacted Richard Markovnikoff, the chairman. They wanted reassurance that the company had fully taken the environmental issues and other risks into account. One fund manager asked if Mr Markovnikoff could explain the sustainability implications of the project to assess whether R&M shares were still suitable for his environmentally sensitive clients. Mr Markovnikoff said, through the company's investor relations department that he intended to give a statement at the next annual general meeting (AGM) that he hoped would address these environmental concerns.

These and other issues were discussed at the last Board meeting where it was agreed that as part of a detailed risk assessment for the project, a preliminary step should be to identify key external stakeholders and assess their claims and potential influence.

As an external consultant you have been approached by the Board to assist with this step.

Required:

Draft a report extract for the Board of R&M that identifies key external stakeholders, describes their claims and evaluates their potential level of influence on the project's success. **(12 marks)**

Professional skills marks will be awarded for demonstrating analysis skills for assessing the relative level of stakeholder interest / influence. **(2 marks)**

(Total: 14 marks)

11 SCIENCE FIRST

In the city of Philo, the closure of a large factory released a large amount of land very close to the city centre which was bought by the Philo local government authority. As an area of high unemployment due to closures of heavy industry including shipbuilding and coal mining, Philo had an unemployment rate higher than the national average. As such, the local government authority was always keen to see new investments which would create high quality jobs. Although the former factory land had a potentially high commercial value if sold to housing developers, the local government authority offered the local university the chance to buy it for a favourable rate due to what it could offer the town as a whole. It was hope that the university would buy the land, creating a new development called 'Science First' on the old factory site which would in turn create 500 jobs.

As a city, Philo was well known for its science and engineering history, with many innovations, inventions and science developments having been made in the city going back over 200 years. Philo University saw investment in science as strategic to its future and as a key part of its competitive advantage. The Philo local government authority discussed the possibility of developing the former factory site with the university. After a series of meetings between the university and the local government authority, the university bought the land, as co-owners with the local government authority, with the full support of the local authority for building laboratories and related buildings on the site.

They agreed the name Science First for the development and jointly formed a company of the same name for the investment.

It was planned to build four large science laboratories on the site for medical, pharmacological and technology research.

Science First Company also wanted to develop a cluster of science-based businesses on the site and offered discounted rents as well as negotiating lower local taxes, to attract these businesses to the site. One of these new businesses, Topscience Company, had received international attention because of a key breakthrough it had made in medical research. Topscience was very concerned about how its building would appear on promotional photographs and it noticed that just beyond the science park, and within a few metres of its new building, were a number of blocks of poor quality social housing, owned by the Philo local government authority and accommodating rental tenants. Topscience asked if the local government authority would require Science First Company to re-landscape the area around the flats and knock them down in favour of green spaces more in keeping, in Topscience's opinion, with the image of a science park. They suggested they would not be able to locate to the Science First development in Philo unless this was done.

Anxious not to be seen to be doing anything to hinder the park's development, the Philo local government authority agreed to Topscience's demands and issued a notice to quit for all of the local residents affected by the potential demolition of the flats. Upon hearing of the plan to demolish the flats, the head of the local residents' association, Ann Tang, was outraged. She criticised the Philo local government authority for a lack of fairness and transparency in their dealings with the residents. She said that the local authority was so concerned about the science park's development that it did not care about social housing residents and that this was a betrayal of the authority's ethical responsibilities. Ann Tang also said that if the flats were demolished, there would be a loss of a 'close-knit, effective and cohesive' community of people who did not deserve to lose their homes in this way, all for the sake of a science development in which they, the local residents, had no say and did not vote for Ann Tang also acquired some figures which showed that, in order to invest in the Science First Company, the local government authority had to take budgeted funding from other services including the cancellation of a proposed new public library in the area where Ann Tang lives. Local residents, who were excited about the new library development, planned to use the new library as a lending library, as a place to study, as a café where people could meet and enjoy time with friends, and as a place for other services to be provided including 'mums and toddlers', 'unemployment clubs' and art classes. The cancellation of this library development would also mean that the ten jobs in the library would not now be created.

In seeking to address the challenges from the residents' association and others, the local government authority asked the finance director of Science First Company, accountant Kathy Wong, to produce a balanced assessment of the contribution of the Science First development to the city and the region. The local government authority, co-owners of Science First Company, insisted that she produce a balanced assessment which could also be published for the benefit of local residents. As a director of the development, however, she felt she ought to produce a report which clearly showed the benefits of the park to the city of Philo. Accordingly, she produced a report which concentrated on the benefits to Philo of the Science First development, in terms of the creation of jobs, marginal revenues and improved reputation for both the university and the city. Kathy Wong's report concluded that the park was of substantial benefit and should be supported by the local government authority, by the university and by local residents, who, she argued, should understand the strategic benefits of the development to the city.

Ann Tang criticised Kathy Wong for not taking into account the costs to residents and other local services of the Science First development. She said that the true social cost of the development was negative because it threatened to destroy homes and it would entail the cancellation of the proposed library. It would also have a negative effect on local infrastructure, including the diversion of roads, footpaths and bus routes.

The Philo local government authority, as a democratic body, is controlled by elected representatives from a range of different political parties, each of whom represents a portion of the total city population. Despite their political differences, the majority of elected representatives strongly supported the Science First development.

Some of the elected representatives on the Philo local government authority decided that it was right to consider the various stakeholders in the Science First development. Some elected representatives, especially those representing residents around the development, wanted to minimise the damage to local communities. They decided that the three main stakeholders to be considered were the Science First Company, the residents' association and the potential library users.

The head of the Philo local government authority, Simon Forfeit, sought to address the concerns of the elected representatives in a meeting of the elected members in which he set out the case for why the Philo local government authority had so strongly supported the Science First development. He said he recognised that in allowing and encouraging the Science First development, it was clear there would be local problems to address, but that the strategic interests of the city of Philo required this development. The city's reputation as a science city would, in his view, be enhanced by the Science First development. He argued that public sector organisations had complicated objective-setting processes which have to prioritise some interests over others. He said that he 'can't please everybody all the time and in any planning decision there are winners and losers.'

Mr Forfeit said that a local government authority had many obligations and had to serve the interests of local taxpayers who fund its work, and also the people who use its services. At the same time, it had to act in the long-term strategic interests of the city, which was why it so strongly supported the Science First development. The quality of jobs attracted by the science site, being highly skilled and highly paid, meant that the local government authority had no choice but to support and invest in the development even though some of the effects on local residents might be perceived as negative. In addition to the 500 new jobs, which will be advertised locally, Mr Forfeit said that the site would also provide space for expansion of the businesses which locate to the site. Mr Forfeit said that in addition to Topscience, other companies attracted to the site included companies producing electric vehicles, advanced medical solutions and other companies in growth sectors.

Required:

(a) (i) **Analyse the stakeholder claims of Science First Company, the residents' association and the potential library users, using the Mendelow matrix to plot these three stakeholders in the Science First development.** **(9 marks)**

    (ii) **Explain how the potential library users and residents' association might attempt to increase their influence as stakeholders in the Science First development.** **(4 marks)**

        Professional skills marks will be awarded for demonstrating analysis skills for assessing the relative level of stakeholder interest / influence. **(2 marks)**

(b) The head of the local authority was criticised by the residents' association for lacking transparency and fairness in its dealings with the residents.

Required:

Draft a statement on behalf of the head of the Philo local government authority, for their website, which covers the following issues:

(i) **Explanations of transparency and fairness and their importance in public sector governance.** **(6 marks)**

(ii) **An analysis of the complexities of performance measurement for public sector organisations and an explanation of how the 3Es model can be a used for this purpose.** **(9 marks)**

(Total: 30 marks)

12 ROSEY AND ATKINS (R&A)

Rosey and Atkins (R&A) is one of the largest institutional investors in the country. Its investment strategy has traditionally been to own a minor shareholding in each of the top 200 companies on the stock exchange. The R&A shareholding is typically between 2% and 10% of each company and it manages funds for over two million clients (people and businesses who buy into share funds managed by R&A).

Established over 200 years ago, R&A has always believed itself to be socially responsible. As part of its CSR strategy, R&A recently purchased 100% of the shares in a national house builder, Natcon, which it owned as a direct holding and did not include in its managed funds. Natcon, in turn, owned a large amount of land suitable for future low cost housing development. The R&A website reported that the reason for this purchase was to address the board's concerns over a shortage of affordable housing in the country which R&A felt they could help to address by having outright ownership of Natcon. R&A reported that there was a large social need for affordable homes, and it hoped to create many hundreds of new low cost homes each year.

Natcon wanted to build a large estate of new homes in the town of Housteads and the local government authority granted the required building permission. But the nearby University of Housteads strongly opposed it because it believed the new houses would ruin what was considered to be a panoramic view from the university campus which helped it to recruit staff and students to the university. Both the Housteads local government authority and the University of Housteads had money from reserves invested as clients (i.e. fund investors) with R&A, but with the university having a substantially smaller investment in the fund than the local government authority. The local government authority also owned shares in R&A, meaning that it was both an investor in funds and a shareholder in R&A.

At a recent board meeting of R&A there was a discussion over whether or not such investments were appropriate and a dispute arose over whether R&A should be focussing more on its CSR strategy or strategic CSR. Some directors were unsure over the distinction and so asked you, as an external consultant, to prepare some briefing notes on the matter.

Required:

Prepare briefing notes that explain the difference between 'corporate social responsibility (CSR) strategy' and 'strategic CSR', and construct the argument that the purchase of Natcon (the house builder) is an example of strategic CSR. **(10 marks)**

13   ZPT

In the 20X9 results presentation to analysts, the chief executive of ZPT, a global internet communications company, announced an excellent set of results to the waiting audience. Chief executive Clive Xu announced that, compared to 2008, sales had increased by 50%, profits by 100% and total assets by 80%. The dividend was to be doubled from the previous year. He also announced that based on their outstanding performance, the executive directors would be paid large bonuses in line with their contracts. His own bonus as chief executive would be $20 million. When one of the analysts asked if the bonus was excessive, Mr Xu reminded the audience that the share price had risen 45% over the course of the year because of his efforts in skilfully guiding the company. He said that he expected the share price to rise further on the results announcement, which it duly did. Because the results exceeded market expectation, the share price rose another 25% to $52.

Three months later, Clive Xu called a press conference to announce a restatement of the 20X9 results. This was necessary, he said, because of some 'regrettable accounting errors'. This followed a meeting between ZPT and the legal authorities who were investigating a possible fraud at ZPT. He disclosed that in fact the figures for 2009 were increases of 10% for sales, 20% for profits and 15% for total assets which were all significantly below market expectations.

The proposed dividend would now only be a modest 10% more than last year. He said that he expected a market reaction to the restatement but hoped that it would only be a short-term effect.

The first questioner from the audience asked why the auditors had not spotted and corrected the fundamental accounting errors and the second questioner asked whether such a disparity between initial and restated results was due to fraud rather than 'accounting errors'. When a journalist asked Clive Xu if he intended to pay back the $20 million bonus that had been based on the previous results, Mr Xu said he did not. The share price fell dramatically upon the restatement announcement and, because ZPT was such a large company, it made headlines in the business pages in many countries.

Later that month, the company announced that following an internal investigation, there would be further restatements, all dramatically downwards, for the years 20X6 and 20X7. This caused another mass selling of ZPT shares resulting in a final share value the following day of $1. This represented a loss of shareholder value of $12 billion from the peak share price. Clive Xu resigned and the government regulator for business ordered an investigation into what had happened at ZPT. The shares were suspended by the stock exchange. A month later, having failed to gain protection from its creditors in the courts, ZPT was declared bankrupt. Nothing was paid out to shareholders whilst suppliers received a fraction of the amounts due to them. Some non-current assets were acquired by competitors but all of ZPT's 54,000 employees lost their jobs, mostly with little or no termination payment. Because the ZPT employees' pension fund was not protected from creditors, the value of that was also severely reduced to pay debts which meant that employees with many years of service would have a greatly reduced pension to rely on in old age.

The government investigation found that ZPT had been maintaining false accounting records for several years. This was done by developing an overly-complicated company structure that contained a network of international branches and a business model that was difficult to understand. Whereas ZPT had begun as a simple telecommunications company, Clive Xu had increased the complexity of the company so that he could 'hide' losses and misreport profits. In the company's reporting, he also substantially overestimated the value of future customer supply contracts.

The investigation also found a number of significant internal control deficiencies including no effective management oversight of the external reporting process and a disregard of the relevant accounting standards.

In addition to Mr Xu, several other directors were complicit in the activities although Shazia Lo, a senior qualified accountant working for the financial director, had been unhappy about the situation for some time. She had approached the finance director with her concerns but having failed to get the answers she felt she needed, had threatened to tell the press that future customer supply contract values had been intentionally and materially overstated (the change in fair value would have had a profit impact). When her threat came to the attention of the board, she was intimidated in the hope that she would keep quiet. She finally accepted a large personal bonus in exchange for her silence in late 2008 as she needed the funds for her ill mother's medical bills. The investigation later found that Shazia Lo had been continually instructed, against her judgement, to report figures she knew to be grossly optimistic.

The investigation found that the auditor, JJC partnership (one of the largest in the country), had had its independence compromised by a large audit fee but also through receiving consultancy income from ZPT worth several times the audit fee. Because ZPT was such an important client for JJC, it had many resources and jobs entirely committed to the ZPT account. JJC had, it was found, knowingly signed off inaccurate accounts in order to protect the management of ZPT and their own senior partners engaged with the ZPT account. After the investigation, JJC's other clients gradually changed auditor, not wanting to be seen to have any connection with JJC. Accordingly, JJC's audit business has since closed down. This caused significant disturbance and upheaval in the audit industry.

Sometime later, Mr Xu argued that one of the reasons for the development of the complex ZPT business model was that it was thought to be necessary to manage the many risks that ZPT faced in its complex and turbulent business environment. He said that a multiplicity of overseas offices was necessary to address exchange rate risks, a belief challenged by some observers who said it was just to enable the ZPT board to make their internal controls and risk management less transparent.

The ZPT case came to the attention of Robert Nie, a senior national legislator in the country where ZPT had its head office. The country did not have any statutory corporate governance legislation and Mr Nie was furious at the ZPT situation because many of his voters had been badly financially affected by it. He believed that legislation was needed to ensure that a similar situation could not happen again. Mr Nie intends to make a brief speech in the national legislative assembly and has asked for your help, as an external consultant, to outline the case for his proposed legislation and draft some of its proposed provisions.

Required:

Draft the speech for Mr Nie to cover the following areas:

(a) **Explain the importance of sound corporate governance by assessing the consequences of the corporate governance failures at ZPT** **(10 marks)**

(b) **Construct the case for the mandatory external reporting of internal financial controls and risks** **(8 marks)**

(c) **Explain the broad areas that the proposed external report on internal controls should include, drawing on the case content as appropriate.** **(6 marks)**

(Total: 24 marks)

14 OLAND

After a recent financial crisis in the country of Oland, there had been a number of high profile company failures and a general loss of confidence in business. As a result, an updated corporate governance code was proposed, with changes to address these concerns.

Before the new code was published, there was a debate in Oland society about whether corporate governance provisions should be made rules-based, or remain principles-based as had been the case in the past.

One elected legislator, Martin Mung, whose constituency contained a number of the companies that had failed with resulting rises in unemployment, argued strongly that many of the corporate governance failures would not have happened if directors were legally accountable for compliance with corporate governance provisions. He said that 'you can't trust the markets to punish bad practice', saying that this was what had caused the problems in the first place. He said that Oland should become a rules-based jurisdiction because the current 'comply or explain' was ineffective as a means of controlling corporate governance.

Mr Mung was angered by the company failures in his constituency and believed that a lack of sound corporate governance contributed to the failure of important companies and the jobs they supported. He said that he wanted the new code to make it more difficult for companies to fail.

The new code was then issued, under a principles-based approach. One added provision in the new Oland code was to recommend a reduction in the re-election period of all directors from three years to one year. The code also required that when seeking re-election, there should be 'sufficient biographical details on each director to enable shareholders to take an informed decision'. The code explained that these measures were 'in the interests of greater accountability'.

Martin Mung believes that Oland should become a rules-based jurisdiction because the current 'comply or explain' approach is ineffective as a means of controlling corporate governance. Martin plans to raise the issue in parliament but is concerned to ensure that he gets his facts straight and is fully aware of any counter arguments that his opponents might use against him. He has therefore come to you, an external consultant, for assistance.

Required:

Draft a set of notes for Martin Mung that explains the difference between rules-based and principles-based approaches to corporate governance regulation, and sets out the counter argument that opponents could use against his belief that 'comply or explain' is ineffective.

(8 marks)

Professional skills marks will be awarded for demonstrating communication skills for constructing a persuasive counter – argument. **(2 marks)**

(Total: 10 marks)

15 LUM CO

Lum Co is a family business that has been wholly-owned and controlled by the Lum family since 1920. The current chief executive, Mr Gustav Lum, is the great grandson of the company's founder and has himself been in post as CEO since 1998.

Because the Lum family wanted to maintain a high degree of control, they operated a two-tier board structure: four members of the Lum family comprised the supervisory board and the other eight non-family directors comprised the operating board.

Despite being quite a large company with 5,000 employees, Lum Co never had any non-executive directors because they were not required in privately-owned companies in the country in which Lum Co was situated.

The four members of the Lum family valued the control of the supervisory board to ensure that the full Lum family's wishes (being the only shareholders) were carried out. This also enabled decisions to be made quickly, without the need to take everything before a meeting of the full board.

Starting in 2016, the two tiers of the board met in joint sessions to discuss a flotation (issuing public shares on the stock market) of 80% of the company. The issue of the family losing control was raised by the CEO's brother, Mr Crispin Lum. He said that if the company became listed, the Lum family would lose the freedom to manage the company as they wished, including supporting their own long-held values and beliefs. These values, he said, were managing for the long term and adopting a paternalistic management style. Other directors said that the new listing rules that would apply to the board, including compliance with the stock market's corporate governance codes of practice, would be expensive and difficult to introduce.

The flotation went ahead earlier this year. In order to comply with the new listing rules, Lum Co took on a number of non-executive directors (NEDs) and formed a unitary board. A number of problems arose around this time with NEDs feeling frustrated at the culture and management style in Lum Co, whilst the Lum family members found it difficult to make the transition to managing a public company with a unitary board. Gustav Lum said that it was very different from managing the company when it was privately owned by the Lum family. The human resources manager said that an effective induction programme for NEDs and some relevant continuing professional development (CPD) for existing executives might help to address the problems.

You have been approached, as an external management consultant, to assist with the transition to the new unitary structure.

Required:

Prepare a report for the unitary board covering the following:

(a) A comparison of the typical governance arrangements between a family business and a listed company, with an assessment of Crispin's view that the Lum family will 'lose the freedom to manage the company as they wish' after the flotation.

(10 marks)

(b) An assessment of the benefits of introducing an induction programme for the new NEDs, and requiring continual professional development (CPD) for the existing executives at Lum Co after its flotation. **(8 marks)**

Professional skills marks will be awarded for demonstrating evaluation skills for assessing the benefits of the proposed induction programme and CPD **(2 marks)**

(Total: 20 marks)

16 OSKAL PETROLEUM

Recent changes to environmental regulations have shifted the onus of responsibility onto companies to prove that their actions did not cause environmental harm, rather than requiring the regulators to prove where fault lies. The board of Oskal Petroleum decided to review its strategic position and how this regulatory change could impact on Oskal Petroleum. The directors concluded that the new regulations potentially exposed their business to considerable costs if they were required to deal with the aftermath of a spillage of any environmentally hazardous substance, such as oil. These costs would be above and beyond any fines or compensation orders which might flow from a related prosecution.

A major spillage from a competitor's oil rig off the African coast several years ago is still under investigation and so far it has resulted in hundreds of millions in related costs, which damaged the business significantly and caused a large and sustained drop in the share price.

Oskal Petroleum, although based in Europe, is a global business with onshore and offshore oil fields in four continents. It has always enjoyed good relations with the host governments in those countries where it has operations, but recently several governments have adopted a more interventionist approach to domestic environmental policy in the aftermath of the African oil disaster. Consequently, the finance director strongly advised the board to set aside an amount of cash equal to 10% of profits, to mitigate against the impact of any costs which might arise if an Oskal oil field suffered a major spillage. The finance director's proposal was approved alongside the decision to undertake a formal environmental risk assessment of all Oskal operational assets throughout the world, particularly in those countries where governments were taking a keen interest in influencing the environmental and social policies of businesses.

In a further attempt to pacify its active stakeholders, and show shareholders that they were taking environmental risks seriously, the board decided to fully adopt the integrated reporting framework. It planned to include the findings from the environmental risk assessment in the next annual report.

Required:

(a) Evaluate the sources of environmental risk which are likely to be identified during Oskal's forthcoming assessment, and suggest ways the company could reduce their impact. **(8 marks)**

(b) Explain the concept of integrated reporting <IR>, and explore how an integrated report covering the six capitals would provide insights for the shareholders and other stakeholders of Oskal Petroleum. **(8 marks)**

(Total: 16 marks)

17   JGP CHEMICALS LTD

At a board meeting of JGP Chemicals Ltd, the directors were discussing some recent negative publicity arising from the accidental emission of a chemical pollutant into the local river. As well as it resulting in a large fine from the courts, the leak had created a great deal of controversy in the local community that relied on the polluted river for its normal use (including drinking). A prominent community leader spoke for those affected when she said that a leak of this type must never happen again or JGP would suffer the loss of support from the community. She also reminded JGP that it attracts 65% of its labour from the local community.

As a response to the problems that arose after the leak, the JGP board decided to consult an expert on whether the publication of a full annual environmental report might help to mitigate future environmental risks. The expert, Professor Appo (a prominent academic), said that the company would need to establish an annual environmental audit before they could issue a report. He said that the environmental audit should include, in addition to a review and evaluation of JGP's safety controls, a full audit of the environmental impact of JGP's supply chain. He said that these components would be very important in addressing the concerns of a growing group of investors who are worried about such things. Professor Appo said that all chemical companies had a structural environmental risk and JGP was no exception to this. As major consumers of natural chemical resources and producers of potentially hazardous outputs, Professor Appo said that chemical companies should be aware of the wide range of ways in which they can affect the environment. CEO Keith Miasma agreed with Professor Appo and added that because JGP was in chemicals, any environmental issue had the potential to affect JGP's overall reputation among a wide range of stakeholders.

When the board was discussing the issue of sustainability in connection with the environmental audit, the finance director said that sustainability reporting would not be necessary as the company was already sustainable because it had no 'going concern' issues. He said that JGP had been in business for over 50 years, should be able to continue for many years to come and was therefore sustainable. As far as he was concerned, this was all that was meant by sustainability.

In the discussion that followed, the board noted that in order to signal its seriousness to the local community and to investors, the environmental audit should be as thorough as possible and that as much information should be made available to the public 'in the interests of transparency'. It was agreed that contents of the audit (the agreed metrics) should be robust and with little room left for interpretation – they wanted to be able to demonstrate that they had complied with their agreed metrics for the environmental audit.

Required:

(a)   Explain 'sustainability' in the context of environmental auditing and criticise the finance director's understanding of sustainability.   **(6 marks)**

(b)   Explain the three stages in an environmental audit and explore, using information from the case, the issues that JGP will have in developing these stages.   **(9 marks)**

(c)   Explain why the environmental risks at JGP are strategic rather than operational.
  (6 marks)

(Total: 21 marks)

18   CHEMCO

Chemco is a well-established listed European chemical company involved in research into, and the production of, a range of chemicals used in industries such as agrochemicals, oil and gas, paint, plastics and building materials. A strategic priority recognised by the Chemco board some time ago was to increase its international presence as a means of gaining international market share and servicing its increasingly geographically dispersed customer base. The Chemco board, which operated as a unitary structure, identified JPX as a possible acquisition target because of its good product 'fit' with Chemco and the fact that its geographical coverage would significantly strengthen Chemco's internationalisation strategy.

Based outside Europe in a region of growth in the chemical industry, JPX was seen by analysts as a good opportunity for Chemco, especially as JPX's recent flotation had provided potential access to a controlling shareholding through the regional stock market where JPX operated.

When the board of Chemco met to discuss the proposed acquisition of JPX, a number of issues were tabled for discussion. Bill White, Chemco's chief executive, had overseen the research process that had identified JPX as a potential acquisition target. He was driving the process and wanted the Chemco board of directors to approve the next move, which was to begin the valuation process with a view to making an offer to JPX's shareholders. Bill said that the strategic benefits of this acquisition was in increasing overseas market share and gaining economies of scale.

While Chemco was a public company, JPX had been family owned and operated for most of its 35 year history. Seventy-five percent of the share capital was floated on its own country's stock exchange two years ago, but Leena Sharif, Chemco's company secretary suggested that the corporate governance requirements in JPX's country were not as rigorous as in many parts of the world.

She also suggested that the family business culture was still present in JPX and pointed out that it operated a two-tier board with members of the family on the upper tier. At the last annual general meeting, observers noticed that the JPX board, mainly consisting of family members, had 'dominated discussions' and had discouraged the expression of views from the company's external shareholders. JPX had no non-executive directors and none of the board committee structure that many listed companies like Chemco had in place.

Bill reported that although JPX's department heads were all directors, they were not invited to attend board meetings when strategy and management monitoring issues were being discussed. They were, he said, treated more like middle management by the upper tier of the JPX board and that important views may not be being heard when devising strategy. Leena suggested that these features made the JPX board's upper tier less externally accountable and less likely to take advice when making decisions. She said that board accountability was fundamental to public trust and that JPX's board might do well to recognise this, especially if the acquisition were to go ahead.

Chemco's finance director, Susan Brown advised caution over the whole acquisition proposal. She saw the proposal as being very risky. In addition to the uncertainties over exposure to foreign markets, she believed that Chemco would also have difficulties with integrating JPX into the Chemco culture and structure. While Chemco was fully compliant with corporate governance best practice, the country in which JPX was based had few corporate governance requirements. Manprit Randhawa, Chemco's operations director, asked Bill if he knew anything about JPX's risk exposure. Manprit suggested that the acquisition of JPX might expose Chemco to a number of risks that could not only affect the success of the proposed acquisition but also, potentially, Chemco itself. Bill replied that he would look at the risks in more detail if the Chemco board agreed to take the proposal forward to its next stage.

Finance director Susan Brown, had obtained the most recent annual report for JPX and highlighted what she considered to be an interesting, but unexplained, comment about 'negative local environmental impact' in its accounts. She asked chief executive Bill White if he could find out what the comment meant and whether JPX had any plans to make provision for any environmental impact. Bill White was able to report, based on his previous dealings with JPX, that it did not produce any voluntary environmental reporting.

The Chemco board broadly supported the idea of environmental reporting although company secretary Leena Sharif recently told Bill White that she was unaware of the meaning of the terms 'environmental footprint' and 'environmental reporting' and so couldn't say whether she was supportive or not. It was agreed, however, that relevant information on JPX's environmental performance and risk would be necessary if the acquisition went ahead.

Required:

(a) Evaluate JPX's current corporate governance arrangements and explain why they are likely to be considered inadequate by the Chemco board. **(10 marks)**

(b) Manprit suggested that the acquisition of JPX might expose Chemco to a number of risks. Identify the risks that Chemco might incur in acquiring JPX and explain how risk can be assessed. **(15 marks)**

(c) Construct the case for JPX adopting a unitary board structure after the proposed acquisition. Your answer should include an explanation of the advantages of unitary boards and a convincing case FOR the JPX board changing to a unitary structure. **(8 marks)**

Professional skills marks will be awarded for demonstrating communication skills in constructing a persuasive argument for the JPX board changing to a unitary structure. **(2 marks)**

(Total: 35 marks)

19   KK

KK is a large listed company. When a non-executive directorship of KK Limited became available, John Soria was nominated to fill the vacancy. John is the brother-in-law of KK's chief executive Ken Kava. John is also the CEO of Soria Supplies Ltd, KK's largest single supplier and is, therefore, very familiar with KK and its industry. He has sold goods to KK for over 20 years and is on friendly terms with all of the senior officers in the company. In fact last year, Soria Supplies appointed KK's finance director, Susan Schwab, to a non-executive directorship on its board. The executive directors of KK all know and like John and so plan to ask the nominations committee to appoint him before the next AGM.

KK has recently undergone a period of rapid growth and has recently entered several new overseas markets, some of which, according to the finance director, are riskier than the domestic market. Ken Kava, being the dominant person on the KK board, has increased the risk exposure of the company according to some investors. They say that because most of the executive directors are less experienced, they rarely question his overseas expansion strategy. This expansion has also created a growth in employee numbers and an increase in the number of executive directors, mainly to manage the increasingly complex operations of the company. It was thought by some that the company lacked experience and knowledge of international markets as it expanded and that this increased the risk of the strategy's failure. Some shareholders believed that the aggressive strategy, led by Ken Kava, has been careless as it has exposed KK Limited to some losses on overseas direct investments made before all necessary information on the investment was obtained.

As a large listed company, the governance of KK is important to its shareholders. Fin Brun is one of KK's largest shareholders and holds a large portfolio of shares including 8% of the shares in KK. At the last AGM he complained to KK's chief executive, Ken Kava, that he needed more information on directors' performance.

Fin said that he didn't know how to vote on board reappointments because he had no information on how they had performed in their jobs. Mr Kava said that the board intended to include a corporate governance section in future annual reports to address this and to provide other information that shareholders had asked for.

He added, however, that he would not be able to publish information on the performance of individual executive directors as this was too complicated and actually not the concern of shareholders. It was, he said, the performance of the board as a whole that was important and he (Mr Kava) would manage the performance targets of individual directors.

Required:

(a) **Explain the term 'conflict of interest' in the context of non-executive directors and discuss the potential conflicts of interest relating to KK and Soria Supplies if John Soria were to become a non-executive director of KK Limited.**   **(8 marks)**

(b) **Assess the advantages of appointing experienced and effective non-executive directors to the KK board during the period in which the company was growing rapidly.**   **(7 marks)**

(Total: 15 marks)

20   'HELP-WITH-LIFE' (HWL)

'Help-with-life' (HWL) is a charitable organisation established ten years ago. Its stated purpose is, 'to help individuals and families with social problems and related issues.' Its work, in a large city with people from many countries and backgrounds, involves advising, counselling, giving practical support to service users (the people who come for help). Over the years it has been operating, HWL has realised that the best outcomes are achieved when the staff member understands and sympathises with the service users' social norms, ethical and cultural beliefs.

40% of HWL's funding comes from local government. This means that HWL has to account for its use of that portion of its funding and comply with several rules imposed by local government. One of these rules concerns demonstrating appropriate diversity amongst the managers of services such as those delivered by HWL. It requires the charity management team to involve the widest feasible range of people and to reflect the demographic make-up of the community.

HWL has recently had to replace a number of executive and non-executive members of its board. The external auditor suggested that setting up a nominations committee would help in these board appointments. The CEO, Marian Ngogo, has always stressed that all directors should share the ethical values of HWL and agree to take reduced rewards because, 'every dollar we pay a director is a dollar less we are spending on service delivery.' She stressed that the culture in a charity was very different from a commercial ('for profit') business and that staff and directors must share the ethical stance of HWL and had to accept a different approach to social responsibility if they joined.

Required:

(a)   Explain the advantages of diversity on the board of HWL.   **(8 marks)**

(b)   Explain 'corporate social responsibility' (CSR) and discuss the ways in which CSR and the ethical stance might differ between HWL and a commercial 'for profit' business.   **(9 marks)**

(Total: 17 marks)

21   VESTEL

Vestel is a drinks manufacturer that specialises in producing wine and spirit products for consumption in its home markets and abroad. The company has been very successful in recent years culminating in its ability to gain listing on the local stock exchange.

Acceptance as a member of the stock exchange has placed pressure on the board of directors to ensure the company is fully compliant with the principles-based governance regime currently in operation. This compliance includes the need for appropriate committee structures and support for all board members in ensuring appropriate skills and expertise are developed over time.

As a relatively small public company Vestel has needed to be innovative and adaptive in order to compete against global competitors that operate in its markets. In addition, it has recently been faced with a number of market challenges that threaten shareholder prospects over the next period. These include the rising price of grapes, molasses and grain due to a series of harsh winters and poor harvests as well as rising costs in energy and transport. At the retail end, government taxation on alcoholic drinks has dramatically increased following public outcry over levels of alcohol abuse amongst the country's citizens.

Ethics, environmentalism, skills in government lobbying and operational infrastructure are all seen as key areas for improvement following a recent review of board performance. In response the current board are discussing whether a nomination committee should be created for the first time in the company's history in order to recruit a number of non-executive directors onto the board. Finding suitable candidates may be difficult in a country where the size of the economy and number of large companies is relatively small.

You have been asked, as an external consultant, for advice on this matter.

Required:

Write a brief report to the Board that

(a)   Explains why a nomination committee is suggested to be essential for effective board operations.   **(6 marks)**

(b)   Explains how the committee might tackle the recruitment process.   **(7 marks)**

(Total: 13 marks)

22   TOMATO BANK

Five years ago, George Woof was appointed chief executive officer (CEO) of Tomato Bank, one of the largest global banks. Mr Woof had a successful track record in senior management in America and his appointment was considered very fortunate for the company. Analysts rated him as one of the world's best bankers and the other directors of Tomato Bank looked forward to his appointment and a significant strengthening of the business.

One of the factors needed to secure Mr Woof's services was his reward package. Prior to his acceptance of the position, Tomato Bank's remuneration committee (comprised entirely of non-executives) received a letter from Mr Woof saying that because his track record was so strong, they could be assured of many years of sustained growth under his leadership. In discussions concerning his pension, however, he asked for a generous non-performance related pension settlement to be written into his contract so that it would be payable whenever he decided to leave the company (subject to a minimum term of two years) and regardless of his performance as CEO.

Such was the euphoria about his appointment that his request was approved. Furthermore in the hasty manner in which Mr Woof's reward package was agreed, the split of his package between basic and performance-related components was not carefully scrutinised. Everybody on the remuneration committee was so certain that he would bring success to Tomato Bank that the individual details of his reward package were not considered important.

In addition, the remuneration committee received several letters from Tomato Bank's finance director, John Temba, saying, in direct terms, that they should offer Mr Woof 'whatever he wants' to ensure that he joins the company and that the balance of benefits was not important as long as he joined. Two of the non-executive directors on the remuneration committee were former colleagues of Mr Woof and told the finance director they would take his advice and make sure they put a package together that would ensure Mr Woof joined the company.

Once in post, Mr Woof led an excessively aggressive strategy that involved high growth in the loan and mortgage books financed from a range of sources, some of which proved unreliable. In the fifth year of his appointment, the failure of some of the sources of funds upon which the growth of the bank was based led to severe financing difficulties at Tomato Bank. Shareholders voted to replace George Woof as CEO. They said he had been reckless in exposing the company to so much risk in growing the loan book without adequately covering it with reliable sources of funds.

When he left, the press reported that despite his failure in the job, he would be leaving with what the newspapers referred to as an 'obscenely large' pension. Some shareholders were angry and said that Mr Woof was being 'rewarded for failure'. When Mr Woof was asked if he might voluntarily forego some of his pension in recognition of his failure in the job, he refused, saying that he was contractually entitled to it and so would be keeping it all.

Required:

(a)   **Criticise the performance of Tomato Bank's remuneration committee in agreeing Mr Woof's reward package.**   **(10 marks)**

(b)   **Explain, with justification, the components of a more balanced package of benefits that should have been used to reward Mr Woof.**   **(10 marks)**

(Total: 20 marks)

23   ABC CO

In a recent case, it emerged that Frank Finn, a sales director at ABC Co, had been awarded a substantial over-inflation annual basic pay award with no apparent link to performance.

When a major institutional shareholder, Swanland Investments, looked into the issue, it emerged that Mr Finn had a cross directorship with Joe Ng, an executive director of DEF Co. Mr Ng was a non-executive director of ABC and chairman of its remunerations committee. Swanland Investments argued at the annual general meeting that there was 'a problem with the independence' of Mr Ng and further, that Mr Finn's remuneration package as a sales director was considered to be poorly aligned to Swanland's interests because it was too much weighted by basic pay and contained inadequate levels of incentive.

Swanland Investments proposed that the composition of Mr Finn's remuneration package be reconsidered by the remunerations committee and that Mr Ng should not be present during the discussion.

Another of the larger institutional shareholders, Hanoi House, objected to this, proposing instead that Mr Ng and Mr Finn both resign from their respective non-executive directorships as there was 'clear evidence of malpractice'. Swanland considered this too radical a step, as Mr Ng's input was, in its opinion, valuable on ABC's board.

Required:

(a)   **Explain FOUR roles of a remunerations committee and how the cross directorship undermines these roles at ABC Co.**   **(12 marks)**

(b)   **Swanland Investments believed Mr Finn's remunerations package to be 'poorly aligned' to its interests. With reference to the different components of a director's remunerations package, explain how Mr Finn's remuneration might be more aligned to shareholders' interests at ABC Co.**   **(8 marks)**

(Total: 20 marks)

C: STRATEGY

24 TMZ

TMZ is a music company based in the developed country of Artazia. It was founded in 1963 when it started to sign emerging rock and roll artists to its record label. TMZ offers a contract in which the artists receive royalties based on the sales of their music. As part of this contract, TMZ record the music, distribute it and promote it. Most of the contracts are for a defined number of songs or records. For example, in 1980, TMZ contracted the heavy metal band, Vortex31, to produce ten albums, to be delivered over seven years. Extracted financial data for the period 1965–2000 is given in Table one. During these years TMZ successfully signed bands offering different and emerging types of music (pop, punk, garage, grunge, patio) and also successfully altered the physical media of distribution, from vinyl records to tape cassette and subsequently to compact disc (CD).

All figures in $million	1965	1970	1980	1990	2000
Revenue	10	70	120	150	170
Gross profit	4	30	45	50	50
Net profit	3	22	30	30	25

Table one: Revenue and profit information: TMZ (1965–2000)

The company remained profitable in this period, despite musicians taking longer to produce albums and senior management adopting a relaxed and indulgent approach to their creative artists.

In 1999, the first file sharing company was formed in Artazia, allowing people to easily share their music files with each other. During the next decade, numerous file sharing and digital downloading companies were launched. As early as 2003, the possible implications of this growth in file sharing and digital downloading were highlighted by a number of employees in TMZ. However, senior management at TMZ were dismissive of this threat, suggesting that the contracts with their artists were 'watertight'. Table two shows revenue and profit information for 2003–2007.

All figures in $million	2003	2004	2005	2006	2007
Revenue	165	150	130	100	80
Gross profit	45	30	10	0	(10)
Net profit	20	5	(15)	(20)	(30)

Table two: Revenue and profit information: TMZ (2003–2007)

Senior management at TMZ believed that this decline in performance was due to them providing the 'wrong music, promoted to the wrong people at the wrong price'. During this period the company signed new artists, increased advertising and cut prices. However, this did not halt its decline.

Losses were also made in 2008 and 2009 and the company was only kept afloat by fresh injections of shareholder capital. During these years, the company took legal action against what they considered illegal downloading and file sharing. It won a number of small cases but its actions angered many music fans, who felt that music labels had been greedy in the past. It also upset some of its artists who now benefited from the opportunity the internet gave them to sell music directly to their fans.

In 2009, a new CEO was appointed from outside the music industry. In 2010 he announced a new strategy. TMZ was no longer interested in contracting new artists to the label. Instead it would focus on deriving profit from its established artists and music catalogue.

He came to licensing agreements with some large digital downloading operators and stores, allowing them to access or sell the music of established artists. However, he continued litigation against others. He also began to generate revenue from licensing the music for use in computer games, television advertisements and personalised ringtones.

In 2011 the company reported a gross profit for the first time since 2005. In each subsequent year it recorded a small net profit. The CEO stated that TMZ was now a 'slimmer, fitter company. We are a learning organisation, developing the resilience needed to trade successfully in the ever-changing digital music age'. However, he warned that TMZ, like others in the industry, would continue to pursue actions against the illegal downloading of music. 'There is a generation where many people consider music and all creative content should be free. However, we see signs that this assumption is becoming less widely held. The next generation is questioning it. Like many others, we continue to seek ways of distributing music which is fair to both the consumer and the artist. We are constantly monitoring trends and patterns in consumer behaviour. We will not get caught out like we were ten years ago. We won't be fooled again!'

Required:

The CEO of TMZ is concerned by the past strategic drift of the company. He wants to learn from the organisations past mistakes.

Analyse the performance of TMZ from 1965 to the present, including any evidence of past strategic drift. **(15 marks)**

Professional skills marks will be awarded for demonstrating analytical skills in considering the causes of the strategic drift. **(2 marks)**

(Total: 17 marks)

25 SWIFT

Ambion is the third largest industrial country in the world. It is densely populated with a high standard of living. Joe Swift Transport (known as Swift) is the largest logistics company in Ambion, owning 1500 trucks. It is a private limited company with all shares held by the Swift family. It has significant haulage and storage contracts with retail and supermarket chains in Ambion. The logistics market-place is mature and extremely competitive and Swift has become market leader through a combination of economies of scale, cost efficiencies, innovative IT solutions and clever branding.

However, the profitability of the sector is under increased pressure from a recently elected government that is committed to heavily taxing fuel and reducing expenditure on roads in favour of alternative forms of transport. It has also announced a number of taxes on vehicles which have high carbon emission levels as well as reducing the maximum working hours and increasing the national minimum wage for employees. The company is perceived as a good performer in its sector. The 20X9 financial results reported a Return on Capital Employed of 18%, a gross profit margin of 17% and a net profit margin of 9.15%. The accounts also showed a current liquidity ratio of 1.55 and an acid test ratio of 1.15. The gearing ratio is currently 60% with an interest cover ratio of 8.

10 years ago the northern political bloc split up and nine new independent states were formed. One of these states was Ecuria. The people of Ecuria (known as Ecurians) traditionally have a strong work ethic and a passion for precision and promptness. Since the formation of the state, their hard work has been rewarded by strong economic growth, a higher standard of living and an increased demand for goods which were once perceived as unobtainable luxuries. Since the formation of the state, the government of Ecuria has pursued a policy of privatisation. It has also invested heavily in infrastructure, particularly the road transport system, required to support the increased economic activity in the country.

The state haulage operator (EVM) was sold off to two Ecurian investors who raised the finance to buy it from a foreign bank. The capital markets in Ecuria are still immature and the government has not wished to interfere with or bolster them. EVM now has 700 modern trucks and holds all the major logistics contracts in the country.

It is praised for its prompt delivery of goods. Problems in raising finance have made it difficult for significant competitors to emerge. Most are family firms, each of which operates about 20 trucks making local deliveries within one of Ecuria's 20 regions.

These two investors now wish to realise their investment in EVM and have announced that it is for sale. In principle, Swift are keen to buy the company and are currently evaluating its possible acquisition. Swift's management perceive that their capabilities in logistics will greatly enhance the profitability of EVM. The financial results for EVM are shown in Figure 1. Swift has acquired a number of smaller Ambion companies in the last decade, but has no experience of acquiring foreign companies, or indeed, working in Ecuria.

Joe Swift is also contemplating a more radical change. He is becoming progressively disillusioned with Ambion. In a recent interview he said that 'trading here is becoming impossible. The government is more interested in over regulating enterprise than stimulating growth'. He is considering moving large parts of his logistics operation to another country and Ecuria is one of the possibilities he is considering.

Figure 1 – Extract from financial results: EVM 20X9

Extract from the statement of financial position

Assets	$million
Non-current assets	
Intangible assets	2,000
Property, plant, equipment	6,100
	8,100
Current assets	$million
Inventories	100
Trade receivables	900
Cash and cash equivalents	200
	1,200
Total assets	**9,300**
Equity and liabilities	$million
Equity	
Share capital	5,700
Retained earnings	50
Total equity	5,750

Non-current liabilities

Long-term borrowings	2,500

Current liabilities

Trade payables	1,000
Current tax payable	50
	1,050
Total liabilities	3,550
Total equity and liabilities	**9,300**

Extract from statement of profit or loss

	$million
Revenue	20,000
Cost of sales	(16,000)
Gross profit	4,000
Administrative expenses	(2,500)
Finance cost	(300)
Profit before tax	1,200
Income tax expense	(50)
Profit for the year	1,150

Required:

(a) Assess, using both financial and non-financial measures, the attractiveness, from Swift's perspective, of EVM as an acquisition target. **(15 marks)**

(b) Examine the factors which could influence Swift's decision to move a large part of its logistics business to Ecuria. **(10 marks)**

(Total: 25 marks)

26   BOWLAND

Bowland Carpets Ltd is a major producer of carpets within the UK. The company was taken over by its present parent company, Universal Carpet Inc., in 20X3. Universal Carpet is a giant, vertically integrated carpet manufacturing and retailing business, based within the USA but with interests all over the world.

Bowland Carpets operates within the UK in various market segments, including the high value contract and industrial carpeting area – hotels and office blocks, etc. – and in the domestic (household) market. Within the latter the choice is reasonably wide, ranging from luxury carpets down to the cheaper products. Industrial and contract carpets contribute 25% of Bowland Carpets' total annual turnover which is currently $80 million. Up until 15 years ago the turnover of the company was growing at 8% per annum, but since 20X2 sales revenue has dropped by 5% per annum in real terms.

Bowland Carpets has traditionally been known as a producer of high quality carpets, but at competitive prices. It has a powerful brand name, and it has been able to protect this by producing the cheaper, lower quality products under a secondary brand name. It has also maintained a good relationship with the many carpet distributors throughout the UK, particularly the mainstream retail organisations.

The recent decline in carpet sales revenue, partly recession induced, has worried the US parent company. It has recognised that the increasing concentration within the European carpet manufacturing sector has led to aggressive competition within a low growth industry. It does not believe that overseas sales growth by Bowland Carpets is an attractive proposition as this would compete with other Universal Carpet companies. It does, however, consider that vertical integration into retailing (as already practised within the USA) is a serious option. This would give the UK company increased control over its sales and reduce its exposure to competition.

The president of the parent company has asked Jeremy Smiles, managing director of Bowland Carpets, to address this issue and provide guidance to the US board of directors. Funding does not appear to be a major issue at this time as the parent company has large cash reserves on its balance sheet.

Required:

Acting in the capacity of Jeremy Smiles you are required to outline the extent to which the distinctive competences of Bowland Carpets conform to the key success factors required for the proposed strategy change. **(10 marks)**

27 **ONE ENERGY PLC** *Walk in the footsteps of a top tutor*

OneEnergy plc supplies over half of the electricity and gas in the country. It is an expanding, aggressive company which has recently acquired two smaller, but significant, competitors.

Just over a year ago, OneEnergy purchased the RitePay payroll software package from RiteSoftware. The recently appointed Human Resources (HR) director of OneEnergy recommended the package because he had used it successfully at his previous employer – a major charity. His unreserved recommendation was welcomed by the board because the company was currently running three incompatible payroll systems. The purchase of the RitePay payroll system appeared to offer the opportunity to quickly consolidate the three separate payroll systems into one improved solution. The board decided to purchase the software without evaluating alternative solutions.

It was felt that payroll rules and processes were relatively standard and so there was no need to look further than a package recommended by the HR director. The software was purchased and a project initiated for converting the data from the current systems and for training users in the features and functions of the new software.

However, it soon became apparent that there were problems with the suitability of the RitePay software package. Firstly, OneEnergy had a wide variety of reward and pay schemes to reflect previous employment in the acquired companies and to accommodate a wide range of different skills and grades. Not all of these variations could be handled by the package. Consequently, amendments had to be commissioned from the software house.

This led to unplanned costs and also to delays in implementation. Secondly, it also became clear that the software was not as user-friendly as the previous systems. Users had problems understanding some of the terminology and structure of the software. 'It just does not work like we do', commented one frustrated user. Consequently users made more errors than expected and training costs exceeded their budget.

Three months ago, another set of amendments was requested from RiteSoftware to allow one of the acquired companies in OneEnergy to pay bonuses to lorry drivers in a certain way. Despite repeated requests, the amendments were not received. Two weeks ago, it was announced that RiteSoftware had filed for bankruptcy and all software support was suspended. Just before this was announced the HR director of OneEnergy left the company to take up a similar post in the public sector.

OneEnergy has engaged W&P consultants to advise them on the RitePay project. An interim report from W&P suggests that OneEnergy should abandon the RitePay package. 'It is clear to us that RitePay never had the functionality required to fulfil the variety of requirements inevitable in a company the size of OneEnergy.' They also commented that this could have been avoided if the project had followed the competitive procurement policy defined in company operating procedures.

W&P also reports that:

- The procurement department at OneEnergy had requested two years of accounts from RiteSoftware. These were provided (see Appendix 1 below) but not interpreted or used in the selection process in any way. W&P concluded 'that there were clear signs that the company was in difficulty and this should have led to further investigation'.

- They discovered that the former HR director of OneEnergy was the brother of the managing director of RiteSoftware.

Required:

W&P concluded in their report 'that there were clear signs that the company (RiteSoftware) was in difficulty and this should have led to further investigation'.

Assess, using the financial information available, the validity of W&P's conclusion.

(13 marks)

Professional skills marks will be awarded for demonstrating professional scepticism in probing and questioning the information provided. **(2 marks)**

(Total: 15 marks)

Appendix 1: RiteSoftware Accounts

Extract from the statement of financial position$000

Assets

Non-current assets	**20X8**	**20X7**
Property, plant and equipment	30	25
Goodwill	215	133
	245	158
Current assets		
Inventories	3	2
Trade receivables	205	185
	208	187
Total assets	453	345
Liabilities		
Current liabilities		
Trade payables	257	178
Current tax payable	1	2
Bank overdraft	10	25
	268	205
Non-current liabilities		
Long-term borrowings	80	35
Total liabilities	348	240
Equity		
Share capital	105	105
Total equity and liabilities	453	345

Extract from the statement of statement of profit and loss

	20X8	20X7
Revenue	2,650	2,350
Cost of sales	(2,600)	(2,300)
Gross profit	50	50
Other costs	(30)	(20)
Finance costs	(10)	(4)
Profit before tax	10	26
Income tax expense	(1)	(2)
Profit for the year	9	24

Extract from the annual report

	20X8	20X7
Number of staff	90	70

28   MOOR FARM

Moor Farm is a large estate in the rural district of Cornaille. The estate covers a large area of forest, upland and farmland. It also includes two villages, and although many of the properties in these villages have been sold off to private homeowners, the estate still owns properties which it rents out. The estate also has a large mansion house set inside a landscape garden designed in the 19th century by James Kent. The garden, although now overgrown and neglected, is the only surviving example of his work in the district. The estate was left as a gift to a charitable trust ten years ago. The trust is based at the estate. A condition of the gift to the trust was that the upland and forest should be freely accessible to visitors.

The estate has a manager, four full-time staff and 45 volunteers. These volunteers undertake most of the work on the estate, including the continuing excavation of Kent's original garden design. They are happy, well-motivated and fully support the current manager who is due to retire in the very near future. Three of the volunteers have become acknowledged experts on land management, through their work on the estate. Government grants for initiatives such as tree planting, protected pasture land and rural employment have been received by the estate in the past. However, a recent change in government means that this funding is unlikely to continue. This will also affect funding for the maintenance of the mansion. It was built almost 80 years ago when the climate of the area was much colder and drier. Recent warm wet winters have caused the fabric of the building to decay and increased the cost of maintaining it.

The estate has appointed a new manager who is due to take over the estate when the current manager retires. She is working alongside the current manager so that she understands her responsibilities and how the estate works.

As a one-off project, she has commissioned a stakeholder survey which has requested information on the visitor experience to help with a planned re-design of the estate's website. The website is generally thought to be well structured and presented, but it receives fewer visitors than might reasonably be expected. It provides mainly static information about the estate and forthcoming events but currently users cannot interact with the site in anyway.

Here are some extracts from the survey:

'I live in one of the villages and I am angry about visitors crowding around the village attractions – the tearooms, the craft shops, the souvenir stalls. We feel that we are prisoners in our own village and the traffic is terrible.' **Homeowner, from a village on the estate**

'We had a good day, but the weather was awful. If we had known it was going to rain all day, then we probably would have postponed the visit until a fine day. It spoilt a family day out.' **Visitor with small family**

'We were very disappointed, on arrival, to find that the family fun day was fully booked.' **Visitor who had travelled 100 kms with two small children to visit a special event**

'We all love it here, but we didn't know you had a website!! We almost had to type in the complete website address before we found it! I am sure more people would come if they could only find the website!' **Visitor aged mid-20s**

'As usual, we had a great time here and took great photos. It would have been nice to be able to share our pleasure with other people. We would recommend it to anyone who loves the outdoors.' **Visitor – family with teenage children**

'We met the volunteers who were excavating the buildings in the landscape garden. They were so helpful and knowledgeable. They turned something that looked like a series of small walls into something so much more tangible.' **Visitor – elderly couple**

'I was disappointed that I was not allowed into the farmland with my dog. As a human being, I have the right to roam. It is a basic human right.' **Visitor – elderly female dog-walker**

'We are regular visitors and we really want to know what is going on! There are many of us who would like to really be involved with the estate and help it thrive. We need more than just occasional questionnaires.' **Visitor – hiking group**

'We came out for a nice walk and ended up dodging cyclists. Next time we will go somewhere where they are not welcome.' **Visitor – hiking group**

'As a farmer, I am appalled with the reckless attitude of some dog walkers. Last week, I lost two sheep, ravaged by dogs that should not have been off their leads.' **Farmer – estate tenant**

'I'm a volunteer and I love it here. We are a happy, social group of people. I hope the new manager is not going to change things.' **Volunteer**

Required:

(a)   Evaluate the strategic position of the estate with specific reference to the expectations of stakeholders, to the external environmental factors beyond the control of the estate and to the strategic capabilities of the estate itself. (15 marks)

(b)   Discuss how the website could be further developed to address some of the issues highlighted in the survey.   (10 marks)

(Total: 25 marks)

29   NOBLE PETS

Noble Pets is one of four companies which dominate the pet food market in the country of Brellia. Between them, these four companies share 90% of the market. Noble Pets was established in 1930 in the market town of Milton. Its factory (plant) was updated in 1970 with new canning and labelling technology. However, further developments and expansion to the factory site were prevented by the rapid growth of housing in Milton. The factory, which was once on the edge of the town, is now surrounded by modern housing development. The town is also relatively remote from the motorway network which has been developed in Brellia since 1960. Trucks transporting goods in and out of the plant have to negotiate relatively minor rural roads and also have to pass through the town centre of Milton, which is often very congested. Furthermore, the large 44 tonne trucks which Noble Pets and its competitors use, wherever possible, to distribute cans of pet food to wholesalers and supermarket distribution centres are banned from the centre of the town. Thus distribution out of the Milton plant is undertaken with smaller 36 tonne trucks, which are less cost-effective. However, residents find even this size of truck too large, complaining that they keep them awake at night.

The Milton plant is solely concerned with the production of moist pet food. Raw foodstuff and empty unlabelled cans are brought into the plant, where the foodstuff is cooked and put into cans which are then labelled and distributed to wholesalers or supermarket distribution centres. Many of these distribution centres, like Noble Pets' competitors, are now located on or near the motorway network. Although the recipe for the pet food is very similar to its competitors, Noble Pets has a reputation for producing a quality product.

This quality has been promoted ever since the company's formation by clever marketing campaigns which stress the importance of giving your pet good food, and the superior nature of Noble Pets' products to its competitors. This has traditionally been supported by free fact guides and information promoting responsible pet ownership and nutrition. The company now has a website dedicated to giving advice and guidance. This advice appears to be unbiased, although recommended solutions to pet problems often involve Noble Pets' products.

Noble Pets is currently reviewing its operations and has asked external consultants to assess the Milton plant from a value chain perspective. It has provided the following table (Table One) to help in that analysis. Average figures for its competitors are also provided.

Production cost of a six can pack of moist pet food	Milton Factory	Competitor A	Competitor B	Competitor C
All figures in $				
Raw foodstuff costs	0.10	0.10	0.09	0.15
Cost of cans	0.05	0.10	0.06	0.05
Direct labour costs	0.25	0.25	0.30	0.24
Production costs	0.30	0.25	0.20	0.26
Transport costs (good inward)	0.15	0.10	0.10	0.12
Transport costs (good outward)	0.10	0.05	0.05	0.08
Sales price (to customer)	**1.25**	**1.15**	**1.10**	**1.20**

Table One: Direct costs of the Milton plant compared to major competitors

Required:

Evaluate the strengths and weaknesses of the Milton plant from the perspective of the primary activities of a value chain analysis. **(15 marks)**

30 INDEPENDENT LIVING

Introduction

IL (Independent Living) is a charity that provides living aids to help elderly and disabled people live independently in their own home. These aids include walkers, wheelchairs, walking frames, crutches, mobility scooters, bath lifts and bathroom and bedroom accessories.

IL aims to employ people who would find it difficult or impossible to work in a conventional office or factory. IL's charitable aim is to provide the opportunity for severely disabled people to 'work with dignity and achieve financial independence'. IL currently employs 200 severely disabled people and 25 able bodied people at its premises on an old disused airfield site. The former aircraft hangars have been turned into either production or storage facilities, all of which have been adapted for severely disabled people.

Smaller items (such as walking frames and crutches) are manufactured here. These are relatively unsophisticated products, manufactured from scrap metal bought from local scrap metal dealers and stored on-site. These products require no testing or training to use and they are packaged and stored after manufacture. IL uses its own lorry to make collections of scrap metal but the lorry is old, unreliable and will soon need replacing.

Larger and more complex items (such as mobility scooters and bath lifts) are bought in bulk from suppliers and stored in the hangars. Delivery of these items to IL is organised by their manufacturers. These products are stored until they are ordered.

When an order is received for such products, the product is unpacked and tested. An IL transfer logo is then applied and the product is re-packaged in the original packing material with an IL label attached. It is then dispatched to the customer. Some inventory is never ordered and last year IL had to write-off a significant amount of obsolete inventory.

All goods are sold at cost plus a margin to cover wages and administrative costs. Prices charged are the same whether goods are ordered over the web or by telephone. Customers can also make a further voluntary donation to help support IL if they wish to. About 30% of customers do make such a donation.

Ordering and marketing

IL markets its products by placing single-sided promotional leaflets in hospitals, doctors' surgeries and local social welfare departments. This leaflet provides information about IL and gives a direct phone number and a web address. Customers may purchase products by ringing IL directly or by ordering over their website. The website provides product information and photos of the products which are supplied by IL. It also has a secure payment facility. However, customers who ring IL directly have to discuss product requirements and potential purchases with sales staff over the phone. Each sales discussion takes, on average, ten minutes and only one in two contacts results in a sale. 20% of sales are through their website (up from 15% last year), but many of their customers are unfamiliar with the Internet and do not have access to it. Goods are delivered to customers by a national courier service. Service and support for the bought-in products (mobility scooters, bath lifts) are supplied by the original manufacturer.

Commercial competitors

IL is finding it increasingly difficult to compete with commercial firms offering independent living aids. Last year, the charity made a deficit of $160,000, and it had to sell some of its airfield land to cover this. Many of the commercial firms it is competing with have sophisticated sales and marketing operations and then arrange delivery to customers directly from manufacturers based in low labour cost countries.

Required:

IL fears for its future and has decided to review its value chain to see how it can achieve competitive advantage.

(a)   Analyse the primary activities of the value chain for the product range at IL.

(10 marks)

(b)   Evaluate what changes IL might consider to the primary activities in the value chain to improve their competitiveness, whilst continuing to meet their charitable objectives. (15 marks)

(Total: 25 marks)

31   MMI *Walk in the footsteps of a top tutor*

In 20X2 the board of MMI met to discuss the strategic direction of the company. Established in 1952, MMI specialised in mineral quarrying and opencast mining and in 20X2 it owned fifteen quarries and mines throughout the country. However, three of these quarries were closed and two others were nearing exhaustion. Increased costs and falling reserves meant that there was little chance of finding new sites in the country which were economically viable. Furthermore, there was significant security costs associated with keeping the closed quarries safe and secure.

Consequently the Chief Executive Officer (CEO) of MMI suggested that the company should pursue a corporate-level strategy of diversification, building up a portfolio of acquisitions that would 'maintain returns to shareholders over the next fifty years'. In October 20X2 MMI, using cash generated from their quarrying operations, acquired First Leisure, a company that owned five leisure parks throughout the country. These leisure parks provided a range of accommodation where guests could stay while they enjoyed sports and leisure activities. The parks were all in relatively isolated country areas and provided a safe, car-free environment for guests.

The acquisition was initially criticised by certain financial analysts who questioned what a quarrying company could possibly contribute to a profitable leisure group. For two years MMI left First Leisure managers alone, letting them get on with running the company. However, in 20X4 a First Leisure manager commented on the difficulty of developing new leisure parks due to increasingly restrictive government planning legislation. This gave the CEO of MMI an inspired idea and over the next three years the five quarries which were either closed or near exhaustion were transferred to First Leisure and developed as new leisure parks. Because these were developments of 'brown field' sites they were exempted from the government's planning legislation. The development of these new parks has helped First Leisure to expand considerably (see table 1). The company is still run by the managers who were in place when MMI acquired the company in 20X2 and MMI plays very little role in the day-to-day running of the company.

In 20X4 MMI acquired two of its smaller mining and quarrying competitors, bringing a further five mines or quarries into the group. MMI introduced its own managers into these companies resulting in a spectacular rise in revenues and profits that caused the CEO of MMI to claim that corporate management capabilities were now an important asset of MMI.

In 20X6 MMI acquired Boatland, a specialist boat maker constructing river and canal boats. The primary rationale behind the acquisition was the potential synergies with First Leisure.

First Leisure had experienced difficulties in obtaining and maintaining boats for its leisure parks and it was expected that Boatland would take on construction and maintenance of these boats.

Cost savings for First Leisure were also expected and it was felt that income from the First Leisure contract would also allow Boatland to expand its production of boats for other customers. MMI perceived that Boatland was underperforming and it replaced the current management team with its own managers. However, by 20X8 Boatland was reporting poorer results (see table 1). The work force had been used to producing expensive, high quality boats to discerning customers who looked after their valued boats. In contrast, the boats required by First Leisure were for the casual use of holiday makers who often ill-treated them and certainly had no long-term investment in their ownership. Managers at First Leisure complained that the new boats were 'too delicate' for their intended purpose and unreliability had led to high maintenance costs.

This increase in maintenance also put Boatland under strain and its other customers complained about poor quality workmanship and delays in completing work. These delays were compounded by managers at Boatland declaring First Leisure as a preferred customer, requiring that work for First Leisure should take precedence over that for established customers. Since the company was acquired almost half of the skilled boat builders employed by the company have left to take up jobs elsewhere in the industry.

Three months ago, InfoTech – an information technology solutions company approached MMI with a proposal for MMI to acquire them. The failure of certain contracts has led to falling revenues and profits and the company needs new investment.

The Managing Director (MD) of InfoTech has proposed that MMI should acquire InfoTech for a nominal sum and then substantially invest in the company so that it can regain its previous profitability and revenue levels. However, after its experience with Boatland, the CEO of MMI is cautious about any further diversification of the group.

Table 1: Financial and market data for selected companies (all figures in $millions)

MMI Quarrying and Mining	20X8	20X6	20X4	20X2
Revenue	1,680	1,675	1,250	1,275
Gross profit	305	295	205	220
Net profit	110	105	40	45
*Estimated Market Revenue	6,015	6,050	6,200	6,300
First Leisure	**20X8**	**20X6**	**20X4**	**20X2**
Revenue	200	160	110	100
Gross profit	42	34	23	21
Net profit	21	17	10	9
*Estimated Market Revenue	950	850	770	750
Boatland	**20X8**	**20X6**	**20X4**	**20X2**
Revenue	2.10	2.40	2.40	2.30
Gross profit	0.30	0.50	0.50	0.60
Net profit	0.09	0.25	0.30	0.30
*Estimated Market Revenue	201	201	199	198
InfoTech	**20X8**	**20X6**	**20X4**	**20X2**
Revenue	21	24	26	25
Gross profit	0.9	3	4	4
Net profit	−0.2	2	3	3
*Estimated Market Revenue	560	540	475	450

*The estimated size of the market (estimated market revenue) is taken from Slott's Economic Yearbooks, 20X2–20X8.

Required:

(a)   In the context of MMI's corporate-level strategy, explain the rationale for MMI acquiring First Leisure and Boatland and assess the subsequent performance of the two companies.   **(15 marks)**

(b)   Assess the extent to which the proposed acquisition of InfoTech represents an appropriate addition to the MMI portfolio.   **(10 marks)**

                                                                    (Total: 25 marks)

32   OCEANIA NATIONAL AIRLINES (ONA)   *Walk in the footsteps of a top tutor*

The island of Oceania attracts thousands of tourists every year. They come to enjoy the beaches, the climate and to explore the architecture and history of this ancient island. Oceania is also an important trading nation in the region and it enjoys close economic links with neighbouring countries. Oceania has four main airports and until ten years ago had two airlines, one based in the west (OceaniaAir) and one based in the east (Transport Oceania) of the island. However, ten years ago these two airlines merged into one airline – Oceania National Airlines (ONA) with the intention of exploiting the booming growth in business and leisure travel to and from Oceania.

Market sectors

ONA serves two main sectors. The first sector is a network of routes to the major cities of neighbouring countries. ONA management refer to this as the regional sector. The average flight time in this sector is one and a half hours and most flights are timed to allow business people to arrive in time to attend a meeting and then to return to their homes in the evening. Twenty five major cities are served in the regional sector with, on average, three return flights per day. There is also significant leisure travel, with many families visiting relatives in the region. The second sector is what ONA management refer to as the international sector. This is a network of flights to continental capitals. The average flight time in this sector is four hours. These flights attract both business and leisure travellers. The leisure travellers are primarily holiday-makers from the continent. Twenty cities are served in this sector with, on average, one return flight per day to each city.

Image, service and employment

ONA is the airline of choice for most of the citizens of Oceania. A recent survey suggested that 90% of people preferred to travel ONA for regional flights and 70% preferred to travel with ONA for international flights. 85% of the respondents were proud of their airline and felt that it projected a positive image of Oceania. The company also has an excellent safety record, with no fatal accident recorded since the merging of the airlines ten years ago.

The customer service of ONA has also been recognised by the airline industry itself. In 20X5 it was voted Regional Airline of the Year by the International Passenger Group (IPG) and one year later the IPG awarded the ONA catering department the prestigious Golden Bowl as provider of the best airline food in the world.

The courtesy and motivation of its employees (mainly Oceanic residents) is recognised throughout the region. 95% of ONA employees belong to recognised trade unions. ONA is perceived as an excellent employer. It pays above industry average salaries, offers excellent benefits (such as free health care) and has a generous non-contributory pension scheme. In 20X4 ONA employed 5400 people, rising to 5600 in 20X5 and 5800 in 20X6.

Fleet

Fleet details are given in Table 1. Nineteen of the Boeing 737s were originally in the fleet of OceaniaAir. Boeing 737s are primarily used in the international sector. Twenty-three of the Airbus A320s were originally part of the Transport Oceania fleet. Airbuses are primarily used in the regional sector. ONA also used three Embraer RJ145 jets in the regional sector.

Table 1: Fleet details

	Boeing 737	Airbus A320	Embraer RJ145
Total aircraft in service			
20X6	21	27	3
20X5	21	27	3
20X4	20	26	2
Capacity (passengers)	147	149	50
Introduced	October 1991	November 1988	January 1999
Average age	12.1 years	12.9 years	6.5 years
Utilisation (hrs per day)	8.70	7.41	7.50

Performance

Since 20X4 ONA has begun to experience significant competition from 'no frills' low-cost budget airlines, particularly in the international sector. Established continental operators now each offer, on average, three low fares flights to Oceania every day. 'No frills' low-cost budget airlines are also having some impact on the regional sector. A number of very small airlines (some with only one aircraft) have been established in some regional capitals and a few of these are offering low-cost flights to Oceania. A recent survey for ONA showed that its average international fare was double that of its low-cost competitors. Some of the key operational statistics for 20X6 are summarised in Table 2.

Table 2: Key operational statistics for ONA in 20X6

	Regional	International	Low-cost competitor average
Contribution to revenue ($m)			
Passenger	400	280	Not applicable
Cargo	35	15	Not applicable
Passenger load factor			
Standard class	73%	67%	87%
Business class	90%	74%	75%
Average annual pilot salary	$106,700	$112,500	$96,500
Source of revenue			
On-line sales	40%	60%	84%
Direct sales	10%	5%	12%
Commission sales	50%	35%	4%
Average age of aircraft	See Table 1		4.5 years
Utilisation (hrs per day)	See Table 1		9.10

ONA have made a number of operational changes in the last few years. Their website, for example, now allows passengers to book over the internet and to either have their tickets posted to them or to pick them up at the airport prior to travelling. Special promotional fares are also available for customers who book on-line. However, the website does not currently allow passengers to check-in on-line, a facility provided by some competitors.

Furthermore, as Table 2 shows, a large percentage of sales are still commission sales made through travel agents. Direct sales are those sales made over the telephone or at the airport itself.

Most leisure travellers pay standard or economy fares and travel in the standard class section of the plane. Although many business travellers also travel in standard class, some of them choose to travel business class for which they pay a price premium.

In the last three years, the financial performance of ONA has not matched its operational success. The main financial indicators have been extracted and are presented in Table 3. In a period (20X4–20X6) when world-wide passenger air travel revenue increased by 12% (and revenue from air travel to Oceania by 15%) and cargo revenue by 10%, ONA only recorded a 4.6% increase in passenger revenue.

Table 3: Extracted Financial Information (All figures in $m)

Extracted from the Statement of Financial Position

		20X6	20X5	20X4
Non-current assets				
Property, plant and equipment		788	785	775
Other non-current assets		60	56	64
	Total	848	841	839
Current assets				
Inventories		8	7	7
Trade receivables		68	71	69
Cash and cash equivalents		289	291	299
	Total	365	369	375
Total assets		**1,213**	**1,210**	**1,214**
Total shareholders' equity		250	259	264
Non-current liabilities				
Interest bearing long-term loans		310	325	335
Employee benefit obligations		180	178	170
Other provisions		126	145	143
	Total	616	648	648
Current liabilities				
Trade payables		282	265	255
Current tax payable		9	12	12
Other current liabilities		56	26	35
	Total	347	303	302
Total equity and liabilities		**1,213**	**1,210**	**1,214**

Extracted from the income statement

		20X6	20X5	20X4
Revenue				
Passenger		680	675	650
Cargo		50	48	45
Other revenue		119	112	115
	Total	849	835	810
Cost of sales				
Purchases		535	525	510
Gross profit		314	310	300
Wages and salaries		215	198	187
Directors' salaries		17	16	15
Interest payable		22	21	18
	Total	254	235	220
Net profit before tax		**60**	**75**	**80**
Tax expense		18	23	24
Net profit after tax		**42**	**52**	**56**

Future strategy

The management team at ONA are keen to develop a strategy to address the airline's financial and operational weaknesses. One suggestion has been to re-position ONA itself as a 'no frills' low-cost budget airline. However, this has been angrily dismissed by the CEO as likely to lead 'to an unnecessary and bloody revolution that could cause the death of the airline itself'.

Required:

(a) Evaluate the strengths and weaknesses of ONA and their impact on its performance. Please note that opportunities and threats are NOT required in your evaluation.

(20 marks)

(b) The CEO of Oceania National Airways (ONA) has already strongly rejected the repositioning of ONA as a 'no frills' low-cost budget airline.

   (i) Explain the key features of a 'no frills' low-cost strategy. (4 marks)

   (ii) Evaluate why moving to a 'no frills' low-cost strategy would be inappropriate for ONA. (16 marks)

   Professional skills marks will be awarded for demonstrating evaluation skills in appraising the issues identified. (2 marks)

(c) Identify and evaluate other strategic options ONA could consider to address the airline's current financial and operational weaknesses. (10 marks)

(Total: 52 marks)

33 LING

Man Lal relaxed in business class as the aircraft skimmed across the Uril Mountains. Generally he considered himself a contented man. He had successfully built his company, Ling, to be the largest light bulb manufacturing company in the world, with global revenues of $750m. From its factories in Lindisztan it supplied a worldwide market for LED (light emitting diodes) light bulbs. Lal congratulated himself on the fact that he had quickly spotted the potential of LED light bulbs and had entered large-scale production whilst his rivals were still focusing their production on candescent and halogen bulbs. The world now realised that LED light bulbs provided a cheaper, more energy efficient, greener solution than all of its alternatives. To that end, many countries had passed legislation requiring domestic and business consumers to replace candescent light bulbs with greener equivalents. In fact, he was on his way right now to Skod, a country which had passed efficient lighting legislation which, from next year, banned the use of candescent bulbs in commercial premises and outlawed their production and importation after that date. Domestic consumers were expected to replace their candescent bulbs with newer technology as their bulbs failed. Man Lal confidently expected that LED would be, for many, the newer technology of choice.

Required:

(a) Analyse the macro-environmental factors affecting the Skod light bulb industry. Your analysis should reflect the fact that Ling might enter this industry directly by setting up a distribution company for its products or through the acquisition of Flick.

(7 marks)

(b) Assess the attractiveness of the Skod light bulb industry. (13 marks)

(c) Ling is considering entering the Skod light bulb industry by acquiring Flick.

Evaluate the potential acquisition of Flick by Ling from the perspectives of suitability and acceptability. **(18 marks)**

(d) The finance director of Ling is concerned that Ling has no expertise in acquiring foreign companies and he is advocating a strategic partnership with Flick instead.

Discuss the appropriateness of such an approach to facilitating Ling's proposed entry into the Skod light bulb market. **(8 marks)**

(Total: 46 marks)

Exhibit 1 – Man Lal's visit to Skod

The visit to Skod was of great significance to Man Lal because it was here that he did his business studies degree at Skodmore University. Indeed, he was due to give a lecture to the staff and students of the university the following day and he felt great personal pride in returning to describe the extent of his success and the fulfilment of his personal ambitions. He was also planning to visit a company called Flick which Ling was considering acquiring. This would be a new growth method for Ling. Up to now its worldwide expansion had been achieved by establishing wholly owned distribution companies in each targeted country. All production had remained in Lindisztan. However, for various reasons, Ling was now considering entering the Skod market by acquiring one of its light bulb producers, Flick.

In fact, remembering this brought a slight frown across Man Lal's face. To help fund his global expansion, he had sold 49% of Ling to institutional investors. These institutional investors required growth and high dividends and he was having difficulty meeting their demands.

There was now very little growth in the domestic Lindisztan market and the distribution approach used to expand into foreign countries was taking a long time to mature. The investors were demanding quicker growth and acquisitions appeared to promise this. Despite paying high dividends over the last few years, the company still had significant retained profits and this was another issue for the institutional shareholders. They felt that this money should be used to promote growth and have agreed to a $400m acquisition fund. So, thought Man Lal, what better place to start those acquisitions than Skod, the place where I studied as a poor overseas student so many years ago. However, he had to admit to himself, he was still much happier with organic growth through setting up his own distribution companies. Ling had made a few acquisitions in Lindisztan, but had never bought a foreign company and he was worried about the risk of failure.

Turbulence buffeted the aircraft as it made its final descent into the capital of Skod. To distract himself, Man Lal picked up the latest copy of Lighting Tomorrow, the research magazine of the light bulb industry. He skim read an article on tubular daylight lighting which promised to reduce the need for electric lighting by introducing more daylight into a building. Effective daylighting (it said) is achieved through the strategic placement of skylights and windows, as well as lighting controls which monitor available daylight and respond as needed to decrease or increase electric lighting. Perhaps I need to look into this, thought Man Lal.

At the airport, Man Lal took a taxi to his hotel. He could not help but notice that Skod was not as neat and tidy as it used to be. A lot of shops and buildings had been closed down and there was graffiti across many buildings and bridges. 'Skod for Skodders', said one, 'Skod jobs for Skod people', said another. Man Lal remembered now that the Skod nationalist movement had become increasingly popular.

He mentioned this to the taxi driver. 'Yes', he said, 'Most people are fed up with Skod being pushed around by the International Financing Consortium (IFC), we want prosperity and jobs for people who grew up here.'

Slightly unnerved, Man Lal, checked in at the hotel. He switched on the television. He watched with interest as Niklas Perch, the newly elected nationalist leader of the Skod government, outlined his plans for the future.

'We are committed to a return to prosperity', he said. 'To achieve this we have to make some short-term adjustments which may be unpopular with our trading partners. We are currently considering the imposition of import taxes as a way of protecting our home industry. We wish to create a protected commercial environment here in Skod in which our companies can prosper.

'We must also ask our citizens to continue with their energy saving measures. As you know, the government has agreed that all street lighting will be turned off from 2300 hours to 0500 hours. I have also decreed that all government offices must proactively embrace energy saving lighting and heating. In the same way, I expect our citizens to look at ways of saving money and energy.

'The government also recognises that the country continues to be in a recession, and that disposable income is falling for all people. However, I cannot condone the recent demonstrations against, and boycott of, foreign goods and food products. We must rebuild our country peacefully and legally. I would ask all citizens to support me in this.'

Just then, the air conditioning failed and the television went off. Another energy failure in Skod. There were three further failures that night. The hotel manager apologised to Man Lal in the morning. 'I am sorry', he said 'but despite higher energy prices, this is an increasing feature of life in Skod.'

Exhibit 2 – Skod electric light bulb industry

All electric light bulbs are largely made out of glass and metal and this is likely to remain the same in the foreseeable future. In Skod, 90% of glass is produced by three companies. However, for all of these three companies, light bulb manufacturers are unimportant customers. Most glass manufacture goes to the construction industry, light bulb manufacturers take less than 0.5% of the country's glass production. Metal manufacture in Skod is dominated by one company, OmniMetal. Most metal is sold to the automobile industry. Light bulb manufacturers take less than 0.1% of OmniMetal's production. However, the quality of glass and metal required by the light bulb manufacturers is quite standard, so switching between suppliers is, in theory, relatively easy. Light bulb manufacture takes place in factories which require substantial initial investment and have no obvious alternative use.

In Skod, light bulbs are low cost commodity products which are replaced infrequently by domestic consumers. Commercial consumers change their light bulbs a little more often and some businesses have recently switched all their bulbs to LED to save energy, reduce costs in the long term and to reflect their aspirations as 'green businesses'. There is very little brand awareness in the light bulb market and all the light bulbs have to fit the standard sockets used in the country.

Electric light bulb manufacture in Skod is dominated by the five companies listed in Table One. Two years ago a large American light bulb manufacturer, Krysal, attempted to enter the market.

The five dominant companies in the industry reacted to this by cutting prices, running marketing campaigns which emphasised the benefits to the country of home-based production and lobbying supermarket groups to not stock products produced by the new entrant. Krysal withdrew from the market after six months. When not focused on fighting new entrants, the five main competitors are regularly involved in price cutting, disruption of competitors' distribution channels and aggressive marketing.

Company	Revenue (20X5)	Revenue (20X0)
Voltface	$85m	$80m
LiteWorld	$80m	$80m
Flick	$70m	$65m
ABC	$65m	$60m
L2L	$60m	$60m
Other companies	$140m	$145m
Total	$500m	$490m

Table One: Skod-based light bulb manufacturers

The products produced by the Skod light bulb industry are largely sold through supermarket groups (50%), household product superstores (30%) and large electrical chains (10%). The rest of the production is sold through small shops, except for a tiny percentage of production (less than 1%) which is sold directly to large organisations, such as government departments. However, light bulbs do not constitute a large sales item for any of these distribution channels. In fact, in a recent report, light bulb sales were one of the products which contributed less than 0.1% of a major supermarket's revenue.

Exhibit 3 – The acquisition of Flick

The light bulb companies in Skod have largely focused on candescent (60% of production) and halogen (30% of production) technologies.

Man Lal intends to fund the updating of the production facilities at Flick to allow the production of LED lights, alongside the continued production of candescent and halogen light bulbs. He wants to achieve this before domestic competitors in Skod gear up their own LED light bulb production. He believes that Ling's competencies in LED manufacture will give Flick a head start. Initial discussions with Flick suggest that the company is open to acquisition and a bid price has been agreed which is acceptable to both parties. Financial information for Flick and the Skod light bulb industry as a whole is shown below:

Financial information for Flick and the Skod light bulb industry

Extract from financial statements (All figures in $millions)

	Flick 20X5	Skod industry totals 20X5
Assets		
Non-current assets		
Property, plant, equipment	190	1,635
Goodwill	10	100
Total non-current assets	200	1,735

	Flick 20X5	Skod industry totals 20X5
Current assets		
Inventory	45	200
Trade receivables	20	250
Cash and cash equivalents	35	115
Total current assets	100	565
Total assets	300	2,300
Equity and liabilities		
Share capital	150	1,000
Retained earnings	50	340
Non-current liabilities		
Long-term borrowings	70	750
Current liabilities		
Trade payables	29	200
Current tax payable	1	10
Total current liabilities	30	210
Total liabilities	100	960
Total equity and liabilities	300	2,300
Revenue	70	500
Cost of sales	(55)	(350)
Gross profit	15	150
Administrative expenses	(4)	(30)
Profit before tax and interest	11	120
Finance cost	(3)	(50)
Profit before tax	8	70
Tax expense	(1)	(12)
Profit for the period	7	58

Note: The Industry total column is for the Skod light bulb industry as a whole (including Flick).

34 NESTA

NESTA is a large chain of fixed-price discount stores based in the country of Eyanke. Its stores offer ambient goods (goods that require no cold storage and can be kept at room temperature, such as cleaning products, stationery, biscuits and plastic storage units) at a fixed price of one dollar. Everything in the store retails at this price. Fixed-price discount chains focus on unbranded commodity goods which they buy from a number of small suppliers, for which the dollar shops are the most significant customers. Profit margins on the products they sell are low and overheads are kept to a minimum. The target price is fixed. The products tend to be functional, standardised and undifferentiated.

NESTA has observed the long-term economic decline in the neighbouring country of Eurobia, where a prolonged economic recession has led to the growth of so-called 'dollar shops'. Three significant dollar shop chains have developed: ItzaDollar, DAIAD and DollaFellas (see Table One). The shops of these three chains are particularly found on the high streets of towns and cities where there is significant financial hardship. Many of these towns and cities have empty stores which are relatively cheap to rent. Furthermore, landlords who once required high rents and long leases are increasingly willing to rent these stores for a relatively short fixed-term lease. The fixed-price dollar shop chains in Eurobia advertise extensively and continually stress their expansion plans. Few weeks go by without one of the chains announcing plans for a significant number of new shops throughout the country.

NESTA has recognised the growth of fixed-price discount retailers in Eurobia and is considering entering this market.

NESTA recently commissioned a brand awareness survey in Eurobia. The survey results showed that NESTA was relatively well-known to respondents who work in the consumer goods retail market. Most of these respondents correctly identified the company as a discount fixed-price company with a significant presence in Eyanke. However, amongst general consumers, only 5% of the respondents had heard of NESTA. In contrast, the three current fixed-price dollar shop discounters in Eurobia were recognised by more than 90% of the respondents.

NESTA itself has revenue of $120,000 million. It has cash reserves which could allow it to lease a significant number of shops in Eurobia and establish a credible market presence. It has recognised competencies in effective supplier selection and management, supported by effective procurement systems. Its logistics systems and methods are core strengths of the company.

There are also many conventional supermarket chains operating in Eurobia. The largest of these has annual revenue of $42,500 million. Supermarkets in Eurobia tend to increasingly favour out-of-town sites which allow the stores to stock a wide range and quantity of products. Customer car parking is plentiful and it is relatively easy for supplying vehicles to access such sites. As well as stocking non-ambient goods, most supermarkets do also stock a very wide range of ambient goods, often with competing brands on offer. However, prices for such goods vary and no supermarkets have yet adopted the discount fixed-price sales approach. In general, the large supermarket chains largely compete with each other and pay little attention to the fixed-price dollar shop discounters. Many supermarkets also have internet-based home ordering systems, offering (usually for a fee of $10) deliveries to customers who are unable or unwilling to visit the supermarket.

The relative revenue of the three main discount fixed-price chains in Eurobia is as follows:

	20X2 ($million)	20X1 ($million)	20X0 ($million)
ItzaDollar	330	300	275
DAIAD*	310	290	250
DollaFellas	290	235	200
Total	930	825	725

*Don't Ask it's A Dollar

Table One: Revenue of three main discount fixed-price chains in Eurobia

Required:

Assess the attractiveness, to NESTA, of entering the discount fixed-price retail market in Eurobia. **(16 marks)**

Professional skills marks will be awarded for demonstrating commercial acumen when applied to the competitive nature of the industry in particular. **(2 marks)**

(Total: 18 marks)

35 YVERN TRINKETS REGIONAL (YTR)

Yvern is large region in the country of Gaulle. It is ethnically and culturally distinct from the rest of the country and it has aspirations for independence. The desire for this independence is reflected by consumers in Yvern preferring to buy products which have been produced in the region.

Yvern Trinkets Regional (YTR) is a manufacturer of giftware products aimed at the Yvern market. Its products are bought primarily by residents of Yvern and visitors to the Yvern region. It is the third largest company of its type in the region, and the 50th largest producer of giftware in Gaulle. Its marketing message stresses the regional identity of the company and its employment of local skills and labour

YTR recently appointed a new managing director, born outside the region. He has been tasked with improving the profitability of the company. After a short period of consultation, the new managing director produced a proposal for the board. Here is an extract of his proposal.

'First of all, we need to be clear about our generic strategy. Strategists have suggested that we have four alternatives. I have reproduced them in this slide (shown here as Table one).

Cost Leadership	Differentiation
Cost Focus	Differentiation Focus

Table one: Generic strategies

My vision for YTR is that we should pursue a cost leadership strategy. I have already established that our products can be produced by an established company in the distant country of Tinglia. My view is that increased profitability can only be achieved if we take advantage of the cheaper production costs now available to us. All four products can be produced more cheaply by the supplier in Tinglia. So, this strategy of outsourcing is the one we should pursue to achieve our cost leadership strategy.

Also, the information technology of YTR is outdated and inefficient. Productivity benefits will follow from harnessing the power of modern technology.'

Required:

Examine the relevance of each of the four generic strategies shown in Table one to the competitive environment in which YTR operates and evaluate the choice of a cost leadership strategy by YTR's managing director. **(10 marks)**

Professional skills marks will be awarded for demonstrating evaluation skills in assessing the appropriateness of each generic strategy. **(2 marks)**

(Total: 12 marks)

D: RISK

36   BTS COMPANY

The BTS Company manufactures and sells chairs and sofas for use in the 'sitting' or 'living' rooms of houses. The company's products are displayed on an internet site and orders received via this site only. Order processing takes place on the company's in-house computer systems along with inventory control and payment to suppliers. The computer systems are managed in-house with no external links other than the Internet for selling.

Production is carried out in BTS's factory. There is little automation and production is dependent on the knowledge of Mr Smith and Mr Jones, the production controllers. Similarly, BTS rely on the Woody company for the supply of 80% of the wood used in the manufacture of BTS products. BTS's supplier policy is to pay as late as possible, providing little information on future production requirements.

Other raw materials purchased include fabrics for chair and sofa covers. However, a minority of sales orders are lost because the correct fabric is not available for the customer. The main reason for these stock-outs appears to be that the procurement manager forgets to order the fabric when inventory levels are low.

BTS's products are distributed by FastCour – a nationwide courier firm. However, due to the size of the chairs and sofas it is essential that the customer is available to take delivery of the goods when the courier arrives at their house. FastCour offer a 2-hour 'window' for delivery although only 55% of deliveries are actually meeting this criteria providing poor publicity for BTS and an increasing number of customer complaints. The board of BTS do not believe a strategic review of courier services is required at this time.

Required:

Identify and explain any strategic, tactical and operational risks affecting the BTS company. For each risk, discuss method(s) of alleviating this risk. **(12 marks)**

37   LANDMASS

Landmass is a property company that is planning to obtain a listing for its shares on the stock market of the country in which it is based. The directors are aware, however, that the company will be required to comply with the corporate governance requirements including an annual review by the directors of the adequacy of its risk management systems. This country has a principles-based system of corporate governance which covers all companies with a listing on the stock market.

At the moment, the company does not have any formal risk management system, and the directors need advice on how such a system might be established. They have been informed that the risks of the business should be categorised, but they do not know how this might be done.

The company operates in three different areas:

1   It manages business property which it rents to business customers under short-term and medium-term lease arrangements.

2   It buys and re-sells office property and property used by retail businesses (such as shopping arcades).

3   It has a subsidiary that specialises in building high-quality residential property.

Required:

(a)   Explain how risks might be categorised by companies, and suggest the risk categories that might be used by Landmass.   (9 marks)

(b)   Recommend how Landmass might establish a risk management system prior to its listing and the introduction of its shares to trading on the stock exchange.

(16 marks)

(Total: 25 marks)

38   REGIONAL POLICE FORCE

A regional police force has the following corporate objectives:

*   to reduce crime and disorder

*   to promote community safety

*   to contribute to delivering justice and maintaining public confidence in the law.

The force aims to achieve these objectives by continuously improving its resources management to meet the needs of its stakeholders. It has no stated financial objective other than to stay within its funding limits.

The force is mainly public-funded but, like other regional forces, it has some commercial operations, for example policing football matches when the football clubs pay a fee to the police force for its officers working overtime. The police force uses this money to supplement the funding it receives from the government.

Required:

(a) Discuss the risks to the achievement of the corporate objectives of the regional police force. **(12 marks)**

(b) Discuss the risks associated with a regional structure for the national police force. **(7 marks)**

(c) Describe the types of internal controls that might be applied by the police force in order to assist with the achievement of its objectives. **(6 marks)**

(Total: 25 marks)

39 MANAGE LTD

Background information

Manage Ltd is a large family-owned private company operating in the UK in the contract services sector. The principle business that Manage undertakes is project management on large, long-term building projects in the UK. Manage Ltd has no overseas customers. The company provides a complete project management service, enabling the customers to deal just with Manage Ltd. Manage deal with all sub-contractors. The business has been very successful in recent years and as a result has become a potential acquisition target for a major international company, Utopia Inc, based in the US. Utopia Inc is listed on the New York Stock Exchange and is interested in furthering its businesses in Europe.

Some of the members of the family that own Manage Ltd (the Inglesons) are keen to dispose of their shares and it is therefore expected they will sell to Utopia if a suitable price can be agreed. The managing director of Manage, Jean Smith (not in the Ingleson family), is currently negotiating with the directors of Utopia over a price for the shares.

Following the negotiation Jean will make a proposal to the Ingleson family. Jean and other selected staff have already been offered positions in Utopia if the acquisition proceeds.

Financing the acquisition

Utopia Inc have a corporate policy of financing their acquisitions through loans. In previous foreign acquisitions, they have used either US or foreign loans depending on their views on economic and political factors in the US and in the foreign markets. They have no strong views on where to raise finance. They expect to need to borrow in 4 months' time to finance the acquisition.

One factor that the directors of Utopia Inc do feel needs to be considered however is that they are considering selling an existing UK division within a year and the proceeds are expected to be in the region of the acquisition price for Manage Ltd. The disposal will definitely occur after the acquisition of Manage Ltd, probably six months later.

Corporate governance

In anticipation of Manage Ltd becoming part of the Utopia Group the group CFO, Bert Bailey, has forwarded to Jean Smith a memo he sent last year to all divisional CEOs on corporate governance. He told Jean that the same process would operate for Manage Ltd, but with the dates about a year on.

MEMO

To:	Divisional CFOs and CEOs
From:	Bert Bailey
Subject:	SOX compliance
Date:	15 January 20X4

As you are all no doubt aware, we are implementing Sarbanes-Oxley (SOX) this year. This memo summarises the timetable; more detail on the processes and procedures required will follow later.

Feb – May	Document key financial reporting systems and controls. Decide key controls and report any material design weaknesses in systems
Jun – July	Divisional management to test key controls to confirm compliance and the effectiveness of the systems
Aug – Sept	Group internal audit to review documentation and testing, and report on each division to the audit committee
Oct – Nov	External audit to conduct the majority of their attestation work
Dec	Management certification and assertions as required by sections 302 and 404.

The control framework the US companies will be using is the COSO framework. Overseas companies can use a local framework, if desired, provided it is approved in advance by the group SOX project team. Documentation must be standard across the group.

Required:

Explain the risks that could exist for Utopia in making the investment in Manage Ltd and discuss how Utopia could assess their likely impact on the company. **(25 marks)**

40   DUBLAND

Because of a general lack of business confidence in Dubland, its major banks had severely restricted new lending. This lack of lending extended to small and large businesses, and also to individuals in society. Press statements from the banks often referred to the need to mitigate financial risks and the need to maintain capital adequacy. Over time, the lower lending produced some negative consequences in the wider Dubland economy.

Responding to these problems, the Dubland finance minister remarked that, 'financial risks may not only cause companies to fail but they can also cause problems in wider society. Banks, in particular, need to be more aware of their financial risks than most other sectors of the economy. They have to manage a unique set of risks and I strongly urge the directors of banks to institute robust risk management systems as part of their corporate governance.

'As finance minister, however, I also believe that banks have a vital role in supporting the economic strength of this country. They hold cash deposits and make short and long-term loans, which are vital to other businesses. Taking risks is a normal part of all business operations and our banks need to accept this risk when it comes to lending.'

Ron Ng, the chief executive of BigBank, Dubland's largest bank, said that continuous and ongoing risk assessment was necessary.

He said that despite the finance minister's call for higher lending, his only duty was to BigBank's shareholders and it was this duty that guided BigBank's reduced lending.

Required:

Explain and evaluate the two statements made by Ron Ng.   **(15 marks)**

41   GHI GROUP

The GHI Group is a major listed travel company based in northern Europe, with a market capitalisation of €200 million. GHI specialises in the provision of budget-priced short and long haul package holidays targeted at the family market. The term 'package holiday' means that all flights, accommodation and overseas transfers are organised and booked by the tour operator on behalf of the customer.

The GHI Group encompasses a number of separate companies that include a charter airline, a chain of retail travel outlets, and several specialist tour operators who provide package holidays. Each subsidiary is expected to be profit generating, and each company's performance is measured by its residual income. The capital charges for each company are risk adjusted, and new investments are required to achieve a base hurdle rate of 10% before adjustment for risk.

The package holiday market is highly competitive, with fewer than five main players all trying to gain market share in an environment in which margins are continually threatened. The key threats include rising fuel prices, last minute discounting and the growth of the 'self-managed' holiday, where individuals by-pass the travel retailers and use the Internet to book low cost flights and hotel rooms directly with the service providers. Also, customer requirements regarding product design and quality are continuously changing, thereby increasing the pressure on travel companies to devise appropriate strategies to maintain profitability.

Sales of long haul packages to North America are relatively static, but the number of people travelling to South East Asian destinations has fallen substantially following the 2004 tsunami disaster. Africa, New Zealand, Australia and certain parts of the Caribbean are the only long haul growth areas, but such growth is from a small base. Sales within the European region are shifting in favour of Eastern Mediterranean destinations such as Cyprus and Turkey as the traditional resorts of Spain and the Balearic Islands fall out of favour. Short 'city breaks' are also growing rapidly in popularity, reflecting higher spending power particularly amongst the over 50s.

The shift in patterns of demand has created some problems for GHI in a number of Eastern Mediterranean resorts over the last two summer seasons. There are not many hotels that meet the specified quality standards, and consequently there is fierce competition amongst travel operators to reserve rooms in them. In addition GHI customers have experienced very poor service from hotels, which has resulted in adverse publicity and high compensation payments.

GHI has recently invested €8 million in purchasing two new hotels in the affected resorts. Sales forecasts indicate demand will grow at approximately 15% per year in the relevant resorts over the next five years. It is anticipated that the hotels will supply 70% of the group's accommodation requirements for the next season.

The package holidays to the GHI owned hotels will be sold as premium all-inclusive deals that include all food, soft drinks and local beers, wines and spirits. Such all-inclusive deals are not currently offered by other hotels in the target resorts.

GHI's local currency is the Euro.

Required:

(a)   **Identify and briefly discuss two risks that are likely to be faced by the GHI Group under each of the following categories:**

- **Financial**
- **Political**
- **Environmental**
- **Economic.**   **(12 marks)**

(b)   **Identify and comment upon the changes in risks to GHI Group that might arise from the decision to sell premium all-inclusive deals, and suggest methods by which these risks might be monitored and controlled.**   **(8 marks)**

(Total: 20 marks)

42 YGT

The board of YGT discussed its need for timely risk information. The consensus of the meeting was that risk consultants should be engaged to review the risks facing the company. One director, Raz Dutta, said that she felt that this would be a waste of money as the company needed to concentrate its resources on improving organisational efficiency rather than on gathering risk information. She said that many risks 'didn't change much' and 'hardly ever materialised' and so can mostly be ignored. The rest of the board, however, believed that a number of risks had recently emerged whilst others had become less important and so the board wanted a current assessment as it believed previous assessments might now be outdated.

The team of risk consultants completed the risk audit. They identified and assessed six potential risks (A, B, C, D, E and F) and the following information was discussed when the findings were presented to the YGT board:

Risk A was assessed as unlikely and low impact whilst Risk B was assessed as highly likely to occur and with a high impact. The activities giving rise to both A and B, however, are seen as marginal in that whilst the activities do have value and are capable of making good returns, neither is strategically vital.

Risk C was assessed as low probability but with a high potential impact and also arises from an activity that must not be discontinued although alternative arrangements for bearing the risks are possible. The activity giving rise to Risk C was recently introduced by YGT as a result of a new product launch.

Risk D was assessed as highly likely but with a low potential impact, and arose as a result of a recent change in legislation. It cannot be insured against nor can it be outsourced. It is strategically important that the company continues to engage in the activity that gives rise to Risk D although not necessarily at the same level as is currently the case.

In addition, Risks E and F were identified. Risk E was an environmental risk and Risk F was classed as a reputation risk. The risk consultants said that risks E and F could be related risks. In the formal feedback to the board of YGT, the consultants said that the company had to develop a culture of risk awareness and that this should permeate all levels of the company.

Required:

(a) Criticise Raz Dutta's beliefs about the need for risk assessment. Explain why risks are dynamic and therefore need to be assessed regularly. **(8 marks)**

(b) Using the TARA framework, select and explain the appropriate strategy for managing each risk (A, B, C and D). Justify your selection in each case. **(6 marks)**

(c) Explain what 'related risks' are and describe how Risks E and F might be positively correlated. **(5 marks)**

(Total: 19 marks)

43   HOPPO

A report was recently published by an international accounting organisation on the future of certain rare chemicals used in industrial processes. The report said that some of these chemicals, crucial to many industrial processes, were now so scarce that there was a threat to supply chains for items such as computer circuitry and the rechargeable batteries used in electronic goods. One of these scarce and rare chemicals, the highly toxic trans-Y13 (TY13), has become increasingly rare and, therefore, very expensive. It requires careful processing and, although used in small quantities in each product, its high cost means that even small inefficiencies in its treatment can disproportionately affect final product costs.

The report's conclusions included this statement: 'Put simply, we are living beyond the planet's means. Businesses that use these materials will experience new risks. It may even become seen as socially unacceptable to use some of these materials. Finally, if supply stops, then manufacturing stops.'

One company which depends on a continuous and reliable supply of TY13 is Hoppo Company. Hoppo is a listed company based in the highly developed country of Essland. It has, for several years, designed and developed its products in Essland and then outsourced manufacturing to another company, Red Co, which is based in the developing country of Teeland. This means that Red Co manufactures Hoppo's products for an agreed price and to Hoppo's designs and technical specifications.

Because Red Co is based in Teeland (a developing country with lower land and labour costs than Essland), working with Red Co has offered Hoppo cost advantages over manufacturing its products in its home country. As a company which outsources many of its functions, Hoppo tries to ensure that in each case of outsourcing, working conditions and environmental responsibility are the same at each outsourcing company as they would be if carried out in its highly-regulated home country of Essland.

Hoppo itself is one of the most valuable companies on the Essland stock exchange and has strategically positioned itself as a company that is seen as a trustworthy and responsible producer that is also responsible in its social and environmental behaviour. In its press statements and annual reports, it has frequently highlighted the high value it places on integrity and transparency as fundamental values in its corporate governance. It has recently considered producing an annual environmental report, as it believes its shareholders would value the information it contains.

Red Co is an experienced producer of electronic circuits and has a long history of working with TY13. It has relationships with the main TY13 suppliers going back many years, and these relationships ensure that it can normally obtain supplies even during periods when world supply is short. Because the supply quality of TY13 varies widely, Red Co has developed finely-tuned methods of ensuring that the TY13 received is of suitable quality.

The performance of the finished product is very sensitive to the quality of the TY13 and so this pre-production testing is considered vital. In addition, TY13's toxicity and high cost mean that other systems are put in place at Red Co to ensure that it is safely stored until needed for manufacture.

Earlier this year, however, two issues arose at Red Co which caused Hoppo to reconsider its outsourcing relationship. The first one was the publication of an international media report showing evidence that, despite Hoppo's claims about having the same working conditions at all of its outsourcing clients, labour conditions were unacceptably poor at Red Co. Because labour regulations were less stringent in Teeland, Red Co had been forcing employees to work excessively long hours without breaks, and other measures that would not have been permitted in Essland. It was reported that workers were being bullied, and threatened with dismissal if they complained about their working conditions.

The second problem was a leakage of unprocessed TY13 from the Red Co factory. Not only was this seen as wasteful and careless, it also poisoned a local river, killing many fish and contaminating local farmland. The community living nearby said that it would be unable to use the contaminated land for many years and that this would affect local food supply.

When a journalist, Bob Hob, discovered information about these two issues, the media interpreted the story as a problem for Hoppo, partly because of its reputation as a responsible company. Hoppo's own research had shown that many of its customers valued its environmental reputation and that some of its key employees were attracted to Hoppo for the same reason.

Some important customers began to associate Hoppo directly with the problems at Red Co, even though it was Red Co which had actually been responsible for the employee issues and also the TY13 leak. Hoppo's share price fell when some investors considered the problems to be important enough to undermine future confidence in Hoppo's management and brand value.

In an effort to protect its reputation in future, Hoppo began to review its outsource arrangement with Red Co. The board considered the options for taking manufacturing under its own direct control by building a new factory in another low-cost country, which would be owned and operated by Hoppo.

It quickly realised that stopping the outsourcing relationship with Red Co would mean the loss of about 1,000 jobs there and could also raise the likelihood of legal action by Red Co against Hoppo for loss of contract. As Hoppo's manufacturing contract is so valuable to Red Co, some people thought it likely that Red Co would sue Hoppo for loss of future earnings, despite the terms of the contract being legally ambiguous. This lack of clarity in the contract arose because of differences in Essland and Teeland law and as a consequence of poor legal advice that Hoppo received when drawing up the contract. It was believed that any legal action would be widely reported because of Hoppo's international profile and that this may result in some unfavourable publicity.

Required:

Briefly explain 'related' and 'correlated' risks. Explore the correlation between legal risk and reputation risk for Hoppo if it were to cancel its contract with Red Co.   (10 marks)

44   H&Z COMPANY

John Pentanol was appointed as risk manager at H&Z Company a year ago and he decided that his first task was to examine the risks that faced the company. He concluded that the company faced three major risks, which he assessed by examining the impact that would occur if the risk were to materialise.

He assessed Risk 1 as being of low potential impact as even if it materialised it would have little effect on the company's strategy. Risk 2 was assessed as being of medium potential impact whilst a third risk, Risk 3, was assessed as being of very high potential impact.

When John realised the potential impact of Risk 3 materialising, he issued urgent advice to the board to withdraw from the activity that gave rise to Risk 3 being incurred. In the advice he said that the impact of Risk 3 was potentially enormous and it would be irresponsible for H&Z to continue to bear that risk.

The company commercial director, Jane Xylene, said that John Pentanol and his job at H&Z were unnecessary and that risk management was 'very expensive for the benefits achieved'. She said that all risk managers do is to tell people what can't be done and that they are pessimists by nature. She said she wanted to see entrepreneurial risk takers in H&Z and not risk managers who, she believed, tended to discourage enterprise.

John replied that it was his job to eliminate all of the highest risks at H&Z Company. He said that all risk was bad and needed to be eliminated if possible. If it couldn't be eliminated, he said that it should be minimised.

Required:

(a)   Assess John Pentanol's understanding of his role.   **(8 marks)**

(b)   With reference to a risk assessment framework as appropriate, criticise John's advice that H&Z should withdraw from the activity that incurs Risk 3.   **(6 marks)**

(Total: 14 marks)

45   SALTOC

After a major fire had destroyed an office block belonging to Saltoc Company, the fire assessment reported that the most likely cause was an electrical problem. It emerged that the electrical system had suffered from a lack of maintenance in recent years due to cost pressures. Meanwhile in the same week, it was reported that a laptop computer containing confidential details of all of Saltoc's customers was stolen from the front seat of a car belonging to one of the company's information technology (IT) mid-managers.

This caused outrage and distress too many of the affected customers as the information on the laptop included their bank details and credit card numbers. Some customers wrote to the company to say that they would be withdrawing their business from Saltoc as a result.

When the board met to review and consider the two incidents, it was agreed that the company had been lax in its risk management in the past and that systems should be tightened. However, the financial director, Peter Osbida, said that he knew perfectly well where systems should be tightened. He said that the fire was due to the incompetence of Harry Ho the operations manager and that the stolen laptop was because of a lack of security in the IT department led by Laura Hertz. Peter said that both colleagues were 'useless' and should be sacked. Neither Harry nor Laura liked or trusted Peter and they felt that in disputes, chief executive Ken Tonno usually took Peter's side.

Both Harry and Laura said that their departments had come under severe pressure because of the tight cost budgets imposed by Peter.

Ken Tonno said that the last few years had been 'terrible' for Saltoc Company and that it was difficult enough keeping cash flows high enough to pay the wage bill without having to worry about 'even more' administration on risks and controls. Peter said that Harry and Laura both suffered in their roles by not having the respect of their subordinates and pointed to the high staff turnover in both of their departments as evidence of this.

Mr Tonno asked whether having a complete risk audit (or risk review) might be a good idea. He shared some of Peter's concerns about the management skills of both Harry and Laura, and so proposed that perhaps an external person should perform the risk audit and that would be preferable to one conducted by a colleague from within the company. Sarah Aston (Sales Director) disagreed and suggested that the company should prioritise embedding risk systems within Saltoc instead.

You have been approached, as an external management consultant, to advise the Board.

Required:

Write a report to the Board of Saltoc covering the following:

(a)   What 'embedding' risk means with reference to Saltoc Company.   (6 marks)

(b)   An assessment of the ability of Saltoc's management culture to implement embedded risk systems.   (8 marks)

(c)   An explanation of the case for an external risk audit at Saltoc Company.   (11 marks)

(Total: 25 marks)

46   P&J

P&J is a long established listed company based in Emmland, a highly developed and relatively prosperous country. For the past 60 years, P&J has been Emmland's largest importer and processor of a product named X32, a compound used in a wide variety of building materials, protective fabrics and automotive applications. X32 is a material much valued for its heat resistance, strength and adaptability, but perhaps most of all because it is flexible and also totally fireproof. It is this last property that led to the growth of X32 use and made P&J a historically successful company and a major exporter.

X32 is mined in some of the poorest developing countries where large local communities depend heavily on X32 mining for their incomes. The incomes from the mining activities are used to support community development, including education, sanitation and health facilities in those developing countries.

The X32 is then processed in dedicated X32 facilities near to the mining communities, supporting many more jobs. It is then exported to Emmland for final manufacture into finished products and distribution.

Each stage of the supply chain for X32 is dedicated only to X32 and cannot be adapted to other materials. In Emmland, P&J is the major employer in several medium-sized towns. In Aytown, for example, P&J employs 45% of the workforce and in Betown, P&J employs 3,000 people and also supports a number of local causes including a children's nursery, an amateur football club and a number of adult education classes. In total, the company employs 15,000 people in Emmland and another 30,000 people in the various parts of the supply chain (mining and processing) in developing countries. Unlike in Emmland, where health and safety regulations are strong, there are no such regulations in most of the developing countries in which P&J operates.

Recently, some independent academic research discovered that X32 was very harmful to human health, particularly in the processing stages, causing a wide range of fatal respiratory diseases, including some that remain inactive in the body for many decades. Doctors had suspected for a while that X32 was the cause of a number of conditions that P&J employees and those working with the material had died from, but it was only when Professor Harry Kroll discovered how X32 actually attacked the body that the link was known for certain. The discovery caused a great deal of distress at P&J, and also in the industries which used X32.

The company was faced with a very difficult situation. Given that 60% of P&J's business was concerned with X32, Professor Kroll's findings could not be ignored. Although demand for X32 remained unaffected by Kroll's findings in the short to medium term, the company had to consider a new legal risk from a stream of potential litigation actions against the company from employees who worked in environments containing high levels of X32 fibre, and workers in industries which used X32 in their own processes.

In order to gain some understanding of the potential value of future compensation losses, P&J took legal advice and produced two sets of figures, both describing the present value of cumulative future compensation payments through litigation against the company. These forecasts were based on financial modelling using another product of which the company was aware, which had also been found to be hazardous to health.

	In 5 years $(M)	In 15 years $(M)	In 25 years $(M)	In 35 years $(M)
Best case	5	30	150	400
Worst case	20	80	350	1,000

The finance director (FD), Hannah Yin, informed the P&J board that the company could not survive if the worst-case scenario was realised. She said that the actual outcome depended upon the proportion of people affected, the period that the illness lay undetected in the body, the control measures which were put in place to reduce the exposure of employees and users to X32, and society's perception of X32 as a material. She estimated that losses at least the size of the best case scenario were very likely to occur and would cause a manageable but highly damaging level of losses.

The worst case scenario was far less likely but would make it impossible for the company to survive. Although profitable, P&J had been highly geared for several years and it was thought unlikely that its banks would lend it any further funds. Hannah Yin explained that this would limit the company's options when dealing with the risk. She also said that the company had little by way of retained earnings.

Chief executive officer, Laszlo Ho, commissioned a study to see whether the health risk to P&J workers could be managed with extra internal controls relating to safety measures to eliminate or reduce exposure to X32 dust. The confidential report said that it would be very difficult to manage X32 dust in the three stages of the supply chain unless the facilities were redesigned and rebuilt completely, and unless independent breathing apparatus was issued to all people coming into contact with X32 at any stage. FD Hannah Yin calculated that a full refit of all of the company's mines, processing and manufacturing plants (which Mr Ho called 'Plan A') was simply not affordable given the current market price of X32 and the current costs of production. Laszlo Ho then proposed the idea of a partial refit of the Aytown and Betown plants because, being in Emmland, they were more visible to investors and most other stakeholders.

Mr Ho reasoned that this partial refit (which he called 'Plan B') would enable the company to claim it was making progress on improving internal controls relating to safety measures whilst managing current costs and 'waiting to see' how the market for X32 fared in the longer term. Under Plan B, no changes would be made to limit exposure to X32 in the company's operations in developing countries.

Hannah Yin, a qualified accountant, was trusted by shareholders because of her performance in the role of FD over several years. Because she would be believed by shareholders, Mr Ho offered to substantially increase her share options if she would report only the 'best case' scenario to shareholders and report 'Plan B' as evidence of the company's social responsibility. She accepted Mr Ho's offer and reported to shareholders as he had suggested. She also said that the company was aware of Professor Kroll's research but argued that the findings were not conclusive and also not considered a serious risk to P&J's future success.

Eventually, through speaking to an anonymous company source, a financial journalist discovered the whole story and felt that the public, and P&J's shareholders in particular, would want to know about the events and the decisions that had been taken in P&J. He decided to write an article for his magazine, Investors in Companies, on what he had discovered.

Required:

(a) **Define 'social footprint' and explain, from the case, four potential social implications of Professor Kroll's discovery about the health risks of X32.** **(10 marks)**

(b) **Describe what 'risk diversification' means and explain why diversifying the risk related to the potential claims against the use of X32 would be very difficult for P&J.**

(10 marks)

(Total: 20 marks)

47 CHEN PRODUCTS

Chen Products produces four manufactured products: Products 1, 2, 3 and 4. The company's risk committee recently met to discuss how the company might respond to a number of problems that have arisen with Product 2. After a number of incidents in which Product 2 had failed whilst being used by customers, Chen Products had been presented with compensation claims from customers injured and inconvenienced by the product failure. It was decided that the risk committee should meet to discuss the options.

When the discussion of Product 2 began, committee chairman Anne Ricardo reminded her colleagues that, apart from the compensation claims, Product 2 was a highly profitable product.

Chen's risk management committee comprised four non-executive directors who each had different backgrounds and areas of expertise. None of them had direct experience of Chen's industry or products. It was noted that it was common for them to disagree among themselves as to how risks should be managed and that in some situations, each member proposed a quite different strategy to manage a given risk. This was the case when they discussed which risk management strategy to adopt with regard to Product 2.

Required:

Using the TARA framework, construct four possible strategies for managing the risk presented by Product 2. Your answer should describe each strategy and explain how each might be applied in the case. **(10 marks)**

E: TECHNOLOGY AND DATA ANALYTICS

48   GOOD SPORTS

Good Sports Limited is an independent sports goods retailer owned and operated by two partners, Alan and Bob. The sports retailing business in the UK has undergone a major change over the past ten years. First of all the supply side has been transformed by the emergence of a few global manufacturers of the core sports products, such as training shoes and football shirts. This consolidation has made them increasingly unwilling to provide good service to the independent sportswear retailers too small to buy in sufficiently large quantities. These independent retailers can stock popular global brands, but have to order using the Internet and have no opportunity to meet the manufacturer's sales representatives. Secondly, UK's sportswear retailing has undergone significant structural change with the rapid growth of a small number of national retail chains with the buying power to offset the power of the global manufacturers. These retail chains stock a limited range of high volume branded products and charge low prices the independent retailer cannot hope to match.

Good Sports has survived by becoming a specialist niche retailer catering for less popular sports such as cricket and hockey. They are able to offer the specialist advice and stock the goods that their customers want. Increasingly since 2000 Good Sports has become aware of the growing impact of e-business in general, and e-retailing in particular. They employed a specialist website designer and created an online purchasing facility for their customers. The results were less than impressive, with the Internet search engines not picking up the company website. The seasonal nature of Good Sports' business, together with the variations in sizes and colours needed to meet an individual customer's needs, meant that the sales volumes were insufficient to justify the costs of running the site.

Bob, however, is convinced that developing an e-business strategy suited to the needs of the independent sports retailer such as Good Sports will be key to business survival. He has been encouraged by the growing interest of customers in other countries to the service and product range they offer. He is also aware of the need to integrate an e-business strategy with their current marketing, which to date has been limited to the sponsorship of local sports teams and advertisements taken in specialist sports magazines. Above all, he wants to avoid head-on competition with the national retailers and their emphasis on popular branded sportswear sold at retail prices that are below the cost price at which Good Sports can buy the goods.

Required:

(a)   **Provide the partners with a short report on the advantages and disadvantages to Good Sports of developing an e-business strategy and the processes most likely to be affected by such a strategy.**   **(15 marks)**

(b)   **Good Sports Limited has successfully followed a niche strategy to date. Assess the extent to which an appropriate e-business strategy could help support such a niche strategy.**   **(10 marks)**

(Total: 25 marks)

49   CRONIN AUTO RETAIL

Cronin Auto Retail (CAR) is a car dealer that sells used cars bought at auctions by its experienced team of buyers. Every car for sale is less than two years old and has a full service history. The company concentrates on small family cars and, at any one time, there are about 120 on display at its purpose-built premises.

The premises were acquired five years ago on a 25 year lease and they include a workshop, a small cafe and a children's playroom. All vehicles are selected by one of five experienced buyers who attend auctions throughout the country. Each attendance costs CAR about $500 per day in staff and travelling costs and usually leads to the purchase of five cars. On average, each car costs CAR $10,000 and is sold to the customer for $12,000. The company has a good sales and profitability record, although a recent economic recession has led the managing director to question 'whether we are selling the right type of cars. Recently, I wonder if we have been buying cars that our team of buyers would like to drive, not what our customers want to buy?' However, the personal selection of quality cars has been an important part of CAR's business model and it is stressed in their marketing literature and website.

Sales records show that 90% of all sales are to customers who live within two hours' drive of CAR's base. This is to be expected as there are many competitors and most customers want to buy from a garage that they can easily return the car to if it needs inspection, a service or repair. Consequently, CAR concentrates on display advertising in newspapers in this geographical area. It also has a customer database containing the records of people who have bought cars in the last three years. All customers receive a regular mail-shot, listing the cars for sale and highlighting any special offers or promotions. The company has a website where all the cars are listed with a series of photographs showing each car from a variety of angles. The website also contains general information about the company, special offers and promotions, and information about its service, maintenance and repair service.

The managing director is keen to examine how the 'interactivity, intelligence, individualisation and independence of location offered by e-marketing media can help us at CAR'.

Required:

Evaluate how the principles of interactivity, intelligence, individualisation and independence of location might be applied in the e-marketing of the products and services of CAR.   **(16 marks)**

Professional skills marks will be awarded for demonstrating professional scepticism skills relevant to the achievability for CAR of the benefits from e-marketing.   **(2 marks)**

(Total: 18 marks)

50   SRO

Shop Reviewers Online (SRO) was founded in 2010 by Amy Needham. She felt that many customers buying from online stores were misled by advertising and that too often, purchased products turned out to be unreliable, faulty or failed to meet the customers' expectations. Amy believed that the online retail industry was increasingly acting unethically, caring only for profits at the expense of the needs and expectations of customers.

Consequently, she set up SRO to 'provide an unbiased review of online stores to ensure the customer has all available information'. The company offers reviews of current online stores and provides direct links for customers to shop at the stores featured on its site. The reviews include price comparisons, provided by SRO, as well as general reviews provided by registered users of the site. The company has two main revenue streams. The first is advertising revenue from online stores who place advertisements on the SRO site.

The second revenue stream is commission from sales by online stores to customers who have clicked on the sponsored links provided on the SRO website. This commission is only paid by stores who have entered into such a commission arrangement with SRO.

SRO relies upon its website being available online 24 hours a day, 7 days a week. For this reason it has backup servers running concurrently with the main servers on which data is processed and stored. The servers are directly linked so that any update to the main servers automatically occurs on the backup. The servers are all housed in the same computer centre in the company head office. The computer centre has enhanced its security by implementing a fingerprint recognition system for controlling access to the site. However, as the majority of staff at headquarters are IT personnel, and often temporary staff are hired to cover absentees, the fingerprint recognition system is not comprehensive and, to save time, is often bypassed. Similarly, to save time needed to set up new permanent staff with passwords to access the company's systems, a general 'administrator' user has been created, with the password 'password'. Many temporary staff access the system in this way.

SRO has an intelligent software application which constantly searches the internet for product price changes, uploading these into the reviews of the online store in question. Sometimes, however, there have been problems. Usually this is when the application has not recognised an outdated page and has replaced the correct latest price with an old price found on the outdated page. Furthermore, this intelligent software application needs permanent continual access to the internet, and SRO has identified a problem with its firewall which has prevented the software application from sometimes updating the internal systems. For this reason, it has removed the firewall protection to help ensure that the correct up-to-date prices of all online stores are shown on the website.

SRO rarely generates other elements of reviews (such as product experience), leaving this to registered users of the site. However, it will, occasionally, submit its own review to help boost a store which pays a higher commission rate than its competitors. SRO is always honest in its reviews, but the more reviews a store has, the higher up the search list it appears, when a customer searches for a specific product.

Registered users can submit as many reviews as they wish. Unregistered users may also submit reviews, which will be published under the name 'anonymous', but these reviewers will be unable to comment on the reviews of others. SRO checks reviews for appropriate content, but does not contact the store to verify the accuracy of the review.

SRO is about to undertake an audit of the adequacy of its general and application IT controls. In addition, SRO is currently undertaking an internal ethical governance audit, which has identified two main areas of concern:

1 **Commercial conflicts of interest**

As mentioned earlier, SRO's business objective is to 'provide an unbiased review of online stores to ensure the customer has all available information'. However, the audit has revealed that both SRO's revenue streams may cause an ethical dilemma with regards to this objective.

2 **Company offices**

SRO has little need for traditional offices, as it does not have a direct customer-facing role. It mainly requires IT technicians to support its automated services. The company has carried out research which suggests that the IT skills it requires could be sourced at a much lower rate overseas. It is considering relocation to one such country. This country has low rates of corporation tax and cheaper labour costs.

However, the country itself is poorly regulated and does not have legislation concerning the quality of information systems or the security of data contained within them, particularly relating to personal data. The culture of the country is such that accepting unauthorised payments for services is also not unusual. Whilst SRO does not condone this in its code of conduct, it is aware that such issues exist in the country under consideration.

Required:

(a) **Evaluate the adequacy of the general and application controls in place within SRO, with respect to its information technology and information systems. Suggest any improvements you consider to be necessary.** **(15 marks)**

(b) **Assess the corporate governance and ethical dilemmas identified by SRO in its possible relocation to the foreign country and discuss the implications of these on organisational mission, purpose and strategy.** **(10 marks)**

(Total: 25 marks)

51 AEC

Introduction

The Accounting Education Consortium (AEC) offers professional accountancy education and training courses. It currently runs classroom-based training courses preparing candidates for professional examinations in eight worldwide centres. Three of these centres are also used for delivering continuing professional development (CPD) courses to qualified accountants. However, only about 30% of the advertised CPD courses and seminars actually run. The rest are cancelled through not having enough participants to make them economically viable.

AEC has developed a comprehensive set of course manuals to support the preparation of its candidates for professional examinations. There is a course manual for every examination paper in the professional examination scheme. As well as being used on its classroom-based courses, these course manuals are also available for purchase over the Internet. The complete set of manuals for a professional examinations scheme costs $180.00 and the web site has a secure payment facility which allows this to be paid by credit card. Once purchased, the manuals may be downloaded or they may be sent on a CD to the home address of the purchaser. It is only possible to purchase the complete set of manuals for the scheme, not individual manuals for particular examinations.

To help the student decide if he or she wishes to buy the complete manual set, the web site has extracts from a sample course manual. This sample may be accessed, viewed and printed once a student has registered their email address, name and address on the web site.

AEC has recently won a contract to supply professional accountancy training to a global accounting company. All students working for this company will now be trained by AEC at one of its worldwide centres.

Web site

The AEC web site has the following functionality:

Who we are: A short description of the company and its products and services.

Professional education courses: Course dates, locations and standard fees for professional examination courses. This schedule of courses is printable.

Continuing professional development: Course dates, locations and standard fees for CPD courses and seminars. This schedule is also printable.

CPD catalogue: Detailed course and seminar descriptions for CPD courses and seminars.

Downloadable study material: Extracts from a sample course manual. Visitors to the site wishing to access this material must register their email address, name and address. 5,500 people registered last year to download study material.

Purchase study material: Secure purchase of a complete manual set for the professional scheme. Payment is by credit card. On completion of successful payment, the visitor is able to download the manuals or to request them to be shipped to a certain address on a CD. At present, 10% of the people who view downloadable study material proceed to purchase.

Who to contact: Who to contact for booking professional training courses or CPD courses and seminars. It provides the name, email address, fax number, telephone number and address of a contact at each of the eight worldwide centres.

Marketing strategy

The marketing manager of AEC has traditionally used magazines, newspapers and direct mail to promote its courses and products. Direct mail is primarily used for sending printed course catalogues to potential customers for CPD courses and seminars. However, she is now keen to develop the potential of the Internet and to increase investment in this medium at the expense of the traditional marketing media. Table 1 shows the percentage allocation of her budget for 20X8, compared with 20X7. The actual budget has only been increased by 3% in 20X8.

Table 1

Percentage allocation of marketing budget (20X7–20X8)

	20X8	20X7
Advertising	30%	40%
Direct mail	10%	30%
Sponsorship	10%	10%
Internet	50%	20%

Required:

(a)   Explain, in the context of AEC, how the marketing characteristics of electronic media (such as the Internet) differ from those of traditional marketing media such as advertising and direct mail. **(10 marks)**

(b)   Evaluate how the marketing manager might use electronic marketing (including the Internet) to vary the marketing mix at AEC. **(15 marks)**

(Total: 25 marks)

52   THE HOLIDAY COMPANY

The Holiday Company (HC) currently offers travel agency services by giving travel advice and making travel bookings for customers who physically visit the offices located in most major towns in the country. However, it is progressively reducing this part of the business while simultaneously trying to achieve a greater proportion of its revenue online.

To help meet this objective, HC is in the process of forming a new business unit to market and sell luxury holidays. The holiday product range marketed by this new business unit will be named Inspirations. It is intended that Inspirations will provide a high quality, bespoke holiday service for discerning clients. HC has decided that this new business unit will have its own mission statement of 'delivering a high quality service for discerning travellers'.

The new managing director of Inspirations has stated that it has an objective of achieving annual revenue of $100m by 2018.

This would be approximately 25% of the total forecast revenue for HC that year, but it is expected to represent only about 5% of the total number of holidays sold by HC. The type of holidays offered by Inspirations is already provided by some of HC's competitors.

Dilip Kharel, the new director of marketing of Inspirations, has stated that the internet should be increasingly used as the main source of marketing and selling the holidays, as 'the days are almost gone when families visit a 'high street' travel agency to plan their holiday; it's all done now from the comfort of the home'. He believes that potential customers of Inspirations will not want to visit high street travel agencies.

HC currently makes extensive use of traditional marketing techniques, sending out travel brochures containing all of its holidays to potential customers. However, as Dilip has recognised, 'the problem is that we don't even know if our customers bother opening these, or if they put them directly into the dustbin.' These brochures are often produced months in advance, and may advertise holidays which are no longer available. Customers will not discover this until they visit one of the travel agents. The company currently does make some use of targeted emails, but it has been accused of sending spam mail in the past and mass mailing a weekly email of all current holiday offers to everyone registered on its database.

Dilip is keen to embrace the opportunities offered by electronic marketing and believes that Inspirations can benefit greatly by exploiting the principles of intelligence, individualisation, interactivity, integration and independence of location which are central to electronic marketing.

Inspirations will offer holidays in a wide variety of locations, including the Caribbean, Africa and Asia, and plan to offer 'themed' trips, such as gourmet food holidays and heritage trips. Different countries may have different requirements for visiting tourists, such as visa regulations. Inspirations does not own hotels or aircraft and therefore the majority of holidays offered will be provided by third-party suppliers, such as hotel and airline companies. This means that Inspirations can lack control over some elements such as passenger taxes.

Inspirations will have representatives on site in all resorts to meet guests at airports and to address any issues they have with the holiday. However, the hotels and excursions will not be solely or exclusively offered to Inspirations guests. For example, there will be other guests at a hotel who have not booked through Inspirations.

Dilip is concerned about this. He feels that the company needs to be able to differentiate itself, either in the overall holiday experience itself or in the marketing of it, so that customers are more likely to book such holidays through Inspirations, rather than through a competitor, or indeed through booking with the hotel directly. He also recognises the importance of adopting an appropriate pricing strategy which meets the needs of the organisation (HC and Inspirations) and customers alike.

Required:

Evaluate how the principles of intelligence, individualisation, interactivity, integration and independence of location could be exploited when marketing the new range of holidays to be offered by Inspirations. **(15 marks)**

53 BA TIMES

The country of Umboria has two professional business analysis associations, both running certification examination schemes for business analysts worldwide. These are the Association of Benefits Consultants (ABC) and the Institute of Consultants, Finance and Commerce (ICFC). Many private and public sector learning providers run accredited training courses to prepare candidates for the examinations.

Some learning providers provide courses for both associations, whilst others focus on niche markets. Umboria itself is a wealthy country with high labour costs and property prices, particularly in the capital city of Ambosium.

Victor Isaacs is the editor of the BA Times, a subscription magazine, published once a month, which provides news and articles preparing students for the examinations of both business analysis associations. The magazine is edited and printed in offices and an adjoining factory in Ambosium. The offices and factory are leased and the magazine currently employs 20 people, all of whom live close to the offices. It is the only independent magazine in the sector. Each association has its own magazine and website, but relatively tight control is maintained over their editorial policy. Victor was the editor of the ABC magazine (Business Analysis Today) for 16 years before establishing the BA Times nine years ago. Because of its independence, the BA Times can be a little more controversial and provocative than its rivals and it is popular with students and well respected by the profession.

However, despite such recognition, the magazine is currently unprofitable due to increased production, distribution and office costs, falling subscriptions and reduced advertising. Changing reading habits in Umboria, particularly amongst the young, has led to less reading of printed media. All of the traditional media providers are experiencing financial problems. The sales of printed magazines and the profits of publishers are both falling dramatically throughout Umboria. Furthermore, advertisers are increasingly unconvinced about the effectiveness of advertising in printed magazines and so the advertising revenues of these magazines are also falling.

The BA Times currently has a website but its role is to convince the visitor to order the printed magazine. The website offers extracts of news and articles, often with provocative headlines, which may only be read in full in the printed magazine.

Recent survey

A recent survey of people who had decided not to renew their BA Times subscription revealed the following comments:

> I quite enjoy reading the news parts, but not the in-depth analysis of examinations that I am not taking.
> *ABC student*

> I have reached the final stage of my examinations. I do not want to read articles about the stages I have already passed. I reckon only about 15% of BA Times is relevant to me now.
> *ABC Final Stage student*

> I became a business analyst to get a job, not just to sit examinations and read about examining bodies.
> *ICFC student*

The examinations are getting more demanding and Victor is under pressure to increase the number of technical examination articles in the magazine, despite the fact that this will make the magazine longer and heavier and so increase print and distribution costs.

Victor is aware that new technology and new media offer opportunities for changing the business model and the financial performance of the BA Times. However, he likes the physical, tactile feel of printed magazines and he feels that some of his subscribers do as well. Also, he cannot see how harnessing new technology will make him money, particularly if it leads to decreasing sales of the printed magazine. He is also concerned about how his subscribers and advertisers will react to technological change. He feels that some subscribers will not have access to online technology and that many advertisers would prefer to continue with display advertisements in a printed magazine.

Required:

Write a short report to Victor which addresses the specific concerns Victor has about the effect of any potential technology or media change on his subscribers, on his advertisers and on the financial viability of his company. **(10 marks)**

54   RETAIL WORLD

Retail World (RW) is a major international retail chain, selling groceries, clothing, electronic items, toiletries and homeware items. It has grown rapidly across a number of different countries, offering a broad product range to suit a wide range of customer segments. Growth has been through the expansion of existing stores, the opening of new stores and on line sales.

The new finance director, whose background is in a non-retail environment, is keen to understand the sales trends of the organisation, as well as the industry, in order to help develop a strategy which can take advantage of these trends in the future. A business analyst has provided summarised internal sales data for this purpose detailing the last three years of trading and detail the growth in the number of stores and average quarterly sales.

The company's IT systems are fully integrated and associated controls are rigorous, allowing the data to be manipulated in many ways. The number of stores has grown annually and the analyst believes that this is a better indicator of the expected future revenue than simply the passage of time. The average number of stores expected to be in operation in 2019 is 3,700 rising to 4,000 in 2020.

The finance director was interested to receive the analysis; however, he also stated that it was not quite as useful as he would have hoped for, commenting, 'I have been hearing a lot about big data at industry meetings I have attended. I think we should investigate the ways in which we could use this, and the benefits we might hope to obtain from it.'

Required:

Prepare a briefing note for the Finance Director which:

(a) **Outlines 'big data' and how it could be used to enhance strategic development within RW.** **(10 marks)**

In a similar context the FD had recently attended a forum of retail consultants who had stressed the future significance of 'blockchain' technology for the enhancement of the retail industry.

The FD would like to present his initial thoughts on this concept to the board at their next scheduled meeting and has asked you to help.

(b) **Prepare two presentation slides, together with accompanying notes, for the FD to be used which outlines why blockchain technology could be beneficial at Retail World and the challenges that the introduction of such technology might present.**

(8 marks)

(Total: 18 marks)

F: ORGANISATIONAL CONTROL AND AUDIT

55 YAHTY

The YAHTY organisation provides investment services to individuals living away from their country of residence. For example, a person may be required to work in a foreign country for two or three years, but will retain an investment portfolio of shares, bank account deposits, pension contributions, etc. in their home country. The YAHTY organisation manages this portfolio for the individual until they return to their country.

YAHTY employs 35 investment accountants to provide the investment services. Each accountant controls the portfolio of up to 200 clients, with an average fund value of €500,000. Decisions regarding the companies to invest in, the pension scheme funds to use, etc. are made by the individual financial accountant. The accountant retains a computer record for each client which shows the funds invested in, the values and recent transfers. As long as the individual requirements of the client are met, then the YAHTY organisation is deemed to have been successful in managing that client. A senior accountant provides additional investment advice should the need arise.

For each client, the investment accountant is the authorised signatory on the client accounts, enabling funds transfers to be made by that individual. Any payment over €100,000 has to be authorised by the senior accountant.

Most transfers are between €10,000 and €50,000 – the senior accountant only checking material transactions. At any time, the list of investments on the computer must agree to share certificates, etc. retained by the accountant. The list of investments is not, however, linked to the payments systems in YAHTY.

Documentation for each transfer has to be retained by each investment accountant. Documents regarding fund transfers are retained in date order within a central filing system. This procedure provides YAHTY with significant savings in storage costs while ensuring that documentation can be obtained when necessary.

When a client returns to their home country, the investment manager transfers all funds back into the client's name. A list of the investments is printed off from the accountant's computer system and this is given to the client along with share certificates, pension scheme reports, etc. Full transaction histories are not available due to the time required for obtaining detailed historical documentation from the filing system already mentioned above.

To ensure completeness and accuracy of transfer, the senior accountant reviews all funds with a value of more than €750,000 by checking the list of investments to the supporting documentation.

Required:

Prepare a report for the directors of YAHTY that evaluates the YAHTY organisation's internal control systems, identifying any weaknesses; assesses the effectiveness of any controls over those weaknesses; and recommends improvements to the system of internal controls.

(15 marks)

56   STEFAN KRANK

Stefan Krank had been the most successful fund manager at Fortune Investments for the past five years. During this time he had earned a large salary, which was supplemented by considerable annual bonuses from the many profitable investment portfolios he had managed for his wealthy private clients. Consequently, he and his family had become accustomed to a very lavish lifestyle, which was threatened when he started to have a run of bad luck on the markets.

Over the past few months he had been unable to deliver the predicted levels of returns for his clients, so he decided to resort to drastic measures. Initially he tried to recover the position by investing funds in high risk securities to generate higher returns, even though his clients had only ever agreed to medium risk levels for their investments. However, even this tactic failed to deliver sufficient profits and some investments actually lost considerable amounts of money. In desperation Krank's behaviour took a very disturbing turn when he started a fraudulent investment operation where he paid returns to his existing investors from new capital paid into the fund by new investors, rather than from profit earned. He enticed new investors into the scheme by offering them far higher returns than were available from other comparable investments, often in the form of short-term profits which were both abnormally high and unusually consistent. Unfortunately in order to maintain this deception of seemingly perpetual high returns, Krank required an ever-increasing flow of money from new investors which was clearly unsustainable. Over time returns became far more volatile simply because of the higher risk investments and reduced amounts of new investment capital becoming available.

James Reynolds, a wealthy client who wanted to extract value from a fund managed by Krank for his impending retirement, noticed that returns on his fund were showing increased volatility. He demanded an explanation from Krank, who responded by advising him that he must have looked at his fund on a bad day. He assured Mr Reynolds he always aimed to maximise returns on his clients' investments even if this meant bending the rules occasionally. He further claimed that Mr Reynold's fund would both grow in value and stabilise very soon. Mr Reynolds was unconvinced by Krank's weak and unsubstantiated explanation; so he referred the matter to Krank's manager.

Required:

(a)   Discuss the extent to which the main objectives of an internal control system were not achieved at Fortune Investments, and criticise how the behaviour of Stefan Krank resulted in a clear breach in his duty to his clients as their fund manager.

(12 marks)

(b)   Explain the importance of good quality information at Fortune Investments, both for the effective management of funds, and their monitoring by investors.   (7 marks)

(Total: 19 marks)

57   DUTTON SUPERMARKET

In pursuit of ever greater profits to satisfy the shareholders, the supermarket chain Dutton had searched overseas for cheaper suppliers. Unfortunately this strategy failed when the following headline appeared in the newspapers:

'Dutton Supermarket poisons customers'

Government inspections of farming facilities in the chosen countries were almost non-existent so Dutton had employed a local inspector to work closely with factory managers and to carry out food hygiene audits. When the news of the disaster was first reported to the board six months after problems begun the inspector simply disappeared and still cannot be traced.

In their defence, the suppliers say they were forced to cut veterinary attention to their herds because of the low rate paid by Dutton for their meat. The result was that large amounts of infected foodstuffs were exported to the supermarket's home country.

When interviewed as part of a review of the failure in control, Dutton store managers said that they had known for some time that there was something wrong with the meat. As part of their routine goods inward inspection they examined the cellophane wrapped cuts and threw out any that seemed discoloured. Most say that they had not received any complaints from customers regarding ill effects following consumption of the product.

The Chief Executive (CEO) of Dutton, Jon Cooper, fears that the repercussions of this event will have a serious effect on this year's profit. Some customers have defected to competitors whilst an environmental group is protesting at some of the larger stores. There are rumours of a government audit of the company's supplier systems and they have, of course, needed to commence a search for a new and hopefully cheaper supplier in another country.

Required:

Examine failures in internal control at Dutton and recommend improvements.   (15 marks)

58 BLUP CO

When Blup Co (a listed company involved in water supply) decided to establish an internal audit function, in line with new listing rules, the board approached Karen Huyer, an external consultant. She explained that internal audit is especially important in highly regulated industries but that it could also offer benefits to companies regardless of the industry context.

Karen was particularly keen to talk to John Xu, the head of the audit committee. John explained that because Blup Co was a water supply company and was thus highly regulated, he considered it important that all of the members of the audit committee were professional water engineers so that they fully understood the industry and its technical challenges. All three members of the audit committee were non-executive directors and all were recently retired members of the Blup executive board. When Karen asked about the relationship with external auditors, John said that they had an 'excellent' relationship, saying that this was because the external audit practice was run by the chairman's son-in-law.

Karen said that one of the essential functions of internal audit is to provide assurance that the internal controls which underpinned financial reporting are effective. She said that effective internal controls are necessary for maintaining the integrity of financial reporting and that the new internal audit function could help with that.

Required:

(a) Discuss the importance of internal audit in a highly regulated industry such as the water industry that Blup Co. operates in. **(7 marks)**

(b) (i) Criticise the ways in which Blup Co's audit committee has failed to meet best practice. **(6 marks)**

(ii) Explain why the audit committee is responsible for overseeing the internal audit function. **(6 marks)**

(Total: 19 marks)

59 CC & J

Audit firm CC & J had worked extensively with the global banking organisation Banco for many years. Senior audit partner, Andrezej Puczynski, had built up a close working and personal relationship with the Chief Finance Officer (CFO), often attending private family barbeques. In return for his diligent support and low fee audit work he had been rewarded with hugely lucrative management consultancy contracts that made his local office profits the envy of senior CC&J partners around the world.

The closeness of the relationship could be seen in the automatic selection of CC & J by the CFO, operating as chair of the audit committee of Banco, despite the existence of cut price tenders from audit firm competitors. Andrezej had only met the other two members of the committee once on a shooting trip organised by the CFO. The other members of the committee had no financial expertise and little, if any, involvement in Banco outside of an annual meeting with the committee chairman.

Last week significant financial impropriety was uncovered at Banco leading to the collapse of the firm and its suspension on the stock exchange. Andrezej knew that many of the accounting treatments he had personally signed off were, at the least, stretching the interpretation of accounting standards to their breaking point.

Required:

Discuss the threats to auditor independence in this case and identify measures that would have helped reduce these threats. **(10 marks)**

60 FRANKS & FISHER

The board of Franks & Fisher, a large manufacturing company, decided to set up an internal control and audit function. The proposal was to appoint an internal auditor at mid-management level and also to establish a board level internal audit committee made up mainly of non-executive directors.

The initiative to do so was driven by a recent period of rapid growth. The company had taken on many more activities as a result of growth in its product range. The board decided that the increased size and complexity of its operations created the need for greater control over internal activities and that an internal audit function was a good way forward.

The need was highlighted by a recent event where internal quality standards were not enforced, resulting in the stoppage of a production line for several hours. The production director angrily described the stoppage as 'entirely avoidable' and the finance director, Jason Kumas, said that the stoppage had been very costly.

Mr Kumas said that there were problems with internal control in a number of areas of the company's operations and that there was a great need for internal audit. He said that as the head of the company's accounting and finance function, the new internal auditor should report to him.

The reasons for this, he said, were because as an accountant, he was already familiar with auditing procedure and the fact that he already had information on budgets and other 'control' information that the internal auditor would need.

It was decided that the new internal auditor needed to be a person of some experience and with enough personality not to be intimidated nor diverted by other department heads who might find the internal audits an inconvenience. One debate the board had was whether it would be better to recruit to the position from inside or outside the company. A second argument was over the limits of authority that the internal auditor might be given. It was pointed out that while the board considered the role of internal audit to be very important, it didn't want it to interfere with the activities of other departments to the point where their operational effectiveness was reduced.

Required:

(a) Explain, with reference to the case, the factors that are typically considered when deciding to establish internal audit in an organisation. **(10 marks)**

(b) Construct the argument in favour of appointing the new internal auditor from outside the company rather than promoting internally. **(6 marks)**

(c) Critically evaluate Mr Kumas's belief that the internal auditor should report to him as finance director. **(4 marks)**

(Total: 20 marks)

61   WORLDWIDE MINERALS (WM)

Worldwide Minerals (WM) is a large listed multinational company that deals with natural minerals that are extracted from the ground, processed and sold to a wide range of industrial and construction companies. In order to maintain a consistent supply of minerals into its principal markets, an essential part of WM's business strategy is the seeking out of new sources and the measurement of known reserves. Investment analysts have often pointed out that WM's value rests principally upon the accuracy of its reserve reports as these are the best indicators of future cash flows and earnings. In order to support this key part of its strategy, WM has a large and well-funded geological survey department which, according to the company website, contains 'some of the world's best geologists and minerals scientists'. In its investor relations literature, the company claims that:

'our experts search the earth for mineral reserves and once located, they are carefully measured so that the company can always report on known reserves. This knowledge underpins market confidence and keeps our customers supplied with the inventory they need. You can trust our reserve reports – our reputation depends on it!'

At the last board meeting, the head of the geological survey department, Ranjana Tyler, reported that there was a problem with the latest report because one of the major reserve figures had recently been found to be wrong. The mineral in question, mallerite, was WM's largest mineral in volume terms and Ranjana explained that the mallerite reserves in a deep mine in a certain part of the world had been significantly overestimated. She explained that, based on the interim minerals report, the stock market analysts were expecting WM to announce known mallerite reserves of 4.8 billion tonnes. The actual figure was closer to 2.4 billion tonnes. It was agreed that this difference was sufficient to affect WM's market value, despite the otherwise good results for the past year.

Vanda Monroe, the finance director, said that the share price reflects market confidence in future earnings.

She said that an announcement of an incorrect estimation like that for mallerite would cause a reduction in share value. More importantly for WM itself, however, it could undermine confidence in the geological survey department. All agreed that as this was strategically important for the company, it was a top priority to deal with this problem.

Ranjana explained how the situation had arisen. The major mallerite mine was in a country new to WM's operations. The WM engineer at the mine said it was difficult to deal with some local people because, according to the engineer, 'they didn't like to give us bad news'. The engineer explained that when the mine was found to be smaller than originally thought, he was not told until it was too late to reduce the price paid for the mine. This was embarrassing and it was agreed that it would affect market confidence in WM if it was made public.

The board discussed the options open to it. The chairman, who was also a qualified accountant, was Tim Blake. He began by expressing serious concern about the overestimation and then invited the board to express views freely. Gary Howells, the operations director, said that because disclosing the error to the market would be so damaging, it might be best to keep it a secret and hope that new reserves can be found in the near future that will make up for the shortfall. He said that it was unlikely that this concealment would be found out as shareholders trusted WM and they had many years of good investor relations to draw on. Vanda Monroe, the finance director, reminded the board that the company was bound to certain standards of truthfulness and transparency by its stock market listing.

She pointed out that they were constrained by codes of governance and ethics by the stock market and that colleagues should be aware that WM would be in technical breach of these if the incorrect estimation was concealed from investors. Finally, Martin Chan, the human resources director, said that the error should be disclosed to the investors because he would not want to be deceived if he were an outside investor in the company. He argued that whatever the governance codes said and whatever the cost in terms of reputation and market value, WM should admit its error and cope with whatever consequences arose. The WM board contains three non-executive directors and their views were also invited.

At the preliminary results presentation sometime later, one analyst, Christina Gonzales, who had become aware of the mallerite problem, asked about internal audit and control systems, and whether they were adequate in such a reserve-sensitive industry. WM's chairman, Tim Blake, said that he intended to write a letter to all investors and analysts in the light of the mallerite problem which he hoped would address some of the issues that Miss Gonzales had raised.

Tim Blake has asked you, as an external consultant, to help him draft the letter.

Required:

Draft a letter for Tim Blake to send to WM's investors to include the following:

(a)   why you believe robust internal controls to be important; and

(b)   proposals on how internal systems might be improved in the light of the over-estimation of mallerite at WM.   (12 marks)

Professional skills marks will be awarded for demonstrating communication skills in constructing a persuasive document to reassure investors and analysts over the mallerite problems.**(2 marks)**

(Total: 14 marks)

62   RG

RG manufactures industrial glues and solvents in a single large factory. Approximately 400 different inputs are used to produce the 35 specialist outputs, which range from ultra-strong glues used in aircraft manufacture to high-impact adhesives that are required on construction sites.

Two years ago, with the company only just breaking even, the directors recognised the need for more information to control the business. To assist them with their strategic control of the business, they decided to establish a MIS. This is now operational but provides only the following limited range of information to the directors via their networked computer system:

•   A summary business plan for this and the next two years. The plan includes details of the expected future incomes and expenditure on existing product lines. It was produced by a new member of the accounting department without reference to past production data.

•   Stock balances on individual items of raw materials, finished goods etc. This report is at a very detailed level and comprises 80% of the output from the MIS itself.

•   A summary of changes in total demand for glues and solvents in the market place for the last five years.

This information is presented as a numerical summary in six different sections. Each section takes up one computer screen so only one section can be viewed at a time.

Required:

(a)   Comment on the weaknesses in the information currently being provided to the directors of the company.   **(11 marks)**

(b)   Suggest how the information may be improved, with particular reference to other outputs which the MIS might usefully provide to the directors.   **(8 marks)**

(Total: 19 marks)

G: FINANCE IN PLANNING AND DECISION-MAKING

63   GRAFFOFF

Emile Gonzalez is an industrial chemist who worked for the government of Pablos for more than 20 years. In his spare time, he continually experimented with formulating a product that could remove graffiti from all surfaces.

Graffiti is a particular problem in Pablos and all previous removal methods were expensive, dangerous to apply and did not work on all surfaces. After many years of experimentation, Emile formulated a product that addressed all these issues. His product can be applied safely without protective clothing, it removes graffiti from all surfaces and it can be produced economically in small, as well as large, volumes.

Three years ago, Emile left his government job to focus on refining the product and bringing it to market. He formed a limited liability company, Graffoff, with initial share capital funded by his savings, his family's savings and a legacy from a wealthy relative. He is the sole shareholder in the company, which is based in a factory in central Pablos.

The company has filed two years of results (see Appendix 1 for extracted information from year (2), and it is expected to return similar net profit figures in its third trading year.

Emile takes a significant dividend out of the company each year and he wishes that to continue. He also wishes to remain the sole owner of the company.

Four years ago, Emile was granted a patent for the formula on which his product is based and a further patent on the process used to produce the product. In Pablos, patents are protected for ten years and so Emile has six further years before his formula becomes available to his competitors. Consequently, he wants to rapidly expand the company and plans to lease premises to create 30 new graffiti removal depots in Pablos, each of which will supply graffiti removing services in its local region. He needs $500,000 to finance this organic growth of his company.

Emile does have mixed feelings about his proposed expansion plan. Despite the apparent success of his company, he prefers working in the laboratory to managing people. 'I am just not a people person', he has commented. He is aware that he lacks business experience and, despite the technical excellence of the product, he has failed to build a highly visible brand. He also has particular problems in the accounts receivables department, where he has failed to address the problems of over-worked and demotivated employees. Emile dislikes conflict with customers and so he often offers them extended payment terms to the dismay of the accounts receivables section, who feel that their debt collecting effectiveness is being constantly undermined by his concessions.

In contrast, Graffoff pays bills very promptly, due to a zealous administrator in accounts payable who likes to reduce creditors. Emile is sanguine about this. 'I guess we have the money, so I suppose we should pay them.'

In Pablos, all goods are supplied to customers on 30 days credit. However, in the services sector that Graffoff is trading in, the average settlement period for payables (creditors) is 40 days. One supplier commented that 'Graffoff is unique in its punctuality of payment.'

Emile is currently reviewing how to finance his proposed organic growth. He is unwilling to take on any further external debt and consequently he has also recently considered franchising as an alternative to organic growth. In his proposed arrangement, franchisees would have responsibility for leasing or buying premises to a specification defined in the franchise agreement. The franchise would have exclusive rights to the Graffoff product in a defined geographical region.

The Equipment Emporium has 57 superstores throughout the country selling tools and machines such as air compressors, generators and ventilation systems. It is a well-recognised brand with a strong marketing presence. It focuses on selling specialist products in bright, well-lit superstores. It has approached Graffoff to ask whether it can sell the Graffoff product through its superstores. Emile has rejected this suggestion because he feels that his product requires proper training if it is to be used efficiently and safely.

He sees Graffoff as offering a complete service (graffiti removal), not just a product (graffiti removal equipment) and so selling through The Equipment Emporium would be inappropriate.

Required:

(a) **Evaluate the franchising option being considered, highlighting the advantages and disadvantages of this approach from Emile's perspective.**   **(10 marks)**

(b) **Evaluate how other forms of strategic alliance might be appropriate approaches to strategy development at Graffoff.**   **(7 marks)**

(c) **A consultant has suggested that Graffoff should be able to completely fund its proposed organic expansion (at a cost of $500,000) through internally generated sources of finance. Evaluate this claim.**   **(8 marks)**

(Total: 25 marks)

APPENDIX 1: Extracted financial data for Graffoff's second year of trading
(All figures in $000)

Extract from the statement of financial position: as at 31 December 20X1		Extracts from the income statement: as at 31 December 20X1	
ASSETS		Revenue	1,600
Non-current assets		Cost of sales	(1,375)
Property, plant and equipment	1,385	Gross profit	225
Intangible assets	100	Administrative expenses	(100)
Total non-current assets	1,485	Finance costs	(15)
Current assets		Profit before tax	110
Inventories	100	Income tax expense	(20)
Trade receivables	260	Profit for the period	90
Cash and cash equivalents	30		
Total current assets	390		
Total assets	1,875		

EQUITY AND LIABILITIES

Share capital	1,500
Retained earnings	30
Total equity	1,530
Non-current liabilities	
Long-term borrowings	250
Total non-current liabilities	250
Current liabilities	
Trade and other payables	75
Current tax payable	20
Total current liabilities	95
Total liabilities	345
Total equity and liabilities	1,875

64 PROTECH-PUBLIC

Ergo city authority administers environmental, social care, housing and cultural services to the city of Ergo. The city itself has many social problems and a recent report from the local government auditor criticised the Chief Executive Officer (CEO) for not spending enough time and money addressing the pressing housing problems of the city.

Since 1970 the authority has had its own internal Information Technology (IT) department. However, there has been increasing criticism of the cost and performance of this department.

The CEO has commented that 'we seem to expand the department to cope with special demands (such as the millennium bug) but the department never seems to shrink back to its original size when the need has passed'. Some employees are lost through natural wastage, but there have never been any redundancies in IT and the labour laws of the nation, and strong trade unions within the authority, make it difficult to make staff redundant.

In the last few years there has been an on-going dispute between managers in the IT department and managers in the finance function. The dispute started due to claims about the falsification of expenses but has since escalated into a personal battle between the director of IT and the finance director. The CEO has had to intervene personally in this dispute and has spent many hours trying to reconcile the two sides. However, issues still remain and there is still tension between the managers of the two departments.

A recent internal human resources (HR) survey of the IT department found that, despite acknowledging that they received above average pay, employees were not very satisfied. The main complaints were about poor management, the ingratitude of user departments, ('we are always being told that we are overheads, and are not core to the business of the authority') and the absence of promotion opportunities within the department. The ingratitude of users is despite the IT department running a relatively flexible approach to fulfilling users' needs.

There is no cross-charging for IT services provided and changes to user requirements are accommodated right up to the release of the software. The director of IT is also critical of the staffing constraints imposed on him. He has recently tried to recruit specialists in web services and 'cloud computing' without any success. He also says that 'there are probably other technologies that I have not even heard of that we should be exploring and exploiting'.

The CEO has been approached by a large established IT service company, ProTech, to form a new company ProTech-Public that combines the public sector IT expertise of the authority with the commercial and IT knowledge of ProTech. The joint company will be a private limited company, owned 51% by ProTech and 49% by the city authority. All existing employees in the IT department and the IT technology of the city authority will be transferred to ProTech who will then enter into a 10 year outsourcing arrangement with the city authority. The CEO is very keen on the idea and he sees many other authorities following this route.

The only exception to this transfer of resources concerns the business analysts who are currently in the IT department. They will be retained by the authority and located in a new business analysis department reporting directly to the CEO.

In principle, the creation of the new company and the outsourcing deal has been agreed.

Required:

Evaluate the potential benefits to the city authority and its IT employees, of outsourcing IT to ProTech-Public.   **(12 marks)**

65   8-HATS PROMOTIONS

8-Hats Promotions was formed twenty years ago by Barry Gorkov to plan, organise and run folk festivals in Arcadia. It soon established itself as a major events organiser and diversified into running events for the staff and customers of major companies. For example, for many years it has organised launch events, staff reward days and customer experiences for Kuizan, the car manufacturer. 8-Hats has grown through a combination of organic growth and acquiring similar and complementary companies.

Recently, it purchased a travel agent (now operated as the travel department of 8-Hats) to provide travel to and from the events that it organised.

Barry Gorkov is himself a flamboyant figure who, in the early years of the company, changed his name to Barry Blunt to reflect his image and approach. He calls all the events 'jobs', a terminology used throughout the company. A distinction is made between external jobs (for customers) and internal jobs (within 8-Hats itself). The company is organised on functional lines. The sales and marketing department tenders for external jobs and negotiates contracts. Sales managers receive turnover-related bonuses and 8-Hats is known in the industry for its aggressive pricing policies. Once a contract is signed, responsibility for the job is passed to the events department which actually organises the event. It is known for its creativity and passion. The operations department has responsibility for running the event (job) on the day and for delivering the vision defined by the events department. The travel department is responsible for any travel arrangements associated with the job. Finally, the finance department is responsible for managing cash flow throughout the job, raising customer invoices, paying supplier invoices and chasing any late payments.

However, there is increasing friction between the departments. The operations department is often unable to deliver the features and functionality defined by the events department within the budget agreed by the sales manager.

Finance is unaware of the cash flow implications of the job. Recently, an event was in jeopardy because suppliers had not been paid. They threatened to withdraw their services from the event. Eventually, Barry Blunt had to resolve friction between finance and other departments by acquiring further funding from the bank. The event went ahead, but it unsettled Kuizan which had commissioned the job. The sales and marketing department has also complained about the margins expected by the travel department, claiming that they are making the company uncompetitive.

There has been a considerable amount of discussion at 8-Hats about the investment appraisal approach used to evaluate internal jobs. The company does not have sufficient money and resources to carry out all the internal jobs that need doing. Consequently, the finance department has used the Net Present Value (NPV) technique as a way of choosing which jobs should be undertaken. Appendix 1 shows an example comparison of two computer system applications that had been under consideration. Job One was selected because its Net Present Value (NPV) was higher ($25,015) than Job Two ($2,090).

'I don't want to tell you about the specific details of the two applications, so I have called them Job One and Job Two' said Barry. 'However, in the end, Job One was a disaster. Looking back, we should have gone with Job Two, not Job One. We should have used simple payback, as I am certain that Job Two, even on the initial figures, paid back much sooner than Job One. That approach would have suited our mentality at the time – quick wins. Whoever chose a discount rate of 8% should be fired – inflation has been well below this for the last five years. We should have used 3% or 4%. Also, calculating the IRR would have been useful, as I am sure that Job Two would have shown a better IRR than Job One, particularly as the intangible benefits of improved staff morale appear to be underestimated. Intangible benefits are just as important as tangible benefits. Finally, we should definitely have performed a benefits realisation analysis at the end of the feasibility study. Leaving it to after the project had ended was a ridiculous idea.'

Required:

(a)   Barry Blunt has criticised the investment appraisal approach used at 8-Hats to evaluate internal jobs. He has made specific comments on payback, discount rate, IRR, intangible benefits and benefits realisation.

   Critically evaluate Barry's comments on the investment appraisal approach used at 8-Hats to evaluate internal jobs.   **(15 marks)**

(b)   **Discuss the principles, benefits and problems of introducing a matrix management structure at 8-Hats.**   **(10 marks)**

   (Total: 25 marks)

Figure 1: NPV calculation for two projects at 8-Hats (with a discount rate of 8%)

Job One $000s

		Year 0	Year 1	Year 2	Year 3	Year 4	
Costs	Hardware costs	50	0	0	0	0	
	Software costs	50	0	0	0	0	
	Maintenance costs	10	10	10	10	10	
	Total	110	10	10	10	10	
		Year 0	Year 1	Year 2	Year 3	Year 4	
Benefits	Staff savings	0	40	5	0	0	
	Contractor savings	0	20	10	10	10	
	Better information	0	0	0	20	30	
	Improved staff morale	0	0	10	20	30	
	Total	0	60	25	50	70	
	Cash flows	−110	50	15	40	60	
	Discount factor at 8%	1.000	0.926	0.857	0.794	0.735	**NPV**
	Discounted CF	−110.000	46.300	12.855	31.760	44.100	25.015

Job Two $000s

		Year 0	Year 1	Year 2	Year 3	Year 4	
Costs	Hardware costs	50	0	0	0	0	
	Software costs	30	10	10	0	0	
	Maintenance costs	10	10	10	10	10	
	Total	90	20	20	10	10	
Benefits	Staff savings	0	30	10	5	0	
	Contractor savings	0	30	15	15	15	
	Better information	0	0	0	10	10	
	Improved staff morale	0	0	10	10	10	
	Total	0	60	35	40	35	
	Cash flows	−90	40	15	30	25	
	Discount factor at 8%	1.000	0.926	0.857	0.794	0.735	**NPV**
	Discounted CF	−90.000	37.040	12.855	23.820	18.375	2.090

66 SATELLITE NAVIGATION SYSTEMS

Satellite Navigation Systems (SNS) installs complex satellite navigation systems in cars, at a very large national depot. The standard cost of an installation is shown below. The budgeted volume is 1,000 units installed each month. The operations manager is responsible for three departments, namely: purchasing, fitting and quality control.

Satellite Navigation Systems Limited purchases navigation systems and other equipment from different suppliers, and most items are imported. The fitting of different systems takes differing amounts of time, but the differences are not more than 25% from the average, so a standard labour time is applied.

Standard cost of installation of one navigation system

	$	Quantity	Price ($)
Materials	400	1 unit	400
Labour	320	20 hours	16
Variable overheads	140	20 hours	7
Fixed overheads	300	20 hours	15
Total standard cost	1,160		

The Operations Department has gathered the following information over the last few months. There are significant difficulties in retaining skilled staff. Many have left for similar but better paid jobs and as a result there is a high labour turnover. Exchange rates have moved and commentators have argued this will make exports cheaper, but SNS has no exports and has not benefited from these movements. Some of the fitters have complained that one large batch of systems did not have the correct adapters and would not fit certain cars, but this was not apparent until fitting was attempted. Rent, rates, insurance and computing facilities have risen in price noticeably.

The senior management team of SNS want the finance department to lend more support for the business and provide information that will help them to understand why costs appear to be spiralling out of control in the last few months and what the organisation can do to improve its position in the future.

The financial results for September to December are shown below.

Operating statement for SNS for September to December

	September $	October $	November $	December $	4 months $
Standard cost of actual output	1,276,000	1,276,000	1,102,000	1,044,000	4,698,000
Variances:					
Materials Price	5,505 F	3,354 F	9,520 A	10,340 A	11,001 A
Materials Usage	400 A	7,200 A	800 A	16,000 A	24,400 A
Labour rate	4,200 A	5,500 A	23,100 A	24,000 A	56,800 A
Efficiency	16,000 F	0	32,000 A	32,000 A	48,000 A
Variable overheads					
Expenditure	7,000 A	2,000 A	2,000 F	0	7,000 A
Efficiency	7,000 F	0	14,000 A	14,000 A	21,000 A
Fixed overheads					
Expenditure	5,000 A	10,000 A	20,000 A	20,000 A	55,000 A
Volume	30,000 F	30,000 F	15,000 A	30,000 A	15,000 F
Actual costs	1,234,095	1,267,346	1,214,420	1,190,340	4,906,201

A = adverse variance F = favourable variance

Required:

(a) Assess the performance of SNS for the period from September to December and suggest probable causes for the key variances. **(15 marks)**

(b) Suggest what extra information could be provided by the finance function and how the finance function can support the business in its development and implementation of new business strategies. **(10 marks)**

(Total: 25 marks)

67 MANTIS & GEAR

Mantis & Gear (M&G) was formed over 50 years ago to manufacture branded electrical and electronic goods for other companies. These goods are made to the specification required by these companies, whose own brand logos are attached to the products during the production process. M&G currently manufactures hundreds of products, although some are very similar in specification, with slight differences due to the requirements of each customer. M&G does not sell its own products to individual domestic consumers. Sales teams therefore focus on high volume sales to large companies.

The electrical and electronic goods market is increasingly competitive, with overseas companies entering the market. M&G's customers have responded to this by demanding lower prices and better quality products from M&G. As the electrical and electronic goods market is technologically innovative, there is also a requirement to continually develop new products or enhance existing ones.

The sales manager, James Slater, has revealed his sales team figures for the year 2014 and is excited to announce that the team has exceeded sales volume targets. However, his enthusiasm is not shared by the business controller, Furzana Khan, who has written a report to the chief executive officer (CEO) suggesting that there are fundamental performance problems in the company. An extract of her report is given below:

Business performance

'In a period of increased competition and growing product ranges, we are failing to keep control of the profitability of our business. Table 1 presents a summary of our performance for 20X4, showing problems with our pricing and/or our cost control. This has affected profitability.

	Budget Units	Actual Units
Sales volume	243,000	270,000

	Budget $000s	Actual $000s
Sales revenue	36,450	36,450
Direct materials	(15,795)	(18,630)
Direct labour	(3,402)	(4,725)
Fixed overheads	(8,250)	(11,450)
Operating profit	9,003	1,645

Table 1 – Budgeted versus actual performance for 20X4

James Slater has seen the report and has angrily confronted Furzana. 'We are in a period of increased competition and have successfully managed to grow our sales in difficult times. We even managed to fulfil some special orders with very short lead times. We should be celebrating these successes, not treating them as poor performance. We should expect some fall in profitability as our customers are able to shop around, so we have to make our products and our prices more attractive to them.'

Required:

It is clear that the business controller and the sales manager have different opinions about the current performance of the company.

Prepare three slides, with supporting notes, for a presentation to these managers which explain the performance of the business in the year both in overall terms and in each relevant business area. **(15 marks)**

Professional skills marks will be awarded for demonstrating communication skills in highlighting the key points to include in the slides and for clear supporting notes. **(2 marks)**

(Total: 17 marks)

68 JONES PACKAGING

You are a business advisor commissioned by the owner of a recently formed gift packaging company.

David Jones is the founder and owner of a recently formed gift packaging company, Gift Designs Ltd. David has spotted an opportunity for a new type of gift packaging. This uses a new process to make waterproof cardboard and then shapes and cuts the card in such a way to produce a container or vase for holding cut flowers.

The containers can be stored flat, in bulk and then simply squeezed to create the flowerpot into which flowers and water are then put. The potential market for the product is huge. In UK hospitals alone, there are 200,000 bunches of flowers bought each year for patients. David's innovative product does away with the need for hospitals to provide and store glass vases.

The paper vases are simple, safe and hygienic. He has also identified two other potential markets.

Firstly, the market for fresh flowers supplied by florists, and secondly, the corporate gift market where clients such as car dealers present a new owner with an expensive bunch of flowers when the customer takes delivery of a new car. The vase can be printed using a customer's design and logo, and creates an opportunity for real differentiation and impact at sales conferences and other high profile PR events.

David anticipates a rapid growth in Gift Designs as its products become known and appreciated. The key question is how quickly the company should grow and the types of funding needed to support its growth and development.

The initial financial demands of the business have been quite modest but David has estimated that the business needs $500k to support its development over the next two years and is uncertain as to the types of funding best suited for the business as it looks to grow rapidly. He understands that business risk and financial risk is not the same thing and is looking for advice on how he should organise the funding of the business to take advantage of this opportunity.

He is also aware of the need to avoid reliance on friends and family for funding and to broaden the financial support for the business perhaps by the use of new forms of funding such as Initial Coin Offerings ICOCs). David has heard the issue of ICOs may remove the need to rely on the more traditional forms of investment but allow (at least potentially) easier access to finance.

Clearly the funding required will also be affected by his personal involvement and he is aware of the need to ensure that those factors critical to the success of the venture and any new opportunities are identified and measured could also be affected by the activities David decides to carry out him and those activities better provided by external suppliers.

David has come to you for advice as although he is keen to grow the business, he is also concerned that his lack of experience and business knowledge background may confuse and cloud any decision that he may take.

Required:

Provide David with a briefing note on:

(a)   The key factors he should take into account for Gift Designs' future strategic growth.

(10 marks)

(b)   Advise on the funding strategy that David should adopt and the key risks for organisations from ICOs.

(10 marks)

(Total: 20 marks)

H: INNOVATION, PERFORMANCE EXCELLENCE AND CHANGE MANAGEMENT

69   ALG TECHNOLOGY *Online question assistance*

John Hudson is the Managing Director of ALG Technology, a medium-sized high tech company operating in several geographic markets. The company provides software and instrumentation, mainly for military projects but it also does have civilian interests. It currently has four key projects – (1) a command, communication and control system for the army's gunnery regiments, (2) avionics for the fighter aircraft within the air force, (3) an air traffic control system for a regional airport and (4) radar installations for harbour authorities in the Middle East. All these projects were expected to have a life expectancy of at least five years before completion. However, Hudson was worried because each of these projects was increasingly falling behind schedule and the contracts which he had negotiated had late delivery penalties.

Hudson is convinced that a significant cause of the problem is the way that the company is organised.

It has been shown that a competitive advantage can be obtained by the way a firm organises and performs its activities. Hudson's organisation is currently structured on a functional basis, which does not seem to work well with complex technologies when operating in dynamic markets. The functional structure appears to result in a lack of integration of key activities, reduced loyalties and an absence of team work. Hudson has contemplated moving towards a divisionalised structure, either by product or by market so as to provide some element of focus, but his experience has suggested that such a structure might create internal rivalries and competition which could adversely affect the performance of the company. Furthermore, there is a risk that such a structure may lead to an over-emphasis on either the technology or the market conditions. He is seeking a structure which encourages both integration and efficiency.

Any tendency towards decentralisation, whilst encouraging initiative and generating motivation may result in a failure to pursue a cohesive strategy, whereas a move towards centralisation could reduce flexibility and responsiveness.

The company is already relatively lean and so any move towards delayering, resulting in a flatter organisation is likely to be resisted. Furthermore the nature of the market – the need for high technical specifications and confidentiality – is likely to preclude outsourcing as a means of achieving both efficiency and rapidity of response.

Required:

(a)   Provide an alternative organisational structure for ALG Technology, discussing both the benefits and problems which such a structure might bring.   **(13 marks)**

(b)   Evaluate the main factors which can influence organisational design relating these, where possible, to ALG Technology.   **(12 marks)**

(Total: 25 marks)

70 COUNTRY CAR CLUB

Introduction

The Country Car Club (3C) was established fifty years ago to offer breakdown assistance to motorists. In return for an annual membership fee, members of 3C are able to phone for immediate assistance if their vehicle breaks down anywhere in the country. Assistance is provided by 'service patrol engineers' who are located throughout the country and who are specialists in vehicle repair and maintenance. If they cannot fix the problem immediately then the vehicle (and its occupants) are transported by a 3C recovery vehicle back to the member's home address free of charge.

Over the last fifteen years 3C has rapidly expanded its services. It now offers vehicle insurance, vehicle history checks (to check for previous accident damage or theft) as well as offering a comprehensive advice centre where trained staff answer a wide range of vehicle-related queries. It also provides route maps, endorses hotels by giving them a 3C starred rating and lobbies the government on issues such as taxation, vehicle emissions and toll road charging. All of these services are provided by permanent 3C employees and all growth has been organic culminating in a listing on the country's stock exchange three years ago.

However, since its stock market listing, the company has posted disappointing results and a falling share price has spurred managers to review internal processes and functions. A Business Architecture Committee (BAC) made up of senior managers has been charged with reviewing the scope of the company's business activities.

It has been asked to examine the importance of certain activities and to make recommendations on the sourcing of these activities (in-house or outsourced). The BAC has also been asked to identify technological implications or opportunities for the activities that they recommend should remain in-house.

First review

The BAC's first review included an assessment of the supply and maintenance of 3C's company vehicles. 3C has traditionally purchased its own fleet of vehicles and maintained them in a central garage. When a vehicle needed servicing or maintenance it was returned to this central garage.

Last year, 3C had seven hundred vehicles (breakdown recovery vehicles, service patrol engineer vans, company cars for senior staff etc) all maintained by thirty staff permanently employed in this garage. A further three permanent employees were employed at the garage site with responsibility for the purchasing and disposal of vehicles. The garage was in a residential area of a major town, with major parking problems and no room for expansion.

The BAC concluded that the garage was of low strategic importance to the company and, although most of the processes it involved were straightforward, its remoteness from the home base of some vehicles made undertaking such processes unnecessarily complicated. Consequently, it recommended outsourcing vehicle acquisition, disposal and maintenance to a specialist company. Two months ago 3C's existing vehicle fleet was acquired by AutoDirect, a company with service and repair centres nationwide, which currently supplies 45,000 vehicles to companies throughout the country. It now leases vehicles back to 3C for a monthly payment. In the next ten years (the duration of the contract) all vehicles will be leased from AutoDirect on a full maintenance basis that includes the replacement of tyres and exhausts. 3C's garage is now surplus to requirements and all the employees that worked there have been made redundant, except for one employee who has been retained to manage the relationship with AutoDirect.

Second review

The BAC has now been asked to look at the following activities and their supporting processes. All of these are currently performed in-house by permanent 3C employees.

- *Attendance of repair staff at breakdowns* – currently undertaken by permanent 'service patrol engineers' employed at locations throughout the country from where they attend local breakdowns.

- *Membership renewal* – members must renew every year. Currently renewals are sent out by staff using a bespoke computer system. Receipts are processed when members confirm that they will be renewing for a further year.

- *Vehicle insurance services* providing accident insurance which every motorist legally requires.

- *Membership queries* handled by a call-centre. Members can use the service for a wide range of vehicle-related problems and issues.

- *Vehicle history checks.* These are primarily used to provide 'peace of mind' to a potential purchaser of a vehicle. The vehicle is checked to see if it has ever been in an accident or if it has been stolen. The check also makes sure that the car is not currently part of a loan agreement.

Required:

(a) The Business Architecture Committee (BAC) has been asked to make recommendations on the sourcing of activities (in-house or outsourced). The BAC has also been asked to identify technological implications or opportunities for the activities that they recommend should remain in-house.

   Suggest and justify recommendations to the BAC for each of the following major process areas:

   (i)   Attendance of repair staff at breakdowns

   (ii)   Membership renewal

   (iii) Vehicle insurance services

   (iv)   Membership queries; and

   (v)   Vehicle history checks.   **(15 marks)**

(b) **Analyse the advantages that 3C will gain from the decision to outsource the purchase and maintenance of their own vehicles.**   **(10 marks)**

                                                                    (Total: 25 marks)

71 STELLA ELECTRONICS

Stella Electronics (SE) owns a chain of electrical retail stores throughout the country of Arborium. The company sells to the general public through its stores and website. It has outsourced three areas of a business process to Terra Call Generale (TCG), a call centre specialist based overseas. They handle, on behalf of SE, the following calls:

- Customers requesting service contracts.

- Customers requesting refunds for goods purchased from the SE website.

- Customers with technical queries about the products they have bought.

SE is currently reviewing the renewal of the TCG contract in the light of customer complaints about:

- The time taken to complete a query

- The frustration caused by the need to provide a reference number and password

- The problem of understanding the accents of the people in the call centre.

Unemployment is rising in Arborium and there is increased resistance to services being outsourced and offshored to companies such as TCG. SE is aware of the growing hostility of customers to such arrangements.

Call centre processing (TCG) – to be read in conjunction with Figure 1 below

1   The process is initiated by a customer phoning the TCG call centre.

2   TCG offers call centre services to a number of companies. The supervisor asks the customer which company they are phoning about. Calls for SE are routed to Stella support. Calls for other companies are routed to other support teams (not shown here).

3   The TCG support operator asks the customer what their call is about. Three transaction types are possible.

4   Callers who wish to discuss a service contract are passed immediately to the contracts section. Service contract options are discussed and if the caller decides to buy a service contract, then this is raised in the next activity in the process (5: Raise service contract).

5   Raise service contract and details are emailed to the customer. If the caller decides not to have a service contract, then the call is terminated.

6   For all other transaction types, Stella support asks the customer for their payment reference number or service contract reference number. If the customer cannot supply either of these, then the call is terminated. If the reference number is provided, then the support team member enters it into the computer system.

7   The computer system retrieves customer details and these are confirmed by the support team member with the customer. These details include a password which the customer has to give. Failure to give the correct password leads to the call being terminated.

8   If the password is correct and the customer requires a purchase refund, then the refund is processed and details emailed to the customer and the call is terminated.

9   If the password is correct and the customer has a technical query, then the call is passed to technical support who log and then resolve (process 10) the query before terminating the call.

Further information:

- TCG provides a 24 hour/7 days per week service. There are 600 calls per 24 hours from SE customers.

- 60% are technical queries, 25% are requests for refunds and 15% are for service contracts.

- 30% of customers do not know their payment/service reference number.

- 5% of customers who do know their payment/service reference number are unable to remember their password.

- TCG charges SE $1 for every call they take (so, typically $600 per day).

- TCG has ten staff dedicated to SE: six in technical support, one in the contracts section and three in SE support.

- SE has calculated that it would cost $50 to employ one equivalent employee in Arborium for an eight hour shift.

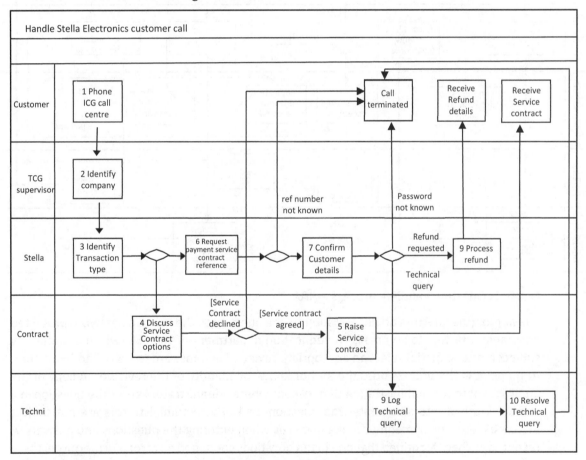

Figure 1: Business process for handling a Stella Electronics customer call

Required:

(a)   **Evaluate the current process for handling SE's customer calls at TCG and suggest improvements to that process at TCG.**   **(15 marks)**

(b)   **Discuss whether SE should continue outsourcing its customer call handling process to TCG or should it bring the process in-house.**   **(10 marks)**

(Total: 25 marks)

72   INSTITUTE OF ANALYTICAL ACCOUNTANTS

The Institute of Analytical Accountants (IAA) offers three certification programmes which are assessed through examinations using multiple choice questions. These questions are maintained in a computerised question bank. The handling process for these questions is documented in Figure 1 and described in detail below. The IAA is currently analysing all its processes seeking possible business process re-design opportunities. It is considering commissioning a bespoke computer system to support any agreed re-design of the business processes. The IAA is keen to implement a new solution fairly quickly because competitors are threatening to move into their established market.

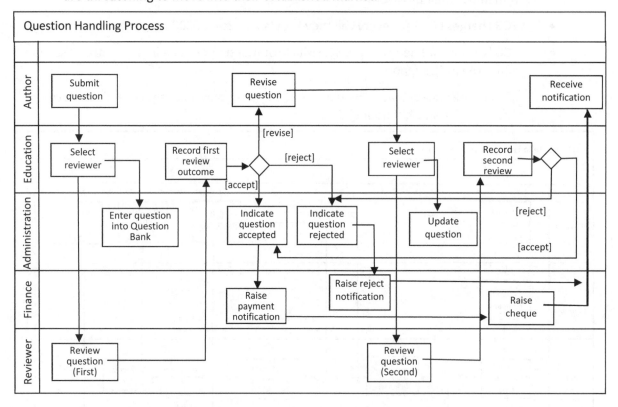

Figure 1: Question handling process at IAA

The author (the question originator) submits the question to the IAA as a password protected document attached to an email. The education department of the IAA (which is staffed by subject matter experts) select an appropriate reviewer and forward the email to him or her. At no point in the process does the author know the identity of the reviewer. A copy of the email is sent to the administration department where administrators enter the question in a standard format into a computerised question bank. These administrators are not subject matter experts and sometimes make mistakes when entering the questions and answers. A recent spot-check identified that one in ten questions contained an error. Furthermore, there is a significant delay in entering questions.

Although five administrators are assigned to this task, they also have other duties to perform and so a backlog of questions has built up. Administrators are paid less than education staff.

The reviewer decides whether the question should be accepted as it is, rejected completely, or returned to the author for amendment. This first review outcome is recorded by the education department before the administration department updates the database with whether the question was accepted or rejected. On some occasions it is not possible to find the question which needs to be updated because it is still in the backlog of questions waiting to be entered into the system. This causes further delay and frustration.

The finance department is notified of all accepted questions and a payment notification is raised which eventually leads to a cheque being issued and sent to the author.

The amended question is returned by the author to the education department who forward this onto the reviewer. A copy is again sent to the administration department so that they can amend the question held on the database.

On the second review, the question is accepted or rejected. Rejected questions (irrespective of when they are rejected) are notified to the finance department who raise a reject notification and send it back to the author.

Currently, 20% of questions are immediately rejected by the reviewer and a further 15% are sent back to the author for revision. Of these, 30% are rejected on the second review.

Required:

The IAA would like to consider a number of re-design options, ranging from very simple improvements to radical solutions.

Identify a range of re-design options the IAA could consider for improving their question handling process. Evaluate the benefits of each option. **(15 marks)**

73 HOMEDELIVER

HomeDeliver is a nationwide company that sells small household goods to consumers. It produces an attractive, comprehensive catalogue which it distributes to staff known as catalogue supervisors. There are 150 of these supervisors in the country. Each supervisor has approximately 30 part-time home-based agents, who then deliver the catalogue to consumers in their homes. Agents subsequently collect the catalogue and any completed order forms and forward these forms to their supervisor. Payment is also taken when the order is collected. Payment is by cash or cheque and these payments are also forwarded to the supervisor by the agent. At the end of the week the supervisor returns completed order forms (and payments) to HomeDeliver. Order details are then entered into a computer system by order entry administrators at HomeDeliver and this starts an order fulfilment process that ends with goods being delivered directly to the customer. The supervisors and the agents are all self-employed. HomeDeliver rewards supervisors on the basis of how many agents they manage. Agents' reward packages are based on how many catalogues they deliver and a commission based on orders received from the homes they have collected orders from.

In August 2010 HomeDeliver decided to replace the physical ordering system with a new electronic ordering system. Agents would be provided with software which would allow them to enter customer orders directly into the computer system using their home personal computer at the end of each day. Payments would also be paid directly into a HomeDeliver bank account by agents at the end of each day.

The software to support the new ordering system was developed in-house to requirements provided by the current order entry administrators at HomeDeliver and managers concerned with order fulfilment and invoicing. The software was tested internally by the order entry administrators. At first, both the specification of requirements and initial software testing progressed very slowly because order administrators were continuing with their normal operational duties. However, as project delays became more significant, selected order administrators were seconded to the project full-time. As a result the software was fully acceptance tested by the end of July 2011, two months behind schedule.

In August 2011 the software was rolled out to all supervisors and agents. The software was claimed to be easy to use, so no formal training was given. A large comprehensive manual with colour screenshots was attached as a PDF to an email sent to all supervisors and agents. This gave detailed instructions on how to set up and use the software.

Unfortunately, problems began to appear as soon as the agents tried to load and use the software. It was found to be incompatible with one particular popular browser, and agents whose computers used that browser were advised to use an alternative browser or computer. Agents also criticised the functionality of the software because it did not allow for the amendment of orders once they had been submitted. It emerged that customers often contacted agents and supervisors to amend their order prior to it being sent to HomeDeliver. This was no longer possible with the new system.

Many agents also claimed that it was not possible to enter multiple orders for one household. However, HomeDeliver confirmed that entering multiple orders was possible; it was just not clear from the software, or from the instructions provided, how this could be achieved.

Most of the agents were reluctant to print off the manual (preferring to read it on screen) and a significant number claimed that they did not receive the email with the manual attachment. Agents also found quite a number of spelling and functionality errors in the manual. At certain points the software did not perform in the way the manual stated that it would. Internal standards at HomeDeliver require both a post-project and a post-implementation review.

Required:

Evaluate the problems and the lessons that should be learned from a post-project review and a post-implementation review of the electronic ordering system at HomeDeliver.

(12 marks)

74 ASW

ASW is a software house which specialises in producing software packages for insurance companies. ASW has a basic software package for the insurance industry that can be used immediately out of the box. However, most customers wish ASW to tailor the package to reflect their own products and requirements. In a typical ASW project, ASW's business analysts define the gap between the customer's requirements and the basic package. These business analysts then specify the complete software requirement in a system specification. This specification is used by its programmers to produce a customised version of the software. It is also used by the system testers at ASW to perform their system tests before releasing it to the customer for acceptance testing.

One of ASW's new customers is CaetInsure. Initially CaetInsure sent ASW a set of requirements for their proposed new system.

Business analysts from ASW then worked with CaetInsure staff to produce a full system specification for CaetInsure's specific requirements. ASW do not begin any development until this system specification is signed off. After some delay (see below), the system specification was eventually signed off by CaetInsure.

Since sign-off, ASW developers have been working on tailoring the product to obtain an appropriate software solution. The project is currently at week 16 and the software is ready for system testing. The remaining activities in the project are shown in figure 1. This simple plan has been put together by the project manager. It also shows who has responsibility for undertaking the activities shown on the plan.

The problem that the project manager faces is that the plan now suggests that implementation (parallel running) cannot take place until part way through week 28. The original plan was for implementation in week 23. Three weeks of the delay were due to problems in signing off the system specification. Key CaetInsure employees were unavailable to make decisions about requirements, particularly in the re-insurance part of the system. Too many requirements in this module were either unclear or kept changing as users sought clarification from their managers. There have also been two further weeks of slippage since the sign-off of the system specification.

The CaetInsure contract had been won in the face of stiff competition.

As part of securing the deal, the ASW sales account manager responsible for the CaetInsure contract agreed that penalty clauses could be inserted into the contract. The financial penalty for late delivery of the software increases with every week's delay. CaetInsure had insisted on these clauses as they have tied the delivery of the software in with the launch of a new product. Although the delay in signing off the system specification was due to CaetInsure, the penalty clauses still remain in the contract. When the delay was discussed with the customer and ASW's project manager, the sales account manager assured CaetInsure that the 'time could be made up in programming'.

The initial planned delivery date (week 23) is now only seven weeks away. The project manager is now under intense pressure to come up with solutions which address the project slippage.

The project plan is presented in Appendix 1.

Required:

(a) Evaluate the alternative strategies available to ASW's project manager to address the slippage problem in the CaetInsure project. **(10 marks)**

(b) As a result of your evaluation, recommend and justify your preferred solution to the slippage problem in the CaetInsure project. **(6 marks)**

(Total: 16 marks)

Appendix 1: Project plan

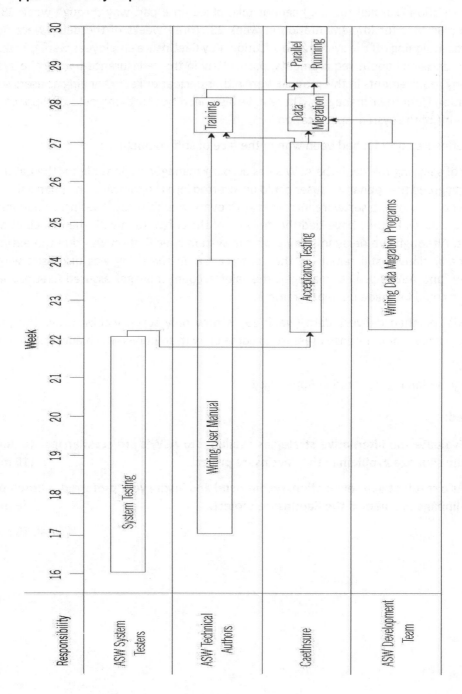

Figure 1: Project Plan – ASW: CaetInsure Contract

75   TKP

This information was taken from an internal newsletter of The Knowledge Partnership LLP (TKP), a company which offers project and software consultancy work for clients based in Zeeland. The newsletter was dated 2 November 20X1 and describes two projects currently being undertaken by the partnership.

Project One

In this project, one of our clients was just about to place a contract for a time recording system to help them monitor and estimate construction contracts when we were called in by the Finance Director.

He was concerned about the company supplying the software package. 'They only have an annual revenue of $5m', he said, 'and that worries me.' TKP analysed software companies operating in Zeeland. It found that 200 software companies were registered in Zeeland with annual revenues of between $3m and $10m. Of these, 20 went out of business last year. This compared to a 1% failure rate for software companies with revenues of more than $100m per year. We presented this information to the client and suggested that this could cause a short-term support problem. The client immediately re-opened the procurement process. Eventually they bought a solution from a much larger well-known software supplier. It is a popular software solution, used in many larger companies.

The client has now asked us to help with the implementation of the package. A budget for the project has been agreed and has been documented in an agreed, signed-off, business case. The client has a policy of never re-visiting its business cases once they have been accepted; they see this as essential for effective cost control. We are currently working with the primary users of the software – account managers (using time and cost data to monitor contracts) and the project support office (using time and cost data to improve contract estimating) – to ensure that they can use the software effectively when it is implemented. We have also given 'drop in' briefing sessions for the client's employees who are entering the time and cost data analysed by the software. They already record this information on a legacy system and so all they will see is a bright new user interface, but we need to keep them informed about our implementation. We are also looking at data migration from the current legacy system. We think some of the current data might be of poor quality, so we have established a strategy for data cleansing (through offshore data input) if this problem materialises. We currently estimate that the project will go live in May 20X2.

Project Two

In this project, the client is the developer of the iProjector, a tiny phone-size projector which is portable, easy to use and offers high definition projection. The client was concerned that their product is completely dependent on a specialist image-enhancing chip designed and produced by a small start-up technology company. They asked TKP to investigate this company. We confirmed their fears. The company has been trading for less than three years and it has a very inexperienced management team. We suggested that the client should establish an escrow agreement for design details of the chip and suggested a suitable third party to hold this agreement.

We also suggested that significant stocks of the chip should be maintained. The client also asked TKP to look at establishing patents for the iProjector throughout the world. Again, using our customer contacts, we put them in touch with a company which specialises in this. We are currently engaged with the client in examining the risk that a major telephone producer will launch a competitive product with functionality and features similar to the iProjector.

The iProjector is due to be launched on 1 May 20X2 and we have been engaged to give advice on the launch of the product. The launch has been heavily publicised, a prestigious venue booked and over 400 attendees are expected. TKP have arranged for many newspaper journalists to attend. The product is not quite finished, so although orders will be taken at the launch, the product is not expected to ship until June 20X2.

Further information:

TKP only undertakes projects in the business culture which it understands and where it feels comfortable. Consequently, it does not undertake assignments outside Zeeland.

TKP has $10,000,000 of consultant's liability insurance underwritten by Zeeland Insurance Group (ZIG).

Required:

(a) Analyse how TKP itself and the two projects described in the scenario demonstrate the principles of effective risk management. **(15 marks)**

(b) Discuss the implications of the triple constraint (scope, time and cost) on the two projects described in the scenario. **(10 marks)**

(Total: 25 marks)

76 A CLOTHING COMPANY

A clothing company sells 40% of its goods directly to customers through its website. The marketing manager of the company (MM) has decided that this is insufficient and has put a small team together to re-design the site. MM feels that the site looks 'amateur and old-fashioned and does not project the right image'. The board of the company has given the go-ahead for the MM 'to re-design the website'. The following notes summarise the outcomes of the meetings on the website re-design. The team consists of the marketing manager (MM), a product range manager (RP), a marketing image consultant (IC) and a technical developer (TD).

Meeting 1: 9 July attended by MM, RP, IC and TD

The need for a re-designed website to increase sales volume through the website and to 'improve our market visibility' was explained by MM. IC was asked to produce a draft design.

Meeting 2: 16 August attended by MM, RP, IC and TD

IC presented a draft design. MM and RP were happy with its image but not its functionality, suggesting that it was too similar to the current site. 'We expected it to do much more' was their view.

Meeting 3: 4 September attended by MM, RP and IC

IC produced a re-drafted design. This overall design was agreed and the go-ahead was given for TD to produce a prototype of the design to show to the board.

Meeting 4: 11 September attended by RP, IC and TD

TD explained that elements of the drafted re-design were not technically feasible to implement in the programming language being used. Changes to the design were agreed at the meeting to overcome these issues and signed off by RP.

Meeting 5: 13 October attended by MM, RP, IC and TD

The prototype re-design was demonstrated by TD. MM was unhappy with the re-design as it was 'moving too far away from the original objective and lacked functionality that should be there'. TD agreed to write a technical report to explain why the original design (agreed on 4 September) could not be adhered to.

Meeting 6: 9 November attended by MM, IC and TD

It was agreed to return to the 4 September design with slight alterations to make it technically feasible. TD expressed concerns that the suggested design would not work properly with all web browsers.

At the board meeting of 9 December the board expressed concern about the time taken to produce the re-design and the finance director highlighted the rising costs (currently $25,000) of the project. They asked MM to produce a formal cost-benefit of the re-design.

The board were also concerned that the scope of the project, which they had felt to be about re-design, had somehow been interpreted as including development and implementation.

On 22 December MM produced the following cost-benefit analysis of the project and confirmed that the word 'redesign' had been interpreted as including the development and implementation of the website.

	Year 1	Year 2	Year 3	Year 4	Year 5
Costs	$50,000	$10,000	$10,000	$10,000	$10,000
Benefits*	0	$15,000	$25,000	$35,000	$35,000

*These benefits are extra sales volumes created by the website's extra functionality and the company's increased visibility in the market place.

On 4 January the board gave the go ahead for the development and implementation of the website with a further budget of $25,000 and a delivery date of 1 March. TD expressed concern that he did not have enough developers to deliver the re-designed website on time.

Meeting 7: 24 February attended by MM, RP, IC and TD

A partial prototype system was demonstrated by TD. RP felt that the functionality of the re-design was too limited and that the software was not robust enough. It had crashed twice during the demonstration. He suggested that the company delay the introduction of the re-designed website until it was complete and robust. MM declared this to be impossible.

Conclusion

The re-designed website was launched on 1 March. MM declared the re-design a success that 'had come in on time and under budget'. On 2 and 3 March, numerous complaints were received from customers. The website was unreliable and did not work with a particular popular web browser. On 4 March an emergency board meeting decided to withdraw the site and reinstate the old one. On 5 March, MM resigned.

Required:

(a) **Explain how a business case and a project initiation document would have helped prevent some of the problems that emerged during the conduct of the website re-design project.** **(15 marks)**

(b) **Analyse how effective project management could have further improved both the process and the outcomes of the website re-design project.** **(10 marks)**

(Total: 25 marks)

77 PSI

Introduction

Retail pharmacies supply branded medicinal products, such as headache and cold remedies, as well as medicines prescribed by doctors. Customers expect both types of product to be immediately available and so this demands efficient purchasing and stock control in each pharmacy. The retail pharmacy industry is increasingly concentrated in a small number of nationwide pharmacy chains, although independent pharmacies continue to survive. The pharmacy chains are increasingly encouraging their customers to order medicinal products online and the doctors are being encouraged to electronically send their prescriptions to the pharmacy so that they can be prepared ready for the patient to collect.

Pharmacy Systems International (PSI)

Pharmacy Systems International (PSI) is a privately owned software company which has successfully developed and sold a specialised software package meeting the specific needs of retail pharmacies. PSI's stated objective is to be a 'highly skilled professional company providing quality software services to the retail pharmacy industry'. Over the last three years PSI has experienced gradual growth in turnover, profitability and market share (see Figure 1).

Figure 1: PSI Financial information

	20X7	20X6	20X5
Turnover ($000)	11,700	10,760	10,350
Profits ($000) (pre-tax)	975	945	875
Estimated market share	26%	24%	23%
Number of employees	120	117	115

PSI has three directors, each of whom has a significant ownership stake in the business. The chief executive is a natural entrepreneur with a past record of identifying opportunities and taking the necessary risks to exploit them. In the last three years he has curbed his natural enthusiasm for growth as PSI has consolidated its position in the market place. However, he now feels the time is right to expand the business to a size and profitability that makes PSI an attractive acquisition target and enables the directors to realise their investment in the company. He has a natural ally in the sales and marketing director and both feel that PSI needs to find new national and international markets to fuel its growth. The software development director, however, does not share the chief executive's enthusiasm for this expansion.

The chief executive has proposed that growth can best be achieved by developing a generic software package which can be used by the wider, general retail industry. His plan is for the company to take the current software package and take out any specific references to the pharmaceutical industry. This generic package could then be extended and configured for other retail sectors. The pharmaceutical package would be retained but it would be perceived and marketed as a specialised implementation of the new generic package.

This proposed change in strategic direction is strongly resisted by the software development director. He and his team of software developers are under constant pressure to meet the demands of the existing retail pharmacy customers. On-line ordering of medicinal products and electronic despatch of prescriptions are just two examples of the constant pressure PSI is under from their retail customers to continuously update its software package to enable the pharmacies to implement technical innovations that improve customer service.

Ideally, the software development director would like to acquire further resources to develop a more standardised software package for their current customers. He is particularly annoyed by PSI's salesmen continually committing the company to producing a customised software solution for each customer and promising delivery dates that the software delivery team struggle to meet. Frequently, the software contains faults that require expensive and time consuming maintenance. Consequently, PSI is being increasingly criticised by customers. A recent user group conference expressed considerable dissatisfaction with the quality of the PSI package and doubted the company's ability to meet the published deadline for a new release of the software.

Required:

(a)   The proposal to develop and sell a software package for the retail industry represents a major change in strategy for PSI. Analyse the nature, scope and type of this proposed strategic change for PSI.   **(10 marks)**

(b)   The success of any attempt at managing change will be dependent on the context in which that change takes place. Identify and analyse, the internal contextual features that could influence the success or failure of the chief executive's proposed strategic change for PSI.   **(15 marks)**

(Total: 25 marks)

78   ZOOMBA

Zoomba is a national chain of restaurants. Zoomba competes with other rival chains by targeting mainly 18–25 year olds and providing healthy food options in a spacious restaurant using organically grown ingredients and served by staff who are in the same age group. It has 100 permanent locations spread across the country. The chain has traditionally performed well and continues to make high levels of profits. However, these profits have levelled off in the last two years and the first quarter of this year saw the first year-on-year, like-for-like drop in sales that the company has experienced in its ten year life.

The company's CEO, Grace Grove, believes that this is due to a number of factors such as a recent downturn in the economy, the market becoming saturated with rivals and limited space for further expansion. She also feels that the company hasn't taken advantage of the growing trend for pop-up restaurants. These restaurants are often created for very short periods, such as during a music festival or national events and public holidays, using temporary locations such as food trucks, disused premises or market stalls. The aim is to maximise sales during a small time frame whilst minimising costs. Reservations are not taken and the restaurants are therefore more accessible to a wider range of customers and can be an important step in breaking into new market segments.

Grace Grove therefore put together a team of staff to manage a project aimed at exploiting this growth opportunity. The team was headed by Elise Hazelwood who had been working in the company's IT function. The project launched in the second quarter of the year and the new pop-up restaurants opened in the third quarter of the year.

The team's first job was to design the process for setting up and running the pop ups. Processes were designed for venue location, asset management, food production, material supplies, marketing and sales. Work was put in to ensure that each process worked as efficiently as possible and, because of Elise Hazelwood's background, there was as much automation and e-processing as possible. Elise was able to ensure that adequate IT systems and controls were in place for elements such as e-procurement, social media marketing, sales recording, staff monitoring and inventory management. Social media marketing was particularly successful as Zoomba gained many followers who would not only act as a feedback and a word of mouth marketing service for the pop ups, but were also useful in suggesting venues and occasions for the pop ups.

Specialist team roles were created for pop up restaurants within the organisational structure. These teams would be managed by a member of the project team who would ensure that the new processes were followed and applied. Staff for the pop ups would be seconded from the nearest permanent location and would return to that location when the pop up closed.

Everything seemed set for success and both Grace Grove and Elise Hazelwood had high expectations for the venture. But having run the first two pop ventures (one to coincide with a large weekend music festival and the other situated at a major tourist resort for three months) profits and feedback have not been as good as expected. Elise Hazelwood was confident that all of the systems were in place to make the pop ups a success. The IT system worked well, premises were sourced and furbished to expectations, all food and service materials were at the venues, and social marketing was a particular success. Onsite project managers understood the processes well and were experienced in team management.

Feedback from customers was no better than average. Many customers were happy that they could now access Zoomba at a point that would not be available to them. But others were unhappy with the level of service provided. Some regular Zoomba visitors complained that the pop ups were disorganised with slower than usual service, whilst first time visitors had comments such as 'surly staff', 'lack of co-ordination' and 'messy premises'.

But the greatest resistance appeared to come from pop up staff. The following are samples of comments gathered as part of a lessons learnt review:

I turned up at my normal location one day but was told I'd be spending the weekend working on the van at the music festival. It took me an extra half hours travel to get there each day.

I volunteered for the tourist resort pop up thinking it would be good for my career. But there was little chance to get involved in decision making and when I returned to my normal location I found that someone else had gotten a promotion that I was hoping for.

I enjoyed my time at the pop up but we seemed to spend most of it learning the new processes which were very different to what we were used to. They worked well once we were used to them but there were many mistakes at first.

Grace Grove is committed to make the pop ups a success and wants to learn from the mistakes of these initial trials. She intends to meet with Elise Hazelwood to discuss how the project can best move forward.

Required:

(a)   **Explain the type of strategic change that Zoomba appear to be going through with the new pop up venture.** **(8 marks)**

(b)   **Analyse the reasons for the failures in the pop up venture.** **(7 marks)**

(Total: 15 marks)

79   WEBFILMS

Webfilms was originally a film rental organisation, offering DVD rentals which were sent to customers and returned using parcel couriers. Webfilms enrolled members who paid a monthly fee and could rent as many films as they liked, receiving their next choice as soon as a previous film was returned.

However, Webfilms found this model was not as successful as it had hoped. It struggled to gain a large customer base and high courier fees made it difficult for the company to make a reasonable profit.

The company underwent a radical strategic change and remodelled itself as an internet television network screening films and drama series. This service is now available in over 25 countries worldwide.

All programmes are original and so have not been previously shown on any television channel in any country. The programmes are all produced by a creative team at Webfilms, headed by Paolo Butterfield, and all are only available in English. Members pay a monthly subscription charge and have access to unlimited viewing. Webfilms relies entirely on member subscriptions for funding as, to enhance the customer experience, its programmes do not carry advertising. Webfilms considers itself to be a focused differentiator, offering only programmes which it feels will attract a younger audience (the teens and twenties).

Until recently, Webfilms had no close competitors in this form of internet television. Indeed, it was the main substitute for traditional television channels, causing a downturn in that industry. However, its success has been noted and this has led to the emergence of a number of competitors in different countries. These competitors have recognised and capitalised on any perceived weakness of Webfilms. So, for example, some of them include programmes which are not in English and others also include popular programmes which have also been shown on other television channels. This means that customers need to only subscribe to one television service.

The CEO of Webfilms, who previously transformed the organisation from a postal to internet-based service, has recognised that strategic change is required in order for Webfilms to continue competing effectively in a dynamic market environment. Her proposal to the board included the following key points:

- The creation of a wider range of new programmes, including documentaries and current affairs programmes

- The inclusion of popular programmes which were created for one country's viewers being shown in other countries

- Broadening the types of programmes so that the company can appeal to all age ranges

- Introduction of on-screen advertisements to create another revenue stream

- Translation of the most popular programmes into languages other than English

- The introduction of new services including broadband provision and online gaming

- A focus on efficiency, using the existing customer base to expand and to gain economies of scale, before any new competitors can gain a large market share

- The drive for efficiency should not be at the cost of quality, allowing the company to operate a hybrid strategy

The CEO stated that it would be imperative to set all the new key points of the strategy in place as soon as possible, to be implemented on a pre-announced date, with a large marketing campaign to support it.

At a meeting with the creative director, Paolo Butterfield expressed concerns about many of the changes being suggested: 'This is an effective demotion for me and my team. Customers pay their monthly fees because they love what we do, and yet you want to change it. Why are we following the crowd, when our existing business model is successful?' The CEO responded, 'There is no demotion. You will still be responsible for the creative element, just not producing all the programmes. This will allow you to take a much more strategic view of what we show, where and in what language.

Argue as much as you like, but this is going to happen, it's up to you whether you want to be involved in deciding how such change will take place.'

The meeting ended with some disharmony and a further meeting was arranged to determine which form of boundary-less working would be the most appropriate for Webfilms.

Required:

Balogun and Hope Hailey developed a change model which examines the contextual features which can influence the success or failure of strategic change. Assess how five of the internal contextual features defined in Balogun and Hope Hailey's model (time, scope, readiness, preservation and power) would influence the likely success or failure of the strategic change proposed by the CEO for Webfilms. **(16 marks)**

80   GREENTECH

greenTech was established in 1990 and is still run by the management team that founded it. The company began by specialising in the supply of low voltage, low emission, quiet, recyclable components to the electronic industry. Its components are used in the control systems of lifts, cars and kitchen appliances. Two medium-sized computer manufacturers use *greenTech* components in selected 'green' (that is, environmentally-friendly) models in their product range. Recent market research showed that 70% of the global electronics industry used *greenTech* components somewhere in its products.

In 1993 the company began a catalogue mail order service (now Internet-based) selling 'green' components to home users. Most of these customers were building their own computers and they required such components on either environmental grounds or because they wanted their computers to be extremely quiet and energy efficient. From 20X5, *greenTech* also offered fully assembled computer systems that could be ordered and configured over the Internet. All *greenTech's* components are purchased from specialist suppliers. The company has no manufacturing capability, but it does have extensive hardware testing facilities and it has built up significant technical know-how in supplying appropriate components.

In 20X8 a television company wrote to *greenTech* to ask whether it would consider taking part in a television programme called 'Company Doctor'. In this programme three teams of consultants spend a week at a chosen company working on a solution to a problem identified by the company. At the end of the week all three teams present their proposal for dealing with the problem. A panel of experts, including representatives from the company, pick the winner and, in theory, implement the winning proposal. *greenTech* agreed to take part in the programme and selected their future strategic direction as the problem area to be analysed. Their cash surplus would then be used to fund the preferred option. The show was recorded in September 20X8 to be transmitted later in the year. Details of the proposals from each team are provided in Exhibit 2.

Required:

(a)   **Evaluate the current strategic position of *greenTech*.** **(10 marks)**

(b)   **The panel selected the proposal of Professor Ag Wan as the winning proposal.**

Write a briefing paper evaluating the three proposals and justifying the selection of the proposal of Professor Ag Wan as the best strategic option for *greenTech* to pursue. **(20 marks)**

Professional skills marks will be awarded for demonstrating commercial acumen in recommending the best strategy to implement. **(2 marks)**

(c)   **Identify deficiencies in the current Internet-based process for ordering and configuring fully assembled green computers. Recommend a new process, together with its implications, for remedying these deficiencies.** **(10 marks)**

(Total: 42 marks)

Exhibit 1 – Finance and revenue

The company has traded profitably since its foundation and has grown steadily in size and revenues. In 20X8, its revenues were $64 million, with a pre-tax profit of $10 million. The spread across the three revenue streams is:

All figures in $million	20X8	20X7	20X6
Component sales to electronics industry	40	36	34
Component sales to home users	20	18	16
Fully assembled green computers	4	3	2
Total	64	57	52

The company has gradually accumulated a sizeable cash surplus. The board cannot agree on how this cash should be used. One beneficiary has been the marketing budget, but the overall spend on marketing still remains relatively modest and, by April 20X8, the cash surplus stood at $17 million.

Marketing budget 20X6–20X8

All figures in $	20X8	20X7	20X6
Internet development and marketing	100,000	70,000	60,000
Display advertising (manufacturers)	50,000	40,000	30,000
Display advertising (domestic customers)	20,000	15,000	15,000
Exhibitions and conferences	30,000	20,000	15,000
Marketing literature	10,000	5,000	5,000
Total	210,000	150,000	125,000

Exhibit 2 – Company Doctor

Three teams presented on the television programme Company Doctor. Each team had a separate proposal for future strategic plans for *greenTech*.

The following diagram, which was shown on the television show, illustrates how each solution came from a different part of an amended Ansoff product/market matrix.

		Products	
		Existing	**New**
Markets	**Existing**	Protect/Build *Lewis-Read (option 1)*	Product development with new capabilities *Fenix (option 2)*
	New	Market development with new uses and capabilities *Professor Ag Wan option 3)*	No team chose this option Diversification

A brief summary of the conclusions of each team of consultants is given below.

The accountants Lewis-Read suggested a strategic direction that planned to protect and build on *greenTech*'s current strategic position. They believed that the company should invest in marketing the fully assembled 'green' computers to both commercial and home customers.

They pointed out that the government had just agreed a preferential procurement policy for energy efficient computers with high recyclable content. 'This segment of the market is rapidly expanding and is completely under-exploited by *greenTech* at the moment', Lewis-Read concluded.

The corporate recovery specialists, Fenix, put forward a strategic direction that essentially offered more services to *greenTech*'s current customers in the electronics industry. They suggested that the company should expand its product range as well as being able to manufacture components to respond to special requirements. They also believed that potential supply problems could be avoided and supply costs could be cut if *greenTech* acquired its own manufacturing capability. 'You need to secure the supply chain, to protect your future position.' They felt that the surplus cash in the company should be used to acquire companies that already had these manufacturing capabilities.

The third team was led by Professor Ag Wan from MidShire University. Their main recommendation was that *greenTech* should not see itself as a supplier of components and computers but as a supplier of green technology. They suggested that the company should look at many other sectors (not just electronics) where quietness, low emissions and recyclable technology were important. 'The company needs to exploit its capabilities, not its products. It is looking too narrowly at the future. To compete in the future you need to develop your markets, not your products', concluded the professor.

In the television programme, the panel chose option 3 (as suggested by Professor Ag Wan's team) as being the most appropriate strategic direction and, much to everyone's surprise, the company began to pursue this direction with much vigour. Objectives and goals were established and a set of processes was designed to facilitate business-to-business transactions with potential new customers. These processes allow customers, by using computer-aided design software, to view the specification of products available, to assemble them and to integrate their own components into the design. This means that they are able to construct virtual prototypes of machines and equipment. This process design, delivered through a web service, is still under development.

Exhibit 3 – Tackling operational problems

In parallel, *greenTech* has decided to make tactical changes to current processes where the company has received poor customer feedback. One of these is the ordering of fully assembled green computers.

The current Internet-based process for ordering and configuring these computers is described below. A swim-lane diagram (flowchart) showing the process is also included as Figure 1.

On-line customers use the *greenTech* web site to enter the specific computer configuration they require. These details are fed through to the sales department at *greenTech* which then e-mails Xsys – *greenTech*'s Korean manufacturer – to ask for a delivery date for the requested computer. Xsys e-mails the date back to *greenTech* which then e-mails the customer with delivery and cost details. The customer then decides whether they wish to proceed with their order. Currently, 40% of enquiries proceed no further, which is of concern to *greenTech* as it means that time and effort have been wasted.

For those enquiries that do proceed, customers are invited to enter their payment details (credit card only). These details are sent directly to Equicheck – a specialist credit checking agency. About 20% of orders are rejected at this point because the potential customer has a poor credit rating. For orders that pass the credit check, a payment confirmation is raised by *greenTech* and sent to the customer and *greenTech* place a confirmed order with Xsys for the computer.

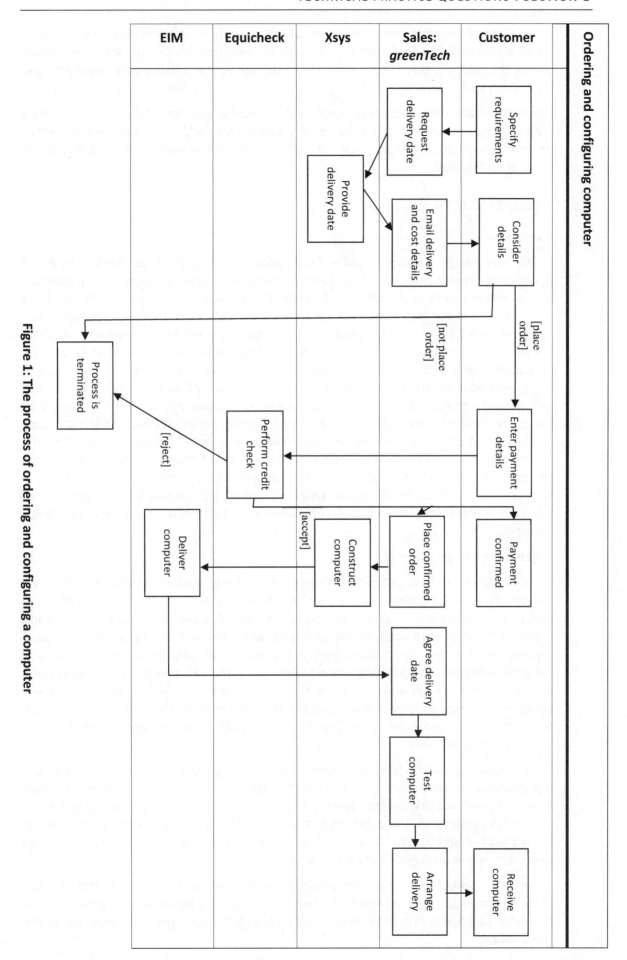

Figure 1: The process of ordering and configuring a computer

When Xsys has completed the construction of the computer it arranges for the international logistics company EIM to deliver the machine to *greenTech* for testing. After acceptance testing the machine, *greenTech* e-mails the customer, agrees a delivery date and arranges for delivery by courier.

Recent feedback from customers suggests that missing promised delivery dates is their biggest complaint. This is because the delivery date agreed early in the order process cannot necessarily be matched by Xsys when it actually receives the confirmed order. Figure 1 shows the process involved.

81 MIDSHIRE HEALTH

Introduction

In 20X1 Terry Nagov was appointed as Chief Executive Officer (CEO) of MidShire Health, a public authority with responsibility for health services in Midshire, a region with a population of five million people in the country of Etopia. Like all health services in Etopia, MidShire Health is funded out of general taxation and is delivered free of charge. Terry Nagov was previously the CEO of a large private company making mobility appliances for disabled people. He had successfully held a number of similar executive positions in companies producing consumer products and goods for the consumer market. He was appointed to bring successful private sector practices and procedures to MidShire Health. Etopia had experienced a prolonged economic recession and such appointments were encouraged by the government of Etopia who were faced with funding increased health care costs. They perceived that private sector expertise could bring some order and greater control to the functioning of public sector services. One of the government ministers publicly commented on the apparent 'anarchy of the health service' and its tendency to consume a disproportionate amount of the money collected through general taxation. The government was keen on establishing efficiencies in the public sector, by demonstrating 'value for money' principles.

Vision and strategic planning

Terry Nagov believed that all organisations need to be firmly focused on a visionary objective. He stated that 'our (MidShire Health) mission is to deliver health to the people of Midshire and, by that, I don't just mean hospital services for the sick, but a wider vision, where health is a state of complete physical, mental and social well-being and not merely the absence of disease or infirmity.' He believed that this vision could only be achieved through a comprehensive strategic planning process which set objectives, policies and standards at a number of levels in the organisation. In the strategic plan, the high-level objectives and policies of the organisation would be cascaded down to operational levels in a series of lower-level plans, where departments and functions had specific objectives that all contributed to the overall strategic vision.

Terry Nagov had successfully implemented such strategic planning systems at previous organisations he had worked for. He believed that centralised, senior management should decide strategy, and that line managers should be given power and responsibility to achieve their defined objectives. This approach had worked well in the heavily automated industries he had worked in, with semiskilled employees closely following standards and procedures defined by senior managers in the organisation.

Terry Nagov believed that a project should be put in place to establish a formal strategic planning system at MidShire Health and that this should be supported by a comprehensive computer-based information system which recorded the outcomes and activities of the organisation.

He immediately engaged the commercial IT consultants, Eurotek, to develop and implement this information system using a standard software package that they had originally developed for the banking sector. The overall strategic planning system project itself would be owned by a small steering group of two senior hospital doctors, two hospital nursing managers and two workers from the health service support sector. Health service support employees provide health services to the wider community in the form of health education and public health information and initiatives. Their inclusion in the steering group was not welcomed by the hospital doctors, but the CEO wanted a wide range of professional input. 'Collectively', Terry declared, 'the steering group has responsibility for delivering health to the Midshire community'.

Initial meeting of the steering group (meeting 1)

The initial meeting of the steering group was not attended by the two senior hospital doctors. In Etopia, it is accepted that hospital doctors, although employed by the health authority on full-time contracts, also have the right to undertake paid private work (practice) where they deliver services for private hospitals to fee-paying patients. This right was negotiated by their professional body, the Institute of Hospital Doctors (IOHD), many years ago. Many of the patients they treat in private practice have paid for private health insurance so that they can be treated quickly and thus avoid the long waiting times associated with the free, public service. The initial meeting of the steering group coincided with a day when both doctors were undertaking private work. In their absence, the steering group approved the overall vision of the CEO and agreed to the initiation of an information system project to generate the detailed planning and control information to support this vision. The exact nature and contents of this information system would be determined by a small multi-disciplinary team reporting to the steering group and referred to as the 'implementation team'. It was made up of three administrative staff employed by MidShire Health supported by four technical consultants from Eurotek, experienced in implementing their software package solution as shown in Figure 1.

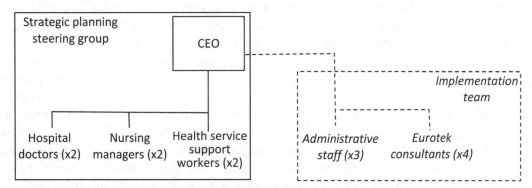

Figure 1: Composition of the steering group and the implementation team

Second meeting of the steering group (meeting 2)

The second meeting was attended by the two senior hospital doctors, but one of the health service support sector workers could not attend. At the start of the meeting, the two hospital doctors questioned the wide definition of health agreed at the previous meeting.

One of the hospital doctors suggested that delivering health in this wider context was completely beyond the resources and capabilities of MidShire Health. 'You have to realise', he said, 'that poor health is often caused by poverty, bad housing and social dislocation. You cannot expect MidShire Health to solve such problems. We can advise and also treat the symptoms, but prevention and cure for these wider issues are well beyond us.' The nursing managers, who had previously approved the wider definition of health, now voiced their support for a narrower definition of health and sided with the hospital doctors.

One of them commented that 'our real work is treating the sick and we must recognise this'. The CEO, outnumbered and outmanoeuvred in the meeting, had to agree to a modification of his initial vision, narrowing the overall objective to 'effectively and efficiently treating disease'. 'And, as we all know', stated one of the doctors, 'efficiency can only be achieved through giving control and budgets to the doctors, not to the administrators who are an unwanted overhead. This is the very first step we should take.' The nursing managers agreed and the meeting came to a slightly acrimonious and early conclusion.

Meeting three of the steering group (meeting 3)

At the third meeting, a presentation was made by the IT consultants, Eurotek, where they demonstrated their software for recording business activities and showed how these activities could be measured against agreed targets. A great deal of discussion took place on the targets that could be set for measuring health efficiency. After a long heated debate, three measures were agreed for hospitals. It was suggested that similar measures should be discussed and developed for health service support services, such as health education. However, at this point, the two senior doctors declared that they had to leave the meeting to 'return to our real job of treating patients'. The CEO agreed that the health service support workers could establish their own measures before the next meeting. One of these representatives commented that 'in my day-to-day job I am confronted by many people who have preventable illnesses. Their problems are due to poor diet and unhealthy habits. Preventing such problems must be better than curing them!' The CEO agreed; this was what he wanted to hear!

Meeting four of the steering group (meeting 4)

The fourth meeting of the steering group began with a discussion of the preventative perspective of health raised by one of the health service support workers at the end of the previous meeting. Both the hospital doctors and nursing managers suggested that this did not come under the revised definition of health used by the steering group, and the CEO quickly agreed. The rest of the meeting was dominated by a discussion of the costs of the Eurotek software solution. A local newspaper had run the headline 'spending money on computers – not patients' and it included a number of quotes attributed to one of the hospital doctors on the strategic steering group where he criticised the appointment of Eurotek and the attitude of the MidShire Health CEO. 'Running a manufacturing company is very different from running a health service', he said. 'We are motivated by service, not products and profit.' Terry Nagov, as CEO, openly questioned the ethics of members of the steering group discussing confidential internal matters with the press. The hospital doctors and the nursing managers fiercely defended their right to do so. 'You have to understand', they said, 'our loyalty is to the profession and to the public. We must act in the public interest.' Nevertheless, the CEO raised the possibility of disciplinary action against the hospital doctor.

At this point, the senior hospital doctors and the nursing managers left the meeting. The health service support workers stayed and pledged their support to the CEO. They revealed that the autocratic behaviour of hospital doctors often resulted in their work being both unrewarding and unrecognised. One commented, 'We have little professional autonomy, we feel controlled by the agenda of the hospital doctors.'

Meeting five of the steering group (meeting 5)

The possibility of disciplinary action against the hospital doctor had been published in the press and the Institute of Hospital Doctors (IOHD) had made a formal complaint about the CEO's behaviour to Etopia's health minister.

Faced with pressure from within the hospital sector, Terry Nagov was forced to retract his threat of disciplinary action and to issue a public apology, but meeting five was boycotted by the hospital doctors and nursing manager representatives due to 'the lack of respect shown by the CEO'. Consequently, meeting five was cancelled.

Meeting six of the steering group (meeting 6)

This meeting received a report from the implementation team working on the specification of the information system for MidShire Health. They reported that the software suggested by Eurotek was excellent for time recording, analysis and reporting, but had very few features to aid the planning and control of activities. 'I suspected this all along', said one of the hospital doctors. 'I think this report shows that you are more interested in finding out what we are doing. The strategic planning exercise is really about cost reduction.' It was agreed that Eurotek should be contacted to provide a price for developing a bespoke solution for the information system requirements envisaged by the MidShire implementation team. 'I realise', the CEO said, 'this will affect the viability of the whole strategic planning project but I ask you all to pull together for the good of MidShire Health and its image within the community.'

Just prior to the next planned meeting, the implementation team specifying the information system reported that Eurotek had quoted a price of $600,000 to develop a software solution that integrated planning and control of hospital activities into their software package solution. This was additional to the $450,000 it was charging for the basic software package. The CEO reacted immediately by cancelling the information system project 'on cost grounds' and disbanding the steering group. He stated that 'from now on, I will personally specify and develop the targets required to bring health to the people of Midshire. I will focus on using the current systems to bring these into place'. Emails were sent to the steering committee members informing them of the dissolution of the steering group, stating that no further meetings would be held and no comments were invited. However, the costs of paying penalty charges to Eurotek were soon released to the press and Terry Nagov resigned from his post as CEO of MidShire Health to return to his previous company as chairman. The Institute of Hospital Doctors (IOHD) took the opportunity to issue the following press release:

'Once again, the government has failed to realise that managing public sector services is not the same as managing a private sector profit making company. Money and time have been wasted, and reputations needlessly damaged. Doctors and nurses, people at the cutting edge of the service, know what needs to be done. But time after time our views are disregarded by professional managers and administrators who have little understanding of health care delivery. The public deserve better and we, the IOHD, remain committed to delivering services in the public interest.'

Required:

(a) Identify and analyse mistakes made by the CEO in the project management process (initiation, conduct and termination) in his attempt to introduce strategic planning, and an associated information system, at MidShire Health. **(18 marks)**

(b) Explain how an understanding of organisational culture and organisational configuration would have helped the CEO anticipate the problems encountered in introducing a strategic planning system, and an associated information system, at MidShire Health. **(18 marks)**

(Total: 36 marks)

82   LEARN TO PASS (L2P)

Learn to Pass (L2P) is the largest driving instructor agency in Eastlandia. Government rules state that all citizens wanting to be able to drive vehicles on public roads must have at least 30 hours of formal tuition and training as well as passing a government set practical exam.

Most learner drivers actually require, on average, around 45 hours of formal training. Trading as L2P, Learn to Pass train around 45% of all learners each year.

L2P has a national network of franchised driving instructors and provides liveried vehicles and marketing material to all driving instructors, who in return pay L2P a fixed fee of $650 per month.

L2P also provides a central booking system. Learners typically book directly through L2P who then allocates the work to driving instructors based on criteria such as location and availability. Learners pay a fee of $40 per hour from which L2P retain 10% before passing the balance onto franchisees. This is the primary source of income for franchisees, though occasionally they may gain work through recommendations or word-of-mouth that is not booked onto the L2P systems.

Franchisees are responsible for all other running costs for their franchise such as fuel and insurance costs. Each franchisee is also responsible for their own taxation and accounting matters. Most franchisees therefore use small accountancy firms to provide these services (at an average annual fee of around $500 per franchisee).

L2P has been approached by a new technology start-up called Eccounts. Eccounts have developed a new financial technology package that can provide the service for franchisees that they would normally outsource to small accountancy firms.

The software can interrogate L2P's booking systems to determine income for each franchisee and digital monitoring systems placed in cars can monitor driving distances and times which link to key expenses such as fuel consumption. Franchisees can input other incidental expenses into the system using a mobile phone app. The software can then electronically provide all necessary accounting and taxation information (as well as sending this information directly to the tax authorities if authorised to do so).

Eccounts have trialled the software with a very small driving instructor business which has only 4 franchisees (L2P has over 8,000 franchisees) and the system worked efficiently and effectively. Eccounts believe that the software can be used in any franchisee business system with central booking systems such as logistics and distribution companies and they see L2P as an opportunity to demonstrate the capabilities of the system before looking for expansion opportunities in other industries.

Eccounts have offered to provide the software to L2P at a cost of $100 per annum per franchisee. L2P could then recharge this to franchisees at a mark-up if they choose to do so. Alternatively, Eccounts have suggested that L2P could buy the software and exclusive rights to use it for $5m.

Required:

Evaluate whether L2P should take up the opportunity provided by Eccounts.   (16 marks)

Professional skills marks will be awarded for demonstrating evaluation skills in appraising this opportunity.   **(3 marks)**

(Total: 19 marks)

TECHNICAL PRACTICE QUESTIONS : **SECTION 1**

83   PIONEER VEHICLES

Company background

Pioneer Vehicles is a manufacturer of high quality off-road vehicles. Founded in the 1930s to meet the needs of armed forces, the company evolved to incorporate other sectors such as farming, science research, and exploration – in fact, any customers that needed a robust vehicle that could cope with the harshest terrains on the planet. Ten years ago Pioneer Vehicles brought out luxury consumer models aimed at wealthy individuals who would appreciate the toughness, performance and quality engineering of the cars, even if they had no intention of ever using them off road.

Disruptive technologies

The Board of Pioneer Vehicles has recently returned from 'The car of the future Expo', a trade conference on trends in the car industry, where the topic of disruptive technologies was the main area of discussion. The main presenter, a leading business analyst, argued that disruptive technology and technology trends were fundamentally changing the relationship between the driver and the car. He suggested that by 2030, 15% of new cars would be fully autonomous and self-driving, with a further 50% highly autonomous, incorporating features such as self-braking, self-parking, adaptive cruise control, accident avoidance and automatic responsiveness to changing road conditions. Given this, he concluded that software competence would become the most important differentiating factors for the industry.

At the Expo Elsie Igbinadola (Pioneer's CEO) was approached by Professor Brian Hughes, a prominent academic at the Department of Artificial Intelligence and Cybernetics at the country's leading university. Professor Hughes had explained to Elsie that his department had developed new advanced AI systems that were capable of so much more than the examples of intelligent cars given by the presenters at the Expo. He explained how his systems could learn about individual drivers' preferences and driving styles, it could interrogate traffic alerts and weather forecasts to enable better route planning and could even adapt to a wider range of road conditions. Professor Hughes had built a prototype jeep that was able to analyse not only road conditions on tarmac but also dirt, sand and gravel – even assessing the structural integrity of road surfaces in order to improve grip and traction. What finally grabbed Elsie's attention was the Professor's claim that his prototype jeep was able to complete a high profile, off road test track 20% quicker than comparable vehicles from the market leaders? The professor was keen to work with Pioneer to exploit the new technology and systems.

Board meeting

At the subsequent Board meeting there was heated discussion over what the Directors had heard at the expo and how it would affect Pioneer Vehicles.

Elsie argued that Pioneer should enter into partnership with the Professor to give them an advantage in an increasingly competitive market. She was supported by Brenda Ng (Sales and Marketing Director) who felt that there was a high risk that Pioneer would get left behind in a changing market if it didn't embrace change.

The opposite viewpoint was typified by Ahmed Kahn (Production Director) who argued that the risks of getting involved with the new technology were just too high and that Pioneer should wait and see how competitors acted first. He added that AI was unlikely to be of importance to most of Pioneer's customers

The Board was unable to reach a consensus, so it was agreed that further research be done prior to the next meeting in two weeks' time.

KAPLAN PUBLISHING   119

Required:

You are a Non-Executive Director of Pioneer with expertise in risk evaluation and risk management. You have been asked by Elsie to prepare some briefing notes evaluating the key risks involved with the proposal from Professor Hughes. **(15 Marks)**

Note: You are not required to make recommendations whether or not to proceed further.

Professional skills marks are available for professional scepticism related to the claims made by the professor. **(2 marks)**

(Total: 17 marks)

84 ABC TEXTILES

ABC Textiles is a manufacturer of soft furnishings including bedding, cushions and curtains.

Alan Cochrane owns all of the ordinary share capital of ABC is owned by who established ABC a number of years ago and immediately acquired a factory, located in the UK, and good quality machinery at low cost from the liquidator of another company.

ABC's business model is based on a cost leadership strategy. Alan ensures this by his personal involvement in maintaining strict operational and financial control over all the company's activities in order to minimise costs. Price competition throughout the supply chain is intense. Whilst design and quality are important, contracts are frequently won and lost on the basis of price.

ABC makes sales to low-price soft furnishings retailers throughout the UK. The main raw material used by ABC is polyester, a cheap synthetic fabric, imported by ABC from a small number of suppliers located in developing nations. ABC uses only a few suppliers to obtain larger quantity discounts and to increase the efficiency of its procurement system. It is the responsibility of suppliers to arrange delivery directly to ABC's factory. The fabric purchased by ABC is of basic quality, but it is fit for the purpose of manufacturing soft furnishings for ABC's customers. The labour-intensive manufacturing process involves colouring, processing and cutting the raw material polyester fabric, before making it into soft furnishings designed by ABC. The colouring and design are particular features of ABC products that have enabled the company to distinguish its products from those of competitors.

The board at ABC believes that the company's cost leadership position is no longer sustainable. It has proposed changing the company's strategic direction with a new business model. This involves moving upmarket by producing better quality soft furnishings in a new range of fabrics. The company will mainly use natural fabrics including cotton, wool, linen and silk. It will still use some polyester fabric, but this will be better quality than the type currently used.

The new business model is likely to require significant change and will include replacing most of the old machinery and increasing automation through the use of advanced robotic machinery operated by an intelligent control system. The board believe that the introduction of the new machinery will lead to significant efficiencies in the manufacturing process.

The change in business model is also likely to require new management roles and reporting structures to be created. The model is planned to be introduced on 1 January 20XX. The change will involve fewer unskilled staff and it is likely that many of these employees will be made redundant. Skilled staff will be need to retrained to upgrade and adapt their skills and there will be a need for to recruit of new staff with specialist skills more relevant to the new automated production facility.

There has been a long-term trend for soft furnishings to be manufactured in developing nations using low cost production and locally produced fabrics. These goods are imported into the UK, and other developed countries, and sold at prices which undercut ABC's prices.

The machinery that Jason originally acquired from the liquidator gave ABC a significant but short term cost advantage. It is now nearing the end of its useful life, becoming unreliable and an increasing number of defects have been found in batches of production. ABC has high standards of customer service and always replaces such items for its customers.

Required:

With respect to the new strategic proposal:

Outline the advantages and disadvantages of such a strategic change and recommend based on your discussion whether ABC should implement the new business model

(14 marks)

Professional skills marks will be awarded for demonstrating evaluation skills in appraising this strategic change. **(3 marks)**

85   TECHWARE LTD

Techware Ltd is a leader in the wearable technology market in the UK, selling fitness trackers and smartwatches to individual customers through its own stores and online.

Wearable technology is an aspect of the 'internet of things' comprising of electronics that can be worn on the body and connected to the internet, enabling data to be both transmitted and received.

Wearables have become increasingly popular and, for example, some 36% of individuals in the UK own more than one wearable device.

The products on offer include the following:

- Fitness trackers – a wrist-worn device that uses a sensor to record the wearer's daily physical activity, heart rate, calorie consumption and sleep patterns. It can provide the user with summary data via an app when connected to a smartphone or tablet.

- Smartwatches – a wrist-worn device with a touchscreen display to receive and respond to emails, texts, calls and social media notifications.

- Smart clothing – clothing (including footwear) that has technology embedded to monitor the wearer's physical condition.

- Smart glasses (the most recent development) – computerised eyewear that uses stored data, images or video to enhance real world images (augmented reality) and adds information to what the wearer sees.

Wearables continue to evolve as individuals increasingly use digital technology to enhance their lives. The industry began with fitness trackers, which employ the least complex technology and typically cost less to produce than other wearables.

Smartwatches that act as a combined wristwatch, fitness tracker and smartphone are increasing in popularity. Smart clothing is also becoming popular as a less intrusive, more effective, way of wearing and using the technology. Geographically, the North American and European wearable technology markets are the most developed in terms of lifecycle.

In addition to the individual customer market, there is a growing corporate market for wearables in sectors such as insurance, fitness, healthcare, industrial and the military. For example, some logistics companies use fitness trackers to support driver healthcare programmes, while other organisations use smart glasses to enhance training or improve customer experience.

Competition in the UK Companies in the UK wearable technology market ranges from small start-ups to global market leaders in information technology (IT). Several major sportswear brands produce wearables for the fitness sector. Competition has increased significantly and there is a lot of choice. Key factors for individual customers include functionality, portability (size and weight), ease of set-up and use, compatibility with existing devices, appearance and durability. Research suggests that within one year, more than two million employees in the UK will be required to wear fitness tracking devices as a condition of their employment.

Some organisations already insist that, if employees wish to use wearable technology while at work, they wear employer-issued devices rather than their own personal devices. This arises from concern about cyber risks if a range of employees' personal devices are connected to the employers' networks.

Techware competes with several large companies in the UK, including some global IT, electronics and telecommunications businesses. Techware's fitness trackers and smartwatches are comparatively cheap. Technological innovation is a critical success factor and Techware spends a lot on research and development to identify new features for its two products.

Techware customers can link their devices to a Techware app which presents their data to them in a user friendly format. Techware does not sell data gathered from the app to other users.

Techware is considering entering the corporate market. This would provide an opportunity for high volume sales contracts. However, Techware has no experience of dealing with large corporate clients which are likely to want detailed and insightful analysis of the data captured about individual users by wearable technology.

New contract proposal

Techware is evaluating a specific corporate contract with C, a large consulting business.

C wants to give its employees the option to wear a Techware fitness tracker. C would purchase the devices from Techware then supply them to the employees free of charge. The trackers would record C employees' heart-rate and exercise and track other indices that affect health and stress levels during the working day.

Techware would aggregate individual employee data and analyse it to produce data relevant to the C workforce as a whole. C would use this to monitor employees' wellbeing, improve its HR policies and healthcare programme and create a safer and healthier working environment.

C's employees have given a mixed reaction to the offer of a free wearable device. Some are keen to accept. Others are concerned that, if they wear their fitness tracker 24 hours a day, C will have access to excessive private information about them. In particular,

C will know their location and activity, both inside and outside of work hours, and how many hours they have slept. Some employees are concerned that this data may be used to deal with poor performance and absenteeism and to discriminate against certain employees on health or lifestyle grounds.

Required:

(a) Identify the advantages and disadvantages of entering the corporate market. Recommend a course of action and justify your choice **(12 marks)**

(b) Discuss the issues relating to ethics, data protection and data security arising from C's proposal to collect and use data from Techware's fitness trackers to monitor its employees. **(12 marks)**

Professional skills marks are available for professional scepticism related to the proposal to offer a free wearable device to C's employees. **(2 marks)**

Section 2

CASE STUDY QUESTIONS

1 DIXON SMITH BURRELL

You are Michael Ling, a recently qualified accountant. You work in the business advisory section of an international firm of accountants. Your manager is Masaki Setsu who has assembled a team together to work on a report for an existing client, Dixon Smith Burrell.

Dixon Smith Burrell (known as 'DSB') is one of the world's largest pharmaceutical companies. It is based in Geeland and is responsible alone for 12% of Geeland's total stock market value. It employs 130,000 people in many countries and is an internationally renowned brand name.

The company is facing a number of problems in some of its locations and is seeking help and advice in overcoming these problems. Masaki Setsu's team has been given the responsibility of preparing a draft of this report.

The team has gathered a number of pieces of information in order to help draft this report. This information includes the following:

Exhibit 1: A report on the pharmaceutical industry in the country of Nearland

Exhibit 2: Extracts from Nearland internal training documents at DSB

Exhibit 3: Extracts from the financial statements of the Nearland division

Exhibit 4: Copy of press article from Farland National Daily

Exhibit 5: Extract from draft DSB Board Meeting Minutes

Exhibit 6: Email trail regarding a new opportunity in Leeland

Following your findings you are now starting to prepare the consultancy report and associated tasks for DSB.

The case requirements are included in the tasks shown below:

TASK 1

DSB is concerned about the downturn in profits in Nearland, a country that the company entered over ten years ago and which has traditionally provided strong returns to the business.

Required:

(a) **Using a suitable model or models, analyse the macro environment for pharmaceutical companies operating in Nearland.** **(12 marks)**

(b) **Evaluate the performance of the Nearland division for the year ended 31 December 20X2.** **(14 marks)**

Professional skills marks are available for demonstrating analytical and evaluation skills relating to the Nearland division's environment and performance. **(4 marks)**

(Total: 30 marks)

TASK 2

The bribery allegations represent a high risk to the future success of DSB.

Required:

(a)   **Briefly explain 'related' and 'correlated' risks. Explore the correlation between legal risk and reputation risk for DSB if the bribery allegations were proved.**   **(10 marks)**

Professional skills marks are available for professional scepticism related to the allegations made against the company.   **(2 marks)**

(b)   **Describe the general purposes of an internal control system and, based on the information presented by Sena Ali in the board meeting, assess the main internal control failings which have led to the bribery allegations in Farland.**   **(10 marks)**

Professional skills marks are available for analytical skills relating to the internal control system.   **(2 marks)**

(Total: 24 marks)

TASK 3

Masaki Setsu wants you to prepare a public statement to use to communicate DSB's response and reaction to the Farland bribery allegations. Nur Saah wants the communication to explain her role as CEO.

Required:

Prepare a public statement for Nur Saah to use to communicate to stakeholders. The statement should:

(a)   **Explain the bribery allegations and the steps taken to ensure such issues do not reoccur.**   **(6 marks)**

(b)   **An explanation of the roles of the chief executive in areas such as communicating with stakeholders, managing the company and controlling operational areas.**   **(6 marks)**

Professional marks for demonstrating communication and commercial acumen skills in ensuring that the statement solves the key issues arising from the bribery allegations and is satisfactory to both the stakeholders of DSB and Nur Saah.   **(4 marks)**

(Total: 16 marks)

TASK 4

DSB has an opportunity to develop new antibiotics in one of its existing markets, Leeland. This project would be partly funded by the Leeland government.

DSB does not currently research into the development of such drugs as there would only be a market for them if a superbug was to develop. Since new antibiotics would be designed to hopefully never be used (and so not be sold to make profits) the project would not normally be of interest to DSB.

You have agreed to put together a short presentation to help DSB in making a decision on the project.

Required:

Create some slides to be used in the presentation to Burak Rom and his colleagues next week.

(a) **Prepare two presentation slides, with accompanying notes, evaluating the strategic and financial risks associated with the opportunity in Leeland.** **(12 marks)**

Professional skills marks are available for illustrating analysis and evaluation skills relevant to the risks in the project. **(4 marks)**

(b) **Prepare three presentation slides which consider the business and ethical arguments for DSB to develop antibiotics to combat superbugs regardless of support from the government of Leeland and which give an overall opinion on whether DSB should proceed with the project.** **(12 marks)**

Professional skills marks are available for demonstrating commercial acumen in determining why this decision may be justified on non-financial grounds. **(2 marks)**

(Total: 30 marks)

EXHIBIT 1

A REPORT ON THE PHARMACEUTICAL INDUSTRY IN THE COUNTRY OF NEARLAND

Source: *Drugs Approval and Regulation Authority of Nearland, June 20X2*

The marketing and sale of new drugs is highly regulated. In Nearland the relevant industry body is the Drugs Approval and Regulation Authority (DARA). DARA closely monitors the testing of drugs and is responsible for licensing drugs for sale in most developed nations.

DARA has strict rules on claimed efficacy of drugs and performs independent tests to ensure that drugs are safe for use and can do what they claim to do. Advertising of drugs is controlled and monitored and action is taken against companies who try to make unsubstantiated claims on the benefits of developed drugs. Sales are regulated regardless of the sales route taken by pharmaceutical companies – whether that is selling in bulk to healthcare providers, selling directly to doctors and clinicians or selling through new e-channels.

Most individuals in Nearland must pay for the drugs prescribed by their doctor. For that reason many Nearland citizens take out medical insurance which will cover any medical expenses that might occur. Employees of public organisations have their medical insurance paid for by the government. This is one of the reasons why the government of Nearland are putting pharmaceutical companies who operate in the country under greater scrutiny.

Nearland has recently experienced an economic downturn brought about by weak international demand for products manufactured in the country. This has led to an increase in unemployment which in turn has led to cuts in discretionary expenditure.

In order to sustain the economy the government have implemented measures such as reductions in state pensions which have had a particular effect on the country's aging population (where a greater proportion of citizens are reliant on state pensions each year). However, the government have aimed to balance this by maintaining free healthcare for all citizens receiving a state pension.

EXHIBIT 2

EXTRACTS FROM NEARLAND INTERNAL TRAINING DOCUMENTS AT DSB

Last updated: December 20X2

Our organisational structure

DSB is a global pharmaceutical company. It has offices in over 50 countries around the world and employs over 125,000 people. But DSB aims to have a local focus for local markets so that we fully reflect the culture, legislation and staffing needs that are unique to each market.

Each country has its own unique division which is a wholly-owned separate legal entity and which is solely responsible for performance in that country. Local managers manage each subsidiary which allows them to exploit local market knowledge and better meet the needs to local customers and staff.

Local managers monitor staff performance against performance targets which are set for reward purposes. This should allow staff to feel that their rewards are better linked to their personal and local performance rather than to the fate of the organisation globally.

Our intellectual property

DSB is an active member of the Nearland Drugs Approval and Regulation Authority (DARA). This means that DSB's drugs have been fully tested for safety and for their ability to do what they claim to do.

All of DSB's products are protected by global and national patents which prevent rivals copying the drug, its brand or its marketing. The length of patents can vary from at least 15 years to up to 25 years and none of DSB's current products has less than 5 years of its patent life left. This gives assurance to employees about the likely ongoing success of the business in the future.

Our rewards

At DSB, staff are our most valued asset. DSB know that to have the best business we need the best staff and our recruitment aims to achieve this. The best staff need to be rewarded to ensure that we retain their services and their motivation.

DSB aims to have incentives that ensure that staff feel highly valued and highly motivated. DSB also has many worker programmes and policies to ensure that staff have a work/life balance that suits their needs.

Rewards are closely linked to the organisational goals and strategies. For example, sales representatives have sales related targets to ensure that they are working in the best interests of DSB. If sales levels increase then the financial rewards for sales representatives increase.

Corporate governance and ethics

As a highly visible company, and a global household name, DSB has long prided itself on its ethical reputation. We believe this to be essential in supporting shareholder value. Our corporate code of ethics, published some years ago, pledges our commitment to the highest standards of ethical performance in the following areas: full compliance with regulation in all jurisdictions; safety and care of all those relying on DSB products; transparency and communication with stakeholders and environmental responsibility.

In addition, DSB has always stressed that it puts patient interests first and considers its responsibility to society to be a priority. DSB drugs are sold to developing countries at lower than usual prices and the company often donates vaccines to vulnerable populations. DSB aspires to be thought of as a well governed company in all the countries in which it operates.

EXHIBIT 3

EXTRACTS FROM THE FINANCIAL STATEMENTS OF THE NEARLAND DIVISION

Extract from the statement of financial position

For the year ended 31st December 20X2

(All figures in $m)

	20X2	20X1
Assets		
Non-current assets		
Intangible assets	6,100	6,400
Property, plant, equipment	3,600	3,900
	9,700	10,300
Current assets		
Inventories	420	450
Trade receivables	2,600	2,300
Cash and cash equivalents	480	560
	3,500	3,310
Total assets	13,200	13,610
Current liabilities	2,660	1,980
Non-current liabilities		
Long-term borrowings	9,000	10,000
Total liabilities	11,660	11,980
Equity		
Share capital	50	50
Retained earnings	1,490	1,580
Total equity and liabilities	13,200	13,610

Key data from the statement of profit or loss for the year ended 31st December

(All figures in $m)

	20X2	20X1
Revenue	6,140	7,200
Cost of sales	1,949	2,160
Research and development costs	600	800
Finance costs	1,000	1,100
Profit for the year after tax and interest	410	586
Dividends paid	500	500

Other company data for Nearland

	20X2	20X1
Number of employees		
Production	815	818
Sales	1,304	1,212
Research and development	246	315
Other	189	204
Number of patents held	16	17

Industry sales

Total pharmaceutical sales in Nearland over the last 5 years are illustrated as follows:

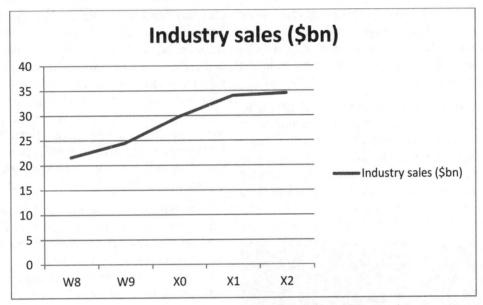

Source: DARA Industry report December 20X2

EXHIBIT 4

FARLAND NATIONAL DAILY	5th February 20X3

DRUGS COMPANY SENDS DOCTORS ON 5 STAR HOLIDAYS WITH YOUR MONEY!
BY EMINE VASIRI

A global pharmaceutical company are bribing doctors to recommend their drugs by offering those doctors a free life of luxury. DSB, the pharmaceutical company responsible for over 20% of drugs prescribed by doctors in Farland, are sending some doctors on all expenses-paid holidays masquerading as conferences.

In return, doctors prescribe these drugs for use by their patients. There is no guarantee that the drugs are needed or that better or cheaper drugs may be available. DSB make over $100,000m from the sales of their drugs.

Our investigations have discovered that payments to doctors in Farland totalling $600m were funnelled as fictional expenses through a travel agent and approved by DSB sales managers locally. The payments were ostensibly for doctor attendances as conferences, but instead doctors were free to use the money to fund luxury lifestyles normally only enjoyed by the superrich.

A yacht similar to the one used by Dr Farzan Ali

One doctor, Farzan Ali, hasn't held surgery for over three weeks. Instead Dr Ali has been spending his time on a yacht in an exclusive foreign resort. Dr Ali, whose official earnings are $200,000 per annum, drives a $400,000 foreign sports car and lives in a $6m mansion with his accountant wife.

Our investigators believe that doctors in Farland are being bribed by DSB to recommend and buy DSB's drugs. The conferences are nothing more than a sham way for doctors to claim for holidays, cars or whatever they like in exchange for giving glowing reviews of DSB products and recommending them to their clients. Many DSB conferences, which in other professions would happen no more than once per year, happen up to 6 times a year in Farland.

We interviewed one senior staff member at DSB who said that the legitimacy of Farland conferences was not checked. When told of the amounts involved the staff member said that she was shocked and embarrassed to be working for a company such as DSB, especially as she has to buy DSB's expensive drugs for her sons medical treatments.

So far DSB have refused to comment on these bribery allegations. New CEO Nur Saah has only been in her role for 2 months so it will be interesting to see whether she is just another fat cat executive or whether her company will put the public first and stop these outrageous actions.

EXHIBIT 5

EXTRACT FROM DRAFT DSB BOARD MEETING MINUTES

26th February 20X3

In attendance:

- Alonzo Far (AF) – Non-executive director

- Burak Rom (BR) – Finance director

- Nur Saah (NS) – Chief Executive Officer

- Sena Ali (SA) – Head of internal audit

- Yusuf Kim (YK) – Sales director

Discussion of recent bribery allegations against DSB:

NS: Like most pharmaceuticals companies we are subject to close scrutiny where controls over the development and testing of drugs are concerned. Many of our shareholders have chosen to invest in DSB because they believe the pharmaceuticals industry to be one of the most highly regulated in the world and that this reduces their exposure to risk. This issue of paying bribes in Farland could have massive repercussions for us.

AF: Do we sell our products to doctors in Farland differently than we do elsewhere?

YK: No, much the same as in other countries, promotion traditionally happens via personal selling, with sales representatives visiting doctors and persuading them to prescribe or recommend our products.

BR: Budgets are available to sales representatives to pay doctors to make speeches about particular drugs at conferences, take them out for meals after such events and even pay for accommodation.

YK: This kind of arrangement has always been a feature of pharmaceutical sales and is a way of 'spreading the word' about new and often innovative products, but it seems that in Farland, doctors were given payments by DSB employees in return for simply prescribing DSB drugs.

SA: DSB does not tolerate corruption in its business. We have many policies, procedures and controls in place to monitor payments given to doctors and take action against any breaches. For example a report of all payments made to doctors over a certain amount (considered excessive) is produced on a monthly basis for management review in each country we operate within (an exception report). Unfortunately in Farland, the amount considered excessive was set at an extremely high level and so the exception report was always without content. Investigations have already taken place into the activities of the sales teams accused of targeting influential doctors with expensive gifts and cash to win business'.

NS: What have you found?

SA: My team have investigated the allegations using external legal and audit advice. Some fraudulent behaviour relating to expense claims were identified as well as evidence of non-existent conferences, and this has resulted in employee dismissals and further changes to monitoring procedures in Farland. For example, all sales representatives are now being asked to take part in an ethical training programme.

AF: I'm horrified by these allegations. Especially as this is not the first time that bribery allegations against DSB have been made. I suggest DSB make an immediate public statement to reassure all stakeholders that patient interests came first and all payments to doctors would be immediately discontinued since controls to ensure legitimacy were obviously not working.

BR: If the allegations are proved by the authority, DSB would probably be fined heavily for breaking local laws and we may find ourselves under scrutiny from authorities in other countries in which we operate. In any case, the publicity generated by any legal proceedings would cause our reputation to suffer.

NS: I think we need to get ahead of these allegations and make a public statement to reassure stakeholders that action had been taken to prevent any reoccurrence.

BR: If the Leeland project went ahead, we could use our involvement to repair any damage done to their reputation by the bribery scandal. Not only that, the government funding could make the project very lucrative.

AF: If the government of Leeland are funding it, why would stakeholders consider it an ethical project on DSB's part?

NS: The government funding need not be mentioned in any publicity related to the project.

BR: I think that if we are going to make an announcement on the bribery allegations we should also use the statement to announce the 'ethical project' in Leeland.

NS: I'd also like to use any public statement to explain my role at DSB as I think this newspaper article amounts to a personal attack on me.

EXHIBIT 6

EMAIL TRAIL ON LEELAND OPPORTUNITY

Ling, Michael

From:	Burak Rom
Sent:	Friday, 17th Mar 20X3, 9:58 am
To:	Michael Ling
Subject:	Leeland opportunity

Hi Michael,

It was nice to meet you along with Masaki Setsu earlier in the week. As discussed at the meeting we have a new opportunity in Leeland that I would like your opinion on before taking it to the board. We agreed that I'd get together a few researchers and myself and that you'd put together a little presentation for us early next week. It doesn't have to be too long, just as long as it covers some of our key concerns.

DSB has an especially strong presence in Leeland because of Leeland's unique state funded health system whereby sophisticated care is given to the population freely at the point of need. This means DSB invests a great deal of time and money ensuring it develops the right products for Leeland's needs and marketing these products to clinicians within the Leeland system.

Government representatives from Leeland have been in discussions with our senior research team at DSB with a view to Leeland's health service subsidising the development of new antibiotic strains. There is a need for new antibiotics to be developed and kept in reserve in case of an outbreak of a superbug which could be devastating to Leeland's population.

I've estimated that the cost of research and development into the new antibiotics would be around $1,000m. The Leeland government have offered to fund 40% of this. But there is only a 5% chance of the research and development successfully developing a usable drug which would gain regulatory approval and a patent for marketing and sales of the developed antibiotic.

If the regulatory approval is granted the Leeland government have suggested that they will make an offer to buy the patent immediately from DSB. The government would pay a fee over 10 years that would give the Leeland government control over all future distribution and sale of the drug.

Alternatively, DSB could retain the patent on the drug which would give it the ability to sell the drug if a superbug was to be discovered. I think we could make upwards of $50bn if that were to happen as we'd get a lot of sales around the world.

But I still think that this is a very big risk for us to take. The researchers seem very keen to proceed due to the challenge that the research would demand, but I'm not sure whether this fits in with DSB's goals and strategies.

I'd like to have your thoughts on this before I make more detailed calculations and take the plan to the board.

I'll see you next week and I look forward to your presentation.

Burak

END OF QUESTION

2   FOODMART

You are a Junior Management Consultant, working for Chen and Company, a medium-sized accounting practice. The firm is based in Upland, a developed economy with a freely-traded currency (the UpMark).

You have worked for Chen and Company since you qualified, and have been a member of several consultancy project teams. Your specialist sector is retail. On your most recent project, you deputised for your manager when she was unable to attend client meetings. You were a member of the project management team and also ran a sub-team.

Following an appraisal meeting with the Consultancy Partner of Chen and Company, it has been agreed that you will manage a small project, as part of your professional development.

A few days ago, you were informed that a suitable opportunity had arisen. You were briefed by the Consultancy Partner (see Exhibit 1), who handed you a file containing Exhibits 2-7.

Exhibit 1: Transcript of briefing given by the Consultancy Partner

Exhibit 2: File note – Position report on FOODMART

Exhibit 3: Extracts from FOODMART 2017 Strategic Plan

Exhibit 4: Press article – Disruptive Technologies

Exhibit 5: Internal Audit report – New Product Development process

Exhibit 6: Organisation chart of FOODMART NPD function

Exhibit 7: Notes from discussions with staff

You have now been with FOODMART for a couple of days, and the Board members are keen to hear your initial impressions.

The case requirements are as follows:

TASK 1

As a first step in your consultancy project, you have been asked to report the findings from your document review to The Board of FOODMART.

Required:

You have been asked to produce a report to the Board of FOODMART, which:

(a)   **Assesses the recent impact of disruptive technologies on FOODMART.**   **(12 marks)**

Professional skills marks are available for demonstrating evaluation skills in estimating the impact of the business environment.   **(3 marks)**

(b)   **Evaluates the importance of New Product Development in enabling FOODMART to deliver its 2017 strategy.**   **(10 marks)**

Professional skills marks are available for demonstrating commercial acumen skills in showing insight into how NPD might affect FOODMART's achievement of its aims.   **(3 marks)**

(c)   **Identifies areas that FOODMART should address, if it wishes to attain 'business performance excellence'. You should use an appropriate theoretical model to structure your answer.**   **(21 marks)**

Professional skills marks are available for demonstrating analysis skills in your consideration of the requirements of the excellence model.   **(4 marks)**

(Total: 53 marks)

TASK 2

After the recent Board meeting, at which your initial findings were presented, the CEO of FOODMART asked you to give some thought to how the threat posed by disruptive technologies might be mitigated. The CEO is particularly keen to hear your views relating to the NPD function.

Required:

You have been asked to produce a confidential report to the CEO of FOODMART, which:

(a) **Evaluates the effectiveness of the current New Product Development processes in FOODMART.** **(16 marks)**

Professional skills marks are available for demonstrating scepticism skills in your questioning of the information provided. **(4 marks)**

(b) **Classifies, using an appropriate theoretical model, the type of organisational process change required in the New Product Development function of FOODMART.**

(5 marks)

Professional skills marks are available for demonstrating commercial acumen skills in using your judgement to classify NPD. **(2 marks)**

(c) **Recommends how the organisation structure of FOODMART, and the internal relationships between the New Product Development function and other functions, should be changed to improve the effectiveness of NPD. You should justify each of your recommendations.** **(16 marks)**

Professional skills marks are available for demonstrating communication skills in persuading the CEO. **(4 marks)**

(Total: 47 marks)

EXHIBIT 1

TRANSCRIPT OF BRIEFING GIVEN BY THE CONSULTANCY PARTNER

"You will be aware of FOODMART. They've been a client of ours for many years, and we've helped them to develop from being a small regional retailer to one of our major supermarket chains.

I can see from your Staff Record that you've become something of an expert in the retail sector, but you haven't yet worked with a supermarket. That's good, as FOODMART's CEO has specifically asked for a 'fresh pair of eyes'. I share their concern that the previous project manager may have become a little too familiar with FOODMART's business model, as he has worked with them on several assignments over the past five years.

The CEO of FOODMART is concerned that its business model may be under threat from new technologies, and that their strategic plan is not robust enough to cope with what might be coming. I was impressed by the work you did on M-commerce, last year, so I naturally thought of you.

I've asked the previous project manager to write a brief position report (Exhibit 2) that explains where FOODMART are now, and how they got there. I've also compiled some other stuff that I hope you'll find useful. It's all in the file here (Exhibits 3-7).

You have a meeting with the CEO of FOODMART tomorrow, when you'll get your detailed terms of reference. I'll let you have an assistant. If you need anything else, just let me know."

EXHIBIT 2

FILE NOTE – POSITION REPORT ON FOODMART

(Provided by your predecessor, the consultancy manager for the past 5 years)

Introduction

FOODMART is Upland's third largest supermarket (by revenue). It was formed in 1978, and listed on the Upland stock exchange in 2002. It currently (May 2018) has 834 stores, and revenues (in 2017) of about UM29 billion. FOODMART retails a full range of food and non-food household products, and is perceived as 'fairly up-market'.

Origins

Before the early 1970s, Upland had not developed a 'supermarket culture'. Food was purchased from specialist retailers, such as bakers and greengrocers, or from small convenience stores. Service was personal, with staff serving individual customers from behind counters.

The first supermarket chain in Upland was Camberwell's, which had been established in a neighbouring country using a US-style discount business model. Camberwell's opened its first store in Upland in 1974, then opened stores at a rate of twenty to thirty each year between 1974 and 1979, leading to the closure of many small food retailers. The three founders of FOODMART were all formerly senior managers with Camberwell's. The founders saw an opportunity for a supermarket chain based on quality of environment and stock, rather than on price. This remains FOODMART's key strategic aim.

FOODMART opened its first 9 stores in 1978, then rapidly gained market share over the following decade. It was rated as the 'best supermarket chain' in Upland every year from 1989 to 2013, in the Retail Federation of Upland (RFU) survey.

Early sector development

By 1985, Upland had nine supermarket chains covering a wide range of price-points. FOODMART and Ultra were seen as the most up-market, while Camberwell's and Unimart occupied the lower end of the price spectrum.

The late 1980s and 1990s saw consolidation in the sector. While FOODMART and Ultra remained independent, Camberwell's acquired Unimart and two mid-point chains. There were further mergers and acquisitions, and the number of major supermarket chains in Upland gradually reduced to the current four.

The last ten years

FOODMART, in common with most other supermarket businesses, has shifted its emphasis away from large 'superstores' very large 'megastores' towards increasing its number of small high-street stores. Branded 'FOODMART Everyday', these stores carry a restricted range of goods and are cheaper to staff and operate than larger stores. Due to their proximity to business districts, the FOODMART Everyday stores are designed around shoppers who visit on their way to work, during the lunch break, or on their way home. The driver for this has been the shortage of suitable 'out of town' sites, and a switch away from frozen and 'convenience' foods towards fresh foods. FOODMART now has 114 Everyday stores, representing just under 10% of revenues.

Unlike many of its rivals, FOODMART does not have its own e-commerce system. Online ordering and home delivery, under FOODMART's brand, are managed by a third-party supplier (MaxDel). FOODMART also does not allow customers to 'self-scan' products, to avoid delays at the checkout, due to concerns about theft.

FOODMART lost its position as 'best supermarket chain', in the RFU survey, in 2014. It has not regained it.

SWOT analysis

My personal assessment of FOODMART is as shown.

<table>
<tr><td align="center">**STRENGTHS**</td><td align="center">**WEAKNESSES**</td></tr>
<tr><td valign="top">

- Excellent management team
- Good reputation for quality
- Dedicated staff

</td><td valign="top">

- Low cash balance (and reliance on debt)
- Reliance on third party e-commerce provider
- No 'self-scan' in stores
- Lack of an ERP system makes detailed analysis of performance difficult
- Little emphasis on development of loyalty programme (only 4% of transactions from programme members)

</td></tr>
<tr><td align="center">**OPPORTUNITIES**</td><td align="center">**THREATS**</td></tr>
<tr><td valign="top">

- Towns and city regions still available for expansion, in some areas of Upland

</td><td valign="top">

- Recession still slowing economic growth
- Foreign competitors believed to be considering development into Upland
- Growth in online ordering (and home delivery)

</td></tr>
</table>

Recent financial performance

UM (Millions)	2017	2016	Change %
Group Revenues	27,534	26,994	2.2
Retail operating profit (ROP)	626	635	(1.4)
Financial Services* operating profit	62	65	(4.6)
Net finance cost	(119)	(121)	1.7
Number of stores	828	801	
Retail space (000 M^2)	1,818	1,796	

* Financial Services comprises FOODMART Credit Cards, Insurance and Personal Loans

EXHIBIT 3

EXTRACTS FROM FOODMART 2017 STRATEGIC PLAN

(Provided by the CEO of FOODMART)

Market analysis and prospects

As Upland recovers from the recession, total spend in the foods sector is expected to remain static until at least 2020, then to grow by only 1-2% each year for the remainder of the period covered by this strategy document. The planned growth in this strategic plan will come from new store openings and increased market share.

Competitors

Ultra is perceived as FOODMART's primary rival. As the current holder of the Retail Federation of Upland (RFU) 'Best Supermarket' accolade, a position held by FOODMART until 2013, it is Ultra that we always aim to beat. Looking at the performance metrics (see below) Ultra is able to invest more heavily in the retail environment than FOODMART, due to its significant cash balance. It also opens more stores each year, and spends more on advertising.

	New store fittings spend (per m² as a multiple of FOODMART)	Refurbishment spend on existing stores (per m² as a multiple of FOODMART)	Advertising spend (as a % of revenue)
FOODMART	1.00	1.00	2.2
Ultra	1.43	2.04	3.9

Camberwell's is very much a mid-range player. Its stores have very strong branding, but fittings and environment are generally of a lower standard than Ultra and comparable to those of FOODMART. It has self-scan checkouts in every store (in common with Ultra). Camberwell's losses due to theft at self-scan are believed to be slightly higher than Ultra's, possibly due to its customers' slightly lower disposable income levels, but still represent less than 0.2% of self-scan revenues (interview in Retail Week Magazine, March 2017).

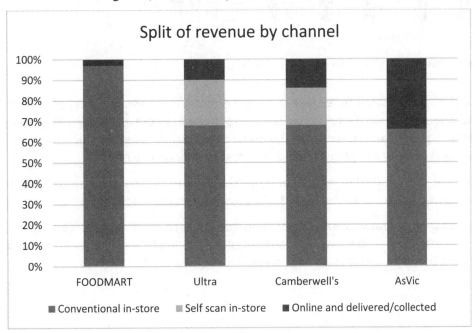

In common with Ultra, Camberwell's markets its customer loyalty programme very aggressively.

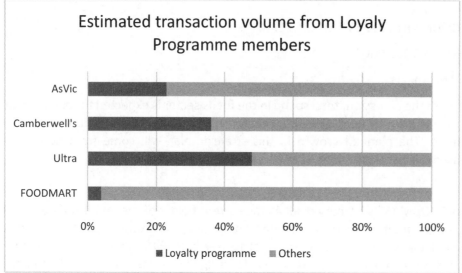

Possibly due to the recession, Camberwell's has achieved the highest growth in revenues of all of the big 4 over the last 5 years. Although it is impossible to judge where this growth has come from, some must have been due to customers down-switching from ourselves and Ultra.

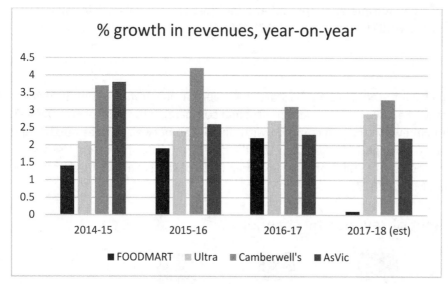

AsVic is more of a discounter than a supermarket. Only 3% of AsVic's revenue comes from High Street locations. Additionally, most of AsVic's stores fall into the 'megastore' category, being more like industrial units than supermarkets. AsVic still has some of its original 'pile them high, sell them cheap' feel: a legacy of its origins as Upland's first discount supermarket chain.

AsVic has been rated as the 'best value' major supermarket chain in Upland (RFU) since 2009. It consistently has the lowest prices, of all the big 4, for a 'basket' of staple foodstuffs.

Others include regional co-operative retail chains, and convenience store groups. Collectively, these account for less than 20% of all spend on foods in Upland. None of these groups is seen as a threat, as they lack the brand presence and financial resources of the big 4.

Branch network development

The target level for new store openings, across the planning period, is maintained at the current target level of 30 per year. While this level was not achieved last year, and will not be achieved in the current year, it has been retained as a fundamental driver on advice from The Board. Without this level of network expansion, the revenue and profit growth expected by shareholders will not be achieved.

As in the recent past, new store openings will concentrate on 'Everyday' stores in key city centre (and business district) locations. We currently have 11 properties acquired (leased or purchased), at various stages of conversion/refurbishment, with a further 13 in the course of negotiation. It is becoming increasingly difficult to identify suitable high-street properties, as most have already been taken by us or our competitors.

In accordance with our strategic aims, we are not planning any developments outside Upland during the current strategic plan timescale. Neighbouring countries each have their own established supermarket chains.

Product and technology development

In addition to all scheduled updates to software and hardware, we plan upgrades to the Electronic Point of Sale (EPOS) systems during 2020. At this point, most of the hardware will have been written down to zero (being over 5 years old) and the software will be nearing obsolescence. A major capital investment proposal will be submitted during 2019.

We plan to continue our margin-sharing partnership with MaxDel, whereby they provide online shopping and home delivery services under the FOODMART brand. The Board still feels that the required investment to bring this activity in-house, and the associated risks, are too great.

We plan to continue to widen the product offering in our larger stores, selecting new products after consultation with customer panels and suppliers. Our own-brand offering will also be widened. All new products must meet targets set for contribution per square metre.

We will continue to revise the 'Everyday' stores product range purely based on improving contribution per square metre. Products will be changed in order to maximise the returns from floor space.

Financial targets

	2017 Actual UMm	2018 Forecast UMm	2019 Target UMm	2020 Target UMm	2021 Target UMm	2022 Target UMm
Group Sales (inc VAT)	29,112	29,332	31,302	32,371	33,440	34,510
Retail operating profit (ROP)	626	630	939	1,295	1,338	1,380
Financial Services operating profit	62	58	60	60	60	60
Number of stores	828	848	878	908	938	968

Risks to achievement of strategy targets

The stagnant economy in Upland means that achievement of the revenue and profit targets relies on the identification of suitable new sites. As previously discussed, this has risks attached. We will continue to investigate suitable sites, and to aggressively negotiate their acquisition (whether by purchase of the freehold, or by long leasehold).

EXHIBIT 4

PRESS ARTICLE – DISRUPTIVE TECHNOLOGIES IN SUPERMARKET RETAILING

(From 'Business Today', 2017)

What is disruptive technology?

Harvard Business School professor Clayton M. Christensen coined the term disruptive technology. In his 1997 best-selling book, 'The Innovator's Dilemma', Christensen separates new technology into two categories: sustaining and disruptive. Sustaining technology relies on incremental improvements to an already established technology. Disruptive technology lacks refinement, often has performance problems because it is new, appeals to a limited audience and may not yet have a proven practical application. It does, however, have the potential to revolutionise.

Think about the impact on our everyday lives of such developments as email, social media, cloud storage and e-commerce. They were all, once upon a time, 'disruptive' technologies.

In this article, we draw upon the work of Professor Max Stelling at the University of Upper Upland (UUU). Stelling and his team, in the University's Innovation Unit, have been looking at the (often secret) work being carried out in technology companies in Upland and elsewhere. We thank Professor Stelling for his contributions to this article, and for granting us permission to quote from our interview with him.

PREDICTED DEVELOPMENTS IN RETAIL

> *"The next decade will see a revolution in the way we shop. Visiting a supermarket once a week, or a fashion outlet once a month, will become a thing of the past. E-commerce has already disrupted the markets for clothing, entertainment and leisure goods. Over the next decade, technologies will do the same for foodstuffs."*

In this article, we look at the 'top five' disruptive technologies predicted by Stelling and his team. Stelling has kindly ranked these developments in terms of likelihood and immediacy, with number one the most likely to impact in the shortest timeframe.

1. Personal shopper applications

> *"Shoppers can spend valuable hours surfing the Internet, comparing prices and availability. With the growth of free home delivery, and the multiplicity of retailers stocking the same products, all this will change. At some point, you will decide that the potential savings from comparison shopping are not justified by any cost savings. Or, maybe, you'll just wish that someone (or something) would do it for you."*

Price comparison websites are nothing new. When we buy flights, holidays or durables we use such sites to try to get the best deal. There are apps available, to make the search easier. Those apps rank the options, and recommend which one we should take. Why shouldn't the same principles work for branded FMCG purchases?

Personal shopper applications will go much further than price comparison. Because of the low unit cost of the items in a typical FMCG shopping basket, the consumer does not want to waste time shopping around for the best deal. Any savings made are really not worth the investment of time.

In a personal shopper app, the app becomes the customer. All the consumer needs to do is to generate a shopping list (or maybe not – see below). The app then scans retailers' online stores to find the best deals, trades off savings against any delivery charges (though these are becoming increasingly rare), schedules deliveries, and places the orders. The consumer receives multiple deliveries, from different retailers, which combine to provide the best value for money.

2. Push-through scanning

"Once you think about the potential of replacing barcodes with passive RFID[1] tags, it's easy to see how retailing might change. While the tags are currently quite expensive, they will become much cheaper as demand rises and technology improves. When they cost little more than printing a barcode, the manufacturers will all use them. RFID is the key to the revolution that's coming. It enables so many new ways of shopping."

Many supermarkets allow loyalty-card holders to scan their own purchases, then pay for their goods at a separate checkout. The self-scan checkouts are un-staffed, and generally have no line to stand in. Security staff very occasionally do a 'spot check' on high value items, but the vast majority of self-scan customers interact with no staff at all during their shop. Losses due to theft are far outweighed by the savings in staff costs. Customers also find self-scan much quicker.

The next logical progression, made possible when barcodes are replaced by RFID tags, is that the customer would scan their loyalty-card and payment card before taking a trolley, do their shopping, then simply walk out of the store to their car. A scanner, sited near the exit, would automatically scan everything in the trolley and charge the relevant payment card. No staff interaction, no scanning of individual products and no standing in line at the checkout.

3. IoT – Home stock control

"The 'Internet of Things' (IoT) is the interconnection, via the Internet, of computing devices embedded in everyday objects, enabling them to send and receive data. This is where we see the greatest impact on retailing. All of the white goods manufacturers are looking at this, as are many of the large food manufacturers. Retailers need to catch up."

Combined with the replacement of barcodes by RFID tags, the IoT opens up a whole new world of opportunities. Imagine if your larder, refrigerator and rubbish bin were all connected via the Internet. For example:

- You would be prompted, by your refrigerator, about foodstuffs that were about to reach their 'best before' date. No more sweaty cheese in the back of the refrigerator, growing mould.

- Your refrigerator could give you menu and recipe suggestions, based on whatever foodstuffs you have 'in stock' in your refrigerator and larder. No more last-minute shopping trips.

- Your rubbish bin could automatically add things to your shopping list, as you use them, by scanning the RFID tag in discarded packaging. No more running out of food.

4. Automatic shopping

Of course, if you are going to allow your kitchen devices to manage your stock, why not let them do your shopping for you? Simply allow your devices to update your shopping list, in your personal shopper app, and anything you use will be automatically replaced. You could even plan your meals for the week, by discussing menu options with your refrigerator, safe in the knowledge that the ingredients would be automatically purchased and delivered in time for the appropriate meal.

5. Drone delivery

"Four years ago, Jeff Bezos promised that Amazon would soon deliver packages by drone. Bezos' primetime announcement sparked a lot of interest – and a media consensus that it was a publicity stunt to get Christmas shoppers thinking about Amazon. After all, the law in most countries prohibited commercial drones from flying over populated areas, and planes were already experiencing close calls with hobbyists' drones. But the drone community is not acting like the prospect of delivering packages by drone is a pipe dream."

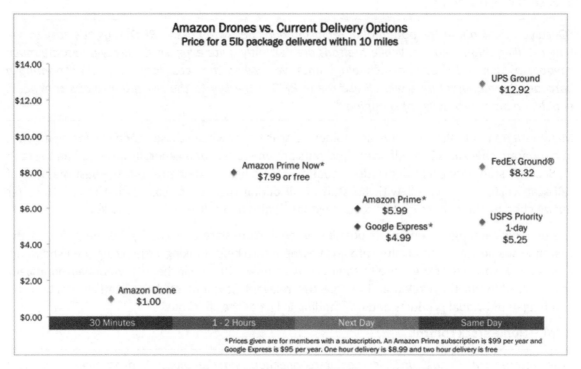

Graph, data, and analysis by ARK Invest (2017)

"But my food shopping weighs WAY more than 5lb, and I'm 20 miles from the nearest supermarket", you cry. True, but you are assuming that your whole weekly shop is delivered at the same time, and that the carrying capacity and economic range of a drone will remain at 5lb and 10 miles.

JD.com, the Chinese retailer, already has drones with a one-tonne carrying capacity and a range of 300 miles. The sky really is the limit!

1 Radio-frequency identification (RFID) uses electromagnetic fields to automatically identify and track tags attached to objects. The tags contain electronically stored information. Passive tags collect energy from a nearby RFID reader's interrogating radio waves. Active tags have a local power source such as a battery and may operate at hundreds of meters from the RFID reader. Unlike a barcode, the tag need not be within the line of sight of the reader, so it may be embedded in the tracked object. RFID is one method for Automatic Identification and Data Capture (AIDC)

EXHIBIT 5

INTERNAL AUDIT REPORT – NEW PRODUCT DEVELOPMENT PROCESS

Introduction

We audited the New Product Development (NPD) processes in May 2016. NPD includes new products, technologies and operations processes. This function had previously been audited in 2011 (see file 2011/34).

The working papers for this audit can be found under reference 2016/41.

Method

1   We first produced a detailed process map, based on observation and interviews with participants. The process map was compared to documented procedures, and any discrepancies noted.

2   A thorough document review was carried out, covering correspondence, working files and meeting minutes. Any issues were noted.

3   Participants were again interviewed, this time to seek their views regarding issues and suggested improvements.

4   A detailed report was made verbally, to the Head of NPD and the Operations Director, of which this report is a summary.

Key findings

Head of NPD makes decisions which activities to prioritise.

Each NPD area (product range; technologies; operations processes) has a manager, who manages any projects in that area. Other staff from within the NPD function join those project teams, as required. If resources are a constraint, Head of NPD decides on priorities.

- New product trends are identified by scanning the trade press. New products are incorporated into the portfolio after discussions with customer panels and suppliers. All new products are assessed against guidelines for contribution per square metre, before selection. Product Range Manager makes recommendations to Head of NPD.

- Competitor analysis is carried out, to identify technological trends. New technologies are incorporated as and when the required investment is predicted to pay back, according to investment policy (currently 'within five years' for operations technologies). Technology Development Manager makes recommendations to Head of NPD.

- Operations processes are revised on an ad-hoc basis, when issues arise or a viable staff suggestion is received. Operations Process Manager makes recommendations to Head of NPD.

Head of NPD meets with the three Managers on the first Tuesday of each month, to plan the month's work. Two days later, Head of NPD meets with Operations Director to discuss work plans and recommendations. Minutes are taken at these meetings (see sample copies in file).

Recommendations

- Improvement required to chasing up action points in NPD meeting minutes.

- NPD area Managers should meet weekly, to discuss resource allocation between projects.

- This process is scheduled to be re-audited in 2021.

EXHIBIT 6

**ORGANISATION CHART OF FOODMART NPD FUNCTION
(SHOWING ONLY OPERATIONS DIRECTORATE)**

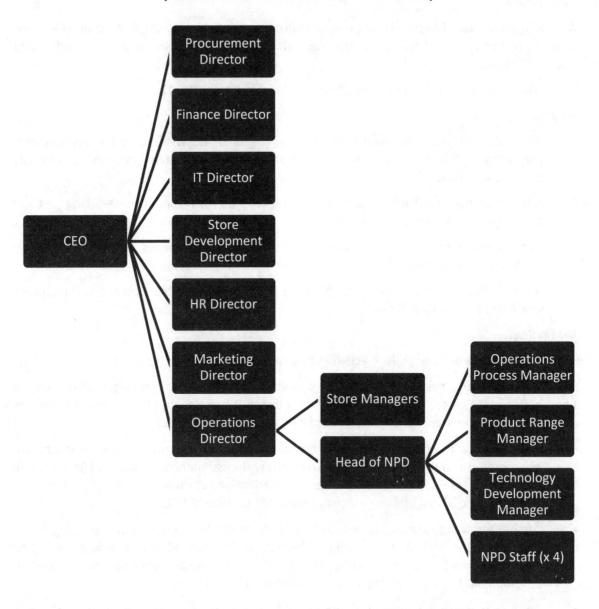

EXHIBIT 7

NOTES FROM DISCUSSIONS WITH STAFF (RELATING TO NPD)

(Provided by your predecessor, the project manager for the past 5 years)

> *I have been speaking to staff, regarding the way the NPD function operates. I have some concerns, which I am happy to share with you later. For now, here are some excerpts from the transcripts...*

"To be honest, I've never met anyone from NPD, other than at social events. They tend to keep themselves to themselves. I know that my Director gets very annoyed with new product decisions being made in Operations." *Procurement Manager*

"I get emails from Head of NPD, telling me what has been agreed. My job is to implement whatever upgrades, modifications or new systems they decide on. It's a bit irritating, to be honest. If only they would ask, before making decisions, I'm sure we could help them. Some of their decisions seem irrational. The Technology Development Manager isn't an IT expert – she used to be a store manager." *Head of IT*

"I like the NPD function to be fairly isolated from the day-to-day operations of the business. It allows them to take an overview, without being influenced by the other functions. Many of the managers elsewhere in FOODMART are very set in their ways, and a bit resistant to change. The role of NPD is to innovate, and I believe that they do that best without outside interference." *Operations Director*

"NPD? They're a law-unto-themselves. I've never had any contact with them. Actually, I hardly ever see Head Office staff. I can't remember the last time I met anyone outside the Operations Directorate, and even our own senior managers seldom visit stores." *Store Manager*

END OF QUESTION

3   SWAN HILL COMPANY (SHC)

Swan Hill Company (SHC) is a global manufacturer of specialist parts for the use in the construction of offshore oil rigs.

Trading as SHC, the company has been in business for over 100 years and is listed on the stock exchange of Eastlandia, the country in which it was originally formed. Although originally owned and managed by a collective group of friends, the company is now managed by a Board of directors responsible for a number of executive areas.

The company provides dozens of different components to hundreds of different construction businesses around the world. Its bestselling product is the CAS4, a necessary component in controlling underwater pressure in offshore oil rigs. SHC is the market leader in this type of product and it provides the majority of SHC's revenue and profit.

A major opportunity for the redesign of the CAS4 has recently presented itself to the company. However, the board of SHC is unsure as to how to proceed with this opportunity.

The following exhibits provide information relevant to SHC.

Exhibit 1: Extract from the SHC website

Exhibit 2: Email regarding the new sink method discovery

Exhibit 3: Ken Bowler's conference call with directors

Exhibit 4: Expected financial returns

Exhibit 5: Key benefits to be achieved from the secrecy option

Exhibit 6: Extract from Business Times Blog

The case requirements are as follows:

TASK 1

The board is still uncertain as to whether or not to disclose the science team's discovery. This will be a major event in the company's history which could fundamentally change its business model.

Assuming the role of financial director Ken Bowler, you have been asked by Nelson Cobar, SHC's chief executive, to assess whether or not to disclose the discovery of the new sink method to rivals. To aid you in this you have gathered and considered a range of information on the business as well as holding a conference call with other directors.

Prepare brief notes for a meeting with Nelson Cobar. The notes should cover the following areas:

Required:

(a)   **Assess the decision to follow the secrecy option from an ethical point of view.**

(10 marks)

Professional skills marks are available for illustrating commercial acumen in demonstrating awareness of organisational and wider external factors affecting the decision.   **(3 marks)**

(b)   **Distinguish between strategic and operational risks, and explain why the secrecy option would be a source of strategic risk.**   **(10 marks)**

Professional skills marks are available for illustrating analysis skills in investigating the risks associated with the secrecy option.   **(3 marks)**

(Total: 26 marks)

TASK 2

Still undecided, Nelson Cobar has decided to draft two alternative statements to explain both possible outcomes of the secrecy/licensing decision to SHC's key stakeholders. Once the board has decided which one to pursue, the relevant statement will be included in a voluntary section of the next corporate annual report.

Working as a senior member of the company's internal public relations team, you report directly to Edwin Kiama, the director of sales and marketing. You have been asked to draft statements that may be used to announce SHC's plans for the new sink method discovery.

Required:

(a)   **Draft a statement in the event that the board chooses the secrecy option. It should make a convincing business case and put forward ethical arguments for the secrecy option. The ethical arguments should be made from the shareholder (or pristine capitalist) perspective.**   **(10 marks)**

(b)   **Draft a statement in the event that the board chooses the licensing option. It should make a convincing business case and put forward ethical arguments for the licensing option. The ethical arguments should be made from the wider stakeholder perspective.**   **(10 marks)**

Professional skills marks are available for illustrating communication skills in effectively informing stakeholders about the company's choice and persuading users of the benefits of each option.   **(4 marks)**

(Total: 24 marks)

TASK 3

You work for Ken Bowler in the finance function of SHC. You helped in the preparation of the financial evaluation of the returns from the two options available to the company.

Unfortunately, when these were presented to Nelson Cobar he didn't really understand them as he does not have a financial background. He was particularly concerned that the secrecy option seems to take longer to make any money, is more expensive yet it is being proposed as the preferred option. Nelson suspects that when he presents the numbers to the board that they will have similar concerns.

You have therefore been asked to provide a short presentation aimed at helping the board understand the numbers produced in your calculations.

Required:

(a)   **In preparation for a presentation to the SHC board, prepare two presentation slides, with accompanying notes, explaining why, from a financial perspective, the secrecy option was chosen and the reason for the differences in the expected returns from each option.**   **(10 marks)**

Professional skills marks are available for illustrating communication skills in clarifying the information and presenting it appropriately to the intended audience.   **(3 marks)**

It was also obvious to Ken Bowler that Nelson wasn't sure as to why all of the benefits of the project had not been included in the evaluation. Ken is particularly worried about the benefits from the secrecy option and has gathered together some of the key benefits expected from that option. He has asked you to prepare an additional hand-out for board members in case anyone else raises this issue at the board meeting.

(b) **Prepare a hand-out for board members explaining the different types of benefits expected from the secrecy option and why some of these benefits have not been included in the net present value calculation.** **(14 marks)**

Professional skills marks are available for illustrating evaluation skills in assessing the benefits identified for the project. **(3 marks)**

(Total: 30 marks)

TASK 4

Assuming the role of Sean Nyngan, chief investment officer, Nelson Cobar has sent you a link to a blog called the Business Times Blog (Exhibit 6). It refers to an increasingly popular term called performance excellence.

Nelson has said that not only is this an area that may need to be exhibited as part of any financing initiative if SHC pursues the secrecy option, but that it is something that SHC should strive for regardless of the need to raise new external finance.

Nelson believes that SHC is an excellent company, but he wants to know whether there are areas where others may not see it as being so. He also wants to consider whether these are areas in which the company should make voluntary disclosures in annual reports in order to enhance SHC's accountability to investors.

Required:

Prepare briefing notes for Nelson Cobar covering the following areas:

(a) **An initial assessment of whether SHC would satisfy the criteria for performance excellence.** **(14 marks)**

Professional skills marks are available for illustrating professional scepticism relevant to questioning and challenging SHC's focus on performance excellence. **(4 marks)**

(b) **Explain why the disclosure of voluntary information in annual reports can enhance the company's accountability to equity investors.** **(3 marks)**

(Total: 21 marks)

EXHIBIT 1

The world's largest supplier to the oil rig construction industry

About us

The Swan Hill Company's history is one of technical excellence, community spirit, strong ethical principles and a constant strive for innovation and improvements.

Our history

The Swan Hill Company was a community effort that resulted in the creation of the company in 1907 in the town of Swan Hill. Jim Swanson had returned with his family having spent twenty years working overseas as the first wave of oil booms hit parts of the western world. Around the same time Jim's close friend, PJ Dixon, created a machine part for local water mills that was able to improve both efficiency and reliability. Jim's experience meant that he soon recognised that this invention could equally be applied to the new drilling processes used by companies looking to extract petroleum from newly discovered oil reserves. Together with funding from other associates based in Swan Hill, the friends created the Swan Hill Company, which was run collectively and successfully by members of the Swan Hill community for over 75 years before listing on the country's international stock exchange.

Throughout our history we have strived for constant innovation and improvements. We strive for excellence in everything that we do. This has led to countless innovation and performance awards.

Today SHC employs over 20,000 people in 100 countries around the world. Together, we expect to be making new history for the next 100 years.

Our Community

Despite having sales and operational locations around the world, SHC continues to have Swan Hill as our base where we retain our head office functions in Swan Hill. We have become a global business, satisfying customers in every corner of the world, but we will always consider ourselves to be a Swan Hill business.

SHC greatly values our relationship with the Swan Hill community. We are the biggest local employer and many of our senior employees were born and raised in Swan Hill. We continue to offer many local community support programmes aimed at maximising the abilities of Swan Hill people and encouraging others to follow in our footsteps.

Over the last 25 years we have grown our community beyond the boundaries of Swan Hill and offer community support programmes in every market where we have a significant presence. We want the communities that we meet around the world to value us as much as we value them. Our communities play a key role in all of our business decisions and we have always sought to maximise the benefit to the workforce and community in all of our business decisions.

Our ethics

SHC greatly values the planet and our environment. We take every care to minimise our impact on the planet and have hundreds of carbon offset programmes in place around the world. We also consult with local communities to ensure that any new expansions or plans have minimal negative impacts and that we have the full support of our communities.

We strive to act ethically in all of our business relationships. We want to act openly and honestly with our business partners and we demand the same from our partners. We would never accept a business partner whose ethical principles do not match our own.

SHC has strong principals managing our relationships with our staff. All staff are valued, trusted and rewarded regardless of religious beliefs, ethnicity or physical ability. We want to be a trusted employer where our staff value us as much as we value them.

We are passionate about ensuring that we build and maintain a strong relationship with our customers, built upon trust and integrity. We strive to ensure that our transactions are fair to both parties and ensure that all staff of SHC follow a code of practice which constantly guides us towards ethical behaviour in our business transactions.

Our current board of directors

SHC has a combination of executive and non-executive directors whose focus is to ensure the ongoing success of the company, sustaining its value for customers, our communities and the world at large. Many of these directors have lived in Swan Hill for all of their lives, but others bring a wealth of knowledge and experience from all around the world.

Our executive directors

Nelson Cobar – Chief Executive Officer

Ken Bowler – financial director

Ali Hamels – human resource director

Li Jang – production and operations director

Edwin Kiama – sales and marketing director

Sean Nyngan – chief investment officer

Sonja Rainbow – chief scientist

Our non-executive directors

Alison Manilla – non-executive chairman

Marti Cabrera

Maria Castellos – employee representative

Mo Gomez

Bryan Keane – shareholder representative

Stephen Pallister

Susan Pierse

EXHIBIT 2

EMAIL REGARDING THE NEW SINK METHOD DISCOVERY

Bowler, Ken

From:	Nelson Cobar
Sent:	Wednesday, 21st Aug 20X7, 10:15 am
To:	Ken Bowler
Subject:	Sink method project

Hi Ken,

Further to our discussions on the phone this morning about an email that I received from Sonja Rainbow, our chief scientist, please see Sonja's email below.

I'd really appreciate your advice on this and the other matters we discussed.

Speak soon

Nelson

------Original message-----------------

From:	Sonja Rainbow
Sent:	Sunday, 18th Aug 20X7, 8:02 pm
To:	Nelson Cobar
Subject:	

Hi Nelson,

I hope that you don't mind me emailing you at the weekend, but I'm really excited by a new discovery and couldn't wait until tomorrow to tell you (never mind waiting until our next board meeting)!

Early last week our scientific team discovered a massive breakthrough for the production of our major product, the CAS4. I won't bore you with the details as I know you're always telling me to keep it simple and avoid the scientific jargon. Basically, we've discovered a way, known as the sink method, which will enable us to produce the CAS4 at a lower unit cost and in much higher volumes than the current process.

It would also produce lower unit environmental emissions and would substantially improve the reliability of the CAS4 product. This has the potential to have a massive impact on CAS4 sales and our share in this market. I've spent the week using my contacts and research skills and I am certain that no-one else in the world has figured out a way to do this. This will completely blow our rivals out of the water.

I've spoken to our sales team and they agree with me that if we do this then we'll take over the entire market. We've currently got 30% of the market (DBC, our next biggest rival, have 25% with the remainder split across 12 much smaller organisations). But with this discovery we could have virtually 100% of the market to ourselves within four years!

DBC have been trying to apply the sink method for years but I'm reliably informed that they are still several years from working out the right way to do it. By the time they do so, it'll be too late. We'll be the single sole supplier in this industry and everyone else will have disappeared.

I've spoken with Mike in the finance function and we came up with two ways to go forward with this. Mike's team have created estimated returns for the two possibilities. I asked them to perform some calculations for me and I'll send you them in the morning, but you'll see that we can make over $200m from this if we follow my recommended option of just keeping this discovery secret and blowing our rivals away.

Mike said that his team could only include the financial benefits in their calculation. But it's not just financial benefits that we'll get from this. There are loads of other benefits – including ones for the Swan Hill community.

There's so much more to discuss with this, but I just couldn't wait to tell you about it. Everyone else is sworn to silence about this and I've tried to limit the amount of people who know about.

I'll come to see you first thing in the morning and we can discuss it further then.

Sonja

EXHIBIT 3

KEN BOWLER'S CONFERENCE CALL WITH DIRECTORS

Ken Bowler Question: Keeping this scientific discovery to ourselves and not releasing it to our rivals could have serious implications for the industry. Have you any thoughts on how we should proceed?

Edwin Kiama: I'm strongly in favour of the secrecy option. The board owes it to SHC's shareholders to take the option that would maximise shareholder value. The sink method should not be licensed to competitors and should be pursued as fast as possible.

Alison Manilla: I'm looking at the issue from an ethical perspective. I wonder whether SHC has the right, even if it had the ability, to put competitors out of business.

Ali Hamels: The secrecy option is the best way to secure long term employment for all of our staff and secure the future of Swan Hill as a manufacturing base.

Ken Bowler Question: Have we the ability to go it alone on this new method?

Li Jang: To gain the full benefits of the sink method with either option would require a complete refitting of the factory and the largest capital investment that SHC has ever undertaken.

Sean Nyngan: Pressing ahead with investment under the secrecy option is not without risks. First, we would have to finance the investment, probably initially through debt, and second, there are risks associated with any large investment. The licensing option would, over many years, involve the inflow of 'massive' funds in royalty payments from competitors using the SHC's patented sink method. By pursuing the licensing option, SHC could retain our market leadership in the short term without incurring risk, whilst increasing our industry dominance in the future through careful investment of the royalty payments that would be obtained from existing rivals being tied in to licensing agreements for the technology.

Ken Bowler Question: Do you think this new sink method will be a success?

Edwin Kiama: Business strategy is all about gaining competitive advantage and this is a chance to do exactly that. Once we've decided on the best way forward I can incorporate this into my regular customer briefings and discussion groups. We can get some vital feedback from them which will be invaluable in marketing this in the right way and making it a success.

Li Jang: This will throw our existing strategic plans into disarray. We've had these plans in place for a long time and we are working towards clear strategic objectives. Those objectives can still be achieved with this new method, but there will be considerable short-term disruption.

Ali Hamels: It's likely that some workforce jobs will have to be redesigned. But we have some of the best staff in the world, and I'm confident that they can make this a success

Sean Nyngan: As you know yourself, Ken, we've grown revenue year on year for the last five years and our shareholders and lenders are very happy. We've proven to be successful and resilient to any business changes and, to me, this is just a chance to continue our tradition of innovating and leading the market. We're constantly benchmarking ourselves against our rivals across a wide range of areas, and we're ahead in most measures already. This new sink method will only help in cementing that.

Ken Bowler Question: Is there anything else that we need to consider?

Alison Manilla: We should recognise that, not only do we as a company strive to act ethically, but many of our investors, some of which are members of my non-executive board, also have a strong ethical process. This shouldn't just be about what's best for the wealth of our shareholders.

Li Jang: We also need to think about whether Swan Hill has the capacity to fit in a factory of this size. It's likely that we may end up with a more geographically diverse workforce if we go forward with the secrecy option. That'll make it harder to monitor areas such as staff motivation, satisfaction and performance.

EXHIBIT 4

EXPECTED FINANCIAL RETURNS

Prepared for Sonja Rainbow by the SHC finance department

Option 1 – the secrecy option

Key assumptions:

- A patent disclosing the nature of the technology would not be filed so as to keep the technology secret within SHC

- SHC go it alone and rivals eventually leave the market

- New external finance is needed (including some newly issued debt)

Expected long term returns:

Period	T_0	T_1	T_2	T_3	$T_4 - \infty$
Net after tax cash flows	0	8	16	32	68
Capital investment	(95)	(24)	(14)	(12)	(10)
Net cash flows	(95)	(16)	2	20	58
Discount factors @12%	1.000	0.887	0.788	0.701	5.392
Present value	(95)	(14.2)	1.6	14.0	312.7

(all figures in $m)

Net present value = **$219.1m**

Option 2 – licensing option

Key assumptions:

- A patent is flied disclosing the nature of the discovery. This will prevent unauthorised use of the method for 20 years

- SHC then offer the use of the discovery to competitors under a licensing arrangement where SHC would receive substantial royalties for the twenty-year legal lifetime of the patent

- The licence contract would include an 'improvement sharing' requirement where licensees would be required to inform SHC of any improvements discovered that made the sink method more efficient or effective

- SHC's internal development can be fully funded from internal funds

Expected long term returns:

Period	T_0	T_1	$T_2 - T_{20}$
Net after tax cash flows	0	1	5
Capital investment	(2)	(1)	(1)
Net cash flows	(2)	–	4
Discount factors @14%	1.000	0.870	6.576
Present value	(2)	–	26.3

(all figures in $m)

Net present value = **$24.3m**

EXHIBIT 5

KEY BENEFITS TO BE ACHIEVED FROM THE SECRECY OPTION

Prepared by: Mike Nixon, Management accountant, finance function

For: Ken Bowler, Finance Director

Based on our initial investigations, discussions with the science team and market analysis we expect that the secrecy option on the CAS4 project would deliver the following benefits:

- Rivals will take too long to copy this innovation so are likely to leave the market as all buyers switch to SHC

- It will be easier to attract staff to SHC and the staff recruitment can focus on recruiting the most able staff

- Environmental emissions from production should be reduced by around 10% per annum

- Product returns should be reduced by around 5%

- Wastage and errors in production will fall by 8%

- Extra sales achieved will be $12m in the first year and should increase each year as more rivals leave the market

- The SHC brand will become more widespread, allowing easier product development in the future and reducing the risk of future product launch failures

- Other products will gain sales of around $1m per annum due to many customers buying these as a package alongside the new product being launched

- Market share will increase each year until year 4, when market share will be close to 100%

- Local house prices are likely to rise which will benefit existing employees

- Staff will be more motivated through working for a larger company offering more responsibility and reputation

- Economies of scale should result in bulk purchasing discounts worth $2m per annum in the first year and growing with production levels in subsequent years

EXHIBIT 6

Business Times Blog

| **Home** | **Forum** | **Archives** | **Contact** | **About** | **Donate** | **Writers** | **Search** |

The pursuit of excellence

By Anji Dia

24th February 20X7

In this blog post we examine the country's seeming obsession with performance excellence. Ever since the government choose this measure as a way of choosing business suppliers 'performance excellence' has become the buzzword in the business community.

Performance excellence is a phrase that probably has its origins in the US. A popular model used there is the Baldridge program which awards a presidential award to organisations which achieve performance excellence.

The Baldridge organisation states that it is "dedicated to help organisations identify, understand, and manage the factors that determine their success". Their program aims to examine the factors which it believes come together to determine excellent performance. Based on empirical data of successful criteria the program can be seen to be a progression of previous studies by the likes of Peters and Waterman.

Performance excellence aims to take a systematic approach to achieving excellence. It looks for total involvement at all levels of the business from the leaders of the organisation, to staff, to process developers. Only if all areas are seen to be excellent can the organisation itself achieve excellence. The result should allow the organisation to efficiently and effectively achieve its mission and goals.

Our own government want to develop a similar award system. It has been at the forefront of the chancellor's business briefings and, not only is it a big determinant in the awarding of business contracts, but the government are looking at awarding funding to organisations who want to pursue their ideals.

The increased presence and prevalence of the term might lead to finance providers using some of the framework measures in determining the provision of finance to organisations. This in turn could lead to organisations performing their own introspections on whether they meet the expectations of their finance providers.

But is performance excellence actually something new? Haven't organisations always strived for excellence. Surely the best indicator of performance excellence is financial performance. If a business performs well for shareholders surely it is performing excellently. Or if a not-for-profit improves its benchmark performance isn't it performing excellently?

Surely, this focus on performance excellence is just more administrative introspection that forms an unnecessary distraction at a time when organisations should be focusing on core activities and results.

What are your experiences with performance excellence? Does your organisation pursue performance excellence? Do you think that this is just the latest, in a likely to be short-lived, trend until the next big thing comes along? Do you understand performance excellence? Hit up the comments and let us know.

END OF QUESTION

4   FISHNET

You are a senior finance manager, working for Fishnet. Your role is to advise the directors on confidential strategic matters. You report to Jane Wills, the Finance Director.

Fishnet is a major manufacturer of fish-based 'recipe dishes', based in Sealand. The main products of Fishnet are 'convenience meals' – complete, cooked food which is sold by supermarkets for heating at home. Fishnet's products are either frozen (for consumption over the next six months), or chilled (for consumption within a week).

Fishnet's operations are sited in Grubsby, a traditional fishing port city on the East coast of Sealand. Fishnet does not own any fishing vessels, but local fishermen and large 'factory ships' deliver to Fishnet's processing plant in the 'Port of Grubsby Enterprise Zone'. Fishnet's processing plant carries out a full range of highly automated manufacturing processes, from the handling of the fresh fish through to the preparation, cooking and chilling/freezing of the recipe dishes. The other ingredients required for the manufacturing process (such as vegetables, flour, fats and spices) are delivered to the processing plant by road.

Fishnet's finished goods are delivered, by rail or road, to the distribution depots of large supermarket chains and independent wholesalers. Fishnet does not get involved in retail activities, nor does it currently export outside of Sealand.

Your days are very varied, with members of the Board approaching you for advice on a wide range of strategic matters. Today, you find three significant requests in your inbox, together with some attachments, as follows:

Exhibit 1: Consultant's report

Exhibit 2: Email from Engineering Director (NPD Strategy)

Exhibit 3: Email from IT director, and notes (proposed CRM upgrade)

The Case requirements are as follows:

TASK 1

The Board recently commissioned an independent marketing consultant to prepare a 'critical review' of Fishnet's market position and strategy. Extracts from the consultant's report are attached (Exhibit 1). The Finance Director, on behalf of the Board, has asked for your assistance.

Required:

You have been asked to produce a report to the Board, which:

(a)   Evaluates the sources of competition in the fish-based recipe dish manufacturing industry.   (10 marks)

Professional skills marks are available for demonstrating *evaluation* skills in appraising the business environment.   **(3 marks)**

(b)   Assesses the implications, for Fishnet, of the 'strategic drift' identified by the consultants.   (8 marks)

Professional skills marks are available for demonstrating commercial acumen skills in demonstrating awareness of the consequences of strategic drift.   **(2 marks)**

(c)   Advises the directors of a suitable 'intrapreneurship' policy and procedure, to exploit strategic opportunities.   (10 marks)

Professional skills marks are available for demonstrating *communication* skills in informing the Directors.   **(3 marks)**

(Total: 36 marks)

TASK 2

As a result of the consultant's report, the Engineering Director of Fishnet was asked to provide a briefing paper to the CEO in advance of the next Board meeting. The paper was to assess whether Fishnet needed a formal 'new product development' strategy and, if so, what such a strategy might cost.

Having received the briefing paper from the Engineering Director, the CEO has asked you to carry out a more thorough assessment of the proposals. The CEO is particularly concerned that the new strategy might have to be 'sold' to stakeholders, as he is concerned that some of the stakeholders may not support the strategy without some persuasion.

Required:

You have been asked to produce a report for the CEO, which:

(a)   **Analyses the stakeholders in the new product development strategy, using an appropriate model.** **(12 marks)**

Professional skills marks are available for demonstrating *analysis* skills in your consideration of the issues. **(3 marks)**

(b)   **Assesses the suitability, feasibility and acceptability of the new product development strategy. You should refer to your stakeholder analysis, where appropriate. *This information should be provided as a series of slides, with accompanying notes, for the CEO to present to the next Board meeting.*** **(10 marks)**

Professional skills marks are available for demonstrating communication skills in informing the directors. **(2 marks)**

(c)   **Assuming that Fishnet decides to proceed with the new product development strategy, advises the CEO how Fishnet should communicate with each of the main stakeholders in the project. You should refer to your stakeholder analysis, where appropriate.** **(8 marks)**

Professional skills marks are available for demonstrating *communication* skills in persuading the CEO. **(3 marks)**

(Total: 38 marks)

TASK 3

The IT director has asked you to assist him in getting final board approval for a capital investment. He plans to upgrade Fishnet's Customer Relationship Management (CRM) system, with the full support of the Marketing Director.

A member of the finance function has already produced a net present value (NPV) analysis (not provided), which shows that the proposal adds shareholder value when discounted at Fishnet's Weighted Average Cost of Capital (WACC). However, a concern was expressed within the finance function that a higher discount rate should have been used.

The CEO is apparently concerned that the risks inherent in some of the proposed system components are 'not well understood'. The Chair of the Risk Management Committee (a non-executive director) has asked that the CEO's concerns be addressed before the proposal comes back to the board for final approval.

Required:

You have been asked to produce an email to the Chair of the Risk Management Committee, which:

(i)   **In the context of the proposed change to the CRM system, evaluates the benefits and risks of 'big data'.**   **(10 marks)**

(ii)   **Advises on the risks of using The Cloud, as an alternative to owned hardware and software technology, in the proposed system.**   **(10 marks)**

(iii)   **Concludes whether the finance function was right to suggest that a higher discount rate should be used in the NPV calculation.**   **(2 marks)**

Professional skills marks are available for demonstrating *scepticism* skills in challenging the Director's views.   **(4 marks)**

(Total: 26 marks)

EXHIBIT 1

EXTRACTS FROM MARKETING CONSULTANT'S REPORT (MARCH 2018)

Consumer market

The Sealand retail market for fish-based recipe dishes is dominated by the four major supermarket chains. Together they represent about 80% of the Sealand retail market, with remaining sales coming via small wholesalers who sell on to small independent retailers and convenience store chains.

In 2017, the fish-based recipe dishes retail market was divided as follows:

Desco	23%
Waitfell	21%
Salisbury	20%
Mattesons	17%
Independents	19%

Customer market

The customer market consists of two different segments – supermarkets and wholesalers.

The supermarket chains demand excellent service levels, faultless delivery according to promise, and significant discounts. They also take between 90 and 120 days' credit, and sometimes pay much later than this. Suppliers are expected to deliver to regional distribution depots as often as three times per day, and also to 'buy' prime shelf position in the stores.

While the wholesalers are much easier to deal with, and offer higher margins, recent mergers have reduced the number of wholesale networks from seven to five. This trend is expected to continue.

Industry share

The Sealand fish-based recipe dish manufacturing industry has changed significantly over the past ten years, as can be seen from the following:

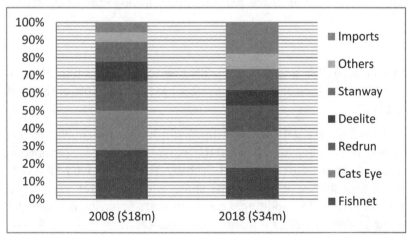

Percentage shares of the fish-based recipe dish manufacturing industry

Notes:

- Fishnet's revenues have grown by 20% over the same period, but margins have fallen year-on-year.

- Deelite and Stanway merged in 2014, but their 2018 shares have been estimated, for consistency.

Recent trends in products

The main sales trends to emerge over the past ten years are as follows:

1   Separation of own-brand into:

- 'Value' own-brand – the production of basic quality, low price-point, recipe dishes to be retailed under the supermarket/wholesaler's own brand name with a value/everyday tag

- 'Elite' own-brand – the production of high quality, high price-point, and recipe dishes to be retailed under the supermarket's own brand name with a quality/finest/special tag

2   **Low in… / Free from…** – products with less or no salt, sugar, gluten, fat or other ingredients where consumer tastes, fashion or health concerns have rendered the ingredient undesirable

3   **Exotics** – recipe dishes based on exotic fish varieties, such as red snapper or cobia

4   **Ethnics** – recipe dishes using influences from 'foreign' cultures and cuisines, such as Middle-Eastern or Caribbean

5   **Home cooking** – more and more customers are now buying raw fish, and creating their own dishes at home. This is possibly due to the high number of cookery programmes on SealandTV. While this has had a significant impact on restaurants and cafés, it has also impacted on recipe dishes.

Fishnet has never been particularly active in the own-brand segments, due to a desire to protect its brand name and reputation. As a result, other manufacturers satisfy most of the demand in this sector. Indeed, Deelite-Stanway is 100% dedicated to producing own-brand ranges (both 'value' and 'elite') for supermarkets, and does not itself have any recognisable brand names.

None of Fishnet's products is explicitly labelled 'low in' or 'free from', except the low calorie 'skinny fish' range. The percentage of revenues from this range has fallen to below 10% of Fishnet's total.

Fishnet does not produce any exotic/ethnic dishes. Many of the producers of these products are smaller manufacturers ('Others', in the market share graphs), often having started as family businesses.

Supply chain

The Sealand fishing fleet has declined by 20% since 2000, mainly due to the imposition of catch quotas and competition from the large "factory' ships. Grubsby now has less than 10% of the fleet size that operated from the port in 1950.

A contributing factor is that factory ships are getting larger making it harder for smaller fishing vessels to compete – forcing many of the smaller vessels out of the market. The increase proportion of factory ships is also putting pressure on the port facilities at Grubsby. The current wharf will only accept about two thirds of the factory ships visiting the East coast, with the larger vessels off-loading at Eastport, further down the coast. The additional transport costs of having fish brought from Eastport by road make it impossible to maintain margins on products using this fish. As you know, Cats Eye has a large processing plant at Eastport. The Grubsby Development Authority has said that no public money is available for development of facilities in the Port of Grubsby Enterprise Zone.

The logistical links for bringing other ingredients into Fishnet are adequate for the current level of manufacturing activity, plus about a 20% increase. Above this point, an upgrade of road and/or rail links would be required.

Fishnet product portfolio

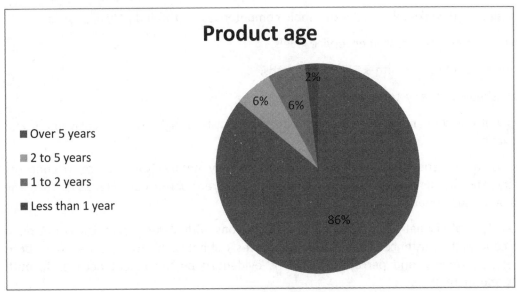

Product age

- Over 5 years
- 2 to 5 years
- 1 to 2 years
- Less than 1 year

2%
6% 6%
86%

Bearing in mind that one of the 'seven core values' in Fishnet's mission statement is 'growth through innovation', it is rather surprising to see that over 85% of Fishnet's revenue comes from products that have remained essentially unchanged since 2013.

While there have been new products in the last five years, most of these have either been new versions of existing products, or extensions to existing product lines. It is eleven years since Fishnet introduced its last completely new product line – the low calorie range branded 'Skinny Fish'. Perhaps due to the success of that product line, which won many innovation awards, Fishnet seems to have lost sight of the need for innovation.

Twenty years ago, Fishnet was regarded among the most innovative companies in the food industry. Now, customer and consumer surveys show that an increasing percentage of the audience see Fishnet's product range as 'boring' or 'traditional'.

Examination of the strategic plans produced over the past decade shows a gradual reduction in the emphasis on new product development, replaced by an increasing focus on cost reduction in production and logistics (to attempt to correct the falling margins). If this were a deliberate shift from a generic strategy of differentiation to one of cost leadership, it would be understandable. However, no such rationale can be seen in the strategic plans. Indeed, 'growth through innovation' has been a core value throughout the decade. This 'strategic drift' seems to have had unintended impact on Fishnet's business model.

As a side note, we are aware that both Cats Eye and Redrun operate formal incentive programmes, and 'intrapreneurship' programmes. These seem to have led to much higher innovation rates at those companies, when compared to Fishnet, and several of the small manufacturers in the 'Others' category are spin-offs from one or other of these programmes.

Conclusion – Threshold and core competences

From discussions with stakeholders, the threshold competences for this industry appear to be:

• provision of excellent customer service levels,

• maintenance of high Health & Safety standards,

• established logistics systems, and

• supply of branded and/or own brand product lines, with a high level of replacement and innovation.

While there is no suggestion that any of these are not currently met by Fishnet, there are concerns that industry expectations may be rising beyond Fishnet's current performance levels (particularly in the area of product innovation).

From the analysis of Fishnet's performance, and discussions with stakeholders, it has not been possible to confirm the existence of any core competences. Fishnet seems to be very average, both in terms of performance and perceptions. This is evidenced by the recent declines in both profitability and share price.

EXHIBIT 2

EXPECTED COSTS AND REVENUES (provided by the engineering director) – NPD STRATEGY

To: **Finance Director**

From: **Director, Engineering**

Date: **Yesterday**

Subject: **Investment in Product Development**

As you are aware, the CEO asked me to investigate the likely financial implications of having a formal 'new product development' department, rather than relying on our team of chefs to find new product lines alongside their routine work.

I spoke to my colleagues, some suppliers of capital equipment and to building contractors. To create a department with five staff, capable of working on three possible new products each year, we would need to spend $1.5m on purchasing capital equipment and converting an existing storage area into a development kitchen. This expenditure would be completed by the end of 2018.

The staff costs of the department would be $300k each year, for the five additional staff required, and other annual overheads would increase by $200k. These expenditures would start at the beginning of 2019.

If a newly-developed product is a success, we estimate that it will generate (on average) $700k in additional net revenue, each year for four years (including the year of 'discovery'). The chances of success, for any individual development, are estimated at 25%. Obviously, any failures will generate no additional net revenue.

We have looked at the expected cash flows over five years (i.e. to 2023) and, in line with company policy, the project achieves the desired 'payback within three years'.

My spreadsheet is attached. Let me know if you need anything else.

Item ($000)	'18	'19	'20	'21	'22	'23
Capital investment	1500					
Additional staff costs		300	300	300	300	300
Additional overhead		200	200	200	200	200
TOTAL COSTS	1500	500	500	500	500	500
Net cash flow from new products		525	1050	1575	2100	2100
NET	−1500	25	550	1075	1600	1600
CUMULATIVE	−1500	−1475	−925	150	1750	3350

EXHIBIT 3

Email:

To: Finance Manger

From: IT Director

Date: Today

CRM System Upgrade

It is our policy to review (and upgrade, if necessary) all 'mission-critical' systems every five years. The existing CRM system was introduced in 2013.

A full investment appraisal has been carried out by the finance function, and they raised a concern about risk.

The proposal requires the final approval of the board, before it can proceed, as the initial investment exceeds the $1m delegated authority limit of the Investment Committee.

This proposal was discussed at the most recent board meeting, and additional information was requested by the Chair of the Risk Management Committee.

I understand that you have been asked to respond to the Chair of the Risk Management Committee, and would be obliged if you would copy me in on your response.

IT Director

ATTACHMENT:

Existing system failings

The current CRM system is creaking at the seams. While it is perfectly capable of recording and reporting on our direct relationships with wholesale and retail customers, it cannot cope with the increasing volumes of consumer-related data that it is being required to handle.

Since the supermarkets started to provide us with consumer transaction data, they increasingly expect us to model consumer behaviour. The supermarkets expect us to analyse product sales data, and advise on forecast demand. In some cases, Fishnet is responsible for advising the supermarket what to buy, and is only paid if the product sells. We are being made responsible for the cost impact of products not selling before their 'best before' dates.

While the current system contains a very basic data mining application, it cannot cope with the volume and variety of the data being provided. The storage capacity of the current system has been increased twice in the last 18 months, and another capacity increase will be required within six months.

Proposed solution

The proposal is to acquire a series of applications from an established third-party developer. The IT department does not have the capability to design and program major applications, nor does it have the experience in developing cloud-based big data solutions. These areas are very complex, and utilise leading edge algorithms that are not in the public domain.

The solution provider is well established, and their applications are 'industry-standard' in FMCG manufacturing outside Sealand. The applications will cover all of the functions of the existing CRM system, as well as allowing further evolution of consumer data analysis.

Big data

The proposed solution makes use of big data analytics, to identify trends, patterns and relationships in the (potentially huge) consumer transaction dataset. These analytical tools should allow CRM to improve the competitive position of Fishnet, as it is believed that none of Fishnet's competitors uses this technology.

Cloud storage and processing

The investment appraisal includes cash flows relating to small savings within the IT function, as we migrate the CRM storage and application processing from our own hardware to The Cloud. The solution provider's quote includes the cost of a scalable cloud solution, to be provided by a highly-regarded international cloud services provider.

Recommendation

This proposal has the support of IT, Marketing and Finance. It supports Fishnet's strategy, and the investment required is included in the 2018 and 2019 budgets.

END OF QUESTION

Section 3

ANSWERS TO TECHNICAL PRACTICE QUESTIONS

A: LEADERSHIP

1   ACADEMIC RECYCLING COMPANY (ARC)

Key answer tips

This question on leadership may be answered in a number of ways. The main focus of the answer should be on Sully Truin's leadership style both before and after the management training course and the effect these styles have on his employees. It is expected that candidates will also comment on the speed of change and its consequences, as well as the principles of a training programme which promotes a particular style as the 'best approach to leadership'.

Report on management style at ARC

From: 100 day review team

To: HR director, Scat

Introduction

ARC has not successfully met all of its first 100 day targets. This report aims to consider whether this is caused by a failure in the management style employed at ARC or whether Scat's own training programme for managers may be at fault.

Management style pre-acquisition

Prior to attending the course, Sully Truin appeared to have, in McGregor's terms, many elements of a Theory X manager about him. He felt that it was necessary to closely control and direct staff in order to get them to do what was needed. He perceived that, in general, employees wished to avoid responsibility and so wanted to be closely directed and controlled. This belief was reflected in work design in the company where employees were increasingly restricted to relatively simple repetitive tasks, for which he had defined well-established procedures. While he was attending the course, Sully still had relatively trivial control issues referred to him and he was exasperated by his employees' inability to take actions to resolve these issues. His initial diagnosis of this reluctance was that this was due to their personal inadequacies rather than the result of the work situation that he had created. In terms of the Tannenbaum and Schmidt model, Sully originally displayed a manager-centred leadership, whereby he made a decision and then announced it.

Finally, in terms of the Blake and Mouton managerial grid, Sully's style is primarily that of authority/obedience. His main concern is task completion, with a leadership style which dictates what should be done and how it should be done.

The impact of Scat's training course

The course questioned Sully's tough-minded management approach, promoting a more democratic style where leadership responsibilities are shared with subordinates, who are also involved in the planning of tasks, not just their execution.

The course essentially suggested that Sully changed his style of leadership, moving to the right on the Tannenbaum and Schmidt model and towards a stereotypical Theory Y manager. Scat's course promotes the benefits of a democratic style of management.

However, contingency or situational theorists have argued that there is no one 'best leadership style' and that style has to be contingent, at least, on the nature of the work to be done and the needs of the people doing that work. For ARC, the choice of leadership style probably depends on three factors:

- The characteristics of the leader. As already discussed, Sully tends towards a Theory X style. However, his willingness to change style as a result of the course might suggest that his approach may be due to a lack of confidence in his subordinates rather than the reflection of deeply held values about leadership.

- The characteristics of those led. It could be argued that Sully's style has necessarily led to him employing people who are comfortable with his style, and demand a work environment which is routine, well-specified and tightly controlled. When Sully changes his style after the course, they are unable to contribute effectively and are left confused and anxious. It is their suggestion that Sully returns to his old style of leadership.

- The situation itself, the nature of the task. For ARC, the task has been increasingly constrained, so that it can be closely defined and controlled by Sully. It is relatively simple but decisions on problems have to be taken quickly. This is why they are referred to Sully. He is good at making an instant decision and has the authority to back it up. When subordinates were asked to take responsibility for these decisions, they felt that they did not have sufficient authority or experience and so they consulted their colleagues, which took time, before arriving at a decision.

Contingency or situational theorists would probably be critical of Scat's training course as it appears to encourage a management style that would be unlikely to be appropriate for all situations. Even the most democratic of managers has to adopt an authoritarian style at some point to get certain things done or problems resolved.

From a contingency perspective, it could be argued that before going on the course, ARC had a relatively good fit between leadership, subordinates and the task. Sully Truin was relatively well-liked, he was trusted by his employees to make decisions, and his power was high. As owner of the company he has the power to reward and punish employees. The tasks required of employees were clearly laid down and were well defined.

Going forward

Reversion to Sully's old style of management might make employees feel more comfortable but it does not solve the fundamental problems. The company is still over-reliant on Sully and, as well as causing him personal health problems, this also severely restricts the company's ability to expand. The company could look more closely at the definition of the task and the competencies required of employees. The speed of change may have also been an important factor in the failure of Sully's new democratic approach.

His sudden conversion from Theory X to Theory Y manager was too much, too soon and left employees anxious and confused.

Conclusion

Much of the blame for the lack of initial success at ARC can be attributed to ARC's training programme attended by Sully Truin. However, there are other factors to be consider such as the speed of change and Sully's confidence in employing a new management style.

Marking scheme – technical marks	
	Marks
1 mark for each relevant point up to a maximum of 15 marks.	**15**

How well has the candidate demonstrated Professional Skills as follows:	Not at all	Not well	Quite well	Very well
Demonstrating commercial acumen in demonstrating awareness of the wider external factors that may have affected the success of ST's new management style	The candidate has failed to consider any wider issues.	The candidate has considered the wider context but the issues addressed are generic and lack relevance to ARC.	The candidate has identified some wider issues relevant to ARC but has failed to link this to the success or failure of ST's management style.	The candidate has identified some wider issues relevant to ARC and explained how these may have contributed to the failure of ST's management style.
	0	1	2	3

2   ICOMPUTE

Key answer tips

The culture of an organisation can be explored from a variety of perspectives and through a number of frameworks and models. This answer uses selected elements of the cultural web as a framework. The use of the cultural web will provide a solid foundation for a pass in this question. The key will be to use the scenario to ensure that the models are made as relevant as possible.

Stories are told by employees in an organisation. These often concern events from the history of the organisation and highlight significant issues and personalities. In the context of iCompute, there is evidence of stories that celebrate the earlier years of the organisation when founder Ron Yeates had an important role. 'Ron used to debate responsibility for requirements changes with the customer.'

In contrast modern management is perceived as weak, giving in too easily in negotiations with customers. Not only is this perceived weakness affecting morale, but it also appears to be affecting profit margins and this is an important consequence for the organisation.

Symbols include logos, offices, cars, titles and the type of language and terminology commonly used within the organisation. The language and symbols of technology appear to dominate at iCompute. Software developers constantly scan the horizon for new technological opportunities. They embrace these technologies and solutions and, as a result, continually distract the organisation. As soon as a technical direction or solution is agreed, or almost agreed, a new alternative is suggested causing doubt and delay. One of the managers claimed that the company was 'in a state of constant technical paralysis'. This paralysis has implications. Furthermore, technological objectives can quickly outweigh business and financial objectives, to the detriment of the company as a whole.

The perceived inability of managers to effectively participate in technological discussions is derided by software developers who suggest that they are technically out of touch. Ownership and understanding of up-to-date mobile phones is perceived to be important, particularly by the software developers who are an important and powerful group within the organisation.

Finally, the language of the manager who suggested that support should be outsourced is very illuminating. Support calls are not from customers but from 'incompetent end users, too lazy to read user guides'. Re-focusing managers on customers appears to be long overdue.

Routines and rituals concern the 'way we do things around here'. At iCompute this involves long working hours and after-work social activities such as football, socialising and playing computer games. The latter of these reinforces the technical focus (discussed in symbols) of employees. The routines and rituals of the organisation are largely male-oriented (football, computer games) and would probably exclude most females. This would almost certainly contribute to the company's inability to recruit and retain women employees. Furthermore, long working hours and after-work activities will also alienate employees who have to get home to undertake family commitments or simply do not wish to be 'one of the lads'. This must contribute to almost one-third of all employees leaving within their first year at the company. The consequence of this culture is an expensive recruitment and training process.

The control systems of the organisation include measurement and reward systems. Within iCompute technical expertise is only rewarded to a certain organisational level. To earn more, technically adept employees have to become managers. Evidence appears to suggest that many are unsuited to management, unable to deal appropriately with their former peers. These managers also seem anxious to show that their technical expertise is not diminishing, emphasising the importance of technology as a symbol within the organisation. Consequently, they often try to demonstrate this expertise (for example, through programming) but are unaware that this brings derision rather than respect. The absence of measurement systems has recently been recognised by management within the company. This has led to the initiation of an in-house project to improve time recording. However, software developers within the company see this as an unwelcome initiative.

Paradigm and discussion

Initially, iCompute was an entrepreneurial organisation with a significant work ethic based on long hours, technical innovation and competitive management. Although the organisation has superficially matured, the stories told by employees and the recruitment and retention of similarly minded people, has led to the continuation of a male-oriented, technologically focused workforce managed by unprepared and unsuitable managers.

Managers' reaction to conflict is to avoid it (agreeing with customers over requirements), outsource it (software support) or put in formal computer systems to control it (the implementation of a time recording system). The failure to recruit and retain female staff appears to be a direct consequence of the organisational culture of iCompute.

The 'work hard, play hard work ethic' is only suitable for employees with certain objectives, characteristics and minimal childcare responsibilities. This culture needs to change if the company is to employ a more balanced and representative workforce that is focused on business rather than technological objectives.

Marking scheme – technical marks	
	Marks
1 mark for each appropriate point up to a maximum of 13 marks.	**13**

How well has the candidate demonstrated **Professional Skills** as follows:	Not at all	Not well	Quite well	Very well
Analytical skills in considering the implications of the issues raised.	The candidate has failed to identify the key issues created by the current culture of iCompute.	The candidate has identified and understood the culture of iCompute but has failed to develop these into issues for future performance.	The candidate has identified and understood the culture of iCompute and some issues have been explored with respect to their longer term impact on the future performance of the business.	The candidate has fully understood the issues raised by the culture at iCompute and has clearly explained how this may be detrimental for the future performance of the business.
	0	**0.5**	**1**	**2**

3 THE NATIONAL MUSEUM (NM) *Walk in the footsteps of a top tutor*

Key answer tips

Part (a)

The use of the PESTEL model would give the correct focus though other similar models were also useful and would have been awarded credit. Make sure you apply the model to the scenario and avoid straying into internal issues (e.g. strengths and weaknesses of the museum).

Part (b)

This part of the requirement wanted students to assess the organisational cultural issues that caused the failure of the museums strategy. As with part (a), the use of an appropriate model will help generate ideas and give a structure to your response. There are a range of cultural models that can be used (Handy, Peters & Waterman, the cultural web), although the cultural web is probably the most easily assessable and familiar model for students.

Apply the model to the scenario. Don't simply explain what the model is. Instead use examples from the case of stories, structure, symbols etc. to explain why the problems arose. Show a link between the parts of the cultural web (e.g. there are clear status symbols for some staff in the museum) and the failure of the strategy (the Director General proposed removing these).

> The main danger here is not focusing enough on culture. Some students may stray into change management but there was not enough material given in the case for 20 marks worth of material on change management. The requirement also clearly stated it wanted the focus to be on cultural issues.

(a) The PESTEL framework may be used to explore the macro-environmental influences that might affect an organisation. There are six main influences in the framework: political, economic, social, technological, environmental and legal. However, these influences are inter-linked and so, for example, political developments and environmental requirements are often implemented through enacting legislation. Candidates will be given credit for identifying the main macro-environmental influences that affect the NM, whether or not they are classified under the same influences as the examiner's model answer.

Political

Monitoring, understanding and adapting to the political environment is absolutely essential for the National Museum. It is currently very reliant on government funding and so is significantly affected by the recently elected government's decision to gradually reduce that funding. The implications of this were recognised by the Board of Trustees and led to the appointment of a new Director General. Unfortunately, senior staff at the museum did not share this perception of the significance of the funding changes. Their opposition to change, which culminated in the Director General's resignation, has led to further political ramifications. The government is now threatening heavier funding cuts and further political trustee appointments. Furthermore, it does appear that the political context has changed for the foreseeable future. The government has only just been elected and the opposition also agrees that the reliance of museums on government funding has to be reduced.

The political appointment of two (and possibly more) trustees is also important to the National Museum. It was significant that it was the two trustees appointed by the government who supported the Director General and his proposed changes. Finally, the continued funding of the government will now largely depend on performance measures – such as accessibility – which have been determined by a political agenda. The museum must strive to meet these objectives even if they are not shared by senior staff. The old ways – built around an assessment of Heritage Collections – appear to have gone forever and senior staff members need to recognise this.

Economic

Up to now the National Museum has been largely sheltered from the economic environment. It has been funded by the government, not the marketplace, and that funding has been largely determined by stable internal factors, such as artefacts in the Heritage Collection. Evidence from the scenario and Figure 1, suggests that this funding is stable, increasing on an annual basis to reflect inflation. However, the progressive reduction of government funding will mean that the museum will be exposed to economic realities. It will have to set realistic admission charges. Resources will also have to be used effectively and new opportunities identified and exploited for increasing income. The Director General included a number of these ideas in his proposals. However, it will be difficult to set a charge that will attract sufficient customers to cover the museum's costs, particularly as visitors have been used to paying only a nominal entry charge.

Social

The social environment is important to the museum from at least two different perspectives. The first is that social inclusion is an important part of the government's targets. The government is committed to increasing museum attendance by both lower social classes and by younger people who they feel need to be made more aware of their heritage. The visitor information shown in Figure 3 suggests that not only are visitor numbers declining in total, but the average age of these visitors is increasing. The percentage of visitors aged 22 and under visiting the NM has decreased from 19% of the total visitors (in 20X4) to just over 12% in 20X7. The museum needs to identify what it needs to do to attract such groups to the museum. The Director General had suggested free admission. This could be combined with popular exhibitions (perhaps tied in with television programmes or films) and 'hands-on' opportunities. It appears that the immediate neighbourhood of the museum now houses many of the people the government would like as visitors and so, from this angle, the location of the museum is an advantage. However, the comment of the Director of Art and Architecture about popularity and historical significance hardly bodes well for the future.

The decay of the neighbourhood and the increased crime rate may also deter fee-paying visitors. The museum is becoming increasingly isolated in its environment, with many of its traditional middle-class customers moving away from the area and reluctant to visit. The extensive reporting of a recent assault on a visitor is also likely to deter visitors. The museum needs to react to these issues by ensuring that good and safe transport links are maintained to the museum and by improving security both in the museum and in its immediate vicinity. Visitors need to feel safe and secure. If the museum believes this to be unachievable, then it might consider moving to a new site.

Technological

It is estimated that only 10% of the museum's collection is on view to visitors. Technology provides opportunities for displaying and viewing artefacts on-line. It provides an opportunity for the museum to become a virtual museum – allowing visitors from all over the world access to images and information about its collections. Indeed, such an approach should also help the museum achieve some of its technology and accessibility targets set by the government. Technology can also be used to increase marketing activity, providing on-line access to products and allowing these products to be bought through a secure payment facility. The appropriate use of technology frees the museum from its physical space constraints and also overcomes issues associated with its physical location.

Environmental

It can be argued that all contemporary organisations have to be aware of environmental issues and the impact their activities have on the environment. These are likely to be exacerbated by the museum being located in an old building which itself requires regular maintenance and upgrading to reflect government requirements. It is also very unlikely that such an old building will be energy efficient and so heating costs are likely to be high and to continue to increase. The museum needs to adopt appropriate policies on recycling and energy conservation, but it may be difficult to achieve these targets in the context of an old building. Consequently, environmental issues may combine with social issues to encourage the possible relocation of the museum to a modern building in a more appropriate location. However, the museum building is also of architectural importance, and so some acceptable alternative use for the building might also have to be suggested.

Legal

Legal issues affect the museum in at least two ways. Firstly, there is already evidence that the museum has had to adapt to legal requirements for disability access and to reflect health and safety requirements. Some of these requirements appear to have required changes in the building which have been met with disapproval. It is likely that modifications will be expensive and relatively awkward, leading again to unsightly and aesthetically unpleasing modifications to the building. Further tightening of legislation might be expected from a government with a mandate for social inclusion. For example, it might specify that all documentation should be available in Braille or in different languages. Legislation concerning fire safety, heating, cooking and food preparation might also exist or be expected.

Secondly, the museum is run by a Board of Trustees. There are legal requirements about the behaviour of such trustees. The museum must be aware of these and ensure that their work is properly scoped and monitored. Trustees have, and must accept, ultimate responsibility for directing the affairs of the museum, ensuring that it is solvent, well-run, and meeting the needs for which it has been set up. The museum is a charity and it is the responsibility of the trustees to ensure that its operation complies with the charity law of the country.

(b) The underlying cultural issues that would explain the failure of the Director General's strategy at the National Museum can be explored using the cultural web. It can be used to understand the behaviours of an organisation – the day-to-day way in which the organisation operates – and the taken-for-granted assumptions that lie at the core of an organisation's culture. The question suggests that it was a lack of understanding of the National Museum's culture that lay at the heart of the Director General's failure.

In this suggested answer the cultural web is used as a way of exploring the failure of the Director General's strategy from a cultural perspective. However, other appropriate models and frameworks that explore the cultural perspective will also be given credit.

A cultural web is made up of a set of factors that overlap and reinforce each other. The symbols explore the logos, offices, titles and terminology of the organisation. The large offices, the special dining room and the dedicated personal assistants are clear symbols of hierarchy and power in the museum. Furthermore, the language used by directors in their stories (see below) suggests a certain amount of disdain for both customers and managers. The status of professor conferred on section heads with Heritage Collections also provides relative status within the heads of collection sections themselves. The proposal of the Director General to close the heads' dining room and to remove their dedicated personal assistants would take away two important symbols of status and is likely to be an unpopular suggestion.

The *power* structures of the organisation are significant. Power can be seen as the ability of certain groups to persuade or coerce others to follow a certain course of action. At present, power is vested in the heads of collection sections, reflected by their dominance on the Board of Directors. Three of the five directors represent collection sections. Similarly the Board of Trustees is dominated by people who are well-known and respected in academic fields relevant to the museum's collections. The power of external stakeholders (such as the government) has, until the election of the new government, been relatively weak.

They have merely handed over funding for the trustees to distribute. The Director General of the museum has been a part-time post.

The appointment of an external, full-time Director General with private sector experience threatens this power base and his suggestion for the new organisation structure takes away the dominance of the collection heads. On his proposed board, only one of six directors represents the collection sections.

The *organisational* structure is likely to reflect and reinforce the power structure. This appears to be the case at the museum. However, it is interesting to note that the collections themselves are not evenly represented. Both the Director of Industrial Art and the Director of Media and Contemporary Art represent five collection sections. However, only two collection areas are represented by the Director of Art and Architecture. This imbalance, reinforced by different symbols (professorships) and reflected in stories (see later) might suggest a certain amount of disharmony between the collection heads, which the Director General might have been able to exploit. Management at the museum are largely seen as administrators facilitating the museum's activities. This is reinforced by the title of the director concerned; Director of Administration.

The *controls* of the organisation relate to the measurements and reward systems which emphasise what is important to the organisation. At the National Museum the relative budget of each section has been heavily influenced by the Heritage Collections. These collections help determine how much the museum receives as a whole and it appears (from the budget figures) that the Board of Trustees also use this as a guide when allocating the finance internally. Certainly, the sections with the Heritage Collections appear to receive the largest budgets. Once this division has been established the principle of allocating increases based on last year's allocation, plus a percentage, perpetuates the division and indeed accentuates it in real financial terms. Hence, smaller sections remain small and their chance of obtaining artefacts for them to be defined a Heritage Collection becomes slimmer every year.

Again, this may suggest a potential conflict between the larger and smaller collection sections of the museum. Finally, up until the election of the new government, there appears to have been no required measures of outputs (visitor numbers, accessibility etc.). The museum was given a budget to maintain the collections, not to attract visitors. The proposal of the Director General to allocate budgets on visitor popularity disturbs the well-established way of distributing budgets in a way that reinforced the current power base.

The *routines and rituals* are the way members of the organisation go about their daily work and the special events or particular activities that reinforce the 'way we do things around here'. It is clear from the scenario that it is not thought unacceptable for directors to directly lobby the Board of Trustees and to write letters to the press and appear on television programmes to promote their views. In many organisations issues within the boardroom remain confidential and are resolved there. However, this is clearly not now the case at the National Museum. The scenario suggests that there are certain *rites of challenge* (exemplified by the new Director General's proposals) but equally there are strong *rites of counter-challenge*, resistance to the new ways of doing things. Often such rites are limited to grumbling or working-to-rule, but at the National Museum they extend to lobbying powerful external forces in the hope that these forces can be combined to resist the suggested changes.

Stories are used by members of the organisation to tell people what is important in the organisation.

The quotes included in the scenario are illuminating both in content and language. The Director of Art and Architecture believes that Heritage Collections have a value that transcends popularity with the 'undiscerning public'. He also alludes to the relative importance of collections.

He suggests that fashion may not be a suitable subject for a collection, unlike art and architecture. Similarly, the anonymous quote about lack of consultation, that includes a reference to the new Director General as 'an ex-grocer', attempts to belittle both management and commerce.

In the centre of the cultural web is the paradigm of the National Museum. This is the set of assumptions that are largely held in common and are taken for granted in the organisation. These might be:

- The museum exists for the good of the nation

- It is a guardian of the continuity of the nation's heritage and culture

- What constitutes heritage and culture is determined by experts

- The government funds the purchase and maintenance of artefacts that represent this heritage and culture.

There are two important elements of the Director General's proposals that are missing from this paradigm; visitors and customers. Changing the current paradigm may take considerable time and effort.

Tutorial note

Candidate answers which considered the cultural web from a perspective of how it might have helped the Director General develop and implement proposals are also acceptable:

- He may have considered deferring one or both of the proposals to remove the head of collection sections' dining room and their dedicated personal assistants. These are important symbols of their status and the financial gains from removing them seem unlikely to outweigh the consequences of their removal.

- He might have considered simply adding directors to the organisational structure, rather than inviting conflict by removing two of the collection directors. For example, replacing the current Director of Administration with the four new directors of his proposed structure (Finance, Visitor Services, Resources, Information Systems) might then have been more acceptable. The actual number of collection related directors remains the same (three), but their relative power in the board would have been decreased.

- An analysis of the cultural web identifies a possible conflict between the collection section heads that could have been exploited. A significant number of sections are not designated as Heritage Collections and so are not headed by professors. These sections are also less well represented on the board and they receive less money, which is allocated in a way that accentuates and perpetuates the relative wealth of the powerful sections. Published stories and deriding fashion, reinforces this division. The Director General could have identified proposals that could have brought the heads of certain sections 'on side' and so destroy the apparently harmonious position of the collection heads.

- He also needed to recognise the structure of the Board of Trustees. Their current composition meant that there was little chance that they would support his proposals.

- Finally, he would have benefited from understanding the paradigm of the National Museum and how at odds this paradigm is with his own vision and with the vision of the incoming government. In this context the cultural web has important implications for the heads of collection sections. Both the power and controls elements of the cultural web are undergoing significant change. The new government is exploiting its position as a major stakeholder and insisting on new controls and measures that reflect their paradigm. Although the heads of collection sections have successfully lobbied for the removal of the Director General, they are very unlikely to change the government's policy. Indeed the sacking of the Director General has strengthened the government's action and resolve. The sacking of the Director General may have been a pyrrhic victory and a much worse defeat now awaits the heads of collection sections.

Marking scheme – technical marks		
		Marks
(a)	Up to 2 marks for identifying appropriate macro-environmental influences in each of the six PESTEL areas – even if it is justifying the lack of influence. A further 8 marks are available for giving credit to candidates who have extended their argument in selected areas of the framework. It must be accepted that each area of the PESTEL will have a differential effect.	20
(b)	Up to 2 marks for each significant cultural factor identified by the candidate up to a maximum of 10 marks. Up to 2 marks for an explanation of how each factor contributed to the rejection of the Director General's proposals, up to a maximum of 10 marks. This includes any ethical issues raised within the cultural analysis.	20
Total		40

How well has the candidate demonstrated Professional Skills as follows:	Not at all	Not well	Quite well	Very well
Demonstrating commercial acumen in applying judgement and insight into the cultural issues of the organisation which have led to its failure..	The candidate has failed to identify the key issues created by the current culture of the NM.	The candidate has identified relevant cultural issues but has failed to identify linkages between the elements of the cultural web and how these may impact on the central organisational paradigm.	The candidate has made some attempt to identify and prioritise the key issues, but there is a lack of insight into how this impact on the central organisational paradigm.	The candidate has shown strong judgement in allocating business problems to the relevant area of the cultural web and has also shown good insight into what may be missing from the cultural paradigm.
	0	0.5	1	2

4   PHARMA

Key answer tips

A key aspect of this question is 'user-focus'. Professor Jones is not a finance professional, so make sure you explain technical issues in sufficient detail for him to understand. Also, make sure you examine different sides of the arguments concerned as requested.

External Consultant

Address line 1

Address line 2

Date

Dear Professor Jones

This letter examines the ethical issues relating to recent trials of a new drug undertaken by you on behalf of Pharma.

Whether being part of an esteemed profession should influence the CFO's behaviour

A profession is an occupation carried out by a privileged body of individuals. It is suggested that a profession has specific characteristics, one of which is the need for members of a profession must act in the interests of the society it is created to serve. This is known as acting in the public interest.

However, the CFO is likely to view 'the public interest' in a narrow sense. As much as doctors work for the health of the social community so accountants work for the health of the business community rather than the broader societal interest.

For example, the CFO could claim that supporting the business community includes monitoring companies and auditing accounts, reporting to regulatory bodies and providing market confidence in the wellbeing of business entities. This assists fraudulent activities to be diagnosed and those perpetrating theft to be uncovered. The accountant becomes the watchdog of commerce ensuring rules are followed and regulation adhered too.

However, you could also argue that the CFO and other professional accountant should recognise a wider value laden role. This relates to an extension to the accountant's current role in order to embrace the remit of the wider society. This suggests an expansion to the stakeholders influencing the accountant's role away from corporate masters towards public health, societal needs, governments, environmentalist, disadvantaged communities and in general the ethical role of a corporate citizen.

The key question behind the wide value laden role is the extent to which accountants such as the CFO believe this is necessary or achievable.

Whilst most appreciate the need for change the egoistical nature of ethical decision making ensure accountants suppress concern for the common good beneath their allegiance to the corporate flag. This seems appropriate since organisations generally pay their wages in one form or another.

Whether publishing concerns would be a breach of confidentiality

Confidentiality relates to the need for secrecy – here, the need for Pharma to keep its research a secret from its competitors in order to ensure they do not steal the company's ideas. Certainly publishing the report would be a breach of contract but the key issue is whether there is an ethical argument in favour of publishing

Confidentiality is a key principle defined in the IFAC code of ethics where members are expected to respect the confidentiality of information acquired as a result of professional and business relationships and not disclose any such information to third parties without proper and specific authority unless there is a legal or professional right or duty to disclose.

Confidentiality leads to confidence in ensuring that any problems identified can be discussed and resolved in a private arena without the issue being disclosed, discussed or acted upon by external groups. Shareholders expect a degree of confidentiality to be shown by managers ensuring that they are the first to know about any issues that relate to their investment and its returns. This is naturally extended to the relationship between the accountant as employee and the executive of the company.

The concept is not without its detractors. The issue of whistleblowers sits very uncomfortably with the need for confidentiality as shown in this case. The need for confidentiality must be weighed against the public good and when the latter is found to be dominant the accountant, or indeed you, must act and not remain silent.

The CFO's use of the concept is entirely inappropriate in the scenario. He likens confidentiality to the need for trade secrets and yet the essence of the secret being kept is that the product may kill children. It is certain that competitors would like to know this but equally certain they would not want to copy the product which is the interpretation given by the ethically misguided executive.

Possible courses of action

In a practical and personal way you could be forgiven for taking no action. The sums of money involved and the effect on your personal career and therefore your family may be devastating if you decide to publish the report.

It is also worth bearing in mind that your findings may be flawed since the product would have been tested by government scientists prior to release. If your report is correct, and you believe that it is, then despite the effect on your personal circumstances you may take a more utilitarian or egalitarian ethical stance where the needs of the many outweigh the needs of the one.

Your first steps would be to seek advice from colleagues, both from an ethical perspective and to review the technical content of your findings. You need to be totally sure of your findings before publicising them. If they are validated by colleagues then you should publish the document and accept the consequences that arise from that action.

Yours Sincerely

A Consultant

Marking scheme	
	Marks
Discussion of consequences of being a professional – 1 mark per point	Max 5
Discussion of confidentiality – 1 mark per point	Max 5
Advice – up to 2 marks per issue	Max 5
Total	**15**

How well has the candidate demonstrated Professional Skills as follows:	Not at all	Not well	Quite well	Very well
Communication skills in addressing the recipient's concerns.	The candidate has failed to address the concerns of Professor Jones.	The candidate has only addressed some concerns of Professor Jones, but without showing both sides of arguments and has over used technical jargon without explanation	The candidate has addressed most of the concerns of Professor Jones, but has not adequately examined issues from different points of view	The candidate has clearly addressed the concerns of Professor Jones, having examined both sides of arguments, presented the information without unnecessary technical terms and having used a letter format
	0	0.5	1	2

5 JOHN MATHERS

BRIEFING NOTES

1 INSIDER TRADING

What is meant by insider trading?

General principle or definition	Mather's behaviour
Insider trading can be described as the illegal purchase of shares by someone who is in possession of useful inside information specific and precise about a company's performance and business prospects, and would affect the share price if made public.	Clearly John Mathers abused his position as finance director at Parkstone to personally profit from the knowledge he had of an impending major contract which would be viewed positively by the financial markets. The sensitive inside information used by Mathers in this crime had not been made public at that time, yet he knew that when it was made public it would have a significant positive effect on the company's share price.

What are directors' responsibilities?

General principle or definitions	Mather's behaviour
Board members have a duty of care to indemnify the company against any losses caused by any negligent behaviour. Directors hold a fiduciary position in relation to the company, so are required to act in good faith and in the best interest of both the company and its shareholders. Directors have a duty not to make a personal profit from the company's business activities.	As the company's FD, Mathers would have both expressed and implied authority to deal in all financial matters which pertain to the ongoing success of the company, acting as an agent for the shareholders and promoting the success of the company. It is apparent that the insider trading perpetrated by Mathers compromised his core duties and responsibilities as a director of a public company in general, and as its finance director in particular.

General principle or definitions	Mather's behaviour
	Apart from breaking the law, there were clear violations of corporate governance provisions which define the role of directors and safeguard the interests of shareholders and other stakeholders.

2 FUNDAMENTAL ETHICAL PRINCIPLES

As a professionally qualified accountant, John Mathers was duty bound to comply with the following five fundamental principles which underpin the code of ethics issued by his professional body:

General principle or definitions	Mather's behaviour
Professional behaviour Accountants must comply with all relevant laws and regulations and shall avoid any action which may discredit the profession.	It is clear from the statement made by the judge in court that Mathers knew that by insider trading he was breaking the law, so when he was caught it would have come as no surprise that he was liable for prosecution by the authorities. The publicity arising from his crime would have identified his professional status as a qualified accountant, and so indirectly brought the accountancy profession into disrepute.
Integrity Integrity requires accountants to be straightforward and honest in all their professional and business relationships. Integrity also implies fair dealing and truthfulness, two characteristics which Mathers clearly failed to display.	He was in effect found guilty of misleading his colleagues, possibly providing them with false statements about his real intentions and actions. The fact that he used a false name to cover his tracks when purchasing shares illegally clearly illustrates his profound lack of integrity.
Professional competence and due care All accountants must act diligently in accordance with applicable technical and professional standards when providing professional services.	The behaviour of John Mathers, although not suggesting a lack of knowledge and skill, was misplaced. He did not act with due care in the interests of Parkstone, but instead proceeded to damage the reputation and standing of the company in the market.
Confidentiality Accountants must respect the confidentiality of information acquired as a result of professional relationships, and shall not disclose such information to third parties without authority or unless there is a right or duty to disclose.	The $120k profit earned by Mathers from insider trading was only possible because he used confidential business information for his own elicit purposes, and so represented a breach of professional confidentiality.

General principle or definitions	Mather's behaviour
Objectivity Accountants should not allow any bias, conflicts of interest or the undue influence of others to compromise their professional or business judgement.	Mathers was placed in a position of trust as the FD of a listed company and he had a fiduciary duty to act in the best interests of its shareholders. However, by using his insider knowledge of the forthcoming contract, he abused this trust placed in him, instead he acted in his own self-interest with greed as his primary motive.

Marking scheme – technical marks	Marks
Up to 2 marks for a description of the insider trading/dealing.	2
Up to 2 marks for a description of how directors' responsibilities are compromised by insider trading.	2
Up to 2 marks for each principle discussed in the context of the insider trading described. Max of 1 mark if the point raised did not specifically refer to the actions of John Mathers and only a maximum of ½ mark available for identifying or listing each of the fundamental principles.	10
Total	14

How well has the candidate demonstrated Professional Skills as follows:	Not at all	Not well	Quite well	Very well
Communication skills in ensuring that the briefing notes are fit for purpose.	The candidate has failed to adequately separate out principles and application and has not explained Mathers' behaviour.	The candidate has only addressed some aspects of Mathers' behaviour, but without distinguishing principle from application	The candidate has addressed most of the issues raised, but has not adequately distinguished between principles and application	The candidate has clearly addressed all of the issues raised and has made clear distinction between principles and application
	0	0.5	1	2

6   HAPPY AND HEALTHY

Key answer tips

Within this requirement a considered, logical approach is necessary.

The normal behaviour for the auditor, regardless of the options available in this situation, would be to initially seek representations from Ivan to establish whether there is an explanation that has so far been overlooked or not known about. Following that, there are two options in Mr Shreeves's dilemma: to tell or not tell Ken and Steffi about Ivan's behaviour. In discussing these options, a number of issues are relevant.

Discussion of dilemma

Mr Shreeves is clearly in a difficult situation but he must be aware of his duty as a professional accountant which includes, in his role as auditor, a duty to the public interest.

He has a *duty of due care and diligence* to society and government as well as the shareholders of a company being audited. Being complicit in Ivan's activity is clearly not an option as this would be incompatible with his duties to the shareholders and to society in his role as auditor. Furthermore, he has realised a disclosure of such transactions is required and it would be unprofessional not to discuss this with his clients.

He feels he owes a debt to the Potter family as a longstanding family friend and this has the potential to cloud his judgement as the company's auditor. The case says that the effect of Ken and Steffi finding out about Ivan's theft could be 'devastating' and this is bound to weigh heavily upon Mr Shreeves's mind. In getting too close to the family, Mr Shreeves has compromised his duty as auditor as he is probably less objective than he should be. He should probably have chosen between being a family friend or being the auditor some years ago and that would have made his resolution of the dilemma somewhat easier.

Ivan has been *unprofessional and has acted fraudulently* in his dealings with 'Happy and Healthy'. In such a situation, the auditor does not have latitude in how he or she deals with such a discovery. It is a very serious breach of trust by Ivan, regardless of whether he is the Potters' son or not, and it would be inexcusable to withhold this information from the owner-managers of the business.

Advise Mr Shreeves

Given that the auditor has a duty to the public interest and the company shareholders, he should *inform the majority shareholders (Ken and Steffi) what he has found during the audit*. To do anything other than this would be to act unprofessionally and irresponsibly towards the majority shareholders of the company. Family relationships or friendships must never be allowed to interfere with an auditor's professional duty and independence. This approach need not be in the form of a blunt confrontation, however, and it would *not be unprofessional to speak with Ivan before he spoke to his parents in order to convey to him the potential seriousness of his actions.*

Marking scheme	
	Marks
2 marks for each relevant issue in the dilemma identified and discussed	Max 6
2 marks for each relevant point made of the 'advise' point	Max 4
Total	**10**

7 AEI

Key answer tips

Make sure you discuss the ethical issues by reference to ACCA ethical principles.

Attempting 'bribery' of P

P, an audit junior, has been offered a free re-fitting of his kitchen with AEI goods.

The manager in charge of the department mentioned that this was standard practice each year as a 'thank you' to the member assigned to carry out the inventory checking and subsequent valuation of that inventory.

P has also discovered that the inventory is materially overvalued.

There appears to be a threat to P's objectivity. P needs to ensure that audit work is being carried out correctly, while at the same time ensuring there are no factors influencing judgment in this respect. The offer of a free kitchen could influence that judgment as P may be being asked to ignore the over-valuation of inventory and consequent over-statement of profits in AEI. However, it is also concerning that this situation appears to be 'normal' and has therefore been the practice for some years.

To remove the threat P needs to:

- Inform you, the audit manager, of the situation and ask for advice. As a junior member of staff P would be expected to refer the issue to senior management for advice.

Actions that the audit manager should then take include:

- Ascertaining the situation from previous years, including contacting the previous audit manager and juniors to determine action taken in previous years.

- Inform the manager of the warehouse that P is concerned about the situation and ask the manager to confirm this is standard practice.

- Inform the audit partner and ask for his or her advice.

- Inform P not to accept any free goods until the situation has been resolved.

It is possible, albeit unlikely, that this is standard practice. However, this does not assist in resolving the objectivity issue. It is more likely that P will have to decline the offer and also recommend the inventory valuation adjustment. At this stage, actions will include:

- The audit partner explaining the need for the adjustment to AEI's directors.

- Where the adjustment is carried out, no further action will be required.

- Where the adjustment is refused, then there will be the requirement for further discussion with the possibility of the audit report being modified, even if this leads to the loss of the audit client.

Q and disclosure requirements, holding of shares in AEI

Q has two ethical issues to resolve:

- Firstly, to determine whether or not disclosure of directors' remuneration is complete

- Secondly, the issue of holding shares in the audit client.

Regarding disclosure of remuneration, statute requires the disclosure of the different elements of remuneration, including share options. The fact that the total remuneration payable cannot be determined when options are granted is not a reason for non-disclosure. In this situation Q appears to be being pressured into disclosing incorrect information. The ethical threat is therefore not behaving with integrity – Q understands what should be disclosed and integrity would be threatened if this disclosure was not made.

The argument from the chair of the audit committee is not valid. While disclosure of information between an audit client and the auditor attracts confidential status, this confidentiality cannot hold where statutory requirements have not been fulfilled. To maintain integrity, Q must recommend that share option information is disclosed.

However, the situation is made more complicated by the fact that Q holds shares in AEI. The ethical threat here is that Q's objectivity may be compromised.

Q may overlook issues which would adversely affect the profit of AEI as this would also affect the share price and dividend that would be obtained as a shareholder.

Furthermore, it is not clear whether Q has disclosed this information to his employer. The 2.5% holding is below the disclosure limit (currently 3% in the UK) for the financial statements, so it is also possible the audit firm is unaware of this conflict. To resolve the conflict, Q should dispose of the audit shares and inform his employer.

The situation is made more complex by the fact that the share price of Q is likely to fall when the results for the year are announced. It could therefore be argued that Q is using inside information and in breach of insider trading rules if shares were sold now. It therefore appears that Q must resign from the audit immediately and make full disclosure of the shareholding and the lack of information in the directors' remuneration statement.

Finally, by resigning now, Q may well face disciplinary action from the employer and/or from the institute for not disclosing the conflict of interest earlier. There is therefore still the temptation to 'keep quiet' about the directors' remuneration disclosure and trust that the chair of the audit committee will not disclose information about Q's shareholding to any third party.

Cross-directorships

The ethical threat here appears to be a lack of independence and self-interest regarding the setting of remuneration for these directors. The chair of the remuneration committee of AEI will be voting on the remuneration of directors in AEI; similarly, one of those directors as chair of the remuneration committee of IEA would be voting on remuneration of that executive director in IEA. There would be a temptation to vote for high remuneration levels in AEI in the knowledge that reciprocal high levels of remuneration would be voted for in IEA.

In corporate governance terms, one ethical safeguard is to ban these cross-directorships. The ban would be enforceable as the directors of companies must be stated in annual accounts; hence it would be easy to identify cross-directorships. The ban would also be effective as the conflict of interest would be removed. However, in principles based jurisdictions, the fact that the rule had been broken would only lead to disclosure of this fact; the actual directorships could continue. It is only by making corporate governance regulations enforceable by statute (as in the USA) that the situation could be removed.

In professional terms, the directors clearly have a conflict of interest. While their professional code of ethics may mention this precisely as an ethical threat. Both directors should follow the spirit of the code and resign their non-executive directorships. This again would remove the threat.

Bank reconciliation

R has not carried out work on the bank reconciliation correctly.

Ethically accountants must have the correct level of knowledge to perform their duties, otherwise audit and other clients will not receive the standard of service they are paying for. It would be unethical therefore to imply knowledge was available when this was not the case.

However, in this situation, it appears that R has simply followed the instructions given; there was no indication that the timing of clearance of cheques was an issue to be identified as an error. The problem, if anything, is therefore lack of appropriate training of R and/or supervision of R by the audit manager. The 'real' ethical threat is that the audit firm are not training their staff correctly decreasing the standard of service provided to their clients.

Actions to be taken to resolve the situation include:

- Ensuring that training within the audit firm does include appropriate knowledge on audit procedures for all levels of staff.

- Contacting the client to determine why the cheques were presented for payment late. If 'window dressing' has taken place then ask the client to amend the financial statements. Lack of amendment may again result in a modification of the audit report.

8 MRA

Key answer tips

In **part (a)** make sure your answer reflects the verb in the requirement and assesses the impact of bribery on MRA.

Email

To: Charlie Desborough

From: NED

Date: Today

Subject: Bribery and Corruption

1 **Corporate governance**

(a) Corporate governance involves establishing trustworthy relationships between various parties in the management and operation of a commercial business. Key to successful governance arrangements is the recognition of fundamental principles upon which both decisions and disclosures should be based. However, bribery and corrupt activities undermine these principles and diminish the value of corporate governance in a number of ways:

1 **Integrity** requires that a firm conducts straightforward and honest dealings with all of it stakeholders. If MRA were to agree to pay the bribe, it would become complicit in a dishonest action purely designed to serve its own interests at the expense of others.

2   **Fairness** suggests that a business respects the rights and views of all stakeholders with legitimate interests. It is difficult to reconcile how by paying a bribe MRA would be serving the interests of all stakeholders in an even-handed way.

3   **Judgement** is concerned with making decisions using objective and reliable information which enhance the firm's prosperity. Although it is not explicitly stated, it could be reasonably be presumed that the directors of MRA would ultimately benefit personally from the award of the $2 billion contract, therefore they need to be very cautious when judging the situation on its merits.

4   **Independence** further develops the principle of judgement by requiring an action to be based on objective criteria which service the interests of the firm, its shareholders and other legitimate stakeholders.

The arguments presented by both the CEO and HR director do appear to be considering the employees and shareholders, but are certainly not giving due regard to the wider public interest.

5   **Openness** suggests that actions, decisions and information should be conducted and presented in a transparent manner. The secrecy under which the MRA board meeting was conducted fundamentally contradicts this principle, and suggests a secret agenda is being pursued. Such secrecy does not inspire confidence and trust.

6   **Probity** requires that individuals act truthfully, and without misleading others. Should the board of MRA eventually decide to pay the bribe, it will have to be done covertly, and by default it will mislead other stakeholders.

7   **Responsibility** involves having an explicit and implied duty to deal with an issue. This means that individual directors at MRA cannot allow others to decide about paying the bribe and assume they are not responsible for the decision.

8   **Accountability** holds that decision-makers are answerable for the consequences of actions. This would in effect mean that the directors of MRA will be jointly and severally liable should they decide to pay the bribe, and this could result in criminal proceedings being taken against them.

9   **Reputation** is the perception or expectation that others hold about a firm, and there is little doubt that the reputation of MRA would be damaged if it paid the bribe and this knowledge were made public.

It is clear that the MRA board faces a challenging dilemma and needs clear guidance and support to ensure that they act both legally and correctly.

2 **Best practice**

(b) The following best practice measures could be employed to both reduce and combat bribery and corruption in MRA:

1 **Top-level commitment.** The board must foster a culture in which bribery is never acceptable and it is understood that the achievement of business objectives should never be at the expense of unethical and corrupt behaviour. Consequently it should not make the $1 million payment to the foreign official.

2 **Proportionate procedures.** Procedures should be implemented which are proportionate to the bribery risks faced by the firm and its activities. These should also be transparent, practical, accessible, effectively implemented and enforced by management.

3 **Risk assessment.** A formal and documented audit of both the internal and external risks of bribery and corruption should be periodically undertaken. This should be incorporated into the firm's generic risk management procedures and reported upon annually to shareholders.

4 **Due diligence procedures.** Bribery risks can be mitigated by exercising due diligence. Any personnel operating in sensitive areas require greater vigilance; this includes all board members and any personnel involved in procurement and contract work.

5 **Communication.** Internal and external communications ensure that bribery prevention policies and associated procedures are embedded into the firm's culture and understood by everyone.

Employees at all levels should undertake regularly anti-bribery compliance training so that they remain constantly aware of the risks.

6 **Monitoring and review.** Internal audit, tasked by the audit committee, should monitor and review bribery prevention procedures and recommend improvements where necessary. This control loop can then gauge if actions taken have been effective in reducing bribery and corruption at MRA.

Marking scheme	
	Marks
(a) 1 mark for each governance principle assessed at MRA.	
½ mark if no reference made to confidence and/or trust at MRA.	8
(b) 1 mark per described best practice measure.	6
	—
Total	**14**
	—

B: GOVERNANCE

9   ROSH AND COMPANY

Key answer tips

The requirement only requires **criticisms** of the situation at Rosh and Company – so do not waste time commenting on anything that it is doing well.

REPORT

To:	Timothy Rosh
From:	External Consultant
Date:	Today
Subject:	Criticisms of Rosh and Company's Corporate Governance arrangements

0   INTRODUCTION

This report examines the weaknesses within the current corporate governance of Rosh and Company. The report does not discuss strengths.

1   WEAKNESSES IN THE EXISTING CORPORATE GOVERNANCE OF ROSH AND COMPANY

Five areas of concern can be identified based on evidence provided.

1.1   Non-executive directors

There are several issues associated with the non-executive directors (NEDs) at Rosh. It is doubtful whether two NEDs are enough to bring sufficient scrutiny to the executive board. Some corporate governance codes require half of the board of larger companies to be non-executive and Rosh would clearly be in breach of such a requirement.

Perhaps of equal concern, there is significant doubt over the independence of the current NEDs as they were recruited from retired executive members of the board and presumably have relationships with existing executives going back many years.

Some corporate governance codes (such as the UK Corporate Governance Code) specify that NEDs should not have worked for the company within the last five years. Again, Rosh would be in breach of this provision.

1.2   Succession planning

Succession planning for senior positions in the company seems to be based on Rosh family membership rather than any meritocratic approach to appointments (there doesn't appear to be a nominations committee).

Whilst this may have been acceptable before the flotation when the Rosh family owned all of the shares, the flotation introduced an important need for external scrutiny of this arrangement. The lack of NED independence makes this difficult.

1.3 Diversity

There is a poor (very narrow) diversity of backgrounds among board members. Whilst diversity can bring increased conflict, it is generally assumed that it can also stimulate discussion and debate that is often helpful.

There is a somewhat entrenched executive board and Mary is the first new appointment to the board in many years (and is the first woman). Whilst experience is very important on a board, the appointment of new members, in addition to seeding the board with talent for the future, can also bring fresh ideas and helpful scrutiny of existing policies.

1.4 Strategic planning

There is no discussion of strategy and there is evidence of a lack of preparation of strategic notes to the board. The assumption seems to be that the 'best' option is obvious and so there is no need for discussion and debate. Procedures for preparing briefing notes on strategy for board meetings appear to be absent. Most corporate governance codes place the discussion and setting of strategy as a high priority for boards and Rosh would be in breach of such a provision.

1.5 Training and development

There is no evidence of training for Mary to facilitate her introduction into the organisation and its systems. Thorough training of new members and ongoing professional development of existing members is an important component of good governance.

2 NOMINATIONS COMMITTEE

2.1 General roles of a nominations committee

It advises on the balance between executives and independent non-executive directors and establishes the appropriate number and type of NEDs on the board. The nominations committee is usually made up of NEDs.

It establishes the skills, knowledge and experience possessed by current board and notes any gaps that will need to be filled.

It acts to meet the needs for continuity and succession planning, especially among the most senior members of the board.

It establishes the desirable and optimal size of the board, bearing in mind the current size and complexity of existing and planned activities and strategies.

It seeks to ensure that the board is balanced in terms of it having board members from a diversity of backgrounds so as to reflect its main constituencies and ensure a flow of new ideas and the scrutiny of existing strategies.

2.2 Usefulness for Rosh and Company

In the case of Rosh, the needs that a nominations committee could address are:

- To recommend how many directors would be needed to run the business and plan for recruitment accordingly.

  The perceived similarity of skills and interests of existing directors is also likely to be an issue.

- To resolve the issues over numbers of NEDs.

  It seems likely that the current number is inadequate and would put Rosh in a position of non-compliance with many of the corporate governance guidelines pertaining to NEDs.

- To resolve the issues over the independence of NEDs.

  The closeness that the NEDs have to existing executive board members potentially undermines their independence and a nominations committee should be able to identify this as an issue and make recommendations to rectify it.

- To make recommendations over the succession of the chairmanship.

  It may not be in the interests of Rosh for family members to always occupy senior positions in the business.

3 CONCLUSION

The corporate governance arrangements at Rosh and Company are far from ideal and need to be addressed to ensure investor confidence. A nominations committee will go some way to resolving these problems but is not the whole solution. If you require more detailed advice on how to implement such changes, then I would be pleased to assist.

Marking scheme – technical marks		
		Marks
Criticisms		
1 mark for identification of each criticism		Up to 5
1 mark for brief discussion of each criticism		Up to 5
	Maximum	**10**
Nominations committee		
1 mark for each relevant role of the nominations committee		Up to 4
1 mark for each relevant point on the usefulness of a nominations committee to Rosh		Up to 4
	Maximum	**8**
Total		**18**

How well has the candidate demonstrated professional skills as follows:	Not at all	Not so well	Quite well	Very well
Scepticism skills in probing the governance arrangements	The candidate has failed to demonstrate any scepticism regarding the described practices. The candidate demonstrated no evidence of challenging or questioning the existing structures.	The candidate has demonstrated some, but limited, scepticism regarding existing practice. The candidate questioned some of the behaviour but the depth of the questioning was limited and the challenge to the current structures was not presented in a professional manner.	The candidate has demonstrated scepticism of the existing governance practices. The challenge could have been presented in a more professional manner.	The candidate has demonstrated deep scepticism of the existing governance practices. The candidate strongly questioned, with evidence, the validity of the practices in a professional and justified manner.
	0	1	2	3

10   ROWLANDS & MEDELEEV (R&M)

Key answer tips

It is not sufficient within SBL to merely describe a scenario – here, stakeholder claims. Instead you must assess and evaluate the situation in order to give relevant advice.

REPORT EXTRACT

To: The Board of R&M

Date: Today

By: External Consultant

Subject: Key External Stakeholders for the Giant Dam Project

2   KEY EXTERNAL STAKEHOLDERS

2.1   Introduction

A stakeholder can be defined as any person or group that can affect or be affected by an entity. In this case, stakeholders are those that can affect or be affected by the building of the Giant Dam Project.

All stakeholding is characterised by the making of 'claims' upon an organisation. Put simply, stakeholders 'want something' although in some cases, the 'want' may not be known by the stakeholder (such as future generations).

It is the task of management to decide on the strengths of each stakeholder's claim in formulating strategy and in making decisions. In most situations it is likely that some stakeholder claims will be privileged over others.

2.2 The Government of the country in which the dam will be built

In many respects it could be argued that key stakeholder in this context is the client, i.e. the government of the East Asian country.

This stakeholder has a high level of interest in the project, wanting completed to budget and on time. It may also be concerned to minimise negative publicity in respect of the construction of the dam and the possible negative environmental consequences.

The government also has a high level of influence as it is paying for the dam and could withhold progress payments if it is unhappy with how the project is proceeding, including the management of risks and publicity.

2.3 Shareholders

The second most important group are shareholders.

The shareholders have the right to have their investment in the company managed in such a way as to maximise the value of their shareholding. The shareholders seek projects providing positive NPVs within the normal constraints of sound risk management. As a result, the interest, particularly of fund managers and other major shareholders should be considered to be high.

Similarly the influence of major shareholders is also high as they have the power to hold directors to account should they feel that the company is not being run in an appropriate manner.

2.4 Stop-the-dam pressure group

The third most important stakeholder is Stop-the-dam, the vocal and well organised pressure group. This stakeholder wants the project stopped completely, seemingly and slightly paradoxically, for environmental and social footprint reasons.

The level of interest can be considered to be high as Stop-the-dam seems very determined to delay and disrupt progress as much as possible.

However, the potential impact and influence of their activities should be assessed as low, as the tunnelling and other 'human' disruption will only cause a short-term delay.

2.5 First Nation

The final external stakeholder that should be considered here is First Nation, the indigenous people group currently resident on the land behind the dam that would be flooded after its construction.

This stakeholder has a high level of interest, wanting the project stopped so they can continue to live on and farm the land. It is thus highly likely that they will protest against the dam. However, overall their potential influence on the project is low as any protests would be unlikely to disrupt the building of the dam.

It is possible that their level of influence could increase if, for example, they gained support from national (or even global) media and organisations in their struggle against 'big business'.

Marking scheme – technical marks	
	Marks
Up to 3 marks for discussion of each stakeholder, including relative importance (and why), assessment of interest and assessment of influence	**12**

How well has the candidate demonstrated Professional skills as follows:	Not at all	Not so well	Quite well	Very well
Analytical skills for assessing the relative power and interest of stakeholders	The candidate merely described the scenario with no attempt to analyse or prioritise stakeholders.	The candidate made an attempt to discuss interest and influence but inadequately used relevant information from the scenario and failed to prioritise claims. However, their prioritisation lacked justification.	The candidate demonstrated good analytical skills by applying scenario information correctly to The problem.	The candidate comprehensively and accurately assessed stakeholder claims and put forward a clear argument to justify their prioritisation
	0	0.5	1	2

11   SCIENCE FIRST

(a)   (i)   Mendelow matrix

The Mendelow matrix is a way of analysing the relative influences of a number of stakeholders in an organisation. In this case, the organisation is the new science park named the Science First development. Influence is conceived of as the result of an estimate of each stakeholder's power and interest. Power is the ability to bring pressure to bear over the objectives and policies of the project and interest is the capital which a stakeholder has invested in the organisation or project (or, an assessment of how much they care or are interested in the development). Higher influence is arrived at by a combination of higher power and higher influence.

Stakeholder claims

Science First Company is seeking to remove any obstacles for the construction of the science park. It believes strongly that the science park is in the strategic interests of the city of Philo and of Philo University. Kathy Wong's report suggested that the board may be unwilling or has become frustrated by local opposition to the development. Science First Company is in a high interest and high power situation and is probably therefore the most influential stakeholder. Its interest is derived from the capital investment in the site, and its power is based on its shareholders including the Philo local government authority, Philo University, both of which are prominent local organisations. The local government authority has control over the planning process and was able to issue a 'notice to quit' notice for residents in the flats affected by Topscience's objection to their presence near the Science First development.

The residents' association represents the interests of local residents affected by the development of the Science First development. The scenario does not say that the residents' association opposes the development of the site, but it feels that the *rights of longstanding residents near the site have not been adequately taken into account.*

Although vocal and with a high degree of interest, it is likely that it has relatively low power. Its interest is based on the fact that the Science First development affects the lives of some residents, especially those whose homes are threatened. The evidence for its low power is based on the observation from the case that it seems unable to resist the proposed demolition of the flats, or any of the other infrastructure changes around the Science First development.

The cancellation of the proposed library was necessitated by the diversion of funds from library services to the Science First development. The loss of the planned library means the loss of a number of community services including a library, a café, and services for parents, art students and others. It will also result in the loss of ten jobs locally which would have been created had the library gone ahead. The potential library users are likely to feel aggrieved at the loss of the planned facility quite intensely and so their interest is likely to be high but, as with the residents' association, their power is relatively low. The low power of the potential library users is suggested by the fact that they were unable to resist the cancellation, and the loss of these important services will be keenly felt locally, especially if residents need to travel away from their local areas to use library services elsewhere in the city of Philo.

(ii) **Increasing low power stakeholdings**

Low power but high interest stakeholders are, when acting separately, unable to influence objectives because they are unable to move into the influential quadrant of the map because of the structural lack of power.

A common way to increase the aggregated influence of high interest but low power stakeholders is to *act together in a type of coalition*. This approach has often been tried when stakeholders oppose certain developments, seek to challenge policy changes and similar change initiatives. Stakeholders, often with little in common except their opposition to a certain initiative, *act in concert, co-ordinating their messages to achieve maximum pressure*, to influence local opinion on that which they both oppose. If they were to include other stakeholder also opposed to the science park, their potential influence would be maximised.

In this way, *many stakeholders act as one* and attempt to mobilise public opinion. In this case, highlighting the local costs of the Science First development on local media and in the streets around the site might serve to challenge the messages conveyed about the site by Philo University, by the Philo local government authority and Science First Company itself. By combining to make their arguments locally, stakeholders with undecided views, such as the local newspapers and some elected representatives, *might be influenced to recognise the wider issues* surrounding the development and the need for wider consultation. In this way, concessions might have been granted which were favourable to the potential library users and the residents.

(b) (i) **Philo local government authority and the Science First development**

The local government authority is aware of some discussion in the city over the building of the Science First development. It is of concern that the local government authority has been criticised for a lack of transparency and fairness, when, in reality, these are essential characteristics of an effective local authority.

As a public sector organisation, funded by central and local taxation, the Philo local government authority operates in a transparent way in order to ensure that local constituents are consulted and informed on key local decisions. If it failed to be transparent and fair in its decisions, a public sector organisation would fail in its public duty and its legitimacy would be called into question. The social contract which a public sector organisation has with its constituencies relies on these characteristics and it would be open to justifiable criticism were it to fail in these ways.

Transparency is a *default position of openness and disclosure rather than concealment*. Democratic bodies such as the Philo local government authority are required to debate in public and so the local authority would strongly contest any allegation that it has been lacking in transparency. Because the Philo local government authority exists for the benefit of local citizens, and can only exist with their continuing support, it is necessary to inform citizens of key issues and changes to their service provision and the reasons behind those changes. The scenario explains that the majority of elected representatives are supportive of the Science First development and, accordingly, it means the development enjoys the support of the local government authority. In Philo, an elected representative may be asked to account for her or his views on the development, perhaps by a constituent or the local media and this helps in local transparency.

Fairness is also a central theme in public sector organisations. To be fair is to *recognise many interests and to weigh each one against others in an equitable and transparent way*. Because a local government authority owes a duty to so many stakeholders, it needs to be fair to all of them. Because they operate using taxpayers' money, public sector organisations need to be fair, and be seen to be fair, in carrying out local policy. It is not always the case that all citizens and causes are treated equally, however, as some interests need to be subordinated for the wider benefit of society, but the local government authority owes a duty to explain any ways in which it balances the interests of different stakeholders over which it has influence.

(ii)   The Philo local government authority recognises that its performance measurement is more complex than for a private sector 'for profit' business. With a business, relatively straightforward financial measures are usually good signifiers of success or failure, including, for example, return on equity or return on sales, efficiency measures and productivity measures. For a public sector organisation like the Philo local government authority, *financial measures are only one type of many other relevant objectives including the availability and quality of service delivery*.

Because public sector objectives *are often contested by a range of different stakeholders* in society, public sector outcomes are often expressed in terms of value for money or in the delivery of public services such as the provision of public housing, health services, refuse collection, provision of jobs or learning opportunities. In a representative democracy such as in Philo, these outcomes are contested by political parties, with some preferring more or less of some provisions than others. So whilst the residents' association was disturbed by the loss of the proposed library and the block of flats, for example, *it was felt by others that these losses were necessary* in order to ensure the development of the Science First development.

The 3 Es framework is a way in which public sector objectives can be considered, with the 3 Es referring to the efficiency of the local authority, its effectiveness and its economic performance.

For the Philo local government authority, it must provide an *efficient* and value-for-money service to local taxpayers. In many cases, its service delivery is prescribed by national government policy whilst other activities, including the support for, and investment in, the science development, are discretionary. We would be very unhappy to run a fiscal deficit (spending more than we receive in tax receipts and block grants) and so we have to observe tight financial limits in delivering the services which our citizens want us to deliver. Efficiency is about delivering outputs for a set level of income, with efficient organisations delivering more on a given level of input than less efficient ones.

The local government authority must also be *effective* in that it must delivery its required services to a high quality and meet the expectations of service users. The Philo local government authority sees its support for the science development as a key part of its effectiveness as it is unlikely that the development would have been established without its support. In many cases, however, as we have seen with the loss of the adjacent building and the proposed library, the total effectiveness of our service delivery is not evenly spread and sometimes cuts in some services are necessary to provide increases in others.

This is always a difficult judgement and public sector bodies are usually very aware of these choices when measuring their performance.

The final E concerns the economic performance or *'economy'* of the local government authority. The Philo local government authority receives an income each year based on a settlement from central government and what it raises in local taxation. Within this budget, we must deliver a wide range of local services and employ the skilled people necessary to deliver those services. There is little scope to run a deficit under most public sector organisation terms of reference and in fact most are encouraged to operate at a slight surplus. This often requires painful choices to remain within budget and accordingly, the political choices are often between the 'good' and the 'very good' in terms of how money is spent and this may be little comfort to the residents and library users around the Science First site, but I hope, at least, that this provides some explanation for the local government authority's actions.

As the chief executive of the Philo local government authority, I very much hope I have been able to clarify some issues for local residents. Citizens can, of course, always contact their local elected representative to discuss these matters further.

Marking scheme – technical marks			
			Marks
(a)	(i)	1 mark for explanation of each stakeholder's claim to a maximum of 3 marks. 2 marks for explanation of each stakeholder's position on the Mendelow matrix to a maximum of 6 marks. **Maximum**	9
	(ii)	2 marks for explanation of coalition arrangements. 2 marks for application to case. **Maximum**	6
(b)	(i)	2 marks for the importance of transparency and fairness in public sector organisations. 2 marks for explanation of transparency. 2 marks for explanation of fairness. **Maximum**	6
	(ii)	Up to 4 marks for understanding of complexity and contestability of public sector objectives. 2 marks for explanation of each of the 3 Es in the context of the case to a maximum of 6 marks. **Maximum**	9
Total			30

How well has the candidate demonstrated Professional skills as follows:	Not at all	Not so well	Quite well	Very well
Analytical skills for assessing the relative power and interest of stakeholders	The candidate merely described the scenario with no attempt to analyse or prioritise stakeholders.	The candidate made an attempt to discuss interest and influence but inadequately used relevant information from the scenario and failed to prioritise claims.	The candidate demonstrated good analytical skills by applying scenario information correctly to The problem. However, their prioritisation lacked justification.	The candidate comprehensively and accurately assessed stakeholder claims and put forward a clear argument to justify their prioritisation
	0	0.5	1	2

12   ROSEY AND ATKINS (R&A)

BRIEFING NOTES

The distinction between CSR strategy and strategic CSR

To have a strategy for CSR is to have a set of policies which guide and underpin CSR activities. This means that some causes or areas of activity are favoured over others, in line with the strategy adopted.

So, for example, a company might have a policy to invest in some communities or charitable causes and not others.

The policy or strategy may be agreed based on a number of issues: perhaps the preferences of the employees, the preferences of senior people in a business, or the preferred outcomes may be chosen based on strategic concerns.

When CSR is undertaken to maximise its effects on the long-term economic benefit of the business, it can be described as strategic CSR.

When CSR activities are strategic, they generally support the main business areas of the business. So a financial company such as a bank might favour financial education causes whilst a medical supplies company might prefer medical or nursing research causes or overseas medical efforts.

It would be seen as strategically wasteful to use CSR to support activities which are not aligned to the core activities. An assumption underpinning strategic CSR is that all assets in a company belong to the shareholders and so all activities, including CSR, should be configured in such a way as to support shareholder value.

Argument that the purchase of the house builder is strategic CSR

The purchase of the house builder is described in the case as a departure from R&A's longstanding strategy of investing in listed companies as part of its holding of passive funds. In arguing that it is nevertheless strategic and therefore in the long-term economic interests of the R&A shareholders, several points can be made.

The case scenario describes a *'shortage' of low cost housing* and whenever demand exceeds supply, prices rise. This has the capacity to make the prices chargeable for the new properties higher than might be expected and the large reserves of land (land bank) are also likely to increase in value over time if demand continues to exceed supply. So although it may be described as a CSR measure by R&A, it is likely that substantial returns may be made on the investment at the same time. Because it serves both ends (CSR and the strategic good), it could be argued to be a good example of strategic CSR.

As with other CSR initiatives, the development of affordable homes may make some *reputational capital for R&A*, especially as it frames its purchase in terms of meeting a social need. If the housing developments are conveyed to the public as R&A exercising its social responsibility, it may increase the company's profile generally, and also enhance the favourable perception by which R&A is viewed. These joint effects may make it more likely that people will invest in R&A either as shareholders or clients, thereby ensuring the company makes an economic return on its CSR.

Because R&A is an investment company which purchases shares but does not control the companies it invests in, the outright purchase of a company represents *a diversification of its business activities.* It could be argued that such a diversification represents a strengthening of the robustness of R&A's business as it means that risk and return become more widely spread.

13   ZPT

SPEECH ON IMPORTANCE OF GOOD CORPORATE GOVERNANCE AND CONSEQUENCES OF FAILURE

Introduction

Ladies and Gentlemen, I begin my remarks today by noting that we meet at an unfortunate time for business in this country. In the wake of the catastrophic collapse of ZPT, one of the largest telecommunications companies, we have also had to suffer the loss of one of our larger audit firms, JJC. This series of events has heightened in all of us an awareness of the vulnerability of business organisations to management incompetence and corruption.

The consequences of corporate governance failures at ZPT

I would therefore like to remind you all why corporate governance is important and I will do this by referring to the failures in this unfortunate case. Corporate governance failures affect many groups and individuals and as legislators, we owe it to all of them to ensure that the highest standards of corporate governance are observed.

Firstly and probably most obviously, effective corporate governance *protects the value of shareholders' investment in a company.* We should not forget that the majority of shareholders are not 'fat cats' who may be able to afford large losses. Rather, they are individual pension fund members, small investors and members of mutual funds. The hard-working voters who save for the future have their efforts undermined by selfish and arrogant executives who deplete the value of those investments. This unfairness is allowed to happen because of a lack of regulation of corporate governance in this country.

The second group of people to lose out after the collapse of ZPT were the *employees.* It is no fault of theirs that their directors were so misguided and yet it is they who bear a great deal of the cost. I should stress, of course, that jobs were lost at JJC as well as at ZPT. Unemployment, even when temporary and frictional, is a personal misery for the families affected and it can also increase costs to the taxpayer when state benefits are considered.

Thirdly, because of the collapse of ZPT, *creditors have gone unpaid and customers have remained unserviced.* Again, we should not assume that suppliers can afford to lose their receivables in ZPT and for many smaller suppliers, their exposure to ZPT could well threaten their own survival. Where the value of net assets is inadequate to repay the full value of payables, let alone share capital, there has been a failure in company direction and in corporate governance so I hope you will agree with me that effective management and sound corporate governance are vital.

The loss of two such important businesses, ZPT and JJC, has *caused great disturbance in the telecommunications and audit industries.* As JJC lost its legitimacy to provide audit services and its clients moved to other auditors, the structure of the industry changed. Other auditors will eventually be able to absorb the work previously undertaken by JJC but clearly this will cause short-to-medium term capacity issues for those firms as they redeploy resources to make good on those new contracts. This was, I should remind you, both unnecessary and entirely avoidable.

Linked to this point, I would remind colleagues that it is important for *business in general and auditing in particular to be respected in society.* The *loss of auditors' reputation* caused by these events is very unfortunate as *auditing underpins our collective confidence in business reporting.* It would be wholly inappropriate for other auditors to be affected by the behaviour of JJC or for businesses in general to be less trusted because of the events at ZPT. I very much hope that such losses of reputation and in public confidence will not occur.

Finally, we have all been dismayed by the case of Shazia Lo that was reported in the press. A lack of sound corporate governance practice *places employees such* as Ms Lo *in impossible positions.* Were she to act as whistleblower she would, by all accounts, have been victimised by her employers. Her acceptance of what was effectively a bribe to remain silent brings shame both on Ms Lo and on those who offered the money. An effective audit committee at ZPT would have offered a potential outlet for Ms Lo's concerns and also provided a means of reviewing external audit and other professional services at ZPT. This whole situation could, and would have been, avoided had the directors of ZPT managed the company under an effective framework of corporate governance.

The case for the mandatory external reporting of internal controls and risks

I now turn to the issue of the mandatory external reporting of internal controls and risks. My reason for raising this as an issue is because this was one of the key causes of ZPT's failure.

My first point in this regard is that *disclosure allows for accountability.* Had investors been aware of the internal control failures and business probity risks earlier, it may have been possible to replace the existing board before events deteriorated to the extent that they sadly did. In addition, however, the need to generate a report on internal controls annually will *bring very welcome increased scrutiny from shareholders* and others. It is only when things are made more transparent that effective scrutiny is possible.

Secondly, I am firmly of the belief that more information on internal controls would *enhance shareholder confidence and satisfaction.* It is vital that investors have confidence in the internal controls of companies they invest in and increased knowledge will encourage this. It was, I would remind you, a *lack of confidence in ZPT's internal controls* and the strong suspicion of fraud that caused the share price to collapse and the company to ultimately fail.

Furthermore, compulsory external reporting on internal controls will *encourage good practice inside the company.* The knowledge that their work will be externally reported upon and scrutinised by investors will *encourage greater rigour in the IC function* and in the audit committee. This will further increase investor confidence.

To those who might suggest that we should opt for a comply-or-explain approach to this issue, I would argue that this is simply *too important an issue to allow companies to decide for themselves* or to interpret non-mandatory guidelines. It must be legislated for because otherwise *those with poor internal controls will be able to avoid reporting* on them. By specifying what should be disclosed on an annual basis, companies will need to make the audit of internal controls an integral and ongoing part of their operations. It is to the contents of an internal control report that I now turn.

Content of external report on internal controls

I am unable, in a speech such as this, to go into the detail of what I would like to see in an external report on internal controls, but in common with corporate governance codes elsewhere, there are four broad themes that such a report should contain.

Firstly, the report should contain *a statement of acknowledgement by the board* that it is responsible for the company's system of internal control and for reviewing its effectiveness. This might seem obvious but it has been shown to be an important starting point in *recognising responsibility.* It is only when the board accepts and acknowledges this responsibility that the impetus for the collection of data and the authority for changing internal systems is provided. The 'tone from the top' is very important in the development of my proposed reporting changes and so this is a very necessary component of the report.

Secondly, the report should summarise the *processes the board (or where applicable, through its committees) has applied* in reviewing the effectiveness of the system of internal control. These may or may not satisfy shareholders, of course, and weak systems and processes would be a matter of discussion at AGMs for non-executives to strengthen.

Thirdly, the report should *provide meaningful, high level information* that does not give a misleading impression. Clearly, internal auditing would greatly increase the reliability of this information but a robust and effective audit committee would also be very helpful.

Finally, the report should contain *information about any weaknesses in internal control* that have resulted in error or material losses.

This would have been a highly material disclosure in the case of ZPT and the costs of non-disclosure of this were a major cause of the eventual collapse of the company.

I very much hope that these brief remarks have been helpful in persuading colleagues to consider the need for increased corporate governance legislation.

Thank you for listening.

Marking scheme		
		Marks
(a)	2 marks for assessment of each consequence of ZPT's governance failures (1 mark for brief explanation only).	10
(b)	2 marks for each argument identified and made.	8
(c)	2 marks for each broad theme identified and explained.	6
		───
Total		**24**
		───

14   OLAND

Key answer tips

Make sure that you set out the key facts that Martin needs and that you argue clearly **against** his belief.

RULES AND PRINCIPLES, AND WHY 'COMPLY OR EXPLAIN' IS EFFECTIVE

1   Context – Rules and principles approaches

Rules

In a rules-based approach to corporate governance, provisions are made in law and a breach of any applicable provision is therefore a legal offence.

This means that companies become legally accountable for compliance and are liable for prosecution in law for failing to comply with the detail of a corporate governance code or other provision.

Principles

A principles-based approach works by (usually) a stock market making compliance with a detailed code a condition of listing. Shareholders are then encouraged to insist on a high level of compliance in the belief that higher compliance is more robust than lower compliance.

When, for whatever reason, a company is unable to comply in detail with every provision of a code, the listing rules state that the company must explain, usually in its annual report, exactly where it fails to comply and the reason why it is unable to comply.

The shareholders, and not the law, then judge for themselves the seriousness of the breach. This is what you meant by markets 'punishing bad practice'.

2   Argument why 'comply or explain' can be effective

Comply or explain is intended to allow latitude in compliance with details of corporate governance provision, but is not 'optional' in the usual meaning of the term.

Listing rules insist on compliance with codes in many countries with 'comply or explain' allowed when compliance with detail is not possible or desirable, usually in the short to medium term.

If the shareholders are not satisfied with the explanation for lack of compliance, they can punish the board by several means including holding them directly accountable at general meetings, by selling shares (thereby reducing the value of the company) or by direct intervention if a large enough shareholder.

Comply or explain is seen as an alternative to a rigid 'rules-based' approach and is effective for the following reasons:

It enables the policing of compliance by those who own the entity and have *a stronger vested interest* in compliance than state regulators who monitor compliance in a legal sense. This places the responsibility for compliance upon the investors who are collectively the legal owners of the company. It makes the company accountable directly to shareholders who can decide for themselves on the materiality of any given non-compliance.

It *reduces the costs of compliance* and recognises that 'one size' does not fit all. There may be legitimate reasons for temporary or semi-permanent non-compliance with the detail of a corporate governance code, perhaps because of size or the company adopting its own unique approach for highly specific and context-dependent reasons.

It *avoids the need for inflexible legislation,* which, itself, is sometimes also ineffective. Whereas the effectiveness of a 'comply or explain' principles-based approach relies on the ability and willingness of shareholders and capital markets to enforce compliance, rules-based approaches rely on the effectiveness of law enforcement officials.

Marking scheme – technical marks	
	Marks
2 marks for distinguishing between rules and principles.	2
2 marks for each argument supporting comply or explain to a max of 6 marks.	6
	——
Total	8
	——

How well has the candidate demonstrated Professional Skills as follows:	Not at all	Not well	Quite well	Very well
Communication skills in formulating a counter argument.	The candidate has failed to formulate a counter argument but has supported Martin's viewpoint	The candidate has only addressed some counter arguments.	The candidate has addressed most of the counter arguments, but their answer is not persuasive.	The candidate has clearly formulated a persuasive counter argument
	0	0.5	1	2

15 LUM CO

Key answer tips

Part (a) required candidates to recognise the difference in governance arrangements and the importance of those changes – the effect of listing and the involvement of institutional investors at the forefront.

Part (b) of the question is not asking for the **content** of induction programmes or CPD. It required an assessment of the **benefits** of both for 'new' NEDs and executives in situ.

REPORT

To: The Board of Lum Co

From: External consultant

Title: Making a successful transition from a two tier system to a unitary board

1   **Introduction**

This report examines the impact on the board structure of Lum Co as a result of becoming listed with particular focus on the freedom of the Lum family and suggestions for managing the transition.

2   **The differences between being a family business and a listed company**

2.1   **Comparing family and listed businesses**

There are a number of differences between the governance arrangements for a privately-owned family business like Lum Co and a public company which Lum Co became after its flotation.

In general, governance arrangements are much *more formal* for public companies than for family businesses. This is because of the need to be accountable to external shareholders who have no direct involvement in the business. In a family business that is privately owned, shareholders are likely to be members of the extended family and there is usually less need for formal external accountability because there is less of an agency issue.

Linked to this, it is generally the case that larger companies, and public companies in particular, are *more highly regulated* and have many more stakeholders to manage than privately-owned, smaller or family businesses.

The higher public visibility that these businesses have makes them more concerned with maintaining public confidence in their governance and to seek to reassure their shareholders. They use a number of ways of doing this.

For example, public companies must comply with regulations that apply to their stock market listing *(listing rules)*. Whilst not a legal constraint in a principles-based jurisdiction, listing rules require listed companies to meet certain standard of behaviour and to meet specific conditions. These sometimes include using a unitary board structure and thus, in the case, would require a change in the governance arrangements at Lum Co.

The more formal governance structures that apply to public companies include the requirement to *establish a committee structure* and other measures to ensure transparency and a stronger accountability to the shareholders. Such measures include additional reporting requirements that do not apply to family firms.

2.2   **An assessment of Crispin's view that the Lum family will 'lose the freedom to manage the company as they wish' after the flotation**

It is likely that the flotation will bring about a change in the management culture and style in Lum Co. Flotations often cause the loss of the family or entrepreneurial culture and this contains both favourable and unfavourable aspects. Whether the company loses the freedom to manage as they wish will depend upon a number of factors.

Firstly, *whether Gustav Lum's 'wishes' (such as the values and beliefs) are known and trusted by the shareholders.* The need for returns to meet shareholder expectations each year often places cost pressures on boards and this, in turn, sometimes challenges a paternalistic management style (such as at Lum Co) which some investors see as self-indulgent and costly.

Second, the company has become *subject to listing rules* such as the governance code, and, because of its higher visibility on the stock market, a range of *other societal expectations* may be placed upon the company. This will have an effect on all aspects of the company's internal systems and norms, including its prior management style. Because of these things, the family will no longer be able to choose how to act in a number of ways, which supports Crispin's view.

Third, the board of Lum Co will be subject to *influence from institutional investors.* They will demand an effective investor relations department, information on a number of issues throughout the year, briefings on final year and interim results and sound explanations whenever performance or behaviour is below expectation. This places the management of Lum Co in a very different environment to when it was privately owned.

Fourth, the board will be under pressure to produce *profits against targets* each year, which may militate against the company's previous long-term and sustainable commercial approach. If, for example, the long-term approach may have meant taking less profit from a particular operation in one year to leave liquidity or cash in place for a future period, this may become more difficult for a listed company, which can sometimes be under pressure to achieve short-term financial targets such as a dividend payment.

3   The benefits of induction and CPD

3.1   Induction for the new NEDs

Induction is a process of orientation and familiarisation that new members of an organisation undergo upon joining.

It is designed to make the experience as smooth as possible and to avoid culture or personality clashes, unexpected surprises or other misunderstandings. In the case of the problems with NEDs at Lum, an effective induction programme will enable the new NEDs to gain *familiarisation with the norms and culture* of Lum. This might be more important for Lum, being at flotation stage and having a deep-seated family culture.

They will be able to gain an understanding of the *nature of the company and its business model.*

This will, as with the culture and norms, be especially relevant for a company like Lum emerging from a long period as a private company with little need to explain its business model to outside parties.

Induction will help NEDs in *building a link with people* in Lum Co and other directors. The building of good quality interpersonal links is important in NEDs working effectively.

This applies to their relationships with other executive and non-executive directors, and also with relevant people in the company itself. This is especially important in NEDs populating the board committees.

Induction will enable the new NEDs to gain an *understanding of key stakeholders* and relationships including those with auditors, regulators, key competitors and suppliers. In order to understand the business model operated by Lum Co, NEDs need to understand its external relationships and how these support the company's operation.

3.2 CPD for the existing executives

The purpose of any programme of CPD is to *update skills and knowledge* as relevant to the professional situation. This will typically involve content on regulation and law, best practice, new developments, etc. Directors should undergo CPD regularly to keep these areas up to date and to ensure they do not 'fall behind' on key skills.

In the case of the changes at Lum Co, another specific benefit of CPD will be *learning about working with NEDs and the new board procedures* that apply to listed companies. For Lum Co this involved creating a new unitary board, employing NEDs and generally taking a more consultative approach to decision-making.

They would also benefit from *learning about compliance requirements* as a listed company. Legal and regulatory frameworks differ between private and public companies. The listing rules that will be imposed by the stock exchange may be seen as an imposition, especially the need to comply with the corporate governance code. This is likely to necessitate a lot of internal change in governance and reporting behaviour and the CPD will help to provide the directors with this support.

After the flotation, the board of Lum Co gained a number of shareholders other than the Lum family. This would have created a new governance environment and so *learning about coping with the expectations of shareholders* would also be a benefit of the CPD. This would include, for example, learning about investor relations, dealing with shareholders at an AGM and similar.

Marking scheme – technical marks		Marks
(a)	4 marks for contrasting family and listed. 2 marks for each relevant point of assessment to a maximum of 6 marks.	
	Maximum	10
(b)	1 mark for each contribution of induction to a maximum of 4 marks. 1 mark for each contribution of CPD to a maximum of 4 marks.	
	Maximum	8
Total		18

How well has the candidate demonstrated Professional Skills as follows:	Not at all	Not well	Quite well	Very well
Evaluation skills in assessing the benefits of the proposed induction programme and CPD	The candidate has not assessed the benefits of each proposal.	The candidate has assessed the appropriateness of each proposal in general terms and has not applied this to Lum.	The candidate has assessed the appropriateness of each proposal to Lum but opinions are not supported by information from the scenario.	The candidate has assessed the appropriateness of each proposal to Lum and this is clearly evidenced from information from the scenario.
	0	0.5	1	2

16 OSKAL PETROLEUM

(a) Environmental risk can be described as a loss or liability which arises from the effects of the natural environment on an organisation, or a loss or liability arising out of the environmental effects of the organisation's operations.

In the case of Oskal Petroleum, the principal risks will arise out of how its oil exploration, extraction and distribution processes could negatively impact [*environmental footprint*] on the natural environment in the vicinity.

This risk would be exacerbated if the operations take place in a sensitive area, such as near a concentration of population or a designated area of significant importance for flora and fauna. A business consequence of environmental risk is that it may suffer significant costs and a loss of reputation if a problem arises.

Therefore during Oskal's forthcoming assessment it is essential that it identifies its sources of environmental risk.

Non-renewables

The core operations of Oskal will result in a steady depletion of non-renewable natural resources, namely oil. However, whilst there is a constant economic demand for oil derived products and services, Oskal has a justification for extracting oil from its onshore and offshore fields. In order to deflect criticism, it could aim to reduce its environmental footprint by implementing complementary measures to promote sustainable development in other areas. It could set a target to reduce the amount of fresh water consumed in its cooling systems; instead it could recycle water through its plant and machinery.

Unplanned spillages

Oil extraction may lead to spillages, most frequently caused by equipment failure, errors committed by employees and extreme environmental [weather] conditions. The environmental consequences of accidental discharges are especially severe when they occur near to shore, or in remote areas which cannot be cleaned up quickly.

Oil spills may seriously impair the functioning of the marine ecosystem by: deterioration in the chemical composition of the water and its physical characteristics, resulting in deaths of living organisms as a result of oil products penetrating the surface layers of the skin and plumage, forced changes in migration routes, spawning and so on.

By undertaking carefully planned maintenance of all facilities, training employees to the highest standard and developing robust early warning systems, the likelihood and impact of any spillage will be significantly reduced.

Atmospheric emissions

Emissions of pollutants into the atmosphere are a common feature of operating oil fields. The most widespread source of such emissions is the burning of surplus quantities of hydrocarbons in the course of testing and exploiting wells. The burning of fossil fuel such as oil has been shown to make a significant contribution to climate change by emitting high quantities of greenhouse gases, which are known to damage the ozone layer and possibly leads to 'global warming'.

Although it would be clearly impossible for Oskal to operate as an oil company without some level of atmospheric emission, the overall effect could be reduced if the firm developed an environmental management system and considered its environmental impacts more holistically, offsetting its greenhouse gas emissions with improved recycling, waste management, etc.

Regulatory non-compliance

Due to the dangerous and environmentally damaging nature of the oil industry it is highly regulated, however, the regulations can vary significantly between countries and regions.

So a firm like Oskal, with global operations, must have systems in place which ensure full compliance with all local and international regulations in all of its oilfields. Failure to do so could result in high financial penalties and the possible removal of operating licences, both of which would badly harm the business.

(b)   Integrated reporting

Integrated reporting <IR> is a more concise communication of an organisation's strategy, governance and performance. It demonstrates the links between the organisation's financial performance and its wider social, environmental and economic context. Additionally, it illustrates how organisations create value from their activities over the short, medium and long term. The main purpose of <IR> is to enable more effective board level decision making, improve the quality of information available to investors, and encourage more integrated thinking and business practices.

The use of <IR> at Oskal will encourage the preparation of a report which shows its performance against strategy, explains the various 'capitals' used and affected, and gives a longer term view of the organisation and enable its stakeholders, like host governments, to make a more informed assessment of the organisation and its prospects.

<IR> capitals

All organisations depend on various forms of capital for their success. These 'capitals' store value which eventually become the inputs to the company's business model.

The capitals will increase, decrease or transform through the various activities undertaken by the organisation. Therefore it is important that a company like Oskal is able to measure and monitor the use of its capitals, which can be incorporated into its annual report.

These capitals are classified under the following six headings under <IR>:

Financial capital is the pool of funds available to a company, including both debt and equity finance. The focus is on the source of funds, rather than its application which results in the acquisition of manufactured or other forms of capital.

Oskal must be able to source sufficient financial resources to deliver its strategy and achieve its objectives, so by providing such information to its investors it will inspire greater confidence.

Manufactured capital is seen as human-created, production-oriented equipment and tools, with a distinction drawn between inventory and plant and equipment. These are the tangible assets which are employed by the company to create value.

In Oskal, this would include the very expensive drilling and extraction equipment.

Intellectual capital is a key element in the company's future earning potential, with a tight link and contingency between investment in R&D, innovation, human resources and external relationships which can ultimately determine the company's sustainable competitive advantage.

The intrinsic value in Oskal lies within its many oil reserves and it is essential that an accurate valuation appears on its statement of financial position, as any significant error could affect its share price. Oil companies usually have a considerable stock of intellectual capital and have large R&D budgets.

Human capital is the individual capabilities, knowledge, skills and experience of the company's employees and managers, as they are relevant to the task at hand.

Oskal is operating in a knowledge-based industry and is highly dependent on the ingenuity of its employees to create and maintain its business value. Therefore reporting information on human capital will give a very valuable insight for the users of annual reports.

Social and relationship capital in a business context include community acceptance, government relations and customer loyalty.

It is only by building relationships that a company can retain its social licence to operate. This is particularly pertinent for Oskal, which must maintain a licence to operate in each country, which is granted by the host governments. So investing in developing a sound business relationship with government authorities will ultimately help it to continue in business.

Natural capital includes naturally occurring resources, such as oil, which can be used by businesses to provide a return.

The extraction of oil is the core business of Oskal, so providing detail about the levels of extraction compared to previous periods, and by area, will give stakeholders a very useful insight into the operation of the company. Oil companies also need to report on their 'environmental footprint' and the impact they have on the wider natural capital such as on the quality of water, causing damage to land and the sub-terrain, or to the atmosphere.

Marking scheme		
		Marks
(a)	Up to 2 marks for an evaluation of each source of environmental risk. (Max 4 marks) Up to 2 marks for each risk reduction suggestion. (Max 4 marks)	
		8
(b)	Up to 4 marks for a detailed explanation of integrated reporting. 1 mark for each capital explained in context. (Max 6 marks) ½ mark if not related to Oskal Petroleum.	
		8
Total		**16**

17   JGP CHEMICALS LTD

Key answer tips

In **part (a)** you need to exercise scepticism when evaluating the FD's understanding.

(a)   **Explain 'sustainability' and criticise the finance director's understanding of sustainability**

Sustainability is the ability of the business to continue to exist and conduct operations *with no effects on the environment that cannot be offset or made good in some other way*. The best working definition is that given by the Gro Harlem Brundtland, the former Norwegian prime minister in the Brundtland Report (1987) as activity that, 'meets *the needs of the present without compromising the ability of future generations to meet their own* needs.'

Importantly, it refers to both the *inputs and outputs* of any organisational process. *Inputs (resources) must only be consumed at a rate* at which they can be reproduced, offset or in some other way not irreplaceably depleted. *Outputs (such as waste and products) must not pollute* the environment at a rate greater than can be cleared or offset. Recycling is one way to reduce the net impact of product impact on the environment. They should use strategies to neutralise these impacts by engaging in environmental practices that will replenish the used resources and eliminate harmful effects of pollution.

A number of reporting frameworks have been developed to help in accounting for sustainability including the notion of triple-bottom-line accounting and the Global Reporting Initiative (GRI). Both of these attempts to measure the social and environmental impacts of a business in addition to its normal accounting.

The finance director has *completely misunderstood the meaning of the term sustainable*. He has *assumed that it refers to the sustainability of the business as a going concern* and not of the business's place in the environment. Clearly, if a business has lasted 50 years then the business model adopted is able to be sustained over time and a healthy balance sheet enabling future business to take place ensures this. But this has *no bearing at all on whether the* business's *environmental footprint is sustainable* which is what is meant by sustainability in the context of environmental reporting.

(b)   **Stages in an environmental audit and the issues that JGP will have in developing these stages**

Environmental auditing contains three stages.

The first stage is *agreeing and establishing the metrics* involved and deciding on what environmental measures will be included in the audit. This selection is important *because it will determine what will be measured against, how costly the audit will be and how likely it is that the company will be criticised for* 'window dressing' or 'greenwashing'. JGP needs to decide, for example, whether to include supply chain metrics as Professor Appo suggested which would be a much more challenging audit. Given that the *board's preference is to be as 'thorough as possible'*, it seems likely that *JGP will include a wide range of measures* and set relatively ambitious targets against those measures.

The second stage is *measuring actual performance against the metrics* set in the first stage. The means of measurement will *usually depend upon the metric being measured.* Whilst many items will be capable of numerical and/or financial measurement (such as energy consumption or waste production), others, such as public perception of employee environmental awareness, will be less so. Given the board's stated aim of providing a robust audit and its need to demonstrate compliance, this stage is clearly of great importance. If JGP wants to demonstrate compliance, then measures must be established so that compliance against target can be clearly shown. This is likely to favour quantitative measures.

The third stage is *reporting the levels of compliance or variances.* The issue here is *how to report the information and how widely to distribute the report.* The board's stated aim is to *provide as much information as possible* 'in *the interests of transparency'.* This would tend to signal the publication of a public document (rather than just a report for the board) although there will be issues on how to produce the report and at what level to structure it. The information demands of local communities and investors may well differ in their appetite for detail and the items being disclosed.

Given that it was the desire to issue an environmental report that underpinned the proposed environmental audit, it is likely that JGP will opt for a high level of disclosure to offset the concerns of the local community and the growing number of concerned investors.

(c) **Explain why the environmental risks at JGP are strategic**

An environmental risk is an unrealised loss or liability arising from the effects on an organisation from the natural environment or the actions of that organisation upon the natural environment. Risk can thus arise from natural phenomena affecting the business such as the effects of climate change, adverse weather, resource depletion, and threats to water or energy supplies. Similarly, liabilities can result from emissions, pollution, and waste or product liability.

In the specific case of JGP, environmental risks are strategic for the following reasons:

First, environmental performance *affects the way in which the company is viewed by some of its key stakeholders.* The case mentions the local community (that supplies employees and other inputs) and investors. The threat of the withdrawal of support by the local community is clearly a *threat capable of affecting the strategic positioning* of JGP as its ability to attract a key resource input (labour) would be threatened.

In addition, the case mentions that a 'growing group of investors' is concerned with environmental behaviour and so this could also have *potential market consequences.*

Second, *as a chemical company, Professor Appo said that JGP has a* 'structural *environmental* risk' which means that its membership of the chemical industry makes it have a higher level of environmental risk than members of other industries.

This is because of the *unique nature of chemicals processing* which can, as JGP found, have a major impact on one or more stakeholders and threaten a key resource (labour supply).

Environmental risk arises from the potential losses from such things as emissions and hazardous leaks, pollution and some resource consumption issues. CEO Keith Miasma referred to this risk in his statement about the threat to JGP's overall reputation. As a major source of potential reputation risk, environmental risk is usually a strategic risk for a chemical company such as JGP.

Marking scheme		Marks
(a)	4 marks for explanation of sustainability. 2 marks for criticism of the FD's understanding. Allow cross marking between the two tasks.	6
(b)	3 marks for each of the 3 stages of the audit (1 for explanation of the stage, 2 for exploration).	9
(c)	2 marks for explanation of each reason why environmental risks are strategic at JGP to a maximum of 6 marks.	6
Total		**21**

18 CHEMCO

Key answer tips

(a) Ensure you explain why the governance arrangements of JPX are inadequate to the Chemco board and not just list the inadequacies of the arrangement.

(b) There are two parts to this requirement: (1) Identify risks – try to find approx. 5 distinct risks. (2) Explain how risk can be assessed. Make sure you clearly answer both parts.

(c) The requirement asks you to construct a case: this means you need to argue for a change to unitary; only positive points for change will receive credit – your examiner is looking for a persuasive argument in order to award the two professional marks available here.

(a) **JPX's current corporate governance arrangements**

Inadequacy of JPX's current corporate governance arrangements

The case highlights a number of ways in which the corporate governance at JPX is inadequate. JPX's history as a privately run family business may partly explain its apparent slowness to develop the corporate governance structures and systems expected in many parts of the world.

There are five ways, from the case, that JPX can be said to be inadequate in its corporate governance although these are linked. There is overlap between the points made.

In the first instance, the case mentions that there were no non-executive directors (NEDs) on the JPX board. It follows that JPX would be without the necessary balance and external expertise that NEDs can provide.

Second, there is evidence of a corporate culture at JPX dominated by the members of the family. The case study notes that they dominate the upper tier of the board. This may have been acceptable when JPX was a family owned company, but as a public company floated on a stock exchange and hence accountable to external shareholders, a wider participation in board membership is necessary.

Third, the two-tier board, whilst not necessarily being a problem in itself (two-tier boards work well in many circumstances), raises concern because the department heads, who are on the lower tier of the board, are excluded from strategic discussions at board level. It is likely that as line managers in the business, the departmental heads would have vital inputs to make into such discussions, especially on such issues as the implementation of strategies. It is also likely that their opinions on the viabilities of different strategic options would be of value.

Fourth, it could be argued that JPX's reporting is less than ideal with, for example, its oblique reference to a 'negative local environmental impact'. However, it might be noted that ambiguity in reporting is also evident in European and American reporting.

Finally, having been subject to its own country's less rigorous corporate governance requirements for all of its previous history, it is likely that adjusting to the requirements of complying with the European-centred demands of Chemco will present a challenge.

(b)   Risks of the proposed acquisition

Risks that Chemco might incur in acquiring JPX

The case describes a number of risks that Chemco could become exposed to if the acquisition was successful. Explicitly, the case highlights a possible environmental risk (the 'negative local environmental impact') that may or may not be eventually valued as a provision (depending on whether or not it is likely to result in a liability). Other risks are likely to emerge as the proposed acquisition develops.

Exchange rate risks apply to any business dealing with revenue or capital flows between two or more currency zones. The case explicitly describes Chemco and JPX existing in different regions of the world. Whilst exchange rate volatility can undermine confidence in cash flow projections, it should also be borne in mind that medium term increases or decreases in exchange values can materially affect the returns on an investment (in this case, Chemco's investment in JPX).

There is some market risk in Chemco's valuation of JPX stock. This could be a substantial risk because of JPX's relatively recent flotation where the market price of JPX may not have yet found its intrinsic level. In addition, it is not certain that Chemco has full knowledge of the fair price to pay for each JPX share given the issues of dealing across national borders and in valuing stock in JPX's country.

All mergers and acquisitions ('integrations') are exposed to synergy risks.

Whilst it is expected and hoped that every merger or acquisition will result in synergies (perhaps from scale economies as the case mentions), in practice, many integrations fail to realise any. In extreme cases, the costs arising from integration can threaten the very survival of the companies involved.

Finally, there are risks associated with the bringing-together of the two board structures. Specifically, structural and cultural changes will be required at JPX to bring it in line with Chemco's. The creation of a unitary board and the increased involvement of NEDs and departmental heads may be problematic, for example, Chemco's board is likely to insist on such changes post-acquisition.

Assessment of risk

The assessment of the risk exposure of any organisation has five components. Firstly, the identity (nature and extent) of the risks facing the company should be identified (such as considering the risks involved in acquiring JPX). This may involve consulting with relevant senior managers, consultants and other stakeholders. Second, the company should decide on the categories of risk that are regarded as acceptable for the company to bear. Of course any decision to discontinue exposure to a given risk will have implications for the activities of the company and this cost will need to be considered against the benefit of the reduced risk. Third, the assessment of risk should quantify, as far as possible, the likelihood (probability) of the identified risks materialising. Risks with a high probability of occurring will attract higher levels of management attention than those with lower probabilities.

Fourth, an assessment of risk will entail an examination of the company's ability to reduce the impact on the business of risks that do materialise. Consultation with affected parties (e.g. departmental heads, stakeholders, etc.) is likely to be beneficial, as information on minimising negative impact may sometimes be a matter of technical detail. Fifth and finally, risk assessment involves an understanding of the costs of operating particular controls to review and manage the related risks.

These costs will include information gathering costs, management overhead, external consultancy where appropriate, etc.

(c)   **Unitary and two-tier board structures**

Advantages of unitary board structure in general

There are arguments for and against unitary and two-tier boards. Both have their 'place' depending on business cultures, size of business and a range of other factors. In general, however, the following arguments can be put for unitary boards.

One of the main features of a unitary board is that all directors, including managing directors, departmental (or divisional) directors and NEDs all have equal legal and executive status in law.

This does not mean that all are equal in terms of the organisational hierarchy, but that all are responsible and can be held accountable for board decisions. This has a number of benefits.

Firstly, NEDs are empowered, being accorded equal status to executive directors. NEDs can bring not only independent scrutiny to the board, but also experience and expertise that may be of invaluable help in devising strategy and the assessment of risk.

Second, board accountability is enhanced by providing a greater protection against fraud and malpractice and by holding all directors equally accountable under a 'cabinet government' arrangement. These first two benefits provide a major underpinning to the confidence that markets have in listed companies.

Third, unitary board arrangements reduce the likelihood of abuse of (self-serving) power by a small number of senior directors. Small 'exclusivist' boards such as have been evident in some corporate 'scandals' are discouraged by unitary board arrangements.

Fourth, the fact that the board is likely to be larger than a given tier of a two-tier board means that more viewpoints are likely to be expressed in board deliberations and discussions. In addition to enriching the intellectual strength of the board, the inclusivity of the board should mean that strategies are more robustly scrutinised before being implemented.

Relevance to JPX in particular

If the JPX acquisition was to proceed, there would be a unitary board at Chemco overseeing a two-tier board at JPX.

The first specific argument for JPX adopting a unitary board would be to bring it into line with Chemco's. Chemco clearly believes in unitary board arrangements and would presumably prefer to have the benefits of unitary boards in place so as to have as much confidence as possible in JPX's governance. This may be especially important if JPX is to remain an 'arm's length' or decentralised part of Chemco's international operation.

Second, there is an argument for making changes at JPX in order to signal a departure from the 'old' systems when JPX was independent of the 'new' systems under Chemco's ownership. A strong way of helping to 'unfreeze' previous ways of working is to make important symbolic changes and a rearrangement of the board structure would be a good example of this.

Third, it is clear that the family members who currently run JPX have a disproportionate influence on the company and its strategy (the 'family business culture'). Widening the board would, over time, change the culture of the board and reduce that influence.

Fourth, a unitary board structure would empower the departmental heads at JPX whose opinions and support are likely to be important in the transition period following the acquisition.

Marking scheme – technical marks		
		Marks
(a)	Up to two marks per valid point made on the inadequacy of JPX's governance	Up to 10
(b)	One mark for identifying and describing each risk to Chemco in the JPX acquisition	Up to 5
	Up to one mark per relevant point on assessing each risk and a further one mark for development of relevant points	Up to 10
(c)	One mark for each relevant point made.	
	(i) Explanation of the advantages of unitary boards	Up to 4
	(ii) Case concerning the advantages of a unitary board at JPX	Up to 4
Total		33

How well has the candidate demonstrated Professional Skills as follows:	Not at all	Not well	Quite well	Very well
Communication skills in formulating a counter argument.	The candidate has failed to formulate an argument FOR the change	The candidate has only addressed some arguments.	The candidate has addressed most of the arguments, but their answer is not persuasive.	The candidate has clearly formulated a persuasive argument
	0	0.5	1	2

19   KK

Key answer tips

Use the requirement to form a structured answer using appropriate headings.

(a)   Conflict of interest

A conflict of interest is a situation in which an individual has compromised independence because of another countervailing interest which may or may not be declared. In the case of non-executive directors, shareholders have the right to expect each NED to act wholly in the shareholders' interests whilst serving with the company. Any other factors that might challenge this sole fiduciary duty are likely to give rise to a conflict of interest. Does the director pursue policies and actions to benefit the shareholders or to benefit himself in some other way?

Conflicts of interest in the case

John has a longstanding and current *material business relationship with KK Limited* as CEO of its largest supplier. This creates an obvious incentive to influence future purchases from Soria Supplies over and above other competitor suppliers, even if the other suppliers are offering more attractive supply contracts as far as KK is concerned. It is in the interests of KK shareholders for inputs to be purchased from whichever supplier is offering the best in terms of quality, price and supply. This may or may not be offered by Soria Supplies. Similarly, a conflict of interest already exists in that Susan Schwab, KK's finance director, is a NED on the board of Soria Supplies. Soria has a material business relationship with KK and Susan Schwab has a conflict of interest with regard to her duty to the shareholders of KK and the shareholders of Soria Supplies.

His appointment, if approved, would create a cross *directorship with Susan Schwab.* As she was appointed to the board of Soria Supplies, any appointment from Soria's board to KK's board would be a cross directorship. Such arrangements have the ability to create a disproportionately close relationship between two people and two companies that may undermine objectivity and impartiality in both cases.

In this case, the cross directorship would create too strong a link between one supplier (Soria Supplies) and a buyer (KK) to the detriment of other suppliers and thus potentially lower unit costs.

John's brother-in-law is Ken Kava, the chief executive of KK. Such a close *family relationship* may result in John supporting Ken when it would be more in the interests of the KK shareholders for John to exercise greater objectivity. There should be no relationships between board members that prevent all directors serving the best interests of shareholders and a family relationship is capable of undermining this objectivity. This is especially important in public listed companies such as KK Limited.

(b)   **Advantages of appointing non-executives to the KK board**

The case discusses a number of issues that were raised as a result of the rapid expansion. An effective NED presence during this period would expect to bring several benefits.

In the case of KK, the NEDs could provide essential input into two related areas: monitoring the strategies for suitability and for excessive risk. In *monitoring the strategies for suitability,* NEDs could have an important scrutinising and advising role to fulfil on the 'aggressive' strategies pursued by KK. All strategy selection is a trade-off between risk and return and so experience of strategy, especially in risky situations, can be very valuable.

NEDs could also *monitor the strategies for excessive risk.* The strategy role of NEDs is important partly because of increasing the collective experience of the board to a wide range of risks. With KK pursuing an 'aggressive' strategy that involved the 'increasingly complex operations', risk monitoring is potentially of great importance for shareholders. There is always a balance between aggression in a growth strategy and caution for the sake of risk management. The fact that some of the other executive directors are both new to the company (resulting from the expansion) and less experienced means, according to the case, that they may be less able and willing to question Mr Kava. Clearly, an effective non-executive presence would be able to bring such scrutiny to the board. They may also place a necessary restraint on the strategic ambitions of Mr Kava.

They could *provide expertise on the foreign investments including,* in some cases, country-specific knowledge. It is careless and irresponsible to make overseas investments based on incomplete intelligence. Experienced NEDs, some of whom may have done business in or with the countries in question, could be very valuable. Experienced NEDs capable of offering specific risk advice, possibly through the company's committee structure (especially the risk committee) would be particularly helpful.

Investors are reassured by an effective non-executive presence on a board. The fact that investors have expressed concerns over the strategy and risk makes this factor all the more important in this case. An experienced and effective NED presence would provide shareholders with a higher degree of confidence in the KK board so that when large overseas investments were made, they would be more assured that such investments were necessary and beneficial.

Finally, through an effective nominations committee, the NEDs could have *involvement in the recruitment and appointment of executive and non-executive directors* through the nominations committee structure. Specifically when the business is growing the need for new people is at its height and the *appointment of specialists at board level in such periods is strategically important.*

Through the use of contacts and through the experience of recruiting directors for many years, experienced NEDs could make a worthwhile contribution.

Marking scheme		Marks
(a)	2 marks for an explanation of conflict of interest.	
	2 marks for each potential conflict of interest identified and explained.	8
(b)	2 marks for each advantage assessed. Maximum	7
Total		**15**

20 **'HELP-WITH-LIFE' (HWL)**

Key answer tips

Part (a) required the advantages of diversity to be clearly linked to the situation in the case. **Part (b)** required an explanation of CSR and then the differences between CSR for a charity and 'for profit' organisation. Some careful thought was required before attempting the second part of this requirement with the fundamental strategic purpose of each organisation being a good starting point.

(a) **Advantages of diversity**

Diversity policy aims to achieve a board which is demographically representative of the community in which it operates, such that no single demographic segment is over or under-represented. In the case of HWL, a diverse board of directors would provide several advantages.

First, it would make the board *more representative of the community* it is serving, including its donors and supporters.

In doing so, HWL would increase its social legitimacy and enjoy a *stronger social contract* with its community and also with the service users. If the board were homogenous with a certain dominant demographic, it would be open to the charge of being aloof and with a weak connection to the local ethnic groups not represented on the board.

Second, diversity on the board will enable HWL to *meet the local government requirements for diversity* and thus to continue receiving that portion of its funding from the local government. With a large proportion of HWL's funding coming from the local government (40%), HWL is effectively required to comply with the diversity requirements as it would be difficult to replace such funding in the short term.

Third, diversity on a board allows the organisation to benefit from a *wider pool of talent* than would be the case with a less diverse board. Having a wide range of demographic segments represented should mean that a wider range of skills, abilities and competences are available. A demographically narrow board would exclude the talents possessed by those outside of the narrow representation and this would be against the board's best interests in seeking to be effective in its duties.

Fourth, a more diverse board would enable a *wider range of views* and opinions to be expressed. The dominant opinion of the majority and the phenomenon of 'group think' can lead to the adoption of positions and policies which can often be shown to be inappropriate in the longer term. So some contrary and challenging voices, especially from those speaking from the perspective of a demographic minority, can be important contributions in policy discussions.

Fifth, a diverse range of people on the board would provide a *greater understanding of the particular values and beliefs* of a wider range of people in HWL's catchment area. Given that HWL's work is most effective when the service providers share some of the values and beliefs of the clients, a board of directors able to understand as wide a range of beliefs as possible is a clear advantage.

Tutorial note

Some countries are beginning to regulate for diversity on boards. Allow this if placed in a particular national context.

(b) **Corporate social responsibility (CSR)**

CSR is a term used to include a series of measures concerned with an organisation's stance towards ethical issues. These include the organisation's social and environmental behaviour, the responsibility of its products and investments, its policies (over and above compliance with regulation) towards employees, its treatment of suppliers and buyers, its transparency and integrity, how it deals with stakeholder concerns and issues of giving and community relations.

Behaviour in all of these areas is largely discretionary and it is possible to adopt a range of approaches from being very concerned about some or all of them, to having no such concern at all.

CSR can be expressed and undertaken in several ways. It has been the case for some time that companies have exercised a social concern for employees (over and above regulatory compliance) and communities, but in more recent times, the idea has emerged that CSR can be integrated into an organisation's strategy. To be strategic about CSR is to undertake CSR initiatives which can have meaning for the organisation as well as those to whom the initiatives are directed. Ethical 'filters' and scrutiny procedures may be installed to ensure that the company acts in accordance with a set of agreed principles, perhaps expressed in a code of ethics. The organisation's ethical reputation may be viewed as a strategic asset and a key part of its competitive positioning.

CSR at HWL and in a commercial business

As a charity, HWL's *central strategic purpose is to be socially beneficial in nature*. The reason why any charity exists is to pursue a benevolent purpose. In the case of HWL, this is 'to help individuals and families with social problems and related issues.' It performs this service for no charge to the service users and seeks to maximise the quality of this service over other concerns of the organisation. A commercial business is likely to have a strategic purpose framed in terms of competitive or financial measures.

Second, HWL *measures its success in social outcome rather than in profits*. The case scenario says that HWL's strategic (i.e. most important) aim is to deliver its charitable services ('to help its service users') whereas a commercial business is more likely to measure success in financial terms such as returns on investment, net or gross margins, etc.

Third, HWL *supports its charitable purpose* through a number of operational measures. It asks those staff members working for it to *espouse certain values and beliefs* (consistent with those service users being helped). HWL also *asks its directors to forgo income* to work for it. Its attitude towards money was that it would rather spend what money it had on service provision than directors' pay. So asking people to accept a personal discount is perhaps made possible because those who help lead the charity (its directors) are more likely to share a belief in the value of what it does. Such an alignment of personal belief with company policy is rarely asked for in a business organisation and few would ask or expect directors to work for a level of remuneration below the market rate. Increasing personal incomes is often a strong concern of directors in commercial businesses, in contrast with the attitude asked for by Marian Ngogo at HWL.

Marking scheme		Marks
(a)	2 marks for each advantage explained.	
	Maximum	8
(b)	3 marks for explanation of CSR.	
	2 marks for each relevant difference discussed. Half mark for identification only.	
	Maximum	9
Total		17

21 VESTEL

Key answer tips

Ensure that you do not simply describe nominations committees but address the issues faced by the company in the scenario. Furthermore be careful of straying into discussing the roles of NEDs rather than the committee that will recruit them.

REPORT

To: The Board, Vestel

From: Consultant

Title: Nominations committees

1   Introduction

This report considers the role of a nominations committee within Vestel and how it go recruit suitable non-executive directors.

2   Nomination committees

Committees form an important part of board operations and, as stated, are generally included within principles laid down by regulatory bodies in order to advise as to appropriate governance structures. In the UK the role of nomination committees is outlined in the Corporate Governance Code. At the very least it would be good practice to set up a nominations committee even if not detailed within domestic stock-exchange listing requirements

Committees allow the expertise and skills of a focused group of individuals to be used in order to form advisory opinion for the board of directors. They usually consist of non-executive directors who have specialist skills in areas such as environmentalism or ethics. The non-executive nature of membership creates a degree of independence from executive management and this in turn suggests that no undue influence has been placed upon them in relation to conclusions drawn.

Skill provision, appropriate balance to membership and the independence of thought suggested will be important for a nomination committee. Their decisions will affect board composition and the independence of non-executives selected will be vital to ensure that shareholder needs are paramount in the decision making process of the board.

The committee structure offers a channel of communication for both executives and external consultants to ensure all relevant views are canvassed.

At the same time they allow the board to off load responsibility for some key areas of decision making so allowing them to focus on other considerations such as strategy definition.

Nomination committees are essential for effective board operations because of the results they produce. The provision of new directors refreshes the board and ensures succession into roles, promoting stability and loyalty of senior management given a route through which promotion on merit can be achieved.

3   Director recruitment

There is no set approach to recruitment of new non-executive directors although certain issues in the case highlight the need for thoughtful and exacting methodology in order to subsequently ensure quality in the outcome.

The scenario suggests there may be a shortage of suitable local candidates for the job. It draws this conclusion through an analysis of the size of the corporate skill base available locally. This raises a number of issues.

Firstly, candidates will need to be carefully sought out and selected possibly through the use of search firms to act as intermediaries, approaching those in senior roles within other companies with a degree of confidentiality.

Secondly, candidates from outside the private sector should be considered, particularly in areas such as ethics and environmentalism. Academics and activists may be a part of the gene pool trawled in this respect.

Thirdly, overseas or foreign candidates should not be excluded, particularly when a large part of the company's business is in the export market.

This will require a benchmarking exercise in order to ensure the company can afford the costs of drawing individuals from their home country in order to serve.

The Chairman's and CEO's view should be canvassed as part of the process. It may be the case that the Chairman takes overall responsibility for the committee. Since it has such a vital role to perform this is likely to be the case.

Standard background checks and interviews should be used as part of the selection process prior to selection of the best candidate and the negotiation over terms and contracts. Critically, the most important aspect of committee operations takes place following selection. The committee must ensure that their operations are appropriately disclosed to shareholders in the form of a separate section within the annual report. This ensures a degree of transparency exists in order to deal with the agency issue.

Performance appraisal is a final aspect to any board operation. The nomination committee must critically appraise the success and failures within the recruitment process used and ensure it continually evolves and improves over time.

22   TOMATO BANK

Key answer tips

(a)   With a verb like 'criticise' careful analysis of the case is required to answer the question successfully. Ensure you read the scenario carefully.

(b)   The first part of this requirement, to describe components, was largely book work and should have posed no problem to well-prepared candidates. The second element is to apply this knowledge to Mr Woof's remuneration: this took a little further analysis.

(a)   Criticisms of remuneration committee

The remuneration committee has demonstrated failures of duty in several areas.

There is evidence of a lack of independence in the roles of the non-executive directors (NEDs) who comprise the committee. One of the main purposes of NEDs is to bring independent perspectives within the committee structure and shareholders have the right to expect NEDs to not be influenced by executive pressure in decision-making (such as from the finance directors). Two of the NEDs on the remuneration committee were former colleagues of Mr Woof, creating a further conflict. The effect of this lack of independence was a factor in the creation of Mr Woof's unbalanced package. That, in turn, increased agency costs and made the agency problem worse.

There was a clear breach of good practice with the remuneration committee receiving and acting on the letter from Mr Woof and agreeing to the design of the remuneration package in such a hasty manner.

Remuneration committees should not receive input from the executive structure and certainly not from directors or prospective directors lobbying for their own rewards. Mr Woof was presumptuous and arrogant in sending the letter but the committee was naive and irresponsible in receiving and acting upon it.

There is evidence that the remuneration was *influenced by the hype* surrounding the supposed favourable appointment in gaining the services of Mr Woof. In this regard it lacked objectivity. Whilst it was the remuneration committee's role to agree an attractive package that reflected Mr Woof's market value, the committee was seemingly *coerced by the finance director and others* and this is an abdication of their non-executive responsibility.

The committee *failed to build in adequate performance related components* into Mr Woof's package. Such was the euphoria in appointing Mr Woof that they were influenced by a clearly excitable finance director who was so keen to get Mr Woof's signature that he counselled against exercising proper judgement in this balance of benefits. Not only should the remuneration committee have not allowed representations from the FD, it should also have given a great deal more thought to the balance of benefits so that bonuses were better aligned to shareholder interests.

The committee *failed to make adequate pension and resignation arrangements* that represented value for the shareholders of Tomato Bank as well as for Mr Woof.

Whilst pension arrangements are within the remit of the remuneration committee and a matter for consideration upon the appointment of a new chief executive, shareholder value would be better served if it was linked to the time served in the company and also if the overall contribution could be reconsidered were the CEO to be removed by shareholders for failure such as was the case at Tomato Bank.

(b) **Components of a suitable rewards package for Mr Woof**

The components of a typical executive reward package include *basic salary,* which is paid regardless of performance; *short and long-term bonuses* and incentive plans which are payable based on pre-agreed performance targets being met; *share schemes,* which may be linked to other bonus schemes and provide options to the executive to purchase predetermined numbers of shares at a given favourable price; *pension and termination benefits* including a pre-agreed pension value after an agreed number of years' service and any 'golden parachute' benefits when leaving; plus any number of other *benefits in kind* such as cars, health insurance, use of company property, etc.

Balanced package is needed for the following reasons:

The overall purpose of a well-designed rewards package is to achieve a *reduction (minimisation) of agency costs.* These are the costs the principals incur in monitoring the actions of agents acting on their behalf.

The main way of doing this is to ensure that executive reward packages are *aligned with the interests of principals* (shareholders) so that directors are rewarded for meeting targets that further the interests of shareholders.

A reward package that only rewards accomplishments in line with shareholder value substantially decreases agency costs and when a shareholder might own shares in many companies, *such a 'self-policing' agency mechanism is clearly of benefit.* Typically, such reward packages involve a bonus element based on specific financial targets in line with enhanced company (and hence shareholder) value.

Although Mr Woof came to Tomato Bank with a very good track record, *past performance is no guarantee of future success.* Accordingly, Mr Woof's reward package should have been subject to the same detailed design as with any other executive package.

In hindsight, a pension value linked to performance and sensitive to the manner of leaving would have been a worthwhile matter for discussion and also the split between basic and incentive components.

Although ambitious to design, it would have been helpful if the reward package could have been made reviewable by the remuneration committee so that a *discount for risk could be introduced* if, for example, the internal audit function were to signal a high level of exposure to an unreliable source of funding.

As it stands, the worst that can happen to him is that he survives just two years in office, during which time he need not worry about the effects of excessive risk on the future of the company, as he has a generous pension to receive thereafter.

Marking scheme		Marks
(a)	2 marks for each criticism identified and discussed (10 marks)	10
(b)	1 mark for each component described to a maximum of 4 marks	
	1 mark for each relevant point of explanation of the benefits of a balanced package for Mr Woof to a maximum of 6	10
Total		**20**

23 ABC CO

(a) Remunerations committees and cross directorships

Remunerations committees

Remunerations committees comprise an important part of the standard board committee structure of good corporate governance.

The major roles of a remuneration committee are as follows.

Firstly, the committee is charged with determining remunerations policy on behalf of the board and the shareholders.

In this regard, they are acting on behalf of shareholders but for the benefit of both shareholders and the other members of the board.

Policies will typically concern the pay scales applied to directors' packages, the proportions of different types of reward within the overall package and the periods in which performance related elements become payable.

Secondly the committee ensures that each director is fairly but responsibly rewarded for their individual contribution in terms of levels of pay and the components of each director's package. It is likely that discussions of this type will take place for each individual director and will take into account issues including market conditions, retention needs, long-term strategy and market rates for a given job.

Third, the remunerations committee reports to the shareholders on the outcomes of their decisions, usually in the corporate governance section of the annual report (usually called Report of the Remunerations Committee). This report, which is auditor reviewed, contains a breakdown of each director's remuneration and a commentary on policies applied to executive and non-executive remuneration.

Finally, where appropriate and required by statute or voluntary code, the committee is required to be seen to be compliant with relevant laws or codes of best practice. This will mean that the remunerations committee will usually be made up of non-executive members of the board and will meet at regular intervals.

Cross directorships

Cross directorships represent a threat to the efficient working of remunerations committees. A cross directorship is said to exist when two (or more) directors sit on the boards of the other. In practice, such arrangements also involve some element of cross-shareholdings which further compromises the independence of the directors involved. In most cases, each director's 'second' board appointment is likely to be non-executive. Cross directorships undermine the roles of remunerations committees in that a director deciding the salary of a colleague who, in turn, may play a part in deciding his or her own salary, is a clear conflict of interests. Neither director involved in the arrangement is impartial and so a temptation would exist to act in a manner other than for the benefit of the shareholders of the company on whose remunerations committee they sit.

It is for this reason the cross directorships and cross shareholding arrangements are explicitly forbidden by many corporate governance codes of best practice.

(b) **Mr Finn's remunerations package**

Different components of directors' rewards

The components of a director's total rewards package may include any or all of the following in combination. The basic salary is not linked to performance in the short run but year-to-year changes in it may be linked to some performance measures. It is intended to recognise the basic market value of a director. A number of benefits in kind may be used which will vary by position and type of organisation, but typically include company cars, health insurance, use of health or leisure facilities, subsidised or free use of company products (if appropriate), etc. Pension contributions are paid by most responsible employers, but separate directors' schemes may be made available at higher contribution rates than other employees. Finally, various types of incentives and performance related components may be used.

Short to medium term incentives such as performance-related annual bonuses will encourage a relatively short term approach to meeting agreed targets whilst long term incentives including share options can be used for longer term performance measures.

Mr Finn's remuneration package

The case mentions that, 'Mr Finn's remuneration package as a sales director was considered to be poorly aligned to Swanland's interests because it was too much weighted by basic pay and contained inadequate levels of incentive.'

The alignment of director and shareholder interests occurs through a careful design of the performance related components of a director's overall rewards. The strategic emphases of the business can be built into these targets and Mr Finn's position as a sales director makes this possible through incentives based on revenue or profit targets. If current priorities are for the maximisation of relatively short-run returns, annual, semi-annual or even monthly performance-related bonuses could be used. More likely at board level, however, will be a need for longer-term alignments for medium to long-term value maximisation.

While Mr Finn may be given annual or even quarterly or monthly bonus payments against budget, longer-term performance can be underpinned through share options with a relevant maturity date or end-of-service pay-outs with agreed targets. The balance of short and longer-term performance bonuses should be carefully designed for each director with metrics within the control of the director in question.

Marking scheme			Marks
(a)	(i)	One mark for each valid point made for demonstrating an understanding of cross directorships	Up to 2
	(ii)	Award up to two marks for each valid point made on roles of remunerations committees	Up to 8
	(iii)	Award up to two marks for each valid point on undermining the roles	Up to 4
		Maximum	**12**
(b)		One mark for each component of a director's remuneration correctly identified	Up to 4
		One mark for each relevant point describing how Finn's remuneration might be more aligned to shareholders' interests	Up to 5
		Maximum	**8**
Total		**Maximum**	**20**

C: STRATEGY

24 TMZ

Key answer tips

This answer will require a combination of some financial analysis of the numbers provided in tables one and two as well as a discussion on strategic drift. It will not be sufficient to discuss strategic drift in general terms, the scenario should be used to illustrate the different phases.

There is considerable evidence to suggest that strategic drift particularly affects organisations which have experienced a long period of relative continuity during which strategy has either remained unchanged or changed incrementally to react to relatively minor changes in the external environment or industry. This appears to be the case at TMZ. It had enjoyed 35 years of success and growth based on contracting musical artists to its record label and recording and distributing their songs and music through an appropriate physical media. Table one shows that revenues increased continuously in the period 1965–2000.

Profit margins fell during the period, reflecting problems in cost control as established musical acts took longer to produce albums and senior staff of TMZ adopted a more relaxed and indulgent approach to their artists. However, even at the end of the period, TMZ remained a profitable company.

Table one: Gross and net profit margin – 1965–2000

	1965	1970	1980	1990	2000
Revenue ($million)	10	70	120	150	170
Gross profit margin	40.00%	42.86%	37.50%	33.33%	29.41%
Net profit margin	30.00%	31.43%	25.00%	20.00%	14.71%

During this period, the company had reacted positively to significant changes in its environment. Sociocultural changes, represented by musical fashion and technology changes (from vinyl, through tape cassette to compact disc (CD)) had been successfully surmounted. However, such success can often lead to complacency, with the organisation continuing to pursue a strategy which progressively fails to address the changing strategic position of the organisation and this failure leads to deterioration in organisational performance. This is known as strategic drift.

Evidence for this strategic drift starts to emerge in 2003, four years after the launch of the first file sharing company. People within TMZ warned about the possible implications of digital downloading of music. However, senior management at TMZ had rejected this warning and believed that the drop in revenue was due to 'the wrong music, promoted to the wrong people at the wrong price'. They adopted a policy of signing new artists, increasing advertising spend and cutting CD prices. In the policy, 2003–2007, revenues dropped significantly and the company made significant losses (see table two).

Table two: Gross and net profit margin – 2003 – 2007

$million	2003	2004	2005	2006	2007
Revenue	165	150	130	100	80
Gross profit	45	30	10	0	(10)
Net profit	20	5	(15)	(20)	(30)
Gross profit margin	27.27%	20.00%	7.69%	0.00%	(12.50%)
Net profit margin	12.12%	3.33%	(11.54%)	(20.00%)	(37.50%)

Johnson, Scholes and Whittington suggest that it is important to realise why strategic drift occurs. They suggest that managers, faced with the complexities of steering an organisation, tend to look for solutions based on the current ways of doing and seeing things, grounded in the existing organisational culture. So, for example, when revenues from compact discs (CDs) started to decline, the senior managers at TMZ instigated relatively conventional responses to falling sales (increased advertising, reduced prices) and also adopted approaches which had worked before (signing new artists). These may have worked if the environmental change had not been so significant. However, what they failed to realise was that the way people were consuming music was fundamentally changing.

The realisation of performance problems is often followed by a period of flux where no clear direction is pursued. When conventional strategies failed, TMZ resorted to litigation, suing the companies who downloaded music to consumers. In effect, TMZ was attempting to preserve the status quo, trying to ensure that the market remained the same as the one they had operated in so successfully for 40 years. However, not only did this not arrest the decline of the company, it also led to problems with both performers and music fans. In 2010, with the very existence of the company threatened, management was able to define a strategy which worked with the digital download and music-sharing community, to establish a completely different business model based on licensing and ring tones.

This illustrates that a period of flux may itself be followed by transformational change, in which there is a fundamental change in strategic direction. TMZ re-defined its business model in 2010.

It was fortunate that it had enough stakeholder investment to see it through a difficult period. In many organisations transformational change takes place too late and the organisation fails.

Johnson, Scholes and Whittington suggest that the challenge for managers is to stand apart from their own experience and organisational culture so that they are able to recognise the emerging strategic issues which they face. They also suggest that a second challenge relates to the management of strategic change. New strategies might require actions outside the scope of the existing culture. Thus people within the organisation are required to substantially change their core assumptions and their ways of doing things. The senior management at TMZ were warned about the possible effect of digital downloading, but they were unable to change their basic assumptions about how the music industry worked.

Marking scheme – technical marks	
	Marks
1 mark for each appropriate point up to a maximum of 15 marks; this could include: – Up to 1 mark for correct GP margin and appropriate comment 1965–2000 – Up to 1 mark for correct NP margin and appropriate comment 1965–2000 – Up to 1 mark for GP margin and appropriate comment 2003–2007 – Up to 1 mark for NP margin and appropriate comment 2003–2007 **Total**	 —— **15** ——

How well has the candidate demonstrated Professional Skills as follows:	Not at all	Not well	Quite well	Very well
Analysing the causes of the strategic drift	The candidate has failed to investigate the root causes of the strategic drift.	The candidate has integrated the financial and qualitative factors but has not linked the environmental changes to the changes in TMZ's performance.	The candidate has integrated the financial and qualitative factors but has not consistently linked the environmental changes to the changes in TMZ's performance.	The candidate has integrated the financial and qualitative factors to clearly illustrate the causes of each phase in the strategic drift of TMZ.
	0	0.5	1	2

25 SWIFT

Key answer tips

In **part (a)**, when performing the analysis you should ensure that you include both financial measures *and* non-financial measures. Try to take a structured approach to your answer by using a strategic model – the answer uses the Johnson, Scholes and Whittington tests for evaluating a strategy, but other models such as the BCG matrix would also have been appropriate and scored marks.

In **part (b)** a good model to use would be Porter's Diamond. This would give structure to the answer.

(a)   The acquisition of EVM can be analysed using the success criteria of suitability, acceptability and feasibility.

Suitability is concerned with whether a strategy addresses the issues identified when considering the strategic position of the company. In general terms the acquisition appears to make sense. The market is mature and competitive in Ambion, pushing down margins. These margins are further eroded by a government that is hostile to road transport resulting in high taxation on fuel, road taxes linked to carbon emission and restricted working practices.

The acquisition of EVM provides an opportunity for Swift to exploit their core competencies in a different geographical market where demand is rising, the national government is investing in road infrastructure and competition is immature. The increased size of the group will further allow Swift to exploit economies of scale when purchasing trucks and other equipment.

Concerns around suitability surround the potential clash of cultures between Swift and EVM. Swift has no experience of acquiring or running foreign companies. It has no experience of trading in Ecuria. Furthermore, although EVM is now in private hands, it may be possible that the work practices and expectations of employees may still reflect the time when they were working for the central government.

Although altering these practices may give scope for even greater profitability, it may lead to labour disputes that harm the service and reputation of the company. Swift wishes to acquire this company and adopt the practices, principles and technology of the Ambion operation. This may lead to conflict that they may find hard to resolve.

Acceptability is concerned with the expected performance of a strategy in terms of return, risk and stakeholder reactions.

Return: EVM delivers a very similar (18%) Return on Capital Employed (ROCE) to Swift Transport. This appears to be a strong performance for the sector, and should certainly be acceptable to the Swift shareholders. The gross profit margin (20%) is higher than Swift, but the net profit margin (7.5%) is lower. This may support some of the concerns discussed under suitability. The company may still be carrying high costs from its days as a nationalised company. Swift presumably believes that it can improve the net profit margin by implementing competences gained in the Ambion market.

Risk: Both the current liquidity ratio (1·14%) and the acid test ratio (1·05%) are lower than the Swift equivalents and Swift will need to look at this. The introduction of Swift's practices may help reduce trade payables. The gearing ratio (30%) for EVM is much lower than Swift and perhaps reflects a more conservative approach to long-term lending and a reflection of the fledgling capital markets in the country. However, the interest cover ratio (5) is half that of Swift, perhaps reflecting lower profitability and higher business taxation.

Stakeholders: Joe Swift and his family are the major stakeholders in what is still a family-run private limited company. It is unlikely that there will be any opposition to the acquisition from shareholders. However, stakeholders such as drivers might be wary of this strategy and also the government, outspokenly criticised by Joe, may also respond in some way. For example, by imposing taxation on foreign investment.

Feasibility is about whether an organisation has the resources and competencies to deliver the strategy. It appears that Swift does, as funds are in place and the competences are what are partly driving the acquisition.

(b) One possible way to assess this scenario is by using Porter's Diamond. This identifies four main determinants of national advantage and arranges these as a diamond, with each of these determinants interacting with and reinforcing each other.

Two further determinants, chance and government, are discussed outside of the diamond in terms of how they influence and interact with the determinants inside the diamond. This model answer uses Porter's diamond as its basis. However, credit will also be given to candidates who use an alternative appropriate framework or model.

The four main determinants are:

- The nation's position in factor conditions, such as skilled labour or infrastructure, necessary for firms to compete in a given industry. The acknowledged work ethic of the people and the investment in transport infrastructure by the government are significant factor conditions in Ecuria.

- The nature of the home demand conditions for the industry's product or service. Home demand influences economies of scale, but it also shapes the rate and character of improvement and innovation. In Ecuria, the move to a market economy has stimulated a rapid growth in the transport of goods.

  The Ecurian people are traditionally demanding in their standards. They have a passion for precision and promptness and this has shaped the operations of EVM.

- The presence or absence of related and supporting industries that are internationally competitive. Competitive advantage in certain industries confers potential advantages on firms in other industries. Porter suggests that the 'Swiss success in pharmaceuticals was closely connected to previous international success in the dye industry'. There is no evidence in the case study that Ecuria has internationally competitive industries related to logistics. Hence, it is the absence of these that is significant when considering this determinant.

- The final determinant is firm strategy, structure and rivalry. This concerns the conditions in the nation governing how companies are created, organised and managed. It also considers the nature of domestic rivalry. EVM was created by nationalising the state-run haulage system. For the first few years of operation it had few competitors. The nature of the capital markets makes it very difficult to raise finance in Ecuria. Consequently, most of EVM's competitors are small, family-run companies who offer a local service. Porter suggests that there is a strong relationship between vigorous domestic rivalry and the creation and persistence of competitive advantage in an industry. There is little evidence of this emerging in Ecuria.

  Porter also recognises the influence of chance and government. Chance events are developments outside the control of firms and the nation's government. Wars, external political developments and a reduction in foreign demand are all examples of chance factors. Government, in effect, helps shape the diamond by enacting policies that influence each of the determinants. In Ecuria, the government's approach to infrastructure investment and policies towards capital markets has affected factor conditions and impacted on firm structure and rivalry.

Marking scheme		Marks
(a)	1 mark for each relevant point up to a maximum of 15 marks.	15
(b)	1 mark for each relevant point up to a maximum of 10 marks.	10
Total		25

26   BOWLAND

Key answer tips

This question can be split into three parts – what are Bowland's existing competencies, what are the key success factors needed in retailing, and the extent to which these two things match up.

An organisation's distinctive competences are those things which an organisation does particularly well. They include the organisation's unique resources and capabilities as well as its strengths and its ability to overcome weaknesses. These competences can include aspects such as budgetary control, a strong technology base, a culture conducive to change and marketing skills.

Key success factors are those requirements which it is essential to have if one is to survive and prosper in a chosen industry/environment.

These can include areas such as good service networks, up-to-date marketing intelligence and tight cost controls where margins are small.

It is not guaranteed that the distinctive competences and the key success factors are always in alignment. A company moving into the retail sector may have an excellent product research and development capability, but this alone will not help if it has no concept of service or poorly sited retail outlets. It is critical to ensure that what the company excels at is what is needed to be successful in that particular area.

The strengths of Bowland Carpets include strong brand names which maintain integrity within the different market segments where the company operates. The company has a balanced portfolio of customers and the range of products is equally balanced, ensuring that any sectorial decline can be compensated for by growth in other markets. Other strengths which the company currently has include a good relationship with distributors and strong support from a powerful parent company. Some of its distinctive competences, such as a strong brand and a reasonable range of products, are critical in the proposed new environment, as will be the financial support of the parent company. However there are some aspects which are cause for concern in the proposed new business environment.

The strength in the contract and industrial carpet segment will not be affected by the proposed vertical integration – sales tend to be through direct sales force. The strong relationship with distributors will however be jeopardised by the opening up of retail outlets. Other retail chains will be unwilling to permit a rival to operate so freely, and therefore there will be a reluctance to stock Bowland Carpets. Unless Bowland Carpets can obtain wide retail market coverage to compensate for this potential problem, sales revenue will be adversely affected. The cost of developing extensive market coverage will be enormous and whether it is in High Street outlets or specialist out-of-town centres the investment may be greater than the parent company has budgeted for. The company also has no expertise in site appraisal and selection. Although the newly-structured value chain will generate greater control there is an associated lack of flexibility along with an increase in the fixed cost base of the business.

Another key success factor is the need for expertise in retailing. It may be that the UK company can import this from the USA but the culture of marketing household durables may not be transferable internationally. Bowland Carpets as the domestic company has no experience in this field.

A critical factor in successful retailing is the ability to provide a comprehensive range of products. Does Bowland Carpets have one? It is unlikely that the competitive carpet manufacturers will provide such a supply to one of their rivals.

It would, therefore, appear that there is no close conformity between the distinctive competences of Bowland Carpets and the key success factors required in the carpet retailing sector.

Marking scheme	Marks
1 mark for each relevant point up to a maximum of 10 marks.	*Marks* **10**

27 ONE ENERGY PLC *Walk in the footsteps of a top tutor*

Tutor's top tips

Financial analysis (13 marks)

Key to success:

Include a broad range of measures

Give opinions (not just calculations)

Give equal weighting to non-ratio information (such as overdraft level, level of non-TFA etc.)

Give an overall opinion which is consistent with the requirement

Key dangers:

Calculating too many ratios

Too much detail in calculations

Only doing ratios

Lack of focus

The judicious use of selected financial ratios should have indicated some cause for concern, leading to further investigation of the company and the industrial sector itself. It would have been very helpful to identify typical financial ratios in the sector that RiteSoftware is operating in. However, in the absence of such information, comparison between the two years will provide some evaluation and a basis for further investigation.

However, before calculating and commenting on the ratios, there are a number of things directly discernible from the financial figures provided by the company.

Firstly, goodwill is the most significant non-current asset. If the company is in the position that it needs further funding, then the extract suggests that there is little to secure this funding against. Most lenders prefer to lend against tangible assets, such as property. The value of goodwill has also increased substantially since 20X7, suggesting an acquisition. It would be useful to investigate this further.

Secondly, although trade receivables year on year have increased, in percentage terms, about the same as revenue, trade payables have increased significantly more. The efficiency ratios should cast more light on this; but it appears that the company may be using trade payables to finance cash flows. This hunch might be supported by the fact that the bank overdraft was actually reduced in 20X8.

Thirdly, although sales revenue increased by 10% in the period, cost of sales grew by a greater percentage, leading to a reduction in profit. It seems reasonable to assume that labour costs largely contributed to this cost of sales increase. The percentage increase in staff was almost 30%, a significant proportion for a small company to integrate and profitably utilise.

Finally, the extract from the accounts shows no retained profit, suggesting that this is being distributed to shareholders. This needs to be investigated.

There are other non-financial factors that should also be considered. OneEnergy could perhaps have requested management accounts or forecasts to ensure that the business was variable in the long term and that the presented figures were not artificially distorted by financial accounting policies. OneEnergy should have considered that RiteSoftware was providing financial figures which were more positive than the true underlying performance.

OneEnergy should also have sought independent verification of RiteSoftware's suitability for the task via references and a review of available data on past levels of customer satisfaction. It should not have been enough to simply accept the financial figures, even if these figures themselves were not properly analysed.

It is difficult to bench mark the figures as only two years have been provided and there is no data for industry or sector ratios. It is difficult, for example, to say that gearing is too high until the average gearing ratio for the industry is known. Industry benchmark ratios are another area that should have had further investigation before a decision was made on RiteSoftware.

In analysing the figures through financial ratio analysis, a number of issues would have been discovered:

Profitability

The ROCE (Return on Capital Employed) has almost halved. Although the actual profit remained the same, it was achieved with significantly higher borrowing.

The net profit margin has also almost halved. The absolute figures are also very low (less than 1% in 20X8). This indicates that any small change in sales is likely to result in a loss making position making the viability of RiteSoftware a major concern.

Efficiency

The general observation about trade payables made above appears to be borne out by the ratios. The average receivables settlement remains the same, suggesting good credit management in an expanding business. However, average payable days have increased significantly and are now beyond the 30 days normal for this business. This will create a cash drain for the business removing the opportunity to fund some internal investment from internally generated funds.

Sales revenue per employee has dropped from $33,500 in 20X7 to under $29,500 in 20X8.

Liquidity

Liquidity (measured through both the current and acid test ratios) has declined slightly during this period. Also, the values are rather low (approximately 0.76:1). This indicates that RiteSoftware's cash problems are resulting in it being unable to meet short-term liabilities.

Financial gearing

The two gearing ratios discernible from the extracted information both give cause for concern. The gearing ratio itself has jumped from 25% to above 43%.

The interest cover ratio has dropped to 2 from 7.5. This should have indicated a potential problem in the financing of RiteSoftware – as retained earnings are there are no retained earnings and cash, it would appear that profits are being distributed rather than being reinvested in the business. Instead, necessary investment is coming via borrowing and this may not be sustainable.

Conclusion

The financial figures of RiteSoftware do suggest that everything was not well and that further investigation was necessary. The figures suggest rising debt, cash flow problems, lowering efficiency and very poor profitability. Further investigation might have revealed that RiteSoftware was typical of the industry. However, it might have also identified the problems that led to the company's eventual demise.

Marking scheme	
	Marks
Up to 1 mark for each non-ratio based observation up to a maximum of	5
Up to 1 mark for each ratio based observation up to a maximum of	5
Up to 3 marks for summary and integration of answer, giving a maximum of	**13**

How well has the candidate demonstrated Professional Skills as follows:	Not at all	Not well	Quite well	Very well
Professional scepticism in probing and questioning the information provided.	The candidate has failed to question the data provided or identify areas where further information should have been sought.	The candidate has made only a brief attempt to explain that the financial ratios will provide only a very narrow opinion on the position of RiteSoftware.	The candidate has focused on the financial ratios that can be calculated but has not explained what further ratios or information would be needed in order to provide a complete picture of organisational performance.	The candidate has identified areas of concern and highlighted where further information should be sought.
	0	0.5	1	2

28 MOOR FARM

Key answer tips

This is an unusual question in that it seems to cover a lot of ground such as external analysis, stakeholders, strategic capabilities and marketing. There may be a temptation for students to bring in a lot of models but students have to be careful with their time management and not to go overboard on one particular area. **Part (b)**, on improving a website, would also need very specific suggestions rather than bland, generic answers.

(a) Many issues will need to be considered in the formulation of a strategy for the estate. However, in the context of the scenario, special attention will have to be paid to the expectations of stakeholders, to external environmental factors beyond the control of the estate and to the strategic capabilities of the estate itself. These are now considered in turn.

Expectations of stakeholders

Any proposed strategy will have to take into account the expectations of many stakeholders, some of which have conflicting objectives. From an internal perspective, the strategy has to take into account the objectives of volunteers who make up 90% of the workforce. Any strategy that alienates volunteers may leave the charity unable to maintain the estate or meet its basic operational obligations. Volunteers have different objectives to a paid workforce and these needs have to be understood. Replacing volunteers is not as straightforward as replacing a paid workforce, where scarce labour can be attracted through improved pay and conditions.

Most organisations have relatively straightforward relationships with their customers. Providing a service or product to one customer rarely conflicts with offering a service or product to another. Where it does conflict, for example in providing audit and consultancy services, a supplier can usually elect not to supply the customer, who then looks elsewhere for a similar service. In the case of Moor Farm, potential customers do conflict. There are documented examples of cyclists clashing with walkers and dog walkers with farmers. Access to the land is free (a stipulation of the charitable bequest) and so it is difficult to exclude potential customers. Consequently, a strategy has to be developed that is sensitive to the conflicting needs of customers, within the constraints of the charitable bequest.

Finally, the Moor Farm estate also surrounds two villages where private homeowners are angry about the increasing number of visitors to certain parts of the estate. Attractions have been created, causing traffic problems. As well as having a moral responsibility to these homeowners, the estate also depends, to some extent, on rental income from some of the houses in these villages. Again, residents need to be considered in the definition of the estate's strategy.

External environmental issues

The estate needs to continually scan the external environment to identify issues that might affect its situation. Strategy may have to be developed to either exploit or reflect these external changes, most of which are outside the control of the estate. At best, it can only lobby those responsible for creating these influences.

In the scenario, mention is made of a changed political landscape where government funding is to be reduced on initiatives such as tree planting, protected pasture land and rural employment. This will affect the income of the estate. Changes in weather patterns are also causing problems for the mansion that is situated in the estate. Built originally to resist cold dry weather typical of the time, it has proved susceptible to the warmer, wetter winters now experienced in this part of the country. This is causing long-term maintenance issues as the fabric of the mansion deteriorates.

Finally, the population of the country is increasingly vocal about the 'rights' of individuals. The survey suggests that individuals believe that they have a 'right to roam' on private land, even when this violates the 'rights' of others, such as farmers and other land users. The estate has to take into account this social trend and potential stakeholder conflicts in its planned strategy.

Strategic capability

Finally, the strategy has to take into account the internal resources and competencies of the estate. The estate has significant tangible resources, such as land and property. It also has a unique resource, the only landscape garden developed by James Kent in the district. This is a unique resource which the strategy should aim to exploit. There are also other internal capabilities that should be recognised. A happy, motivated volunteer workforce must be properly utilised by any strategic change, not alienated. Amongst these are volunteers with exceptional skills in land management which could be used to exploit other opportunities on similar estates in the country. Leadership style also needs to be considered. The previous manager was well-liked and successful. Any sudden change in style may cause disruption and a fall in morale. The new leader has to be sensitive to her predecessor's leadership style, whilst building on the success of the previous leader by improving the visitor experience.

The estate has valuable and, in some cases, unique resources, which it needs to exploit with a varied set of stakeholders who sometimes come into conflict with each other. A stakeholder analysis, leading to appropriate stakeholder management policies, seems key here, and may provide some insights into how the website might be improved (part (b) of this question). One of these stakeholders, the government, needs to be particularly monitored, as their policies threaten the funding of the trust.

(b) There is little point in having a well-designed website if it is difficult to find. The role of search engines is significant here. Moor Farm needs to be near the top of the search engine listings for search terms that are directly relevant. The estate needs to discuss what these terms might be. 'Moor Farm' is an obvious one, but searches such as 'walking in rural Cornaille' may bring in visitors who are not aware of the estate's existence. There is conflicting advice on how to structure a website to achieve a high position in a search engine listing. One fool-proof way is to buy sponsored links which are shown as such at the top of the displayed page. Some commercial organisations are dubious about the value of such links, but they seem completely appropriate in the context of a charitable estate.

Although the website is well regarded and well presented, it does not appear to have weather feeds that would avoid people coming on days when the weather was so poor that it might be dangerous, or, as in the quote, when it might spoil a family's enjoyment. The website may have a weather forecast, a feed on current conditions, and perhaps webcams showing the actual weather at a number of agreed locations. Of course, these feeds and webcams will also show good weather conditions as well, perhaps enticing people to the estate who were prevaricating about their visit.

The website currently shows information about events, but it does not allow customers to book these events. The *interactivity* of the site has to be improved, allowing customers to book and pay in advance, so that they can be sure that they will be able to attend the event and avoid the disappointment of the family who travelled 100 km only to find the event fully booked. Such a facility also has advantages for the estate. For example, it has some feel about the popularity of the event before it is run, so that the scale of the event can be altered to reflect the likely demand. Furthermore, payment is received in advance, thus improving cash flow.

Feedback from satisfied customers can be an important factor in attracting new customers. At present the site does not appear to allow visitors to post comments, photographs and recommendations. This means that an effective marketing tool, unsolicited recommendations, do not appear on the site.

Comment has also been made about the enthusiasm and knowledge of the volunteers. This could be harnessed on the site by asking volunteers to write blogs, explaining what they are doing and what is going on. This could be linked through to Twitter and other social networking sites.

Finally, there is obviously a group of regular visitors to Moor Farm who wish to become more involved. As the quotation suggests 'we really want to know what is going on!'. The website can be used to develop a community that supports and promotes the estate. This could be achieved by asking users to register with their email address. They will then receive newsletters, special offers and information about forthcoming events. Special events can be offered to this community and part of the website can be set aside for members of this community. Not only will this provide the estate with valuable resource, it will also allow them to build up a marketing profile of likely visitors and, through surveys and questionnaires, continue to understand what different types of visitor want from the estate.

Marking scheme	
	Marks
1 mark for each appropriate point up to a maximum of	15
1 mark for each relevant point up to a maximum of	10
Total	**25**

29 NOBLE PETS

Key answer tips

It will be important that only primary activities are considered as no marks will be awarded for any discussion on the support activities. When discussing each activity students must bring in relevant information from the scenario rather than describe simple, generic activities.

There are five primary activities in the value chain: inbound logistics, operations, outbound logistics, sales and marketing and service. Each of these is now considered in turn.

Inbound logistics are activities associated with receiving and storing the inputs to the production process. In terms of the costs identified in the scenario, inbound logistics are concerned with raw foodstuff costs, the costs of cans and the transport costs (goods inward). In two of these areas (raw foodstuff costs and can costs) Noble Pets appears to be competitive. However, goods inward costs are higher than any of its competitors. The fact that raw foodstuff costs and can costs are competitive makes it seem unlikely that the high goods inward costs are due to procurement failings. What seems more likely is that the location of the factory makes transport costs higher. Travelling on relatively minor rural roads and negotiating the congested town centre and the growing suburbs of Milton will affect the fuel economy of the trucks which make deliveries to the plant. This will place Noble Pets at a disadvantage compared with competitors who may be located adjacent to major motorways. There is also some reputational damage caused by complaints from local residents kept awake by the trucks.

Operations are concerned with the production activities associated with turning inputs into their final form, outputs.

Production at Noble Pets involves the processing of the raw materials, canning and labelling. In the context of the scenario, these are represented by production costs and direct labour costs. Direct labour costs are roughly in line with its competitors. However, production costs are higher. This is probably associated with the ageing technology of the plant itself. Although it was innovative when it was installed 40 years ago, technology changes have meant that there are more reliable and efficient alternatives available. The physical site is also constrained by housing developments which were built subsequent to the plant. Thus the original plant could not be expanded to obtain any further economies of scale.

Outbound logistics are the activities involved with distributing the product to the customer, in this instance the wholesalers and supermarkets. This area is represented by transport costs (goods outward) included in the table given in the scenario. Like inward logistics, these transport costs are higher than Noble Pets' competitors. This is again partly due to the nature of the roads which lead to the factory and to the congestion in Milton. It also seems very likely that most of the company's customers have relocated to locations which have good road links. Wholesaler and supermarket distribution centres are relatively flexible and footloose and most locate to easily accessible locations. A further problem with outbound logistics is the size of the trucks which can be used to carry the final product. The larger 44 tonne vehicles are banned from Milton town centre, so the company has to continue using the less cost-effective 36 tonne trucks. Again, it is likely that its competitors will be benefiting from the lower unit transport costs offered by the larger trucks.

Sales and marketing is concerned with the activities which make the buyer aware of the product (marketing) and also provide a means by which the buyer can purchase the product (sales). No details of the costs of sales and marketing are provided in the table. However, marketing is an acknowledged strength of the firm and has allowed the company to command a premium price for its products. The term 'noble' itself has positive connotations and appeals to the buyers' sense of duty to feed their pets with what appears to be a superior product. This is significant, because the firm is targeting the buyers of a product who are, in this case, not the consumers of that product.

In fact, the consumers' feedback is probably restricted to the pet's reluctance to eat the food. So advertising campaigns which stress the need for people to give their pets the best and that the best is provided by Noble Pets are very effective. Interestingly, the trend to move from moist foods to dry foods (discussed in part (b)) has been driven by buyers wanting more convenient foods rather than the preferences of the pets themselves.

Service activities are designed to support or enhance the product. Normally, these include services such as installation, repair, training and part supply. In the context of Noble Pets, this can be perceived as the factual information sheets and website designed to promote responsible and appropriate pet ownership. Although the advice is product neutral, its association with Noble Pets enhances the reputation of the company and makes it more likely that consumers will buy its products. The apparently unbiased advice which Noble Pets gives to the community is again an acknowledged strength of the company.

Summary

Noble Pets is a company trapped by its location and its technology. These have led to high transport costs and uncompetitive production costs. It may be possible to address the latter by installing new equipment which is more efficient and reliable, but the business case for replacing all the moist food production facilities depends on future trends in the relative popularity of dry and moist foods. However, it is difficult to see how the company can reduce its transport costs if it remains at the current site.

Perhaps it has to continue relying on strong branding and praiseworthy service to allow it to charge a premium price for a product to buyers who are unaware that its content is really very much the same as its competitors' cheaper alternatives.

Marking scheme	
	Marks
1 mark for each relevant point up to a maximum of 15 marks.	**15**

30   INDEPENDENT LIVING

Key answer tips

In **part (a)** the key to success is to apply the model to the scenario. Be careful to focus on primary activities and avoid the secondary/support activities. This will also be important in **part (b)**. In this part there are 15 marks available spread over the 5 primary activities. So you should aim to make three suggestions for improvements in each of the five areas.

(a)   IL supplies both manufactured products (crutches, walking frames) and bought-in products (mobility scooters, bath lifts). The value chain for these two sets of products is different and this is reflected in the following analysis.

The primary activities of the value chain are:

Inbound logistics

These are activities associated with receiving, storing and disseminating inputs to the product. Typical examples are materials handling, warehousing and inventory (stock) control.

For manufactured products this concerns collection of material from scrap merchants and the storage of that material prior to use. For bought-in products, inbound logistics is handled by the supplying manufacturers. Products are stored in the warehouse.

Operations

This is concerned with transforming inputs into the final product. This includes machining, assembly, testing and packaging. In the context of manufactured products this covers the production of crutches and walkers (and other simple aids), their testing and packaging. For bought-in products, operations is concerned with the careful opening of packaging, the addition of an IL transfer logo, the testing of the equipment and the re-packaging of the product into its original packaging.

Outbound logistics

These are activities associated with storing and then physically distributing the product to buyers. Finished goods warehousing, order processing and delivery is considered here.

At IL, both manufactured and bought-in products need to be stored prior to delivery. Distribution is undertaken by a national courier company. Orders are placed by telephone or through the website.

Marketing and sales

These are activities by which customers can learn of the existence of and then purchase the products. It includes advertising, promotion, sales and pricing.

At IL this covers leaflets in hospitals and surgeries, a website catalogue and order taking and the giving of advice.

Service

These are activities associated with providing a service to enhance or maintain the value of the product. It includes installation, repair, training, parts supply and product adjustment. The simple nature of the manufactured products means that service is inappropriate. For bought-in product, service is undertaken by the original manufacturer.

(b) The value chain is used as a basis for answering the question. Many of the potential re-structuring suggestions produce cost reductions. However, it must be acknowledged that the charity also has the objective of providing jobs for severely disabled people. Suggestions for change have to reflect this fact. It is also clear from the scenario that some customers are prepared to pay price premiums for the goods by making donations to the charity as part of their purchase of these goods.

Inbound logistics

For bought in products, IL could explore the possibility of reducing scrap metal storage costs by requesting dealers to store the metal until it is required. Furthermore, dealers may also be able to offer competitive delivery costs. This would remove the need for IL to maintain (and eventually replace) the lorry it uses for collection of this material. For bought in products, IL could explore the cost of using a specialist logistics company to carry out both its inbound and outbound logistics. This should produce economies of scale leading to reduced costs. Many of these logistics companies also offer storage facilities. However, IL already has storage at an airfield site and the employment of severely disabled labour is one of its objectives.

Operations

It seems vital that IL retains its manufacturing capability to help achieve its goal of providing work and income for severely disabled people. It could probably gain cost savings by outsourcing manufacture to cheaper countries (like its commercial competitors) but this would not meet its core objective. IL marketing could stress the location of the manufacture as an important differentiator. Customers might then perceive it as an ethical choice.

The operations part of the value chain for bought-in products is relatively labour intensive (see later notes) and could be simplified in two ways.

1   Asking manufacturers to affix the IL logo and label prior to despatch to IL. The testing of the products could also be delegated to the manufacturer as they provide post-delivery support.

2   Reducing inventory by arranging for bought in goods to be supplied to the customer directly by the manufacturer. Not only would this cut delivery costs but it would also reduce inventory costs, and eliminate the costly write-off of obsolete purchased inventory.

Employees in the warehouse could be reallocated to order processing and other administrative tasks.

Outbound logistics

The ordering of products through the website appears to be extremely effective. The site includes a product catalogue and a secure payment facility. However, although use of the website is growing, most orders are still placed by telephone.

IL might consider ways of encouraging further use of the website, for example by offering discounts, cheaper prices and a wider range of products. It might also consider how it could make its website more available to potential consumers, perhaps by placing dedicated terminals in hospitals and surgeries.

The telephone ordering process is currently too complex because sales staff have to describe the products available and also provide purchasing advice and guidance. IL needs to consider ways of making details of their product range available to customers before they place the order (see below).

Marketing and sales

Relatively little sales and marketing takes place at IL which is probably due its charitable status. Charities are usually very keen to minimise their overhead costs. Traditional marketing appears to be very limited, restricted to leaflets in hospitals and surgeries. IL could consider replacing its current leaflets (which just give a phone number and a website) with a leaflet that effectively doubles as a catalogue, showing the products on offer. This should help improve the efficiency of the telephone ordering service. Display advertising in magazines and newspapers with coupons to request a catalogue would also increase the profile of the brand.

Many charities use Customer Relationship Management (CRM) systems to manage their donors. IL should explore the potential of this. It already has records of purchasers and also those purchasers that have made extra donations.

All sales and marketing material needs to stress the charitable status of the organisation. This effectively differentiates it from commercial competitors. There is already evidence that some customers are willing to reflect this by increasing the price they pay for goods by including a donation to support the charity.

Service

Because of the nature of the product, little direct support is required. However, IL could expand its website to give general support and advice on mobility problems and independent living.

Marking scheme		Marks
(a)	Up to 1 mark for identifying each primary activity (for example, inbound logistics) and up to 2 marks for discussing its application to IL in both contexts (metal scrap collection, supplier delivery) up to a maximum of 10 marks.	10
(b)	Up to 1 mark for each significant point (for example, arrange bought in products to be delivered directly to the customer from the manufacturer) up to a maximum of 15 marks.	15
Total		**25**

31   MMI *Walk in the footsteps of a top tutor*

Tutor's top tips

Part (a): *This part of the question asked students to explain why two acquisitions had taken place and assess their post-acquisition performance.*

Key to success:

Models such as Porter's acquisition tests or the BCG matrix will give structure to the answer.

*As is usual with financial analysis the key to getting the marks will be to explain **why** a ratio has changed and **what** the implications of such a change might be. There wasn't much financial information provided so use as much of it as possible.*

Dangers:

Not using the financial analysis

Not recognizing that the requirement had two elements (explain why the acquisitions had happened, and assessing their performance).

Part (b): *Having assessed two acquisitions that had already taken place, students were asked to assess a third proposed acquisition.*

Key to success:

Apply the same techniques that were used in part (a). So use a model if possible and include financial analysis. Students could also have used the suitability, feasibility, and acceptability approach suggested by Johnson, Scholes and Whittington.

Make a recommendation as to whether the acquisition should proceed and justify it. It doesn't matter whether you think the acquisition should go ahead or not, as long as you have an opinion one way or the other and can back it up with sensible analysis.

(a)   **First Leisure**

The initial motivation for the acquisition of First Leisure was the need to diversify out of a declining market place (falling 5% over the recorded period) into an expanding one (increasing over 25% in the recorded period). The cash generated by the quarrying company was used to purchase a profitable, well-run company in an expanding market. Diversification was a direct response to environmental changes. Increased costs and falling reserves meant that there was little chance of finding new sites in its core market. MMI initially played no managerial role in First Leisure, allowing the managers who had made it successful to continue running the company. However, buying a company concerned with leisure appeared to be an example of unrelated diversification and there were some negative comments about the financial wisdom of this acquisition.

After a period of consolidation, certain unexpected synergies emerged that had not been clear at the time of acquisition. These came from the conversion of disused or unprofitable quarry sites into leisure parks. This conversion was doubly advantageous.

In the first instance it reduced the operating costs of MMI, allowing it to shed costs associated with running unprofitable mines and maintaining security and safety at disused sites.

Secondly, it allowed First Leisure to acquire sites relatively easily and cheaply in an environment where it was becoming more expensive and harder, because of planning restrictions, to purchase new sites. Johnson, Scholes and Whittington discuss the principles of economies of scope where an organisation has underutilised resources that it cannot effectively use or dispose of. It makes sense to switch these if possible to a new activity, in this instance leisure parks.

The turnover of First Leisure has doubled in six years. The figures summarised in table 1 suggest an expanding company in an expanding market and its market share continues to grow (up from 13% to 21% in the recorded period). Furthermore, gross profit margins have remained fairly constant but recent increases in the net profit margin suggests that costs appear to be under control, despite the recent issues concerning the supply of boats from Boatland. In corporate management terms MMI probably perceived that it would initially be playing a 'portfolio management' role at First Leisure.

However, the discovery of unexpected synergies has led to it adopting (and perhaps claiming in hindsight) a synergy manager role. In terms of the BCG matrix, First Leisure exhibits all the characteristics of a star business unit and so it should be retained in the portfolio. It has a high market share in a growing market and increasing margins means that even if it has spent heavily to gain this share (and there is no direct evidence of this in the scenario), costs are now beginning to fall.

Boatland

The synergies that emerged from acquiring First Leisure appear to have been unexpected. However, the acquisition of Boatland in 20X6 was largely justified on the grounds of synergy. Synergies were expected with First Leisure and with MMI itself. By this time the directors felt that they had built up significant managerial competencies that could be successfully applied to acquired companies. These managerial competencies could be used to drive extra value from underperforming companies and so deliver benefits to shareholders.

In the case of Boatland the expected synergies with First Leisure were as follows:

- First Leisure had experienced difficulties in the supply and maintenance of boats for their leisure parks. Boatland seemed to offer a way out of this problem. First Leisure would become a preferred customer of Boatland, taking priority over other customers. MMI also perceived that cost savings could be found by bringing boat manufacture and maintenance into the Group. In this instance, MMI was pursuing a policy of backward integration, producing one of the inputs into First Leisure's current business activities.

- Secondly, Boatland itself appeared to be undervalued. The management team appeared to lack ambition, focusing on producing a limited number of craft to high specification. It was felt that the production of boats for First Leisure would help the company expand, allowing it to increase market share partly based on guaranteed orders from First Leisure.

In this instance MMI probably thought of itself as a synergy manager, helping Boatland develop strategic capabilities and exploiting synergies with both MMI and First Leisure. However, the acquisition has not brought the expected benefits.

The boats provided for First Leisure have not been appropriately constructed for their purpose and, paradoxically, because of the way they are misused by holiday makers, maintenance costs and 'downtime' has increased. Furthermore, the status of First Leisure as a preferred customer has led to delays in boat manufacture and maintenance for established customers.

Orders have fallen and so has the reputation of the company. This is reflected in the data provided in table 1. Revenue and market share has fallen in a static market place. More worrying is the significant fall in gross and net profit margins. The net profit margin has fallen from 13.04% in 2002 to just 4.29% in 20X8. Furthermore, difficulties also have been created for First Leisure, which are also disturbing its relationship with MMI. The problem at Boatland appears to be cultural and this is reflected not only on the results but in the loss of experienced boat building employees. When the company was bought it concentrated on building a small number of high quality boats to discerning customers who valued and cherished their boats. In contrast, First Leisure required a large number of simple, robust boats that could be used and abused by holiday makers. The products and markets are different and the perceived synergy was an illusion.

In BCG terms Boatland has a very small share of a static market which would class it as a dog. Although there is no evidence of it being a cash drain on MMI the conflict between the culture of Boatland and the cultures of MMI and First Leisure probably used up a disproportionate amount of company time and resources. It seems sensible to divest Boatland from the portfolio. However, the supply implications of this to First Leisure will have to be investigated and so divestment may have to wait until First Leisure has built up a relationship with an alternative supplier.

(b)   **Introduction**

Since 2002 MMI have built up a small portfolio of businesses that reflect different strategic directions. It has consolidated in its own market by shedding unprofitable or closed quarries and purchasing smaller competitors. This is reflected in the data given in table 1. During a period when the marketplace has declined by 5%, MMI has increased its market share from 20% to 28%. Gross profitability has remained fairly steady during the period, but the net profit margin has increased significantly since 2004. The increase in market share is probably due to the acquisition, in 2004, of two smaller competitors. The increase in the net profit margin can largely be traced to the disposal of redundant and unprofitable quarries to First Leisure. MMI's attempts at diversification have had mixed success. First Leisure, acquired in 2002, turned out to be an inspired acquisition as unexpected synergies emerged which assisted MMI's profitability. However, the expected synergies from the Boatland purchase have not materialised and MMI appear to have destroyed rather than created value in this acquisition.

In 2004 MMI acquired two of its smaller competitors, bringing five further mines or quarries into the group. MMI introduced its own managers into these companies resulting in a spectacular rise in revenues and profits that caused the CEO of MMI to claim that corporate management capabilities were now an important asset of MMI. So there appears to be evidence that MMI management can successfully improve the performance of an acquisition. However, Boatland is in a significantly different industry to these earlier acquisitions. MMI managers are familiar with the management of mines and quarries and probably found that the employees of these companies shared the culture of an industry they were familiar with. In contrast, at Boatland the sought after synergy was with First Leisure, not MMI, and so the MMI managers entered an industry and an environment they were unfamiliar with.

Evidence from the First Leisure and Boatland acquisitions suggests that MMI is more successful when it employs a 'hands-off' approach to managing acquisitions which are not directly related to its core mining and quarrying operations. The incumbent management team are left to get on with the job with minimal interference from MMI.

InfoTech

The current financial position of InfoTech suggests that its management team may not be able to deliver the turnaround required. Market share and gross and net profit margins have fallen over the recorded period. Revenues have decreased by 16% at InfoTech in a period where the size of the market has increased by almost 25%. If MMI acquires InfoTech then the preferred 'hands-off' approach will be very risky, particularly considering the financial investment the company requires. MMI appears to have two alternatives if it goes ahead with the acquisition.

The first is to learn from its experience at Boatland and install managers who are more sensitive to the culture of the organisation and the industry as a whole. To do this, they will have to recognise that their perceived value adding managerial capabilities actually turned out to be value destroying at Boatland. MMI could recruit managers with established track records in the information technology industry. However, there is no evidence that MMI has successfully adopted this approach before.

The financial position alluded to above also needs to be considered. Boatland and First Leisure were both successful, profitable companies when they were acquired. In contrast, Infotech is making a loss and appears to require investment which it has failed to secure in its own right. This is a controversial reason for acquisition and in this context MMI is playing the role of a portfolio manager, one it has never played for a failing company. In terms of the BCG matrix, InfoTech is a business unit in a growing market but with a low market share. It would be defined as a question mark or problem child.

Suitability is one of the three success criteria Johnson, Scholes and Whittington use to judge strategic options. An approach which evaluates whether the acquisition addresses the situation in which MMI and InfoTech are operating would be a perfectly valid approach to answering this question.

	Marking scheme	
		Marks
(a)	**First Leisure**	
	Up to 2 marks for recognising that this unrelated diversification was driven by environmental change; supported by appropriate data.	
	Up to 2 marks for issues concerning economies of scope	
	Up to 3 marks for interpreting the financial and market data.	
	Up to 2 marks for recognising the likely parenting role and for locating First Leisure on an appropriate analysis matrix.	
	Boatland	
	Up to 2 marks for recognising the synergies expected from Boatland.	
	Up to 2 marks for interpreting the financial and market data.	
	Up to 3 marks for explaining the failure of the acquisition.	
	Up to 2 marks for recognising the likely parenting role and for locating Boatland in an appropriate analysis matrix.	15
(b)	Up to 3 marks for interpreting the financial performance of MMI and summarising its acquisition strategy.	
	Up to 2 marks for recognising that a 'hands-off' approach has been more successful when MMI has pursued unrelated diversification	
	Up to 2 marks for recognising the difficulty of pursuing this approach at InfoTech	
	Up to 2 marks for interpreting the financial and market data	
	Up to 2 marks for recognising the likely parenting role and for locating InfoTech in an appropriate analysis matrix	10
Total		**25**

32   OCEANIA NATIONAL AIRLINES (ONA) *Walk in the footsteps of a top tutor*

Tutor's top tips

Overview of the requirement

From the first paragraph in this question you can discover:

- *there are 2 distinct markets – tourists and business users*

- *the company runs an airline business*

- *they aim to exploit the growth in business and leisure travel*

Requirement

(a)   Evaluation of strengths and weaknesses

The key too many requirements is to choose an appropriate model to give structure and focus. The key will be to choose the most appropriate model, build an answer around that model, and then, if you have time, to briefly show how other models could have been useful.

The question clearly states that opportunities and threats are not required, so the SWOT model would be inappropriate. However, the first part of the model (SW) could have been used – this is what the answer does. An assessment of strengths and weaknesses is an internal assessment and therefore an internal tool such as the resource audit or the value chain would have been most appropriate.

It is important to choose the model with which you are most comfortable. For the purpose of this walkthrough the resource audit (sometimes called the 'M's model') is chosen. A brief plan of the resource audit could be set up on a blank page with space for each of the key areas (i.e. manpower, machinery, markets, money etc.). This can be used to record key information in the question as you read it, and also it should ensure that you do not miss anything important from your answer.

(b)   Strategy evaluation

The question asks for an explanation and evaluation of a 'no frills' strategy. One approach is to use three criteria: feasibility, suitability and acceptability. So again, these headings can be recorded on a planning page and you can add points to them as you read the question.]

(c)   Strategic choice

The key again will be to determine which model will be most appropriate. There are 3 choices: Porter's generics, the strategic clock or Ansoff. The first two models will be important if ONA want to improve their position, the second would be most appropriate if ONA are looking for new ways to grow. It is not entirely clear which goal is most relevant at this stage, so part of the task when reading the question should be to determine which model is most relevant.

Reading the exhibits

The key issues to pick out from the question as are as follows:

- *ONA serve two markets – the regional and international sectors. Therefore, when choosing strategies in part c), you should choose a strategy for each sector.*

- *The company's strengths seem to be laid out clearly in the section on image, service and employment. Weaknesses are less apparent and it is therefore very likely that they will arise from numerical analysis of the three sets of data that have been provided.*

- *The market is very competitive and there have been lots of new entrants (especially at the 'no frills' part of the market).*

- *Sales channels appear to be a critical success factor and it will be important that answers discuss the issues between using website sales and travel agent sales.*

- *In the section on future strategy it appears that ONA want to solve their existing problems rather than try new markets or diversify, so for part c) of the question Porter's generics or the strategic clock may be more important than the Ansoff matrix.*

Answering the question

Part (a) Strengths and weaknesses

This is the analysis part of the question and therefore one of the most important things to remember will be to include an analysis of the numbers that have been provided in Exhibits 2 and 3. There are no marks for illustrating, explaining or calculating ratios so don't get bogged down on these. Also, you should only need to calculate the ratios for 20X4 and 20X6 rather than doing the calculations for all three years which would add little to your answer. Instead, allocate around half of the total marks for quantitative analysis (therefore 10 marks) and work on the basis of around 2 marks for each well explained point. This means that you should choose 5 or 6 key ratios and explain why they might have changed and whether they create a strength or weakness for the company.

For example, there has been a 2.5% fall in net profit margin which could be down to poor control of overheads (e.g. wages and salaries) and this indicates a weakness of the business.

For other strengths and weaknesses, go through as many of the 'M's' in the resource audit as possible. Remember for each one that you should explain why it is a strength or weakness. If we take 'manpower' as an example; the service provided and motivation of staff can be seen as a strength of ONA. But on the other hand, the fact that salaries are above industry average and have attached expensive benefits will create a weakness for the company.

This is just one part of the resource audit, but all of the elements can be considered in the same manner in order to create a complete answer to this part of the question when combined with the quantitative analysis.

Part (b) Strategy evaluation

Explaining what a 'no frills' strategy is should be relatively straight forward for all students.

For the second part it is very important to reach the same conclusion as the company – that this is an inappropriate strategy for ONA.

If you use the feasibility, suitability and acceptability model suggested by Johnson, Scholes and Whittington you should achieve a good, well balanced answer. Some of the key issues might be as follows:

(i)   *Feasibility*

This examines whether a strategy is possible based on a company's current resources and position. Therefore it will be important to link it back to some of the issues discovered in part a).

The key issues to discuss might be:

- *ONA have higher wage rates than rivals*

- *because ONA have older aircraft their maintenance costs are likely to be higher*

- *it would be easier to achieve if the sales channels were changed so that more sales were made via a website than through the travel agents*

- *ONA may need to seek out alternative airports with lower landing fees and baggage handling costs etc.*

- *it should be possible to copy the ideas of successful 'no frills' airlines and avoid their past mistakes*

(ii)   *Suitability*

This examines whether the strategy is appropriate for the company's environment and whether it will solve the businesses problems.

The key issues to discuss might be:

- *there is already significant competition in this part of the market who will have lower cost bases and more experience at offering a no frill service*

- *these rivals may also react aggressively to any attempt by ONA to enter the market*

- *in order for ONA to achieve this strategy greater economies of scale would be necessary. This would mean an investment in more aircraft, more destinations etc. but it is likely that ONA would still be behind the scale of rivals*

(iii)   *Acceptability*

This area examines whether the strategy will be acceptable to the key stakeholders of the business.

The key issues to discuss might be:

- *this is likely to require a reduction in customer service – something that ONA prides itself on. This may be unacceptable to both customers and shareholders*

- *moving to alternative/cheaper destinations may not be acceptable to business users*

- *a change of selling channels may not be acceptable to the citizens of Oceania who have a culture of using travel agents to make their bookings.*

Overall, there are 16 marks available which allows for about 5 marks for each of the three evaluation criteria. So you should aim to cover 3 issues under each of the headings above and finish with an overall conclusion that this is an inappropriate strategy.

Part (c) Strategic choice

As already stated it will probably be more relevant in this section to use a competitive strategy model, such as Porter's generics or the strategic clock, than to use the Ansoff matrix. Also, as there are 2 market segments (regional and international) then the answer can choose strategies for each segment. There are around 4/5 marks available for each segment so you should only have to make 2 points for each one. The key will be to make the points relevant to the company in the question and to avoid suggesting a no frills approach that has already been discarded in part b).

Overall

The key points to take away from this question and apply to other compulsory, strategic questions are:

- *find the requirements before reading the full question*

- *for each part of the question, choose one key model and apply it to the scenario*

- *include quantitative analysis in all analysis answers*

- *allocate your time appropriately between all sections of the requirement.*

(a)   Strengths

1   Strong brand identity particularly with the citizens of Oceania. A quoted recent survey suggested that 90% of people preferred to travel ONA for regional flights and 70% preferred to travel ONA for international flights. 85% of respondents were proud of their airline and felt that it projected a positive image of Oceania.

2   ONA have an exemplary safety record. There have been no fatal accidents since its formation in 1997.

3   Excellent customer service recognised by the Regional Airline of the Year award and the Golden Bowl as provider of the best airline food in the world.

4   High business class load factors, particularly in the regional sector. This appears to suggest that ONA are particularly strong in the business market.

5   Relatively strong cargo performance. In the period 20X4–20X6 when passenger air travel revenue had increased by 12% (and air travel to Oceania by 15%) and cargo revenue by 10%, ONA increased cargo revenue by 11%, just above the industry average.

6   Financially, although the net profit margin has fallen (see weaknesses), the gross profit margin remains relatively stable. Hence the cost of sales (excluding wages, salaries and financing) has moved roughly in line with revenue. The gross profit margin for 20X4 is 37.04% and for 20X6 it is 36.98%, very little change.

7   The settlement of debt is an important issue for an organisation. The average settlement period for receivables is concerned with how long it takes for customers to pay the amounts owing. This is low at ONA (29 days) and reducing, suggesting effective credit control and an industry where many customers pay before they are able to use the service. It is likely that much of the debt is tied-up with commission sales and cargo services.

8   The gearing ratio measures the contribution of long-term lenders to the long-term capital structure of the business. Gearing for ONA remained relatively stable during the period 20X4–20X6. It stood at 71.13% in 20X6, a marginal increase on the 20X4 figure of 71.05%.

9   Conveniently scheduled flights to business travel for the regional sector. Allows business to be conducted in one day, with a flight out in the morning and a flight back in the evening. Most cities in this sector also receive an extra flight in the middle of the day.

10   Highly motivated, courteous employees.

Weaknesses

1   High cost base. The most tangible evidence of this is the average pilot salary given in Table 1. Pilot salary costs appear to be over 10% higher than their competitors. The scenario also suggests that ONA pay above industry average salaries, offer excellent benefits (such as free health care) and have a generous non-contributory pension scheme. Other hints of high costs (insourced non-core activities such as catering, highly unionised) are also mentioned in the scenario. High costs are also hinted at in Tables 1 and 2, with ONA having relatively older aircraft, presumably requiring more maintenance, and lower utilisation hours than their competitors. The average wage of an employee rose by about 7% during the period under consideration.

2   Poor growth rate. The scenario makes the point that in the period 20X4–20X6, passenger air travel revenue has increased world-wide by 12% (and revenue from air travel to Oceania by 15%). However, ONA only recorded a 4.6% increase in passenger revenue in this period.

3   Low frequency of flights in the international sector, where there is on average only one flight per day to each destination. This makes it very difficult for the airline to gain any operational economies of scale in this sector.

4   The mixed airliner fleet is largely a result of the merger of the two airlines that formed ONA. The airframes for the bulk of the fleet are from two competing manufacturers (Boeing and Airbus). The information given in Table 1 suggests that the two aircraft types (Boeing 737 and A320) are very similar. The need to service and maintain two aircraft types creates an unnecessary cost.

5   Although the airline offers on-line booking, it does not currently offer on-line check-in. Hence overheads still remain in the embarkation process. Business travellers particularly favour on-line check-in as it means they can leave their homes and meetings later. In 20X6 the New Straits Times reported a recent global survey that showed that air travellers spend an average of four days in a year in queues at airline check-in counters.

6   Table 2 shows below average load factors in standard class seating. This is particularly significant on international sector flights.

7   Return on capital employed (ROCE) and return on ordinary shareholders' funds (ROSF) are important measures of profitability. Both of these ratios show a significant fall in 20X6. The fall can be largely attributed to a decline in net profit due to increases in costs outstripping increases in revenue.

8   The reduction in profitability is also revealed by the net profit margin which has reduced from 12.10% in 20X4 to 9.66% in 20X6. However, the gross profit percentage remains relatively stable and so it appears that it is the increased cost of wages, salaries and borrowing that has caused ONA profitability problems.

9   Efficiency ratios are used to examine how well the resources of the business are managed. The sales revenue per employee has reduced during the period, perhaps suggesting a reduction in productivity that needs to be investigated. In contrast, the average settlement period for payables shows a marginal rise.

Trade payables provide a free source of finance, but extending the average settlement period too far can lead to loss of goodwill with suppliers. ONA already have a high settlement period for payables, although this may be typical in this industry.

10   Liquidity (both current and acid test ratios) fell significantly in 20X6. This may affect the ability of the company to meet its short-term obligations.

11   Finally, the interest cover ratio has declined considerably during the period covered in Table 1. In 20X4, it was 5.44, but by 20X6 it had declined to 3.73. The lower the level of profit coverage, the greater the risk to lenders that interest payments will not be met.

Credit will also be given to points which are discernible from the scenario but have not been covered above. The extent of unionisation and the percentage of sales made through commission sales might be thought of as strengths or weaknesses depending upon perspective.

(b)   **(i)**   A 'no frills' strategy combines low price with low perceived benefits of the product or service. It is primarily associated with commodity goods and services where customers do not discern or value differences in the products or services offered by competing suppliers. In some circumstances the customer cannot afford the better quality product or service of a particular supplier. 'No frills' strategies are particularly attractive in price-sensitive markets. Within the airline sector, the term 'no frills' is associated with a low cost pricing strategy. In Europe, at the time of writing, easyJet and Ryanair are the two dominant 'no frills' low-cost budget airlines. In Asia, AirAsia and Tiger Airways are examples of 'no frills' low-cost budget carriers. 'No frills' strategies usually exist in markets where buyers have high power coupled with low switching costs and so there is little brand loyalty.

It is also prevalent in markets where there are few providers with similar market shares. As a result of this the cost structure of each provider is similar and new product and service initiatives are quickly copied. Finally a 'no frills' strategy might be pursued by a company entering the market, using this as a strategy to gain market share before progressing to alternative strategies.

(ii)   'No frills' low-cost budget airlines are usually associated with the following characteristics. Each of these characteristics is considered in the context of Oceania National Airlines (ONA).

- **Operational economies of scale**

  Increased flight frequency brings operational economies and is attractive to both business and leisure travellers. In the international sector where ONA is currently experiencing competition from established 'no frills' low-cost budget airlines ONA has, on average, one flight per day to each city. It would have to greatly extend its flight network, flight frequency and the size of its aircraft fleet if it planned to become a 'no frills' carrier in this sector. This fleet expansion appears counter to the culture of an organisation that has expanded very gradually since its formation. Table 1 shows only three aircraft added to the fleet in the period 20X4–20X6.

It is likely that the fleet size would have to double for ONA to become a serious 'no frills' operator in the international sector. In the regional sector, the flight density, an average of three flights per day, is more characteristic of a 'no frills' airline. However, ONA would have to address the relatively low utilisation of its aircraft (see Tables 1 and 2) and the cost of maintenance associated with a relatively old fleet of aircraft.

- **Reduced costs through direct sales**

On-line booking is primarily aimed at eliminating commission sales (usually made through travel agents). 'No frills' low-cost budget airlines typically achieve over 80% of their sales on-line. The comparative figure for ONA (see Table 2) is 40% for regional sales and 60% for international sales, compared with an average of 84% for their competitors. Clearly a major change in selling channels would have to take place for ONA to become a 'no frills' low-cost budget airline. It is difficult to know whether this is possible. The low percentage of regional on-line sales seems to suggest that the citizens of Oceania may be more comfortable buying through third parties such as travel agents.

- **Reduced customer service**

'No frills' low-cost budget airlines usually do not offer customer services such as free meals, free drinks and the allocation of passengers to specific seats. ONA prides itself on its in-flight customer service and this was one of the major factors that led to its accolade as Regional Airline of the Year. To move to a 'no frills' strategy, ONA would have to abandon a long held tradition of excellent customer service. This would require a major cultural change within the organisation. It would also probably lead to disbanding the award winning (Golden Bowl) catering department and the redundancies of catering staff could prove difficult to implement in a heavily unionised organisation.

Johnson, Scholes and Whittington have suggested that if an organisation is to 'achieve competitive advantage through a low price strategy then it has two basic choices. The first is to try and identify a market segment which is unattractive (or inaccessible) to competitors and in this way avoid competitive pressures to erode price.' It is not possible for ONA to pursue this policy in the international sector because of significant competition from established continental 'no frills' low-cost budget airlines. It may be a candidate strategy for the regional sector, but the emergence of small 'no frills' low-cost budget airlines in these countries threaten this. Many of these airlines enter the market with very low overheads and use the 'no frills' approach as a strategy to gain market share before progressing to alternative strategies.

Secondly, a 'no frills' strategy depends for its success on margin. Johnson, Scholes and Whittington suggest that 'in the long run, a low price strategy cannot be pursued without a low-cost base'. Evidence from the scenario suggests that ONA does not have a low cost base. It continues to maintain overheads (such as a catering department) that its competitors have either disbanded or outsourced. More fundamentally (from Table 2), its flight crew enjoy above average wages and the whole company is heavily unionised. The scenario acknowledges that the company pays above industry salaries and offers excellent benefits such as a generous non-contributory pension. Aircraft utilisation and aircraft age also suggest a relatively high cost base. The aircraft are older than their competitors and presumably incur greater maintenance costs. ONA's utilisation of its aircraft is also lower than its competitors.

It seems highly unlikely that ONA can achieve the changes required in culture, cost base and operations required for it to become a 'no frills' low-cost budget airline. Other factors serve to reinforce this. For example:

- Many 'no frills' low-cost budget airlines fly into airports that offer cheaper taking off and landing fees. Many of these airports are relatively remote from the cities they serve. This may be acceptable to leisure travellers, but not to business travellers – ONA's primary market in the regional sector.

- Most 'no frills' low-cost budget airlines have a standardised fleet leading to commonality and familiarity in maintenance. Although ONA has a relatively small fleet it is split between three aircraft types. This is due to historical reasons. The Boeing 737s and Airbus A320s appear to be very similar aircraft. However, the Boeings were inherited from OceaniaAir and the Airbuses from Transport Oceania.

In conclusion, the CEO's decision to reject a 'no frills' strategy for ONA appears to be justifiable. It would require major changes in structure, cost and culture that would be difficult to justify given ONA's current position.

Revolution is the term used by Balogun and Hope to describe a major rapid strategic change. It is associated with a sudden transformation required to react to extreme pressures on the organisation. Such an approach is often required when the company is facing a crisis and needs to quickly change direction. There is no evidence to support the need for a radical transformation. This is why the CEO brands the change to a 'no frills' low-cost budget airline as 'unnecessary'. The financial situation (Table 3) is still relatively healthy and there is no evidence of corporate predators. It can be argued that a more incremental approach to change would be beneficial, building on the strengths of the organisation and the competencies of its employees. Moving ONA to a 'no frills' model would require seismic changes in cost and culture.

If ONA really wanted to move into this sector then they would be better advised to start afresh with a separate brand and airline and to concentrate on the regional sector where it has a head start over many of its competitors.

(c) Within the strategy clock, ONA might consider both differentiation and focus. A differentiation strategy seeks to provide products or services that offer different benefits from those offered by competitors. These benefits are valued by customers and so can lead to increased market share and, in the context of ONA, higher seat utilisation. Differentiation is particularly attractive when it provides the opportunity of providing a price premium. In other words, margins are enhanced through differentiation. Air travellers may be willing to pay more to travel with an airline that offers seat allocation and free in-flight food and drinks.

However, such a broad-based differentiation strategy may be inappropriate for ONA because of the need to service both business and leisure travellers. Consequently, the potential strategy also has to be considered in the context of the two sectors that the company perceives that it services. In the regional sector a focused differentiation strategy looks particularly attractive. Here, the strategy focuses on a selected niche or market segment. The most obvious focus is on business travel and building the company's strengths in this sector. This focus on the business traveller might be achieved through:

- Ensuring that flight times are appropriate for the business working day. This is already a perceived strength of the company. This needs to be built on.

- Providing more space in the aircraft by changing the seating configuration – and the balance between business and standard class. ONA currently has a low seat occupancy rate and a reduction in seat capacity could be borne.

- Fewer passengers in the aircraft may also lead to improved throughput times. Loading and unloading aircraft is quicker, minimising the delays encountered by the traveller.

- Providing supporting business services – lounges with fax and internet facilities.

- Speeding the process of booking and embarkation (through electronic check-in), so making the process of booking and embarkation easier and faster.

- Providing loyalty schemes that are aimed at the business traveller.

Although this focused differentiation is aimed at the business customer it is also likely that particular aspects of it will be valued by certain leisure travellers. Given the strong regional brand (people from Oceania are likely to travel ONA) and the nature of the leisure travel in this sector (families visiting relatives) it seems unlikely that there will be a significant fall off in leisure travel in the regional sector.

In the international sector, the strategic customer is less clear. This sector is serving both the leisure and business market and is also competing with strong 'no frills' competitors. The nature of customer and competition is different. A strategy of differentiation could still be pursued, although perhaps general differentiation (without a price premium) may be more effective with the aim of increasing seat occupancy rate. This sector would also benefit from most of the suggested improvements of the regional sector – providing more space in aircraft, faster passenger throughput, electronic check-in etc. However, these small changes will not address the relatively low flight frequency in this sector. This could be addressed through seeking alliances with established airlines in the continental countries that it services. Simple code share agreements could double ONA's frequencies overnight. Obviously, ONA would be seeking a good cultural fit – the 'no frills' low-cost budget airlines would not be candidates for code shares.

ONA's perception of market segmentation, reflected in splitting regional from international travel and distinguishing leisure from business appears to be a sensible understanding of the marketplace. However, it might also be useful for them to consider on-line customers and commission customers (travel agents) as different segments. Perceiving travel agents as the strategic customer would lead to a different strategic focus, one in which the amount and structure of commission played an important part.

Finally, whichever strategy ONA adopts, it must continue to review its operational efficiency. An important strategic capability in any organisation is to ensure that attention is paid to cost-efficiency. It can be argued that a continual reduction in costs is necessary for any organisation in a competitive market. Management of costs is a threshold competence for survival. ONA needs to address some of the weaknesses identified earlier in the question. Specific points, not covered elsewhere, include:

- Improved employee productivity to address the downward decline in efficiency ratios.

- Progressive standardisation of the fleet to produce economies of scale in maintenance and training. This should reduce the cost base.

- Careful monitoring of expenditure, particularly on wages and salaries, to ensure that these do not exceed revenue increases.

Marking scheme – technical marks		
		Marks
(a)	Up to 2 marks for each identified strength up to a maximum of 10 marks for strengths	
	Up to 2 marks for each identified weakness up to a maximum of 10 marks for weaknesses	20
(b)	(i) Up to 1 mark for each relevant point up to a maximum of 4 marks	
	(ii) Up to 2 marks for each relevant point concerning the inappropriateness of a no-frills solution, up to a maximum of 16 marks	20
(c)	Explanation of alternative strategies: Up to 2 marks for each significant point up to a maximum of 10 marks.	10
Total		**50**

How well has the candidate demonstrated Professional Skills as follows:	Not at all	Not well	Quite well	Very well
Evaluation skills in appraising the issues identified	The candidate has failed to consider whether the strategy is or isn't appropriate.	The candidate has concluded that the strategy is appropriate for ONA.	The candidate has concluded that the strategy is inappropriate for ONA but has a weak argument to support this.	The candidate has a rational argument to support a conclusion that the strategy is inappropriate.
	0	0.5	1	2

33 LING

Key answer tips

Part (a) of this question should be very comfortable for students. But, many students are likely to ignore the fact that there are only seven marks available and therefore induce undue time pressure for the rest of the question.

Part (b) is more likely to suit student expectations on the marks available for this type of requirement. The use of an appropriate model should provide some structure and focus to answers.

For **parts (c) and (d)** the key to success will be ensuring that answers are related to the scenario rather than being a simple regurgitation of study notes.

(a)   Environmental analysis

A PESTEL analysis identifies the main drivers in the external environment which are largely outside the control of the company. The relevance of these factors may depend upon whether Ling decides to enter the light bulb market directly or to enter it by acquiring a Skod-based company. In some instances the driver affects the industry wherever it is based.

Political

The government is considering the imposition of import taxes. This would be a threat if Ling decides to enter the market place using the distribution company approach and keep manufacturing in Lindisztan. However, it presents an opportunity if Ling decides to acquire Flick and continue to run it as a Skod-based company.

Economic

Although the country of Skod is in recession and consumer disposable income is falling, it seems unlikely that such a low cost commodity product will be greatly affected. This is an industry which is unlikely to be touched by changes in economic prosperity. The only minor issue may be the effect of switching off street lights. This may lengthen the life span of the bulb. However, overall, this is likely to have very little effect on total light bulb demand.

Sociocultural

There is a growing nationalist movement in Skod who are keen to keep jobs within the country. There have been instances, in other industries, where imported goods have been boycotted. It seems unlikely that a backlash against foreign goods would affect such an unglamorous product as a light bulb. However, it is possible, and any potential consumer backlash can be avoided by buying a Skod-based company and manufacturing light bulbs in the country.

Technical

Ling has so far benefitted from technological innovations which has put it ahead of competitors who have focused on candescent and halogen bulbs. However, other lighting initiatives, such as the tubular daylighting devices discussed in the Lighting Tomorrow article need to be continually monitored. This monitoring is required whether Ling enters the Skod market directly, or acquires a company such as Flick.

Legal

The 'efficient lighting' legislation due to become law in Skod in 2017 is an opportunity for Ling to enter the market with its innovative LED products. This is an opportunity whether the company enters the market directly or buys a home-based company such as Flick.

Environmental

Businesses and consumers in Skod are increasingly aware of energy issues. This is partly due to increasing energy prices as well as more frequent breaks in the electricity supply (such as the power cuts which affected Lal's hotel).

The LED bulbs offered by Ling are greener and more efficient than candescent and halogen bulbs, which are still widely made in the home industry. In the case of businesses, many are quickly moving to LED light bulbs to reduce running costs and boost their environmental credentials. The environmental attractions of its products is important to Ling but again this is independent of whether they are made by a home-based company or one based abroad.

(b)   Market attractiveness

Porter's 5 forces model has been used to assess the attractiveness of the industry.

Bargaining power of buyers

In this scenario, the buyers of the industry's products are large supermarket groups, household product superstores and large electrical chains. These buyers, particularly the supermarket groups, purchase a large volume of the industry's products (90%) and so, on the face of it, they can demand favourable prices. However, the products the buyer purchases from the industry represents a relatively insignificant fraction of the buyer's costs or purchases. A recent report suggested that light bulb sales contributed less than 0.1% of a supermarket's revenue. Light bulbs are much less important to supermarket groups than food and drink. When the product sold by the industry is a small fraction of the buyers' total costs, then buyers are less price sensitive. They are more likely to bargain with food suppliers than light bulb suppliers.

Buyers' bargaining power in the light bulb industry is strengthened by the product being undifferentiated, with low customer switching costs.

However, the buyers are extremely unlikely to move backwards in the supply chain to manufacture their own light bulbs and so this potentially limits their bargaining power. Again, their focus is likely to be elsewhere.

Some of the factors which concern the buyer also relate to the consumer (end customer) as well. To the end customer, light bulbs are undifferentiated and there are no switching costs. Light bulbs are an insignificant fraction of their total spend and so they are unlikely to shop around to get the lowest price.

Bargaining power of suppliers

A supplier group is more powerful if it is dominated by a few companies and is more concentrated than the industry it sells to. This appears to be the case in Skod, where 90% of glass production is accounted for by three companies and metal production is largely concentrated in the hands of one very large company, OmniMetal. The customers (such as Flick) are large but they are more fragmented than the suppliers. Furthermore, the supplier group is, by and large, not obliged to contend with other substitute products for sale to the industry. Light bulbs are largely made of glass and metal and it seems unlikely that this will change in the near future. This lack of substitutes increases the power of the supplier.

The industry is not an important customer of the supplier group. Most glass is sold to the construction industry. Most metal is sold to the automobile industry. The light bulb manufacturers use less than 0.5% of the country's glass production and less than 0.1% of its metal production. This lack of importance increases the supplier group's power, because suppliers' fortunes are not closely tied to the industry and they will not need to protect it through reasonable pricing. Another factor increasing suppliers' power is that the products (glass and metal) are a vital part of the buyers' (customers) light bulb business.

On the other hand, the supplier group's products are largely undifferentiated and switching costs between suppliers appears to be reasonably low. Finally, it seems unlikely that the supplier group poses a credible threat of forward integration into light bulb manufacture and this will be a factor which reduces supplier bargaining power.

Threat of new entrants

Ling is considering entering this market and so the barriers to entry and the potential reaction of current suppliers is important to consider here. The main barriers to entry appear to be:

Economies of scale: The five large dominant companies in the industry should be enjoying economies of scale which force any potential new entrant to come into the market with large scale production, which carries with it a high risk of failure. This is not an issue for Ling who also currently enjoys economies of scale in its manufacture. However, it will deter many other entrants.

Capital requirements: The manufacture of light bulbs requires new entrants to invest large financial resources into production plants. Although capital may be available, the risk associated with large-scale entry may lead to high premiums on borrowed capital.

Access to distribution channels: This may be very significant, as the distribution channels are very specific (supermarket groups, large home products superstores and major electrical chains). The new entrant will have to persuade these channels to accept its products, perhaps through offering price discounts.

It seems unlikely that the new entrant can create a completely new channel. Selling directly to the consumer seems unlikely in this industry where individual purchases are both infrequent and low value.

The reaction to new entrants of existing firms in the industry is likely to be relatively forceful as they have a history of vigorous retaliation to prospective entrants. The upsurge of nationalism in the country will also give them a powerful card to play in this retaliation.

Threat of substitute products

Substitute products are products which can perform the same function as the product of the industry under consideration. It is hard to envisage any potential substitute for light bulbs except for candles which, in the long term, are likely to be much more expensive. Another possible substitute is to do without. This is the approach taken by government policy on street lighting. It is turned off from 2300 hrs to 0500 hrs. However, it seems unlikely that many consumers will prefer to sit in the dark instead of using a relatively cheap lighting product. In the short term, the threat of substitute products seems very low. However, in the long term, the tubular daylight lighting initiative described in Lighting Tomorrow is a possible substitute product as it aims to reduce the need for electric lighting.

Competitive rivalry in the industry

Equally balanced competitors. When an industry is dominated by a few firms and these firms are relatively well balanced in terms of size, it creates potential instability because they may be prone to fight each other. This appears the case in Skod where five fairly similar sized firms produce 72% (20X5) of the light bulbs sold in the country and wage short-term price cutting wars, disrupt competitors' supply lines and react aggressively to potential new entrants.

Slow industry growth. Despite the switch to new technologies, there is little market growth. From 20X0 to 20X5 the market only grew by just over 2%. In such a situation, the only way a firm can increase market share is to take it from one of its competitors. Consequently, slow industry growth increases competitive rivalry.

Lack of differentiation or switching costs. Competitive rivalry is increased where the product is perceived as a commodity. In such circumstances the buyer's decision is largely based on price and service and pressures for intense price and service competition result. Light bulbs are definitely a commodity product in Skod.

High exit barriers. Exit costs are high because of the investment required in plant and the fact that light bulb factories cannot easily be adapted for other uses. When exit costs are high, companies hang on in the industry often resorting to extreme tactics which weaken the profitability of the industry as a whole.

(c)   **Evaluation of an acquisition**

One of the elements of **suitability** is a consideration of how well the strategy fits with future trends and changes in the environment. This environment has already been considered in the PESTEL and five forces analysis. Acquiring Flick is particularly appropriate in the context of the government's threat to impose taxes on imported goods. The increasingly nationalistic Skod population can also be acknowledged if the acquisition is carefully handled. Ling can stress that it is investing in Flick to secure its future and to create jobs for the people of Skod. The impending efficient lighting legislation also provides an opportunity for Ling, but this is irrespective of whether the company enters the market directly or acquires Flick.

However, it is better placed to quickly meet this demand through acquisition. Direct entry is generally a slower approach to growth, as Man Lal has acknowledged.

Entering the market through acquisition also means that it can use the effective distribution channels which are already in place. There is no guarantee that the established distribution channels would welcome a new entrant into the market and indeed they may demand price reductions in exchange for distribution access. Acquisition also means that no new capacity is brought to the market. Ling can then focus on increasing market share in a competitive, relatively slow-growing market. Entering directly is likely to prompt a hostile reaction from competitors currently in the market. Acquiring Flick might also invoke a hostile reaction, but it is likely to be more muted because it does not immediately alter the balance of power in the market.

However, in the longer term, the worldwide size of Ling may affect the bargaining power of suppliers and buyers in the Skod market. As a group, it has revenues which exceed the Skod market total, so there may be possibilities for negotiating reductions in raw material costs and the profit margins of suppliers. If these savings are not passed on to the end consumer, then Ling's profitability will inevitably improve. If these savings are passed on, then Ling will begin to dominate a commodity market place.

A further element of suitability is whether the acquisition provides an opportunity to exploit the strategic capability of Ling. In one sense it does, as it provides an opportunity for it to exploit its technical capability in LED lighting, before the domestic industry can gear up its production levels. However, in another sense the strategy is not suitable because Ling does not have strategic capability in acquiring foreign companies. All of its growth has been achieved through setting up wholly owned distribution subsidiaries. Its only production factories are in Lindisztan.

Acquisition also has to meet the expectations of the stakeholders. In terms of the institutional stakeholders who hold 49% of Ling's shares, the acquisition promises the rapid growth which they are lobbying for. They have been critical of Ling's slow, cautious foreign growth and the maturity of the Lindisztan market means that there is little opportunity for growth there. The institutional shareholders have also been critical of the high levels of retained earnings and they wish to see a significant portion of it invested back into the company to fuel growth. The size of the retained earnings makes the acquisition financially feasible, although of course there is always the possibility that such funds could be better invested elsewhere.

The acquisition of Flick is also of personal significance to Lal himself. It provides him with an opportunity to show the country where he received his business education that he has succeeded. This tangible proof of his success and ambition is important to him. Acquisition is a speedy approach to growth, but it can raise issues of culture clash. This needs further investigation and will be one of the challenges which Ling faces, because it does not have any previous experience of this method of growth. It seems unlikely that the business culture of Skod and Lindisztan is exactly the same and so cultural issues can be expected. Perhaps this is contributing to Man Lal's unease about the acquisition policy.

The **acceptability** of the acquisition can also be considered in the light of Flick's financial performance in its market sector.

The profitability of Flick is currently below average for the industry sector. Gross profit margin in 20X5 was 21.43% (industry average 30%), net profit margin 15.71% (industry average 24%) and ROCE 4.07% (industry average 5.74%).

This may suggest to Ling's shareholders that there are short-term profits to be gained by reducing the cost of sales and overheads to a point where the company at least achieves the average performance of its sector.

In contrast, liquidity is higher than the industry averages. The current ratio is 3.33 (compared with 2.69 for the industry as a whole) and the acid test ratio is 1.83 (1.74 for the industry as a whole). It is possible that the high current ratio reflects a lack of investment in plant and equipment. At Flick, property, plant and equipment accounts for 63.33% of its assets, compared with an industry average of 71.09%. Inventory holding appears unnecessarily high and perhaps shows a lack of good inventory management practice. 15% of the total assets are held in inventory, compared with an industry average of 8.7%. Flick's liquidity is boosted by the amount of money it holds in cash or cash equivalents. This accounts for 11.87% of the asset base, more than double the industry equivalent.

Gearing is relatively low. The gearing ratio is 25.9% (compared with an industry average of 35.9%) and the interest cover ratio is 3.7 (compared to an industry average of 2.4). This points towards a cautious approach to investment and borrowing. It may again suggest that Flick has been reluctant to borrow money to invest in production machines and processes which, in the long term, contribute to more profitable products. It has preferred a lower risk strategy which leads, in turn, to the company making lower profits.

However, one area where Flick appears to excel is in its management of receivables. At an average of 104.3 days this is much lower than the industry norm. Its industry payables is broadly in line with the industry norm (192.5 days compared to 208.6 days).

Conclusion

The acquisition of Flick is, potentially, an excellent way of entering the Skod light bulb market. It appears to be a cautiously run company which has reported lower profitability, perhaps as a result of failing to invest in efficiency initiatives. The threat of import controls makes direct entry very risky and there is sufficient evidence to suggest that Ling's input will improve Flick's position in a very competitive market.

One reservation might be the lack of experience the company has in acquiring and managing foreign companies. Thus a comprehensive due diligence process to purchasing the company and a non-intervention approach to managing Flick when it is acquired is recommended, particularly while Ling gets to grip with the cultural differences which are bound to exist. Such an approach is also likely to partly appease any nationalist critics. Even in the short term, there appears to be improvements which can be made to Flick and profitability will improve by just bringing company performance into line with the national average. Although it is expected that Ling will supply most of the funding for expansion and equipping the factory to produce LED bulbs, liquidity and gearing data suggest that Flick itself has unlocked financing potential which could be used to help finance growth.

(d) **Strategic alliance**

There are many documented cases where acquisitions have been unsuccessful and so the caution of Ling's financial director is understandable. Strategic alliances appear to offer a less risky way of entering a market place.

A strategic partnership is where two or more organisations share resources and activities to pursue a strategy.

The basis for an alliance between Ling and Flick would be co-specialisation, allowing each partner to focus on their core capabilities. Johnson, Scholes and Whittington suggest that 'alliances are used to enter new geographical markets where an organisation needs local knowledge and expertise in distribution, marketing and customer support'. This is exactly the situation Ling finds itself in. In such an alliance it could exploit a new market, retain all production in its own country and save itself the costs of acquisition and due diligence. In return, Flick would gain new energy-efficient products for its home market which would allow it to fulfil the requirements of impending legislation. Crucially, however, the profit of the alliance would have to be split, on some agreed basis, between the two companies.

There are different types of strategic partnership. In a joint venture a new organisation is created which is jointly owned by the parents. The parent companies remain independent trading companies. This is unlikely to be attractive in the Ling/Flick situation. It seems more likely that Flick would wish to sell the product as its own and not confuse the market place with an offering from a related company. A joint venture is probably more appropriate where the participating companies are entering into a different market place. For example, Ling and Flick combining their expertise to enter the energy management consultancy business. At the other end of the spectrum, a network of firms might collaborate without too much formality. For example, Flick could agree to brand and distribute Ling's products, paying a fraction of the sales price (or profit margin) back to Ling. This is in effect a licensing agreement, and this might eventually stretch to the company making the LED bulbs in Skod under licence, after testing the market first through branding and distributing them.

Different levels of formality of the alliance lead to different characteristics.

For example, if speed to market is important, then an opportunistic alliance would be preferred to a joint venture. Indeed a joint venture might easily take longer to agree and legally establish than to complete an acquisition.

The form of the strategic alliance can be shaped to take into account the environmental factors which affect the industry and the different capabilities of the participants. It can also be made responsive to cultural differences. However, in the Ling/Flick situation, it is difficult to see how a strategic alliance will address the needs of the institutional stakeholders for growth and Lal's personal desire for acknowledged success and prestige. Furthermore, there may be concerns about the long-term viability of any such alliance. Trust is probably the most important ingredient of any alliance and it seems likely that Ling will be reluctant to licence a product which could be easily imitated by the licensee. Furthermore, just as Ling has limited expertise in acquisitions, it also has no experience of strategic alliances at all. Success requires expertise in setting up and monitoring clear goals, governance, financial arrangements and other organisational issues. There is no evidence in the scenario that Ling has this expertise.

	Marking scheme	*Marks*
(a)	Up to 1 mark for each relevant point up to a maximum of 7 marks.	7
(b)	Up to 1 mark for each relevant point up to a maximum of 13 marks.	13
(c)	Up to 1 mark for each relevant point (accurate calculation of financial ratios and for correctly interpreting their implications).	18
(d)	Up to 1 mark for each relevant point up to a maximum of 8 marks.	8
Total		**46**

34   NESTA

Key answer tips

A good model to use in assessing industry attractiveness is Porter's 5 forces, though other models would be acceptable. For each force, try to highlight one or two relevant issues which will make the force a threat (or not as the case may be) and explain how this will impact on the attractiveness of the industry for Nesta.

For the professional skills marks, not how more relevance to the scenario is required in order to achieve a 'quite well' or 'very well' mark.

The Eurobian market has been assessed from NESTA's point of view using Porter's 5 Forces model to assess market attractiveness.

The *bargaining power of NESTA* appears to be very strong. There are several factors that contribute to this:

- The products supplied by the supplier earn a relatively low profit margin for the buyer. Low profits provide a great incentive to buyers to pursue lower purchasing costs.

- Switching costs are relatively low as the products are largely unbranded commodity goods. The buyer should find it relatively easy to switch supplier.

- The purchased products are standard and undifferentiated. Buyers should always find it relatively easy to find alternative suppliers and can play companies off against each other in their search for better prices and other terms of supply.

- The products purchased from suppliers represent a significant fraction of the buyer's cost. Buying is price sensitive and the company is likely to spend a great deal of effort trying to ensure the best terms of supply.

- Purchasing companies are fewer and larger than potential suppliers. Suppliers may have alternative customers but their scope is limited. In contrast, the buying companies have many smaller supplying companies competing for their business.

Supplying companies are fragmented and the fixed-price discount channel represents a significant customer group. None of the suppliers appears to offer a credible threat of *forward integration* whereby they might become competitors of their current customers. From NESTA's perspective their high bargaining power is an attractive aspect of the discount fixed-price channel in Eurobia. Furthermore, effective purchasing systems, supplier selection and excellent logistics are perceived as core strengths of NESTA. There is a good match between the nature of the market and the core competencies of NESTA.

Within Eurobia there are currently three dominant competitors. The three fixed-price discount chains compete on profit margins (the target price is fixed at $1), on brand name and on expanding the number of outlets in the chain. The *intensity of the rivalry amongst existing competitors* is largely caused by their ambitious expansion plans. Apparently, few weeks go by without one of the companies announcing plans to extend their chain of shops. It is likely that a new arrival into the market will be *resisted,* particularly when it is a potential entrant as well-known (in the retail market) as NESTA. Resistance will probably be through tightened supplier contracts (better prices, agreement not to supply competitors), increased marketing and rapid store expansion.

However, evidence from Table One also suggests that the market sector is continuing to grow. Year on year growth in the last two years has been around 13%, in an economy that is in recession. In such circumstances, companies competing in the market can continue to improve their results simply by keeping up with industry performance. It gives all competitors greater breathing space. Furthermore, perhaps the arrival of NESTA in the market may help grow the market (by giving it greater legitimacy) and by NESTA exploiting geographical areas not yet comprehensively served by existing competitors.

NESTA should experience a very little competitive pressure from existing rivals in Eurobia. NESTA has turnover of $120,000 million which means that new rivals (even when combined) will be less than 1% of the size of NESTA overall. This should give NESTA the ability to outspend rivals in areas such as marketing and allow NESTA to absorb any short term losses when entering the market. This will add to the attractiveness of the industry from NESTA's point of view.

The main *barriers to entry* to any potential entrant is the capital required to rent, stock and staff the number of stores required to realise the required economies of scale and to establish a credible market presence. It appears that NESTA has both the capital and expertise, particularly as the economic recession has led to reduced shop rents and greater shop availability. Furthermore, possible *exit costs* have also been reduced by the willingness of landlords to consider short fixed-term leases. NESTA's main problem could be quickly establishing a brand name in a country where it is relatively unknown (5% awareness), and competing with three incumbents who are very well known. The survey showed that all three established brands were recognised by more than 90% of the consumers in Eurobia. Finally, there may also be barriers to entry erected by the government to prevent foreign companies opening.

The threat of *substitute products* is probably best considered in terms of alternative channels of supply. The scenario notes that the large supermarkets do supply ambient goods, but have so far resisted competing on price. They are differentiating through product (a wider range of branded goods) and through place (providing the convenience of purchasing a wide range of other goods, including food, in one location). Their sheer scale may mean that they have been willing to overlook the discount fixed-price market niche up to now. The largest discount fixed-price company has revenue of $330m, a fraction of the size of the largest supermarket group ($42,500m). However, the arrival of NESTA, an established global player, in the market may change the dynamic and cause the established supermarkets to take another look.

The supply of ambient goods is also well-suited to the internet and the growth of internet-based competitors has to be considered. The current market is firmly based around high street shopping. The internet might be a substitute channel, and indeed might be considered by NESTA as a way of differentiating itself on its entry into the market. The current internet home delivery service offered by the supermarkets is unlikely to be much of a threat as long as they continue to charge a significant fee for using it. It is clearly aimed at a different market segment.

Marking scheme – technical marks	
	Marks
1 mark for each relevant point up to a maximum of	**16**

How well has the candidate demonstrated Professional Skills as follows:	Not at all	Not well	Quite well	Very well
Professional acumen skills relevant to the competitive nature of the industry	The candidate has not considered the competitive nature of the industry at all.	The candidate has considered the competitive nature of the industry but has failed to make use of the data provided in Table One.	The candidate has considered the competitive nature of the market, including reference to the data provided in Table One. However, this data has not been referenced to the size and potential spending power of NESTA.	The candidate has considered the data provided in Table One relevant to the size of NESTA and concluded that the potential rivals in Eurobia are significantly smaller than NESTA and therefore likely to offer a greatly reduced competitive threat.
	0	0.5	1	2

35   YVERN TRINKETS REGIONAL (YTR)

Key answer tips

The four key generic strategies are clearly provided. A brief evaluation of each option was required where the key will have been making points which were relevant to the company in the scenario.

The managing director states that he wishes to follow a generic strategy of cost leadership. However, it seems likely that he has misunderstood the term or that he is knowingly using it as a euphemism for cost reduction. His slide missed out important information.

Strategic advantage

Target	Low cost	Unique
All customers	Cost Leadership	Differentiation
Market segment	Cost Focus	Differentiation Focus

A generic strategy of cost leadership means being the lowest cost producer in the industry as a whole.

It seems unlikely that the company can pursue such a strategy. It has larger rivals (who will be able to obtain better economies of scale) both within the region and within the country as a whole. There is no evidence of technical advantage, and indeed the managing director has commented on outdated information technology. There is no suggestion, either, of other factors which would allow the company to achieve cost leadership, such as having favourable access to sources of supply, or raw materials or labour.

A differentiation strategy assumes that competitive advantage can be gained, in the industry as a whole, through particular characteristics of a company's product. Companies which pursue such a strategy worry less about costs and seek, instead, to be perceived in the industry as unique. For example, the product may be innovative or superior in some way. Again, this does not appear to apply to YTR, in the context of the industry.

Both cost leadership and differentiation require superior performance, which does not appear to be a characteristic of YTR.

A focused or niche strategy takes place when a firm concentrates its attention on one or more market segments or niches. In doing so it could aim to be a cost leader for a particular segment. This is the cost focus strategy identified in the managing director's slide. This is often associated with an environment where 'broader scope' companies exhibit an element of over-performance, offering a particular segment much more than it wants, at a price which reflects this. This may be a possible strategy for YTR if their products are largely indistinguishable from other producers in Yvern. However, outsourcing production does not appear to be the right way of pursuing this strategy.

Alternatively, a company might pursue differentiation for a particular segment; a differentiation focus strategy. This strategy seeks to provide a perceived high quality product to a selected market segment or niche. Such products may be heavily branded and sold at a substantial price premium. There is evidence to suggest that YTR has a strong brand and meets a demand for regional, locally produced products.

A better strategy for YTR is focus, where it can serve a particular niche where it can largely insulate itself from the competition. Porter suggests that a company must pursue one of these strategies. Both cost leadership and differentiation require superior performance and some form of focus strategy is easier, as it is simpler to dominate a niche market.

Marking scheme – technical marks	
	Marks
1 mark for each appropriate point up to a maximum of 10 marks	**10**

How well has the candidate demonstrated Professional Skills as follows:	Not at all	Not well	Quite well	Very well
Evaluation skills in assessing the appropriateness of each strategy	The candidate has not assessed the appropriate of each generic strategy.	The candidate has assessed the appropriateness of each strategy in general terms and has not applied this to YTR.	The candidate has assessed the appropriateness of each strategy to YTR but opinions are not supported by information from the scenario.	The candidate has assessed the appropriateness of each strategy to YTR and this is clearly evidenced from information from the scenario.
	0	0.5	1	2

D: RISK

36   BTS COMPANY

Key answer tips

This question requires you to look for risks within the scenario and then to move onto discuss suitable controls. There is plenty of information in the scenario to work from in doing this.

Risks affecting BTS Company

Risks that the BTS company should be aware of include:

Strategic – IT failure

The company is heavily dependent on its IT systems. Failure in this area would mean that the company cannot sell its products via the website, or indeed process orders or make payments to suppliers.

To mitigate this risk, BTS needs to ensure that mirrored servers are available (so if one breaks then the second server starts processing immediately from exactly the same place) There is also the need to ensure that appropriate disaster planning and backup facilities are implemented.

Strategic – distribution systems

BTS is also heavily dependent on the reliability of its distribution system to maintain customer confidence in the company. Given the increasing number of customer complaints, it appears that confidence in the FastCour firm is decreasing. However, at present there is no evaluation of alternative couriers or systems to use.

To mitigate this risk, the board should investigate alternative delivery solutions e.g. use of a different courier firm or even purchase of their own vans for delivery. If the service from the existing couriers continues to fall then switching delivery methods should be seriously considered.

Tactical – key staff

Production of chairs and sofas is under the supervision of two key members of staff, Mr Smith and Mr Jones. While it is essential to have skilled members of staff available to maintain production efficiently, there is the risk that one or both of these staff members could leave the company. If this happens the ability of BTS to continue production at current levels could be jeopardised.

To mitigate this risk, the knowledge of the production controllers should be codified into a production manual which means it will be possible for another staff member to take over production duties. Mr Jones and Mr Smith must be made aware that this step is being taken, not because they are not trusted, but simply so BTS has a full record of all its activities.

Tactical – suppliers

BTS is very dependent on the Woody company for supply of wood for its products.

However, the relationship with the supplier appears to be inappropriate – late payment and lack of warning regarding future orders means that Woody cannot plan supplies to assist BTS and may not be inclined to help anyway given the late payment. If Woody decide to stop supplying BTS then production would be adversely affected while a new wood supplier is located.

To mitigate this risk, BTS should attempt to enter into more of a partnership with Woody. Providing future wood requirements and paying on time would help Woody to look on BTS more favourably and help BTS guarantee supply of wood.

Operational – lack of fabric

Occasionally, BTS is unable to sell a specific chair or sofa because the customer's choice of fabric is unavailable. Lack of fabric is caused primarily by human error at BTS – the procurement manager forgets to re-order fabric. While lack of fabric on an occasional basis is not threatening for BTS, an increase in errors would mean loss of more orders which will start to affect sales significantly.

To mitigate this threat, BTS should either implement a computerised re-ordering system or possibly try and ensure that the procurement manager is trained in memory techniques or implements some other system to identify low fabric stock levels.

37   LANDMASS

Key answer tips

The syllabus does not specify which corporate governance codes you need to be familiar with. However if you do know the details of the UK's Corporate Governance Code this should give you an understanding of the typical requirements of such systems for **part (b)**.

(a)   Risks should be categorised by companies according to the circumstances in which the company operates and according to how it perceives its risks.

   (i)   A distinction might be made between business risks and governance risks. Business risks relate to the risks of failing to achieve objectives in business operations. Governance risks would relate to the risks of failing to comply with best practice in corporate governance, a failure of internal controls, or a failure to comply with legislation or regulations.

   (ii)   Broad categories of risk should be divided into sub-categories: for example, business risks might be categorised into strategy risks, competition risks and environmental risks (political risks, legislation risks, economic risks, technology risks, and so on).

   (iii)   If a company consists of several independent investment centres, each investment centre might be responsible for its own risk classification and risk management.

   (iv)   There might be established classifications of risk within a particular industry. For example, in banking, risks are classified for risk assessment and capital management purposes into credit risk, traded market risk, operational risk and other risks.

In most situations, however, companies should carry out regular assessments of the risks that they face, using risk categories that seem appropriate to their individual circumstances.

The risk categories that may be appropriate for Landmass are as follows:

   (i)   *Compliance risk.* Landmass is a planning to become listed company and hence will be subject to the listing rules of the stock exchange. These rules can change, and non-compliance met with penalties or, ultimately de-listing.

   (ii)   *Product risk.* A risk to any business is that the demand for its product may fall, or rise. With three different product lines, Landmass may hope to reduce this risk.

   (iii)   *Economic risk.* The property business is highly affected by the overall state of the economy, benefiting in times of boom, and suffering in times of recession. GDP, economic growth and unemployment will all be major risk factors for Landmass.

   (iv)   *Interest rate risk.* No information has been given of how Landmass finances its business, so it may or may not be directly affected by movements in interest rates. However, it is highly likely that its customers will be adversely affected if interest rates rise, and hence their demand for the property that Landmass offers could fall.

Tutorial note

The above categories are by no means the only risk categories that Landmass faces. To identify categories, it may have been helpful to brainstorm the risks facing the business, and then see which are major, or which can be grouped together under a single category heading.

(b)   This answer assumes that the corporate governance guidelines which Landmass will be subject to are similar to those in the UK's Corporate Governance Code.

When Landmass becomes a listed company, it will be expected to comply with corporate governance guidelines. The board of directors will be required to carry out an annual review of the system of internal control and risk management, and report to the shareholders that they have done so.

In order to do this, a formal system of risk management should be put in place. An appropriate approach would be to establish one or more risk management committees. The risk management committee(s) should be responsible for the supervision of risk management within the company. The role of a risk management committee might be to:

- identify and assess risks regularly, and provide information to the board of directors and executive management

- formulate risk management policies, for submission to the board of directors for approval

- communicate with executive management, to ensure that risks are taken into consideration in decision-making.

Since many of the specific business risks and internal control risks will differ for each of the three business areas of Landmass, it might be appropriate to establish risk committees at a divisional level. However, other risks might apply to the group as a whole (for example, risks arising from changes in the value of land, or changes in legislation relating to property rights) and it might therefore be appropriate to have a risk committee at group level, to consider broader strategic risks facing the company.

The management of risk, and the implementation of risk controls, is the responsibility of the management who make decisions for the company. This responsibility might remain at board level (for example, in assessing strategic risk, or making decisions about acquisitions or major capital investments), or might be delegated to senior management.

A risk management committee should assess business risks and strategic risks, but there will also be a requirement to assess the system of internal control in the company. In the UK, guidelines for the review of internal control systems were provided in the Turnbull guidelines, which were based on the review structure proposed by COSO. It is recommended that the management and review of internal control should be based on five elements:

(i)   creating a suitable control culture and risk management environment within the organisation

(ii)   the regular review of risks, including procedures for identifying, assessing and prioritising risks

(iii) selecting suitable internal controls to contain or prevent the risks

(iv)   communicating information about risks and risk controls throughout the organisation to the individuals affected by them

(v)   monitoring the effectiveness of controls, with a view to rectifying weaknesses in control that might be discovered.

This continual review of internal control could be made a responsibility of the risk management committee(s).

The board of directors should assess the adequacy of internal control and risk management systems each year. In addition, the company might be required to publish an operating and financial review (OFR) each year in which the significant risks facing the company are explained to the shareholders, together with information on how the company is managing these risks. The board of directors should therefore also consider a system for reporting on risks, based on the information provided by its risk committee(s).

It might also be appropriate to consider the role of an internal audit department within a risk management system. If a company has an internal audit department, the audit staff can provide a means of monitoring risks and controls, and reporting their findings to operational managers, possibly the finance director (or the person to whom the internal audit department reports) and the risk committee(s).

38   REGIONAL POLICE FORCE

Key answer tips

This question is completely focused on the area of risks and controls, but it has been placed in a non-listed company environment. The key to success here will be practical, precise suggestions entirely related to the information provided in the scenario.

(a)   There are several significant risks to the achievement of the corporate objectives of the regional police force.

   •   The police force has several different stated objectives, which means that there will have to be some prioritisation of objectives, given limited resources to carry out the police work. For example, how should decisions be taken about allocating resources to tasks that reduce crime and those that promote community safety (such as road traffic safety or anti-terrorist measures).

   •   The objective of reducing crime and disorder is a very broad one, given that there are many different types of crime and lawlessness. Priorities will have to be assigned to the reduction in different types of crime, and efforts to deal with some types of crime will not receive adequate police resources.

- There might also be a temptation for the police force to divert resources away from 'normal' police work to money-earning activities such as policing football matches. There is a risk that money-earning activities will divert too many resources away from normal police work, and the amounts of money earned will be insufficient.

- Since the police force is a public body, there is a high risk of political interference. Political decisions are taken about specific priorities for dealing with crime, setting targets for achievement, and allocating money from taxation. Political decisions might increase or decrease the funds available to the police.

- There might be some conflict between the objectives of the police force. For example, if tough police measures are taken to reduce rates of crime or to deal with public disorder, public confidence in the police force might be adversely affected if the police tactics are too aggressive. Excessive violence in dealing with political demonstrations is a particular source of risk to public confidence.

- Risks to the achievement of the corporate objectives might also arise from a lack of public support. The police force are accountable to the general public as well as to politicians, and success in dealing with crime and improving community safety depends heavily on public support for the police – for example in reporting crimes and being willing to give evidence in criminal trials.

(b) The risks in a regional structure for the police force are as follows:

- The regional management will want to set its own targets for the achievement of corporate objectives, but these might conflict with national targets set by government.

- A regional police authority might formulate its own strategies for dealing with crime that are different from the strategies adopted by other regional authorities. As a result, different crimes might be dealt with in completely different ways in different regions.

  The resulting lack of consistency in policing around the country could have an adverse effect on public opinion and public confidence in the police force.

- Crime is not restricted to regional boundaries, and regional forces rely on co-operation from other regional forces to carry out their work. Operational difficulties might arise that reduce the efficiency and effectiveness of inter-regional co-operation.

- Some crimes are of such potential importance, and operate on a national or international basis, that they need to be dealt with on a national or international basis, and not at regional level. Without national and international structures and organisation, much police work would be ineffective.

- Information will have to be shared between regions. There might be some risk that information held in one region might not be properly accessible to another region.

Tutorial note

In a question such as this it is acceptable to suggest risks that are not directly referred to in the scenario, but can be drawn from your experience of such a situation. However, ensure that your risks (and subsequent controls) are explained very clearly so that the marker can award you points for relevant suggestions.

(c)   In broad terms, the internal controls that should apply within a police force are similar to the internal controls that should operate in any large organisation. The aim of internal controls should be to ensure that the policies of the organisation are properly applied and that operations are conducted efficiently and effectively.

- There must be procedural controls, to ensure that activities are carried out in accordance with policy and legal requirements. Police work is subject to extensive procedural controls.

- There should be adequate management and supervisory controls. Supervisors should monitor the work of their subordinates, and should be accountable to their own superiors for the actions of the individuals in their charge.

- There should be controls over recruitment and training (personnel controls), to ensure that appropriate individuals are employed and that these individuals are given sufficient training to do their work properly.

- Organisational controls should ensure that there is sufficient accountability for police work that is carried out. Although there will be accountability through normal reporting lines in the organisational hierarchy, the work of a police force should also be subject to external assessment, for example from public or political bodies.

- There must be procedures for the authorisation and approval of police activity, including the commitment of expenditure to activities. Decisions to commit resources and spending to various activities should be taken at an appropriate level within the management hierarchy.

39   MANAGE LTD

Key answer tips

Make sure that you explain your risks precisely and clearly, don't just stop at things like 'interest rate risk'. Note the careful wording of the requirement: you are asked to discuss how they could assess impact on the company. As such you are not required to formulate a view on the impact or likelihood, but discuss how Utopia could assess these. Be careful that you answer the question set.

A number of risks exist for Utopia Inc in making the acquisition of Manage Ltd. The following explains some of the main risks.

Strategic risks – understanding market

The investment in Manage Ltd is a strategic investment and there is the chance that the investment will not generate the returns expected. The reason for this could be that Utopia has not understood the market in which Manage Ltd operates and therefore predicts growth that may not actually arise. There is perhaps a danger of this in the scenario as Manage Ltd has been very successful in recent years and Utopia could be paying a price based on the growth continuing, which it may not.

Carrying out market research will enable Utopia to assess the likelihood of the sales revenue failing to grow as expected. The use of scenario planning to assess the outcome of different levels of sales would enable the company to quantify the impact on the business.

Loss of staff

There is a danger that key staff in Manage Ltd will leave after the acquisition and as a result there will be a loss of goodwill and customer support.

If staff leave, they may join competitors or set up in competition with Manage. It appears that Utopia Inc is attempting to reduce this risk by offering positions to Jean Smith and other selected staff.

Utopia may be able to assess the probability of staff leaving based on the experience from previous acquisitions. Feedback from discussions with selected staff could also give an indication of the likelihood that staff will leave. The company will also be able to estimate the cost of replacing staff who leave.

Culture

There is a serious risk of a cultural issue in Utopia investing in Manage. It is possible that Utopia's management style will not fit with the style of Manage. This could result in the existing Manage staff being demotivated and therefore either leaving or not putting their full effort into making Utopia a successful business.

There is also a risk that Utopia will not understand the UK culture and therefore as a result they might operate in a way which is unacceptable to UK customers.

It may be possible for Utopia to gain an understanding of the culture of Manage and assess how different it is and the likely problems from the conversations it is having with staff. Utopia should also be able to draw on the company's experience of previous acquisitions of UK companies to make an assessment of the risk of losing customers due to differences between the cultures in the US and the UK.

Financial risk

There are distinct financial risks for Utopia in different areas. One area is interest rate risk. As Utopia is planning to finance the acquisition of Manage through loans, there is the chance that interest rates will increase meaning that the loans become more expensive.

In addition there is currency risk. Even though Manage does not have any foreign suppliers or customers and therefore is not exposed to currency risk in the Manage business, Utopia will be exposed to translation risk as they will have a foreign asset and economic risk as they are now exposed to the UK economy affecting exchange rates. The final area to consider with currency risk is the issue of remitting funds to the US. If sterling weakens in the future against the dollar, the value of the dollar profits made by Manage Ltd will fall, as will the level of dividends Manage Ltd could remit to the US.

If Utopia is planning to use the proceeds from the sale of an existing UK division to finance this acquisition or repay any loan, then there is a risk that if the sale does not achieve the price expected or takes place later than anticipated. This will affect the amount of finance required and the level of interest paid.

To assess the risks arising from the disposal of the division, Utopia needs to ensure that sufficient research has been carried out to give as much information as possible about the likely timing and proceeds. The company should then evaluate the different financial options, varying the level of factors such as interest and exchange rates.

Political and regulatory risks

There is an increased political and regulatory risk if operations are conducted in overseas countries as it is unlikely Utopia will understand the political and regulatory environment in the UK as well as the environment in the US. This may not be a significant extra risk because Utopia is continuing to employ key staff of Manage and it already has operations in the UK.

40   DUBLAND

Key answer tips

The context of this question is the reduction of bank lending in Dubland – a topical issue in many countries over the last decade, emphasising the need for the well prepared candidate to read and keep up to date with current affairs.

STATEMENT 1: RISK ASSESSMENT

Explanation of risk assessment

Risk assessment is the process of evaluating the importance of a risk by making an estimate of two variables: the probability of the risk event being realised and the impact that the risk would have if it were realised. Probability refers to the likelihood of the risk materialising and is expressed either as a percentage or as a proportion of one (e.g. a 0.5 risk is considered to be 50% likely). The impact refers to the value of the loss if the risk event were to materialise. The estimated values of these two variables can be plotted on a risk assessment 'map', where the two axes are impact and probability. Then, different risk management strategies can be assigned depending upon the area of the map the risk is plotted in.

Risks assessed at low probability and low impact can be accepted or tolerated, those with high impact but low probability are often transferred or shared, risks with low impact but high probability are typically reduced and those with high impact and high probability are typically avoided. Risks that are known to be more likely to occur in the near future ('proximate' risks) may be assessed as higher probability and have more urgent strategies applied for managing them.

Whether risk assessment should be continuous and ongoing

The first reason why there needs to be a continuous and ongoing risk assessment is because of the strategic importance of many risks *and because of the dynamic nature* of those risks being assessed. Some risks reduce over time and others increase, depending upon changes in the business environment that organisations exist in. Accordingly, it should not be seen as a 'once and for all' activity. If there is a risk that companies who borrow money become less able to repay their loans than previously, this is a negative change in the business environment (thereby affecting liquidity risk). When business recovers and bank customers' ability to repay large loans improves, the liquidity risk for the banks is reduced.

Second, it is necessary to always have accurately assessed risks *because of the need to adjust risk management strategies* accordingly. The probabilities of risk occurring and the impacts involved can change over time as environmental changes take effect. In choosing, for example, between accepting or reducing a risk, how that risk is managed will be very important. In reducing their lending, the banks have apparently decided to reduce their exposure to liquidity risk. This strategy could change to an 'accept' strategy when the economy recovers.

For BigBank, changes in the economic environment of Dubland mean that liquidity risks have increased. As business confidence rises and falls in Dubland, the probabilities and impacts of different risks will change.

In this case, BigBank has decided that a reduction in lending is a suitable response to mitigate its financial risks, but this measure is likely to change as business confidence improves and, indeed, the finance minister has asked the banks to consider this.

STATEMENT 2: FIDUCIARY DUTY

Explanation of fiduciary duty

A fiduciary duty is an often onerous *duty of care and trust* that one party owes to another, mainly defined in terms of a financial duty of care in a business context. It can be either a legal duty or a moral duty (or both). In the case of a legal duty, it is legally required, for example, for a solicitor to act in the best interests of a client, or a nurse to act in the best interests of a patient. In other situations, the legal responsibilities are more blurred but an ethical duty may remain. Many would argue, for example, that people owe a fiduciary duty to certain ancient monuments or to the preservation of a unique landscape. The issue here is the fiduciary duty owed by Mr Ng, the chief executive of BigBank. In terms of his agency relationship with the BigBank shareholders, he is *legally correct in his belief* that he has a pre-eminent duty to the shareholders. The problem arises when the effects of his duty to the bank's shareholders is taken into account and this raises a number of potential issues.

Critical evaluation of Ron Ng's belief

In support of his belief about his 'only duty' being to shareholders (a pristine capitalist perspective) is the fact that as an agent of the shareholders, he is employed by them and *legally and morally bound to act primarily in their economic best interests*.

It will often be the case that one strategy favours one constituency (e.g. the shareholders) whilst disadvantaging another, but this does not warrant him adopting a course of action that would increase the bank's risk exposure or reduce shareholders' returns. Such an action would be a *de facto theft of company value* and hence very unethical. If he were to weaken the bank's risk management in order to reduce the harmful effects on borrowers (and satisfy the finance minister's requirements), he would not be acting in the best interests of the shareholders, who have every right to expect him to *protect their interests* over all other claims upon the bank.

Arguments against his remark arise from the belief that he is being naïve and short-sighted by suggesting that his only duty is to the shareholders. There are both strategic and ethical reasons why, in this case, assuming a narrow and short-term focus on shareholder value is wrong. The finance minister mentioned the importance of banks in wider society and the fact that the lack of lending *has had negative effects on the Dubland economy*. Not only might this be *unfair to other businesses* and individuals unable to gain loan capital, but it might have a *longer term effect on BigBank itself*, and its shareholders, if the economy shrinks and there is less demand for lending when the economy recovers.

Marking scheme	Marks
1 mark for each relevant point describing risk assessment to a maximum of 2 marks.	2
2 marks for each relevant point, in context, on the need for 'ongoing' to a maximum of 6 marks.	6
1 mark for description of fiduciary duty	1
1 mark for each relevant argument in favour of Ron Ng's statement to a maximum of 3 marks.	3
1 mark for each relevant argument against Ron Ng's statement to a maximum of 3 marks.	3
Total	**15**

41 GHI GROUP

Key answer tips

The categories of risk used here in **part (a)** may include one or two which you have not specifically studied – however you should be able to use your general knowledge and information in the question to suggest examples.

The requirement to **part (b)** is precise in focusing solely on risks arising from the decision to sell all-inclusive deals. You will get no marks for including more general risks.

(a) **Risks faced by GHI Group**

The following risks are faced by the GHI Group:

Financial risks

(i) GHI is based in its home country, but organises holidays abroad. Its revenues will be in its home currency, but it will have to pay its suppliers of overseas accommodation and transport services in countries which do not use the Euro in their local currencies. The group is therefore exposed to currency risk given the mismatch of currencies between revenues and costs. It will be possible to charge customers in local currency for services they buy while on holiday (e.g. excursions, wines and spirits at meals, etc.), so some matching of revenues and costs is possible, but there will still be a large mismatch. The risk is that, if the Euro depreciates against the foreign currencies, then more pounds will have to be paid to overseas suppliers, and the profitability of the holiday products may be undermined.

(ii)   There will be a cash flow risk arising from the uncertainty about how many people will actually take the holiday that they originally book. The traditional pattern is for holidaymakers to pay a modest deposit when they book a holiday, with the balance payable (say) a month before the departure date. The company must contractually book a room in a hotel once the initial booking is made, and will be liable to pay the hotel, but in practice a proportion of holidaymakers will be unable to take up their holiday due to illness, family bereavement, etc. They may forfeit the deposit they have paid, but the company must pay for the hotel rooms it has booked, and will lose the profits they had hoped to gain from selling excursions, etc. This uncertainty about the actual number of customers who will turn up leads to the cash flow risk of the company.

Political risks

(i)   The risk of terrorist acts in countries that are popular with GHI's customers may have a severe impact on sales. Overseas holidays are often a discretionary purchase so, if a bomb goes off in Egypt or Turkey or New York, then some holidaymakers will avoid that destination and choose either to holiday in their home country or perhaps just stay at home. It is difficult for a company such as GHI to predict when the next terrorist act will occur, but it is possible to buy insurance against the adverse effects that a major incident would cause the company.

(ii)   GHI is planning to buy two new hotels in the Eastern Mediterranean. The question does not state the countries in which these purchases are to be made, but there will be a discrimination risk that the local government authorities may disapprove of foreign owners of local assets and may make things difficult for the company. The nature of this risk may depend on the political relationship between the two governments.

Environmental risks

(i)   An increasing number of people are using the internet to book 'self-managed' holidays directly, rather than visiting a travel agent. This development in technology has created the risk to GHI that customers will no longer visit its retail travel outlets, and will no longer buy its packaged products. GHI must react quickly by offering its products on the internet at a competitive price, otherwise it will get left behind as the market develops.

(ii)   The growth in divorce rates and in people remaining single means that the traditional family 'bucket and spade' beach holiday with two parents and two children will become less of the norm. This social change means that GHI must offer products of interest to single people, older people and lone-parent families. The 'weekend break' trips to European cities are an example of products popular with the over 50s which will continue to grow in the future as the number of older people in society steadily increases.

Economic risks

(i)   GHI has decided to purchase two new hotels in the Eastern Mediterranean. These will be overseas assets whose cost is denominated in an overseas currency, therefore their translated value in the group's statement of financial position will fluctuate from year to year. This translation risk could mean that the statement of financial position appears weaker if the pound strengthens against the relevant overseas currency, which could have implications for the cost of borrowing charged by future providers of debt finance.

(ii)   GHI must decide on the currency in which it will pay its suppliers in overseas countries. It may be that anyone in the Americas or the Far East is happy to be paid in US dollars, while anyone in Europe or Africa can be paid in Euros. However, there is a currency selection risk in that, if GHI decides to pay African suppliers in Euros while its competitors pay their similar suppliers in dollars, say, then GHI's relative competitive position will depend on the dollar's performance against the Euro.

Tutorial note

The risks given here are by no means the only risks you could have identified. And, it is equally possible to put some risks under different category headings. So don't worry about this, just ensure that you are discussing your risks in plenty of detail to earn the full marks.

(b)   GHI has decided to move from offering traditional 'room-only' or 'bed and breakfast' holidays to offering 'all-inclusive' holidays where the customer pays a larger sum up-front but all food and drink, sports facilities, entertainments, and so on in the hotel are then free. The risk is that:

(i)   customers may not be willing to pay the higher price; and

(ii)   the costs of the additional items may exceed the incremental revenues, so that GHI is worse off after the decision.

The willingness of customers to pay more for a product depends on the elasticity of demand for the product. The demand for package holidays is price elastic, in the sense that higher prices will reduce demand, given the competitive nature of the market. GHI must therefore send a clear message in its marketing literature about the premium quality nature of the holidays it is offering. Services such as free magazines and drinks on aeroplanes are cheap to organise, but may differentiate GHI's offering from the competition.

The risk is that customers will compare the more expensive GHI holiday with a cheaper holiday offered by a competitor, and decide that the extras offered by GHI are not worth the premium price. GHI can combat this risk by describing long lists of facilities that are included in the price, e.g. use of the hotel gym, swimming pool, tennis courts, etc. In reality the likelihood of a customer using all these facilities is low, but they will impress the potential customer in demonstrating the added value in an all-inclusive holiday.

Keeping tight control of costs is also important.

The risk is that customers and staff will not place any value on goods and services that are handed out for free in the all-inclusive environment. Customers might take several different desserts from a free buffet, eat the one that tastes best, and throw the others away. Portion control must be stressed to staff in their training: all portions of food and drink should be the minimum possible to dissuade customers from throwing large amounts away. A training and audit regime for hotel staff should be implemented to monitor and control all portions offered to customers.

A final method of monitoring the success of the all-inclusive packages is to ask customers to fill out questionnaires at the end of their holiday, asking for their feedback. After all, there is no point marketing a premium product that customers are not happy with. Their suggestions for improvements should be taken very seriously and fed back as inputs into the planning process for the future.

42   YGT

Key answer tips

Part (a) needed awareness that risks are dynamic and subject to environmental change and an ability to criticise beliefs. **Part (c)** required an application of related and, in particular, 'positive' related risk and how risks can rise and fall together.

(a)   **Criticism of Raz Dutta's beliefs**

Raz Dutta is wrong in both of her assertions. The belief that risks do not change very much is only true in static environments. In reality, the changeability of risks depends upon the organisation's place on a continuum between highly dynamic and completely static.

The case mentions changes in some of YGT's risks and this suggests that there is some dynamism in its environment. Clearly then, her belief is very difficult to defend.

Her belief that risks 'hardly ever' materialise may be historically true (but this is also unlikely) but the risk assessment highlighted at least two 'likely' risks which could well materialise. Risk D was assessed as 'highly likely' and Risk B was also likely with a high potential impact. Neither of these variables would be known were it not for intelligence gained as part of the risk assessment. Importantly, Risk B was a 'high/high' risk meaning that it is a likely risk with a high impact once it materialised. Being unaware of this could have caused great damage to the organisation.

Why risk assessment is dynamic

Risk assessment is a dynamic management activity because of changes in the organisational environment and because of changes in the activities and operations of the organisation which interact with that environment. At YGT, the case describes Risk C as arising from a change in the activity of the company: a new product launch.

The new product has obviously introduced a new risk that was not present prior to the new product. It may be a potential liability from the use of the product or a potential loss from the materials used in its production, for example.

Changes in the environment might include changes in any of the PEST (political, economic, social, technological) or any industry level change such as a change in the competitive behaviour of suppliers, buyers or competitors.

In either case, new risks can be introduced, existing ones can become more likely or have a higher impact, or the opposite (they may disappear or become less important). The case describes Risk D as arising from a change in legislation which is a change in the external environment.

(b)   **TARA**

The strategies for each risk assessment are as follows:

Risk A is *accept*. This means that the likelihood is low and the impact is low such that even if the risk materialised, it would not have a high severity. The case says that the activity giving rise to Risk A is capable of making good returns so given that both likelihood and severity are low, there is no obvious reason to pursue any of the other strategies with regard to this risk.

Risk B is *avoid*. When the likelihood and impact are high, it would be irrational to accept the risk and so the risk should be avoided. This may involve changing behaviour or discontinuing a certain activity. The case says that the activity giving rise to Risk B is capable of making good returns, but importantly, it is not strategically vital. Given this, and because the case information does not mention the possibility of viably transferring the risk, there is no reason to bear the risk unless the potential return is very large and the company has a high risk appetite.

Risk C is *transfer*. YGT says that the activity giving rise to the risk must not be discontinued (so avoidance is not an option) and specifies that it can be transferred ('alternative arrangements for bearing the risks are possible'). To transfer risk is to share it with another party. The most common way to do this is to insure against losses or to outsource or licence the activity to a third party thereby transferring that risk to that third party.

Risk D is *reduce*. The case emphasises that the risk cannot be transferred (by insurance or outsourcing) but that the activity that gives rise to the risk can be reduced.

Reduction involves reducing the risk exposure by carrying out the activity in a different way, doing less of the activity that gives rise to the risk or adopting behaviour that, whilst still exposing the company to the risk, results in a lower impact if the risk is realised.

(c)   **Related and correlated**

Related risks are risks that vary because of the presence of another risk. This means they do not exist independently and they are likely to rise and fall in importance along with the related one. Risk correlation is a particular example of related risk.

Risks are positively correlated if the two risks are positively related in that one will fall with the reduction of the other and increase with the rise of the other. They would be negatively correlated if one rose as the other fell. In the case of environmental risks and reputation risk, they may be positively correlated for the following reasons.

Environmental risks involve exposure to losses arising from an organisation's consumption of resources or impacts through its emissions. Where an environmental risk affects a sensitive situation, (be it human, flora, fauna or other), this can cause negative publicity which can result in reputation damage.

These two risks can have a shared cause, i.e. they can arise together and fall together because they depend upon the same activity. They are considered separate risks because losses can be incurred by either of both of the impacts (environmental or reputational).

Activities designed to reduce environmental risk, such as acquiring resources from less environmentally-sensitive sources or through the fitting of emission controls, will reduce the likelihood of the environmental risk being realised. This, in turn, will reduce the likelihood of the reputation risk being incurred. The opposite will also hold true: a reduction of attention to environmental risk will increase the likelihood of reputation loss.

	Marking scheme	Marks
(a)	2 marks for each evaluation point made to a maximum of 4 marks 2 marks for each point identified and explained on dynamic to a maximum of 4 marks.	
	Total	8
(b)	Half mark for correct strategy selection for each risk. 1 mark for each risk strategy correctly explained and justified.	
	Total	6
(c)	2 marks for explanation of related and correlated risks. 2 marks for each description of why correlated to a maximum of 4 marks.	
	Total	5
Total		19

43 HOPPO

Related and correlated risks

Related risks are risks that vary because of the presence of another risk or where two risks have a common cause. This means when one risk increases, it has an effect on another risk and it is said that the two are related. Risk correlation is a particular example of related risk.

Risks are positively correlated if the two risks are positively related in that one will fall with the reduction of the other, and increase with the rise of the other. They would be negatively correlated if one rose as the other fell.

Legal risk and reputation risk

At Hoppo, legal risk and reputation risk are likely to be positively correlated because it is likely that as legal risk rises, then, for the reasons explored below, so will reputation risk. Were the legal risk to recede, then risk of reputational damage would also recede. In the case of legal and reputation risks at Hoppo, legal risk is the independent variable and reputation risk is the dependent variable. This is because the reputation risk incurred will largely depend on the legal risk.

The legal risk in this case is the possibility that, if Red Co's outsourced manufacturing contract is cancelled, Red Co will pursue a legal case against Hoppo. Because so many jobs (about 1,000) and a lot of future earnings for Red Co are at stake, Red Co may vigorously pursue the case and seek to gain damages for the loss of a valuable contract and employee termination costs. It is not certain that Red Co would take this option, though, and so the probability of this occurring is not known.

The reputation risk is the loss to Hoppo if issues were to be raised in the public consciousness that might cast the company in a negative light. It is hard to know in advance how a legal challenge would be reported but Hoppo could be accused, justly or unjustly, of several things.

Legal cases sometimes raise issues in the public consciousness that the company would have otherwise not had exposed. Some of these may be perfectly legitimate in business terms but may offend one or more stakeholders.

In the case of Hoppo, they may be accused of incompetence in drawing up the outsourcing contract with Red Co. The fact that the *legal agreement is considered by some to be ambiguous* suggests incompetence and this may erode Hoppo's reputation for competence. The *loss of about 1,000 jobs at Red Co*, arising from the loss of the Hoppo contract, is likely to be widely reported, particularly in Teeland. Although jobs are likely to be created in Yuland if the new facility is built there, some may interpret this re-location as a breach of good faith with Red Co and demonstrating a lack of business integrity on Hoppo's part. The effect of any loss of reputation for Hoppo could be serious.

Hoppo may also be portrayed as an *unreliable business partner* and this may affect future outsource opportunities, especially where the other company is in another jurisdiction and legal complications may consequently arise. In addition, any loss of reputation is probably quite important for Hoppo, as the case makes clear that both *customers and some key employees interact* with the company partly based on its favourable social and environmental reputation. In that case, an eroded reputation may affect product sales and also recruitment.

44 H&Z COMPANY

Key answer tips

In the SBL exam you will not earn marks for definitions or for describing issues – higher level skills are required – so make sure in **part (a)** you answer the question. In **part (b)** focus on the most popular risk assessment framework of an impact/likelihood matrix. However, do not take this as the invitation to draw and describe the matrix in detail, since this will not earn you marks.

(a)   **John Pentanol's understanding of his role as a risk manager**

A risk manager typically has four main roles:

- **Providing overall leadership, vision and direction**

    This involves the establishment of risk management (RM) policies, establishing RM systems and seeking opportunities for improvement or tightening of systems.

    Whereas the establishment of RM policies is usually the most important first step in risk management, *John launched straight into detailed risk assessments* (as he saw it). It is much more important, initially, to gain an understanding of the business, its strategies, controls and risk exposures. The assessment comes once the policy has been put in place.

    Furthermore, he told Jane Xylene that his role as risk manager involved eliminating 'all of the highest risks at H&Z Company' which is an incorrect view. Jane Xylene was correct to say that entrepreneurial risk was important, for example.

- **Developing and promoting RM competences, systems, culture, procedures, protocols and patterns of behaviour**

  It is important to understand that risk management is as much about instituting and embedding risk systems as much as issuing written procedure.

  The systems must be capable of accurate risk assessment which seems not to be the case at H&Z as he didn't account for variables other than impact/hazard.

- **Reporting on the above to management and risk committee as appropriate**

  Reporting information should be in a form able to be used for the generation of external reporting as necessary.

  John's issuing of 'advice' will usually be less useful than full reporting information containing all of the information necessary for management to decide on risk policy.

  The risk manager is an operational role in a company such as H&Z Company and it will usually be up to senior management to decide on important matters such as withdrawal from risky activities. John was being presumptuous and overstepping his role in issuing advice on withdrawal from Risk 3. It is his job to report on risks to senior management and for them to make such decisions based on the information he provides.

- **Ensuring compliance with relevant codes, regulations, statutes, etc.**

  This may be at national level (e.g. Sarbanes Oxley) or it may be industry specific. Banks, oil, mining and some parts of the tourism industry, for example, all have internal risk rules that risk managers are required to comply with.

  There is insufficient information in the case to assess whether John understood this.

(b) **A criticism of John's advice**

The advice is based on an incomplete and flawed risk assessment. Most simple risk assessment frameworks comprise at least two variables of which impact or hazard is only one. The other key variable is probability. Risk impact has to be *weighed against probability* and the fact that a risk has a high potential impact does not mean the risk should be avoided as long as the probability is within acceptable limits. It is the *weighted combination* of *hazard/impact and probability* that forms the basis for meaningful risk assessment.

John appears to be very certain of his impact assessments but the case does not tell us on what information the assessment is made.

It is important to recognise that 'hard' *data is very difficult to obtain on both impact and probability*. Both measures are often made with a degree of assumption and absolute measures such as John's ranking of Risks 1, 2 and 3 are not as straightforward as he suggests.

John also overlooks a key strategic reason for H&Z bearing the risks in the first place, which is the *return achievable by the bearing of risk*. Every investment and business strategy carries a degree of risk and this must be *weighed against the financial return* that can be expected by the bearing of the risk.

Marking scheme

			Marks
(a)	(i)	1 mark for evidence of understanding in each type of role (half mark for identification and half for description)	Up to 4
	(ii)	1 mark for each relevant assessment comment on John's understanding of the role	Up to 4
		Maximum	**8**
(b)		2 marks for evidence of understanding of risk assessment (impact/hazard and probability)	2
		2 marks for recognition of uncertainties over impact and probability information and description	2
		2 marks for importance of return and recognition of lack of return/benefit information and description	2
		Maximum	**6**
Total			**14**

45 SALTOC

Key answer tips

(a) To ensure good marks in this requirement it is vital to refer to Saltoc.

(b) The Turnbull Guidance on Embedding Risk into Culture would give a good answer structure here

(c) This requirement should have been relatively easy marks for the well prepared student, as this topic is raised in an examiner's article titled 'Risk and Environmental Auditing' dated March 2009.

REPORT

To: The Board of Saltoc

Subject: Risk Management

By: External consultant

0 Introduction

This report considers two approaches to managing the current problems with risk management – firstly, embedding risk and, secondly, the case for an external risk audit.

1 Embedding risk

Good internal controls start with a full risk assessment and this control should be introduced and amended to respond to changes in the risk profile as appropriate on an ongoing basis. To have risk awareness and risk systems embedded implies a number of things. It means that risk management is *included within the control systems of an organisation* – for example, Saltoc's budgetary control system will need to reflect the risk metrics in the embedded system.

When risk is embedded, the budgetary control and reward systems would recognise the need for risk awareness in them by including risk-related metrics. When embedded, risk is *interconnected with other systems* so that risks must be taken into account before other internal controls will work effectively. So a given job description, for example, might have a particular risk check included in it which is then assessed annually in the job-holder's appraisal.

This would typically be a part of an operation manager's job description (Harry Ho at Saltoc) where, for example, the accident rate could be a metric built into his annual appraisal.

In an embedded risk system, risk is *not seen as a separate part of internal control but is 'woven in'* to other internal controls and is a *part of the organisation's culture.*

The cultural norms in the IT department, for example, would be an implicit understanding that sensitive data is not transferred to portable laptops and that laptops are not left in unattended cars. This is a part of the taken-for-grantedness of embedded risk systems when woven into culture.

Finally, the management of risk is *'normal' behaviour at all levels.* Behaviour concerned with risk management is never seen as 'odd' or 'interfering' but as much a part of the normal business activity as trading and adding shareholder value.

2   Saltoc's management culture and implementing embedded risk systems

On the evidence of the case, the existing management culture at Saltoc would not be suitable for the introduction of embedded risk systems for four reasons.

There is evidence of a *lack of unity and some mutual distrust within the board.* Some of the members plainly dislike one another and the lack of trust in colleagues is likely to frustrate efforts to change systems and culture throughout the whole organisation. The fact that Peter believes Harry and Laura should be removed is ample evidence of the discord that exists.

Linked to this is the *blame culture.* Rather than seek to resolve the risk problems at Saltoc, the board's first instinct appears to have been to blame others for the problems. Peter blamed Harry and Laura whilst they blamed Peter for his budgetary allocations to their departments. There is no evidence of a consensus, or even a willingness to work together on new systems.

There is a *lack of leadership and understanding from CEO* Ken Tonno. He is clearly most concerned with short term financial measures and cash flow. The tone of his remarks is sceptical, referring as he did to 'even more' administration on risks and controls. It seems unlikely that he would personally lead an effort to redesign structures, systems and culture to embed risks at Saltoc.

The case makes reference to *problems with departmental leadership* among board members. Any change to systems or practice needs departmental directors to be able to lead their departments and this may not be possible if respect is lacking.

3   The case for an external risk audit at Saltoc Company

External risk auditing is an *independent review and assessment of the risks,* controls and safeguards in an organisation by someone from outside the company. Internal risk auditing also occurs in many organisations. It involves an *identification of the risks* within given frames of reference (the whole company, a given area of activity, a given department or location) and *advice on managing those risks in terms of a risk assessment.*

The first argument in favour of an external risk audit at Saltoc Company is the *'fresh pair of eyes' effect* that applies to the use of any external consultant. It seems evident that the existing management is unaware of all of the risks faced by the company and a new person coming in might identify new risks.

An external person would *take responsibility away from the squabbling directors* who are unlikely to work together on it.

There is obviously enough tension and discord among board members to threaten any audit where collaboration would be needed to provide information and implement any recommendations.

An external risk auditor would provide an *unbiased view of the causes of poor risk management* in Saltoc and hence be able to give advice on where things can be improved. This will be important when recommending changes to systems to account for risks as it may impact some departments more than others. If there is any validity to Peter's claims about Harry and Laura then their departments may be disproportionately affected and an independent auditor would be able to comment on this from an objective viewpoint.

In some countries, (i.e. under Sarbanes Oxley), an element of independent assessment is necessary for compliance. In any event, encouraging independent scrutiny is good practice and *reassures external stakeholders (such as shareholders)* in the same way that an external financial audit does. At a time when the effectiveness of internal risk controls have been questioned (such as recently after the fire and the laptop theft), investor confidence is especially important.

Saltoc needs to demonstrate a robust response to the incidents in order to *restore customer confidence*. They have already lost some customer confidence and so the implementation of risk systems following the risk audit, might assume strategic importance. The appointment of an external risk auditor would help in this regard.

Marking scheme		Marks
(a)	1 mark for each relevant point describing embeddedness to a maximum of 3 marks.	
	1 mark for each relevant point of application to case to a maximum of 3 marks.	6
(b)	2 marks for each issue identified and discussed in context	
	(1 for recognition only)	8
(c)	1 mark for each point of explanation of external risk auditing up to a maximum of 3.	
	2 marks for each relevant point in the construction of the argument (1 for recognition, 1 for development and application to the case).	11
Total		**25**

46   P&J

Key answer tips

This scenario and question covered a company making a product which proved to be a health risk. The requirement then examined a broad range of topic areas in this context:

Part (a) required students to define 'social footprint' and then 'explain' the implications. The issues were noted in the scenario and the prepared and practised candidate would have noted this.

Part (b) was concerned with the diversification of risk requiring the candidates to explain why it would be difficult for P&J rather than list the aspects of TARA. The examiner commented that this part was not done well.

(a)   Social footprint and potential social implications

Social footprint

The term 'footprint' is used to refer to the impact or effect that an entity (such as an organisation) can have on a given set of concerns or stakeholder interests. A 'social footprint' is the impact on people, society and the wellbeing of communities. Impacts can be positive (such as the provision of jobs and community benefits) or negative, such as when a plant closure increases unemployment or when people become sick from emissions from a plant or the use of a product. Professor Kroll's findings have both positive and negative impacts upon society and communities in the case of P&J.

Potential implications

The discovery by Professor Kroll will lead, whether by a tightening of controls or by a reduction in P&J's activities, to lower exposures to X32 in Aytown and Betown, and hence there will, over time, be *less X32-related disease.* There will, in consequence, be fewer people suffering, and, accordingly, less misery for the affected families and friends of sufferers. *A lower mortality* from X32-related disease will benefit communities and families as well as those individuals directly affected. However, as they are continuing to manufacture the product, if Professor Kroll's findings prove correct, larger numbers of people using the product will ultimately be affected worldwide.

Loss of jobs in the various stages of the P&J supply chain. The forecast losses, even in the best case scenario, would be likely to involve the loss of jobs and employment levels at P&J plants and its suppliers. The worst case scenario, in which the company itself would be lost, would involve the loss of the 45,000 P&J jobs plus many more among suppliers and in the communities supported by the P&J plants (such as in local businesses in Aytown and Betown).

Loss of, or serious damage to, communities in which the operations are located. This includes the economic and social benefits in the developing countries and a very high level of social loss in Aytown and Betown (in Emmland), where both towns are highly dependent on a single employer. It is likely that Aytown, effectively a 'company town' with 45% of the jobs at P&J, will be very badly affected and the good causes in Betown, such as the nursery and adult education classes, will no longer be able to be supported.

The loss of a major employer from a town can lead to a loss of community cohesion, net outward migration and a loss of, or deterioration in, community facilities.

There will be a loss *of economic value for shareholders,* and a reduction in the standards of living for those depending upon the company's value for income or capital growth. This might result in a reduction in pension benefits or endowment values, where P&J shares are a part of the value of such funds. Individuals holding P&J shares may lose a substantial proportion of their personal wealth.

Tutorial note

Allow other relevant impacts such as loss of taxes to fund states services, increases in state funding to support unemployed/sick workers, etc.

(b)   Risk diversification

Diversification of risk means adjusting the balance of activities so that the company is less exposed to the risky activities and has a wider range of activities over which to spread risk and return. Risks can be diversified by discontinuing risky activities or reducing exposure by, for example, disposing of assets or selling shares associated with the risk exposure.

Problems with diversification of risks

In the case of P&J, the case highlights a number of issues that make P&J particularly vulnerable and which would place constraints on its ability to diversify the X32 legal risk.

A key risk is that the company's portfolio of activities is heavily skewed towards X32 with *60% of its business in* X32 when Kroll's findings were published. This is a very unbalanced portfolio and makes the company structurally vulnerable to any health threat that X32 poses. It means that a majority of its assets and expertise will be dedicated to a single material and anything that might be a risk relating to sales of that material would be a risk to the whole company.

The case says that the *plant cannot be adapted to produce other materials.* A mine, for example, cannot suddenly be 'adapted' to produce a safer alternative. The case also says that processing plants are dedicated exclusively to X32 and cannot be modified to process other materials. This means that they either continue to process X32 or they must be completely refitted to work on alternative materials.

As a result of that, P&J is *unlikely to be able to dispose of X32 assets profitably* now that Kroll's findings are known about and the reasons for the health concerns have been identified. The reaction of society to X32 was highlighted by Hannah Yin as a key factor in determining the likelihood of the risk and this might make it difficult to sell the assets on to others.

Finally, the obvious way to diversify the risk is to expand the remaining 40% of the portfolio to become more prominent. However, the company has *little by way of retained earnings and is already highly geared* with little prospect of further borrowing. This is likely to limit its options for developing new products as a means of diversification. Share issues would be a possible way of re-financing, but with such a high exposure to X32 losses, this would be problematic.

Marking scheme		
		Marks
(a)	2 marks for definition of social footprint. 2 marks for each implication identified and discussed.	10
(b)	2 marks for description of risk diversification. 2 marks for each problem with diversification.	10
Total		**20**

47 CHEN PRODUCTS

Key answer tips

The four aspects of the TARA model can provide the basis for your answer though the key is to ensure that you explain **how** these strategies may be applied to the case.

RISK MANAGEMENT STRATEGIES AND CHEN PRODUCTS

Risk transference strategy

This would involve the company accepting a portion of the risk and seeking to transfer a part to a third party. Although an unlikely possibility given the state of existing claims, insurance against future claims would serve to limit Chen's potential losses and place a limit on its losses. Outsourcing manufacture may be a way of transferring risk if the outsourcee can be persuaded to accept some of the product liability.

Risk avoidance strategy

An avoidance strategy involves discontinuing the activity that is exposing the company to risk. In the case of Chen this would involve ceasing production of Product 2. This would be pursued if the impact (hazard) and probability of incurring an acceptable level of liability were both considered to be unacceptably high and there were no options for transference or reduction.

Risk reduction strategy

A risk reduction strategy involves seeking to retain a component of the risk (in order to enjoy the return assumed to be associated with that risk) but to reduce it and thereby limit its ability to create liability. Chen produces four products and it could reconfigure its production capacity to produce proportionately more of Products 1, 3 and 4 and proportionately less of Product 2. This would reduce Product 2 in the overall portfolio and therefore Chen's exposure to its risks. This would need to be associated with instructions to other departments (e.g. sales and marketing) to similarly reconfigure activities to sell more of the other products and less of Product 2.

Risk acceptance strategy

A risk acceptance strategy involves taking limited or no action to reduce the exposure to risk and would be taken if the returns expected from bearing the risk were expected to be greater than the potential liabilities. The case mentions that Product 2 is highly profitable and it may be that the returns attainable by maintaining and even increasing Product 2's sales are worth the liabilities incurred by compensation claims. This is a risk acceptance strategy.

Marking scheme	
	Marks
Half mark for identification of each strategy	2
One mark for definition of each strategy	4
One mark for application of each strategy to Chen Products	4
	—
Total	**10**
	—

E: TECHNOLOGY AND DATA ANALYTICS

48   GOOD SPORTS

Key answer tips

Part (a) wants you to discuss fairly generic advantages and disadvantages of e-business and, as such, is not representative of the SBL exam. This part has been included, however, as useful revision. **Part (b)** is more typical of SBL, asking for an application of these benefits and problems to Good Sports. A key issue to pick up on in part (b) will be the loss of competitive advantage that Good Sports gets from its personal contact with customers.

(a)   To: **Good Sports Limited**

From: **xxxxx**

E-Business strategy

Clearly, the markets that Good Sports operates in are being affected by the development of e-business and its experiences to date are mixed to say the least. In many ways the advantages and disadvantages of e-business are best related to the benefit the customer gets from the activity.

- First, through integrating and accelerating business processes, e-business technologies enable response and delivery times to be speeded up.

- Second, there are new business opportunities for information-based products and services.

- Third, websites can be linked with customer databases and provide much greater insights into customer buying behaviour and needs.

- Fourth, there is far greater ability for interaction with the customer, which enables customisation and a dialogue to be developed.

- Finally, customers may themselves form communities able to contact one another.

There is considerable evidence to show how small operators like Good Sports are able to base their whole strategy on e-business and achieve high rates of growth. The key to Good Sport's survival is customer service – in strategic terms they are very much niche marketers supplying specialist service and advice to a small section of the local market. The nature of the business means that face-to-face contact is crucial in moving customers from awareness to action (AIDA – awareness, interest, desire and action). There are therefore limits to the ability of e-business to replace such contact.

ANSWERS TO TECHNICAL PRACTICE QUESTIONS : SECTION 3

(b)   Good Sports has pursued a conscious niche or focus differentiation strategy, seeking to serve a local market in a way that isolates it from the competition of the large national sports good retailers competing on the basis of supplying famous brands at highly competitive prices. Does it make strategic sense for Good Sports to make the heavy investment necessary to supply goods online? Will this enhance its ability to supply their chosen market?

In terms of price, e-business is bringing much greater price transparency – the problem for companies like Good Sports is that customers may use their expertise to research into a particular type and brand of sports equipment and then simply search the Internet for the cheapest supply.

Porter in an article examining the impact of the Internet argues that rather than making strategy obsolete it has in fact made it more important. The Internet has tended to weaken industry profitability and made it more difficult to hold onto operational advantages. Choosing which customers you serve and how are even more critical decisions.

However the personal advice and performance side of the business could be linked to new ways of promoting the product and communicating with the customer. The development of customer communities referred to above could be a real way of increasing customer loyalty. The partners are anxious to avoid head-on competition with the national retailers. One way of increasing the size and strength of the niche they occupy is to use the Internet as a means of targeting their particular customers and providing insights into the use and performance of certain types of equipment by local clubs and users. There is considerable scope for innovation that enhances the service offered to their customers. As always there is a need to balance the costs and benefits of time spent. The Internet can provide a relatively cost effective way of providing greater service to their customers. There is little in the scenario to suggest they have reached saturation point in their chosen niche market. Overall there is a need for Good Sports to decide what and where its market is and how this can be improved by the use of e-business.

Marking scheme		Marks
(a)	1 mark for each appropriate point up to a maximum of	15
(b)	1 mark for each relevant point up to a maximum of	10
Total		**25**

49   CRONIN AUTO RETAIL

Key answer tips

Candidate answers do not have to be strictly classified within each of the factors identified below. In reality, suggestions will cross the boundaries of these factors.

To score well in this area, students would have had to make their points as relevant as possible to the scenario. Weaker students may simply regurgitate their study notes and explain the approaches rather than applying them to the scenario and this is unlikely to score well, if at all.

KAPLAN PUBLISHING   297

Interactivity concerns the development of a two-way relationship between the customer and the supplier. The traditional display advertising and mail-shots used by CAR are examples of 'push media' where the marketing message is broadcast to current and potential customers. Their current website continues this approach, with the stock listing essentially representing a continually updated, but widely accessible, display advertisement. Supplementing mail-shots with e-mails could be immediately considered by CAR and would be a cheaper alternative to mail-shots. However, it still remains a 'push technique' with little dialogue with the customer.

Here are three ideas that CAR could consider to improve the interactivity of its site. Other legitimate suggestions will also be given credit.

1   Encouraging potential buyers on their website to ask questions about any car that they are interested in. Both questions and answers are published. This may provide someone with the vital information that clinches the sale. It also creates a great enthusiasm around the car. Buyers may move quickly so that they do not lose the opportunity to buy the car.

     On e-bay, customers are encouraged to 'ask a question' of the seller and this often leads to long threads where the supplier and potential buyers interact.

2   Many buyers would like to test drive a car before they purchase it. CAR could provide the opportunity for customers to book a test drive over the Internet.

3   Once a purchase had been complete, CAR might encourage feedback which could be published on the website. In this instance, customers are actually providing information that is commercially useful to buyers. This may be in the form of testimonials, or in the form of more structured feedback that e-bay encourages. Suppliers who have 100% positive feedback backed up by testimonials from previous buyers are powerfully reinforcing their marketing message.

Intelligence is about identifying and understanding the needs of potential customers and how they wish to be communicated with. It is traditionally the area of market research and marketing research. Currently CAR does very little research. It relies on a database that only consists of people who have actually bought cars from the company. Collecting email addresses through promotions and interactivity initiatives (see above) provides a much greater pool of potential customers who can be kept up-to-date through email.

It can also give CAR significant intelligence about the type of cars that they are interested in and at what price. At present, the buyers for CAR use their experience when buying cars at auction and there is some concern that they buy what they would like to drive, not what the customers want to drive. It would be useful to support this experience with quantitative information about the type of cars potential buyers are really interested in. This may lead to a change in buying policy.

Individualisation concerns the tailoring of marketing information to each individual, unlike traditional media where the same message tends to be sent to everyone. Personalisation is a key element in building an effective relationship with the customer. In the context of CAR, individuals who have shown interest in a certain model or type of car may be selectively emailed when a similar car becomes available. This approach may also be used for current customers. For example, someone who purchased a particular car two or three years ago might be e-mailed about an opportunity to upgrade to an updated model. For individualisation to be successful, sufficient details must be collected through the intelligence and interactive facets of the '6 Is'.

Individualisation will also be key in offering relevant after-sales service.

This may concern inviting customers to return their cars for servicing at the correct dates or offering services only appropriate to that type of car. For example, circulating details of air-conditioning renewal only to customers with air conditioned cars.

Independence of location concerns the geographical location of the company. Electronic media increases the geographical reach of a company. For many companies this gives opportunities to sell into international markets which had previously been inaccessible to them.

This facet of the new media is unlikely to be appropriate to CAR. Most sales are to customers who are within two hours' drive of the CAR premises.

The commodity nature of the cars that CAR are selling means that similar cars will be available throughout the country, often from garages that offer local service and support. Furthermore, the long term lease on CAR's current premises makes it unlikely that they will be able to locate to a cheaper site and hence exploit the independence of location offered by the new media.

Marking scheme – technical marks	
	Marks
Up to 1 mark for appropriate point that applies the 4 areas to the scenario, up to a maximum of	16

How well has the candidate demonstrated Professional Skills as follows:	Not at all	Not well	Quite well	Very well
Professional scepticism skills relevant to the achievability for CAR of the benefits from e-marketing.	The candidate has not determined that the elements requested are potential benefits of using e-marketing within the business.	The candidate has failed to show any scepticism about the e-marketing benefits and has assumed that all benefits will be derived.	The candidate has identified that the benefits from e-marketing are not automatic and that some may not always be derived. But the candidate has not identified which of these may not be derived by CAR.	The candidate has identified that, due to the nature of the business, it is unlikely to derive any benefits from the independence of location.
	0	0.5	1	2

50   SRO

Key answer tips

The key in **part (a)** will be to recognise that there are four components needed in an answer – problems in both application and general controls, as well as necessary improvements for both. Given 15 marks for all four elements only 2 or 3 problems in each area will have needed to have been identified.

Part (b) concerning corporate governance and ethics is examined in a strategic manner rather than the more technical manner that students may be accustomed to from lower papers.

(a) SRO has recognised the importance of the need for functioning systems at all times, and so have ensured that a backup is available. This is key, as any loss of functionality will affect its ability to operate, given that the entire operations are carried out online. However, there are some problems with its general controls, which could severely disrupt business.

General controls

These are controls which relate to the computer environment and, hence, could affect any or all applications in use. These may be policies with regards to the treatment of hardware or procurement, for example, or could be specific security procedures which are in place. SRO appears to recognise the need for general controls by having a separate computer centre, with secure access, a firewall and a password system to protect against unauthorised access. However, despite this recognition, there are a number of areas where the general controls are inadequate.

The computer centre is not secured despite the capability to do so. The reason given is not sufficient to risk security controls for. Although the 'majority of staff' at headquarters are IT support personnel, there are still some staff who should not have access to the computer centre. Indeed, not all IT staff need access to the main servers. Temporary staff should not fulfil roles which are strategically important and so, to risk the entire operations by providing them with unrestricted access, SRO is not showing adequate control. Similarly, the use of a general user id and simple password means that they have access not just to the hardware, but to the entire system too. The user id and password would be simple to guess should anyone be attempting to hack into the system. SRO must immediately revert to the fingerprint access system, and must ensure that all staff are aware of the importance of preventing unauthorised access. The 'administrator' user should be removed immediately, and only those with administrator rights should be afforded them in conjunction with their unique user ID.

Temporary staff should be issued with unique user ids so that SRO can ascertain who has carried out any transactions on the system. In addition, users should be reminded of the necessity of changing passwords regularly and not writing them down anywhere. This could be enforced in training and by the provision of a procedures document.

The firewall has been turned off to allow the intelligent software to upload its finding onto SRO's system. Unfortunately, turning off the firewall not only allows this to happen, it also opens the systems to the threat of hackers. The firewall should be immediately re-installed. If it is finding difficulties with the application, it may be that there is a security risk with that. This should be thoroughly investigated and corrected.

SRO has taken precautions to have a backup system in place as contingency against disasters. However, the system should be in a remote location, rather than in the same location as the main servers. If there were a fire, for example, both the main servers and the backup servers would be affected. Similarly, by having a direct link between the servers, any data corruption or unauthorised access would affect both the servers and their backups. There should be a slight time delay in the connection to prevent this from happening, so immediately a problem is detected the link could be terminated, allowing the backup to be unaffected.

The controls mentioned above would affect all systems. There are some controls which affect only specific applications used by the organisation. These are known as application controls and help ensure that transactions are authorised, and are completely and accurately recorded, processed and reported.

Application controls

There are some issues with the application controls on the review system, which form a threat to the accuracy and reliability of the information provided on the system.

The intelligent software itself appears to provide out-of-date information and there is, currently, no way of assessing whether this is the case. A verification check may be necessary to ascertain the date of the initial posting of information and whether this is earlier or later than the date of information already held.

The reviews posted by users may, or may not, be a fair representation of the service offered. SRO does not verify that the information is correct, nor do they verify whether the users are who they claim to be. Indeed, the ability for users to post anonymously means that they could post whatever they like. There is a possibility that the users may be employed by the stores being reviewed, and giving positive reviews in order to benefit from them. Alternatively, they may be posting negative reviews about their competitors, again compromising the reliability and independence of the reviews. If this were happening, and were to be discovered, it could threaten the entire existence of SRO. It may be that a control needs to be included whereby reviewers can only submit a review if there has been an actual transaction with the store. Similarly, the stores should have the opportunity to respond to a review, made simpler if there is a transaction identifier available.

Overall, it appears that, despite having many of the tools in place, SRO is not using them adequately. Procedures should be clearly defined and adhered to in order to protect from such risks.

(b) **There are two areas of concern identified by SRO:**

Commercial conflicts of interest

SRO's business objective is to 'provide an unbiased review of online stores to ensure the customer has all available information'. So, to meet this objective they should focus on both the terms 'unbiased' and 'all available information'. The fact that SRO provides some reviews itself, which, although honest, seek to show certain stores in a positive light, goes against this objective.

The dilemma for SRO is that the online stores themselves provide both sets of revenue streams for SRO. It is in SRO's interest that the reviews are accurate, otherwise they will lose its users who rely on SRO for an honest and truthful review. Should they use another comparison site, or shop around themselves, SRO will no longer gain commission or advertising revenue. However, if the reviews are negative, it is also unlikely that the store in question will advertise in future on SRO's site and commission sales will also fall, as users of SRO's site will not follow links towards a store with negative reviews.

SRO either needs to change its business objective to remove the terms 'unbiased' and 'all available information', or they need to consider how to do this whilst maintaining their revenue streams. Ideally, the provision of honest reviews should encourage the stores to provide a good service at all times and then this would no longer be an issue.

Relocating company operations

SRO is considering moving its operations to an overseas country with tax and cost benefits. Whilst this may seem to be an attractive option from a financial perspective, there are other elements which should be considered.

The dilemma is that the benefits obtained financially may be counteracted by operational problems. The country they are considering relocating to is poorly regulated and does not have legislative controls with regards to the quality of information systems or security of data contained within them, even for personal data.

This could lead to the risk of loss of personal data of the registered users, which could cause great reputational damage, should it occur. SRO has already recognised some control issues with its systems and it is likely that these would be worsened in a poorly regulated country.

It is mentioned that the country's culture is such that accepting unauthorised payments is considered acceptable, even if it is not publicly acknowledged. SRO would have the dilemma of whether to behave within the culture of the country, even though such business behaviour may be seen as illegal or considered unethical in its home nation, or whether to take a stance against it, and thus put themselves at a competitive disadvantage. The latter would be in line with their current code of conduct, but it may be difficult to convince locally sourced staff of this.

Given that Amy created the company quite recently, in 2010, with the aim of overcoming the unethical behaviour she perceived to exist in the online retail industry, it would appear that both of the dilemmas considered above would risk the entire paradigm of the company, its reason for existence.

Marking scheme		Marks
(a)	Up to 1 mark for each appropriate point up to a maximum of	15
(b)	Up to 1 mark for each appropriate point up to a maximum of	10
Total		25

51 AEC

Key answer tips

Part (a) will be much more straightforward if you choose an appropriate model to add structure and generate ideas – in this case the best model is McDonald and Wilson's 6I's model. It is important to distinguish that in this section you are not being asked to create an e-marketing plan (that is required in part b) of the question), you are merely asked to **explain the differences that e-marketing** has to traditional marketing media. The 6I's model best achieves this .You could set up a planning page with the 6I's listed out and then add points to this plan as you read the question.

In **part (b)** you are asked **to use e-marketing**. You should be able to distinguish this clearly from part a) of the question and not mix your answers together – part a) wants you to explain e-marketing (this will focus on its differences and benefits), part b) then wants you to use it (this will focus on practical suggestions for AEC). A useful model will be the 7P's model and you could approach this in the same way as part a) – set could set up a planning page with the 7P's listed out and then add points to this plan as you read the question.

(a) A key characteristic of traditional marketing media such as advertising and direct mail is that it is predominantly a 'push' technology where the media is distributed to customers and potential customers. There is limited interaction with the customer and indeed, in the case of advertising and to a lesser degree direct mail, there is no certainty that the intended recipient actually received the message. In contrast, the new media, particularly the Internet, is predominantly a 'pull' technology – the customer having initiated the visit to the web site.

This may lead to subsequent push activities, such as sending e-mails to people who have registered their interest on the site, but the initial communication is a pull event. The marketing manager must be careful that, by switching so much of her budget to pull technologies, she does not forego opportunities to find new customers – or reinforce her message – through established push technologies. She must ensure that the company's web site is established in such a way that sufficient people find it, and that when they do, they are prepared to record enough details to allow subsequent push activities.

Dave Chaffey examines the difference between traditional and new marketing media in the context of six 'I's; interactivity, intelligence, individualisation, integration, industry restructuring and independence of location. Four of these are used in this answer.

Interactivity is a significant feature of the new media, allowing a long-term dialogue to develop between the customer and the supplier. In the context of the web site, this is likely to be through e-mails, providing the customer with information and special offers for their areas of specific interest. To initiate this dialogue the web site must capture information such as e-mail address, name, age, gender and areas of interest. The AEC site only collects such information for people who wish to view downloadable study material. This is too restrictive and it will probably exclude all the potential CPD customers. AEC needs to consider ways of making it easier and worthwhile for visitors to the site to register their details. There is no evidence of AEC contemplating the potential use of interactive digital TV or mobile phones to establish long-term dialogues with their customers.

Intelligence has also been a key feature of the new media – allowing the relatively cheap collection of marketing research data about customers' requirements. This is routinely available from web logs and these logs need to be viewed and analysed using appropriate software. This type of analysis is rarely available in the traditional media. For example, AEC does not know how often their training course catalogue is accessed and which pages are looked at. It only knows which training courses are eventually bought. With the new media the company is able to see which services and products are accessed and also to measure how many of these are turned into actual sales. This conversion rate may be an important source of information – for example, why are certain web pages often visited but few sales result – is it a problem with the web page? – is it a problem with the product? An understanding of visit patterns allows the organisation to focus on particular products and services. This analysis should already be available to AEC but there is no evidence that it uses it or is even aware of it.

The new media also permit the marketing to be *individualised*, geared to a particular market segment, company or individual person. In the context of AEC this individualisation could be achieved in at least two ways to reflect clear market segmentation. AEC has recently won a contract to supply professional accountancy training to a global accounting company. All students working for this company will now be trained by AEC in one of its worldwide centres. At present this company and its students will be served through a generic web site.

However, the flexibility of the new media means that a site could be developed specifically for this requirement. The whole site would be geared, and branded, towards the requirements of the global accounting company. Information that is irrelevant to that customer, such as CPD, would not appear on the site. This individualised approach should strengthen the relationship with the customer.

Similarly, individuals may have their own access customised as a result of the profile that they have entered. So, for example, if they have already stated that they are currently sitting the professional stage of an examination scheme then only information relevant to that stage will be presented to them when they log in. This is an example of the principle of mass customisation that was only available in a limited form in the traditional media. AEC does not exploit this at present, but uses a generic web site that looks and feels the same, whoever the user is.

Finally, the new media provide *independence* of location allowing the company to move into geographical areas that would have been unreachable before. The Internet effectively provides a worldwide market that is open 24 hours per day, seven days per week. It is difficult to think of any traditional media which would have permitted this global reach so cheaply.

Furthermore, the web site might also omit the actual physical location of the company because there is no requirement for information to be physically sent to an address. It should also be impossible for the potential customer to gauge the size of the supplying company. AEC has exploited this to some extent as it serves a world-wide market from no clear geographical centre. However, the absence of on-line course booking means that certain physical contact details have to be provided and these might undermine the global perspective.

(b)   In the context of this question, the Ps, whether there are 4 or 7, provide a good framework for the answer, although such a framework is not mandated. The model answer below actually uses '5Ps', relating them to both technology and the situation at AEC.

Product

The product is a fundamental element of the marketing mix. If the product is not 'right' it is unlikely that the marketers will be able to persuade customers to buy the product or, if they do buy it, to convince them to become repeat buyers. In the context of the new technology, an organisation may seek opportunities for developing the product or service. These opportunities emerge from re-considering the core product or identifying options for extending it.

In the context of AEC the consideration of the product is complicated by there being at least three products promoted on their web site; training courses and training manuals for students studying for professional qualifications and training courses for qualified accountants undertaking continuing professional development (CPD). The course training manual is a tangible physical product that can be handled before purchase. Potential customers can try before they buy because a sub-section of a manual is available for inspection. This is an admirable policy. Potential customers do not have to believe that the manuals are comprehensive and well-written; they can make their own judgement based on a sample. In contrast, the training courses are services, bought on the promise of satisfaction.

AEC might profitably consider delivering elements of both student and CPD training courses through web casts and pod casts. Such courses might be fully on-line or the new technologies might be integrated with older ones, such as workshops and offline assignments, to provide a blended approach to learning.

This may be particularly appropriate for student tuition where competence is assessed by a formal examination, not by attendance at a course. AEC is already distributing course catalogues and course schedules through the Internet. However, there is no physical evidence to support the customer's evaluation of such courses. AEC might consider having sample videoed sessions available on the web so that prospective customers can assess the content and approach to training.

Although training documentation is currently available through the web site it could benefit from re-focusing. At present students pay a fixed fee which gives them access to the whole set of manuals. However, manuals for modules at the end of the scheme will only be relevant if the student passes the earlier modules. Lack of confidence may deter the student from committing to the whole manual set at the beginning of his or her studies. Similarly, candidates who become aware of AEC products only after they have passed the first few modules are unlikely to pay a fee for a manual set which includes manuals for modules that they have already passed or for which they are exempted. Consequently, it would appear more sensible to allow candidates to select the manuals they require and pay a fee per manual, with a discounted fee for buying the whole set.

AEC might also wish to consider *product bundling* where it offers further products and services to complement its core products. For example, travel booking, accommodation services and entertainment bookings might be offered to qualified accountants attending CPD courses. AEC is also in a market place where the product needs to be continually updated and developed to reflect changing or clarified requirements. For example, new training manuals may need releasing every year.

Price

The Internet has allowed pricing to be much more transparent to potential customers. They can easily visit the sites of competing companies and compare prices for similar products and services. Such accessibility may deter AEC from using the web site to offer *differential pricing*. The Internet makes products available worldwide but candidates in poorer countries are often unable to afford prices set in richer parts of the world. Consequently, AEC should consider the potential of differential pricing, making prices reflect local currencies and conditions. There is a risk of alienating people in richer countries but it may be a risk worth taking and it is possible that candidates in these richer countries may perceive differential pricing as ethical practice. Web sites produced in national languages using domain names registered in that country might not be discovered or accessed by candidates in the developed world and so differential pricing is never uncovered. However, there is still a risk that customers buying at a lower price will then sell to buyers in the segments that are charged a higher price – so AEC will have to monitor this.

The ability to continually update information on the Internet makes the dynamic pricing of products and services attractive. It is extensively used by airlines (booking early attracts large discounts) and hotels (auctioning off rooms they cannot fill that night). It appears that AEC should also consider differential pricing, particularly using early booking discounts to get the CPD courses up and running. It may also be possible to provide cheap 'late booking' offers to fill the last few places on a course.

However, there is the possibility that this will alienate people who have already booked and paid the standard fee. Hence, this will also have to be given more detailed consideration.

AEC might also wish to consider an alternative pricing structure for the documentation.

At present manuals are purchased and this might still be the case if it adopts the more modular approach suggested in the previous section. However, there may be large areas of the manual that the student is familiar with. An alternative approach is to charge the student only when they access the material.

Hence, students pay for a web service on demand – rather than through purchased download. This 'on demand' payment for actual use is becoming an increasingly popular model of delivering products.

Finally, because off-line booking incurs administrative costs and overheads it is usual to offer on-line customers a significant discount. Hence the pricing structure must recognise this. People booking through an on-line channel now expect to get a discounted price.

Place

It has been argued that the Internet has the greatest implications for place in the marketing mix because, as a distribution channel, it has a global reach, available 24 hours per day, seven days per week. AEC is already exploiting this global reach, although it has to ensure that its products make sense in a global perspective. The training manuals are easy to exploit globally as they are downloaded products which can be printed off throughout the world.

The dates and locations of training courses, in their current format, is also globally accessible but is only really relevant to people living in the geographical regions near to the eight training centres. This is particularly true of CPD courses which are only run in three centres worldwide. The global reach of the Internet can only be exploited in the context of the courses if they use the technology discussed in the *product* section of this answer, perhaps exploiting the *price* differentials discussed in the previous section.

Promotion

Although AEC has an established web site it has not actively promoted it. The promotion of the web site may involve both technology and established marketing media. From the technology perspective, AEC might consider the following to increase its web site visibility.

1   Search Engine registration. This remains the primary method of users finding products and services. Over 80% of web users state that they use search engines to find information. There are five main parameters on which search engines base the order of their ranking.

- Title – keywords in the title of a web page

- Meta tags

- Frequency of keyword in the text

- Hidden graphic text

- Links from other sites.

AEC must ensure that their web site is constructed in such a way that it has a good chance of appearing on the first page of search engine listings.

2 Building links with other web sites should increase traffic to the site as well as improving search engine ranking. The current AEC site does not appear to link (or be linked) to any other sites.

3 Viral marketing is the term used when e-mail is used to transmit a promotional message to another potential customer.

It enables a customer browsing the site to forward a page to a colleague. There is no evidence that the AEC site supports this.

4 On-line advertising includes banner advertising. As well as potentially driving customers to the site, the banner advert also builds brand awareness and reminds the customer about the company and its services. AEC must consider this.

Off-line marketing should also be concerned with promoting the web site in established media such as print, TV and radio. Key issues to communicate are the URL and the online value proposition. It may also be used for special sales promotions and offers to attract visitors to the site. 50% of the marketing manager's budget is being spent on off-line marketing media. She must consider how to integrate the web site into this part of the promotional mix.

Process

This concerns the processes used to support the customer's interaction with AEC. At present the training course part of the web site is predominantly an information site. It provides information about the product and the location and cost of the product. However, it is not used for either purchase or post-sales support. Hence if a student or a qualified accountant wishes to book on a course they have to physically contact a person who then takes booking and payment details.

There is no evidence that post-sales support such as sending joining instructions, answering queries and receiving course feedback is supported by the web site. It would be useful for AEC to consider whether training purchase and post-sales processes could be integrated into its web site. After all, a payment process has already been set up for the training manual part of the site. The automation of routine processes and answers to common questions might help free up the company's administrative resources as well as providing a better service to customers and exploiting the Internet's *independence of location*.

	Marking scheme	Marks
(a)	Up to 2 marks for recognising the distinction between push and pull technologies in the context of the scenario	2
	Up to 2 marks for issues concerned with interactivity	2
	Up to 2 marks for issues concerned with intelligence	2
	Up to 2 marks for issues concerned with individualisation	2
	Up to 2 marks for issues concerned with independence	2
	Credit will also be given for candidates who focus on Chaffey's other 'I's – industry restructuring and integration	
(b)	Up to 4 marks for issues concerned with product	4
	Up to 3 marks for issues concerned with price	3
	Up to 2 marks for issues concerned with place	2
	Up to 4 marks for issues concerned with promotion	4
	Up to 2 marks for issues concerned with process	2
	Credit will also be given for candidates who focus on other 'p's' – physical evidence and people	
Total		25

52   THE HOLIDAY COMPANY

Key answer tips

Each suggestion should be justified in terms of what it can bring to The Holiday Company.

Dilip is justified in his decision to attempt to exploit the principles of electronic marketing, as companies can benefit greatly from this approach. The five principles referred to in the question requirement may be exploited as follows:

(i)   Intelligence

The internet can be used as a low cost option of gathering intelligence about customers and potential customers. The website could use cookies to track the customers' mouse clicks, and see what has been of interest to them, and at what point they leave an area of the site. For example, do they get as far as looking at availability of a holiday and then leave the site when the price is displayed, or do they move on to another area on reading details about the hotel being offered? This can help to determine new product lines and other elements of the marketing mix.

If customers register on the site, then the company can also track their individual preferences over time, and this can help to exploit individualisation. As Dilip says, the company currently has no idea whether customers even read their brochure.

The use of e-marketing will allow analysis of who visited which part of the site, how long they stayed there, whether they went on to get more information and how many times they re-visit the same page.

(ii)   Individualisation

The current approach of sending the same marketing, covering all holidays, to every client is not appropriate for the luxury, bespoke service which Inspirations wishes to offer.

Inspirations should ensure it makes use of the features of promotion which offer individualisation, given that they are offering a bespoke service, which is, by its nature, individual. This is only possible if the company also exploits the use of intelligence, as previously mentioned. For example, if a customer has shown interest in gourmet food holidays, information relating to these can be shown on the home page. It may then offer a personalised home page when that customer visits again, with specific suggestions for them.

Customers should be able to save information on holidays which they are interested in and return to these. Inspirations could send emails if there is anything similar which may be of interest to those customers. Or, if a customer has booked a specific holiday in the past, such as a river cruise, the company may send them an email in the future with similar holidays.

(iii) Interactivity

This principle works on the idea of a 'pull' marketing approach, whereby the customers are driving the marketing and selling process, rather than the company 'pushing' its holidays at them. Given that the company wishes to sell bespoke holidays, this element is crucial.

The interactivity should begin with the use of search engines, such that when a potential customer types 'luxury holidays' or 'bespoke holidays', for example, Inspirations is one of the first to appear in the search results.

Once on the website, the customer should be able to search from easy menus, such as 'destination' or 'holiday type'. The customer should then be shown a range of options, and further action on their part may lead them to further details regarding the holiday being viewed. In this way, the customer will only view holidays and further information which is of interest to them.

Further interactivity may be provided in the form of a two-way dialogue with a holiday adviser, through an online chat function. This could work well with HC's new business unit if the adviser is knowledgeable and able to offer enhanced services, such as managing the overall booking. This could be a valued differentiator for Inspirations: offering a personalised service, as if in-store, without the customer having to be inconvenienced by visiting the store.

(iv) Integration

Holiday companies could make great use of integration, which is about sharing knowledge and marketing activity between different parts of the company. For example, if customers switch to Inspirations holidays, having previously been a customer of HC, this information could be shared such that there is already some knowledge of the customers' preferences.

Inspirations could also integrate the different elements of the holiday experience and the databases of different companies supplying the services. For example, it may be possible for the customer to book hotels, flights, car hire and excursions. Inspirations could integrate the information, such that once a customer has booked a holiday, marketing information could be sent for the elements which have not been included. Once a holiday has been booked, the website may offer suggestions for upgrades and further options.

If, for example, a holiday is booked at a particular destination, then trips available at that destination may be marketed. Depending upon the holiday purpose, different add-ons could be offered. For example, the gourmet trips for food lovers could forward details of excursions to food production facilities, with booking offers if combined with an existing holiday.

(v) Independence of location

Independence of location allows the possibility of selling into global markets. Provided Inspirations has access to flights departing from different countries, there is nothing to stop it operating as a global travel provider. It is intending to make more use of online sales, with the internet being the main source of marketing this new business, therefore high street branches are not necessary in this instance.

In order to exploit the global market, Inspirations must ensure that it offers the ability to view holiday prices, and pay, in foreign currencies. It should also ensure that it considers the current trends of holiday destinations for different markets worldwide.

Marking scheme	
	Marks
1 mark for each relevant point up to a maximum of 15 marks.	**15**

53   BA TIMES

Key answer tips

The requirement is very open ended. To gain focus in your answer, use the specific issues that the editor was concerned about in the scenario.

REPORT THE POTENTIAL IMPACT OF NEW TECHNOLOGY

From: AN Consultant

To: Victor Isaacs, BA Times

Introduction

You have some concerns about the effect of any potential technology or media change on your subscribers, on your advertisers and on the financial viability of BA Times. Your report aims to address these concerns.

You yourself are a potential barrier to the extensive use of new technology and media. Your background is in printed magazines and this is a product that you feel comfortable with. You like the physical, tactile feel of magazines and evidence suggests that your product is well liked and respected in the industry. But, increasing costs and changing reading habits mean that the future of the printed magazine industry looks bleak. However, even if you can overcome your preference for printed media, you have a further problem in understanding how new technology is going to turn round the fortunes of the *BA Times* and return it to profit.

The options

A simple option is to *just employ new technology to reduce costs*. This might give you some breathing space in which to develop a future business strategy or plan your retirement. Alternatively, you could consider an option to embrace the new technology more extensively and re-position the printed *BA Times* as just one channel to your target market. It is possible that the introduction of a comprehensive web resource may lead to a further fall in the circulation of a printed copy version of the *BA Times*. However, this would have to be researched. Perhaps your readership contains people like yourself who would still want to receive a physical copy of a magazine.

If a more radical shift to new technology and new media is to be justified, then you would have to be convinced of the possibility of generating income from at least three sources. These would offset a fall in income from the printed magazine and also address the issue of the financial viability of the company.

Benefits of the new technology

Increased advertising: The very breadth of the *BA Times* (news, articles, three associations, many examinations) probably makes display advertising only attractive to the larger learning providers which provide courses at all levels across all qualifications. Targeted advertising is much easier on the web and so the new resource may attract advertising from a wider range of learning providers. An extended product range (for example, recruitment resources) made available on the website should also bring in new advertisers from different sectors. If you can establish the *BA Times* website as the premier one-stop resource for business analysts, then attracting significant advertising should be no problem.

Subscription services within the website: Many websites contain both free and subscription resources. High quality free services can be a taster for attracting customers to the resources which are only available for a subscription. This is an established approach in web-based services and is particularly relevant in a competitive environment like examinations. Candidates may believe that investing relatively small amounts of money in extra services might give them an edge in preparing for examinations.

Income from selling intelligence: The facility of websites to capture information about visitors and their interests can bring massive benefits to an organisation in terms of marketing, customer engagement, personalisation of content etc. Also, this information will be of potential use to other organisations and with the person's consent can be forwarded and sold.

Other concerns

You are also concerned about the reaction of advertisers to any proposal to adopt new technology within the *BA Times*. However, it is likely that you will receive a positive response from advertisers. At present, advertising revenue is falling. In general, there is a growing disenchantment with push marketing technologies, where advertisers cannot be sure that their message has reached the intended market. Advertising on a comprehensive website has many advantages. Advertisements can be made specific and individualised, they can be quickly and easily updated, and the effectiveness of an advertisement or a campaign can be relatively easily analysed through the responses received from the website.

Finally, you are concerned about the effect on subscribers who cannot access a website or, like you, value a printed copy and wish to still receive one. At this stage, there is no reason why a smaller run of the printed version cannot be maintained by exploiting technology to reduce printing, distribution and office costs. Contribution to overheads will be reduced, but income from other sources (see above) should compensate. Some advertisers may also wish to continue advertising in the printed edition to supplement their web-based marketing.

The nature of the web resource also allows you to reconsider the range of products you have to offer. At present the magazine is focused on news and preparing candidates for examinations. Income is derived from learning providers advertising in the pages of the magazine. You might consider moving into related business areas that would appeal to your readership. From the feedback given, the most obvious candidate is probably recruitment. One of the respondents to the survey commented that, 'I became a business analyst to get a job, not just to sit examinations and read about examining bodies.' You might have lost focus here. For many candidates, taking examinations is a means to an end, not an end in itself, and job opportunities and careers do not seem to be considered in the *BA Times* at present. Articles about certain job roles and interview advice might be provided and a potential new income stream should open up for you from recruitment agencies placing advertisements for jobs which they have been contracted to fill.

Conclusions

The use of new technology does not mean the death of the *BA Times* in print form. Instead it opens up opportunities for new growth areas that may result in stronger financial success in the future.

Marking scheme	
	Marks
1 mark for each relevant point up to a maximum of	**10**

54 RETAIL WORLD

(a) **Briefing note:**

To: FD

Date: Today

Subject: Big data

Big data

Big data is a generic term used to describe the exponential growth of data, provided from numerous sources, available to organisations. The data is not useful in itself; it is the analysis of such data which provides valuable insights to an organisation. The finance director is right to be interested in this, as it can lead to an in-depth insight into trends and the driving forces behind those trends.

Big data can be sub analysed as the 'three vs' i.e. volume, velocity and variety. These three categories can be examined to determine their contribution towards strategic development at RW.

Volume can enhance the understanding of customer requirements and behaviour. The more data available, the greater the reliability of the trends and relationships discovered. In the analysis provided, there was a limited volume of data, spanning less than three years and incorporating only two variables. The use of big data would allow multivariate analysis over a greater time period or a greater number of shorter time periods to understand purchasing patterns better. This could help RW to create better strategies to capitalise on discovered trends.

Velocity refers to the speed of use of real-time data. As the majority of business transactions are now carried out using technology, these transactions can be captured and processed in real time if sufficient processing capacity is available. This ensures that strategies can be continually updated, in order to deliver competitive advantage. For example, as a new product is trending on social media, RW may then ensure they stock this product and aggressively market it in order to capture greater market share. Similarly, when customers are shopping online, RW could analyse their transactions in real time and use current and historic customer information to make recommendations for further purchases.

Variety refers to the different sources from which data is provided. As sources take different forms and include those not in RW's control, this is a challenging aspect of big data. However, if managed correctly, the variety provides the most detailed understanding of the market place, segmentation and individual customers. This could include competitor and industry information, sourced through key words online, to hashtags on social media and discussion forums.

There are many potential benefits which could be obtained through the analysis of big data. RW could use the results to determine where to locate their new stores. By accessing customers' shopping habits from credit and debit card records, they could determine which competing stores are used, and in which locations. This could help in the strategic planning of store locations, especially as RW is intending to continue to grow store numbers, at least over the next two years. This could help maximise the additional revenue to be gained from new stores.

RW are clearly trying to identify trends and maximise the use of them. The use of big data will provide more reliable and robust trend analysis and could lead to the discovery of previously unsuspected trends, allowing RW to capitalise on these before its industry competitors have even recognised the trend.

Further revenue streams are also available through the selling of data. Given the industry RW is in, there will be a number of branded items on offer to customers. Manufacturers of these brands are keen to carry out their own analysis and will pay for information to help with this. RW could capitalise on this new revenue stream.

Conclusion

Overall therefore, it would seem that the finance director is right to consider the use of big data. Indeed, RW may well find itself at a competitive disadvantage if it fails to do so.

However, as with all decisions, the cost-benefit implications would need to be considered before any project leading to implementation is considered.

(b)   **Slides**

> **SLIDE 1**
>
> **Blockchain technology**
>
> - **Why** blockchain **is useful for retail**
> - **Benefits**
>   - Profitability – Identifying counterfeits
>   - Profit margin – Workers' rights and ethical benefits
>   - Tracking stock – Enhancing and managing customer information
>   - Product safety – Enhancing customer loyalty programs
>   – Link with Fintech

Notes:

- **Why blockchain** – often referred to as a distributed ledger, it is basically a decentralised, digital sequence of records shared on a public network that cannot be easily tampered. the key qualities of blockchain that makes it ideal for retail networks is its transparency and immutability (unchangeable) which removes the need for a party on the supply chain to trust another party.

- **Tracking stock** – blockchain can help retailers such as RW to better track their shipments and in formal stock-taking as the entire inventory is visible at every point of the supply chain. Participants can know in real-time the level of stock and the status of new shipments. Understanding where your stock is e.g. in your supply chain or in the store or online – and then matching that with the right customer will provide a key advantage

- **Product safety** – blockchain networks allow products to be traced from the source to the end point on the supply chain making it easy to track the safety of the product. Since the chain is updated in real-time parties on the network can identify the point where an unsafe product goes into the supply chain. For example, the food traceability initiative by Walmart and IBM is a perfect illustration of this benefit. The initiative will enable Walmart, for example, to trace the origin of leafy greens back to their source in about 2 seconds. It took one week to do this historically with less accuracy. This will be of considerable benefit for RW with regard to its grocery business.

- **Identifying counterfeits** – retailers and popular brands are often burdened with the problem of counterfeit products especially of clothing, cosmetics, and luxury products. With a transparent network that links all points on the supply and delivery of product, retailers such as RW can verify the authenticity of their products and the sources whether they are new or used items. Ideal for RW given their clothing, electronic items and toiletry ranges.

- **Workers' rights** – a lot has been in the news about the poor welfare of workers along the supply chain whether it is in the cash crop farms in Africa and Asia or the manufacturing plants in Asia. to address these concerns Coca-Cola, for example, in partnership with the US department of state agreed to use blockchain technology to check the forced labour used along the supply chain for the company's products. Coca-Cola believes the transparency afforded by blockchain will curb issues of child labour, forced labour, and land rights at the source of its raw materials.

- **Ethical bene**fits – in the same vein, blockchain is also helping ensure ethical practices along these supply chains, by giving an accurate and immutable record of where a product came from and where it passed through to get to the retailer and finally the end user.

- **Managing customer information** – retailers deal with a lot of customer information some of which are personal and are best kept private. Normally, this information is used to tailor adverts to these customers and manage their preferences. However, as has been seen with the Cambridge Analytica example, there's need for a better way of storing and managing personal data. Blockchain allows retailers to tailor services and marketing to its customers without having their data on a central server.

- **Customer loyalty** – popular brands and retail outlets can use blockchain to improve customer loyalty programs. This can be through the issue of loyalty tokens on a blockchain network or leveraging blockchain for its digital sales information with ease while maintaining the security and privacy of customers.

- **Link with Fintech** – an area where blockchain is making probably the biggest impact is in the Fintech sector where major payment facilitators are considering the tech for real-time cross-border payments. RW could benefit greatly from this especially for its international customers. Using blockchain, retailers can bypass credit cards and the high processing fees that come with them. Retailers such as RW can charge customers directly; significantly increase their profit margins and will be able to sell at lower prices.

SLIDE 2

The adoption of blockchain technology

- Challenges
    - Participation
    - Reliance on human-computer interface
    - Operability
    - Skills shortage
    - Conclusion

Notes:

- **Participation** – as a network technology, blockchain requires that all points related to the supply and retail process participate in data feeding so there is no gap. Right from the start of the chain, members would input every new transaction, whether it is a product leaving the port or reaching the shelves. These transactions (or info) are linked with all others on the network and stored on multiple devices making it almost impossible to be manipulated. This reliance on participation can be a significant challenge to manage.

- **Reliance on human-computer interface** – as noted above, this dependence on input from participating entities is one of the weaknesses of blockchain because every point has to be active. Accurate records must be fed into the system which means a human-computer interface as well as an analog or digital interface. Any inaccuracies may undermine the solution offered by blockchain.

- **Operability** – the retail sector is not immune to the major barriers of blockchain adoption which include problems of interoperability between blockchain networks, scalability issues, and regulatory uncertainty.

- **Skills shortage** – RW would need to build in skills to develop such technology. This would clearly come at a cost and would rely on the availability of such skilled personnel

- **Conclusion** – blockchain has very important implications for the retail sector. The technology is impacting the supply chain and transaction aspects of retail business, areas the general public may not easily notice. These are nonetheless very crucial to the transformation of the sector and major players are considering adopting blockchain. As blockchain technology continues to mature, retailers both big and small can benefit from the transparency, trust and transaction efficiency it offers.

Marking scheme		
		Marks
(a)	Up to 1 mark for each appropriate point up to a maximum of	10
(b)	Up to 1 mark for each appropriate point up to a maximum of	8
		———
Total		**18**
		———

F: ORGANISATIONAL CONTROL AND AUDIT

55 YAHTY

Key answer tips

In this question there is no theory or framework to assist. You are advised to tackle each aspect of the control systems evident in YAHTY separately. Each should be evaluated using the three sub-headings provided (and discussed above). All your comments need to be well-explained and evidenced from the scenario, with recommendations relevant to this type of business.

REPORT

To: Board of YAHTY

From: An accountant

Subject: YAHTY's Internal control systems

Date: DD MM 200X

The purpose of this report is to evaluate YAHTY's internal control systems and make recommendations for improvement.

Advice provided by investment accountants

Each investment accountant can provide/recommend the individual investment services for their clients. Whilst some accountants may be skilled and have appropriate knowledge, this may not be the case for all accountants. The internal control system appears to be weak in two respects:

- firstly, training of accountants, and

- secondly, ensuring funds are invested to produce a high return, not simply to meet the general investment requirements of clients.

The control of the senior accountant providing investment advice if required is ineffective for two reasons:

- Firstly, the span of control is excessive; with 35 investment accountants having 200 clients each, this could relate to over 7,000 different clients to provide advice to. Given a 200-day working year, this equates to about 12 minutes for each client pa. Control cannot be exercised on a timely basis.

- Secondly, there appears to be no necessity for any client account to be reviewed anyway. The senior accountant only acts on a request basis.

These control weaknesses could result in individual client accounts providing a financial performance well below optimum.

Controls that should be implemented include:

- decreasing the span of control by employing more senior accountants

- standard review of a percentage of client accounts each year

- more detailed investigations where any investment account shows poor investment decisions.

Payment authorisations

Each investment accountant is allowed to make fund transfers relating to investments for their clients. This is appropriate as the accountant will understand the specific client requests and therefore be able to ensure that investments are being made in the appropriate funds.

However, only transfers above €100,000 require a second signatory. This amount is potentially excessive, given that the average fund value is €500,000 and most transfers are below €50,000 anyway. The authorisation limit means that almost all transfers are not checked. Control weaknesses include:

- The investment accountant could make an inappropriate investment decision.

- Funds could be transferred to the investment accountant's own bank account. This could occur because the list of investments is not linked to the bank account – so the list can be manually amended by the accountant to exclude specific investments.

Controls that should be implemented include:

- Lowering the authorisation limit for second signatories to €25,000.

- Providing for a random check on other transactions to ensure they are valid and relate to appropriate funds.

- Linking the list of investments to the payment systems in the company. When a payment is made the list is updated, thus precluding manual updating by the accountant.

Storage of documents

YAHTY is quite correct to retain evidence of the funds transfers carried out by the investment accountants. This will be needed in case of dispute regarding the amount of transfer or the funds transferred to.

However, there is a control weakness in keeping the transfer documents in date order. While this assists initial filing, document retrieval may be extremely difficult. The normal method of searching for a document is likely to be by client name; the date of the transaction may not be immediately available. Working through all documents relating to one date will also be time consuming.

To improve the control, the ordering of the documents should be changed to storage by client name. Investment accountants may undertake this task if necessary as they will be raising the documents.

Alternatively, control would be improved by using pre-numbered documents and retaining the document number on individual client accounts on the computer system. Filing of documents by document number would then provide a quick and efficient filing and retrieval system.

Closing of client accounts

The closure of a client account provides the good control of a list of investments supported by the appropriate documentation. The weakness in the control is confirming the completeness of the list of funds being transferred. If a fund is omitted from the list, there does not appear to be any way to identify this omission. This is a similar issue to the manual updating of the list of investments already noted above.

The control of the senior accountant reviewing the list of investments and agreeing the source documents will be ineffective in identifying omissions. Similar controls are again required for the payment authorisations mentioned above.

56   STEFAN KRANK

(a)   The main objectives of any internal control system are to manage the inherent risks faced by the organisation as far as is reasonably practicable. They comprise the following:

1   Business activities should be conducted in an orderly and efficient manner, with internal procedures and practices strictly adhered to. It is apparent that Stefan Krank showed very little regard to both internal procedures and the wishes of his clients when he circumvented internal controls in order to deliver higher returns.

2   However, by acting as he did, Krank put those funds which he managed at a far higher level of risk than that authorised by his clients, who were totally unaware of his unauthorised actions. The internal control system failed to ensure that he acted in line with client's instructions.

3   The assets of a business need to be adequately safeguarded, a prime consideration for a business like Fortune Investments whose basic role is to manage funds on behalf of its wealthy clients. Unfortunately, the actions of Krank directly threatened the value of the funds he had under his control, with riskier investments actually resulting in lost value.

4   By failing to safeguard his clients' funds, Krank's behaviour could have vicariously damaged the reputation and financial standing of Fortune Investments. This would have arisen if the funds he managed had incurred losses which the company were unable to cover.

5   Fraudulent activities or material errors should be both detected and prevented by the internal control system. Significant errors and any fraud could be detected through management checks and by the audit of internal procedures; neither of which seem evident in the case of Fortune Investments.

6   The fact that Krank had been the most successful fund manager for the company, delivering the best results for his clients possibly elevated him to a status which went unchecked, a clear weakness in the company's internal control system. It was only because James Reynolds escalated his concerns about his investment fund to Krank's manager that any action would have been instigated; and this was far too late.

7   Accounting records must be both complete and accurately maintained. This could not have been the case at Fortune Investments because Krank tried to confuse Mr Reynolds with statements which revealed little resemblance to the reality of his investment fund. The company directors have obligations under corporate governance provisions and legal responsibilities to maintain accurate accounting information. Therefore as Krank failed to record the true value of clients' funds, they are at risk of charges of false accounting and the criminal consequences which might arise.

8   Financial information must be prepared and available in a timely fashion. In the case of Fortune Investments, the information on the performance of individual investment funds must be available as and when the client requires it. To suggest that Mr Reynolds looked at his fund on a bad day which did not accurately represent its true performance infers that clients are reliant on Krank to furnish them with information at a time of his choosing. This arrangement is open to abuse and manipulation, as demonstrated by Krank.

Krank's behaviour

Stefan Krank's behaviour clearly breached the duty of care he owed to his clients. He was placed in a position of trust as their fund manager, which he abused in order to satisfy his own personal need to maintain his lifestyle by earning large bonuses. The clients unwittingly believed that their investments were being managed in a fund within their risk profile, when Krank was acting quite recklessly with their money.

Krank was employed by Fortune Investments to use his knowledge and skills to deliver high returns to their clients but within a controlled environment by following procedures and adhering to the expressed wishes of the investors. However, by disregarding company procedures, he failed to act in the best interest of his clients. This was compounded by the confused and wrong information which he gave to Mr Reynolds, further demonstrating a lack of care and diligence in the performance of his duties.

(b) **Funds management**

Good quality information is necessary so that management can monitor business performance. In the case of Fortune Investments, this would have ensured that they were able to understand the level of risk the business was being exposed to by the actions of Stefan Krank. They could then have taken necessary mitigating actions to reduce the risk to an acceptable level.

However, for this to be possible, the information used would require certain distinguishing characteristics:

1   It would need be accurate particularly because of the nature of the business under consideration. Complete knowledge of how individual funds are performing would allow senior managers to initiate appropriate procedures should they become suspicious about the performance of any individual fund manager. If the board had taken a more proactive stance and obtained accurate information about the funds which Krank managed, then the resultant losses and damage to clients' investments could have been avoided.

2   The information would have to be readily available in real time rather than being reliant on data compiled and submitted periodically by the fund managers. As the individual funds are invested on open capital markets, it should be possible to directly monitor their performance continuously, with alerts set up for any funds which appear to be performing outside agreed parameters. Fortune Investments should have invested in a management information system which enabled real time access to financial markets.

3   The board needs to maintain a comprehensive view of all clients' investments so that they can appraise how the business is performing holistically. Consequently investments information must be complete since any gaps would provide both a confusing and distorted picture which could possibly lead to the wrong decisions being taken.

Investor monitoring

Similarly individual investors, like James Reynolds, should be able to monitor constantly the performance of their funds so that they can be reassured that their investments are safe and delivering expected levels of returns in a risk managed way. This information would allow investors to decide whether to withdraw their money from the fund, maintain their fund as it is, or even invest further.

However, such decisions are only possible if the information can be relied on for accuracy and be continuously available.

The current arrangements at Fortune Investments means that investors are overly reliant on their fund managers to supply them with information about the performance of their investments. This allows fund managers like Stefan Krank, acting as the investors' agent, to filter information ensuring that only positive results are reported and so deflecting any criticism of their own performance.

Marking scheme		Marks
(a)	Up to 2 marks for each internal control objective evaluated in relation to Fortune Investments. 1 mark only if the fact that objectives were not achieved is not included. (Max 10 marks) Up to 2 marks for each criticism of Krank's behaviour. (Max 4 marks)	
		12
(b)	Up to 2 marks for each characteristic of good information for fund management if applied to the scenario. (Max 6 marks) Up to 2 marks for each characteristic of good information for investor monitoring if applied to the scenario. (Max 4 marks) Give no marks if the point lacks detail or application.	
		7
Total		**19**

57   DUTTON SUPERMARKET

Key answer tips

The COSO model of an effective internal control system is helpful in questions where you are asked to evaluate a control system. Ensure that any recommendations you make for improvements are practical and cost-effective.

FAILURES IN THE EXISTING SYSTEM

Failures in internal control can be categorised using a recognised formal framework. COSO is such a structure, recommended in the Sarbanes-Oxley Act and commonly used in the UK and elsewhere.

Control environment

There are both systematic failures and human errors in judgement that have combined to create the problems faced by the organisation. COSO identifies a control environment as the ethical, structural and cultural foundation to a control system. In this respect failure would relate to the ethical policy of the organisation in pursuing profits to the detriment of quality and public safety. This is also a cultural and leadership issue that goes through the spine of the organisation to the board and the CEO. The CEO must accept that he has a personal responsibility for the failure and should act accordingly.

Control activities

Control activities within the value chain are also a cause of failure. This COSO category investigates the practical controls that exist as part of operations and seeks to identify problematic areas. Suppler selection processes and criteria are one such failure.

The criteria seem to be driven by price above all other issues and will, almost inevitably lead to ever increasing problems in quality. The lack of government control in the region should also have highlighted the potential risks involved in sourcing from this location.

Another control activity is the goods receipt process at the stores. This seems ill equipped to carry out any form of quality control except that of a cursory nature. Quality control without fully examining food stuffs will be inappropriate unless it relies on previous quality control carried out at some point higher in the value chain. Since this does not exist it suggests a system wide or systematic failure through the company.

Control reporting

Control reporting or *information and communication* is a third category in the COSO framework. There are two examples of failure in relation to this. Firstly, the failure of store managers to report upwards the problems they were finding with the foodstuffs delivered to them. This failure has continued for some time and so suggests senior management with the power to correct the fault were unaware of it. Secondly, the protracted failure of senior managers to take action down the chain for the last six months is clearly unacceptable and suggests another control environment or ethical failure.

Monitoring

The final category of COSO is *monitoring*. This relates to the audit function or the control over the control. Failure seems to relate to the local auditor who has possibly colluded with the factory managers in order to bypass hygiene regulation and standards. Independence of such individuals must be assured as part of future recommendations to the company.

IMPROVEMENTS

The most important improvement is the need to balance cost against control and risk reduction. This need must begin at the board level with a reassessment of objectives and standards for operations. The threat to the public health cannot be ignored on commercial and ethical grounds.

There may be no need to search for alternative suppliers if quality standards can be improved although it is more likely that current suppliers are tainted with the stain of the scandal and so really should be replaced. Supplier selection processes need to be tightened, using suitable board level non-executive (NED) expertise to assist. Experts within proposed countries of origin may also be employed to identify potential suppliers and assist in future local audits.

The seeming complacency of local store managers must be eradicated. Much more stringent control over quality must take place at each and every step in the supply chain ending with a detailed procedural check carried out by local store manager prior to food stuffs being paced in the shelves. The usual controls over sell by dates and stock rotation should be in place.

Lines of communication including the creation of whistleblower channels to the audit committee should be put in place in order to ensure the swift and effective communication of sensitive and commercially damaging data to the appropriate authorities.

Finally, it is important for this organisation to ensure that it is responsive to external stakeholder issues. There seems to be a failure to consider the needs of suppliers and certainly, through the store managers comment regarding the minor number of complaints, customer safety. Human life is of paramount importance and it is staggering that such comments are accepted by senior management as being appropriate. The reference to the environmental group and government action reinforces the need to consider all stakeholders that impact on the organisations part of a formal review of internal control.

The conclusion must relate to the responsibility of the board in implementing these changes swiftly and effectively.

58   BLUP CO

Key answer tips

The question requires candidates to consider key themes of the importance of internal audit, audit committees and effective internal controls in a highly regulated industry. As such it is important to apply the knowledge of these areas when answering the question.

(a)   Introduction to internal audit

Internal audit is an independent appraisal function established within an organisation to examine and evaluate its activities as a service to that same organisation. The objective of internal audit is to assist members of the organisation in the effective discharge of their responsibilities.

To this end, internal audit furnishes them with analyses, appraisals, recommendations, advice and information concerning the activities reviewed. The main functions of concern to internal audit are reviews of internal controls, risk management, compliance and value for money.

Internal audit in regulated industries

Internal audit is generally considered to be more important in highly regulated industries (utilities, such as water or energy, and pharmaceuticals, defence equipment, etc.) because there is a need, not only to deliver an internal service to aid organisational efficiency, but also to *ensure compliance* with externally-imposed requirements. These may involve a range of technical product compliance issues, product safety issues, hygiene issues, production facility issues or other, similar regulations. They may be legal in nature or may be enforced by an industry regulator at 'arm's length' from government.

Where requirements are imposed by external regulation, the company must usually provide compliance information to that external regulator. This involves the establishment of *systems for collecting and analysing* that data, and also producing *reports to demonstrate the levels of compliance*. Because compliance information may not always report 'good news', it is important that the auditor is independent of those being audited and, for this reason, a formal internal audit function is usually more necessary in such circumstances.

In regulated industries, the *assurance of compliance is a strategic asset* and is somewhat more important than (merely) a desirable outcome.

Compliance failure may mean that the company loses its licence to operate, or it may be subjected to punitive fines. In either case, it could be unable to continue to conduct normal business and so internal audit's role is a key part of the company's strategic success.

(b) **(i)** **Criticisms of Blup Co's audit committee**

There are three ways in which Blup Co's audit committee fails against best practice criteria. First, it is likely that it is *not sufficiently independent* of the executive board, with its entire membership being retired executives. Some jurisdictions place a time limit (after retirement) before a former executive member can take up a non-executive director (NED) position. This is because of the likely lack of independence and objectivity that such a person would have.

Second, because the audit committee is required to monitor and review the company's accounts and internal controls, it is often required that *at least one member has recent, relevant financial experience* (in Singapore, this requirement is more stringent). In Blup Co, *all three members are water engineers*. Although clearly an important area to understand in the case of Blup, this does not appear to provide the level of financial literacy that the committee needs to perform its roles.

Third, the audit committee has allowed, and possibly encouraged, the *appointment and retention of an external auditor who appears to lack independence*. The fact that the head of the external audit practice was a member of the chairman's extended family could give the appearance of a lack of independence (even if not actually true) and is clearly a familiarity threat. Shareholders rely on external auditors to provide a rigorous and independent scrutiny of the company. The audit committee is responsible for recommending external auditor appointments to the board and in doing so, should ensure that there are no factors that might threaten their independence from the company being audited.

(ii) **Audit committee overseeing internal audit**

There are several reasons why internal audit is overseen by, and has a strong relationship with, the audit committee.

The first reason is to ensure that internal audit's remit *matches the compliance needs of the company*. The internal audit function's terms of reference are likely to be determined by strategic level objectives and the risks associated with them. The audit committee, being at the strategic level of the company, will frame these for implementation by the internal audit function.

Second, the audit committee will be able to ensure that the work of the internal audit function *supports the achievement of the strategic objectives of the company*. Whilst this applies to all functions of a business, the supervisory role that the audit committee has over the internal audit function means that this responsibility rests with the audit committee in the first instance.

Third, oversight by the audit committee *provides the necessary authority* for the internal audit function to operate effectively. This means that no-one in the company can refuse to co-operate with the internal audit function and that members of that function, whilst not being necessarily senior members of staff themselves, carry the delegated authority of the audit committee in undertaking their important work.

Fourth, by reporting to the audit committee, *internal auditors are structurally independent* from those being audited. Because they and their work is sanctioned and authorised by the audit committee, the IA function should have no material links with other departments of similar hierarchical level which might compromise independence.

Marking scheme		
		Marks
(a)	Up to 2 marks for explanation of internal audit anywhere in the answer. 2 marks for each point on regulated industry to a maximum of 6 marks.	
	Maximum	7
(b)	(i) 2 marks for each relevant criticism to a maximum of 6 marks. (ii) 2 marks for each relevant issue of AC and IA to a maximum of 6 marks.	
	Maximum	12
Total		19

59 CC & J

Key answer tips

The threats to auditor independence may be evaluated by reference to the categories of self-interest, self-review, advocacy, familiarity and intimidation threats, or considered through a practical reflection on the detail of the scenario.

Threats to auditor independence

The most obvious problem is the level of familiarity that existed between the auditor and Banco. The auditor has overstepped his professional relationship with the company and as such his ability to exclude personal considerations from professional decision making has been severely compromised.

His attendance at family gatherings affects his ability to deal with the executive and his inclusion in the shooting trip has a similarly detrimental effect on his relationship with other members of the audit committee, even if they are not effective in their position. Strict guidelines in relation to this area may have assisted had they been issued through head office.

A related point is how independence weakens over time. The relationship between the partner and the firm has existed for many years and this in itself suggests objective decision making may be compromised. The company should have a clear policy regarding auditor rotation, as required by governance regimes and auditing standards.

The contractual relationship between the two companies is another problematic area. Reliance due to size of revenues generated from single client is one area of concern. This can be coupled with the amount of non-audit work carried out and the level of profits gained through this. Such financial interest reduces the ability of the auditor to operate without concern as to financial consequence. The limited size of the audit fee may in itself compromise the ability to carry out a full audit with the allowable budget.

Fees should be set with reference to head office management and policy determined as to whether any non-audit work can be carried out. It is well known that Sarbanes-Oxley specifically prohibits non-audit work for financial auditors demonstrating the importance of the issue in global governance.

The existence of competitors and the strength of competition for lucrative work may affect the willingness of the auditor to make decisions that negatively affect client relationships. This is difficult to deal with except through reliance on the professionalism of the individual partner. It is clear in the case that such professionalism is in short supply at CC & J. This in turn brings into question the quality of recruitment and training practices at the firm. Head office cannot ignore their own culpability in what has happened. The seeming isolation of the individual involved and the lack of head office involvement in policy making is at the heart of the problems that have occurred.

60 FRANKS & FISHER

Key answer tips

Aspects of Internal audit will always be a well-examined area. Ensure you read the requirement carefully and in part (c) only argue for external appointment.

(a) **Factors to consider**

There is an obvious cost involved in setting up internal audit in an organisation and so it is typical to ask what factors signify the need for internal audit before one is established. Several factors influence the need for internal audit:

The scale, diversity and complexity of the company's activities. The larger, the more diverse and the more complex a range of activities is, the more there is to monitor (and the more opportunity there is for certain things to go wrong).

The number of employees. As a proxy for size, the number of employees signifies that larger organisations are more likely to need internal audit to underpin investor confidence than smaller concerns.

Cost-benefit considerations. Management must be certain of the benefits that will result from establishing internal audit and it must obviously be seen to outweigh the costs of doing so.

Changes in the organisational structures, reporting processes or underlying information systems. Any internal (or external) change is capable of changing the complexity of operations and, accordingly, the risk.

Changes in key risks could be internal or external in nature. The introduction of a new product, entering a new market, a change in any of the PEST/PESTEL factors or changes in the industry might trigger the need for internal audit.

Problems with existing internal control systems. Any problems with existing systems clearly signify the need for a tightening of systems and increased monitoring.

An increased number of unexplained or unacceptable events. System failures or similar events are a clear demonstration of internal control weakness.

The case on Franks & Fisher highlights three factors that would underpin its need to establish internal audit.

There has been growth in number of products, activities and (presumably) processes in recent times, thereby complicating the internal environment and introducing more opportunity for internal control failure. There have been problems with internal control systems (the line stoppage and Mr Kumas's comment that, 'problems with internal control in a number of areas').

Finally, there was an unacceptable event (the line stoppage) that was attributed to poor internal control. Mr Kumas confirmed this with his opinion about a 'great need' for internal audit.

(b) Benefits of external appointment

In practice, a decision such as this one will depend on a number of factors including the supply of required skills in the internal and external job markets. In constructing the case for an external appointment, however, the following points can be made.

Primarily, an external appointment would bring detachment and independence that would be less likely with an internal one.

Firstly, then, an external appointment would help with independence and objectivity (avoiding the possibility of auditor capture). He or she would owe no personal loyalties nor 'favours' from previous positions.

Similarly, he or she would have no personal grievances nor conflicts with other people from past disputes or arguments. Some benefit would be expected from the 'new broom' effect in that the appointment would see the company through fresh eyes. He or she would be unaware of vested interests.

He or she would be likely to come in with new ideas and expertise gained from other situations.

Finally, as with any external appointment, the possibility exists for the transfer of best practice in from outside – a net gain in knowledge for Franks & Fisher.

(c) Why internal audit should not report to the Finance Director

The first thing to say is that Mr Kumas's belief is inappropriate and it would be unacceptable for the internal auditor to report to a divisional director who might be the subject of an internal audit.

The reasons put forward in favour of his request are spurious. All of Mr Kumas's information and expertise would be available to the internal auditor in any event, with or without his oversight of the function. Reporting to Mr Kumas would be a clear threat to the independence of the internal auditor as he or she would not be objective in auditing the accounting and finance department.

The advice from relevant codes and guidelines would also strongly counsel against Mr Kumas's proposal. The Cadbury code is typical where, point (g) under the 'role of the internal audit committee' emphasised the independence of the internal audit function from management. Mr Kumas's request should be refused.

	Marking scheme		Marks
(a)	1 mark for each factor identified and briefly discussed		Up to 7
	1 mark for each factor applicable to Franks & Fisher		Up to 3
		Maximum	10
(b)	1 mark for each relevant point identified and briefly described		Up to 6
		Maximum	6
(c)	1 mark for each relevant point made		Up to 4
		Maximum	4
Total			20

61 WORLDWIDE MINERALS (WM)

Key answer tips

Consider what the main concerns of investors and analysts would be and seek to address them in the letter.

Letter for Tim Blake to send to WM's investors

Worldwide Minerals plc

Address line 1

Address line 2

Address line 3

Date

Dear Shareholders,

Estimation of mallerite reserves

You will be aware of the importance of accurate resource valuation to Worldwide Minerals (WM). Unfortunately, I have to inform you that the reserve of mallerite, one of our key minerals in a new area of exploration, was found to have been overestimated after the purchase of a mine. It has been suggested that this information may have an effect on shareholder value and so I thought it appropriate to write to inform you of how the board intends to respond to the situation.

In particular, I would like to address two issues. It has been suggested that the overestimation arose because of issues with the internal control systems at WM. I would firstly like to reassure you of the importance that your board places on sound internal control systems and then I would like to highlight improvements to internal controls that we shall be implementing to ensure that the problem should not recur.

(a)   **Importance of internal control**

Internal control systems are essential in all public companies and Worldwide Minerals (WM) is no exception.

If anything, WM's strategic position makes internal control even more important, operating as it does in many international situations and dealing with minerals that must be guaranteed in terms of volume, grade and quality. Accordingly, your board recognises that internal control underpins investor confidence. Investors have traditionally trusted WM's management because they have assumed it capable of managing its internal operations. This has, specifically, meant becoming aware of and controlling known risks. Risks would not be known about and managed without adequate internal control systems.

Internal control, furthermore, helps to manage quality throughout the organisation and it provides management with information on internal operations and compliance. These features are important in ensuring quality at all stages in the WM value chain from the extraction of minerals to the delivery of product to our customers. Linked to this is the importance of internal control in helping to expose and improve underperforming internal operations. Finally, internal control systems are essential in providing information for internal and external reporting upon which, in turn, investor confidence rests.

(b)   **Proposals to improve internal systems at WM**

As you may be aware, mineral estimation and measurement can be problematic, particularly in some regions. Indeed, there are several factors that can lead to under or overestimation of reserves valuations as a result of geological survey techniques and regional cultural/social factors. In the case of mallerite, however, the issues that have been brought to the board's attention are matters of internal control and it is to these that I would now like to turn.

In first instance, it is clear from the fact that the overestimate was made that we will need to audit geological reports at an appropriate (and probably lower) level in the organisation in future.

Once a claim has been made about a given mineral resource level, especially one upon which investor returns might depend, appropriate systems will be instituted to ask for and obtain evidence that such reserves have been correctly and accurately quantified.

We will recognise that single and verbal source reports of reserve quantities may not necessarily be accurate. This was one of the apparent causes of the overestimation of mallerite. A system of auditing actual reserves rather than relying on verbal evidence will rectify this.

The purchase of any going concern business, such as the mallerite mine, is subject to due diligence. WM will be examining its procedures in this area to ensure that they are fit for purpose in the way that they may not have been in respect of the purchase of the mallerite mine. I will be taking all appropriate steps to ensure that all of these internal control issues can be addressed in future.

Thank you for your continued support of Worldwide Minerals and I hope the foregoing goes some way to reassure you that the company places the highest value on its investors and their loyalty.

Yours faithfully,

Tim Blake – Chairman

Marking scheme		Marks
(a)	1 mark for each relevant point made on importance of internal control	Up to 6
(b)	Up to 2 marks for each relevant point identified and examined	Up to 6
Total		12

How well has the candidate demonstrated Professional Skills as follows:	Not at all	Not well	Quite well	Very well
Communication skills to reassure investors.	The candidate has failed to address investor concerns and has avoided key issues	The candidate has only addressed some investor concerns.	The candidate has addressed most of the issues, but their answer is not persuasive.	The candidate has clearly formulated a persuasive argument
	0	0.5	1	2

62   RG

Key answer tips

In **part (a)** think about what information the directors would like, and then see where the information provided does not meet these expectations. Other statements such as 'without reference to past production data' also imply some weakness. In this example, think how a budget would normally be produced, and the weakness becomes apparent.

Improving the information in **part (b)** then becomes relatively easy. There are two comments to make in this section; firstly to state how the weakness will be overcome, and secondly stating the other information that the directors may need. In other words the MIS does not provide all of the required outputs and so the missing information must be identified and commented on.

(a)   Weaknesses in the information currently provided

The directors want information which helps their strategic control of the business. Information used at the strategic level normally has the following characteristics:

- It is highly summarised.
- It does not need to be as accurate as operational information.
- It will often be used in making poorly-structured, non-programmable decisions.
- The information will often be forward-looking.
- Non-routine information and reports will often be required.
- It will contain a high amount of probabilistic information (estimates).

The output from the current system has the following weaknesses:

Summary business plan

This would appear to be an unreliable document as it has been prepared by an inexperienced person who seems to have ignored the information content of past production data. The plan is forward looking, though two years would be an absolute minimum for most strategic planning.

Because historical data is not shown on the report, it will be difficult for the directors to assess the assumptions lying behind the report. This is very important when dealing with future estimates where judgement will play a large part and will be especially important here where the author of the report is inexperienced.

Stock balances

This report is much too detailed for the directors and should be presented in a much more summarised form. As it stands, the report would be of use to people much further down the hierarchy in the firm who are making day-to-day operational decisions.

Changes in demand

This may be too detailed, but the directors may well want to have access to this information on demand. Five years is probably going back too far as there will have been many market changes over that time and early trends may no longer be relevant.

The report seems to be poorly presented being purely numerical and not allowing the directors to compare different sections.

(b)   **Improvements in information**

The information could be improved as follows:

Additional outputs

In addition to the existing reports the following could be useful in strategic planning:

- Financial model which allows the directors to see the effects of different inputs and assumptions.

- Summary accounting information. Though this is historical, future projections may depend on an analysis of past trends.

- Sales analyses by product, customer, type of customer, geographical area, sales rep.

Sales value, volume and gross profit percentages should be shown.

In addition, the existing reports could be improved as follows:

Summary business plan

This should:

- look further ahead

- show historical data

- show the assumptions on which the projections are based

- show income and expenditure on likely new product lines

- contain market and competitor information.

Stock balances

This should:

- be summarised much more

- highlight important data, such as large variances

- be arranged in ways which are of importance to the management of the business.

Summary of changes

- Information about all sections should be available on the same screen to allow comparisons to be made.

- Graphics would help the directors to identify important trends and significant events.

- It might be possible to omit data from over three years ago.

- Industry statistics, market growth and the changes in market share would be useful.

Tutorial note

You need to be very precise and specific in your suggestions in this part of the question, always ensuring that any improvements you suggest are cost-effective to implement.

G: FINANCE IN PLANNING AND DECISION-MAKING

63   GRAFFOFF

Key answer tips

The regurgitation of study notes will not score well – students need to apply their knowledge to the scenario and consider the problems that the company in the scenario are likely to experience.

(a)   Johnson and Scholes have identified franchising as a form of strategic alliance in their classification of methods of strategy development. In this approach, franchises are independently run businesses that would enter into a licence agreement with Graffoff to purchase training, equipment and materials in return for an exclusive geographical franchise area. The proposal is that the franchisee would buy or lease appropriate premises, not Graffoff as in Emile's organic expansion plan. Most franchises are required to make a large up-front payment, which would provide Emile with significant funds for investment or, indeed, for further dividend payments. There are also a number of avoided costs as franchisees usually pay for all the operating costs of the franchise.

Running their own business is usually sufficient to motivate the franchise owners and the motivation of any staff they employ is also their responsibility.

Emile has already acknowledged that he is not a people person and so franchising neatly sub-contracts this issue. Thus, Emile could continue running Graffoff more or less as it is currently and he would avoid the problem of raising significant finance and managing a difficult period of expansion.

However, it is possible (but not inevitable) that the long-term returns to Graffoff might be lower than through directly owned or leased depots. Franchisees will take most of the profits and Graffoff will be dependent for income from materials supply and, usually, from a relatively small percentage of the franchise's annual sales specified in the licence contract. There are also important issues to consider in the appropriate selection and control of franchises. Although the initial fee will be received by Graffoff irrespective of the franchise's success, continuing income (and brand awareness) is dependent upon the success of the franchise. Graffoff has no experience in selecting appropriate franchisees, neither is there any evidence that it has systems in place to control quality and audit performance.

These would be needed to ensure that the product is being used correctly and that the correct percentage of sales is being paid to Graffoff. Such systems will need investment and development and need to be in place before the franchise scheme is launched.

Furthermore, the success of franchises is often determined by the visibility of the brand. Emile himself recognises that Graffoff has a very low profile and he acknowledges that he has very little expertise in this area. Also, it would be obvious to potential franchisees that it may be difficult to maintain sales volumes once the patent has expired. Thus, there may be problems in attracting franchisees, particularly those willing to invest a significant amount for a product which, they may consider, has a relatively short lifetime and whose brand awareness is low.

Emile could address the first of these issues by employing marketing expertise and launching vigorous campaigns. He might also address the patent issue by looking at improving the product. Thus focusing on product development (what he is good at) and not business expansion, where he has little experience and interest.

Although franchising appears to reduce financial risk, it is unlikely to produce the financial returns as quickly as the internal growth option. Emile must not underestimate the time taken to draw up the licence agreement, develop systems to support the franchise and recruit and appoint franchisees. He must also accept that some franchises are likely to fail and that returns will be low in the early years of operation as the fledgling franchises seek to establish themselves as viable independent companies.

(b) Strategic alliances take place where two or more organisations share resources and activities to pursue a strategy.

Many organisations recognise that they need to acquire materials, skills, innovation, finance or access to markets, and increasingly recognise that these may be more readily obtained through cooperation rather than ownership. The franchising option is a type of alliance, and Emile sees it as a way of funding his expansion without incurring employee motivational and management issues that he is not confident in addressing.

332

KAPLAN PUBLISHING

In terms of Graffoff, the motivation for an alliance is likely to be *co-specialisation,* where each partner concentrates on activities that best match their capabilities. Graffoff specialises in product design and product development. Its weaknesses, in the context of the planned expansion, appear to lie in marketing, retail and finance. Franchising has already been considered as a type of alliance.

Another type of alliance that Emile might consider is *a joint venture,* where a new organisation is set up jointly owned by its parents. It is often used by companies to enter a new geographical market where one of the companies provides the expertise and the other local knowledge and labour. This is not the case here, where expansion is within the country. Furthermore, there is no obvious candidate for a joint venture and, even if a partner could be found, it would take time to establish a contractual relationship. Emile, as an entrepreneur, might also find it difficult to work within a framework of a joint venture where he would need to cede a certain amount of control.

In *a network arrangement,* two or more organisations work in collaboration without a formal relationship. The Equipment Emporium already has 57 superstores in the country selling tools and machines. Emile rebuffed their initial advance offering to sell his product in the store, because of the need for mandatory product training. However, he might return to them and offer to set up small in-store outlets where his product could be demonstrated and its services sold. The Equipment Emporium would be paid a fee, but such an approach would, in essence, be the same as his organic growth plan but without the need for large scale capital investment. Furthermore, the locations already exist and are backed up by significant marketing expertise and high brand awareness. This kind of *opportunistic alliance* is a quick way of achieving the expansion that Emile requires and it draws on both partners' expertise. There is a concern in such a loose arrangement that one partner might steal the other's ideas or products, but that seems unlikely here. Graffoff is not interested in becoming a general machine superstore and The Equipment Emporium is primarily focused on products not services. From Emile's perspective, this *opportunistic alliance* provides a potential way of piloting his proposed organic growth expansion strategy before moving into dedicated premises or, indeed, offering the outlets to franchisees.

(c) The consultant has suggested to Emile, that the company has internal sources of finance it can exploit to fully meet it's required funding for organic growth. Typical sources of internal finance are retained profits, tighter credit control, reduced inventory and delayed payment to creditors. Given that Emile is committed to high dividend payments and that no information is given about inventory, two of these are relevant here.

Tightening up credit control makes it possible to release money for funding. The average settlement period for receivables can be calculated as (trade receivables/sales revenue) × 365. For the second year trading this is (260/1,600) × 365 = 59 (59.31) days. Thus, customers take, on average, 59 days to pay their debts, despite agreeing to a 30 day payment term.

Reducing this to the agreed 30 days would realise about $128,500, which could be used to invest in the business. Reducing it to 40 days (the sector-wide standard) would realise approximately $84,500.

However, these gains would only be achieved through implementing better procedures in accounts receivable. Emile realises that this section is poorly motivated and under-staffed. Thus some of the proposed savings may be offset by increased staffing costs.

He is also very sensitive to upsetting his customers and so the need to strictly adhere to payment terms may create initial difficulties and strain customer relations.

He will have to refrain, in future, from intervening in the debt collection process, and not offer the generous terms of payment that currently undermine the debt collection efforts of the accounts receivable department.

This approach might be allied to delaying payments to creditors. Given the limited information, a crude estimate of the average settlement period for payables (creditors) can be calculated by (trade payables/cost of sales) × 365. In this instance this is (75/1,375) × 365 = 20 (19.91) days. Thus Graffoff pays its creditors within 20 days, whilst 40 days is common in this sector. Bringing the company in line with this practice would realise up to a further $75,500 which again could be used for investment. There is no suggestion that this will cause a problem. The current fast payment of invoices seems to reflect the zeal of the administrator in accounts payable, rather than any policy of the company. If Graffoff elects to pay within 30 days (the normal credit terms for the country), this will still realise about $38,000.

This means that up to approximately $204,000 could be raised by Graffoff if customers adhered to payment terms and suppliers accepted sector-wide practice. This would result in a short-term, one-off acceleration of cash inflow.

Finally, the acknowledged problems with credit control might also cause Emile to consider factoring the company invoices. Debt factoring involves a third party taking over the businesses debt collection. Most factoring companies are willing to pay 80% of approved trade receivables in advance. At current values, this should lead to an immediate cash input of $208,000 and this might be an attractive alternative to trying to manage receivables internally. It might also address the problems of motivation and staffing in the accounts receivables section. Factoring might be very valuable in a period of expansion, improving cash flow and removing, from the company, responsibility for credit investigation and debt chasing.

Whichever options are chosen, internal finance resources cannot completely raise the $500,000 required for the organic growth plan and so the consultant is incorrect in his assertion. Emile would have to seek external sources of finance to make up the shortfall. However, the amount raised through internal sources may be sufficient to effectively finance either the franchising option or the building of an opportunistic alliance with The Equipment Emporium.

Marking scheme		
		Marks
(a)	1 mark for each appropriate point up to a maximum of	**10**
(b)	1 mark for each relevant point up to a maximum of	**7**
(c)	1 mark for each relevant point up to a maximum of	**8**
	The evaluation of the claim may include:	
	– Receivables calculation:	1
	– Value of reducing receivables to norm:	1
	– Creditors calculation:	1
	– Value of increasing this to norm:	1
Total		**25**

64 PROTECH-PUBLIC

Key answer tips

An answer that simply regurgitates generic issues with regards to outsourcing will not score well. Issues need to come from the scenario and be explained with examples from the scenario.

The scenario suggests a number of reasons why outsourcing should be beneficial to the city authority.

Firstly, over the last decade there have been fluctuations in demand for IT staff. The authority has recruited to meet short-term demand but, because of the problems of shedding labour, the IT department has not proportionally contracted once that demand has passed. The implication is that, as a result, IT staff costs are higher than they should be. The outsourcing model provides a way of matching supply to demand. Employees are only brought in when there is a specific project for them to work on.

There has been a history of conflict between managers in the IT department and managers in the Finance Department. The Chief Executive Officer (CEO) has spent a significant amount of time trying to resolve this conflict. Employee surveys by the HR department have reported that morale is low in the IT department, despite above average pay and relatively secure employment. Outsourcing IT would appear to offer the following advantages to the authority.

The chief executive and his team would be able to focus on delivering services to the city, rather than spending time and energy on resolving internal problems. The chief executive has recently been criticised for failing to tackle the housing problems of the city. Outsourcing IT would give him more time to address external issues and services, which are the primary objectives and responsibilities of the authority.

Although the problems of low morale may be in part due to management problems, it must also be recognised that promotion opportunities and recognition will probably be lower in an organisation where IT is a relatively small support, rather than core activity. This is reflected in the ingratitude of users towards IT staff ('we are always being told that we are overhead, not core to the business of the authority'). It can be argued that IT staff might be better motivated in an organisation where IT is the core activity and where there should be greater scope for learning new skills and gaining promotion.

Finally, the dispute between IT managers and finance managers has still not been resolved. Outsourcing the IT department will, at best, eliminate the problem and, at worst, make this someone else's problem. In reality, the inability to resolve internal political problems is often given as an important reason for outsourcing.

The director of IT is keen to exploit the opportunities of web services and cloud computing but has not been able to recruit someone of sufficient calibre. As he says, 'there are probably other technologies that I have not even heard of that we should be exploring and exploiting'. An outsourced IT supplier should have a much greater range of knowledge and skills that it can then make available to its customers. It will be keen to be at the leading edge of technologies, because these technologies offer it possible competitive advantage, and so it will bear the cost of recruiting and retaining specialist employees.

Finally, the chief executive recognises that outsourcing IT is likely to be a model followed by other authorities. The formation of a separate company in which the city authority has a significant stake might provide an appropriate vehicle for gaining contracts with other authorities. They might be particularly attracted to working with a company which has significant public sector expertise and ownership. Profits made by the company may be distributed by dividend to the authority, bringing in income that can be used to reduce taxes or improve services.

Marking scheme	
	Marks
1 mark for each relevant point up to a maximum of 12 marks.	**12**

65   8-HATS PROMOTIONS

Key answer tips

In **part (a)** time management will be critical as there were 5 elements to discuss in 15 marks and weaker students may overrun on some or all of these parts at the detriment of part (b). In **part (b)** the biggest problem for students is likely to be in leaving enough time for this section.

(a)   In the scenario, Barry Blunt commented on simple payback (and its supposed advantage over discounted cash flow), the selection of the discount rate, the role of the IRR, the importance of intangible benefits and the realisation of benefits. Each of these five themes is elaborated on below:

Simple payback calculation (time to payback)

Job One All figures in $000

C/F	0	−110	−60	−45	−5
	Year 0	**Year 1**	**Year 2**	**Year 3**	**Year 4**
Total costs	110	10	10	10	10
Total savings	0	60	25	50	70
Cumulative	−110	−60	−45	−5	55
C/F	0	−90	−50	−35	−5

Job Two all figures in $000

C/F	0	−90	−50	−35	−5
	Year 0	**Year 1**	**Year 2**	**Year 3**	**Year 4**
Total costs	90	20	20	10	10
Total savings	0	60	35	40	35
Cumulative	−90	−50	−35	−5	20

Figure 1: Payback calculations for 8-Hats

The calculations (Figure 1) show that Barry Blunt's assertion is not true, both jobs payback early in year 4. If payback (time to payback) had been used, Job One would probably still have been selected because it pays back more in Year 4 than Job 2.

Barry also seems to misunderstand the limitations of payback. It ignores all cash flows beyond the payback period, which in longer projects can be very significant.

In this example, payback ignores the fact that Job 1 has a significantly higher net cash flow inflow on year 4 than Job 2.

The discount rate

Inflation is taken into account in setting the discount rate. However, interest forgone, the cost of capital (if money is being borrowed to fund the investment) and risk will also have an influence. Interest forgone is concerned with the opportunity cost of investing the money in a bank deposit account and earning interest. The cost of capital is concerned with the cost of borrowing money to fund investment. A risk premium would reflect the perceived risk associated with these two internal projects. The discount rate used will incorporate an allowance for risk which will determine the required rate of return or 'hurdle rate' that a project must exceed for it to be viable. Information about risk-free interest rates during the period, the risk profile of the company and the company's cost of capital (using the Capital Asset Pricing Model) would also have been of relevance.

Even if there was an economic logic to changing the discount rate to 3% or 4% this would have no overall effect on the selection of the projects. In fact it is likely to have made Job 1 even more attractive than Job 2, as the cash flows in year 3 and 4 would have been discounted less. In fact, if a discount rate of 4% is used (and this calculation is not expected of the candidate) then the gap in NPV between Jobs 1 and 2 increases.

The Internal Rate of return (IRR)

The IRR is basically the discount rate that produces an NPV of zero for net project cash flows. If the selection is between two projects with the same scale of investment (which is the case here), then it has no effect on which project is selected. The project with the greatest NPV will usually produce the higher IRR. However, the IRR does become important when any project selected has to achieve a pre-specified company rate, or where projects with different scales of investment are being compared. This is not the case at 8-Hats.

Tangible and intangible benefits

The fundamental problem with investment appraisal generally is the reliability of cash flow estimates made for future cash inflows and outflows. For both jobs there seems to be an inclusion of specific monetary values for what appear to be intangible benefits – better information and improved staff morale. As Barry Blunt says, these are important, but it is very unlikely that either of these could be predicted with any certainty, particularly at the start of the project. Estimating for later time periods in the project is also very difficult and it is significant that these benefits increase as the project progresses. These intangible benefits amount to $110,000 for Job One and $50,000 for Job Two. If these intangible benefits are deducted from the analysis then, in fact, Job Two has a higher NPV than Job One. However, both are negative, suggesting that neither project should be attempted.

Benefits realisation

Finally, Barry has a fundamental misunderstanding of benefits realisation. The feasibility study is concerned with establishing the business case of a project and it should identify the project's benefits and costs. Benefits realisation is concerned with establishing whether the predicted benefits in the business case have been realised once the product or service delivered by the project has been in place for some time. It compares actual costs and benefits with those predicted in the business case.

It cannot take place after the feasibility study of the project because at that point the project has not been completed and so any predicted benefits could not, at that stage, have been realised.

(b) 8-Hats Promotions are currently structured in functional departments, with each function representing activities of the company that have either been acquired (for example travel) or organically developed. Each job is passed between functions, with each function focusing on optimising its part of the transaction. Thus the sales department concentrates on winning the job by fiercely reducing prices because the sales managers are rewarded on turnover, not profit. The events department focuses on providing the most rewarding client experience and the travel department on selling travel options with the best profit margin. The focus of the travel department can cause conflict with the sales and marketing department and the operations department has the problem of trying to profitably deliver an event at a price agreed by sales and marketing department but with the functionality promised by the events department. The finance department has responsibility for managing the cash flow of the job and the payment of invoices and collection of money owing. There have been occasions where a job has been jeopardised by the failure of the company to pay key suppliers on time.

The problems described above are typical of a functional structure and the 'silo effect' caused by departments sub-optimising based on their own objectives and interests. The job, which is effectively being passed across the silos, suffers due to lack of co-ordination. Conflicts between two silos can often only be dealt with by managers who are above the silos. There is an example in the scenario where Barry Blunt has to intervene to arrange extra funding to pay supplier invoices when those suppliers threaten to boycott a folk music festival.

The matrix structure is an attempt to manage key elements of the company across the functional departments. This might be a product, project or a clearly defined client sector. In the context of 8-Hats it is jobs, which are effectively projects, and potentially, key accounts (such as Kuizan) that need to be managed across the functional silos.

Each job has the characteristics of a project. It has an established start, it runs for a few months, and then has a specified finish which is often the event itself (such as the folk festival or a Kuizan customer experience event). A multi-disciplinary project team drawn from all of the functional sections would allow continuity and focus on delivering a successful and profitable project. Because much of the company is project-based, a set of profitable projects should lead to a profitable company. Decisions within the project will, to some extent, reflect a consensus view of all concerned. The sales manager responsible for agreeing the deal would still be involved at event realisation and would also contribute to the management of cash flow through the complete project. This commitment to the project goal should lead to a more rewarding client experience. The need to keep clients satisfied is another potential element to the matrix, with account managers being appointed to key accounts with the responsibility of managing clients across both silos and projects.

The need for project teams to reflect a consensus view often means that decisions may take longer in a matrix structure and tension within the multi-disciplinary team may lead to a large amount of conflict. This conflict is more likely when cost and profit responsibilities are either unclear or counter-productive. At 8-Hats, the practice of rewarding sales managers on a turnover basis will have to be reviewed, otherwise there will be significant tension between the line (function) and the project.

It has also been claimed that job and task responsibilities are unclear in a matrix structure and so the company will have to address this. Johnson, Scholes and Whittington make the point that 'one arm of the matrix has to lead in the sense that it dictates some key parameters within which the other arm must work'.

In the context of the case study scenario it seems reasonable to devolve profit responsibility and work allocation to the project, leaving the functions to provide technical support and (perhaps) appraisal and competence definition responsibilities. The line manager becomes primarily responsible for the person and the project manager for the project. Such a change would require key cultural changes at 8-Hats.

Marking scheme		Marks
(a)	Up to 1 mark for each appropriate point up to a maximum of	15
(b)	1 mark for each appropriate point up to a maximum of	10
Total		**25**

66 SATELLITE NAVIGATION SYSTEMS

Key answer tips

It is important in **part (a)** to link the variances reported to the possible causes, many of which were alluded to in the scenario. Similarly in **part (b)** – make your answer as relevant as possible to the scenario.

(a)   Report on performance

Production and sales

Production and sales were 1,100 units in September and October, 950 units in November and 900 units in December. There has thus been a marked decline over the four-month period. This good performance in the first two months and poor performance in the latter two months may be due to a seasonal variation. If this is the case, it would be good for the budget to reflect the expected seasonal variation, rather than just being a flat 1,000 units per month.

Tutorial note

The output was calculated by taking the standard cost of actual output and dividing by the standard cost per system, i.e. $1,276,000/$1,160 = 1,100 units, $1,102,000/$1,160 = 950 units and $1,044,000/$1,160 = 900 units.

Materials

The material price variance was favourable for the first two months, and then very adverse for November and December. This was possibly due to the exchange rate movement if the systems are imported. The effect of the exchange rate variations should be quantified.

Any remaining adverse variances may be due to inefficient purchasing by the purchasing manager. It should be investigated as to whether there are alternative suppliers for the systems.

The material usage variance was adverse in every month, but was particularly bad in October and even worse in December.

In October the variance was $7,200 A and as the material cost was $400 per unit, this meant that an extra $7,200/$400 = 18 units were used on a production of 1,100 units. In December, the variance was $16,000/$400 = 40 extra units on production of 900 units. This variance could possibly be due to the large batch of systems which did not have the correct adaptors.

Labour

The labour rate variance was adverse in September and October and substantially adverse in November and December. Expressing the variances as percentages, for September the standard labour cost was $320 × 1,100 units = $352,000 and thus the variance was $4,200 A/$352,000 = 1.1% A. In November the variance was $5,500 A/$352,000 = 1.6% A. These minor variances could be explained by more overtime than expected being worked, especially as production was high in the first two months. Then things were much worse in the latter two months, for November the variance was $23,100 A/($320 per unit × 950 units) = 7.6% A and in December the variance was $24,000 A/($320 per unit × 900 units) = 8.3%. These substantial variances are almost certainly due to higher wage rates being offered in order to retain the staff and lower the labour turnover.

The labour efficiency variance was $16,000 favourable in September ($16,000/$352,000 = 4.5% F), zero in October and $32,000 adverse in November and December ($32,000 A/$320 per unit × 950 units) = 10.5% A, and $32,000 A/$320 per unit × 900 units) = 11.1% A). It would be expected that some of this variance was due to the large batch of systems which did not have the correct adaptors. This problem was not apparent until fitting was attempted, thus involving the fitters in extra work. If this were the case then we would expect the labour efficiency variance to tie up with the material usage variance, but it does not. We are also told that there is a fluctuation of ± 25% in the fitting times, so even the substantial variances for November and December fall within this range and thus might not represent inefficiency, but simply the fitting of a higher proportion of more labour intensive systems.

It would be very useful to have information on the number of staff leaving the business. Overtime is unlikely to be the cause for the labour variances in November and December as production was lower than budget.

Variable overheads

The variable overhead efficiency variance is based on labour hours and thus simply moves in line with the labour efficiency variance.

The expenditure variance was $7,000 A in September, improved to $2,000 A in October and then $2,000 F in November. It was zero in December. For this variance to have any meaning it must be sub-analysed into its different components in order to determine which ones are being overspent and which ones underspent.

Taking the variable overheads as a whole, the variance gets worse as production levels fall, perhaps indicating that the variable overheads are not entirely variable but may include a fixed element.

Fixed overheads

The fixed overhead volume variance simply reflects the better than expected production in the first two months and the worse than expected production in the latter two months.

The fixed overhead volume variance has no significance as it does not represent a cash flow (if we make more or less units than expected then the fixed overheads do not change), but is simply a mathematical device to reconcile budgeted profit with actual profit in an absorption costing system.

The fixed overhead expenditure variance is $5,000 A, $10,000 A, $20,000 A and $20,000 A over the four months and thus shows a worsening pattern, but again in order to understand where things are going wrong we need to sub-analyse the fixed overhead into their different components. We have been told that rent, rates insurance and computing costs have risen in price noticeably; these costs may be regarded as uncontrollable. Managers' attention should be devoted to investigating the controllable costs and reducing any overspend.

Conclusion

Overall the actual cost was 4.4% worse than expected (($4,906,201 − $4,698,000)/ $4,698,000). Whilst this variance might not be regarded as significant, the individual variances in many cases are much bigger and should be investigated. There is a marked decline in performance in November and December. It is important that the individual variances are investigated and their causes understood so that future performance improves.

(b) **The finance function**

The finance department's role has moved beyond simply providing information on performance and results. Increasingly the finance function plays a core role in the support and implementation of strategic decision making.

Decision support

The first role it can offer is in decision support. For example, the finance department could attempt to quantify the effect of the exchange rate variations on material. This may be supplemented by qualitative information of expectations of future changes in exchange rates. This could support a change in purchasing strategy to one that considers overseas purchasing and this might ultimately lead to a change in competitive strategy if SNS believes that it could achieve a low cost strategy from such a position.

The material variance needs careful investigation in order to find out where the excess units were used, which systems and which teams of fitters were involved. This could change operational strategies and plans.

Strategy development

The finance function might even play a key role in the development of new strategic choices not consider by SNS. For example, it could investigate whether material variances are instead due to inefficient purchasing by the purchasing manager. This could lead to a change in the supply chain of the system, with either alternative supplier's users or even a switch towards e-procurement. The finance function could perform cost-benefit analysis on each of the opportunities.

Strategy implementation

The finance function could consider whether the use of different systems, the training and recruitment of new staff, and the job design of existing staff is adequate. It would be useful to have information on the standard times for different systems and the numbers of the different systems, instead of treating all systems alike. The high labour turnover also means that experienced workers are leaving and that new workers are constantly having to be trained.

The efficiency of the new workers would be lower than existing staff and this could be harming the implantation of many of SNS's plans.

Performance measurement

As can be seen in part (a), the finance function can play a role in the assessment of performance within an organisation. But this role has been expanded upon by organisations to include the development of new performance measures and associated KPI's and targets for these measures. For example, staff morale, SNS's competitiveness, levels of innovation etc., might be measures that the finance function suggest should be measured within SNS. It should also be noted that many of these measures will be non-financial in nature and yet the finance function will still be responsible for their creation and measurement.

Conclusion

The role of the finance function is expanding and it is playing a much more fundamental role in the development of the business. Accountants need to be skilled in working on a wide range of decision support and strategic initiatives.

Marking scheme		Marks
(a)	Up to 3 mark for the discussion of each area of variance	15
(b)	Up to 3 mark for each area where information may be needed/useful	10
Total		**25**

67   MANTIS & GEAR

Key answer tips

This requires the calculation of some (reasonably simple) variances and a discussion of their causes. Students should look for the key triggers for this type of requirement: they have been provided with a budget, an actual set of results and the requirement was to analyse the performance. This should always trigger the calculation of variances.

Slides and notes:

SLIDE 1

Overall performance

Area	Performance
• Sales volume	• Up by 27,000 units
• Profitability	• Down $7,358
• Profit margin	• 4.5% actual vs 24.7% budgeted

The sales manager is correct in that the sales volume has outperformed budgeted sales volume by 27,000 units, or 11.1% over budget. This is a positive sign in a situation where there is increased competition and more demanding customers.

However, profitability is much lower than budgeted at 4.5% rather than the 24.7% budgeted, or the 27% expected if the budget was flexed to represent actual sales volume. This could have a serious impact on the future sustainability of the business.

Overall, M&G should have made a budgeted profit of $10.92m on the actual sales, but instead made a profit of $1.645m, a difference of $9.275m.

SLIDE 2

Variance analysis

	Budget units	Actual units	Flexed budget	Variance to flexed
Sales volume	243,000	270,000	270,000	
	Budget	**Actual**		
	$000	$000		$000
Sales revenue	36,450	36,450	40,500	4,050 Adverse
Direct materials	15,795	18,630	17,550	1,080 Adverse
Direct labour	3,402	4,725	3,780	945 Adverse
Overheads	8,250	11,450	8,250	3,200 Adverse
Operating profit	9,003	1,645	10,920	

The flexed budget can be analysed to determine where performance has been worse than expected. Differences between expected and actual performance can then be investigated. The flexed budget and variances are as follows:

One of the problems of using a standard costing system is that standard costs are based on historical information, and in a changing environment these are unlikely to remain accurate for long. It may be that the standards used in the budget are simply no longer realistic, and these need analysing before the blame is placed upon any particular department within the organisation.

SLIDE 3

Potential variance causes

Area	Performance
• Sales price	• Extra competition
• Sales volume	• Linked to sales price
• Materials	• Better materials to make more attractive products
• Labour	• Overtime to meet short lead times
• Overheads	• Difficult to tell

Sales price and volume

The average selling price per unit was budgeted at $150, but the average actual selling price per unit was $135, a decrease of 10%.

It may be that this was reduced in order for the sales team to hit targets, especially if their commission is based on sales volume rather than revenue. Alternatively, it could be that the price was necessarily reduced in order to cope with increased competition. This reduction in price is likely to have been a major contributor in the increase in volume.

Direct materials

It was stated that customers wanted 'more attractive' products, which may have led to more advanced component parts, thus increasing costs.

Direct labour

If orders were satisfied at short notice, this may have required overtime, which could affect the labour rate variance causing it to be higher due to enhanced overtime payments. In addition, special and customer-specific orders may require longer than standard hours as they may not yet have benefitted from the learning curve effect associated with standard, repeat orders.

Fixed overheads

This is clearly a major problem and suggests that either the standard absorption rate of overheads is incorrect, or that overheads have not been controlled throughout the year. The focus on meeting increased orders may have distracted management attention from overhead control, thus leading to inefficiencies related to these costs. Overheads include those indirect elements of cost which are not specifically attributed to a product, such as cleaning materials, machine maintenance, supervisor salaries and factory rent and rates, heating and lighting. By treating them as fixed overheads, the suggestion is that they should not change with a variation in activity volumes. It is vital that the company analyses the overhead spend urgently, as this has had a major impact on profitability.

Marking scheme – technical marks	
	Marks
4 marks for analysing overall performance – 1 for the slide and 3 for the associated notes.	
6 marks for analysing the performance by area (using variances) – 4 for the slides and 2 for the associated notes.	
5 marks for the causes of the variances – 1 for the slide and 4 for the notes.	15

How well has the candidate demonstrated Professional Skills as follows:	Not at all	Not well	Quite well	Very well
Communication skills in highlighting the key points and for clear supporting notes.	The candidate has failed to use a slide format to communicate the performance of the business in the year.	The candidate has only loosely used a slide presentation format, but has either far too many or too few points or has failed to focus on the performance of the business. The candidate has produced some notes but they are either too long or fail to adequately explain the main points.	The candidate has used a slide format and has covered the performance of the business for the year and by revenue or cost, but slides are either overly detailed or are poorly presented. There are slide notes, but they are not always clearly linked to the points on the slide.	The candidate has slides which clearly cover the performance of the business for the year and by revenue or cost. Calculations are not illustrated on slides. The candidate has notes which can be clearly related to the information in the slides.
	0	0.5	1	2

68   JONES PACKAGING

Briefing note:

To: David Jones

From: Advisor

Date: Today

Subject: Business growth and financing

(a)   Key factors for future strategy

At this early stage you need to identify the critical success factors and related performance indicators that will help demonstrate that the concept is turning into a business reality. Many of the success factors will be linked to customer needs and expectations and where the business must excel in order to outperform the competition; these are the critical success factors.

As an innovator one of these critical success factors will be your personal involvement and time taken to develop and launch the new vase; being first-to-market will be a key factor in the success of the new venture. Your ability to generate sales revenue from demanding corporate customers will be a real indicator of that success.

You will also need to ensure that the appropriate patent protection is in place for the product. Similarly it will be important to recognise that the new innovation will be subject to the constraints of the product life cycle. As such there will be a need for future product enhancements and/or developments as the business develops and competition increases.

There are a number of alternative markets and customers, for example the different demands of the public and private sector when dealing with hospitals and the corporate gift market. The ability to customise the product to reflect their needs will also be a CSF. Given these alternatives, one of the key problems as the business progresses may be to decide what type of business you want to be in. There are many different stages a growing business goes through and the different problems associated with each stage will need to identified and addressed.

From the information presented, it looks as if you are aiming to carry out most of the functions yourself. This may well only achievable in the short term and there will be a need to decide what you have the capacity to do and what you may require to get others to do for you, for example using your skills as an innovator and entrepreneur rather than as someone who is too involved in the manufacture and distribution of the product.

Gift Designs may develop most quickly as a firm that creates new products and then licences them to larger firms with the skills to penetrate the many market opportunities that are present. It is therefore important for you to recognise that turning the product concept into a viable and growing business may result in a business and a business model very different to what you anticipated.

Gift Designs needs to have the flexibility and agility to take advantage of the opportunities that will emerge over time.

(b)   Funding strategy for Gift Designs Ltd

You have identified a real business opportunity and face both business and financial risks in turning the opportunity into reality.

As mentioned earlier, one possible model you can use in that context is that of the product life cycle which for a one-product firm is effectively the life cycle for the company. Linking business risk to financial risk is important – in the early stages of the business the business risk is high and the high casualties among new start-ups is well publicised; consequently, there is a need to go for low financial risk. Funding the business is essentially deciding the balance between debt and equity finance, and equity offers the low risk that you should be looking for. As the firm grows and develops so the balance between debt and equity will change.

A new business venture like this could, in Boston Consulting Group analysis terms, be seen as a problem child with a non-existent market share but high growth potential. The business risks are very high, and consequently the financial risks taken should be very low. The financing method adopted therefore should avoid taking on large amounts of debt given the resulting commitment to service the debt.

You need to take advantage of investors who are willing to accept the risks associated with a business start-up – venture capitalists and business angels accept the risks associated with putting equity capital in but may expect a significant share in the ownership of the business. This they will seek to realise once the business is successfully established.

As the business moves into growth and then maturity so the business risks will reduce and access to debt finance becomes feasible and cost effective. In maturity the business should be able to generate significant retained earnings to finance further development. Dividend policy will also be affected by the stage in the life cycle that the business has reached.

Risks to organisations from ICOs

An ICO is a fundraising mechanism in which new projects sell their underlying crypto tokens in exchange for bitcoin and ether. ICOs are a relatively new phenomenon but have quickly become a dominant topic of discussion within the blockchain community.

An Initial Coin Offering (ICO) is the cryptocurrency rough equivalent to an IPO in the mainstream investment world. ICOs act as fundraisers of sorts where a company looking to create a new coin, app, or service launches an ICO. Interested investors buy in to the offering, either with fiat currency (government-issued currency that is not backed by a physical commodity, such as gold or silver) or with pre-existing digital tokens like ether.

In exchange for their support, investors receive a new cryptocurrency token specific to the ICO. The company holding the ICO uses the investor funds as a means of furthering its goals, launching its product, or starting its digital currency. ICOs are used by start-ups to bypass the rigorous and regulated capital-raising process required by venture capitalists or banks.

The key risk revolves around the increase in activity from regulators in response to the surge in Initial Coin Offerings. Regulators have issued consistent warnings of the inherent risks in ICOs and reminders of the need to understand the underlying nature of individual investments. For example, the rapid ICO surge in 2017 incurred regulations from a series of governmental and non-governmental bodies. In early September 2017, for example, the People's Bank of China officially banned ICOs, citing it as disruptive to economic and financial stability.

Concerns over ICOs, the potential for increased scrutiny and additional regulation mean that it may be harder, and more expensive, for start-ups to position an ICO and bring their innovation to market. ICOs are often seen as a route to for projects that would not receive funding through traditional financing, but nevertheless are potentially introducing viable, innovative ideas. In that context the project may suffer from a lack of credibility and affect future business development.

The ICO concept extends the options available for raising finance and accessing a group of participants that appreciate the ideas emerging around new products and new technology. Many ICOs have enabled start-ups to raise much larger amounts than would have been possible through traditional financing and therefore their viability has been more quickly tested.

Regulators consider that some ICOs constitute securities offers, and therefore have an associated requirement to fulfil the related regulatory criteria. The possibility that an ICO may be a security will mean additional unanticipated cost for the promoter. There is also a risk that business start-ups may wrongly consider that their ICO is not a security and face severe penalties, at a later date, should regulators consider that they are.

Marking scheme		Marks
(a)	Up to 2 marks for the discussion of each key area	10
(b)	Up to 2 mark for aspect of funding strategy and risk of ICO	10
Total		**20**

H: INNOVATION, PERFORMANCE EXCELLENCE AND CHANGE MANAGEMENT

69   ALG TECHNOLOGY *Online question assistance*

Key answer tips

The scenario explicitly rejects a divisional structure so this would not score marks as a suggested structure in part (a).

(a)   ALG Technology is a company operating in a number of fields of complex technologies and in several dynamic markets. Its current organisational structure based upon a functional division of work is not providing the necessary integration of activities, nor is it responding sufficiently to market needs. It is likely that a **matrix structure** or one **based on project teams** might work better but there will also be disadvantages associated with such a structure. The basis of such a structure is a multi-functional project team. The team is often small, flexible and temporary. It is often set up when management do not wish to set up separate divisions but are looking for increased co-operation among all their staff. It generally has two reporting lines – one to functional departments and one devoted to specialist products or teams.

In the case of ALG Technology there will be a team focused around each specialist product group and each team will have representations from the various functional areas.

The **advantages** of a matrix or project team structure are as follows:

- The teams do not lose sight of their long-term objectives. They can remain more focused.

- There is more integration between the differing functional specialists – they become inter-disciplinary, resulting in greater co-operation and understand opposing or alternative opinions.

- Such a team is more responsive and flexible to environmental and technical change, so important for a company such as ALG. Because the team is now less bureaucratic and more focused, outcomes are much quicker as the bureaucracy is now replaced by a direct interplay between specialists – the interested parties.

- No one single functional area is likely to dominate. In a company such as ALG there is a danger that the views of scientists and engineers may triumph at the expense of prudent financial advice and market needs may also be ignored. There is a danger of the company becoming too product-orientated.

- Because staff are more directly involved in planning, control and decision making they become more motivated and committed – a key benefit for any company.

- Junior staff experience a wider range of inputs from a broad spectrum of areas. They lose their specialised isolation and become more valuable and 'rounded' employees. This provides a good training platform for future general managers.

- Experiences from one project team can easily and quickly be transmitted to other teams.

There are also **disadvantages**:

- Because of the dual representation within the teams there is a potential for conflict between project managers and functional heads.

- The two reporting lines can lead to confusion for members of the team. Where does their long-term future lie and where is it being determined?

- There is increased complexity in reporting, making such a structure costly to administer.

- Decision making can be slower and not be more responsive if every participant insists on full participation. This is a problem with all democratic and participatory organisations, as has been experienced by a number of Japanese companies.

- Because of dual reporting, there is a problem of allocating responsibilities. Who is in charge?

- This proposed new structure may lead to a dilution of priorities, particularly in resource allocation.

As a guideline for organising innovative project teams it is essential that structures should be flexible so as to encourage experts to break through conventional boundaries into new areas. There should also be leadership within the team of staff with a good technical background (**expert power**) and the team should not be dominated by superiors armed only with authority (**position power**).

(b) **Organisational design can be influenced by many factors which can generally be** divided into two categories – internal and external influences.

The internal influences comprise:

- Poor performance in the past. If a company has had difficulties such as are currently being experienced by ALG Technology then it is not surprising that it is considering a change in its organisational structure.

- If a company is now heavily influenced by entrepreneurs and innovators, a more flexible structure would be welcome. A 'machine bureaucracy', which might be what ALG Technology has become, would not be sympathetic to this type of employee. An adhocracy or an entrepreneurial structure might be more appropriate. (*Mintzberg*)

- A change in organisational ownership would inevitably have given the new shareholders a greater say on matters such as organisational design. Design will be more influenced by their management philosophy.

- There may have been a change in organisational goals. If quality of delivery is now given greater priority than product performance, as in the case of ALG, a structure more oriented to marketing might now be encouraged.

- A change in strategy will also help to influence the design of the organisation. If the company intends to compete with low prices then costs will now become critical. It is likely that there will be a more mechanistic approach to the structure with less focus on the individual. However with a differentiation strategy there is a potential for more informality, with more decision making being devoted to junior managers. This will be reflected in a less bureaucratic organisational structure.

The external factors that might influence organisational design are as follows:

- A change in knowledge available to a company. An increase in the availability and application of information technology (IT) now enables organisations to have greater control and communication within an organisation while having a smaller infrastructure to accomplish these functions.

- Economic opportunities may change: the globalisation of markets will necessitate a change in organisational structure to reflect and respond to these changes. In certain parts of the world barter has been re-introduced because of shortages of liquidity within the banking system. Organisations must build into their structures recognition of this 'problem'. Certain companies have had to create whole departments to respond to this condition.

- Socio-demographic changes: as organisations now operate in different parts of the world, each with different demographic and social regimes then differences such as attitudes to older people working, women in management, educational abilities matching requirements and labour force availability can all influence the design of organisational structures, resulting in more flexible and responsive organisations suiting local needs and cultures.

- Ecological considerations: 'Green' issues are becoming more significant in importance. Decisions on purchasing and distribution will be influenced by this and these, in turn, may affect the organisational structure. 'Just-in-time' supply techniques may be affected here (although just-in-time may be driven more by economic rather than ecological consideration).

- The prevailing ideological beliefs may also influence organisational design. In some countries planning may still be more dominant than a market culture. This could affect the organisational infrastructure with a greater reliance on planning departments than on a marketing and customer service. There has been much discussion on the differences between Japanese and Western-based companies. Concepts popular in Japan in the 1970s and 1980s such as jobs for life, promotion by seniority, job rotation have all affected the way in which organisations are configured. However it is also true to say that with the recent increased tendency towards globalisation these ideological differences are being reduced.

As can be noted from the above discussion, a number of these factors can be used to justify ALG Technology's need to change its organisational structure. Probably the most pressing reason for the change is its current poor performance. Resulting from this, there will probably be changes in both objectives and strategies. Although the environmental factors may have limited relevance here, the fact that ALG is now operating in a dynamic and global market place means that it has to be more responsive to market needs. With improved IT, it can now control its enterprises from a distance without sacrificing responsiveness. It can do so with a relatively flat organisation without the need for an extensive supportive infrastructure.

Marking scheme	
	Marks
(a) Up to 4 marks for the explanation of an alternative structure	
Benefits of this structure (maximum 5 marks)	
Problems with this structure (maximum 5 marks)	13
	(maximum)
(b) Up to 2 marks for each relevant issues discussed	12
Total	**25**

70   COUNTRY CAR CLUB

Key answer tips

Although the question does not explicitly ask for it, the process-strategy matrix suggested by Paul Harmon would provide an appropriate context for the answer to this question. However, other appropriate models or frameworks could be used by candidates to answer this part of the question.

In **part (b)**, it will be important to avoid generic points that simply regurgitate knowledge. Instead the scenario should be used to derive more relevant issues for Country Car Club.

(a)   Management of processes

(i)   Attendance at breakdowns

This appears to be of high strategic importance and, although some breakdowns are bound to be simple to fix, it requires the repairer to be knowledgeable, flexible and diplomatic. Consequently, it appears to be a candidate for the upper right quadrant of the process-strategy matrix. Hence it is suggested that the service should remain in-house and attention should be paid to improving the competency of the 'service patrol engineers'.

Information technology should be harnessed to seek improvements in response time to breakdowns by improving the organisation and distribution of these engineers. Systems might also be developed to technically support engineers and to help them diagnose and fix roadside problems.

(ii)   Membership renewal

This should be a relatively straightforward process, so it sits in one of the two lower quadrants. It can be argued that it is a process that is core to the business and is not one (like payroll) which can be found across all businesses. It appears to be a candidate for the lower right quadrant. Hence it is a candidate for automation to gain efficiency. The organisation already has a bespoke system operated by in-house permanent employees. This seems an appropriate way of delivering this process. However, it might benefit from revisiting the way the bespoke system works. The scenario suggests that the current system sends out membership renewals on receipt of a confirmation from the member. The system might benefit from being built around a presumption of renewal, so that the member only contacts the organisation if he or she does not wish to renew.

(iii)   Vehicle insurance services

These appear to be a relatively complex process which is of little strategic importance to 3C. It appears to inhabit the top left hand quadrant of the matrix. Insurance is not only technically complex, it carries large risks and substantial regulatory requirements. It is likely that these regulatory requirements will undergo frequent changes. It would appear attractive to 3C to outsource this service to a specialist provider who would then badge it under 3C's name. This is relatively common practice and 3C's venture into insurance must have been very expensive. Outsourcing provides it with opportunities for providing a wider service with reduced in-house costs.

(iv) Membership queries

Membership queries are of unpredictable complexity. They are also an important contact point between the company and their members. Failure to handle queries courteously and correctly could have important consequences for membership renewal. It is suggested that this is an upper right hand quadrant process – potentially complex and of high strategic importance to the company. Investment is required in people supported by innovative and speedy IT systems that allow the 3C staff to respond quickly and accurately to a wide range of questions. It is suggested that membership queries continue to remain in-house although the physical location of the call centre might reflect certain financial opportunities – such as low property rents and cheaper labour.

(v) Vehicle history checks

Vehicle history checks appear to be of relatively low strategic importance to 3C.

Automation should make such checks relatively straightforward, although the combination of accident damage, stolen vehicles, finance agreements and time when the vehicle was voluntarily taken off the road may make determining this history more complex then it first appears. Furthermore, the consequences of providing inaccurate or incomplete information may be quite severe. Someone who has unsuspectingly purchased a car which has been damaged and repaired might claim for damages against 3C when this was revealed.

These damages might be extensive if someone died in the vehicle as a result of a botched repair. Consequently it is suggested that this is predominantly an upper left hand quadrant process which should be outsourced to an organisation which is already in this field.

Table 2.1 summarises the advice to the BAC.

Table 2.1

Attendance at repairs	Remains in-house. Improve competency of repair staff. Support them with IT systems
Membership renewal	Remains in-house and revisit basis of automation
Vehicle insurance	Outsource
Membership queries	Remains in-house. Improve competency of call centre staff. Support them with IT systems
Vehicle history	Outsource

(b) Outsourcing

In the question scenario the decision to outsource the purchase and maintenance of 3C vehicles is justified by its low strategic importance and its low to medium complexity. However, this only makes it a *candidate* for outsourcing and so tangible and intangible benefits would have to be attached to this suggestion in a subsequent detailed analysis. This part of the question asks candidates to analyse the advantages of outsourcing the process of the purchase and maintenance of 3C vehicles. It is suggested that advantages would include:

Purchasing benefits from economies of scale

AutoDirect purchase thousands of cars and vans for their customers each year. They should be able to negotiate substantial discounts from manufacturers, some of which can be passed on to their customers.

Predictable costs

The vehicle lease payments with AutoDirect are monthly and they include full maintenance of the car, including tyres and exhausts. Hence 3C will have predictable costs for budgeting purposes. Previously, costs would have been variable and unpredictable, depending upon the reliability of the vehicles.

Reduced overhead costs – garage and purchasing

The overhead costs associated with the garage and the garage and purchasing employees have been lost (except for the one manager retained to manage the contract with AutoDirect). There may also be an opportunity for realising income from the sale of the garage site. It is described as being in a residential area with no room for expansion and severe parking congestion. It may be possible to sell the garage for residential development.

Higher vehicle availability

The central garage itself is a bottleneck. Vehicles have to be driven or transported to this garage from all parts of the country and left there while they are serviced or repaired. They then have to be driven back to their operational area. AutoDirect has repair and servicing centres throughout the country and so it will be possible for vehicles to be taken locally for services and repairs – thus reducing vehicle downtime.

Freeing cash to use for other investments – from purchase to lease

The policy of purchasing vehicles meant that a considerable amount of cash has been tied up in fast depreciating assets. Switching to leasing will release this cash for investment elsewhere in the company.

Access to expertise and legislation

It is likely that vehicles will become increasingly subject to legislation designed to reduce carbon emissions. This, together with the increasing technical complexity of vehicles, will mean that vehicles will become increasingly difficult to maintain without specialist monitoring and repair equipment. It is unlikely that 3C can maintain such a level of investment and so outsourcing to a specialist makes good sense. AutoDirect will have to monitor legislation, advise on its implications and implement its requirements for its large customer base.

Concentration on core business

Although this issue is not explicitly considered in the scenario it is something that impacts on all organisations. The management of the garage does not appear to be a core strategic requirement. It must consume some elements of senior management time. Outsourcing frees up that time so it can be used to focus on issues directly relevant to the customer and the business as a whole.

Marking scheme		
		Marks
(a)	Up to 3 marks for the recommendation and its justification in each of the process areas required by the question	
	Five process areas required giving a maximum of 15 marks	15
(b)	Up to 2 marks for each appropriate advantage identified by the candidate up to a maximum of 10 marks	10
Total		**25**

71   STELLA ELECTRONICS

Key answer tips

For **part (a)**, candidates should focus on identifying problems in the scenario and suggesting solutions for each one. In **part (b)**, weaker candidates might focus on the textbook advantages and disadvantages of outsourcing rather than to make points that are relevant to this scenario (such as using some of the financial data that was provided).

(a)   **Issues with the current process**

- There are too many handoffs in the current process, particularly given the need to connect to each section by telephone. It seems likely that bottlenecks will form around these handoffs.

- The role of the supervisor is particularly redundant from the perspective of Stella Electronics (SE). Enquiries for other companies should not be part of their process and, from their perspective, the supervisor adds no value.

- The payment or service contract reference number and the password are requested relatively late in the process. The need to have these available could have been flagged earlier in the process, perhaps at first contact with the supervisor.

- On average, 153 people per day (600 calls × 0.85 × 30%) do not know their reference number. This means that SE is billed $153.00 per day for calls which are not resolved. It also wastes the end customer's time and money and is a potential source of complaint and dissatisfaction.

- On average, 18 people (17.85) per day ((600 – 90 – 153) × 5%) do not know their password. This means that SE is billed $18 per day for calls which are not resolved. It also wastes the end customer's time and money and is, again, a potential source of dissatisfaction and complaint.

- Although the split of staff across the sections seems reasonable at first sight (six people in technical support for 60% of queries, three people in Stella support for 25% refunds, and one person in the contracts section for 15% of queries), this masks two problems. Firstly, the contracts section is disproportionately understaffed (it should have 1.5 staff) and, secondly, and, more importantly, 100% of the calls have to pass though the three people in Stella support. This must be a bottleneck, and is likely to be the main reason for the poor service experienced by the end customer.

Potential solutions

Tutorial note

There are a range of potential solutions. Some ideas are presented below, but other legitimate answers will be given credit.

- A dedicated phone number could be given to SE customers to eradicate the need for a TCG supervisor.

- Different phone numbers could be given to SE customers for the three different types of query. Thus there will be a dedicated refund line, a dedicated contracts line and a dedicated technical support line.

- Staffing levels could be changed to reflect the frequency of calls. For example, an extra person could be provided in the contracts section, although this does not address the support bottleneck.

- The role of routing calls could be performed by an automated telephone system. For example, option 1 could be refunds, option 2 for technical queries and option 3 for service contracts. This would also provide a mechanism for handling other types of queries (option 4), which could be the responsibility of the supervisor if his or her role is retained.

- Customers requesting refunds or requiring technical support could be informed earlier in the process of the need to have their contract reference number and password ready. This could be given in the automated reply (see point above) to the initial phone call or menu choice selected or it could be requested by the supervisor, if this role is retained. The need for this could also be prominently displayed on their company's website.

- Multi-skilling staff so that they could effectively handle any part of the process would reduce handoffs. It may be difficult to include technical support in a multi-skilled role, but it certainly seems feasible to merge the refund and service contract roles. Reducing the number of swim lanes is an effective way of improving a business process.

(b) The financial case for outsourcing still remains very strong. At present, the cost to SE is $600 per day for a service provided by 10 people, giving a 24 hour service. SE has calculated that it will cost $50 to employ a person with similar competencies in Arborium for an eight hour shift. This produces a 24 hour cost of $150. If SE continues to employ 10 staff, then the total cost will be $1,500 per day. There would also be capital costs of re-establishing the infrastructure to provide the support service, including telephones, office furniture and training costs. There will also be operational costs, such as electricity and office rent and property charges.

So a like-to-like switch back to an in-house support unit seems impossible to justify on cost grounds. However, SE could consider alternative ways of dealing with calls. Technical queries could be addressed by improving support documentation (reducing the demand for queries) and by publishing frequently asked questions (FAQs) on its website. Email support could also be offered. The processing of refunds and the handling of service contracts could be provided by an online process. This seems particularly suited to refund processing. Contracts, which appears to require a dialogue between the customer and SE, seems less of a candidate for this. Improvements in query handling might also allow SE to reduce the number of people working in the centre to a level where the cost of the service would be roughly the same as the outsourced equivalent.

The cultural context of outsourcing needs consideration. Outsourcing, and particularly offshoring, appears to have a negative impact on customers who, as well as having difficulty in understanding the call centre staff based in different countries, increasingly view offshoring as a way of exporting employment. As the number of people out of work in Arborium continues to grow, so the pressure increases on companies to bring work back in-house. SE might be able to make some marketing or public relations capital out of bringing support back in-house and into the country.

Service is a primary activity on the value chain. It is a key point where customers interact with an organisation and form their opinions about it. At present, many customers have a negative view of SE informed by their contact with the TCG call centre. Queries take too long to process and there are problems in understanding the call centre staff. SE needs to consider whether it is wise to outsource such a customer-focused activity. Perhaps the support activities (information technology, procurement) of the value chain are better candidates for outsourcing.

However, it also has to be recognised that support is not a core activity of SE. It is primarily an electronics retailer. It might be reasonable to conclude that a company such as TCG, dedicated to providing call centre support, should give a better service, leaving SE time to focus on its core competencies and activity.

In the short term, it would seem sensible to introduce improvements at the TCG call centre. The service is already relatively cheap and could be made cheaper by reducing the number of calls (through improved documentation and website support) and by reducing the number of calls which are not resolved. In the longer term, SE might wish to re-consider the wisdom of outsourcing a customer-facing service and they may, on ethical grounds, wish to invest in jobs in the country where most of their customers are. Publicising this socially responsible decision might also boost sales.

Marking scheme		Marks
(a)	1 mark for each relevant point up to a maximum of 8 marks for evaluation of the problem. 1 mark for each relevant point up to a maximum of 8 marks for suggested improvements. A maximum of 15 marks for this part question.	15
(b)	1 mark for each relevant point up to a maximum of 10 marks. 1 mark will be allocated for the correct calculation of the daily cost of delivering the service in-house.	10
Total		**25**

72 INSTITUTE OF ANALYTICAL ACCOUNTANTS

Key answer tips

This process has many elements, but this should provide students with plenty of areas to discuss in their answer. The best approach is to identify a problem, explain it, suggest a solution for this problem and justify this solution.

There is an acknowledged bottleneck in the task 'Enter question into Question Bank' (administration). The volume of questions received is too great for the number of administrators assigned to the task of entering them. This often means that questions received back from reviewers cannot be found on the database to have their outcome noted because they have not yet been entered into the system. This causes further frustration and delay. The simplification pattern assumes that most established processes have redundancies and duplication. It focuses on tackling bottlenecks and unnecessary tasks and unnecessary loops.

The backlog of question entering also seems to have had an effect on the quality of data entry. A recent check noted that one in ten questions had an error, making them unfit for purpose. The problem is accentuated by the fact that the administrators are not subject experts and so do not understand the content and context of the questions and answers they are inputting. Furthermore, the current process does not have any subsequent checks on the quality of the questions entered onto the system. This is potentially very serious, with students receiving questions which have spelling mistakes or answers where none of the solutions is correct.

One obvious solution is to increase the number of administrators entering questions into the question bank. However, this will be costly and the quality problems are likely to remain.

One of the potential ways of reducing the bottleneck is to delay question entry until the question has been accepted. Currently, 20% of questions are immediately rejected by the reviewer and a further 15% are sent back to the author for revision. Of these, 30% are rejected on the second review. This approach would also mean that the administrators would not have to enter the suggested amendments (Update Question), where further errors are almost certainly made.

Reducing the number of swim lanes is often advocated by proponents of business process change. It is a central tenant of the gaps and disconnects redesign pattern. Handoffs between departments are often a source of problems and bottlenecks.

One possibility is to move the tasks currently performed in the administration department into the education department where the employees have a greater understanding of the question subject matter and so are unlikely to make as many errors in data entry.

This could be combined with the suggestion outlined in the previous paragraph. However, it seems unlikely that the education department would welcome the suggestion and there seems likely to be staff issues and changes, reducing the number of people in administration and employing higher-cost employees in education.

Changing the sequence of tasks may also bring benefits. For example, the Select Reviewer process (Education) could be performed before the questions are submitted. Therefore all questions from a particular author are automatically sent to a specific reviewer. The need for anonymity would seem to preclude the direct despatch of questions from the author to the reviewer and this could reduce the efficiency of the proposal. However, the time taken to forward the proposed questions to reviewers would probably be reduced by this pre-selection approach.

The inclusion of the finance department as a swim lane also raises certain possibilities. This may be due to some agreed separation of duties between administration/education and the processing of payments. However, the inclusion of 'raise a reject notification' on this swim lane seems a poor fit. It is essentially an administrative process (as it has no apparent financial implications) and so should be performed by either administration or education. So, this task needs to be relocated in the proposed business process.

The re-engineering pattern essentially starts with a blank sheet of paper and the process is re-designed from the beginning focusing on its goals. At the IAA, the goal might be 'to have reviewed questions accurately entered into a computer system at the cheapest cost possible'.

Whether or not it qualifies for the term 're-engineering', a radical solution is to implement a workflow-type system where the author enters the question into a computer system and the question is routed automatically (through anonymously preassigning reviewers to authors) to the specified reviewer. If the author enters the question, he or she is unlikely to make many errors in data entry. Furthermore, if they do, these can be corrected by the reviewer. From the perspective of the IAA, the cost of entering the questions is transferred to the author and so the bottleneck is removed and administrative costs are reduced at one stroke.

The indication of the acceptability of the question is now the responsibility of the reviewer. Accepted responses can lead to the automatic raising of a payment notification which is sent to Finance. Rejection would lead to the automatic raising of a reject notification which is sent electronically to the author. Questions that need revising would also automatically be returned to the author to make amendments prior to re-submission to the second review process.

This re-engineered solution potentially removes IAA departments from the process completely, except for payment by Finance and even this could be automated. The need for administrative staff would be greatly reduced and it is difficult to see how this would not lead to redundancies. There may also have to be fewer employees in Education, although they could perhaps be redeployed on more strategic issues.

The implications for IAA staff of such a solution may mean that it is internally unpopular and difficult to implement, despite the financial and time benefits it will bring to the organisation.

Marking scheme	
	Marks
1 mark for each relevant point up to a maximum of	**15**

73   HOMEDELIVER

Key answer tips

There are effectively four elements to this requirement. Problems in the project need to be identified and lessons learnt need to be determined from this, then problems need to be identified in the implementation of the new software and these too need to have associated lessons learnt.

Post-project review at HomeDeliver

The following issues could have been raised at the HomeDeliver post-project review. They are presented here with lessons learned that should be fed back into the project management process.

- The late allocation of HomeDeliver order administrators full-time to the project. Initially, employees were allocated part-time to the project. However this hampered project progress as these administrators also needed to undertake their normal operational duties. Consequently, the project began to significantly slip. Even though selected order administrators were added full-time to the project it was too late and the software was delivered two months behind schedule.

  Lessons learned: it is likely that deadlines will slip if appropriate employees are not allocated full-time to the project.

- The failure to consult catalogue supervisors and agents. There is evidence in the scenario that internal stakeholders were identified and consulted throughout the project. However, external stakeholders, such as the catalogue supervisors and agents, were not consulted at all. This meant that they had little understanding of the software prior to its implementation. It also meant that their requirements were not taken into consideration when developing the software. Hence the need to amend an order was not included in the software solution.

  Lessons learned: ensure that stakeholder analysis includes both external and internal stakeholders and make sure that external stakeholders are included in the requirements gathering process where appropriate.

- The scope of implementation, implementing all supervisors and agents immediately. In retrospect, implementing all supervisors (and their agents) was too ambitious and risky. It would have been wiser to establish a pilot project where only selected supervisors and agents used the new system. Experience from this pilot could have been used to modify the software and fix faults and omissions before rolling out to the rest of the organisation. The scope should have been defined in the project initiation document and this should have been risk assessed.

  Lessons learned: the risk assessment of the scope of projects is important and project managers should look to mitigate risk by reducing scope.

Post implementation review at HomeDeliver

The following issues could have been raised at the HomeDeliver post-implementation review. They are presented here with recommendations that should be fed back into the software development process.

- Faults and omissions in the computer software. The omission of the order amendment facility has already been considered. However, the failure of the software to work with a popular browser needs investigating. Testing should consider a range of browsers. The post-implementation review should also consider why these faults were not found before the software was released. A possible reason is that the software was tested by full-time employees of HomeDeliver in a controlled office environment. It was not acceptance tested by the part-time, home-based agents who were actually going to use the software. These people were likely to be less familiar with computer applications and were also likely to use a wide variety of hardware and software.

  Lessons learned: acceptance testing should be undertaken by real business users in the hardware and software environment they are actually working in. Testing across multiple browsers must be considered.

- Faults in the documentation. The documentation supporting the implementation was both inappropriate and inappropriately distributed. Distributing the user manual as a PDF file raises at least two issues. Firstly, whether the email, and its attached file, had actually been received by the agent. A significant number of them claim that they did not receive the email. Secondly, it seems unreasonable to expect self-employed agents to print out a large, colour manual at their own cost. A failure to print out and study the manual probably contributed to agents being unable to use the software to enter multiple orders for one household. Spelling and functionality faults in the manual undermine confidence in both the documentation and the software it supports.

  Lessons learned: documentation must be carefully inspected before software release and its physical distribution should be carefully considered. Distributing documentation electronically may seem easy and cheap, but it may have important unanticipated consequences.

- Training of employees. It was perceived that the software was easy to use and so no formal training was given to agents. However, this missed the opportunity to find early faults (for example, not running under a certain browser). The inability of many agents to claim that the system could not support multiple orders from one household also suggests that the software was not as easy to use as its developers claimed.

  Lessons learned: As well as imparting skills, training provides an opportunity to build rapport with users and to identify possible issues and faults with the software at an earlier stage.

Marking scheme	
	Marks
1 mark for each relevant point up to a maximum of	**12**

74   ASW

Key answer tips

In **part (a)** suggest a range of options rather than focusing on just one and try to give as many specific details applying your answer to the scenario as possible. In **part (b)** make sure you justify your choice referring back to key issues identified in part (a).

(a)   The project manager could request an extension to the deadline. The case study scenario suggests that early delays in the project were caused by the absence of key CaetInsure staff and changes in user requirements in the re-insurance module. These delays meant that the full system specification was signed off three weeks later than initially agreed. Unfortunately, the delivery date of the whole project was not re-negotiated at this point as it was suggested that 'time could be made up' during the programming stage. Furthermore, the marketing department of CaetInsure had already announced the launch of a new product to coincide with the implementation of the software and they did not want to change these dates. However, the project manager could now return to CaetInsure and inform them that it had not been possible to catch up with the proposed schedule and to remind them that the initial slippage had been caused by them. Although the deadline date is associated with a product launch it is unlikely that this is crucial. It is not a matter of life and death.

It might be irksome to delay the launch by a few weeks, but it is unlikely that many people will notice or indeed care about it. There are many significant successful products which have been released long after their intended release date. In many ways it is an artificial deadline.

However, there are at least three problems associated with this suggestion. The first is that the delay is now longer than the three weeks incurred at the specification stage. Consequently, the project manager will have to explain that there have been further delays to the project. Secondly, the project manager will have to be very confident about his revised delivery date. The project plan does not explicitly contain any time for programmers fixing faults found in system and acceptance testing and it seems very likely that faults will be found in this testing. Finally, some negotiation will have to take place on the late delivery penalty clause charges the sales account manager agreed in the initial contract. If some (or all) of these clauses are enacted then the profitability of the project will be significantly affected.

The project manager could consider a functional reduction in the scope of the software solution

The scenario suggests that the re-insurance functionality has been a problem throughout the project. There may also be unresolved issues in other parts of the software. However, it must be remembered that the ASW product is a proven software solution, bespoke development is only concerned with customising the basic product to fulfil certain customer requirements. Therefore it is likely that there are large areas of the software that can be successfully delivered to the customer. The key issue here is whether this reduced functionality will fulfil the requirements associated with the proposed new product which CaetInsure intends to launch. If it does then the delivery of a partial solution does not have a significant business impact and the product launch can go ahead as planned. The project manager needs to discuss this with the customer as quickly as possible.

He has to be sure that the reduced scope does indeed fulfil these requirements and, if it does, to focus testing, migration and document production on these parts of the software. He will also have to estimate the delivery time of the second phase of the software that fulfils the complete user requirement.

There are three elements of this suggestion that the project manager should bear in mind. Firstly, the impact of reduced scope on the penalty clauses of the contract. It would appear harsh to deliver a part solution but to still be fully penalised for not delivering the total solution. Consequently some contract renegotiation is necessary. Secondly, there will be an unexpected overhead associated with delivering a second phase which contains the full product.

This is the overhead of *regression testing*, making sure that changes made to the product in the second release do not unintentionally affect the software solution that has already been delivered. Finally, the specification of data migration programs will have to be reviewed to see if they need to be changed in the light of the reduced functionality. Any changes will affect data migration programs which are currently being written or tested.

The project manager could consider taking steps which might reduce the quality of the product

A number of options might be considered around the testing of the software. One option is to considerably reduce system testing and hand over the software to acceptance testing ahead of the proposed schedule. The point has already been made that the software is essentially a package that has to be tailored for specific functions.

Consequently, large areas of the software have been tested before, much of it by actual users out in the businesses that are using this solution. Programs for the CaetInsure version will have been unit tested by programmers before they have been released to system testers and so no area of the system is *untested*, although there will be areas that have not been *independently tested*. Another option is to reduce the scope of system testing, focusing it on testing functionality rather than usability (which will be one focus of acceptance testing) and performance (which can be difficult to perform effectively in a software house environment where the user's actual hardware configuration cannot be easily mimicked). A further option is to execute system and acceptance testing in parallel.

There are a number of issues with this approach which the project manager needs to consider. The first is that the acceptance testers are likely to find significantly more faults than they would if full system testing had preceded acceptance testing. This can lead to a reduction in customer confidence which could jeopardise the whole project. Secondly, faults identified by both system and user acceptance testers have to be carefully managed. Configuration management becomes a very significant issue and appropriate version control of the software is an essential overhead. Confidence is undermined by the constant releases of new versions of the software, some of which, due to poor configuration management, contain faults which have already been reported and fixed in earlier versions of the software.

The project manager might consider requesting more resources

Finally the project manager may request further resources for the project. The current project plan is at a high level of detail. It does not show how many system testers are actually working on the system or how many technical authors are writing the documentation. It may be possible to add more resources and so reduce the elapsed time of the activity. Resources might also be asked to work smarter or work longer.

For example, testing might be prioritised so that the most important areas of the software from the user's perspective are tested first. It may also be possible to automate certain areas of testing or to outsource it to specialist testing companies. Programmers might be asked to focus more on static testing (which is particularly effective at finding faults) and to work overtime to beat their deadlines.

However, the project manager must be aware that adding resources to a late running project often slows the project down as established members of the project team explain requirements, standards and procedures to any newcomers. A key factor here will be the precision of the requirements. If these are well specified then it should be possible to add testing staff reasonably effectively, or indeed to outsource testing to countries where it can be conducted relatively cheaply.

It may also be possible to bring in technical authors and automated testing tools specialists who can speed up these activities. Programming is more of an issue. It will be very difficult to bring new programmers up to speed. However, it may be possible to transfer resources from other projects and to support the established programmers by providing appropriate hardware and software.

Finally, the addition of resources to the project will have an impact on project profitability. The project estimate will have assumed a certain commitment of resources. Adding resources will reduce the profit margin and indeed, in the extreme, may make the project itself unprofitable.

(b) There is no correct answer for this part of the question. However, it is suggested that a combination of the above strategies would be appropriate. The deadline is not crucial in the wider scheme of things and there is no statutory requirement to deliver on time.

However the deadline is significant to the customer and a failure to meet this deadline may cause internal problems and a 'loss of face'. This is particularly significant in this context because ASW is an external supplier. It might have been easier to negotiate an extended deadline if the software were being supplied by an internal IT department. Hence, it might be suggested that, in these circumstances, the deadline should not be extended for an initial release. However, it may be possible to negotiate the scope of this release, making sure that the key functions are in place and tested when the software is delivered. The customer might accept this reduction in scope as recognition of the delays caused earlier in the project when, due to the absence of key personnel, the full system specification was signed off three weeks late.

It could be argued that the current tasks of ASW, system testing and writing the user manual, could be shortened by adding further resources to the project. Effective testing will depend upon the quality of the specifications but it may be possible to add more resources and back this up with reduced test coverage. The amount of testing performed is driven by risk. There has to be a balance between the cost and time of more testing and the consequences of failure. Although the insurance system appears to be mission-critical to CaetInsure, there is a robust current system that could be reverted to during the planned parallel running.

It would also appear that more resources could be added to writing the user manual. There is already slack between the scheduled completion of the user manual and its use in the training course.

ASW might also consider starting writing the data migration programs before week 22. It appears from the project plan that ASW are waiting for system testing to be complete before writing these programs.

It may be possible to start beforehand, writing migration routines for the parts of the system that have already passed system testing.

The acceptance testing is outside the control of ASW. It is being performed by CaetInsure. However, again CaetInsure might consider reducing the time taken for acceptance testing by adding more resources to the task and by accepting a greater risk of failure during parallel running.

On balance, it might be suggested that further resources are quickly added to the project and that the test coverage is reduced. Hence the solution is largely concerned with adding resources and potentially reducing quality. If the customer is happy to slightly reduce the scope of the initial release to reflect past delays then this is a bonus. However, it is suggested that in this project the delivery date should remain fixed. Relaxing this is not an appropriate strategy in this instance.

Marking scheme		
		Marks
(a)	Up to 1 mark for each relevant point up to a maximum of 3 marks for each strategy	10
(b)	Up to 2 marks for each relevant point up to a maximum of 6 marks for this part of the question.	6
Total		**16**

75 TKP

Key answer tips

In **part (a)** make sure you don't limit the scope of your answer to just the two projects – the requirement asked you to analyse TKP as well.

(a) The first stages of risk management are the identification, descriptions and assessment of the risk. This assessment is primarily concerned with the *likelihood* of them occurring and the *severity of impact* on the organisation or project should they occur. Sometimes the likelihood is a subjective probability, the opinions of experienced managers or experts in the field. On other occasions, there is some statistical evidence on which to base the assessment. For example, in project 1, TKP identified that 20 IT software companies with annual revenues between $3m and $10m went out of business last year. This represented 10% of the total number of software companies reporting such revenues. Its report to the client suggested that there was a 10% chance of the current preferred supplier (who had a turnover of $5m) ceasing business and this would have a significant short-term support implication. This compared to a business failure rate of 1% for software companies with an annual revenue exceeding $100m. The client felt that the probability of supplier failure was too high, so eventually bought a software solution from a much larger, well-known, software supplier. In this case, the likelihood of the risk led the client to changing its procurement decision. The risk itself does not go away, large companies also fail, but the probability of the risk occurring is reduced.

The *avoidance (or prevention) of a risk* is a legitimate risk response. In project 1, the client could avoid the risk 'failure of the supplier' by commissioning an in-house bespoke solution. Similarly, TKP itself avoids the risks associated with trading in different cultures, by restricting its projects to clients based in Zeeland.

There are three further responses to risks.

Risk mitigation (or risk contingency) actions are what the organisation will do to counter the risk, should the risk take place. Mitigation actions are designed to lessen the impact on the organisation of the risk occurring. In project 2, TKP recommends that the producers of the iProjector should establish an escrow agreement with the company which produces the chip which enhances the quality of the projected image. It was agreed that design details of this chip should be lodged with a third party who would make them available to the producers of the iProjector should the company which owned the enhanced image technology cease trading. This is a mitigation approach to the risk 'failure of the supplier'. The supplier is relatively high risk (less than three years of trading, inexperienced management team), and the product (the iProjector) is completely dependent upon the supply of the image enhancing chip. The failure of the business supplying the chips would have significant impact on iProjector production. If the escrow agreement had to be enacted, then it would take the producers of the iProjector some time to establish alternative production. Consequently (and TKP have suggested this), it might be prudent to hold significant stocks of the chips to ensure continued production.

In such circumstances, the need to mitigate risk is more important than implementing contemporary just-in-time supply practices. In some instances a mitigation action can be put in place immediately. In other instances risk mitigation actions are only enacted should the risk occur. The risk has been recognised and the organisation has a rehearsed or planned response. For example, in project 1, TKP has identified 'poor quality of current data' as a risk associated with the migration of data from the current systems to the proposed software package solution. It has established a strategy for data cleansing if that risk actually materialises. Importantly, the client knows in advance how to respond to a risk. It avoids making a hasty, ill-thought out response to an unforeseen event.

Risk transfer actions are concerned with transferring the risk and the assessment and consequences of that risk to another party. This can be done in a number of ways. TKP itself has liability insurance which potentially protects the company from the financial consequences of being sued by clients for giving poor advice. TKP has identified this as a risk, but is unlikely to be able to assess either the probability of that risk occurring or establishing meaningful mitigation measures to minimise the effect of that risk. Consequently, the responsibility for both of these is transferred to an insurance company. They establish the risk, through a series of questions, and compute a premium which reflects the risk and the compensation maximum which will have to be paid if that risk occurs. TKP pays the insurance premiums. TKP itself also transfers risks in project 2. It is unsure about how to establish patents and so it refers the client to another company. Transferring avoids the risk associated with 'establishing the patent incorrectly' and the financial consequences of this.

Finally, risk may be identified but just accepted as part of doing business. *Risk acceptance* is particularly appropriate when the probability of the risk is low or the impact of that risk is relatively insignificant. Risks may also be accepted when there are no realistic mitigation or transfer actions. In project 2, the producers of the iProjector are concerned that there is 'a risk that a major telephone producer will launch a product with features and functionality similar to ours'. This is a risk, but there is little that can be done about it. Risks of competition are often best accepted.

The discussion above is primarily concerned with deciding what action to take for each risk.

Once these actions are agreed, then a plan may be required to put them into place. For example, establishing an escrow agreement will require certain activities to be done.

Risks must also be monitored. For example, in project 2, the risk of supplier failure can be monitored through a company checking agency. Many of these companies offer a continuous monitoring service which evaluates financial results, share prices and other significant business movements. Reports are produced, highlighting factors which may be of particular concern. Risks will also disappear once certain stages of the project have been completed and, similarly, new ones will appear, often due to changes in the business environment. Many organisations use a risk register or risk log to document and monitor risks and such logs often specify a risk owner, a person responsible for adequate management of the risk.

(b)   Every project is constrained in some way by its scope, time and cost. These limitations are often called the **triple constraint**. The scope concerns what has to be delivered by the project, time is when the project should deliver by, and cost is concerned with how much can be spent on achieving the deliverable (the budget). Quality is also an important feature of projects.

Some authors include quality in their triple constraint (instead of scope), others add it as a further constraint (quadruple constraint), whilst others believe that quality considerations are inherent in setting the scope, time and cost goals of a project. How a particular project is managed depends greatly on the pressures in the triple constraint.

In project 1, the reluctance of the company to re-visit the business case means that the budget (or cost) of the solution is fixed. The implementation date might be desirable, but it does not seem to be business critical. It is an internal system and so any delays in implementation will not affect customers. It will also be a relatively seamless transition for most employees in the company. They already record the time record details which the new system will collect and so all they will see is a changed user interface. Only the direct users of the output (account managers and the project office) will be affected by any delay. The scope of the software package is also pre-defined. If it fails to meet requirements, then the users will have to adjust their expectations or business methods. There is no money to finance customisation or add-on systems, so in this sense the scope of the solution is also fixed. The quality of the software, in terms of its reliability and robustness, should also be good, as it is a popular software solution used in many large companies.

In project 2, the launch date is fixed. It has been heavily publicised, the venue is booked and over 400 attendees are expected, including newspaper journalists. Thus the time of the project is fixed. However, although orders will be taken at the launch, the product is not expected to ship until a month after launch. Thus the scope of the product shown at the launch date might be restricted and inherent quality problems might not yet be solved. Any defects can be explained away (this is a pre-production model) or, more effectively, they may be avoided by ensuring that the product is demonstrated to attendees, not used by them. The project manager must ensure that key functionality of the product is available on launch date (such as producing an image of a certain quality), but other functionality, not central to the presentation (for example, promised support for all image file formats) could be delayed until after the presentation. The company should make extra funds available to ensure that the launch date is successful.

Marking scheme		Marks
(a)	1 mark for each relevant point up to 15 marks.	15
(b)	1 mark for each relevant point up to 2 marks for principles. 1 mark for each relevant point up to a maximum of 4 marks for each project. Maximum of 10 marks in total.	10
Total		**25**

76   A CLOTHING COMPANY

Key answer tips

Part (a) is on project initiation (and the PID in particular), whilst **part (b)** is on project management and how a manager can attribute to this. Don't mix the parts up and ensure that you put the right elements in the right part (your pocket notes should help here). After that you have to remember to apply your knowledge to the scenario.

(a)   The production of initial documentation concerning the business case and initiation of the project would have addressed many of the issues that subsequently arose in the website re-design. This documentation would typically include:

- A summary of the business justification of the project. These are the business objectives that have been defined in the business case to justify the project.

- The scope of the project, defined in terms of project objectives and ultimate deliverables.

- Constraints and targets that apply to the project.

- Project roles and responsibilities, for example; the definition of the project sponsor and the project manager. It is useful if this part of the document specifies the level up to which named individuals (or roles) can authorise:

- The commitment of resources

- The sign-off of deliverables

- Changes to project objectives and deliverables

- Changes to constraints

- Resources committed to the project

- Risks and assumptions associated with the project. These are considered below in the context of the clothing company's website re-design project.

The business justification of the project

The MM does specify business objectives such as 'increase sales revenue' and 'improve market visibility' (see meeting 1) but these are poorly defined objectives in that they are not quantified. A formal cost-benefit analysis undertaken at the start of the project would have forced the MM to quantify how much sales would increase and by when. The MM would also have been required to document the assumptions behind these predictions and to demonstrate a causal link between the functionality of the website and sales volume. The other suggested objective, improve market visibility, also requires further specification and quantification. The MM provides no evidence of current market visibility (and what this actually means) and how its improvement will be measured.

Some research is needed to quantify market visibility and to set realistic targets for its improvement. The statement of the project's business benefits is an important issue in contemporary project management. It is suggested that these benefits are kept constantly under review to ensure that the project has not strayed from its original justification. Furthermore, at the end of the project, the business benefits have to be reviewed to assess whether they have been realised. Because the MM has not specified measurable objectives in advance, the success of the project is impossible to assess. There is no benchmark to assess it against.

The scope of the project

On at least two occasions there appears to be confusion about the scope of the project. The TD originally produces a design that is too like the current site, 'We expected it to do much more' (meeting 2). However, the most significant misunderstanding about scope is between the board and the MM. It concerns the interpretation of the scope of the word 're-design'. The board appears to perceive that re-design does not include the development and implementation of the software, while the MM holds the opposite view. The scope of the re-design would have been clarified in a project initiation document.

Constraints that apply to the project

Constraints are often defined in terms of cost and time. The absence of a formal cost-benefit analysis for this project has already been recognised, so costs (and budget) were not formally agreed at the start of the project. There is also no evidence that a projected delivery time for the project was agreed at the start of the project. Indeed, it was the elapsed time, as well as the escalating cost, that first caused the board to be alarmed about the website re-design project. It also appears that the TD had technical constraints in mind which were also not articulated. These emerged in meeting 4 and caused delays documented in meetings 5 and 6. Again, technical constraints should have been documented in the project initiation document.

Project roles and responsibilities

Although it is not clearly stated, it appears that the sponsor of the project is the MM. However, at one critical point of the project the RP makes a decision to accept a design (meeting 4) which is subsequently overturned by the MM. This confusion of responsibility causes both cost and delay. If project roles and responsibilities had been properly defined, then it would have been recognised that the RP did not have sufficient authority to sign-off deliverables. Furthermore, the formal allocating of roles would have also meant that a project manager would have been nominated with the responsibility of delivering the project. In the scenario there is never any clear indication of who is playing the role of project manager and this is a major flaw.

Resources committed to the project

There is no evidence that the resources available to the project had been identified and documented at the start of the project. Problems only begin to emerge late in the project when the Board's decision to launch on 1 March prompts the TD to express concern that there are not enough developers to deliver the system on time.

Risks and assumptions associated with the project

Most project management methods suggest that risks should be formally documented and managed. Each risk is identified and its potential effect quantified.

For each significant risk, avoidance actions are suggested which are steps that can be taken to prevent the risk from occurring.

Mitigation actions are also defined for each risk. These are steps that can be taken to reduce the impact of the risks if they occur. Again there is no evidence to show that this has been done. As problems emerged in the project they were dealt with on an ad hoc basis. A consideration of risk at the outset of the project can lead to changes in how the project is conducted. For example, the risk of poor scoping of requirements could have prompted a more formal definition of requirements scope (an avoidance action).

Initial project structure and arrangements for management control

This is an initial project structure describing how the project will be broken down into stages with an associated list of project milestones. It is a very high-level plan which provides a context for the detailed plans that will follow. There is no evidence of such a structure in the website re-design project and so the absence of detailed planning (see below) goes unnoticed. The project initiation document might also include management control information concerning, for example, progress reporting and monitoring arrangements. If these had been defined in advance then their absence (see below) would have been clear in the actual project.

(b) Effective project management could have improved the conduct of the website re-design project in the following ways:

Detailed planning

During the delivery of the project the lack of a formal detailed plan means that there is no baseline for review and control. The absence of monitoring progress against that plan is also very evident. The meetings are events where, although progress appears to have been made, it is unclear how much progress has been made towards the delivery of the final re-designed website. Effective project management would have mandated the production of a detailed plan. There is no mention of a project plan, a critical path analysis, a Gantt chart or supporting project management software.

Effective monitoring and control

The board were not kept up to date about progress and were only alerted to potential issue when the finance director became concerned about spiralling costs. This is a failure of monitoring and control, aggravated by the fact that there is no project plan to monitor against. Effective project management would have required formal progress to the sponsor (in this case the board). Such monitoring should lead to project control, where suggested actions are considered and implemented to deal with project slippage.

The planning, monitoring and controlling aspects of project management are completely absent from the scenario and so none of the usual project management monitoring and reporting structures were in place to alert the board.

Mandating of substitutes

Initial progress is hampered by the absence of key personnel at meetings 3 and 4 and the inappropriate sign-off by the RP (already discussed above) of the technical design. The requirement for the TD to produce a technical report also slows progress. These problems could have been addressed by ensuring that substitutes were available for these meetings who understood their role and the scope of their authority. Effective project management would have ensured that progress would not have been delayed by the absence of key personnel from the progress meetings.

Standards for cost-benefit analysis

The cost-benefit analysis provided by the MM is flawed in two ways. Firstly, the assumptions underpinning the benefits are not explained. There is no supporting documentation and it appears, at face value, that year four and five benefits have been greatly inflated to justify the project. Secondly, it would be usual to discount future costs and benefits using an agreed discount rate. This has not been done, so the time value of money has not been taken into account. Effective project management would have defined standards for the cost-benefit analysis based on accepted practice.

Estimating, risks and quality

The reaction of the board to the cost-benefit analysis also appears unrealistic. They appear to have suggested a budget and a timescale which does not take into account the complexity of the remaining work or the resources available to undertake it. The estimating part of the project management framework appears to be lacking. It is clear at the final meeting that the website will not be ready for launch. However, the MM decides to take the risk and achieve the imposed deadline and take a chance on the quality of the software. This decision is made against the advice of his TD and without any information about the quality of the software. Effective project management would have mandated a framework for considering the balance between risk and quality.

The MM does not inform the board of the TD's advice. The MM, like many project managers (because the MM now appears to have adopted this role) finds it politically more acceptable to deliver a poor quality product on time than a better quality product late. Unfortunately the product quality is so poor that the decision proves to be the wrong one and the removal of the software (and the resignation of the MM) ends the project scenario.

Marking scheme		Marks
(a)	Up to 2 marks for each relevant point relating to the scenario	15
(b)	Up to 2 marks for each relevant point relating to the scenario	10
Total		**25**

77   PSI

Key answer tips

(a)   The first part of the question asked candidates to analyse the nature, scope and type of strategic change at PSI. This should have been straightforward if students were aware of the different categories in the text – evolution v revolution, adaptation v reconstruction.

(b)   The second part of the question asked candidates to identify and analyse the internal contextual features that could influence the success or failure of the chief executive's proposed strategic change at PSI. The terms used pointed to the Balogun and Hope Hailey model. However, even if students were not aware of this model, there were many easy points that could have been made form issues identified in the question.

(a)   The proposal to develop and sell a software package for the general retail industry represents a major strategic decision for PSI. Up till now it has been relatively successful in identifying and servicing the software needs of a specialist niche market – the retail pharmacy market. In Michael Porter's terms it is currently a focused differentiator. Its proposed entry into the general retail market represents both a new product and a new market and so, using the perspective of Ansoff's growth matrix, it is a diversification strategy with high levels of risk. The proposal would lead to significant strategic change and, perhaps not surprisingly, is meeting resistance from the software development director who is responsible for a key activity in this change.

Johnson, Scholes and Whittington (JSW) argue that there is a danger in believing that there is 'only one way, or one best way, to change organisational strategies'. They believe that most strategies are profoundly influenced by earlier strategies and their success or failure. Consequently, strategies are often incremental in nature, adding to or adapting, previous or existing strategy. Rarely is the proposed change so fundamental that it challenges the existing business model and the processes and activities that support it.

JSW make use of a model developed by Balogun and Hope Hailey, which identifies four types of change which have very different degrees of impact. It is suggested that there are two key measures of change. Firstly, the *nature of change* – how big is it? *Incremental* or 'step-by-step' change does not challenge the existing way of doing things and may indeed reinforce the organisation's processes and culture. It is therefore likely to meet less resistance than *Big Bang* or quantum change, which represents significant change to most or all the organisation. Often this *Big Bang* change is necessary to respond to a crisis facing the firm, such as a major fall in profitability, and/or the appointment of a new chief executive.

Secondly, the *scope* of change process is important – how much of the firm's activities are to be changed? If the change does not alter the basic business model (or 'paradigm' in JSW's terms) then it is regarded as 'a *realignment of strategy* rather than a fundamental change in strategic direction' (JSW). However, if the proposed change is a radical challenge to the existing business model or paradigm then it is regarded as a *transformational* change.

The consideration of the two key measures of change enables the identification of four types of change. These four types are used in this answer but other models and approaches would be acceptable.

	Scope of change	
Nature of change	Realignment	Transformation
Incremental	**Adaptation**	**Evolution**
Big Bang	**Reconstruction**	**Revolution**

- *Adaptation* is a change that can be made within the current business model (realignment) and it occurs incrementally. JSW argue this is the most common form of change in organisations.

- *Reconstruction* represents significant change in the organisation, often prompted by a crisis, such as an unwelcome takeover bid, but it does not require a fundamental change to the business model. Turnaround strategies where the aim is to rapidly reduce costs or increase revenues to ensure business survival may affect the whole organisation, but not change the basic business model.

- *Evolution* is a change in strategy, which requires the business model to be significantly changed over a period of time. The perceived need for 'transformation' may be as result of careful business analysis leading to a planned evolutionary change. Alternatively, change may take place through an emergent process where the scope of change only becomes apparent once it is completed.

- *Revolution* affects the whole of the organisation and the scope of change requires a fundamental shift in the business model – the way the firm chooses to compete.

Viewed dispassionately, it appears that PSI's proposed move into the general retail market represents an evolutionary change.

It is incremental because it will build on the skills, routines and beliefs of those in the organisation. However, it is transformational because the proposed move away from the current market niche to a market which requires a generic solution is a fundamental change in strategic direction. It is likely that internal processes and activities will need to significantly change for the company to successfully develop and sell the new packages. In PSI's case, the evolution is driven top-down, by the chief executive's desire to create a company which is an attractive acquisition, at which point he can realise some or all of his investment in the company.

Interestingly, the three directors may not all perceive the change as evolutionary. The entrepreneurial chief executive and the sales and marketing director may see the proposal as adaptive change, realigning the company to take advantage of a business opportunity which will lead to realising their personal goals. Indeed they may see the current product as just the specific implementation of a generic retail software solution. In contrast, the software development director is more likely to agree with our assessment of the change as evolutionary.

(b) JSW argue that successfully managing change depends on context. This context is made up of a number of factors or contingencies peculiar to the organisation under consideration. How change is managed in a relatively small privately owned firm like PSI is very different to how it might be managed in a large international firm of accountants with hundreds of partners.

JSW again use the work of Balogun and Hope Hailey to consider the contextual features that need to be taken into account in deciding how a strategic change programme should be managed.

In the context of PSI, the following observations could be made.

- *Time* – the company is not facing any immediate financial or business problems and so there is no apparent need for rapid change. Figure 1 suggests a company that is slowly consolidating in its market place. There is no evidence of a crisis that requires urgent remedial action. It is likely that it will take a relatively long time to develop the new generic software package, particularly when the current pressures on the software development team are taken into account. They are already having problems meeting deadlines for the current product. The only urgency is that injected by the impatience of the chief executive who may want to quickly introduce change to achieve the objectives of realising his investment in the company.

  The natural inclination of the software team and their director will be to use any available time to consolidate the current product and to improve its quality. In contrast, the chief executive will want to use available time to produce the new generic product.

  This will almost certainly lead to conflict, both within the organisation and with customers pressurising the software team for fault rectification and new requirements. The increased concentration of pharmacies into nationwide chains may also increase the power of certain customers.

- *Scope* – the degree of change should not be underestimated in a relatively small firm like PSI. Supplying a clearly defined segment supported by a vertical marketing strategy is very different to the horizontal marketing strategy required for the proposed move into the general retail market. The company has built up expertise in a niche market. It is unlikely that it will have comparable expertise in the generic retail market as well as in the other niche retail markets that it intends to target with its configurable software package.

- *Preservation* – clearly software development skills are a crucial resource and capability and must be preserved to enable the proposed strategic change. The retention of the software team's expertise and motivation is essential. If they are upset by the proposed change and disturbed by the further pressures it is likely to create then it is unlikely that they will support it. The agreement of the software development director to the change is also vital and some way of securing this must be explored. Although the proposed change is largely based on the competency of current personnel, it is likely that they will be disturbed by the increased pressure imposed on them and so there is a high probability that key employees will leave the company.

- *Diversity* – Change may be helped if there is a diversity of experience. However, change may be hampered if the organisation has followed a particular strategy for a number of years. The relative stability of the last three years and the company's stated objective to be a 'highly skilled professional company providing quality software services to the retail pharmacy industry' seem at odds with the chief executive's vision of expansion. There is also evidence to suggest that the goals of the sales force and those of the software developers are already conflicting and there seems even more opportunity for this to occur in the context of a generic retail software package. Change will be hampered by the current conflict between sales and development.

- *Capability* – The chief executive and sales and marketing director are entrepreneurial in outlook and want change to fuel growth and their personal aspirations. The software development director is much less enthusiastic as he can clearly see the implications of the proposed change in strategic direction. Furthermore, over the last three years the workforce has been relatively settled and has not been subject to much significant change. In some ways the small size of the business may make change easy to facilitate (see power), but there may also be significant barriers to change. The software development director and his staff control and implement the key activity of the new strategy. It may be difficult to overcome their lack of enthusiasm for the proposed change.

- *Capacity* is concerned with resources such as people, finance and information. More detailed analysis will be necessary to see if PSI has the necessary resources to implement the proposed change. However, evidence from the scenario is not encouraging. For example, the company has recently been criticised at a user group conference for failing to meet its proposed release deadlines. The acquisition of necessary resources will take both time and money. There is no evidence that the company has the finances to support the acquisition of new resources. It is a private company and so it will not be able to raise money through the stock market.

  It will rely on further investments from the current shareholders (and the software development director may be reluctant to participate in this) or on bank finance. Furthermore, it usually takes a long time to integrate software developers into a business. There is a long learning curve during which they have to learn not only how the product works, but how it is designed. Hence they are unlikely to be productive until several months after appointment and this lack of progress might again clash with the impatience of the chief executive.

- *Readiness* – There is no evidence that the organisation is ready for the type of change proposed by the chief executive. In fact the current pressure on the software development team suggests that they may not welcome the proposed new strategy.

  What they might be ready for is a strategy that leads to a consolidation of the pharmaceutical product so that faults are fixed and new requirements released on time.

- *Power* – the chief executive has the ultimate power in this organisation, reinforced by (through combining with the sales and marketing director) ownership of the majority of the shares. However he must secure the co-operation of the software development director to make progress. The fact that he has power may lead to him forcing through a strategy which is essentially wrong for the organisation.

Overall, an analysis of the context for change at PSI should provide warning signs to the chief executive. Although the chief executive has the power to impose change, there are concerns about the scope and capacity for change which may make it very difficult for the company to preserve its current resources and competencies. There is a real concern that these will actually be destroyed by the proposed change and this will lead to major difficulties in their current market. There is already evidence of this from the scenario. The company has been criticised at a user group conference for quality failures and there are doubts about whether planned new features will be released on time. The product is fundamental to the efficient purchasing and stock control required in contemporary pharmacies. Customers may switch to a competitor if they feel that their emerging requirements are not met with sufficient promptness and quality.

The workforce is neither ready for change nor diverse enough to welcome change. There are current conflicts between sales and development which are likely to be escalated by the proposed strategic change. Finally, there are also grave doubts about the capacity of the company to deliver the proposed change within the likely time scale required by the chief executive.

There is a concern that the chief executive will rely on managing change through coercion, which 'is the imposition of change or the issuing of edicts about change'. This is not unusual in small firms where the chief executive also has a large ownership stake in the business. It is most appropriate in crisis situations where time is of the essence and clear direction is imperative. However, PSI does not appear to be in a crisis situation. Unfortunately, however, it looks like the chief executive is about to create one!

Marking scheme		
		Marks
(a)	Up to 2 marks for recognising that PSI is pursuing a diversification strategy	2
	Up to 2 marks for explaining the nature of change	2
	Up to 2 marks for explaining the scope of change	2
	Up to 4 marks for exploring the types of change with particular reference to the situation at PSI	4
(b)	Up to 3 marks for an analysis of each feature that could influence the success or failure of the proposed strategic change at PSI up to a maximum of 15 marks	15
	Eight possible features are described in detail in the model answer	
	A possible mark allocation (1 mark per point up to a maximum of 3 marks) for one of these features (time) is given below.	
	– Explanation of possible effect of time	
	– Recognition that time is not an issue at PSI – there is no evidence of a crisis that requires remedial action	
	– Relatively long time to develop a new product given current time pressures	
	– Impatience of the chief executive imposes arbitrary urgency	
	– Conflict between chief executive and software development director over time allocation.	
Total		**25**

78   ZOOMBA

Key answer tips

The key in this question will be try to use the models that are contained in this area of the syllabus rather than relying on common sense which typically results in an answer that lacks structure and does not have suitable breadth.

The key models to use are the JSW change matrix and the POPIT model.

(a) **Type of change**

JSW make use of a model developed by Balogun and Hope Hailey, which identifies four types of change based on two key measures of change. Firstly, the *nature of change* – how big is it? *Incremental* or 'step-by-step' change does not challenge the existing way of doing things and may indeed reinforce the organisation's processes and culture. It is therefore likely to meet less resistance than *Big Bang* or quantum change, which represents significant change to most or all the organisation. Often this *Big Bang* change is necessary to respond to a crisis facing the firm, such as a major fall in profitability, and/or the appointment of a new chief executive.

Secondly, the *scope* of change process is important – how much of the firm's activities are to be changed? If the change does not alter the basic business model (or 'paradigm' in JSW's terms) then it is regarded as 'a *realignment of strategy* rather than a fundamental change in strategic direction' (JSW). However, if the proposed change is a radical challenge to the existing business model or paradigm then it is regarded as a *transformational* change.

The consideration of the two key measures of change enables the identification of four types of change:

	Scope of change	
Nature of change	Realignment	Transformation
Incremental	**Adaptation**	**Evolution**
Big Bang	**Reconstruction**	**Revolution**

It appears that Zoomba's attempt to enter the pop up market represents an adaptation. Adaptation is a change that can be made within the current business model (realignment) and it occurs incrementally. JSW argue this is the most common form of change in organisations.

It is incremental because it will build on the existing skills, routines and beliefs of those in the organisation. There may be some changed processes, but these are likely to be small in nature. Zoomba is seeking to realign itself with the social changes that are happening in the market and take part in an emerging opportunity. There is unlikely to be a need for a complete business transformation as Zoomba continues to perform well despite increased market competition and a downturn in the economy. There will be no need for a radical redesign of the business model and, ideally, the pop ups should look and feel exactly like the product and service provided at the permanent locations.

(b) **Reasons for the project failure**

A useful model for explaining the failures in the system is the POPIT model. The POPIT model provides four views of a business system that must be considered for the successful implementation of business change.

These elements must work together and be aligned for successful change to be realised. A failure in one area can lead to a failure across the entire business system. The areas to be considered are as follows:

Processes must be well defined, efficient, documented and understood. Zoomba appears to have done this. Elise Hazelwood appears to have sought efficiency in areas such as venue location, food production, material supplies, etc. The lessons learnt review appears to highlight that these areas have worked well in the project.

Information Technology needs to support the changes that are taking place within the system. It needs to provide the relevant information at the point that it is needed. Elise Hazelwood's previous IT experience appears to have helped here. The IT system worked well and controls were considered to ensure that risks were reduced.

There was some attempt made on the *organisation* for success. Project team staff were appointed as managers at the pop ups and arrangements were put in place for the secondment of staff. But this could have been much better organised. Job roles were unclear, visitors observed disorganised service and staff appeared to be unaware of potential secondments to the pop ups. This is related to the final view on the business system – its people.

People in the organisation need to have the right skills and motivation to carry out the tasks. This is an area that Elise Hazelwood appears to have ignored almost entirely. She has put managers in place at the pop ups but hasn't really considered the people that they will be managing. There is evidence of poor motivation in the poor service provided to customers and some of that may be down to a lack of consideration of job design. Seconding staff into pop ups without prior notice or explanation needs to be better planned and organised.

There also appears to be evidence of a lack of staff training (service was slower than usual and staff complained of spending too much time learning new, temporary processes) as well as a failure to consider staff development (one staff member complained of a lost development opportunity rather than an enhanced experience).

These are problems that can be rectified for future pop ups. But they highlight that a business system is made up of many components, and a failure to consider one of these views can harm the successes made in other areas.

Marking scheme		Marks
(a)	1 mark for each appropriate point up to a maximum of	8
(b)	1 mark for each appropriate point up to a maximum of	7
Total		**15**

79 WEBFILMS

Key answer tips

In the SBL exam you will not be required to use a specific model. However, the Balogun Hope Hailey model is so useful for examining the cultural aspects of change, that this questions gives you no choice but to practice using it.

The Balogun and Hope Hailey model is used to explore the contextual features of change which need to be considered if that change is to be successful. Five of those contextual features were explored in this question.

Time – This looks at how quickly change is needed. There does not appear to be an immediate need for change as the business is doing well, but is looking at how to successfully compete in the future. Therefore there should be sufficient time to adequately plan the change, leading to a greater chance of success. Indeed, the actions leading towards the change are likely to be incremental, at least internally. However, the CEO has suggested that the entire switchover to the new strategy needs to take place in a single event. From an external perspective, this may be viewed as a 'Big Bang' change, which may lead to greater resistance from those external stakeholders affected by the change. However, if the marketing campaign is well-planned, then change may appear incremental, as customers will have time to get used to the changes which will be implemented.

Scope – This refers to the degree of change required. This may be considered a realignment of existing processes, or a transformational strategic change. Webfilms is planning to move from being a focused differentiator to a hybrid company operating with a broader customer base and a greater focus on cost efficiencies. This is a leap in strategy which needs to be very well planned in order for it to be successful. It is not impossible for a company to move around the strategy clock, but it may take time to gain acceptance from its customers. The continuing focus on quality, which may also be considered under preservation, should help with the success of the strategic change.

Scope also considers the type of business being carried out. This is being expanded to include services which have not previously been offered (e.g. broadband provision). The way in which business is to be carried out (boundary-less working) is also changing.

These are areas unfamiliar to Webfilms and may influence the success of the change unless appropriate expertise is acquired.

Readiness – This examines how ready the workforce is for change. Webfilms has successfully undergone transformational change in the past and so its workforce may be well prepared for it to happen again. However, it appears there is resistance from a key player in this strategy. The creative director and his team are important to the success of the change and their resistance could jeopardise the strategy. The CEO will need to bring them on board for it to be successful.

Preservation – This looks at the organisational resources and characteristics which will be maintained throughout the change. The main business of the company will stay the same: offering programmes through the internet.

This should ensure that the existing customer base remains, as long as it is still done successfully. However, the failure to preserve the advertisement-free approach may alienate existing customers.

Power – This looks at the power the change leader has to impose the change on the organisation. The CEO is the person driving the change and has the power to do so by virtue of her position in the organisation. She also has the experience, as she transformed the company from a postal-based to internet-based provider. However, it appears she plans to do this using force rather than consensus ('this is going to happen. It's up to you whether you want to be involved...'). This use of power may initially deter resistance, but it may have the opposite effect in the long term, demotivating the critically important creative development team.

There seems little doubt that the CEO is again suggesting transformational change as the company reinvents itself. Whether it is incremental or big bang depends on perspective. As mentioned before, internally it could be perceived as incremental and so the change would be classified as evolution. However, to external stakeholders it might appear as big bang, and hence represents revolutionary change.

Marking scheme	
	Marks
Up to 1 mark for each relevant point up to a maximum of 3 marks for each contextual factor. Five contextual factors giving a maximum of 15 marks plus 1 mark in classifying the change as per the Balogun and Hope Hailey model.	16

80 GREENTECH

Key answer tips

There are many ways in which **part (a)** can be approached. The best approach would use a recognised model to provide structure to the answer. The answer provided uses the SWOT model. Make sure points are explained / justified – For example, when discussing strengths a weaker student might simply write that 'The company is in a good financial position'. But the better student will write a more specific answer such as 'The company has a good financial position having built up $17m of surplus cash.'

Part (b) asks you to 'evaluate.....the strategy options'. This is likely to be a regular exam requirement. A good approach is to use the Johnson, Scholes and Whittington criteria of suitability, feasibility and acceptability to assess strategies and answer such requirements. Make sure that you answer the question and justify your selection – all 3 are likely to be feasible, but Ang's is MOST suitable, and the only one that's likely to be acceptable.

With **part (c)** you need to be comfortable with interpreting diagrams. You will never have to draw them, but you need to be able to look at one and spot the problems. Try to link problems and solutions. For example we discover a problem: 20% of orders are rejected late in the process; therefore we need to develop a solution to this problem: move credit checks to earlier in the process.

(a) The current strategic position of *greenTech* could be summarised in a brief SWOT analysis.

Strengths

The company has a good financial position, with, by April 20X8, a cash surplus of $17 million.

The company has explicitly positioned itself as a focused differentiator in a very competitive market place.

The company has a stable, successful management team that has been in place since 1990.

The company has important core competencies in the production of green technology. It was the development of these competencies that formed the basis of Professor Ag Wan's suggestion.

Weaknesses

Despite recent increases, marketing as a whole is under-funded. It currently stands at about 0.3% of turnover.

None of the marketing budget is specifically aimed at the sale of fully assembled green computers. This was recognized by Lewis-Read, who believed that the company should invest in marketing these computers to both home and corporate customers.

The current process for ordering and configuring computers has a number of efficiency problems. This leads to low conversion of enquiries into accepted orders.

Opportunities

The Lewis-Read proposal points out that the government has just agreed a preferential procurement policy for energy efficient computers with high recyclable content.

The general public is increasingly conscious of the need to conserve the environment. 'Green consumers' are increasing both in numbers and visibility.

Other industrial sectors are looking for opportunities to provide products that are quiet, recyclable and have low emissions.

Web-based technology now exists that allows customers to construct virtual prototypes of machines and equipment.

Threats

Although sales are increasing, the company is still relatively small in global terms and so it is unlikely to be able to compete with the established global suppliers of fully assembled computers. There are significant barriers to entry to this market.

Lack of manufacturing capability is a threat as it makes the company vulnerable to problems in the supply chain. The acquisition of a manufacturing company to address this is part of Fenix's proposal.

(b) The team from the accountants Lewis-Read has suggested a strategy that protects and builds on the company's current position. Johnson, Scholes and Whittington identify two broad options within this approach. The first concerns *consolidation* which may include downsizing or withdrawal from certain activities.

The second is *market penetration* where an organisation gains market share, usually by increasing marketing activity. This seems to be what Lewis-Read has in mind.

However, their proposal appears to envisage market penetration in only one of the three specific sectors served by *greenTech*, the provision of fully assembled green computers. This focus is probably based on a perception of high potential demand coupled with low current marketing investment in this area. Trends suggest that the overall market for this type of computer should be growing rapidly. Domestic customers and companies are increasingly aware of their carbon footprint and wish to reduce consumption both on ethical and economic grounds. The scenario also states that the government is promoting energy efficient computers with high recyclable content in their procurement policy. Consequently, demand should be growing. On the other hand, *greenTech*'s marketing spend suggests that not only is the overall budget relatively small, but that none of it appears to be specifically aimed at the green consumer. In contrast, over half of the budget is currently specifically targeted at the electronics industry or home buyers of components. This lack of marketing investment may explain the relatively small growth in sales in the fully assembled green computer's revenue stream. Thus it appears that the company is failing to address a growing market because its marketing spend is too small, with none of it specifically focused on that sector.

It is possible that *greenTech*'s reluctance to market their computers directly to domestic and commercial companies is due to their perception that they will be seen to be competing with two of their commercial customers. This will require careful consideration. However, withdrawal from some activities is a legitimate tactic within a 'protect and build' strategy. Perhaps the loss of some commercial customers will be more than compensated for by direct computer sales to customers.

The second proposal, from the team representing the corporate recovery specialists, Fenix, is to develop products to offer a more comprehensive service to the electronics industry. This is a strategic direction of *product development,* where organisations deliver modified or new products to existing markets. Fenix's suggestion is primarily focused on adding new products (expanded product range) and services (special requirements) beyond current capabilities. The scenario suggests that 70% of the electronics industry currently use *greenTech* components somewhere in their products. However, there may be scope for supplying more products and services to these established customers as well as supplying to those who do not currently use *greenTech's* products.

Fenix also makes the point that buying a manufacturing capability will protect the supply chain. *greenTech* currently has no manufacturing capability of their own and so they are at the mercy of their suppliers. These suppliers might raise prices, supply competitors, fail to meet demand or go out of business. A manufacturing facility could avoid all of these as well as perhaps providing an opportunity to cut supply costs. Furthermore, it could be argued that supplying a more comprehensive range of products to established customers may help protect current business with these customers.

However, Fenix recognise that manufacturing is beyond *greenTech's* current capabilities. Consequently, there is the issue of how these capabilities will be acquired. Their proposal is for the company to spend its cash surplus acquiring companies that already have these capabilities. It would be costly, risky and time-consuming to develop these capabilities organically. So, although *greenTech* has no experience of making acquisitions and making them work, Fenix's suggestion of acquisition seems very sensible.

The final proposal from Professor Ag Wan is for *greenTech* to look for opportunities where the company could use its core competencies with green technology within other industries and products. This is the strategic direction of *finding new* uses *for existing products and knowledge.* Johnson, Scholes and Whittington provide an example: 'manufacturers of stainless steel have progressively found new applications for existing products, which were originally used for cutlery and tableware. Nowadays the uses include aerospace, automobile exhausts, beer barrels and many applications in the chemical manufacturing industry.' For the company itself, this is probably quite a radical way of looking at itself. Instead of being seen as essentially a components supplier it becomes a supplier of ideas and technology. Professor Ag Wan's suggestion makes *greenTech* re-consider what industry they are in and this reflection should allow them to see a potentially much bigger market (green technology) in which they have already demonstrated capabilities in one sector (electronics).

Contemporary social trends also support Professor Ag Wan's suggestion. All industries will have to find greener ways of working if they are to satisfy three important forces. The first is the 'green consumers' who wish to purchase from companies with demonstrable sustainability policies. The second is governments who are increasingly likely to pass laws on emissions and responsibility for waste disposal. The third force is the increasing cost of disposal as the number of potential disposal sites decreases. Thus the market *for greenTech's* products, know-how and testing should be large and increasing.

The problem facing *greenTech* is how they will find these markets and exploit them. Professor Ag Wan's suggestion is that the surplus cash should be spent on finding these markets using market research.

The scenario states that *greenTech* opted for the third option (from Professor Ag Wan) and put it into operation. This briefing paper suggests why this option was selected by the company. Although all three of the suggestions are feasible it argues that Ag Wan's proposal is a more suitable fit.

The first suggestion, from Lewis-Read, appears to address the imbalance between a large potential market (green computers) and an under-promoted and under-sold product (fully assembled green computers). However, the supply of computers is a very competitive market and the money that *greenTech* has to spend on marketing is probably insufficient for it to make a serious impact. There are already global brands supplying computers at highly competitive prices. It must be recognised that *greenTech's* products could be sold initially at a premium price to reflect its niche position. However, if the market-place demands it, the major suppliers will have little difficulty in producing machines that directly compete with *greenTech.* The product can easily be imitated. Indeed the scenario reveals that *greenTech* already supplies two medium-sized computer manufacturers with components for green products in their range.

These manufacturers might feel uneasy about *greenTech* becoming a significant competitor and consequently withdraw their business, so weakening this revenue stream. *greenTech* may be better advised to position their fully assembled computers as a complete kit, just as kit car manufacturers are prepared to provide assembled cars to customers without the time or expertise to assemble them.

Overall, Lewis-Read's proposal does not appear to be a particularly *feasible* strategy. Johnson, Scholes and Whittington suggest that an assessment has to be made about the extent to which the organisation's current capabilities (resources and competences) have to change to reach the *threshold* requirements for a strategy.

In the case of *greenTech,* major investment would be required to overcome entry barriers and maintain market share. It is unlikely that the cash available would be sufficient to cope with the global players who already supply fully assembled computers.

The second suggestion, from Fenix, has many good points. *greenTech* is currently reliant on its suppliers because it lacks a manufacturing capability. It appears to make sense to move upstream in the supply chain to secure supply. Flexibility in the products supplied and reduced costs are also attractive bonuses. However, the company has grown organically and it is still run by the management team that formed it in 1990. It has no experience in acquiring companies, integrating them and running them successfully. All evidence suggests that many acquisitions do not deliver the benefits that had been claimed for them, even when they are acquired by experienced managers. Furthermore, it is likely for cost reasons that the acquired company would be in another country, perhaps creating both language and cultural difficulties. Overall, *greenTech* appears to be a relatively conservative, risk-averse company and so it is the unfamiliarity and risk associated with this proposal that means it should be rejected. In the terms of Johnson, Scholes and Whittington, the Fenix proposal is not a particularly *acceptable* strategy to the existing management because of the risk involved with acquisition.

Professor Ag Wan's suggestion may have won by default; after all the television show has to have a winner! However, it also has two significant strengths. The first, central to his proposal, is that it allows the company to see itself in a new and exciting way. The recognition of these core green technology and know-how competencies and their significance in an important and expanding market should be very motivating to *greenTech's* management and employees. Secondly, it has to be recognised that most of *greenTech's* current business activities are with fellow electronics companies or enthusiasts. Professor Ag Wan's proposal continues that tradition. Transactions will be business-to-business, often at quite a technical level. *greenTech* is comfortable with and experienced in such transactions. Professor Ag Wan's suggestion appears to be suitable, in that the strategy addresses the situation in which the company is operating. It is acceptable because it is in line with the expectations and values of the shareholders. Finally, it appears to be feasible as it does not require excessive funding and most of this funding is focused in one specific area: market research. The proposal is an excellent cultural fit and so was justifiably selected as the winner in the programme.

(c)   A number of issues can be identified in this process.

First of all, 40% of enquiries do not proceed after the delivery and payment details have been sent to the customer. The scenario suggests that this is of concern to *greenTech* because it wastes time and effort.

However, it also impacts upon Xsys and for both of these companies this wastage means the loss of significant selling opportunities. The reason for this high wastage rate is not specified. Three possibilities include:

The cost of the computer was more than expected. In this case it would be useful to supply the cost as soon as delivery details have been completed. This means making sure that the web site has access to Xsys pricing details.

The delivery date was later than required. Although it would be tempting to automatically show the delivery date on the screen alongside cost details, this might not be commercially sensible. It would be better to direct effort at reducing the delivery time so that it was no longer an issue.

Finally, the delay gives the customer time to reflect and change their mind. It would be preferable to get customer commitment much earlier in the ordering process.

The credit check is performed too late in the ordering cycle. 20% of orders are rejected at this point. Hence *greenTech* and Xsys have wasted time and money communicating with the customer. The suggestion again is to bring payment and credit checking forward to the start of the ordering process. This would remove two processes from the *greenTech* swim lane: 'request delivery date' and 'e-mail delivery and cost details'.

Bringing ordering, payment and payment checking to the start of the process eradicates the need for Xsys to provide two delivery dates, one on initial ordering and a second on confirmation.

The problem of delivery time could be addressed by using EIM (or a similar courier company) to deliver directly to the end customer. This would remove two further processes from the *greenTech* swim lane – 'agree delivery date' and 'arrange delivery to customer'.

Making the changes proposed above now only leaves 'place confirmed order' and 'test computer' in the *greenTech* swim lane. 'Place confirmed order' can be automatically triggered near the start of the ordering process. If responsibility for testing was given to Xsys (and there are good reasons why it should be), then there would be nothing left in the *greenTech* swim lane. *greenTech* becomes a virtual supplier and the sales department can get on with making sales rather than processing orders.

Marking scheme – technical marks		
		Marks
(a)	Up to 1 mark for each significant point up to a maximum of	10
(b)	Up to 1 mark for each significant point in the evaluation of each proposal up to a maximum of 4 marks for each proposal.	12
	Up to 1 mark for each significant point in the justification of the winning proposal up to a maximum of 8. 2 marks for a conclusion	8
(c)	Up to 1 mark for each identified deficiency, suggestion or implication.	10
		——
Total		**40**
		——

How well has the candidate demonstrated Professional Skills as follows:	Not at all	Not well	Quite well	Very well
Commercial acumen in supporting the recommended strategy	The strategic option recommended by the candidate was purely based on the application of academic theory, rather than any display of sensible and practical commercial acumen.	The candidate demonstrated only superficial commercial acumen when evaluating the strategic options, to the extent that it really did not contribute to the recommendation.	The candidate has demonstrated some limited commercial acumen when determining which of the three options to recommend, but it was not explicitly mentioned in the answer.	The candidate has demonstrated incisive commercial acumen when determining which of the three strategic options to recommend. This was clearly evidenced in the answer.
	0	0.5	1	2

81   MIDSHIRE HEALTH

Key answer tips

There is plenty of scope to score marks as long as candidates focus on the actual problems in the scenario and don't make their answers overly theoretical. In **part (b)** the answer uses some structural terminology developed by Henry Mintzberg, but other brought forward knowledge from earlier papers would have been just as appropriate.

(a)   Project initiation

It is good practice to establish a Project Initiation Document (PID) or Terms of Reference (ToR) at the start of the project defining the objectives, scope, constraints, authority (owner, sponsor) and resources of the project. In the context of the case study scenario, there appears to be confusion around the objectives, scope and ownership of the project.

Project objectives and project scope: what is the project?

The objectives and scope of the project appear to be at different levels. The project might be 'to establish a formal strategic planning system at MidShire Health', or, it might be more restricted to the development of a 'comprehensive computer-based information system recording the outcomes and activities of the organisation'. Certainly the implementation team set up to undertake the detailed work appears to be primarily concerned with the functionality of the software package and the presence of Eurotek support consultants would tend to support this focus. The assertion from the CEO that the objective of the steering group is 'to deliver health to the Midshire community' adds further confusion. Although this objective is amended later in the project, restricting it to 'effectively and efficiently treating disease', both of these objectives really concern the organisation as a whole, not a specific project within that organisation. It is preferable that the project objectives should be more restricted.

The immediate employment of consultants with a potential software solution will inevitably skew the project towards a particular technical solution designed to support the planning system. There needs to be a distinction at the initiation of the project between the business objectives of the project and the technical objectives of the software system required to support those business objectives. The CEO confuses the two, a confusion accentuated by the early selection of a technical solution, before the business requirements have been defined (see later).

A failure to define a consistent achievable objective often results in projects lacking focus, leading to confusion amongst the project participants about what they are supposed to be doing. Terry Nagov really needed to establish a proper project objective within a formal Project Initiation Document.

The role of the steering group: who owns the project?

All projects should have a sponsor or authority that makes decisions about the project and supports it throughout its lifecycle. Ideally, this should be one person. It is possible for a group of people to play this role, but it is important that they promote a united front.

Even if the objectives and scope of the project can be defined (see previous paragraph), the steering group is disunited in the context of project sponsorship. There are clear conflicts within the group and some of these have been made public. Projects without a well-defined committed sponsor are likely to be unsuccessful as they lack clear leadership and support. Furthermore, if the sponsor is a group, then the focus of the project will veer to reflect changes in interest and power in the make-up of the group. The sponsor (owner) role should have been given more thought at the start of the project and responsibility should have been documented in the Project Initiation Document.

Conduct of the project

Two aspects in the conduct of the project deserve scrutiny. The first concerns the procurement process. The second is group and stakeholder management.

Procurement process

The Eurotek solution was selected before the requirements of the strategic planning process had been defined. Once these requirements had been developed, it became clear that the software package was a poor fit and that a considerable amount of bespoke work was needed to make it fit-for-purpose. The cost of these developments effectively led to the end of the project. This was a poor process. The information system requirements of the strategic planning process should have been developed before a potential software package solution was selected. The selection process should have involved more than one company and should have been transparent, so that the reasons for selecting a particular solution were documented and auditable. It is unclear from the scenario why the Eurotek solution was selected so early in the process, particularly as their expertise appeared to lie in the banking industry, rather than health care. Most public sector organisations have to follow strict procurement guidelines and it is surprising that these were not in place at MidShire Health.

Group and stakeholder management

Terry Nagov appears to believe that the three employee sets within the steering group (senior hospital doctors, hospital nursing managers and health service support staff) are equally powerful within the project context.

However, this is clearly not the case. The hospital doctors resent the inclusion of the health service support staff in the steering group. The hospital nursing managers side with the hospital doctors at key points. The objectives of the health service support staff appear to be aligned with those of Terry Nagov, but this support is not as effective as it may appear because it comes from the weakest set within the steering group. In Tuckman and Jenson's terms the group is fractional, stuck in a storming stage. Differences in power and culture will make it extremely difficult for the group to move beyond this stage. However, the person who could make it happen (Terry Nagov) undermines possible progress by choosing to openly question the ethics of one of the hospital doctors. This appears to destroy the possibility of group harmony and also brings into play a significant actor (Etopia's health minister) who, although very powerful, had hitherto had no obvious interest in the project.

Project cancellation procedures

The CEO did not explore opportunities for negotiating the $600,000 quoted development cost or look for alternatives. Eurotek might have been flexible on price, particularly if the developed software could have potentially been used in other health authorities.

In such circumstances, MidShire Health might have negotiated a royalty fee, to help them recoup their investment. Perhaps this was also the point when alternative suppliers could have been sought, providing solutions which were closer to the requirements of the organisation. This would have led to the investment in Eurotek being written off, but this was also a consequence of project cancellation. No post-project review was conducted, and lessons learned were not fed back into the project management process. In fact, the email sent to the steering group members specifically stated that there would be no further meetings. As someone once wrote, the 'only unforgiveable failure was the failure to learn from failure'.

(b)   Organisational culture

Johnson, Scholes and Whittington suggest that the culture of an organisation consists of four layers. Firstly, *values* which are often written down as statements of the organisation's mission. The visionary objective of the CEO might be an example of a value. The 'mission is to deliver health to the people of Midshire and, by that, I don't just mean hospital services for the sick, but a wider vision, where health is a state of complete physical, mental and social well-being and not merely the absence of disease or infirmity'. *Beliefs* are more specific and concern issues which people in the organisation can talk about. The hospital doctors appear to firmly believe that the visionary objective of the CEO is unobtainable. 'You have to realise that poor health is often caused by poverty, poor housing and social dislocation. You cannot expect MidShire Health to solve these problems. We can advise and also treat the symptoms, but prevention and cure for these wider problems are well beyond us.' *Behaviours* are the day-to-day way in which the organisation operates. Certain aspects of these become clear in the scenario describing the strategic planning project. Finally there are the *taken-for-granted assumptions* that are at the core of an organisation's culture. In the scenario there is a contrast between the CEO's vision of delivering health and the perception of hospital doctors and nursing staff that the real work is really about treating the ill.

The *behaviours* of the organisation can be explored further through selected facets of the cultural web.

The *stories* told by the hospital doctors are primarily concerned with belittling the role of the professional administrator.

'As we know', stated one of the doctors, 'we all agree that efficiency can only be achieved through giving control and budget to the doctors, not to the administrators *who are an unwanted overhead.* This is the first step we should take.' We can assume that the chief administrator (the CEO) present at the meeting could not have missed this slight. Secondly, the planning process does not appear to be perceived as real work. During one of the meetings the hospital doctors stated that they had to leave to get back to their *real job of treating patients.* It almost appears that the hospital doctors have agreed to participate in the planning process as a damage limitation exercise, trying to protect their power and status, rather than because they have any real interest or belief in the planning process and its goals.

A definite hierarchy in the *power structures* appears to exist during meetings. When the senior hospital doctors are present, the nursing representatives side with them and provide a powerful block to any of the initiatives proposed by the CEO. When the hospital doctors are not present, the nursing representatives appear to be more conciliatory, agreeing to actions and objectives that they renege on in subsequent meetings. The opinions of the support staff are clearly not valued by the hospital doctors. The hospital doctors showed their disdain by leaving one of the meetings when the objectives and role of the support staff were discussed.

Their ideas, for example for preventative care, are quickly dismissed by the powerful coalition of the hospital doctors and the nursing managers.

The activities of MidShire Health are affected by the hospital doctors who, through their powerful professional organisation, have negotiated very favourable terms of employment. Not only do they enjoy high salaries for full-time positions, but they also have the right to undertake private practice where they deliver services for private hospitals to fee-paying patients. This almost unprecedented degree of freedom is tolerated by the government and is a parameter that the CEO has to work within.

As Mintzberg observed, such organisations are 'the one place in the world where you can act as if you were self-employed yet regularly receive a pay check (cheque)'. Such flexibility does not seem to stretch to the nursing staff, but long-term loyalties seem to bond them to the hospital doctors. In contrast, the support workers appear to work under difficult circumstances, expected to serve the whims of professionals, but with little recognition of their contribution and little autonomy in undertaking their work. Probably as a result of this, they appear to be the most receptive group to the changes proposed by the CEO.

The lack of *control* the organisation has over the powerful hospital doctors is shown by the fact that one of the doctors perceives that it is perfectly acceptable to criticise his employer in public, disclosing private information from meetings to the press. This behaviour is excused as being in the 'public interest' and the doctor receives support from his colleagues. The CEO, although appalled by the behaviour, cannot pursue any disciplinary action because of threats from nurses and doctors.

Organisational configuration

Organisations tend to configure in a number of ways. The attributes or building blocks of the organisation relate to each other in different ways.

Terry Nagov was formerly the CEO of a company making mobility appliances. As well as having a profit motive (unlike MidShire Health), the company developed its business strategy through a centralised management structure, with line managers given the power and responsibility to achieve defined objectives and targets.

Production itself was heavily automated, administered and controlled through semiskilled employees who followed standards and procedures defined by senior managers. In terms of Mintzberg's configurations, the company appears to exhibit many aspects of a *machine bureaucracy.* The work it undertook appears to be routine, with much of it being simple and repetitive, allowing the company to establish efficient highly standardised processes. Within machine bureaucracies much of the power resides with the managers at the top of the organisation.

To outsiders such organisations can often appear to be an example of a focused, structured organisation which, as Mintzberg himself concedes, 'can be enormously efficient and provide an unmatchable reliability of service'. To a government struggling with rising costs in an economic recession, such organisations contrast starkly with, as the government minister put it, 'the anarchy of the health service'. To an outside agency, such as the government, appointing a CEO such as Terry Nagov to bring order and control must have seemed an attractive step. Nagov had an excellent record in the private sector and bringing such skills to the public sector would seem to have self-evident benefits.

In Mintzberg's terms, MidShire Health is probably *a professional bureaucracy.* Although the work is still relatively standardised, its complexity means that judgements are usually required. The type of work undertaken in the professional bureaucracy is quite different to that of the machine bureaucracy.

Considerable discretion is required in the application of skills that have been gained over years of training. MidShire Health depends on its professional staff and, consequently, like all professional bureaucracies, gives them considerable control over their own work. A machine bureaucracy generates its own standards internally and enforces them through its line managers. This is the approach that the CEO is familiar with. However, in contrast, the standards for a professional bureaucracy originate from self-governing associations that the professionals belong to.

Hence the intervention of the Institute of Hospital Doctors (IOHD) would be viewed legitimately by the hospital doctors, who believe that authority comes through expertise, not through a management hierarchy. In questioning the legitimacy of such advice, the CEO failed to recognise the central role that professional associations play in such bureaucracies. It was bound to cause offence to the professional staff on the working party.

A recognition of MidShire Health as a professional bureaucracy should also have helped the CEO predict the hospital doctors questioning the value of having support staff on the working party. In such organisational configurations, such employees are seen as largely subservient to the professionals delivering the fundamental activities of the organisation. In fact, many support staff are managed in a machine, top-down way, and so their enthusiasm for the formal planning initiative might be expected. It closely matches their experience, as well as providing an opportunity to potentially undermine what they consider to be the comfortable, capricious existence of the powerful professionals.

Similarly, the request of the CEO for the doctors to consider the 'good of MidShire Health and its image within the community' is likely to fall on 'deaf ears'. As Mintzberg comments, 'most professional focus their loyalty on their profession, not on the place where they happen to practice it.'

The problem of introducing change in professional bureaucracies is explicitly considered by Mintzberg.

He states that 'change in the professional organisation does not sweep in from new administrators taking office to announce wide reforms or from government officials intent on bringing the professional under technocratic control'. This, of course, exactly describes the situation at MidShire Health. Rather, he sees change as seeping in through a slow process of changing the professionals themselves, through altering recruitment policies and training. In the short term, he would probably suggest that the government would be better off placing pressure on the professional associations that influence their member (such as the IOHD), rather than tamper with the professional bureaucracies directly.

Finally, it has to be recognised that MidShire Health is a public sector organisation funded by general taxation, rather than by its specific users or customers. In principle the provider of the funds (government) provides resource inputs into a service that is competing with other services funded by general taxation – such as national security. Thus health services, in principle, need to show that they are providing value for money so that politicians support further funding. Such an approach appears to give the government a lot of power. However, the existence of powerful professions and the willingness of press and public to defend health service principles dilute this power, leading to the kind of frustration explicitly articulated in the case study scenario.

Marking scheme		Marks
(a)	1 mark for each relevant point up to a maximum of	18
(b)	1 mark for each relevant point up to a maximum of.	18
Total		**36**

82   LEARN TO PASS (L2P)

Key answer tips

Whenever asked to evaluate a strategic option, it is always considering whether to use the 'suitability, feasibility, acceptability' framework as it is helps generate a breadth of factors to include and gives a clear answer structure

This opportunity represents a potential strategic diversification for L2P. L2P has never offered accountancy services to franchisees and this new product development needs to be considered carefully. The strategy can be assessed across three criteria:

Acceptability

From a financial perspective there would appear to be an opportunity here for L2P to make a high financial return from the software. If, say, L2P were to charge franchisees $250 for the service (representing a 50% reduction on franchisee's existing accountancy fees) L2P would make a profit of $150 per franchisee. This represents an annual profit of around $1.2m (based on 8,000 franchisees). If, alternatively, the second option of paying a one-off fee of $5m were taken then the payback period would be less than three years.

L2P should, however, consider whether this is a product that it wants to get involved with. It is outside L2P's core competencies and new technology typically has a high degree of risk (from replication, failures and obsolescence etc.). But the potential financial returns may outweigh these risks.

The acceptability to franchisees will also be a key determining factor in the decision on whether to pursue the strategy. The new software would appear to provide an opportunity for franchisees to make a significant saving per annum. But the software won't, for example, be able to pick up on bookings that franchisees receive from outside the L2P systems (such as from word-of-mouth). Franchisees may also be resistant to in-car monitoring systems on their driving. It therefore should not be assumed that all franchisees will use the software – thus reducing the potential financial returns to L2P.

Feasibility

A key concern for this strategy will be the feasibility of making the software work for L2P. Scaling up from a demonstration on 4 franchisees to over 8,000 franchisees will present a significant challenge.

Eccounts is a new start-up which implies that it has not successfully managed this scale of project before. L2P needs to carefully consider areas such as Eccounts' staffing plans, access to finance to fund expansion, guarantees, ongoing maintenance plans etc.

The problems will be greater if L2P take up the option to take exclusive rights to the software. L2P will need to recruit the staff and obtain the necessary expertise to operate and manage the system. It may be possible to retain some of Eccounts staff to do this.

If L2P decide to take up the opportunity, it may be best for L2P to gradually roll out and scale up the software. It could be tested on a sample of franchisees (such as new joiners) before being rolled out nationally. L2P could attempt to have an option to make a full acquisition of the software in one year's time when there should be much less uncertainty over the feasibility of the software.

Suitability

This software has the potential to significantly disrupt the small accountancy business sector. This is a large market with high potential financial returns. L2P will have a significant competitive advantage in terms of access to the software, a closed client base and state-of-the-art technology. Small accountancy businesses will not be able to launch and offer similar technology as they will not have access to L2P's booking systems to obtain revenue.

L2P may find that franchisees from rival companies want access to the software (which may in turn drive more business to L2P). The potential financial returns will not therefore be limited simply to L2P's existing franchisee base.

On top of this, if the software scales well to L2P's business then there would appear to be significant opportunities to disrupt other industries such as accountancy services for logistics and distribution companies. These industries are likely to be very large and there may even be opportunities to exploit the technology internationally. L2P would only benefit from these opportunities if it was to pay the $5m for exclusivity on the software.

Conclusions

This disruptive technology represents a massive opportunity to L2P. It would appear to be very suitable and acceptable. The key test is in feasibility. L2P should ultimately aim to gain exclusivity to the software but it needs to firstly confirm that the software works and be scaled up. An initial trial period should be sought with Eccounts before a final decision is made.

Marking scheme – technical marks	
	Marks
2 mark for each relevant point up to a maximum of 16 marks.	**16**

How well has the candidate demonstrated Professional Skills as follows:	Not at all	Not well	Quite well	Very well
Demonstrating evaluation skills in appraising the opportunity	The candidate has failed to consider both risks and benefits in the strategy and to reach a supported conclusion	The candidate has considered some risks and benefits but the recommended action is unsupported or justified.	The candidate has considered both risks and benefits of the project but these are not always weighed against each other so that the conclusion has overly focused on only one side of the argument.	The candidate has objectively weighed up the risks and benefits of the strategy and reached a justified and reasoned conclusion.
	0	**1**	**2**	**3**

83   PIONEER VEHICLES

Key answer tips

There are a number of ways this question could have been asked such as to evaluate the proposal or to discuss advantages and disadvantages. Instead the requirement asked for an evaluation of key **risks**, so make sure your answer is worded and framed appropriately.

BRIEFING NOTES

Whether Pioneer should embrace new disruptive technologies

Key risks are as follows

1   The risk of doing nothing and getting left behind

Given that Pioneer has built its reputation on engineering and design expertise, it could be argued that there is no need to incorporate new technologies such as AI.

However, the key issue is whether Pioneer's customers value and want the new technology. In this respect the risk of getting left behind may vary from one segment to another:

Consumers

Consumers who use the vehicles just like any other car – say, for shopping and commuting – are unlikely to value the enhanced off-road capability that the new AI would give but might value personalisation aspects.

However, such customers will be making comparisons with rival luxury 4WD offerings from Porsche, Range Rover, BMW, etc. – all of whom will be increasing the connectedness, intelligence and semi-autonomous capabilities of their cars. Given this, a certain level of new technology such as self-parking, accident avoidance and so on, may be considered essential by customers. Failure to incorporate such factors could result in Pioneer being viewed as old fashioned and left behind in this market segment.

Note: Acquiring such attributes would not necessitate developing a working relationship with Professor Hughes but could be purchased from other vendors in the market. Furthermore, such technologies have already been extensively tested, so would involve less risk.

Specialist users

Other customers such as the military, farmers or scientific expeditions will be more interested in enhanced off-road capability as it would improve their operational efficiency and effectiveness.

However, such users may be more interested in reliability and would be wary of new technology compromising this.

In summary, further research is thus needed to prioritise the needs of customers.

2   Risks associated with the new technology

There are a number of significant risks associated with the new technology and AI systems:

Does it work as well as claimed?

Firstly there is the risk that the systems do not work to the standard expected. While this is less of a concern if the AI dos not make the car as fast as it could be, say, but could have a devastating impact on Pioneer's reputation if the AI actually resulted in more accidents.

We do not know the extent to which Professor Hughes' systems have been tested and whether they are still ironing out any problems. Either because he wants to generate income, or simply due to academic enthusiasm, the Professor may have downplayed such snags when discussing his ideas. While his theoretical expertise is undoubtable very high, being a professor at a prestigious university, he may underestimate the practical difficulties involved in developing additional claimed features in the future.

How much will it cost?

At this stage it will be very difficult to estimate the final cost per car of implementing the new technologies. Firstly there are still major development costs to incur. Next there will be the costs of hardware, such as servos to operate the steering, IT computer processors new tyres with built in sensors and so on. There may also be hidden costs such as any payments that might be due to radio stations for scanning their broadcasts and using their information.

A strategy of waiting to see which technologies become market leaders and then approaching those companies might be more expensive overall but would certainly be less risky.

3   Risks associated with the relationship established with Professor Hughes

At this stage it is unclear who Pioneer would be developing a relationship with – would it be Professor Hughes as an individual or the Department of Artificial Intelligence and Cybernetics or with the university or would the plan be to set up a new company to develop the technology and run it as a joint venture? It is vital that this is clarified as each of these options will have its own problems to resolve.

The key issue here is who owns the intellectual property (IP) and ideas relating to the new systems – clearly Pioneer would not wish to invest heavily in the ideas only to find that it has no way of preventing rivals using the same AI. It appears that the professor feels that the work is 'his' but that may not be the case – for example, his contract with the university may mean that the IP associated with work carried out within the department belongs to the department. Furthermore, key elements may already have been published in scientific journals making it very difficult to establish patent or other protection.

There would also be a concern over how crucial Professor Hughes' involvement would be to the ongoing development of the systems – as stated above, it is unclear the extent to which the AI can currently be consider to be a finished product. Professor Hughes is currently very keen to develop the current research but how would Pioneer ensure that he stays committed to the project rather than being distracted by other new and exciting research ideas? Similarly, are there key personnel – research students, say – who would be vital to the venture but who might leave for a different university once their current tenures are finished – say when a doctorate is completed?

Marking scheme – technical marks	
	Marks
Up to 2 marks for each relevant point subject to the following maxima:	
– 'Wait and see' v 'getting left behind'	5
– Risks associated with the capabilities of the technology	5
– Risks associated with the business vehicle to be used	5
	___
Total	**15**

Professional skills may be additionally rewarded as in the following rubric:

How well has the candidate demonstrated Profession Skill as follows:	Not at all	Not well	Quite well	Very well
Professional scepticism skills relating to the professor's proposal.	The candidate has not considered the validity of the claims put forward by the professor and has instead taken the claims as fact.	The candidate has questioned the validity of the professor's claims but no justification has been provided as to why.	The candidate has questioned the objectivity of the professor but has not probed deeper into his expertise, IP and other issues	The candidate has questioned the validity of the professor's claims and probed (with justification) the wider implications of the claims made.
	0	0.5	1	2

84 ABC TEXTILES

The new strategy consists of two key changes, firstly abandoning the current model of low cost production and its associated markets; secondly entering a new position in a related market with revised production techniques, improved procurement quality.

The key risk here for ABC is the lack of experience in a differentiated market place

Advantages

The current market is one of cost leadership according to Porter's generic strategies. It appears to be an unsustainable strategy due to low margins and increasing costs. The new strategy offers higher prices with the potential for increased margins.

The new strategy would be a move to be a differentiator in Porter's generic strategies by creating tangible and intangible product features that consumers are willing to pay for and therefore to create margin.

The new strategy is to launch a new product in the existing market (Ansoff's product development), so there is likely to be some overlap of market knowledge and networking contacts. However, it could be argued that the new strategy is in a different sector of the same market.

The ABC brand name for soft furnishings is still relevant to the industry under the new business model. If competition in the new sector of the market is more about quality, design and service, and less about cost and price, then there is an opportunity to compete on more favourable terms with imported goods by taking advantage of proximity to customers.

Whilst rival companies in developing nations may benefit from lower wage costs and lower production costs compared with ABC they may suffer from the fall in the value of the £. Rivals' products will have become more expensive in £ terms and the revenue generated for these rival in £s is less attractive when converted back into their own currencies.

Whilst the new natural products are largely a departure from existing production and markets, the continued use of polyester (albeit of better quality) may give ABC a continued foothold in existing markets and production techniques as a transition to the new business model.

The new strategy requires the purchase of advanced robotic machinery which is to be operated through the use of an intelligent control system. As highlighted by the ABC board, the introduction of the new machinery should enable ABC to achieve significant efficiencies in the manufacturing process. This is a considerable benefit as its existing manufacturing machinery is nearing the end of its useful life, and has resulted in an increasing number of defects in batches of production. As such the introduction of the new machinery and intelligent control system should help support ABC as it transitions from its current business model to its new strategy.

Disadvantages

- The new strategy, despite some overlap may involve new skills (e.g. in processing natural fabrics) which may not be primarily within the existing core competences of ABC.

- The move upmarket may mean that new relationships need to be established with an entire range of new customers. The existing customer relationships may be largely lost as the new quality products may be outside the price range for their customers' range of products

- Whilst the ABC brand name may continue to have some relevance, it may send the wrong signal in suggesting a low-cost product when the firm is trying to promote the opposite, upmarket image.

- One of the reasons that a low-cost operation has been sustainable is that the factory and machinery were acquired at low cost from the liquidator. Now that this initial machinery is failing, the proposed purchase costs of the new automated robotic machinery and intelligent control system will need to be considered.

- The advanced nature of the new machinery proposed for use in manufacturing is likely to require significant capital expenditure. This has a number of risks: – The increased costs of the new machinery and intelligent control system will increase overall costs and this may mean that the new business model may not be competitive even at higher prices. – The increase in machinery costs are fixed costs which raise operating gearing further and increases operating risk. – Any new investment would be a sunk cost and may not be recoverable if ABC's new strategy becomes unviable. – The associated costs of maintaining the intelligent control system infrastructure also need to be factored into the proposed new strategy. Again, due to the technologically advanced nature of this type of system these costs will most likely be significant.

Conclusion/recommendation:

The new strategy is extremely risky and a better response to the demise of existing markets may be to exit the industry. Much will depend on market research and the ability to establish a new range of customers in sufficient quantity to make the new business model viable.

Marking scheme	
	Marks
1 mark for each relevant point up to a maximum of	**14**

Professional skills may be additionally rewarded as in the following rubric:

How well has the candidate demonstrated Professional Skills as follows:	Not at all	Not well	Quite well	Very well
Demonstrating evaluation skills in appraising the strategic change	The candidate has failed to consider both risks and benefits in the strategy and to reach a supported conclusion	The candidate has considered some risks and benefits but the recommended action is unsupported or justified.	The candidate has considered both risks and benefits of the strategy but these are not always weighed against each other so that the conclusion has overly focused on only one side of the argument.	The candidate has objectively weighed up the risks and benefits of the strategy and reached a justified and reasoned conclusion.
	0	1	2	3

85 TECHWARE

(a) The advantages and disadvantages of Techware entering the corporate market Corporate market are shown below

Advantages:

- Offers a potentially lucrative market – research suggests that by 20X2 more than 2 million employees in the UK will be required to wear a fitness tracker.

- There may be economies of scale in high volume contracts

- Since the corporate market is growing it may be less competitive so easier for Techware to operate in

- It will take less time to grow the business as Techware only have to persuade one significant company to buy, compared to lots of individual buyers

- It will enhances Techware's reputation if is seen to be supplying well-known blue-chip companies

- There may be less user drop-out in the corporate market

Disadvantages:

- Techware has no experience of this market and no expertise in it so this increases risk

- Techware is likely to be smaller in relation to some large corporates so customers may have greater bargaining power and the ability to dictate terms, prices, quality standards etc

- Corporate clients are likely to want to pay lower prices or receive volume discounts

- Techware will need to implement high quality customer relationship management systems

- Corporate customers may be looking for a greater analytical service in which Techware has no expertise

- Techware would need to consider timing and capacity to ensure it has the ability to produce for the corporate market without affecting existing sales

- There may be barriers to entry due to existing contracts held by competitors

On the face of it the corporate market, which is growing, appears to merit further consideration and may make up for the decline in sales of fitness trackers to individuals

Marking scheme	
	Marks
1 mark for each relevant point up to a maximum of	**12**

(b) The following issues are relevant:

Data ownership

This is likely to present a challenge. If C provides Techware's device to an employee, it may not always be clear who owns the data held – Techware, C or the employee.

Also data ownership affects whether C has the right to share the customer data with third parties e.g., for analytical purposes.

Data security

Data security is a key concern. Techware's devices capture, store and transmit sensitive personal data about users, which is confidential. Users need to be sure that their data can only be accessed by an authorised user with the appropriate password etc. and Techware must take steps to manage cyber security risks and provide effective data security to prevent information being obtained by hackers.

Reliability/accuracy

Another concern is the reliability/accuracy of the data that is captured by the wearables if they are to be used to monitor and assess employees.

The General Data Protection Regulation (GDPR) strictly regulates the confidentiality, storage and use of personal information. C employees should be informed about the purposes for which their data is going to be used and the processing of data must have employee consent.

As well as data protection issues, there are rules about monitoring and surveillance in the workplace. Employees should be informed about the extent of monitoring and how it might be carried out and what the information will be used for.

The Data Protection Act (DPA) means it is illegal for companies to sell on people's details without their consent or for uses other than those they were originally told about. It is clearly not in C's interests to breach the DPA as it will face consequences in terms of damaged reputation and lost customers.

As a minimum therefore C needs to ensure that it is compliant with data protection legislation.

Ethical considerations

Concerns have been raised about the ethical issues associated with C's use of the fitness trackers for employee monitoring. There is concern that any data captured may be misused or that employees' privacy will suffer.

Key questions are:

- how much data is it reasonable to collect

- and what is acceptable use

One ethical argument is that collection of the data is an invasion of privacy and that it could be abused if it falls into the wrong hands - the scenario refers to C using data from outside of work hours which some might think is spying on their employees. However employees are being given the option to take a device.

Effectively, an employee who accepts device one does so on the basis that their data will be collected. It would be hard to argue that this is an invasion of their privacy if they have a free choice over the matter, although this may not be a very real choice – employees could be subject to an intimidation threat/ penalised if they do not agree.

Key issues will be whether C is behaving in a fair and transparent manner and the likely effect on its employees.

Some employees may not be aware of the data and security issues, and may take advantage of free devices without realising what personal information they are giving away or how it might be used against them.

C should have a stated policy explaining what data is collected and how it is used/shared (transparency) plus an option for employees to tick a box to say they are happy for their data to be used/shared in this way.

Critics might argue that employees are aware generally that their personal data is being captured but lack awareness of how much other data is subsequently captured and how it is used/combined with other information.

The key ethical issue here is therefore transparency and whether informed and willing consent has been given by C's employees.

It could be argued that employees will benefit as a result of the strategy as the motives for introducing the devices to the workplace appear to be positive: "to improve HR policies and procedures, create a safer, healthier working environment and tailor healthcare and flexible working packages".

Marking scheme	
	Marks
1 mark for each relevant point up to a maximum of	**14**

Professional skills may be additionally rewarded as in the following rubric:

How well has the candidate demonstrated Profession Skill as follows:	Not at all	Not well	Quite well	Very well
Professional scepticism skills relating to the proposal.	The candidate has not considered the validity of the claims put forward by C's employees and has instead taken the claims as fact.	The candidate has questioned the validity of C's employee's claims but no justification has been provided as to why.	The candidate has questioned the objectivity of C's employee's claims but has not probed deeper into the wider ethical and other issues	The candidate has questioned the validity of C's employee's claims and probed (with justification) the wider implications of the claims made.
	0	0.5	1	2

Section 4

ANSWERS TO CASE STUDY QUESTIONS

1   DIXON SMITH BURRELL

TASK 1

(a)   Macro environment

The macro environment for pharmaceutical companies in operating in Nearland is explored using PESTEL analysis. The key issues follow.

Political Factors

The government in Nearland appear to have a keen interest in the industry, not only because of their concern for the welfare of their citizens, but also because of the fact that the government must pay for the medical treatments that many public sector workers might need. This has put pharmaceutical companies under greater scrutiny which could lead to even greater levels of regulation which may reduce the chances of gaining approval for new drug developments. This would ultimately make it harder for pharmaceutical companies to grow within Nearland if they cannot get access to patents for new drugs.

On top of this, with the recent economic downturn, the government will be seeking even greater value for money from drug treatments. There have already been cuts to pensions and other public spending cuts may see policies shifting towards reductions in medical treatments and prescriptions and there may even be price limits set on the amounts that drugs companies can charge for their drugs. These measures would further harm future growth prospects for pharmaceutical companies in Nearland.

Economic Factors

The economic downturn may also reduce consumer spending on health insurance and make citizens in Nearland reluctant to seek out medical treatment that they must pay for themselves. This would further harm growth in the sector.

Social Factors

Medical treatment and medical insurance are likely to be seen as a necessity for most citizens of Nearland. For that reason there should always be a strong core demand within the sector which will help protect pharmaceutical companies against short-term economic downturns.

There is also evidence of an ageing population. Older people are more likely to need more medical treatments and this is likely to create growing demand for drugs in the future.

Technological Factors

The key technological factors are likely to come from the development of new drugs. Pharmaceutical companies are likely to invest very heavily in R&D and if a patent is granted then this is likely to create strong growth for successful companies in the future.

There is evidence in the case of a new distribution channel from e-business. Pharmaceutical companies may be able to sell directly to consumers rather than via doctors and clinicians, but there may be large political and legal obstacles to this new growth area.

Environmental Factors

There is a growing demand for environmental and social responsibility from pharmaceutical companies. Strong corporate social responsibility (possibly extending to strong corporate governance) could be key to the success of individual organisations. This may cause particular problems for DSB. Buyers in Nearland may become aware of DSB's bribery allegations in Farland and this could adversely impact on DSB's reputation in Nearland.

Legal Factors

The sector is highly regulated. The key threat from growth will come from DARA failing to approve new drugs. It will be vital that pharmaceutical companies have extensive testing and assurance procedures in order to meet the requirements for obtaining a patent. Once a patent has been achieved then this should provide a high element of economic security to the organisation.

There is also a growing level of litigation in many countries around the world and pharmaceutical companies in particular are likely to face a high level of claims with respect to the side effects and efficacy of their drugs. It will be important that these are managed well in terms of providing clear guidance on drugs use and side effects, not overstating the efficacy of the drugs and having clear terms and conditions on all packaging. Failure to do so may lead to very public high value claims that may have a major detrimental impact on a firm's reputation.

Overall

The government spending cuts and economic downturn experienced in Nearland are likely to create short term issues for the growth of pharmaceutical companies in Nearland. But there is likely to be a strong core demand for drugs and, as long as organisations are successful in gaining new patents, there should continue to be strong long term demand in the sector.

(b) **Analysis of performance and position**

Much of the drop in sales could be attributed to the short term macro environment issues discussed in the first part of this report. However, this does not fully reflect the poor performance that the Nearland division has experienced in the year.

The chart of industry sales show that there has been an industry slowdown in Nearland in 20X2 but that there was still some marginal growth. DSB's sales on the other hand fell by 14.7%. This is at odds with the industry trend and will mean that DSB are losing market share in Nearland. With industry sales of around $35bn DSB would appear to have seen a fall in market share of around 3% to 17.5%. This suggests that DSB's performance is not solely caused by the macro environmental factors and must instead be down to a poor business performance in the market.

Some of the downturn could be attributed to the reduction in the number of patents held by DSB in Nearland. It could be that the downturn in sales was caused by the coming to the end for a patent that was generating a high amount of sales. But it is unlikely that a patent near the end of its life would be generating a higher than average sales per patent. The total drop in sales was $1.06bn whilst sales per patent held has fallen from $424m to $384.

This might reflect that more recent patents are less valuable than older ones or that not enough investment is being made in developing new patents. Although the number of patents held has only fallen by 1, in an industry where innovation and new patent creation are likely to be critical success factors this should be a worry for the main board of DSB.

There appears to have been a reduction in the number of people employed in research and development where staff numbers have fallen by 22%. This may be a short-term policy aimed at maintain bottom line profit performance (R&D costs are down by 25%) but it is likely to have serious detrimental effects on the business in the longer term. The value of intangibles has declined illustrating further that there has been no new investment in drugs patents.

Conversely, there has been an increase in the number of sales staff (up 7.6%) which does not appear to have borne fruit given the decline in sales. Sales per sales employee has fallen by 21% to $4.7m. Such a fall is likely to affect sales team bonuses and may lead to the kind of unscrupulous practices being experienced in Farland.

There has been a fall in the gross profit percentage of from 70% to 68.25%. It may be that some of these costs are fixed in nature (such as depreciation on production property, plant and equipment) but some cost reductions should have been gained in wages and salaries given the increasing unemployment being experienced in Nearland.

Despite reductions in R&D and other staff members the net profit is now not sufficient to cover the normal level of dividend. This can be accepted in the short term where there are enough retained reserves and cash to cover the downfall, but in the longer term DSB will either have to either accept a lower level of dividend from Nearland or invest funds in order to help it solve some of the poor performance issues in order to return to higher levels of dividends. DSB may decide to forgo dividends in the short-term in order to free up finance for the division to solve its problems.

The Nearland division appears to have lots of assets and a reasonable amount of cash that can be used for investment. However, $480m in cash and cash equivalents may not be sufficient to develop a new drug (the new opportunity in Leeland is expected to cost over $1,000m, for example).

It is therefore likely that any new finance will come in either the form of new debt or from a capital injection from the main board. The gearing ratio stands at 85% (down slightly from 86%) in the previous year. High gearing in this type of industry is not unusual as pharmaceutical companies are likely to have high levels of assets to offer as security.

If, however, intangible assets are ignored in the gearing ratio as they may be less valuable as security for providers of debt finance the gearing ratio rockets to 203%. There is also a very low level of interest cover and therefore new debt providers may be unwilling to provide more debt finance.

The Nearland division has performed poorly in the year and appears to have gone backwards. There is evidence of underinvestment in R&D and in order to turn the business around significant new investment may be needed in the future. Long term industry prospects are good, but it may take a large equity investment from the main board in order for the division to exploit this.

TASK 2

(a)   Bribery allegations

Before reacting to the allegations of bribery DSB should consider the validity of the press article presented by the Farland National Daily. The newspaper has not provided any real evidence and much of the article could be judged to be supposition and exaggeration.

For example, the allegations against Dr Ali suggest that he has paid for extravagant trips. But these may not necessarily have been funded by bribes – it is just as likely that his wife or other relatives have funded the trips.

The amounts involved do appear to be high and at least one member of staff is under the impression that conferences are not always genuine. But DSB should not use this article as the sole piece of evidence that bribery is widespread in the Farland division.

Related and correlated risks

Related risks are risks that vary because of the presence of another risk or where two risks have a common cause. This means when one risk increases, it has an effect on another risk and it is said that the two are related. Risk correlation is a particular example of related risk. Risks are positively correlated if the two risks are positively related in that one will fall with the reduction of the other, and increase with the rise of the other. They would be negatively correlated if one rose as the other fell.

Legal risk and reputation risk

At DSB, legal risk and reputation risk are likely to be positively correlated because it is likely that as legal risk rises, then, for the reasons explored below, so will reputation risk. Were the legal risk to recede, then risk of reputational damage would also recede. In the case of legal and reputation risks at DSB, legal risk is the independent variable and reputation risk is the dependent variable. This is because the reputation risk incurred will largely depend on the legal risk.

The legal risk in this case is the possibility that, if the bribery allegations in Farland are proved, DSB will be fined heavily for breaking local laws. According to Burak Rom there would also be a risk that authorities in other countries where DSB operates would investigate whether they needed to bring legal action against the company for similar offences. The probability of this occurring is however not known.

The reputation risk is the loss to DSB if issues were to be raised in the public consciousness that might cast the company in a negative light. It is hard to know in advance how a legal challenge would be reported but DSB could be accused, justly or unjustly, of several things. Legal cases sometimes raise issues in the public consciousness that the company would have otherwise not had exposed. Some of these may be perfectly legitimate in business terms (for example the payments to doctors for conference appearances) but may offend one or more stakeholders.

In the case of DSB, they may be accused of incompetence in controlling the activities of sales staff.

The fact that fraudulent behaviour has been found by DSB's own investigations suggests incompetence and this may erode DSB's reputation as a well governed company. Stakeholders may assume that the same business practices are occurring within all of DSB's sales teams (since this is the latest in a series of bribery scandals) suggesting a total lack of integrity and leadership from the board.

The effect of any loss of reputation for DSB could be serious. DSB could be portrayed as an unethical business partner and this may affect relationships such as that the company has with Leeland. Reputation is important for DSB since it has long prided itself on its ethical stance. With relationships like that with Leeland, a loss of reputation may affect product sales and also recruitment.

(b)   General purposes of an internal control system

Internal control systems should cover all the activities of the company to include, operations, marketing, sales, compliance etc. This will ensure that the directors have met their obligations under corporate governance and that the internal control system will support the maintenance of a robust risk management process, facilitating investor confidence.

This obligation will be assisted by the application of a sound system of internal control which should safeguard the assets of the business, prevent and detect fraud and error, provide accurate and complete accounting records and the timely preparation of financial information.

The maintenance of such a sound system is important to DSB given its stated commitment to maintain the highest standards of ethical performance by putting patient interests and its responsibility to society as strategic and operational priorities. DSB prides itself on its reputation in this context and aspires to be a well governed company in all the countries in which it operates.

A sound system of internal control will be essential for DSB given these commitments and its status as a highly visible company. The internal control system will enable DSB to enhance its prestigious brand name and maintain investor confidence in Geeland where it is responsible for some 12% of total stock market value.

Internal control failings in DSB which have led to accusations of bribery

It would seem that despite DSB having an internal audit function, controls over sales staff in Farland were weak.

Farland sales representatives were able to make up fictitious conferences without senior staff checking that the events actually took place. A lack of checking led to gifts and excessive cash payments not being picked up which meant sales staff could easily bribe medical staff to boost their own sales targets without being found out.

The amount considered as an excessive payment was set very high in Farland so that the exception report of payments considered too great was always without content. Management may have assumed that the payments to doctors were within the usual parameters and not taken any action to check monetary sums paid further. The fact that the exception reports were empty would suggest no large sums were paid. This was in fact not the case.

The bribery payments to doctors were funnelled as fictional expenses through a travel agent and approved by sales managers locally in Farland. This collusion between staff and managers meant that although a control was present (the approval) in actual fact it was not working.

TASK 3

(a) **Public Statement by Nur Saah, CEO of DSB**

Action taken in respect of Bribery Allegations

DSB has recently found itself in the centre of bribery allegations relating to our sales teams in Farland. This has been widely reported in the media and as CEO I wish to take this opportunity to explain the allegations and also give our many stakeholders reassurance that DSB continues to pledge its commitment to the 'highest standards' of ethical performance as stated in our corporate code of ethics. In particular we are dedicated to ensuring full compliance with regulation in all jurisdictions, the safety and care of all those relying on DSB products, transparency and communication with stakeholders and environmental responsibility.

The allegations surround payments made to clinicians to persuade them to prescribe DSB products. In the pharmaceuticals industry it is common practice to compensate doctors for learning about our medications and speaking at conferences in order to educate their colleagues. By adopting this process, knowledge of new and innovative drugs can be quickly spread and many patients can benefit. It would seem that in Farland, this practice was perhaps taken too far by certain employees who are alleged to have made payments to doctors without conference speeches being planned.

At DSB, we do not tolerate corruption in any part of our business. Although the allegations have not yet been proved, we have taken the opportunity to tighten up controls so we can be sure all payments to clinicians are above board and in line with our policies. We have taken external audit and legal advice and undertaken thorough investigations. As a result there have been employee dismissals in Farland. In addition, all of our sales representatives are being asked to complete ethical training to ensure they fully understand what is acceptable in order to raise awareness of our products.

(b) **The roles of the CEO**

As chief executive, you will understand that it is my job to lead the company and to protect shareholder interests above all others. These are responsibilities I take very seriously.

In particular, and in explaining the issues surrounding the bribery allegations, I would like to briefly outline my roles. It is my role to develop and implement policies and strategies capable of delivering superior shareholder value and to assume full responsibility for all aspects of the company's operations. It was I who approved the expansion of DSB sales teams into Farland. The correctness of that decision is shown by the significant presence we have been able to develop there in a relatively short time.

I must also manage the financial and physical resources of the company, monitor results, and ensure that effective operational and risk controls are in place. DSB is a profitable company and I personally took an interest in ensuring sales representatives were rewarded for increasing sales in their area. This however, must be done in conjunction with the highest ethical standards and strict controls. It is up to me to ensure the company wide review of these controls is an ongoing process from now on.

My role also involves overseeing the management team, co-ordinating the interface between the board and the other employees in the company, and assisting in the appointment of senior management. I am pleased to have the expertise of DSB's internal audit team to call upon, in particular Sena Ali, The Head of Internal Audit, who has worked tirelessly to ensure DSB's sales controls are robust and sound.

Finally, it is my role to relate to a range of external parties including the company's shareholders, suppliers, customers and relevant authorities. I hope this statement has satisfied the information needs of DSB's stakeholders in respect of the recent issues in Farland.

TASK 4

(a)   Risks

SLIDE 1 – Strategic risks	
Risk	**Evaluation**
• Loss of focus on current strategies	• May mean that existing strategies are not achieved
• Unlikely growth opportunities	• There is only a small chance of any growth from this strategy
• Retaining the patent may upset government	• May not fit their goal of free care

Notes:

Strategic risks focus on the impact on areas such as growth, competitive position and the achievement of organisational goals.

DSB have a strong position in Leeland and this new strategy may mean that this is lost if resources are relocated to a strategy that Leeland clinicians do not value in the short term.

The chance of success is very small and therefore the likely impact on DSB's strategic position is also small.

The government may prefer to own the patent to ensure that the drug will be available without any premium price added by DSB.

SLIDE 2 – Financial risks	
Risk	**Evaluation**
• Unlikely to recover initial investment	• Shareholder wealth will suffer
• Future returns are unspecified	• Estimated returns are very uncertain
• Costs are upfront, returns are very late	• This may mean that other projects can't be funded
• May be difficult to raise finance	• Debt finance is unlikely to be available

Notes:

Strategic risks focus on the impact on areas such as growth, competitive position and the achievement of organisational goals.

DSB have a strong position in Leeland and this new strategy may mean that this is lost if resources are relocated to a strategy that Leeland clinicians do not value in the short term.

If developed, these drugs would not be immediately profitable since they would hopefully never be needed. The cost of developing the drugs would be high with no government subsidy.

The chance of success is very small and therefore the likely impact on DSB's strategic position is also small.

The government may prefer to own the patent to ensure that the drug will be available without any premium price added by DSB.

(b)   **Development of new antibiotics by DSB**

SLIDE 3 – Business benefits	
Benefit	**Rationale**
• Improved reputation	• May attract customers
• More attractive to clinicians/employees	• Will match their own ethical goals
• Have the expertise	• DSB may be only company who can do this

Notes:

DSB should go ahead and develop the drugs in order to enhance their reputation as an ethical organisation. An improved reputation may attract customers, the clinicians DSB market their products to would probably be impressed by the company's commitment to developing new antibiotics since they would be only too aware of the potential devastation an outbreak of a superbug would cause.

In addition, DSB may attract talented employees because of the project. These employees may welcome the chance to work on new antibiotic strains for the reasons outlined and their skills could be used by DSB on many other projects.

DSB has the capacity and expertise to develop new strains of antibiotics which could be used in the event of a superbug outbreak. DSB are one of the largest pharmaceutical companies in Leeland and have international support. They may be the only company with the capacity to create this defensive drug.

SLIDE 4 – Ethical arguments	
Issue	**Rationale**
• Matches DSB's code of ethics	• Puts patients before profits
• Ties in with other ethical activities	• Such as helping developing nations

Notes:

The company has a corporate code of ethics in which it pledges its commitment to the highest standards of ethical performance, putting patient interests first and prioritising its responsibility to society. It is clear that society is in need of new antibiotic strains, if only to be kept for emergencies. DSB has the knowledge and capability develop new drugs which may be called upon to save many lives in the event of a superbug outbreak. Not to use this knowledge would not only go against DSB's stated objectives but it would also potentially lead to devastating consequences.

DSB already sells drugs to developing countries at lower than usual prices and often donates vaccinations to vulnerable populations. Whereas the development of new antibiotics is clearly on a much larger scale than these projects, it is nonetheless in keeping with activities already undertaken.

SLIDE 5 – Conclusions

Benefits	**Risks**
• Better reputation	• Requires significant investment
• More sales = more profits	• High risk of failure
• Ethically the right thing to do	

Notes:

The business case for developing new antibiotics regardless of securing external funding revolves around enhancing the reputation of DSB leading to greater sales, more sophisticated products and ultimately more profits.

MARKING SCHEME

TASK 1

(a) Up to 4 marks for each element of the PESTEL framework affecting DSB.

(Up to a maximum of 12 marks)

(b) Up to 3 marks for each area of financial performance or position discussed, including any relevant calculations. **(Up to a maximum of 14 marks)**

Professional skills may be additionally rewarded as in the following rubric:

How well has the candidate demonstrated Profession Skill as follows:	Not at all	Not well	Quite well	Very well
(a) Analytical and evaluation skills relating to the Nearland division's environment.	The candidate has failed to use the PESTEL model and has therefore not identified or analysed the key elements of the macro environment.	The candidate has used the PESTEL model but has mainly focused on identifying issues rather than analysing them. The consequences for DSB/pharmaceutical companies have not been explored.	For many areas of the PESTEL the candidate has not only identified relevant issues but explained how these might impact on DSB/ pharmaceutical companies.	For most areas of the PESTEL the candidate has analysed the key issues. The candidate has also explored how this might impact on the growth of DSB/pharmaceutical companies.
	0	0.5	1	2

(b) Analytical and evaluation skills relating to the Nearland division's environment.	The candidate has focused mainly on the production of financial ratios without exploring why these ratios may have changed or what they say about the performance of DSB	The candidate has performed some financial analysis which aims to relate changes to the scenario. But some KPI's such as R&D changes or financial position have been ignored and no use has been made of operational data.	The candidate has performed some ratio analysis and related changes in ratios to the scenario. But the candidate has failed to make use of the operational data on market size and employee numbers.	The candidate has provided comprehensive financial analysis that incorporates the operational data on market size and employee numbers. Reasons for changes and consequences for the business are fully explored.
	0	0.5	1	2

TASK 2

(a)   1 mark for explaining related risks

1 mark for explaining correlated risks

1 mark each for evidence of understanding of legal and reputational risk

1 mark for each issue identified from the case (max 3 marks)

1 mark for each issue from the case which explores the link between legal and reputation risk (max 3 marks)   **(Total: 10 marks)**

(b)   1 mark for each purpose of an internal control system to a maximum of 4

Up to 2 marks for each assessed failing. 1 mark only if described but not assessed.

(Total: 10 marks)

Professional skills may be additionally rewarded as in the following rubric:

How well has the candidate demonstrated **Profession Skill as** follows:	**Not at all**	**Not well**	**Quite well**	**Very well**
(a) Professional scepticism skills relating to the newspaper article provided.	The candidate has not considered the validity of the claims put forward in the newspaper article and has instead taken the articles claims as fact.	The candidate has questioned the validity of the newspaper article but no justification has been provided as to why.	The candidate has questioned the validity of the newspaper article, but no justification has been provided as to why, and subjectivity of the article has been probed.	The candidate has questioned the validity of the newspaper article and challenged (with examples of where the article may not be accurate) the accuracy of the claims made.
	0	0.5	1	2
(b) Analytical skills relating to the internal control failings at DSB.	The candidate has failed to identify internal controls relating to the case scenario and has instead focused on generic issues unrelated to the scenario.	The candidate has identified internal control failings related to the case scenario but not assessed/analysed these.	The candidate has occasionally related internal control failings at DSB to the bribery allegations but has not done so consistently.	The candidate has analysed the internal controls failings and fully related them to the allegations that have been made against DSB.
	0	0.5	1	2

TASK 3

(a) 2 marks for explanation of bribery allegations. 2 mark for each well explained step taken to prevent reoccurrence (max 6 marks) **(Total: 6 marks)**

(b) 2 marks for each well explained role of the CEO using the issues in the case (max 6 marks) **(Total: 6 marks)**

Professional skills may be additionally rewarded as in the following rubric:

How well has the candidate demonstrated Profession Skill as follows:	Not at all	Not well	Quite well	Very well
Demonstrating strong communication in ensuring that the statement solves the key issues arising from the bribery allegations.	The candidate uses poor, unprofessional language. The candidate provides arguments that lack logic and solutions are ambiguous and/or illogical.	The candidate's language is professional but lacks clarity. The candidate repeats themselves and arguments are unpersuasive. The candidate's discussion of the role of the CEO is unrelated to the bribery allegations.	The candidate has clarified the role of the CEO in a manner which relates to the bribery allegations. The candidate's language is occasionally complex and solutions are not always persuasive.	The candidate uses a professional tone and language. The candidate uses positive and authoritative language which is unambiguous. Arguments are simple but persuading.
	0	**0.5**	**1**	**2**
Demonstrating commercial acumen in ensuring that the statement is satisfactory to both the stakeholders of DSB and Nur Saah.	The candidate regurgitates the issues at hand without providing assurance to stakeholders. The candidate seeks to deflect blame away from DSB without suggesting how issues will be/have been resolved.	The candidate's arguments lack fact and the key issues are simply regurgitated without adequate solutions or understanding of their importance and relevance to key stakeholders.	The candidate understands some of the key issues well and the potential impact on stakeholders is considered. Some attempt is made to avoid these problems recurring in the future.	The candidate has a strong understanding of the key issues and how they would impact on key stakeholders. The statement made considers wider and longer term issues and provides confidence to stakeholders that there will be no long term detrimental impact on DSB.
	0	**0.5**	**1**	**2**

TASK 4

(a)   3 marks for each slide (x2)

3 marks for each set of notes (x2)   **(Total: 12 marks)**

(b)   2 marks for each slide (x3)

2 marks for each set of notes (x3)   **(Total: 12 marks)**

Professional skills may be additionally rewarded as in the following rubric:

How well has the candidate demonstrated Profession Skill as follows:	Not at all	Not well	Quite well	Very well
(a) Analytical and evaluation skills relating to the risks in the project.	The candidate has failed to identify key or their impact on DSB.	The candidate has identified some key risks but they are rarely evaluated and there is some confusion between strategic and financial risks.	The candidate is clear on the difference between strategic and financial risks. Risks are properly classified and some have clear evaluations.	The candidate is clear on the difference between strategic and financial risks. All risks are properly classified and have clear evaluations.
	0	1	2-3	4
(b) Commercial acumen applied to justifying the decision on non-financial grounds.	The candidate has not related the analysis to the scenario and has made no attempt to consider longer term impacts on DSB.	The candidate has considered some impacts on DSB but these mainly relate to the bribery allegations and have not considered other longer-term impacts or DSB's code of ethics.	The candidate has considered some longer-term impacts on DSB but has not considered wider stakeholders or the organisation's mission.	The candidate has used judgement to consider longer-term impacts on DSB and has also considered the organisation's mission and concern for putting patients first.
	0	0.5	1	2

2   FOODMART

TASK 1

REPORT

To:	The Board of FOODMART
From:	Consultant
Date:	Today

RESPONDING TO DISRUPTIVE TECHNOLOGIES

(a)   Impact of disruptive technologies (requirement part a)

It is impossible to tell, for certain, how much of the recent decline in FOODMART's position is due to disruptive technologies. However, it is fairly certain that the failure to adopt such developments as online shopping and self-scan checkouts must have contributed to that decline.

FOODMART's loss of 'best supermarket' position to Ultra (in 2014) may also have been partly as a consequence of FOODMART's reluctance to adopt online shopping and self-scan. Online and home deliveries now represent 10-35% of rivals' revenues (compared to 3% of FOODMART's). Self-scan represents 15% of Camberwell's revenue, and 20% of Ultra's. It looks very much like FOODMART is ignoring the shopping preferences of up to a third of the market.

FOODMART's year-on-year revenue growth (of between 0 and 2%) lags behind that of all major rivals (2-4%). It seems highly unlikely that all of this competitor growth has been at the expense of small local retailers. Some must have come from FOODMART customers switching their loyalty to a rival chain. With such a low take-up of FOODMART loyalty programme membership (4% of transactions), it is impossible for management to identify customers ceasing to shop at FOODMART, let alone to tempt them back with promotional offers.

Limiting technology investment to maintenance, and spending relatively little on store fittings, indicate a reluctance to invest. FOODMART's retail technologies are old (5 years) and fully written down. This may improve short term profitability, but leads to problems as technology becomes unstable and capabilities lag behind those of rivals. Ultra spends 40% more on fitting out a new store, and over double on refurbishments, when compared to FOODMART. This must make FOODMART stores look less appealing to customers, and have an impact on market share.

Although FOODMART is still investing in opening new stores, this leaves little cash for investments in fittings, refurbishments and technologies. This becomes a self-fulfilling prophesy, as low levels of investment lead to losses in market share and consequently a fall in profitability and cash flow. A quick assessment of revenue and profitability shows some worrying trends:

	2016	2017	2018
Sales per m²*	15,030	15,145 (+1%)	15,993 (+6%)
Profit (ROP) per m²*	354	344 (−3%)	343 (0)
ROP margin %	2.35	2.27	2.08

*Based on 814 m² per new store in 2018, as per the average for the new stores opened in 2017

Retail is a business based on utilisation. Failing to make significant improvements in revenue and profit per square metre indicates that any growth in the business has come from opening new stores, not from improvements in performance.

Conclusion

In conclusion, it appears highly likely that a failure to respond to disruptive technologies has significantly weakened FOODMART's position.

(b) **The importance of New Product Development**

FOODMART's New Product Development (NPD) function includes 3 key areas – products, technologies and processes. These are all core competences in retail. Get them right, and you gain a competitive advantage. Get them wrong, and you lose out. FOODMART appears to be losing out.

Of the three areas, products is probably the least important at present. It is assumed that FOODMART stocks pretty much the same as its rivals, and there is no evidence to suggest that new product innovation rates are high throughout the industry. However, new product decisions should not be made simply on the basis of increasing contribution per square metre. To do this limits the opportunity for promotional activity, and may make FOODMART's product range look tired. New product decisions should consider the customer. Stocking new products brings in customers, who buy other things during their visit. Customers generate profits, not products.

Process improvement is quite important, as relates to customer service, but many retail processes depend on technology. It is difficult (or impossible) to make step-change improvements in processes without investing in the technological infrastructure to support such change. An example of this is self-scan, where staff processes need to be re-designed from scanning purchases to assisting customers and performing random checks. The whole process depends on an investment in self-scan checkouts and code readers. The technology is the enabler of the process change.

Technology is the most significant area of NPD, as it gives opportunities to develop core competences, but appears most neglected. It appears that Electronic Point-Of-Sale (EPOS) was the last major technology implemented in FOODMART, and that this was more than 5 years ago. A lot of disruptive technology has appeared since EPOS, and there is much more coming. Just as electric cars will be the norm within a decade or two, so the supermarkets of the future will bear little resemblance to the supermarkets of today.

FOODMART will need to invest in such technologies as Radio Frequency Identification (RFID), and exploit the opportunities associated with this technology, or risk becoming obsolete. For the first major supermarket chain to introduce this technology, it will be a core competence. However, in line with most technological innovation, others will adopt it and it will become a core competence. FOODMART already appears old-fashioned. Without RFID, it risks becoming obsolete.

The reduced number of industry players implies that the Upland supermarket industry is experiencing increased rivalry. In such circumstances, rivals need to differentiate in order to succeed. Technology is at the heart of innovation in retailing. Lagging behind rivals reduces the levels of investment required, which improves apparent performance in the short term. In the long term, it limits returns and can lead to obsolescence of the business model.

Conclusion

NPD should be proactive not reactive. FOODMART needs to re-consider its approach (see later).

(c) **Business performance excellence**

An indication of the areas that FOODMART should address, if it wishes to achieve excellence and meet its aim of being "a supermarket chain based on quality of environment and stock", can be seen from a simple application of the Baldrige Business Performance Excellence model.

The model considers seven core values and concepts:

1 **Leadership**

Examines how senior executives guide and sustain the organisation and how the organisation addresses Governance, ethical, legal and community responsibilities.

FOODMART has very clear aims (becoming "a supermarket chain based on quality of environment and stock" and achieving "increased market share"), but appears to lack the strategic direction required to achieve them. It has been allowed to become a follower in its industry, rather than a leader. The Board seems preoccupied with the risks attached to new technologies, rather than looking at the bigger picture. Risks can be managed.

2 **Strategic planning**

Examines how the organisation sets strategic directions and how it determines and deploys key action plans.

FOODMART needs a clear (and realistic) strategy to achieve its aims. The current strategic plan has very optimistic financial targets (such as a 19% increase in revenues, and 120% increase on ROP, over 5 years) but little in the way of real change to support the achievement of this. It may be possible to 'buy' revenue growth, by opening new stores, but improvements in profitability require clear strategy and investment in systems and processes. Setting over-optimistic targets may keep shareholders quiet in the short term, but continually failing to achieve them will lead to a significant loss of confidence in The Board.

3 **Customer focus**

Examines how the organisation determines requirements and expectations of customers and markets; builds relationships with customers; acquires, satisfies, and retains customers.

FOODMART has failed to develop its customer loyalty programme, with only 4% of transactions being linked to a loyalty programme. This compares very badly with Ultra, which gets an estimated 50% of its revenue from loyalty programme members. Loyalty programmes are not about giving away discounts – they are about understanding customer behaviour, getting feedback, and targeting promotions on a personal level. A good loyalty programme opens up the opportunity for huge benefits from Big Data analytics.

4   **Measurement, analysis, and knowledge management**

Examines the management, use, analysis, and improvement of data and information to support key organisation processes as well as how the organisation reviews its performance.

FOODMART seems a little 'blind' to the realities of its performance. The strategic plan is happy to highlight headline growth figures, but lacks any analysis of underlying performance. While revenues are growing, profit per square metre is falling. The lack of an Enterprise Resource Planning (ERP) system must make it difficult and expensive to provide detailed analysis of performance, as well as limiting insight into the business and opportunities. This is another indication of FOODMART's reluctance to invest in technologies.

5   **Workforce focus**

Examines how the organisation engages, manages, and develops all those actively involved in accomplishing the work of the organisation to develop full potential and how the workforce is aligned with the organisation's objectives.

FOODMART seems to ignore its staff, particularly where NPD is concerned. NPD operates in isolation from the rest of the organisation, and staff are not consulted. Operations senior management are seldom seen in stores. If this is representative of the wider organisation, FOODMART is missing an opportunity. Front-line staff almost always know how to fix problems and improve the business.

6   **Process management**

Examines aspects of how key production/delivery and support processes are designed, managed, and improved.

In FOODMART, "operations processes are revised on an ad-hoc basis, when issues arise or a viable staff suggestion is received" (Internal Audit report). This does not indicate proactive management and planned improvement. I am sure that FOODMART's competitors are using Business Process Re-engineering (BPR) and Process Innovation (PI). These techniques have been common practice for decades.

7   **Results**

Examines the organisation's performance and improvement in its key business areas: customer satisfaction, financial and marketplace performance, workforce, product/service, and operational effectiveness, and leadership. The category also examines how the organisation performs relative to competitors.

FOODMART's results, after a little analysis, speak for themselves. ROP per square metre static or falling. ROP margin falling. Revenue growth the slowest, by far, of the big 4 supermarket businesses.

Conclusion

FOODMART has a long way to go, if it wishes to achieve 'excellence'.

TASK 2

REPORT

To: CEO, FOODMART

From: Consultant

Date: Today

STRICTLY CONFIDENTIAL – NEW PRODUCT DEVELOPMENT

Introduction

This report examines the effectiveness of the current NPD processes in FOODMART, and makes suggestions for improvement.

(a) Effectiveness of NPD

The strategic objective of FOODMART – to be "a supermarket chain based on quality of environment and stock" and aim of "increased market share" imply that FOODMART should be leading the industry.

Logically, the supporting goal of NPD should be to make improvements to the quality of the retail environment and the quality of stock. Instead, the NPD function, possibly with leadership from above, has been limiting investment in the retail environment to a much lower level than Ultra, and making stock decisions based solely on the level of returns.

To determine the effectiveness of NPD, we have to ask whether its operations support the strategic aims of FOODMART. The answer is clearly not. FOODMART has become a technology follower (loyalty programme), or avoider (self-scan, e-commerce). It makes product decisions based on returns, not on customer needs. Any process improvement is made on an ad-hoc basis, rather than being based on strategy or benchmarking against competitors.

FOODMART is definitely not prepared to face the threats posed by disruptive technologies. It must change in two ways: Firstly, FOODMART must recover its position and adopt the technologies and processes now considered core competences within the Upland supermarket sector. Secondly, FOODMART must look to exploit disruptive technologies and differentiate its offering.

Conclusion

The NPD function needs to embrace change, and enable FOODMART to lead. However, this will require significant investment. FOODMART is short of funds, so may have to raise capital.

(b) Organisational process change in NPD

Harmon's process strategy matrix can be used to identify the type of process change required in NPD. The matrix looks at two dimensions:

1 the complexity of the process being considered, and

2 the strategic importance of that process

The process being considered is rated either 'high' or 'low' on each axis, and the matrix recommends four approaches based on the outcome.

NPD is highly complex. It includes technological change, and responses to the business environment and competition. NPD is also fundamental to the achievement of FOODMART's strategic aim. It therefore rates 'high-high', on the Harmon matrix, and is an example of a "complex dynamic process that may provide competitive advantage".

Conclusion

For processes in the 'high-high' category, the Harmon matrix recommends Business Process Re-engineering, process improvement, and process innovation.

(c)   NPD structure and relationships

Note: *You could equally recommend leaving NPD as one function, but radically changing its operations, or recommend moving it to a different Directorate. Your recommendations are opinions, and the marks you earn depend on the quality of your justification.*

The current structure assumes that NPD only impacts on Operations, whereas its influence should be company-wide. The Operations Directorate may not be the most appropriate home for all areas covered by NPD.

NPD currently operates in an insular manner, and does not involve/include other stakeholders or departments in the decision-making process or development projects. The Operations Director claims that this is to avoid influence from within the organisation, and says that staff outside NPD are resistant to change.

The 'insular' approach to NPD means that decisions may be short-sighted, opportunities and consequences overlooked, and solutions subject to greater levels of resistance to change (as staff are not involved in the development process).

Based on the analysis in this report, I recommend raising the profile of NPD within FOODMART, changing the organisation structure, and investing heavily to recover strategic position. My detailed recommendations are:

Structure

- NPD should be split into its three component parts. There are few synergies between the three areas, so there are no valid arguments for keeping them together. Process change is really a consequence of technological change, so its role in NPD is secondary.

- Process improvement should remain in Operations, as this is the logical home for it. It should be responsible for BPR exercises, and the implementation of innovations.

- Technology Development should be moved to the IT Directorate. It will benefit from being based in an 'expert' environment, and future developments will integrate better with other IT systems.

- Product Development should be moved to the Procurement Directorate. It is illogical for new product decisions to be made anywhere else. Procurement staff have the best knowledge of what is available, and what suppliers are developing.

Relationships

- All developments are to be based on stakeholder consultation. Staff from other functions, and external stakeholders like customers and suppliers, should be allowed to express their opinion.

- All development teams are to include staff from outside the relevant development function. This will ensure that developments are capable of being implemented, and overcome resistance to change.

- All three NPD areas need to be proactive, and to be guided by The Board through the strategic planning process. This will allow FOODMART to catch up with its competitors, and to start to lead rather than follow. FOODMART needs to investigate emerging technologies, in order to develop new core competences.

- The development areas should also be audited differently. Audits should be based on assessing effectiveness, not on compliance to procedure. Audits should be carried out every two or three years, not every five (as at present).

Conclusion

All of this requires significant investment, but FOODMART must make funds available if it is to catch up with its rivals, then move towards leading the industry.

MARKING SCHEME

TASK 1

(a)   Up to 2 marks per relevant point made, based on evidence or calculation.

1 mark for each relevant calculation (up to a maximum of 5)

(Up to a maximum of 12 in total)

(b)   Up to 2 marks for each valid point made.   **(Up to a maximum of 10 in total)**

(c)   1 mark for theoretical explanation of each part of the framework.

Up to 3 further marks for direct application of each part to FOODMART.

(Up to a maximum of 21 in total)

Professional skills may be additionally rewarded as in the following rubric:

How well has the candidate demonstrated professional skills as follows:	Not at all	Not so well	Quite well	Very well
(a) Evaluation skills in estimating the impact of the business environment	The candidate has demonstrated no evaluation skills. The answer is largely theoretical, or superficial.	The candidate has demonstrated some evaluation skills in assessing the impact of disruptive technologies on FOODMART. However, the answer lacks insight and evidence is taken at face value.	The candidate has demonstrated some sound evaluation skills in assessing the impact of the emergent technologies on FOODMART. Value has been added to the information provided.	The candidate has demonstrated excellent evaluation skills. The candidate has used significant professional judgement to evaluate the impact of the disruptive technologies.
	0	1	2	3

How well has the candidate demonstrated professional skills as follows:	Not at all	Not so well	Quite well	Very well
(b) Commercial acumen skills in showing insight into how external factors might affect FOODMART's achievement of its aims	The candidate has demonstrated no commercial acumen. The candidate has merely restated the information presented, and has showed no commercial awareness of the factors affecting the business, or the role of NPD in addressing those factors.	The candidate has demonstrated some commercial acumen. The candidate has demonstrated a limited commercial awareness of the factors impacting upon the business, or the role of NPD in addressing those factors.	The candidate has demonstrated some sound commercial acumen. The candidate has demonstrated some good commercial awareness of the factors impacting on business, and the role of NPD in addressing those factors.	The candidate has demonstrated excellent commercial acumen, using the exhibits provided to demonstrate the impact on FOODMART, and the role of NPD.
	0	1	2	3
(c) Analysis skills in your consideration of the requirements of the excellence model	The candidate has demonstrated very limited analysis skills. The answer is either common sense (with no reference to the model) or theoretical (with no application to FOODMART)	The candidate has demonstrated some analysis skills in using scenario information to apply the model; however this application is often superficial.	The candidate has demonstrated analysis skills in using scenario information to apply the model. However, a few instances lack depth or clarity.	The candidate has demonstrated excellent analysis skills in using scenario information to apply the model. Arguments are clear and valid.
	0	1	2	4

TASK 2

(a)   Up to 3 marks per relevant point made, based on evidence.

(Up to a maximum of 16 in total)

(b)   Up to 2 marks for explanation of the model.

1 mark for an appropriate classification of NPD.

2 marks for recommendation of an appropriate change method.

(Up to a maximum of 5 in total)

(c)   Up to 3 marks for each recommendation, justified in relation to the position and strategy of FOODMART.   **(Up to a maximum of 16 in total)**

How well has the candidate demonstrated professional skills as follows:	Not at all	Not so well	Quite well	Very well
(a) Scepticism skills in your questioning of the information provided	The candidate has failed to demonstrate any scepticism regarding the opinions and assertions made. The candidate demonstrated no evidence of challenging or questioning the information provided.	The candidate has demonstrated some, but limited, scepticism regarding the information provided. The candidate questioned some of the views. However, others were not challenged	The candidate has demonstrated scepticism of the information provided. The opinions expressed were reasonably sound.	The candidate has demonstrated deep scepticism of the information provided. The candidate strongly questioned the validity of the opinions in a professional and justified manner.
	0	1	2	4
(b) Commercial acumen skills in using your judgement to classify NPD	The candidate has demonstrated no commercial acumen. The candidate has failed to classify NPD in the context of the framework.	The candidate has demonstrated some commercial acumen. The candidate has classified NPD, but the arguments are invalid and the classification inappropriate	The candidate has demonstrated some sound commercial acumen. The candidate has classified NPD appropriately, but failed to justify their view.	The candidate has demonstrated excellent commercial acumen, classifying NPD appropriately and supporting this with clear and valid justification
	0	0.5	1	2
(c) Communication skills in persuading the CEO	The candidate has demonstrated poor communication skills. They have failed to present the required information in a clear, objective and unambiguous way. The answer is not communicated in an appropriate format (report) or tone (to persuade the CEO)	The candidate has demonstrated some basic communication skills in presenting an appropriate report format. Some relevant information is contained in the answer but the tone is not persuasive.	The candidate has demonstrated good communication skills in the presentation of the report to the CEO. The candidate has presented most of the relevant issues and has done so concisely and in most cases, clearly.	The candidate has demonstrated excellent communication skills. The report was correctly structured, covered all of the relevant points needed by the CEO in understanding the issues and was set at the correct tone. A persuasive response.
	0	1	2	4

3   SWAN HILL COMPANY (SHC)

TASK 1

(a)   Secrecy option

A suitable model to use when assessing this decision is Tuckers model which applies a number of criteria to decision making:

Is the decision profitable?

For SHC, the answer to this question is yes. The secrecy option is forecast to create almost ten times as much wealth for shareholders as the licensing option.

Is this decision legal?

The secrecy option poses no legal problems as it is a part of normal competitive behaviour in industries. In some jurisdictions, legislation forbids monopolies existing in some industries but there is no indication here that this restriction applies to Swan Hill Company.

Is this decision fair?

The fairness of the secrecy option is a moral judgment. It is probably fair when judged from the perspective of SHC's shareholders but the question is the extent to which it is fair to the employees and shareholders of SHC's competitors.

Is this decision right?

Again, a question of ethical perspective. Is it right to pursue the subjugation of competitors and the domination of an industry regardless of the consequences to competitors? The secrecy option may be of the most benefit to the local community of Swan Hill that the company has traditionally valued.

Is this decision sustainable or environmentally sound?

The sink method emits at a lower rate per unit of output than the existing process but this has little to do with the secrecy option as the rates of emissions would apply if SHC licensed the process. This is also an argument for the licensing option; however, as environmental emissions would be lower if other competitors switched to the sink method as well. There may be environmental implications in decommissioning the old plant to make way for the new sink method investment.

Tutorial note

The last of Tucker's questions is sometimes mistakenly interpreted. Sustainable is referring to the environmental impact of the decision in question, not the continuing existence of the business.

(b)   **Strategic and operational risks**

Strategic risks

These arise from the overall strategic positioning of the company in its environment. Some strategic positions give rise to greater risk exposures than others. Because strategic issues typically affect the whole of an organisation and not just one or more of its parts, strategic risks can potentially concern very high stakes – they can have very high hazards and high returns. Because of this, they are managed at board level in an organisation and form a key part of strategic management.

Operational risks

Operational risks refer to potential losses arising from the normal business operations. Accordingly, they affect the day-to-day running of operations and business systems in contrast to strategic risks that arise from the organisation's strategic positioning. Operational risks are managed at risk management level (not necessarily board level) and can be managed and mitigated by internal control systems.

The secrecy option would be a strategic risk for the following reasons.

- It would radically change the environment that SHC is in by reducing competition. This would radically change SHC's strategic fit with its competitive environment. In particular, it would change its 'five forces' positioning which would change its risk profile.

- It would involve the largest investment programme in the company's history with new debt substantially changing the company's financial structure and making it more vulnerable to short term liquidity problems and monetary pressure (interest rates).

- It would change the way that stakeholders view SHC, for better or worse. It is a 'crisis issue', certain to polarise opinion either way.

- It will change the economics of the industry thereby radically affecting future cost, revenue and profit forecasts.

- There may be retaliatory behaviour by SHC's close competitor on 25% of the market.

Tutorial note

Other reasons, if relevant and well argued, will attract marks.

TASK 2

(a)   **STATEMENT ON THE SECRECY OPTION**

Important developments at SHC

This is an exciting time for the management and shareholders of Swan Hill Company. The research and development staff at SHC have made a ground breaking discovery (called the 'sink method') that will enable your company to produce its major product at lower cost, in higher volumes and at a much higher quality than our competitors will be able to using, as they do, the existing production technology. The sink process also produces at a lower rate of environmental emissions which, as I'm sure shareholders will agree, is a very welcome development.

When considering the options following the discovery, we, as a board, decided that we should press ahead with the investment needed to transform the production facilities without offering the use of the technology to competitors under a licensing arrangement. This means that once the new sink production comes on stream, we believe that SHC shareholders can look forward to a significant strengthening of our competitive position.

The business case for this option is overwhelming. By pushing ahead with the investment needed to implement the sink method, the possibility exists to gain a substantial competitive advantage over all of SHC's competitors. It will place SHC in a near monopolist position in the short term and in a dominant position long term. This will, in turn, give the company pricing power in the industry and the likelihood of superior profits for many years to come. We would expect SHC to experience substantial 'overnight' growth and the returns from this will reward shareholders' loyalty and significantly increase the value of the company. Existing shareholders can reasonably expect a significant increase in the value of their holdings over the very short term and also over the longer term.

Ethical implications of the secrecy option

In addition to the overwhelming business case, however, there is a strong ethical case for the secrecy option. SHC recognises that it is the moral purpose of SHC to make profits in order to reward those who have risked their own money to support it over many years. Whilst some companies pursue costly programmes intended to serve multiple stakeholder interests, SHC recognises that it is required to comply with the demands of its legal owners, its shareholders, and not to dilute those demands with other concerns that will reduce shareholder returns. This is an important part of the agency relationship: the SHC board will always serve the best economic interests of its shareholders: its legal owners. The SHC board believes that any action taken that renders shareholder returns suboptimal is a threat to shareholder value and an abuse of the agency position. Your board will always seek to maximise shareholder wealth; hence our decision to pursue the secrecy option in this case. The secrecy option offers the possibility of optimal shareholder value and because shareholders invest in SHC to maximise returns, that is the only ethical action for the board to pursue. Happily, this option will also protect the employees' welfare in SHC's hometown of Swan Hill and demonstrate its commitment to the locality. This, in turn, will help to manage two of the key value-adding resources in the company, its employees and its reputation. This will help in local recruitment and staff retention in future years.

(b)   STATEMENT ON THE SECRECY OPTION

Statement from Nelson Cobar, Chief Executive Officer, SHC

Important developments at SHC

SHC's board was recently faced with a very difficult business and ethical decision. After the discovery by SHC scientists of the ground breaking sink production method, we had a choice of keeping the new production technology secret or sharing the breakthrough under a licensing arrangement with our competitors. After a lengthy discussion, your board decided that we should pursue the licensing option and I would like to explain our reasons for this on both business and ethical grounds.

In terms of the business case for licensing, I would like shareholders to understand that although the secrecy option may have offered SHC the possibility of an unassailable competitive advantage, in reality, it would have incurred a number of risks. Because of the speed with which we would have needed to have acted, it would have necessitated a large increase in our borrowing, bringing about a substantial change in our financial structure. This would, in turn, increase liquidity pressures and make us more vulnerable to rising interest rates. A second risk with the secrecy option would involve the security of the sink technology 'secret'. If the sink process was leaked or discovered by competitors and subsequently copied, our lack of a legally binding patent would mean we would have no legal way to stop them proceeding with their own version of the sink process.

As well as avoiding the risks, however, the licensing option offers a number of specific business advantages. The royalties from the licences granted to competitors are expected to be very large indeed. These will be used over the coming years to extend our existing competitive advantage in the future. Finally, the 'improvement sharing' clause in the licensing contract will ensure that the sink process will be improved and perfected with several manufacturers using the technology at the same time. SHC's sink production may, in consequence, improve at a faster rate than would have been the case were we to have pursued the secrecy option.

Ethical implications of the secrecy option

In addition to the business case, there is also a powerful ethical case for the decision we have taken. As a good, responsible corporate citizen, Swan Hill Company acknowledges its many stakeholders and recognises the impacts that a business decision has on others. Your board recognises that in addition to external stakeholders having influence over our operations, our decisions can also affect others. In this case, we have carefully considered the likelihood that keeping the new technology a secret from our competitors would radically reshape the industry. The superior environmental performance of the sink process over existing methods will also mean that when fully adopted, the environmental emissions of the entire industry will be reduced. SHC is very proud of this contribution to this reduction in overall environmental impact.

There seems little doubt that the secrecy option would have had far-reaching and unfortunate effects upon our industry and our competitors. The licensing option will allow competitors, and their employees and shareholders, to survive. It is a compassionate act on our part and shows mercy to the other competitors in the industry. It recognises the number of impacts that a business decision has and would be the fairest (and most just) option given the number of people affected.

TASK 3

(a)   **Presentation slides**

SLIDE 1	
Expected returns from each option	
• Secrecy option	$219.1m
• Licensing option	$24.3m

Notes:

This is the overall expected returns from each project after taking account of all costs and revenues as well as the expected cost of finance (capital).

It represents the expected amount that could, in theory, be distributed to shareholders after all finance costs are met. Therefore, this would be the total amount that shareholder wealth will increase by if each project was pursued.

If the company's objective is to maximise shareholder wealth it should invest in the secrecy option.

SLIDE 2		
Differences in the options		
Area	**Secrecy option**	**Licensing option**
Duration	Foreseeable future	20 years
Inflows	Generating $68m p.a. from year 4	Generating $5m p.a. from year 2
Capital	$95m today, falling to $10m p.a. by year 4	$2m today, $1m p.a. thereafter
DF	12%	14%

Notes:

This is the key data used in determining the NPV of each option.

The period gives an idea of the expected duration of returns from each option. The inflows will represent the financial benefits less the financial costs (including tax) each year. The secrecy option takes four years before returns are maximised but these are then expected to continue into the foreseeable future. The licensing option's returns reach a peak as soon as year 2 but only last for the duration of the patent (20 years).

The capital investment will represent investment in areas such as plant and machinery. It can be seen that both options require ongoing investment and that both the initial investment and ongoing investment in the secrecy option is significantly higher. However, the returns in the secrecy option far outweigh this level of investment (as illustrated by the NPV).

DFs (discount factors) are used to take account of the time value of money. The higher the cost of finance the lower this figure and therefore the lower present value of cash flows received in the future. The secrecy option uses a 12% cost of capital, possibly due to the new debt reducing the overall cost of finance for SHC. Because the debt interest will be tax deductible and result in a lower tax bill for SHC, this is lower than the 14% cost for the licensing option of using the internally generated funds.

(b)   **BOARD HAND-OUT**

Project benefits

Project benefits can fall into four possible categories as explained below:

Observable benefits

These benefits are often intangible and difficult to objectively measure. Their value is often determined by the views of appropriately qualified observers.

Examples of observable benefits from this project for SHC are:

- the ability to attract more able staff

- further brand awareness

- improved staff motivation

Measurable benefits

These types of benefits can be objectively measured. But whilst SHC may know where it is at the moment, it will not be able to reliably estimate how the measure will change. The direction of the change may be estimated, but the value of the change will be difficult to assess and usually the value of the change can only be determined retrospectively.

Examples of measurable benefits from this project for SHC are:

- the number of rivals leaving the market

- the associated increase in market share

- increases in local house prices

Quantifiable benefits

These benefits can be reliably forecast in advance (unlike measurable benefits which can only be quantified when later in the project's life). The forecasting may be based upon historical data, testing or benchmarking against industry experience. The financial value of these quantifiable benefits may be difficult to forecast as they may be external to the company or the financial value may be variable.

Examples of quantifiable benefits from this project for SHC are:

- reduction in environmental emissions

- reduction is wastage

- reduction in product returns

Financial benefits

These are quantifiable benefits that can be given an objective financial value – either in terms of a revenue increase or a cost reduction.

Examples of financial benefits from this project for SHC are:

- extra sales

- extra sales for other products

- savings from economies of scale

Determination of the financial value of the project

Only financial benefits should be included in the financial evaluation of the project. The other benefits may lead to financial benefits in the longer term (meaning that the actual value of the project may be worth substantially more than the values calculated), but because they cannot easily and objectively be given a financial value they are not included in the financial valuation.

TASK 4

(a)   BALDRIDGE PERFORMANCE EXCELLENCE

Use of performance excellence

Firstly, it should be noted that there are a number of issues in using this approach to assess the performance and/or excellence of SHC:

The business blog provided may be showing a bias towards this measure and a wider source of opinion should be considered before we press ahead with a full commitment to this process

Baldridge's framework is only one way to assess excellence and we may need to consider other measures

The blog indicates that this is a vital component in the award of government funding, but we are not seeking government funding and it may be that other finance providers do not actually use this framework

If we decide to press ahead with Baldrige's framework it considers the combination of the following areas in assessing business performance excellence:

Leadership

SHC's shows strong leadership from the top. The current strategic decision is being made inclusively, with all stakeholders being considered, and there appears to be a focus on the objectives of constant innovation, ethical behaviour and community support. There is good corporate governance on the board with an equal balance of executive and non-executive directors and the non-executive directors representing a wide range of stakeholder groups. Functional areas are covered well with no evidence of disputes between functions.

Strategy

We have strong strategic planning and a strong competitive advantage. The discovery of the sink method should provide evidence of continuing focus on the objective of innovation and improvements. The strategy is supported by strong action plans and past strategy implementation has shown a successful level of success for the company.

Customers

We have regular briefings and discussion groups with customers. But this is one area where we may need to provide more evidence of excellence. We need to show that we are measuring customer satisfaction, segmenting customers, improving customer retention and effectively dealing with customer complaints. The sales and marketing team will have to work on providing evidence in this area.

Measurement, analysis and knowledge management

We benchmark ourselves against industry averages, we have regular customer briefings and discussion groups and the sink method discovery should evidence strong knowledge management. These should give assurance in this framework measure.

Workforce

Our history provides evidence of our workforce engagement. We have always sought to engage, improve and empower our workforce – particularly in the Swan Hill community. The impact on job design is already an early consideration in the new strategic development which should provide further evidence of a focus on workforce efficiency and engagement. Ali Hamels is confident that we have some of the best staff in the world and we perhaps should look at measures to evidence this.

Operations

We should be able to exhibit that SCH's processes are strong. We have a history of successful innovation and the discovery of the new sink method should illustrate that this process in particular continues to be a source of strength for the company. There is also a good decision making process (as evidenced by how the sink method decision is being made) as well as good support processes in areas such as human resources.

Results

The market, existing and potential investors should be aware of our strong financial results. We should be able to supplement this with non-financial benchmarks which will show that we are ahead of the industry in most measures. We may, however, need to supplement this with wider results in areas such as customer satisfaction and workforce engagement, but these should be readily evidenced from within the business.

(b) Voluntary disclosures

Voluntary disclosures are an effective way of redressing the information asymmetry that exists between management and investors. In adding to mandatory content, voluntary disclosures give a fuller picture of the state of the company.

- More information helps investors decide whether the company matches their risk, strategic and ethical criteria, and expectations.

- Makes the annual report more forward looking (predictive) whereas the majority of the numerical content is backward facing on what has been.

- Helps transparency in communicating more fully thereby better meeting the agency accountability to investors, particularly shareholders.

- There is a considerable amount of qualitative information that cannot be conveyed using statutory numbers (such as strategy, ethical content, social reporting, etc.).

- Voluntary disclosure gives a more rounded and more complete view of the company, its activities, strategies, purposes and values.

- Voluntary disclosure enables the company to address specific shareholder concerns as they arise (such as responding to negative publicity).

Tutorial note

For illustration purposes, more than three issues are covered in the provided answer. But only three points would be necessary to score all of the marks available.

MARKING SCHEME

TASK 1

(a)   1 mark for evidence of understanding of each of Tucker's criteria.

1 mark for application of each to case (giving a total of 2 marks for each of the five criteria).   **(Total: 10 marks)**

(b)   1 mark for each relevant point demonstrating understanding of operational risk
(max: 3 marks)

1 mark for each relevant point demonstrating understanding of strategic risk
(max: 3 marks)

1 mark for each reason explaining why the secrecy option is a strategic risk
(max: 4 marks)

(Total: 10 marks)

Professional skills may be additionally rewarded as in the following rubric:

How well has the candidate demonstrated Professional Skill as follows:	Not at all	Not well	Quite well	Very well
(a) Commercial acumen in demonstrating awareness of organisational and wider external factors affecting the decision	The candidate's answer lacks any relevance to SHC or its wider industry context.	The candidate's answer shows some relevance to either SHC or its environment but is not focused on the secrecy option.	The candidate has shown some relevance to the secrecy option but the factors are focused on either internal relevant factors OR external wider issues.	The candidate has shown strong relevance to the secrecy option and the factors are a mixture of both internal relevant factors and external wider issues.
	0	1	2	3
(b) Analysis skills in investigating the risks associated with the secrecy option.	The candidate has identified risks which bear no relevance to the option under consideration.	The candidate has identified some relevant risks, but has failed to consider possible strategic impacts for those risks.	The candidate has identified risks relevant to the secrecy option, but some of these are operational	The candidate has focused solely on strategic risks, and all are relevant to the secrecy option.
	0	1	2	3

TASK 2

(a)   1 mark for each relevant point making the business case   **(max: 5 marks)**

1 mark for each relevant point making the stockholder (shareholder) moral case up

(max: 5 marks)

(Total: 10 marks)

(b)   1 mark for each relevant point making the business case (max: 5 marks)

1 mark for each relevant point making the stockholder (shareholder) moral case up

(max: 5 marks)

(Total: 10 marks)

Professional skills may be additionally rewarded as in the following rubric:

How well has the candidate demonstrated **Professional Skill** as follows:	**Not at all**	**Not well**	**Quite well**	**Very well**
Communication skills in informing stakeholders about the company's choice and persuading users of the benefits of each option.	The candidate's statements use complex terms, are not persuasive and lack depth and/or logic.	The candidate's statements are sometimes confused and lack focus on each discrete option. The statements are ambiguous and do not make it clear as to why the board has chosen the relevant option.	The candidate's statements show a clear focus but the arguments are not fully explained and may confuse some users.	The candidate's statements are objective, unambiguous, logical and compelling.
	0	**1**	**2**	**4**

TASK 3

(a)   2 marks for each slide (x2)

3 marks for each set of notes (x2)   **(Total: 10 marks)**

(b)   3 marks for the explanation of each type of benefit (x4)

2 marks for explaining why only financial benefits are included   **(Total: 14 marks)**

Professional skills may be additionally rewarded as in the following rubric:

How well has the candidate demonstrated **Profession Skill** as follows:	**Not at all**	**Not well**	**Quite well**	**Very well**
(a) Communication skills in clarifying the information and presenting it appropriately to the intended audience	The candidate uses complex terms and does not explain all of the financial differences between the projects.	The candidate attempts to explain all relevant terms, but many of these are either framed in complex and technical language or lack the depth required to help users understand the numbers.	The candidate explains all terms in non-complex, professional language, but the slides are overly complex and do not always link to the notes.	The candidate's notes and slides are clearly linked. Slides are simple and all terms are explained in non-complex, professional language.

How well has the candidate demonstrated Profession Skill as follows:	Not at all	Not well	Quite well	Very well
	0	**0.5**	**1**	**2**
(b) Evaluation skills in assessing the benefits identified for the project	The candidate has merely restated the benefits provided without any attempt to classify or evaluate them.	The candidate has made some attempt at explaining the types of benefits that may be derived from the project, but no attempt has been made to explain whether each type of benefit should/should not have been included in the financial evaluation.	The candidate has evaluated some of the benefits provided in the scenario, but not all benefits have been classified.	The candidate has exercised judgement in determining which benefits might fall into each type of benefit classification.
	0	**1**	**2**	**3**

TASK 4

(a)   2 marks for each area of the Baldridge frame work   **(Total: 14 marks)**

(b)   1 mark for each briefly explained point (max: 3)   **(Total: 3 marks)**

Professional skills may be additionally rewarded as in the following rubric:

How well has the candidate demonstrated Professional Skill as follows:	Not at all	Not well	Quite well	Very well
Scepticism relevant to questioning and challenging SHC's focus on performance excellence in part (a)	The candidate has not questioned the use of the Baldridge framework and has also not questioned the focus on performance excellence.	The candidate has questioned only one of either the use of the Baldridge framework or the focus on performance excellence.	The candidate has questioned the use of the Baldridge framework and the focus on performance excellence, but has taken the business blog on trust.	The candidate has questioned the use of the Baldridge framework and the focus on performance excellence as well as the potential bias in the provided blog.
	0	**1**	**2**	**4**

4   FISHNET

Strategic Leader Exam Answers

At the Professional Level, it is not always possible to publish suggested answers which comprehensively cover all the valid points which candidates might make. Credit will be given to candidates for points not included in the suggested answers, but which, nevertheless, are relevant to the requirements. In addition, in this integrated case study examination, candidates may re-introduce points made in other questions or parts of questions if these are made in the specific context of the requirements of the question being answered.

The suggested answers presented below inevitably give much more detail than would be expected from most candidates under examination conditions, and include most of the obvious points evidenced from the case information. The answers are therefore intended to provide a structure of the approach required from candidates, and cover the range and depth of knowledge relating to each task which might be demonstrated by the most well prepared and able candidates. They are also intended to support revision and tuition for future examinations.

TASK 1

(a)   To: The Board

   From: Senior Finance Manager

   Subject: Strategic Issues

Introduction

As requested, this report clarifies key issues arising from the Marketing Consultant's report.

COMPETITION

The competitive forces acting on our industry have been analysed using Porter's 'five forces' model. This model has been chosen as it takes a very diverse view of 'competition', and is very good for identifying potential threats.

Rivalry

From the consultant's report, we can see that the industry is dominated by four rivals of roughly equal size.

While we know that the industry has grown by 100% in a decade, some of this may be due to inflation. The characteristics of the industry seem to imply that it might be in the mature stage of its life cycle – consolidations (such as the merger between Deelite and Stanway) are an indication of this, as is the fragmentation of the industry into sub-groups (such as own brand, branded, exotic and ethnic).

Large-scale automated manufacturing is capital-intensive, so exit barriers are likely to be high. However, capital requirements do not deter small-scale entrants (see below).

Recipe dish manufacturers are forced (by customer bargaining power – see below) to augment the product with service add-ons.

All of this implies that rivalry is high.

Bargaining power of customers

Supermarket retail is a commonly-cited example of high customer bargaining power. We can see many indications of this in that the supermarkets are:

- demanding excellent service and logistics,

- taking discounts,

- paying very slowly, and

All of these are evidence, according to Porter, of high bargaining power.

While the bargaining power of wholesalers may have been weak in the past, this situation will change as they consolidate. The large size of customers, and relatively low number, increases their bargaining power. As an individual (wholesale) customer represents a larger percentage of Fishnet's revenues, the power of that wholesaler increases. This is particularly so if alternative suppliers are available.

Bargaining power of suppliers

It is difficult to make fish-based recipe dishes without fish. While other ingredients are generic, and can be obtained from many different suppliers, fish is the one critical 'component' supporting the whole of Fishnet's product portfolio.

The number of small suppliers (independent fishermen) has declined significantly, implying that Fishnet has less choice of supplier than previously. While it might be assumed that there are very low switching costs, it is quite possible that relatively few factory ships might visit Grubsby at any point in time. If Fishnet requires a specific fish species on any particular day, it may have little or no choice of supplier.

This situation is made worse by the capacity constraints in the port. These introduce switching costs, as road transport is an additional cost if fish cannot be sourced in Grubsby.

The bargaining power of suppliers appears high.

Threat of new entrants

A high level of 'up-front capital costs', and established brand names, are normally effective barriers to entry.

However, two factors seem to imply that the industry is becoming more attractive to new entrants:

1   The growth of own-brand products, which undermines the effectiveness of brand names as a barrier.

2   A proliferation of new entrants in 'niche' areas, such as exotic or ethnic dishes. These producers seem to be able to avoid high capital costs, by remaining quite small.

The threat of new entrants seems to be increasing.

Threat of substitutes

Four major substitutes to Fishnet's branded products can be identified:

1   The supermarkets' 'elite' own brand products directly compete with high quality branded products.

2   Non-fish-based recipe dishes are not direct rivals, but offer an alternative which meets the same customer need.

3   Home cooking is a substitute, as it directly affects the market volume for recipe dishes.

4   Eating out (in a restaurant or cafe) is also an alternative.

Substitution is high.

Conclusion

All of the competitive forces seem to provide a significant threat to margins, making this an unattractive industry for large-scale incumbent manufacturers like Fishnet. The only way to address these issues is to develop (or re-develop) core competences such as innovation. Fishnet must then differentiate its products, which will reduce each of the competitive forces.

(b)   STRATEGIC DRIFT

Fishnet is showing clear symptoms of strategic drift. This is the situation where an organisation's strategy gradually and incrementally moves away from its intended strategy.

Despite having a 'core value' of innovation, new product development seems to have slowed to almost a standstill. The combination of falling market share, pressure on margins and a lack of innovation have worsened margins. If nothing is done to correct this situation, profitability will probably continue to fall.

This complacency may have been caused, in part, by previous success. 'Skinny fish' was introduced more than a decade ago, and it may be that Fishnet has been reaping the rewards from this range, rather than thinking about what comes next. The Engineering Director made a telling statement, in the capital investment proposal (see below), that our team of chefs is focused on 'routine work'. This suggests that innovation is now left to chance, rather than being treated as, and protected as, a core competence.

The consultant's summary of competences is possibly the most telling evidence of the consequences of strategic drift. From a position of being regarded as among the most innovative, Fishnet is now struggling to achieve the threshold competences for the industry. These are standards of performance that are essential for survival, so the very future of Fishnet is under threat.

If threshold competences are not met, Fishnet will fail. A significant fall in share price may make Fishnet vulnerable to a hostile takeover.

(c)   INTRAPRENEURSHIP

While the CEO has asked the Engineering Director to investigate a formal new product development (NPD) strategy, an alternative (or supplement) would be to introduce an intrapreneurism culture. Staff would be encouraged, by the provision of management time and financial resources, to develop their innovations into potentially viable solutions. These innovations might not be limited to new products, but also to new methods.

Fishnet would have to create a policy governing the allocation of resources, and establish a committee to oversee the process. Fishnet will also need a procedure for the assessment of possible development projects.

The procedure might be:

1   The employee produces a business case, outlining the innovation and justifying an initial investment.

2   The business case is reviewed by an innovation committee, probably a group of senior managers. If the proposal is believed to have merit, the employee is given the resources (including, perhaps, a sabbatical from their normal work) to conduct further investigation and, if the innovation is a product, produce a prototype.

3   The innovation committee then assesses the idea or prototype, and makes a recommendation to the Board that either:

   (a)   the idea be incorporated into existing practice, or

   (b)   a new business unit (or NPD project) should be established, headed by the intrapreneur, to develop the new product through the introduction and growth phases, or

   (c)   the innovation be offered to the intrapreneur as a new business (if it does not 'fit' with Fishnet's strategy), and 'seed capital' provided on preferential terms, or

   (d)   the proposal be rejected, because no commercial future can be seen.

Knowing that Fishnet may invest in their innovation will motivate staff, and make them more likely to follow it up. Even if Fishnet is not interested in the innovation, the prospect of having a possible business opportunity will motivate employees to be innovative.

Once the policy and procedure have been designed and agreed, Fishnet will need to change the culture of the organisation to one where innovation is encouraged, and seen to be part of everyone's job description. Innovation has to be 'business as usual', rather than an occasional and optional activity.

TASK 2

(a)   Stakeholders in the NPD strategy

(**Note:** Any six stakeholders, appropriately classified and analysed, would be sufficient for full marks.)

The main stakeholders in the NPD project are as follows. They have been classified according to Mendelow's 'power/interest' model:

The Board/CEO/Engineering Director – these three (which could be regarded as separate stakeholders) each has high power over, and interest in, the strategic decision. They have high power because, ultimately, the final decision is theirs. They have high interest because the NPD strategy (and/or the intrapreneurship strategy, above) is 'mission-critical' to Fishnet (it relates to core competences). These are 'Key Players', in Mendelow's matrix.

Shareholders – will only have high interest in the project if it fails to add value. They may not even know about the NPD project until it is nearing completion, as the details are commercially sensitive. They have significant power as, if they do not like the outcome, they may start selling shares. This will lower the share price still further, and make Fishnet vulnerable to hostile takeover. They are 'Keep Satisfied' in the Mendelow matrix.

Suppliers of capital equipment and local contractors – these have high interest in the project, as it will directly affect their work. However, they have low power as they do not participate in, and cannot influence, the decision. They are therefore 'Keep Informed'.

Current staff (the chefs) – these have high interest in the project, as it will directly affect their work. However, they have low power as they may only be consulted as part of the preparation of the proposal. It is very unlikely that the recruitment (or re-allocation) of five staff would prompt industrial action. They are also 'Keep Informed'.

Potential development staff – the new employees (from inside or outside Fishnet) have no influence over the decision, and are possibly unaware of the details of the strategy. They are therefore 'Minimal Effort'.

Customers – it is unlikely that the supermarkets have been consulted. Although they may become 'Key Players' in any future decisions relating to new product launch, in terms of the NPD strategy they are 'Minimal Effort'.

(b)   **Slide 1 – Evaluation of the NPD strategy**

- Senior Finance Manager review

- 3 'tests': Suitability, Feasibility, Acceptability

- Conclusion

Notes: I asked the Senior Finance Manager to review this proposal, and these are their findings.

The framework used to assess the proposal is that put forward by Johnson, Scholes and Whittington – Suitability, Feasibility and Acceptability. A proposal must meet ALL of these criteria, to be viable.

A conclusion is given, at the end of this presentation.

Slide 2 – Suitability

- Test against position

- Test against environment

- Test against mission

Notes: Suitability is concerned with whether the strategy addresses the circumstances in which an organisation is operating – its strategic position, environment and mission.

In terms of position, we can see that the product portfolio of Fishnet contains an increasingly ageing population of products. In recent years, Fishnet has not been innovating at the rate required to balance its portfolio.

Innovation rates in the industry are generally higher than previously, and the industry is fragmenting with the growth of ethnic, exotic and 'free from' products.

Innovation is one of our core values, and we seem to have forgotten that.

Slide 3 – Feasibility

- Skills and resources

- Time

- Financial

Notes: Feasibility is concerned with whether the strategy could be made to work in practice and, as such, looks at more detailed practicalities of strategic capability.

Fishnet has the skills and resources required. We have talented staff, and we may well be able to recruit internally the five staff needed. We also have premises that can be converted into a development facility. Local contractors are available to do this.

Other than a general sense of urgency, there is no time deadline or constraint on this project.

The Engineering Director has provided a cash flow forecast that shows a payback within the required three years. However, we need to test the various assumptions used to predict the cash flows, in particular those relating to success rates and net cash flow generation. I propose setting up a small project team, to look at our own records and to gather research evidence relating to what is 'normal' for this industry. Staff from Engineering, Finance, Marketing and Operations will be involved.

Slide 4 – Acceptability

- Stakeholder analysis conducted

- All stakeholders should support proposal

Notes: Acceptability is concerned with the expected performance outcomes (such as return or risk) of a strategy and the extent to which these would be in line with the expectations of stakeholders.

Having conducted a stakeholder analysis, the Senior Finance Manager advises me that there should be no issues. All the key stakeholders are likely to support the proposal, and a communication strategy has been developed.

Slide 5 – Conclusion

- Suitable – YES

- Feasible – MAYBE

- Acceptable – YES

Notes: I conclude that a little further work is required to test the financial feasibility of the project. Subject to that, the project should be considered at the next Board meeting.

(c)   Communicating with stakeholders

Assuming that the NPD proposal is approved, I propose the following communication strategy:

1   **Key Players:**

(a)   The Board will receive all the information they require at meetings. They should be briefed on progress and issues at every meeting.

2   **Keep Satisfied:**

(a)   Shareholders should probably be sent a briefing about the project, once work is completed. Relatively few details should be given, as this project is commercially sensitive. Shareholders simply require reassurance that Fishnet is aware of the issue and taking appropriate action.

3   **Keep informed:**

(a)   Suppliers and contractors can be contacted by email. Once the key suppliers have been identified, they will become Key Players in the conversion project, and should be brought onto the project team.

(b)   Current staff could be shown a 'virtual tour' of the new facilities, and briefed by senior management on the background to, and need for, the investment. Internal applications for the new posts should be invited.

4   **Minimal Effort: No action required.**

Failing to communicate effectively with the stakeholders will increase the risk that one or more of them might not support the NPD project, or may take action that prejudices the outcome of the project.

TASK 3

(i)   To: Chair of Risk Management Committee

From: Senior Finance Manager

Date: Today

Subject: Upgrading the CRM system

Big data

Big Data is a term for a collection of data which is so large that it becomes difficult to store and process using traditional databases and data processing applications. Big Data often also includes more than simply financial information and can involve other organisational data (both internal and external), or third-party data, which is often unstructured.

Benefits of big data

The opportunity to incorporate Big Data into the proposed CRM system has the following potential benefits to Fishnet:

•   Big data can drive innovation by reducing the time taken to answer key business questions and therefore make decisions. Fishnet will be able to forecast demand, and better meet the expectations of the supermarkets.

•   It may be possible for Fishnet to gain competitive advantage by identifying trends or information that have not been identified by rivals. This might allow Fishnet to build a new core competence, something it lacks at present.

Risks of big data

- There is a risk that valuable time and money will be spent measuring relationships and information that has no value for the organisation. A database of consumer transaction data may be huge, depending on the time period it covers. Fishnet is not in a position to pass the cost of CRM on to its customers.

- Customer transaction data will rapidly grow, as sales are made, so there is a risk that the costs of storage and processing may spiral out of control. Fishnet's customers may also raise their expectation levels, and ask for more and better analysis.

- Fishnet needs to consider how to keep its data secure from viruses and hackers. There is a risk to data security, though this should be mitigated if storage and processing are outsourced to a reputable supplier (see 'the cloud', below).

- There may be a question over the ownership of the data that the supermarkets have collected on individuals. There may be legal (Data Protection) risks if it holds large amounts of data on consumers, without their consent.

It appears that the IT Director may be unaware of the risks of Big Data, and the level of expertise required to exploit its benefits. Fishnet is a relatively small organisation, with limited IT resource. The IT Director gives the impression that developing a Big Data approach will be simple. This is unlikely to be the case, and simply engaging a supplier will not mitigate many of the risks. Fishnet will need to manage the supplier, but it lacks the expertise to ensure that the supplier's solution avoids or mitigates the risks.

(ii) **'The cloud'**

Cloud computing is a type of Internet-based computing that provides shared computer storage and processing resources to computers, and other devices, on demand. Cloud computing solutions provide users and enterprises with various capabilities to store and process their data in either privately owned, or third-party, data centres that may be located far from the point of data use.

Risks of using (third-party) cloud services

The main risks to Fishnet of using a third-party cloud service are as follows:

- Cloud computing poses integrity risks because the service provider can access the data that is in the cloud at any time. It could accidentally or deliberately alter or even delete information.

- There are also security risks. Many cloud providers can share information with third parties, if necessary for purposes of law and order, even without a warrant. That is permitted in their privacy policies, which users must agree to before they start using cloud services. However, Fishnet could encrypt data that is processed or stored within the cloud, to mitigate the risk.

- There is a further security risk due to unauthorised access. The cloud service provider has to be trusted to put in place an adequate firewall. Fishnet's customers, and their consumers, would react badly to any security breach.

- In cloud computing, the control of the back-end infrastructure is limited to the cloud vendor. Cloud providers often decide on the management policies, which moderates what the cloud users are able to do with their data. There is a risk that Fishnet may not be able to meet the changing needs of their customers.

- Cloud users are also limited in the control and management of their applications, data and services. This includes data caps, which are placed on cloud users by the cloud vendor allocating certain amount of bandwidth for each customer. There is therefore a risk that Fishnet's solution may not be 'scalable' enough to keep up with the growth of the dataset and increasingly complex applications.

Once again, it appears that the IT Director may be unaware of the risks of Cloud Storage. While the level of expertise required to exploit its benefits is nowhere near as great as for Big Data, Fishnet again lacks experience with this technology. The adoption of cloud computing will also require significant risk management effort.

(iii) Choice of discount rate

The business risk inherent in the CRM project is clearly different from the business risk of Fishnet's core business. The proposal to use cloud services and to add big data analytics capabilities increases the project risk.

Fishnet needs to assess the scale of the proposed project, in comparison to the total asset value of the organisation. If the investment is relatively small, it could be argued that use of the current WACC is appropriate.

However, if the investment is substantial, it would be more appropriate for Fishnet to use a risk-adjusted WACC or even a risk-appropriate marginal cost of capital. Both of these are likely to be significantly higher than Fishnet's WACC, so the project might not achieve the positive NPV required to add shareholder value.

MARKING SCHEME

TASK 1

(a) Up to two marks per relevant point for evaluating each of the five forces.

(Up to a maximum of 10 in total)

(b) Up to two marks for each valid point made, in assessing the implications for Fishnet.

(Up to a maximum of 8 in total)

(c) Up to two marks for each valid argument made.　　**(Up to a maximum of 10 in total)**

How well has the candidate demonstrated professional skills as follows:	Not at all	Not so well	Quite well	Very well
(a) Evaluation skills in appraising the business environment	The candidate has demonstrated no evaluation skills. The answer is largely theoretical, or shows little or no understanding of the theoretical model and is therefore just common sense.	The candidate has demonstrated some evaluation skills in appraising the competitive forces on Fishnet. The candidate has used little professional judgement to assess the strength of each force, or has not done so.	The candidate has demonstrated some sound evaluation skills in appraising of the competitive forces on Fishnet. The candidate has used some professional judgement to evaluate the strength of each of the forces.	The candidate has demonstrated excellent evaluation skills. The candidate has used significant professional judgement to evaluate the strength and impact of the forces.
	0	1	2	3

How well has the candidate demonstrated professional skills as follows:	Not at all	Not so well	Quite well	Very well
(b) Commercial acumen skills in demonstrating awareness of the consequences of strategic drift	The candidate has demonstrated no commercial acumen. The candidate has merely restated the information presented and has showed no commercial awareness of the consequences. No use was made of the exhibits provided.	The candidate has demonstrated some limited or naïve commercial acumen. The candidate has demonstrated a limited commercial awareness of the consequences for Fishnet. The candidate made limited reference to the exhibits provided.	The candidate has demonstrated some sound commercial acumen. The candidate has demonstrated some good commercial awareness of the consequences.	The candidate has demonstrated excellent commercial acumen, using the exhibits provided to demonstrate the impact on Fishnet. The candidate has demonstrated strong awareness of the consequences.
	0	0.5	1	2
(c) Communication skills in informing the directors	The candidate has demonstrated poor communication skills. They have failed to present the required information in a clear, objective and unambiguous way. The answer is not communicated in an appropriate format (report) or tone (advice to the Board)	The candidate has demonstrated some basic communication skills in presenting an appropriate report format. Some relevant information is contained in the answer but the steps required are not logical.	The candidate has demonstrated good communication skills in the presentation of the report to Board. The candidate has presented most of the relevant issues and has done so concisely and, in most cases, clearly and logically.	The candidate has demonstrated excellent communication skills. The report was correctly structured, covered all of the relevant points needed by the Board in understanding the issues and was set at the correct tone.
	0	1	2	3

TASK 2

(a) Up to TWO marks for each relevant stakeholder: One mark for identifying and referencing to the strategy; half a mark for an appropriate view of power and interest; a further half mark for the classification ('key player' etc.).

(Up to a maximum of 12 in total)

(b) Up to two marks each for Suitability and Acceptability – the former to reference SWOT or position and environment, the latter the analysis carried out above. Up to 1 mark for each aspect of Feasibility, other than financial. Up to 2 marks for financial feasibility, including the use of the information provided in the spreadsheet.

(Up to a maximum of 10 in total)

(c) Up to TWO marks for each stakeholder, clearly referenced to the analysis carried out above. Communication methods must be specific (e.g. have a meeting with…) not generic (e.g. speak to).

(Up to a maximum of 8 in total)

How well has the candidate demonstrated professional skills as follows:	Not at all	Not so well	Quite well	Very well
(a) Analysis skills in considering the issues	The candidate has demonstrated very limited analysis skills. The candidate has failed to analyse the information carefully. The candidate has simply identified stakeholders.	The candidate has demonstrated some analysis skills in classifying the stakeholders. However, there is only some evidence of reflection on how these might affect the strategy.	The candidate has demonstrated analysis skills in classifying the stakeholders. The candidate has made a reasonable attempt to comment and reflect on how these might affect the NPD strategy.	The candidate has demonstrated excellent analysis skills in classifying the stakeholders. The candidate has also demonstrated sound evidence of high levels of reflection on how these might affect the NPD strategy.
	0	1	2	3
(b) Communication skills in informing the directors	The candidate has demonstrated poor communication skills. They have failed to present the required information in a clear, objective and unambiguous way. The answer is not communicated in an appropriate format (slides) or tone (to inform the directors)	The candidate has demonstrated some basic communication skills in presenting an appropriate presentation format. Some relevant information is contained in the answer but the tone is not appropriate to the audience.	The candidate has demonstrated good communication skills in the presentation. The candidate has presented most of the relevant issues and has done so concisely and in most cases, clearly.	The candidate has demonstrated excellent communication skills. The presentation was correctly structured, covered all of the relevant points needed by the board in understanding the issues and was set at the correct tone.
	0	0.5	1	2
(c) Communication skills in persuading the CEO	The candidate has demonstrated poor communication skills. They have failed to present the required information in a clear, objective and unambiguous way. The answer is not communicated in an appropriate format (report) or tone (to persuade the CEO)	The candidate has demonstrated some basic communication skills in presenting an appropriate report format. Some relevant information is contained in the answer but the tone is not persuasive.	The candidate has demonstrated good communication skills in the presentation of the report to the CEO. The candidate has presented most of the relevant issues and has done so concisely and in most cases, clearly.	The candidate has demonstrated excellent communication skills. The report was correctly structured, covered all of the relevant points needed by the CEO in understanding the issues and was set at the correct tone. A persuasive response.
	0	1	2	3

TASK 3

(i) Up to TWO marks for each relevant benefit (up to four of) and risk (up to four of). Each must be evaluated – an opinion should be expressed as to the significance or impact – in order to earn two marks. **(Up to a maximum of 10 in total)**

(ii) Up to two marks for each relevant risk. **(Up to a maximum of 10 in total)**

(iii) Up to two marks for discussion of the discount rate.

How well has the candidate demonstrated professional skills as follows:	Not at all	Not so well	Quite well	Very well
Scepticism skills in challenging the director's views	The candidate has failed to demonstrate any scepticism. The candidate demonstrated no evidence of challenging or questioning the statements or opinions of the Director.	The candidate has demonstrated some, but limited, scepticism regarding the opinions and assertions made by the Director. The candidate questioned some of the statements. However, the depth of the questioning was limited and the challenge to the opinions was not presented in a professional manner.	The candidate has demonstrated scepticism of the opinions and assertions made by the Director. The challenge of the Director's opinions was reasonably sound. The challenge to the opinions could have been presented in a more professional manner.	The candidate has demonstrated deep scepticism of the opinions and assertions made by the Director. The candidate strongly questioned, with evidence, the validity of the opinions, in a professional and justified manner.
	0	1	2	4

Section 5

SPECIMEN 1 EXAM QUESTIONS

1 HOI LUI

You are Hoi Lui, a management consultant leading a small team which has been commissioned to prepare a consultancy report for the Data Communications Services (DCS) Company directors to help them plan for the next three years. DCS Company has two product areas. The largest area is the manufacture of data communications components which it mainly sells to original equipment manufacturers (OEM). The other smaller and less developed area is based on supply and support contracts for specialist IT management network systems, mainly to domestic medium-sized enterprises. You are a qualified accountant and your colleagues are Danny Leman, a company researcher, and Freddie Lithium who is a part-qualified finance professional. You and your team have collected and analysed the following information about DCS Company to help you prepare the consultancy report.

Exhibit 1: A report on DCS Company's organisational overview, the external environment and the business model sourced and prepared by Danny Leman, your colleague

Exhibit 2: A transcript from interview which was held between you and Java Peraya, the CEO of DCS Company.

Exhibit 3: Summary of financial and business performance of DCS Company extracted from the Integrated Report (2012–2015) presented to you by the finance director of DCS Company

Exhibit 4: The October board report, a recent board meeting notes which include strategic choices facing DCS Company – presented to you by the marketing manager of DCS Company

Exhibit 5: An evaluation of alternative future strategies being considered by the DCS Company board, prepared and presented to you by your colleague, Freddie Lithium

Exhibit 6: Minutes from the focus group meeting you held with middle management of DCS Company

Following your findings you are now starting to prepare the consultancy report and associated tasks for DCS Company.

The case requirements are included in the tasks shown below.

TASK 1

(a)   From the information you have collated, draft a section of the consultancy report for the directors of DCS Company to include the following:

   (I)   An analysis of the industry and market which DCS Company is competing in, using an appropriate model.   **(15 marks)**

   (II)   An evaluation of the overall performance of DCS Company between 2012 and 2015 from an integrated reporting perspective.   **(12 marks)**

   Professional Skills marks are available for demonstrating evaluation skills relating to DCS Company's environment and performance.   **(4 marks)**

(b)   You are now reviewing the transcript of the interview you held with Java Peraya, the CEO of DCS Company and you identify some key weaknesses relating to the governance of DCS Company which you want to include in the consultancy report.

Required:

Explain the key weaknesses of the current governance structure of DCS Company since it became a public limited company, recommending how they should be addressed. **(12 marks)**

Professional Skills marks are available for demonstrating scepticism skills in identifying key weaknesses from the information given.   **(2 marks)**

(c)   Under the Strategy and resource allocation heading in the October board report, the possibility of DCS Company supplying and supporting such technologies as cloud computing and big data analytics is referred to. To accompany the consultancy report a presentation is needed about the exploitation of such new technologies.

Required:

Prepare information for two presentation slides to be presented to the DCS Company board, including relevant bullet points and supporting notes, highlighting the key benefits and identifying the main opportunities presented by big data analytics to DCS Company and its customers. **(6 marks)**

Professional Skills marks are available for demonstrating communication skills in highlighting the key points to include in the slides and for clear supporting notes.
(2 marks)

(d)   You have noted from information you have gathered that DCS Company has an increasing carbon footprint, which it estimates in total, but is failing to control adequately. As part of the consultancy report you are considering recommending to DCS Company that it commissions a specialist environment and sustainability consultancy company to assess these issues at DCS Company.

Required:

Draft a concise section of the consultancy report which constructs the case for commissioning an environmental and sustainability audit of DCS Company, from both a financial and environmental perspective, suggesting ways in which the consultants might assist DCS Company managers to become more sustainable in the management of the DCS Company carbon footprint. **(5 marks)**

Professional Skills marks are available for demonstrating commercial acumen in identifying how DCS Company could benefit from the findings of the audit.   **(2 marks)**

(Total: 60 marks)

TASK 2

In the October board report, the executive directors refer to a number of factors affecting DCS Company and the need to choose one of two alternative strategic options. You now need to do the following:

Required:

(a) Draft a section of the report to identify and briefly discuss THREE main risks which DCS Company currently faces and plot them on a heat map, recommending appropriate strategies to manage those risks using an appropriate risk management framework. **(6 marks)**

Professional Skills marks are available for demonstrating commercial acumen in identifying and locating the risks appropriately. **(2 marks)**

(b) You are reviewing the spreadsheet prepared by your colleague Freddie Lithium which evaluates the strategic choices facing DCS Company in the next three years, to ensure its validity in supporting your recommendation in the consultancy report.

Required:

(i) Critically evaluate the contents of the spreadsheet including any assumption made by the DCS Company board. **(5 marks)**

Professional Skills marks are available for demonstrating scepticism skills in analysing the spreadsheet and any supporting assumptions. **(2 marks)**

(ii) Prepare some key recommendations for the consultancy report, using appropriate supporting evidence to advise which of the two strategies, re-focus or re-align, DCS Company should implement. **(5 marks)**

Professional Skills marks are available for demonstrating commercial acumen skills in justifying the recommendations. **(2 marks)**

(Total: 22 marks)

TASK 3

You have highlighted from your interview with Java Peraya and from your notes from the middle management focus group meeting, that there are some key stakeholder management and engagement issues at DCS Company.

You are now preparing working notes, with relevant visual aids, which will form a key part of your presentation of the overall consultancy report.

Required:

(a) Using appropriate stakeholder analysis, evaluate how the relative power and interests of the following three stakeholder groups and the strategies for engaging with them should have changed after DCS Company became a public limited company.

- Shareholders;
- Employees;
- Lenders. **(9 marks)**

Professional Skills marks are available for analytical skills for assessing the relative power and interest and how to engage with these stakeholders before and after flotation. **(2 marks)**

(b)   **Criticise the CEO's and HR director's ethical and professional behaviour relating to the design, conduct, and reporting of the staff satisfaction survey.   (5 marks)**

Professional Skills marks are available for scepticism skills in identifying ethical and professional issues in the conduct of the survey and communicating these criticisms to the client in a way that is appropriate.   **(2 marks)**

(Total: 18 marks)

EXHIBIT 1

BACKGROUND REPORT TO THE DCS COMPANY

To:	Hoi Lui
From:	Danny Leman
Subject:	Organisational overview, the external environment and the DCS business model
Date:	20 November 2015

Notes:

Organisational overview

Data Communications Systems (DCS), a publicly listed company on the small companies' capitalisation (SmallCap) index of a national stock exchange, used to be a privately owned high technology company established in 1997 by computer engineer, Java Peraya. Due to a rapid expansion over the following years, DCS needed to source additional capital to fund its future growth and was floated on the national stock exchange in 2006. This allowed Java Peraya to realise his majority shareholding in the private company. 30% of the flotation was purchased by institutional investors and DCS also borrowed long-term funds to leverage the newly issued share capital. Before flotation, the company was almost exclusively financed from the founders' share capital, retained earnings and short-term finance.

External environment

DCS has its headquarters in Prydain, a prosperous developed nation with a stable and well established political system and which has highly developed labour laws including a national minimum wage and a newly introduced obligatory contributory pension scheme. The government, like many governments worldwide, has invested heavily in a national telecommunications infrastructure which has led to a significant growth in social media and where virtually 75% of the population are connected to the internet through a range of devices including mobile technology. The government is also proposing a new carbon tax which will affect companies which manufacture and provide IT network services such as data communications components and systems. The electronics and IT industry has recently been identified as a sector with an increasing carbon footprint caused by their applications, such as component cooling devices, complex telecommunications network components and cloud computing technology. Although DCS Company can approximately estimate its total carbon footprint from the manufacture and supply of components from its factory, it has not yet developed formal systems and processes to manage its carbon footprint throughout the value chain.

Business model

DCS has two distinct product/service areas – data communications components manufacture and the supply and maintenance of network management systems, including technical support.

The DCS employees are a mixture of technically qualified engineers, working in research and development (R&D), factory staff manufacturing and assembling products and an IT sales and service support team. Since the flotation of the company, 60% of production employees in the data communications components factory joined a major trade union. In 2012 the country suffered an economic downturn which led many companies to postpone technological investment and by then DCS employed 150 full-time employees.

The main revenue source for DCS is the high-volume low cost data communications component manufacture part of the business and it has 1% of the total market share, which accounts for approximately 65% of DCS's total turnover. DCS mainly sells and supplies large volumes of data communications components to original equipment manufacturers (OEMs), 30% of which are based outside Prydain on a continent which has a single currency which is devaluing against the Prydain dollar. Success in the data communications components sector comes from the economies of scale achieved by producing high volumes of reliable components and keeping prices low. DCS Company has achieved this despite producing components in a country where there is significant employment legislation setting minimum wage rates and conditions.

The second product area is much smaller and is based on supply and support contracts for specialist IT management network management systems, mainly to domestic medium-sized enterprises, which currently yields a relatively higher gross profit margin than the data communications component products. A key aspect of this second product area is the installation and support of big data analytics capability along with cloud computing storage, which can be used to replace existing costly IT architectures such as unsophisticated data warehouses to allow business clients to collect and analyse more targeted and timely data about their own customers and purchasing patterns. Much of this can be obtained from data held within social and business networking software.

EXHIBIT 2

TRANSCRIPT FROM INTERVIEW HELD BETWEEN YOU AND JAVA PERAYA, THE CEO OF DCS COMPANY.

You: Thank you very much Mr Peraya for showing me around the offices and factory. I found your staff and their comments very interesting.

First of all, could I ask you to tell me how you would describe how your company is structured and managed?

Java: I would describe DCS as fairly highly centralised. I suppose in 'management speak' we would describe the DCS management structure as a 'functional bureaucracy'. We prefer not to allow too much managerial or departmental autonomy, for their own good of course, to ensure that they act in the best interest of DCS and to avoid irresponsible risk taking, which unfortunately has happened occasionally in the past.

We expect middle managers to respect and respond positively to senior management requests or directives and not to question these unless they are very sure of their facts. This is probably a legacy from the pre-flotation era, where much of the strategic direction was always decided by me and my closest senior directors, most of whom were my family and trusted friends.

You: Would you mind explaining how your company is directed by describing your corporate governance arrangements to me please?

Java: Yes I can – please look at this chart.

Java hands you an extract of the organisational chart represented below:

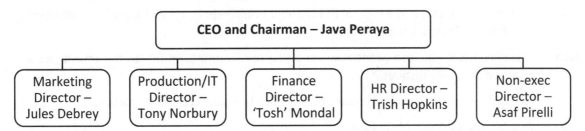

Java: Since 2006 DCS has been governed by a board of directors with me acting as CEO and chairman, giving me sufficient control to effectively direct the company and take strong leadership over the board, encouraging debate and driving the agenda. The board comprises a marketing director, Jules. He was my original sales manager employed by the company, who I have known a long time now. We also have a production and IT director, Tony, who has been with the company for over 10 years. He has a strong background in data communications hardware components. Tosh is our finance director. He joined the company just before the company was listed on the national stock exchange. Trish Hopkins is our female HR director and we also benefit from an independent non-executive member of the board. We were very fortunate to appoint Asaf because he is a very talented businessman and also an executive director of one of our two largest suppliers. This means that he has a really good knowledge of our business and of the data communications industry.

You: That is really useful background Mr Peraya. So what about standing governance committees which presumably report to the board?

Java: We have an audit committee constituted of three experienced network engineers who focus on and investigate internal control and quality failures when they arise. To promote more independence, we have also appointed a non-executive director as chairman on this committee who is a former compliance officer at an airport, whose background is in air traffic control and aviation regulation, but she is also a telecommunications expert.

You: What about a risk committee and do you have nominations or remunerations committees?

Java: DCS has no separate board appointed risk, remuneration or nominations committees. All strategic and long-term planning initiatives are initiated and decided upon by the main board led by myself and, of course, our management structure and culture is such that we embed risk management through having that close control over staff that I mentioned to you previously. As for salary, we strongly believe that all board members should be on a fixed salary to encourage them to take a longer term perspective rather than rewarding them with short-term performance bonuses.

As far as recruitment, remuneration and succession planning is concerned, I personally approve and manage all middle to senior staff recruitment and staff promotions, so there is no need for formal induction processes for our directors or senior management.

You: Now that you are a listed company, how do you report to and engage with your shareholders, particularly institutional shareholders?

Java: DCS does not have special governance or reporting structures to engage with shareholders, including institutional shareholders, but of course we do meet our minimum company law obligations in relation to statutory reporting to shareholders, shareholder democracy, voting and other constitutional rights.

You: That was all very useful Mr Peraya, but what I would like now is more data on the overall performance of DCS and a copy of the October board report, which I know was considering the strategic options facing DCS.

Java: Certainly, I will ask Tosh Mondal to send you our summarised integrated reporting data attached on a spreadsheet.

I will also ask the marketing director to send you the board report for October.

You: Thank you very much Mr Peraya.

EXHIBIT 3

EXTRACTS OF THE INTEGRATED REPORTING DATA (2012–2015) FROM THE FINANCE DIRECTOR – TOSH MONDAL

Financial performance: (all figures in $m)

Financial periods:	2015	2014	2013	2012
Sales revenue (domestic and international)	6.95	7.40	6.80	4.75
Cost of sales	4.97	4.85	4.25	2.62
Gross profit	1.98	2.55	2.55	2.13
Overhead expenses	1.12	1.51	1.41	1.30
Profit before tax and finance costs	0.86	1.04	1.14	0.83
Finance costs	0.69	0.38	0.37	0.14
Tax expense	0.02	0.06	0.08	0.15
Profit for the year	0.15	0.60	0.69	0.54

Other data:	2015	2014	2013	2012
Number of employees	127	135	143	150
Staff turnover (%)	10%	7%	5%	4%
% of orders delivered late	10%	8%	7%	5%
Forward contract order book (number of orders)	2,500	3,750	4,150	3,505
Customer complaints as a percentage of total orders and existing contracts	3.4%	2.4%	2.0%	1.5%
Employee satisfaction survey score (100% max)	61%	65%	68%	72%
Investment in non-current manufacturing equipment as a percentage of sales revenue	7%	8%	8%	10%
R&D expenditure as a percentage of sales revenue	3%	5%	5%	6%
Carbon emissions in kg per $1,000 sales revenue	80	75	65	60

EXHIBIT 4

THE OCTOBER BOARD REPORT FOR DCS COMPANY

To:	The Board of Directors – DCS
Subject:	Strategic overview – DCS Company
From:	Jules Debrey (marketing director)
Date:	12 October 2015

Introduction

This report is based on information obtained from all the executive directors of DCS, under several main headings. The report highlights risks, opportunities and the future outlook for DCS. It also focuses on strategy and resource allocation, highlighting a key strategic decision which the board will need to make in the near future.

Risks and opportunities: What are the specific risks and opportunities which affect DCS's ability to create value over the short, medium and long term, and how is the organisation dealing with them?

By 2014, the international market for data communication components started to saturate and decline.

For the supply and support of contracts for specialist IT network management systems, we are now finding it increasingly difficult and costly to maintain the required level of network support. It is getting harder to recruit high calibre staff to DCS. The headquarters of DCS, although a modern site, is in a geographical location which is unattractive for key personnel to relocate to. Our specialists in the systems support side of the business are currently overstretched because many key staff have been 'head hunted' or taken early retirement.

Lenders have until recently been quite willing to lend DCS additional long-term funds at competitive interest rates, but are now tightening their credit lines to the company and placing covenants on us to keep financial gearing within acceptable limits. They are also increasing their interest rates to compensate for the additional financial risk. It is unlikely that any future growth or investment can be financed from further debt and we would need to use our considerable cash reserves or utilise internally generated funds. Currently, DCS has a geared cost of equity capital of 12%.

Future outlook: What challenges and uncertainties is DCS likely to encounter in pursuing its strategy, and what are the potential implications for its business model and future performance?

DCS currently manufactures approximately 50% of all data communications components used in its own products. The rest of the complete components, including semiconductors and microprocessors, are bought in from two multi-national global suppliers. These suppliers have since 2006 become the key players in the market through a succession of acquisitions and mergers, where previously there were many more suppliers, all with a much smaller market share. Recently, serious production problems have resulted from periodic component shortages from these key suppliers, creating significant delays in manufacturing, assembly and customer deliveries. One of our recently acquired OEM customers accounts for 40% of our sales in this area.

Marketing forecasts for 2016 and beyond indicate stronger growth from the supply and sales support for specialised IT management services to currently installed networks in the domestic financial sector, rather than from the manufacture of components to OEMs or for the installation of new networks to large companies. The other potential growth area is in providing cloud computing and big data analytics capability to the SME sector. Including DCS, there are currently only three companies which provide these specialist services in Prydain.

Strategy and resource allocation: Where does DCS want to go and how does it intend to get there?

As executive directors, we need an appropriate strategy for the next three to five years. On current trends we are looking at approximately a 10% year on year decline in our revenues for the next three years. At this forthcoming board meeting we need to discuss and decide on the best strategy for us as a company.

We need to decide between two strategies. Do we re-align the business to make it less reliant on the high volume, low margin components segment and re-allocate resources from the data communications segment into this higher added-value sector of network management and support? To do this we will need to further exploit technologies such as cloud computing and, in particular, big data analytics which seem to offer lower cost data storage, better understanding of consumer preferences and ability to develop more bespoke products and services. Alternatively, should we re-focus on our core capability in the data communications components manufacturing area, where we have such expertise, experience and where most of our turnover is currently generated?

Conclusions

The DCS board should now evaluate the risks and opportunities and take a key decision. DCS also needs to consider how it will implement its chosen strategy and how it will finance it. See further information below.

Forecast tangible benefits and costs resulting from various potential scenarios

In 2015 we have estimated that the net cash contribution from the data communications components segment of the business is $1.55m and the net cash contribution from the network supply and support is $0.85m. These are after interest and tax. The expectation is that total cash flow contribution will continue to decline by about 10% each year if we do nothing.

Re-focus strategy

We can implement this strategy by re-organising our sales and support teams, making manufacturing cost efficiencies and targeting our data communications component customers more effectively. If we are successful, we estimate that we can at least maintain the total cash contribution of DCS at the current level of $2.4m for the next three years.

Re-alignment strategy

With a re-alignment of the business towards the network supply and support segment, the net cash contribution from the communications components sector is forecast to decline by 10% per year for the following three years. This is regardless of how the net cash contribution from the network and IT systems support business is expected to grow under any of our assumptions. Forecast annual fixed costs and working capital savings from the decline in the data communications manufacturing area are expected to be $0.35m from general costs and will also result in annual carbon tax cost savings of $0.15m, giving a total saving of $500,000 per annum for the next three years (2016–18). Note that these forecast savings are independent of which growth forecast below emerges.

Table 1 below shows the projected growth in the cash flow from the network supply and support segment in the next three years; the additional fixed costs of this investment; and the savings to be made in the data communications division, should the re-alignment and additional investments take place.

Table 1: Alternative growth forecasts for DCS Company under the re-alignment strategy

Re-alignment strategy and probabilities for growth	Probability of growth materialising	Forecast annual increase in cash fixed costs	Forecast annual savings from decline in data communications segment
	(%)	($m)	($m)
Additional cash contribution from the network support business will grow by 25% each year for the next three years from the 2014 level	60	+0.75	−0.5
Additional cash contribution from network support business will grow by 15% each year for the next three years from the 2014 level	30	+0.45	−0.5
Additional cash contribution from network support business will grow by 10% each year for the next three years from the 2014 level	10	+0.25	−0.5

EXHIBIT 5

AN EVALUATION OF STRATEGY CHOICES FACING DCS COMPANY

You asked your colleague Freddie Lithium to evaluate the alternative strategies based on the information contained in the October board report. Freddie has now given you his work in the spreadsheet below:

Strategy evaluation for DCS, using payback method						
Strategy 1: Re-focus strategy:			2015	2016	2017	2018
With total cash contribution maintained:			$m	$m	$m	$m
Data communications			1.55			
Network supply and support			0.85			
(1) Total for Strategy 1:			2.40	2.40	2.40	2.40
Strategy 2: Re-alignment strategy	Growth:		Probability:			
Network supply and support ($0.85m)	25%		0.60	1.063	1.328	1.660
	15%		0.30	0.978	1.124	1.293
	10%		0.10	0.935	1.029	1.131
(2) Expected value from network growth:				1.024	1.237	1.497
(3) Data communications ($1.55m)	10%	decline	1.55	1.395	1.256	1.130
(4) Total cash contribution from Strategy 2: (2 + 3)				2.419	2.492	2.627
(5) Incremental cash contribution (4 − 1):				0.019	0.092	0.227
Additional annual fixed costs based on expected growth:						
	Growth:	$m	Probability:			
Network supply and support ($0.85m)	25%	0.75	0.60			
				0.450	0.450	0.450
	15%	0.45	0.30	0.135	0.135	0.135
	10%	0.25	0.10	0.025	0.025	0.025
(6) Expected value of additional cash fixed costs:				0.610	0.610	0.610
(7) Cash fixed cost savings (Data comms)				0.500	0.500	0.500
(8) Net additional cash fixed costs:				0.110	0.110	0.110
Incremental cash contribution from Strategy 2: (5)				0.019	0.092	0.227
Incremental cash fixed costs (8)				0.110	0.110	0.110
Incremental net cash contribution from Strategy 2 compared with Strategy 1				−0.091	−0.018	0.117
Cumulative payback period = 2 years and eleven months						

EXHIBIT 6

NOTES FROM THE MIDDLE MANAGEMENT FOCUS GROUP MEETING

Having read the integrated reporting data and studying the transcript of the conversation you had with Java Peraya, you needed more background information about some of the key issues which had come to your attention. You therefore invited a representative team of middle managers to a focus group meeting and asked them key questions, from which the following comments were noted:

Quote 1 from a management accountant in the finance directorate

"When undertaking capital investment appraisal we have a strict policy of evaluating investments or projects over a maximum of three years and to ignore cash flows beyond that date, to ensure that any investment we make must pay back within that time period. This ensures that we do not accept unviable projects."

Quote 2 from an engineer in the network supply division:

"What really annoys me is the fact that in 2011, the CEO and HR director introduced an annual staff survey. Although they promised anonymity, the survey required us to give details of our age, ethnicity, length of service and the department in which we are employed. I was called to a meeting last year by the production manager who implicitly threatened me and made comments such as 'if you don't like working here, why not look for another job?' It was made very clear to me that this meeting was private and was to be kept confidential. I was not permitted to discuss the existence or outcomes of these meetings with other members of staff, or there would be consequences."

Quote 3 from a technician in the data communications components division:

"I felt the staff satisfaction survey was designed in a way which dissuaded negative feedback and key issues known to be of concern to staff obtained from the informal 'grapevine' were deliberately omitted from the survey questions. In addition, the way the results were presented by managers, and the visual graphics used, seemed to play down the negative feedback and concentrated only on the positive factors. For example, emphasis was made of how well staff regarded their own performance, and that of their team members, which seemed to have more favourable feedback, compared with other questions about confidence in the leadership of the company. I didn't think this presented the true picture of our feelings."

Quote 4 from a sales support engineer:

"We are rushed off our feet. Due to key staff leaving, our sales areas are getting larger and it is difficult to get around to all our customers. This means we have difficulty getting our orders in on time and are often late to appointments. Although sales productivity might be improving, because fewer of us are covering a greater geographical area, customers are not as satisfied as they used to be and are making more complaints."

After this meeting you went back to your office and scheduled a meeting in the following week with Danny and Freddie, to start preparing the consultancy report findings for DCS Company.

END OF QUESTION

Section 6

SPECIMEN 1 EXAM ANSWERS

1   HOI LUI

TASK 1

(a)   Background section of consultancy report

One mark per relevant point for discussing any relevant environmental model such as Porters five forces, or PESTLE.

Introduction

The first part of this report analyses DCS Company's market and the industry using the Porter's Five Forces model.

(i)   Bargaining power of buyers

DCS is competing in two markets. In the data communications component market which is more mature and where it has less than 1% of the market share, it is a supplier of marginal significance, despite 65% of its gross profit or cash contribution being generated in this segment. Its customers in the neighbouring single market (30%) with its own currency are likely to demand low prices, high quality and reliability. They may not accept late delivery of orders. It appears that alternative sources of supply are readily available and that switching costs are relatively low. Multinational OEMs have significant bargaining power in this market, particularly the OEM which accounts for 40% of DCS's current data communications component sales.

In the second market, where network management systems are supplied to mainly domestic, SMEs and a few larger companies, the buyers appear to have less bargaining power. DCS is catering for each customer's specific needs and so each solution is, to some degree, a bespoke solution. This makes it much harder for buyers to compare products and prices of potential suppliers. Alternative sources of supply are much more difficult to find as there only three companies (including DCS) in this specialist marketplace.

The bargaining power of suppliers

Although DCS manufactures 50% of all components used in its data communications products, reducing its overall reliance on suppliers in this sector, it seems unlikely that DCS will be able to exert much influence on its suppliers, which provide the other 50%. As a relatively small player in the data communications market, the company does not have the power to exert buyer pressure on its two large suppliers, either in terms of price or delivery. Current problems associated with the delivery of components are having a significant impact on the company's ability to meet customer deadlines and expectations.

Suppliers of financial capital, namely lenders, have gained more bargaining power as DCS has had to borrow more to sustain their recent growth.

If labour is seen as a supplier, then evidence again suggests that DCS is in a relatively weak position particularly since there has been a limited trade union membership since 2006. However, the union members are mainly in the data communications components division where employee remuneration and employment rights are already compliant with Prydain's national employment laws. The scenario also indicates the difficulty of finding high calibre network staff with DCS's small size and location making it difficult to attract the key personnel necessary for future growth in this sector.

Threats from new entrants

DCS is operating in an industry where the costs of entry are significant because it is capital and knowledge intensive. Economies of scale compel new entrants to enter at significant output levels or suffer a cost disadvantage. Furthermore, the need to offer comprehensive aftersales support, although a problem for DCS, does also create a significant barrier to new entrants. Finally, the exit costs and barriers such as industry-specific knowledge, skills and assets, reduce the attractiveness of the marketplace to new entrants.

Threats from substitutes

There is evidence that large, successful, high technology companies are particularly vulnerable to ignoring the challenge from disruptive new technologies which can replace the need for certain high technology products and services overnight. However, the relatively small size of DCS may give it a competitive advantage in its ability to respond quickly and flexibly to change, as long as it can attract the right calibre of expertise to achieve this.

Rivalry amongst competitors

Very different levels of competition are being experienced in the two market places DCS is operating in. It is clear that the high volume, low-margin component business offers intense competition with buyers who are able to use their size to extract favourable prices. DCS only has 1% of this market. The ability of DCS to generate better market share and volumes through product innovation in this market seems highly unlikely.

The intensity of rivalry in the network management systems sector is significantly less in this specialist market. DCS is dealing with a smaller number of large and medium-sized users, designing products specific to their needs. In Porter's terms, DCS is adopting a focused differentiation strategy. In these low-volume high-margin markets, the emphasis has to be on increasing the volume side of the business, but at the same time making sure that they have the resources to attract and support new customers.

(ii) The following is an evaluation of the performance of DCS against the six capitals of <IR> and how these are being transformed at DCS between 2012 and 2015.

Financial capital

The financial data shows revenue reaching a peak in 2014, before falling away (by just over 9%) in 2015.

Although 2014 was a record year for revenues, increased cost of sales meant that gross profit declined significantly. The gross profit margin has declined every year in the period under consideration, and the reasons for this need to be investigated. The rapid fall in 2015 suggests that operating costs have not been brought under control to reflect the sudden sales decline.

	2015	2014	2013	2012
Gross profit margin (gross profit/revenue)	28.49%	34.46%	37.50%	44.84%

In 2015, although DCS seems to have made reductions in overhead costs, finance costs have increased despite the fall in revenue, leading to a progressive decline in net profit margin in the period under consideration.

	2015	2014	2013	2012
Net profit margin (net profit before interest and tax/revenue)	2.16%	8.11%	10.15%	11.37%

The overall financial picture is of a company which has failed to control its core operating and finance costs as it generated increases in revenue until 2014 and as revenues fell in 2015. Finance costs are increasing as a proportion of net profit before interest and tax (NPBIT) as shown below:

	2015	2014	2013	2012
Interest cover ratio (finance costs/NPBIT)	1.26	2.74	3.08	5.93

Manufacturing capital

Working manufacturing capital seems to be reducing. This is confirmed by the forward contract order book. This has fallen from 3,505 in 2012 to 2,500 which will require fewer components, work-in-progress and finished products needed at the factory. It is also clear that capital budgeting and investment is slowing from 10% to 7% of turnover over the period. The R&D budget is also falling and is at 3% of turnover in 2015 compared with 6% in 2012, which is a 50% decline. These statistics indicate a clear depletion of the manufacturing capital of DCS.

Human capital

DCS seems to be seeing a depletion of high value human capital and morale may be seen as low. Recruitment and succession planning seem to be poorly planned and coordinated – leading to insufficient skilled people being recruited or promoted to replace staff either leaving the company or retiring early. There is just over 15% fewer staff at DCS in 2015 compared with 2012.

However, human capital has performed reasonably well from a productivity perspective. Analysing the data, productivity reached a peak in 2014 and has only fallen slightly in the last financial year:

	2015	2014	2013	2012
Sales revenue per employee (000)	54.72	54.81	47.55	31.66

The sales support element of human capital is not performing well, however. The number of late contracts has doubled since 2012 and the number of complaints from customers has increased from 1.5% of orders to 3.4%.

Social and relationship capital

Social capital measures cultural health within the company and one of the ways this can be assessed is by using staff satisfaction surveys. The case indicates that employee satisfaction has been declining between 2012 and 2015. The increase in trade union membership may be a symptom of this. The case indicates that the survey measures such aspects as confidence in the leadership, opinions about personal growth and individual wellbeing. Each year since the surveys were launched, the satisfaction ratings have fallen by more than 15%.

Intellectual capital

Another area where DCS seems to be failing is in its maintenance and transformation of intellectual capital. There has been a depletion of intellectual capital, through skilled staff being either underutilised or leaving the company. This can be related to two areas:

– Staff turnover

– R&D.

Clearly the stock of intellectual capital is closely correlated to the stock of human and cultural capital. DCS seems to be depleting all three of these and its staff turnover has increased by 150% since 2012.

Natural capital

It is clear that DCS has a growing carbon 'footprint' and that it is unable to identify where precisely in its value chain the carbon footprint is most problematic. The information in the case shows that the overall carbon emissions are increasing. Carbon emissions have risen by 1/3 since 2012.

The case clearly indicates that the main cause of the carbon footprint is in the data communications components manufacturing division. This is already a high volume and relatively lower margin sector of the business which will be subject to additional carbon taxes under the government proposals. There is also likely to be a greater carbon cost with this sector as a significant proportion of these components are exported to the nearby continental trading community.

Conclusions

DCS needs to be aware of the dynamics relating to its market and industry, particularly the power of key customers and over reliance on two main suppliers. It must also be aware of and manage the threats from substitutes and new entrants in its two main business segments.

On the company's performance against the six capitals of <IR>, DCS's performance in several areas is weak and indicates a strategic drift which will need to be addressed.

(b) **Governance and internal control Introduction**

In DCS's case there seem to be significant shortcomings in regard to the governance structures against broad principles of good governance. In particular, as a listed company, the board of DCS Company will be accountable to institutional investors. This formal investor relations function seems to be lacking at DCS and should be formalised. However, there are general weaknesses in a range of governance arrangements at DCS and these include weak internal controls, which are a key responsibility of the audit committee and these may have led to the poorly managed R&D policy and the ineffective capital budgeting process.

These specific shortcomings are as follows:

Non-separation of the role of chairman and CEO

This is a serious weakness and leads to lack of independence within the board by vesting too much power in one individual who may be able to dominate the board of DCS. The two roles are very different in nature. The CEO is responsible for directing and implementing strategic plans and for leading the executive team. The chairman is responsible for ensuring that the board of directors operates effectively, that it is properly constituted and is managed impartially to encourage open and transparent discussion. These roles should be separated.

Lack of independent non-executive directors and diversity

DCS only has one independent NED to scrutinise the executive directors and to exercise independence of judgement and scepticism where appropriate. DCS's independent NED is an executive director of one of DCS's two main suppliers which is inappropriate. The company should appoint NEDs who are 'independent' and increase the diversity of the board, both in terms of functional expertise and business acumen and to benefit from the broader experience of those who have worked for other companies. The gender balance on the board needs addressing. Only the HR director is female.

No director or senior management induction policy

There seems to be no director induction process at DCS which is important in ensuring that directors and senior managers understand the mission, strategic objectives and cultural values of the organisation. Introducing such a programme will help integrate new senior staff into DCS and help them make more immediate and valuable contributions.

Lack of risk, nominations and remuneration committees

DCS seems to have no formal board appointed committees for the above. A public limited company is expected to have a committee which identifies, assesses and recommends strategies to mitigate risk. There is also no independent committee to consider board appointments or their pay structure. A particular problem related to appointments and rewards is evident from the case. At the senior level, this could have been avoided by having a formal nominations and remunerations committee to consider such appointments. A key shortcoming is the failure to adequately align director pay with the longer-term interests of the shareholders. No-one on the board is allowed share options and all are on a fixed salary meaning that company performance is not aligned to their rewards. A nominations committee would also have addressed some of the problems regarding poor selection and appointment of senior candidates, and the lack of succession planning.

Poorly constituted audit committee

The audit committee seems to be unsatisfactory for a number of reasons. First there seems to be no-one with any real financial expertise and this may be why costs are getting out of control. Most of the members are technical managers from the operating core of the business. There is only one independent NED when generally accepted principles of corporate governance would recommend at least two, if not more. The audit committee does not seem to have proper oversight over the capital budgeting of the company or scrutinise significant expenditure on capital expenditure or R&D. DCS should therefore change the constitution of the audit committee to include more NEDs and members with more financial expertise. It should also review the remit of the audit committee to include induction and responsibility for oversight of the capital budgeting process, and to scrutinise the effectiveness of the financial reporting process, and its relationship with external auditors.

Inadequate reporting and engagement with institutional shareholders

There is a block of 30% institutional investors who seem to be largely ignored or treated as if they were like any other private individual shareholder. This is a key weakness as the institutional block vote is significant and if the shareholding is withdrawn or sold, this could create uncertainty in the market and a serious reduction in the share price. DCS needs to create formal reporting and communication channels with its institutional investors to ensure that they continue to engage with and invest in DCS.

(c) *Candidates may well approach these slides differently but the main benefits and opportunities they should identify should fall under the following main headings:*

- Cost reduction

- More sophisticated analysis of customer data including customer behaviour, sentiments and preferences

- Faster and better decision-making

- Research and development analysis for new products and services

---

SLIDE 1 – Benefits of big data analytics

- Sentiment analysis

- Soft surveillance and consumer behaviour tracking

- Open communication channels with clients

- Predictive analytics (which can monitor inventory levels and ensure product availability)

- Analysis of customers' purchasing behaviours

Notes: As DCS operates in a country with 75% of the population connected to the internet and presumably purchasing a significant proportion of their products and services online, DCS can sell data analytics capability to its clients. It can do this by showing them how to use this capability to capture, store and process data from their customers. By developing sophisticated marketing analytics with big data, DCS's clients can properly evaluate their own marketing performance, gain insight into their customers' purchasing patterns, discern key market trends and permit them to make evidence-based marketing decisions.

SLIDE 2 – Further opportunities to DCS customers of big data analytics

Further opportunities offered by big data analytics for DCS's customers, include the following:

- Potential to unlock significant value

- Big data allows ever-narrower segmentation

- Big data can be used to develop the next generation of products and services

- Ability to collect more accurate and detailed performance information

- Sophisticated analytics can substantially improve decision-making

---

Notes: Big data analytics makes information about DCS customers' clients more transparent and allows DCS's customers to collect more accurate and timely information at a fraction of the costs of hosting expensive architectures such as data warehouses and allows DCS's clients considerable cost savings using cloud computing capability or open source software such as 'Hadoop clusters' for storing and processing large amounts of data. Using this, and through 'data mining' using social and business networking data, DCS's clients can undertake a much more sophisticated analysis of their customers and therefore much more precisely tailor their products or services allowing valuable insights which would otherwise remain hidden and unlock more customer value. The other key opportunity is to allow DCS's clients to develop bespoke products for their customers based on their precise needs and consumer behaviours.

(d)   Recommendations about sustainability issues

Environmental and sustainability issues should have more prominence at DCS. When it was a private company, there would have been more flexibility regarding 'corporate citizenship' and a private company is not as visible to the general public as far as its social and environmental policies are concerned. However, a public limited company is expected to take into account environmental capital in its strategies and policies. DCS has a reputational stake in this. It also has a financial stake, because a carbon footprint which is not properly controlled usually leads to financial inefficiencies as well as environmental costs.

DCS would gain benefits from the expertise of a reputable consultancy firm which specialises in environmental and carbon control. They would need to ensure that DCS is not accused of 'greenwashing' by paying 'lip-service' to green issues but visibly reducing their carbon footprint. They would analyse DCS's value chain from its suppliers, its in-bound logistics to its manufacturing processes and to its outbound logistics. These consultants would examine from top to bottom the policies, processes and procedures of the company. They can advise on the carbon content of raw materials and components and on how to be more fuel efficient in ordering, in production, avoiding or reducing waste and improving their quality control and recycling capabilities. They could advise on carbon offset programmes, ethical sourcing, green manufacturing, more sustainable travel policies and about the logistics of delivering their products and providing their services to customers. For example, having to send staff all over the country and to the nearby continent has a carbon cost, but also a financial cost.

Another explicit financial cost which DCS must take into account is the proposed carbon tax which will add further costs to its already relatively narrow margins on the data communications components business. These consultants could end up helping DCS not only to reduce and control their carbon footprint at the micro level, but to reduce their tangible costs and potential tax liabilities at the same time.

TASK 2

(a)   The potential risks which the company could face whether or not it re-aligns its business are as follows:

(**Note:** Candidates only need to discuss any three of these to gain maximum marks)

Strategic risk, business risk, financial risk and environmental risk.

(**Note:** Markers can give additional credit for any reasonable risks identified from the case information and give a Professional Skills mark for a reasonable positioning of the risks in the heat map)

Heat map for key risks faced by DCS Company

Strategic risk

The key strategic risk which DCS faces is the increased competition in the data communications components manufacturing market, the reduced margins and potential decline in the future. At the same time DCS faces the risk of missing an opportunity to use its competencies to develop the potentially more profitable area of its business. DCS currently faces lower market share and declining shareholder value and this is projected to be a 10% decline year on year for the next three years. To reduce or avoid these risks, DCS could re-align its business towards the more profitable domestic market by investing in the network support business in terms of increased R&D, fixed asset investment and improvements in policies relating to staff retention and recruitment to support this potential growth area. This would also reduce its general cost base.

Business risk

As already explained in the five forces analysis, apart from heavy dependence on its main business sector of data communications (65% of its total turnover), DCS is facing economic risk from overdependence on key customers (one of the OEM customers accounts for 40% of its sales). DCS is also over-reliant for its supplies of data communications sub-components on two large multinational suppliers from which it currently faces serious supply shortages. It also risks further losses of staff and greater recruitment difficulties caused by poor staff morale and due to the unattractive location of DCS's headquarters. Under the TARA framework, it is advisable to reduce these risks by widening the supplier and customer base. From a supply perspective, the benefits of this strategy would be to spread the risk of a disruption to the supplies from one or both of the two current suppliers. The strategy would also help DCS in terms of bargaining power, particularly if it is not getting favourable terms from them. Similarly, widening the customer base, or concentrating on a higher value strategy will reduce its dependence on the data communications business and also the bargaining power of their main OEM customer and help their profitability. DCS can reduce the staff retention and recruitment risk by adopting tactics and implementing policies to improve the culture of the organisation and the morale of their key staff. This could be achieved through offering greater empowerment and devolving more authority to middle managers. An improvement in intrinsic rewards and in pay and conditions, or allowing staff to relocate, or work from other geographical locations which are more attractive to them, may also help to mitigate this risk.

Financial risk

The main risk is the devaluing currency in the main market into which DCS sells a significant proportion of its data communications components. A weakening currency in the economic community from which customers settle their payments means that DCS is facing a currency translation exposure as monies received in the devaluing currency will effectively reduce the turnover collected from customers in these markets. Under the TARA framework, the risk could be reduced or transferred by using foreign currency hedging instruments or by taking out loans in the denomination of the weaker foreign currency, using the payments from the continental customers to offset the liability. The other main financial risk is the high level of gearing and the risk of breaking bank covenants and of default. This risk could be mitigated by either converting some of the debt into equity or by repaying or redeeming loans from DCS's considerable cash reserves, or by issuing more shares.

Environmental risk

DCS is not itself at risk of potential environmental impact, but is facing a risk of creating an increased carbon footprint or environmental impact which it is not effectively managing and which may itself create environmental costs and incur a carbon tax liability. This risk could be transferred through carbon offset strategies, avoided by ceasing to manufacture or distribute goods in a way that creates such a significant carbon footprint, or reduced through pursuing tactics or strategies to avoid waste and reduce emissions.

(b) (i) Table 1 of exhibit 4 makes a number of assumptions. These are as follows:

The 'do nothing' strategy is not considered an option by the board. A reasonably quick financial analysis would confirm that this is not a viable option, but that confirmation has not been included in the October board report or in Freddie Lithium's spreadsheet.

Therefore, a financial evaluation of the 'do nothing' option against the other two options would give a more complete picture. In fact, are there any other strategic options available to DCS? These do not seem to have been considered by the board.

Is it reasonable to extrapolate that a recent decline of 10% in total DCS revenues is indicative of future trends in cash contribution by segment? There seems to be no explanation of how the relative cash contribution of each segment in 2015 was arrived at, other than being calculated after interest and tax. The definition of cash contribution also needs to be investigated further to verify whether it is calculated before capital expenditure or is a free cash flow, because the forecasts might differ, depending on how this cash flow is defined.

Is it possible to assume that annual additional fixed costs will be constant in each year of the forecast planning period as stated? In reality, there might be greater fixed cost expenditure in the first year of the new strategy and less in the subsequent years.

Is it reasonable to assume that fixed cost savings in the data communications plant would be the same regardless of which growth forecast emerges? This seems unreasonable as potential savings in that division would probably depend to some extent on the level of growth which materialises from Strategy 2, if implemented.

The calculations within the spreadsheet all seem accurate, but time value for money has not been taken into account. If the cash flows after interest and tax were discounted, they would need to be discounted by the geared cost of capital, which is estimated at 12%. Making this adjustment to the cash flow will yield a net present value for the project and will change the payback estimate. This is shown below:

	2016 ($m)	2017 ($m)	2018 ($m)
Net incremental cash flow from re-alignment	−0.09	−0.02	+0.12

Net present value = (−0.09 × 1/1.12) − (0.02 × 1/1.1.122) + (0.12 × 1/1.1.123)
= (−0.08 − 0.016 + 0.085)
= −0.011

This means that Strategy 2 (the re-alignment strategy) has a negative NPV of $11,000 which means it does not pay back in the three-year planning horizon.

(ii) **Recommendations to the DCS board**

The purely financial evaluation in (b) above shows that DCS should not re-align towards the higher-value more differentiated network support segment, although undiscounted payback would indicate that it just repays for itself within three years.

However, the strategic and broader business benefits to be gained from re-aligning in this way are that it will help DCS become a differentiator, concentrating on higher value, lower volume business, rather than continuing to maintain an increasingly challenging cost focus. This might be preferable to remaining as active in the high volume low margin data communications manufacturing business, particularly as the company is so reliant on two key suppliers, where supplies are being disrupted and where 30% of their OEM customers are representing an increasing risk of higher currency translation costs.

From the performance data in the <IR> spreadsheet, it seems that manufacturing cost control is one of the key problems for DCS, so the business benefits will include the ability to transfer resources from the manufacturing to the support side and the potential to make labour cost savings in the manufacturing area which is more labour intensive and where labour and employment costs in Prydain are high. DCS can also reduce its carbon footprint further and reduce its environmental impact.

The IT benefits for DCS will be that it will develop greater capability in the new emerging technologies of cloud computing and big data processing services which will give it a competitive advantage over traditional players in the data electronics market.

The strategy to re-align the business will make a small negative net present value of −$11,000 over the next three years, which on the face of it would not justify the strategy on financial grounds alone, assuming that the forecasts were valid. However, while DCS directors were unable or unwilling to consider the cash flows beyond a three-year planning period, due to subjectivity and prudence, it is reasonable to assume that there would be additional positive net cash flow benefits accruing to DCS, well beyond the planning horizon. These seem to be rising exponentially from the trend observed. It could also be assumed, particularly in such a competitive and innovative sector as data communications, that the ability of DCS to maintain its current market share and overall turnover over time could be questioned, should no investment or re-alignment of the business take place.

Therefore considering both strategic and wider business reasons, DCS would be advised to implement the re-alignment of the business and focus on expanding the network support side of the business and invest in the necessary fixed costs, staff recruitment and working capital required, by using internally generated funds or issuing more shares.

TASK 3

(a)   Working notes with relevant visual aids

Using the Mendelow matrix it can be established that before DCS was listed or quoted on the national stock market, it had the following stakeholder groups:

Before flotation:	**Described follows:**
Shareholders	• these were private shareholders comprising the founder's majority holding and possibly those of family and close business associates
Employees	• mainly non-unionised and loyal to a smaller family oriented business
Lenders	• insignificant borrowings before flotation – presumably overdraft and other short-term loans
After flotation:	**Described as follows:**
Shareholders	• wider group of public individual investors and a 30% holding by institutional investors Employees
	• more skilled staff, but operating core staff mostly unionised
Lenders	• much more powerful and interested – higher gearing and covenants in place

The following table shows the Mendelow matrix positioning and strategies for these groups before and after flotation:

(**Note:** Alternatively a grid could be presented where arrows could be used to indicate where stakeholders had moved within and between quadrants after being publicly listed)

Stakeholder groups	Mendelow grid position and strategy before flotation	Mendelow grid position and strategy after flotation
Shareholders	High power/high interest – actively involve	Lower power/high interest – keep informed (particularly institutional shareholders)
Employees	Low power/high interest – keep informed	Higher power/high interest – keep satisfied or involve more actively
Lenders	Low power/low interest – minimal effort	Higher power/high interest – keep well informed and keep satisfied

The strategies DCS Company management would adopt pre- and post-flotation would differ as determined by the changed positions on the Mendelow matrix. The main change in strategies would be as follows in relation to the above stakeholders:

Shareholders: Clearly before the flotation, private shareholders, being the owner and his family or close friends, would have far more interest and power than the majority of shareholders after the flotation, so the need to actively involve is less necessary, but evidence from the case suggests that there is a lack of engagement with institutional shareholders which could be problematic as this group has far more power than other shareholders, so DCS should develop reporting and communications channels with this important group.

Employees: Before flotation most employees were non-unionised and the culture of DCS was not to involve, engage or inform employees and expect them to follow instructions. After flotation 60% of the data communications workforce are now unionised and additional employment legislation such as minimum wage and mandatory company pensions are being introduced which will force DCS to not only keep employees and their representatives informed and fairly well satisfied, but also to more actively involve them– in particular regarding the pension arrangements.

Lenders: Before flotation DCS was predominately funded from shareholders' funds and had few borrowings, so this stakeholder had little power or influence and possibly little interest in DCS, particularly if the loan capital represented an insignificant proportion of the lender's total portfolio. After the flotation, DCS has become increasingly more highly geared in order to expand into new markets and therefore the risk faced by the lender is greater and this increases the lenders' level of interest in DCS and its ability to sustain this level of borrowing and to repay the original capital. As lenders have placed legally binding covenants on the company preventing it from exceeding its current gearing levels, it also has more power over DCS, meaning that DCS will have to keep lenders well informed and certainly keep them satisfied.

(b) Professionally and ethically, there are some issues relating to how the staff satisfaction survey has been conducted, which we would like to highlight.

In theory, such surveys are beneficial to organisations and to staff if conducted properly as they help management gain a better understanding of how staff are thinking, what their attitudes and opinions are and can act as a sounding board from which management can act and make the necessary changes which can improve the culture and productivity of staff.

Lack of integrity – Unfortunately it appears that staff may have been misled in that there were assurances given that the survey responses would be anonymous, but the personal information required gives the impression to staff that management can identify the respondents of the survey.

Lack of objectivity – From discussions with staff representatives, it is possible that key areas known to be of concern to staff (obtained from the informal grapevine) may have been omitted from the survey and the survey could have dissuaded people from giving negative feedback, particularly about confidence in management. From a statistical perspective, the results were presented in quite a subjective way by using graph styles which may have misrepresented the true findings, focusing more on the aspects which staff found most positive.

Professional competence and due care – The design of the survey and the way in which results were presented may be viewed as being somewhat unprofessional and may not have achieved what it was intended to achieve. This could have been avoided if more care had been taken with its design.

Confidentiality – One matter of serious concern relates to the fact that some employees were identified and interviewed by senior managers as a result of their apparent negative responses to the survey. This action appears to have breached the fundamental principle of confidentiality.

Professional behaviour – DCS Company management should not attempt to identify 'dissident' staff or schedule and conduct interviews with these individuals, as it could be described as demonstrating unprofessional behaviour. This is particularly worrying when some interviewees perceive that they have been intimidated or even threatened by the comments made at some of these meetings. Another point we would wish to raise is the danger of operating 'double standards' when the survey was supposed to be anonymous, but staff identified for interview were themselves required to keep confidential the fact that they had been identified and interviewed.

MARKING SCHEME

Note: Markers have the latitude to award Professional Skills marks for Professional and behavioural skills demonstrated in the answers given throughout the paper as described below:

- **Communication**
  Inform
  Persuade
  Justify

- **Commercial acumen**
  Demonstrate awareness
  Use judgement
  Show insight

- **Analysis**
  Investigate
  Scrutinise
  Reflect

- **Scepticism**
  Probe
  Question
  Challenge

- **Evaluation**
  Assess
  Estimate
  Appraise

TASK 1

(a)　(i)　Up to four marks per element of Porter's five forces affecting DCS.
(Up a maximum of 15 marks in total)

　　(ii)　Up to three marks per capital or for possibly discussing the elements of integrated reporting, including any relevant calculations – using data from the performance table. **(Up to a maximum of 12 marks in total)**

(b)　One mark per relevant point for criticising or identifying the key weaknesses in the current governance structure of DCS and one mark per relevant point, up to a maximum of four marks, for suggesting how the governance arrangements could be improved. **(Up to a maximum of 12 marks in total)**

(c)　One mark per relevant point for identifying customer benefits of big data analytics.
(Up to a maximum of 6 marks)

(d)　One mark per relevant point for making the case for DCS commissioning environmental and sustainability consultants to help it better understand how to measure and control its carbon footprint and one mark per relevant point for briefly explaining why DCS should have a better awareness of sustainability and environmental impacts, from both a carbon footprint and financial perspective.
(Up to a maximum of 5 marks in total)

Professional skills may be additionally rewarded as in the following rubric:

How well has the candidate demonstrated Professional skills as follows:	Not at all	Not so well	Quite well	Very well
(a) Evaluation skills in assessing the environment and performance of DCS Company	The candidate has failed to select an appropriate environmental scanning model or to analyse the performance of the company against any of the six capitals of <IR>. The candidate has therefore failed to adequately evaluate either the strategic position or the overall performance of the company meaningfully.	The candidate has demonstrated some basic evaluative skills in the environmental scanning model selected. The candidate has only identified one or two of the six capitals of <IR> and has omitted many of the key performance indicators (KPI) or ratios in their evaluation of company performance.	The candidate has demonstrated good evaluative skills in the environmental scanning model selected, using key facts from the case. The candidate has also selected some of the most important KPIs or ratios when evaluating company performance against most of the six capitals.	The candidate has demonstrated comprehensive evaluative skills in the environmental scanning model or models selected, using most of the key facts from the case. The candidate has also selected comprehensive and appropriate KPIs or ratios when evaluating company performance against all of the six capitals.
	0	1	2	4

How well has the candidate demonstrated Professional skills as follows:	Not at all	Not so well	Quite well	Very well
(b) Scepticism skills in identifying the main CG deficiencies and how to remedy	The candidate has failed to demonstrate any scepticism of the CEO's answers given in the interview and has therefore failed to make any meaningful recommendations for CG improvement.	The candidate has demonstrated some limited scepticism in analysing the CEO's responses in the interview by identifying some CG failures, but has only made a few recommendations for CG improvement.	The candidate has demonstrated scepticism of the CEO's responses in the interview by identifying several of the key CG failures. The candidate has also made some sensible recommendations for CG improvement.	The candidate has demonstrated deep scepticism of most of the CEO's responses in the interview by identifying many of the key CG failures. The candidate has also made all of the obvious recommendations for CG improvement.
	0	**0.5**	**1**	**2**
(c) Communication skills in highlighting the key points and for clear supporting notes	The candidate has failed to use a slide format to communicate the benefits of big data for either the business or their customers.	The candidate has only loosely used a slide presentation format, but has either far too many or too few points or has failed to identify benefits for both the business and customers. The candidate has produced some notes but they are either too long or fail to adequately explain the main points.	The candidate has used a slide format and bullet points, and has covered both benefits to the customers and the business, but there may be too many of them or they have not been expressed succinctly enough. There are slide notes, but they only loosely explain the bullet points selected.	The candidate has appropriately selected and prioritised the key points about benefits to the customer and to the business in a logically flowing bullet list and has produced clear supporting notes which relate closely to the points selected.
	0	**0.5**	**1**	**2**
(d) Commercial acumen skills in identifying how DCS could benefit from the findings of the environmental audit	The candidate has demonstrated no appreciable commercial acumen for identifying any reasonable grounds for commissioning an environmental audit on either environmental or financial grounds.	The candidate has demonstrated some commercial acumen in identifying a few reasonable grounds for commissioning an environmental audit but has missed some of the most important justifications on either environmental or financial grounds.	The candidate has demonstrated commercial acumen in identifying several reasonable grounds for commissioning an environmental audit and has identified some of the most important justifications on both environmental and financial grounds.	The candidate has demonstrated astute commercial acumen in identifying many if not most of the reasonable grounds for commissioning an environmental audit and has strongly justified them on both environmental and financial grounds.
	0	**0.5**	**1**	**2**

TASK 2

(a)   Up to a maximum of two marks per risk for identifying and describing three key risks which DCS faces and plotting them on some form of heat map, whether or not they re-align their business or not. A further one mark per relevant point can be awarded for explaining how each of these three risks can be mitigated using the TARA framework.   **(Up to a maximum of 6 marks)**

(b)   (i)   Up to five marks to be awarded for questioning any assumptions in Table 1 of the October board report, including the recommendation that the cash flows should be discounted.

       (ii)   Up to five marks may be awarded for recommending a strategy for DCS with reasoned arguments which may or may not contradict the financial evaluation of the cash flow forecasts undertaken.

Professional skills may be additionally rewarded as in the following rubric:

How well has the candidate demonstrated Professional skills as follows:	Not at all	Not so well	Quite well	Very well
(a) Commercial acumen skills in identifying and locating risks appropriately on a heat map	The candidate made no attempt to construct a heat map so they failed to illustrate the probability and impact of the categories of risk detailed in the scenario.	The candidate attempted to construct a heat map as required. However, either the accuracy of plotting the risks was wrong or the presentation of the diagram was below standard so it did not help to support the candidate's answer.	The candidate constructed a good heat map, plotting the main risks identified in the scenario correctly. However, the candidate did not reference the heat map to their answer so its usefulness was very limited.	The candidate constructed an accurate heat map, plotting all of the main risks identified in the scenario correctly. The heat map was carefully referenced to the answer thereby constituting part of an effective risk management framework.
	0	**0.5**	**1**	**2**
(b) (I) Scepticism skills in analysing the spreadsheet and supporting assumptions	The candidate showed no evidence of scepticism, and accepted both the content and underlying assumptions of the spreadsheet without question.	Although the candidate displayed a cursory level of scepticism, they failed to challenge the assumptions which underpinned the analysis contained within the spreadsheet.	The candidate displayed evidence of some professional scepticism when analysing the spreadsheet and supporting assumptions. However, this scepticism was not evident in the required critical evaluation of Freddie Lithium's spreadsheet.	The candidate demonstrated strong professional scepticism of the content of Freddie Lithium's spreadsheet in Exhibit 5 together with its supporting market growth assumptions. This provided authority to the critical evaluation of the strategic choices presented.
	0	**0.5**	**1**	**2**

How well has the candidate demonstrated Professional skills as follows:	Not at all	Not so well	Quite well	Very well
(ii) Commercial acumen skills in recommending strategic option to implement	The strategic option recommended by the candidate was purely based on the application of academic theory, rather than any display of sensible and practical commercial acumen.	The candidate demonstrated only superficial commercial acumen when evaluating the strategic options, to the extent that it really did not contribute to the recommendation.	The candidate has demonstrated some limited commercial acumen when determining which of the two options to recommend, but it was not explicitly mentioned in the answer.	The candidate has demonstrated incisive commercial acumen when determining which of the two strategic options to recommend. This was clearly evidenced in the answer.
	0	**0.5**	**1**	**2**

TASK 3

(a) Up to one mark per stakeholder group for identifying and briefly explaining where each of the three stakeholder groups is situated in the Mendelow matrix before and after the company was quoted and listed on the national stock exchange in 2006, including how strategies to manage them would need to have changed.

(Up to a maximum of 6 marks in total)

(b) Up to one mark per relevant point about the professional ethics or fundamental principles relating to the introduction, conduct and reporting of the staff satisfaction survey. **(Up to a maximum of 6 marks)**

Note: Candidates need not refer to all five of the fundamental principles to gain all six marks on offer.

Professional skills may be additionally rewarded as in the following rubric:

How well has the candidate demonstrated **Professional skills** as follows:	**Not at all**	**Not so well**	**Quite well**	**Very well**
(a) Analytical skills for assessing the relative power and interest and how to engage with these stakeholders before and after flotation	The candidate was unable to identify that Mendelow's matrix was the correct analytical framework to use in this instance. By failing to select the correct model the candidate was unable to effectively analyse the stakeholders detailed in the scenario.	The candidate was able to demonstrate a basic understanding of Mendelow's matrix, but inadequately used relevant information from the DCS scenario in this analytical framework. In effect, the candidate was unable to apply their knowledge of a major syllabus model in a meaningful and useful way.	The candidate demonstrated good analytical skills by applying scenario information correctly to Mendelow's matrix. However, they did not use this analysis to determine the most appropriate way to engage with the three stakeholder groups.	The candidate comprehensively and accurately demonstrated how to apply Mendelow's matrix to a changing business situation. The candidate correctly mapped out the position of each of the three stakeholder groups both before and after the DCS floatation, and as a result was able to explain how best the company could engage with each of them.
	0	0.5	1	2
(b) Scepticism skills for identifying ethical issues in the survey and for explaining these diplomatically in writing	The candidate failed to sceptically assess the behaviour of those conducting the survey against the five core ethical principles defined in the 'ACCA Code of Ethics and Conduct' to structure their criticism of the CEO and HR director's behaviour.	The candidate correctly identified the five core ethical principles from the 'ACCA Code of Ethics and Conduct', but the ability to sceptically apply and criticise behaviour against business ethics was quite superficial.	The candidate has demonstrated scepticism of director behaviour against the five core ethical principles and used these to criticise the CEO and HR director's ethical and professional behaviour. However, the answer did not focus specifically on the issue of the conduct of the survey	The candidate has demonstrated very good sceptical skills when discussing failure to comply with the five core ethical principles and used these to comprehensively criticise the CEO and HR director's ethical and professional behaviour. The answer makes specific reference to the way the staff satisfaction survey was conducted.
	0	0.5	1	2

Section 7

SPECIMEN 2 EXAM QUESTIONS

2   RAIL CO

Rail Co is a public sector rail company responsible for delivering passenger rail services within Beeland.

Rail Co is governed by a supreme governing committee known as the Rail Co Trust Board. This board is responsible to the Ministry of Transport for ensuring that the Rail Co board of directors make the best use of public money and maintain effective and efficient services to the public. Figure 1 below shows the governance structure of Rail Co.

Figure 1

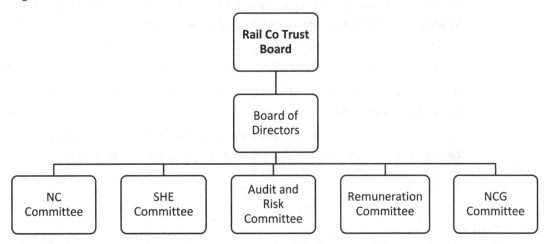

The National Audit Authority (NAA) of Beeland is a national government audit authority with responsibility for evaluating and reporting to the government of Beeland on public spending, suggesting improvements to and benchmarking against the performance of a wide range of publicly funded organisations. The NAA also has a responsibility to advise on the value for money (VFM) obtained from publicly owned enterprises and on the performance of the boards of such organisations, including the senior executives of these boards.

Rail Co has in the recent past received negative publicity in the media and from a variety of other sources relating to its poor services and performance. This has prompted the Minister for Transport of Beeland, to commission the NAA to undertake an urgent investigation of the issues facing Rail Co.

The following exhibits (1–6) provide information relevant to Rail Co.

Exhibit 1: Website page for Rail Co leadership and governance.

Exhibit 2: Transport report published in the Beeland Herald newspaper.

Exhibit 3: Passenger survey results and performance analysis spreadsheet for Rail Co and its competitors (three years data).

Exhibit 4: Rail Co board meeting minutes.

Exhibit 5: Outline person specification and summary CVs for two candidates for the new chief executive position

Exhibit 6: Ticket sales, passenger usage data and fraud analysis at stations in towns within Region 1 – Beeland network – prepared by the financial controller of Rail Co.

The case requirements are as follows and you will be told which role you are taking in each task:

TASK 1

You are a non-executive member and chairman of the nominations and corporate governance (NCG) committee.

The recently appointed chairman of the Rail Co Trust Board has requested that you provide him with information relating to the governance of Rail Co and the roles and responsibilities of the non-executive directors.

Required:

You have been asked to prepare a briefing paper for the Rail Co Trust Board which:

(a)   **Identifies and explains the agency relationship of the parties involved in Rail Co and discusses the rights and responsibilities of those parties.   (8 marks)**

Professional skills marks are available for demonstrating communication skills in clarifying the agency relationships involved in Rail Co.   **(2 marks)**

(b)   **Assesses the role and value of non-executive directors on the board of Rail Co, as a public sector company.   (6 marks)**

Professional skills marks are available for demonstrating evaluation skills in assessing the role and value of non-executive directors in a public sector environment.

(2 marks)

(Total: 18 marks)

TASK 2

You are an assistant auditor reporting to Alex Reed, the senior audit officer of the NAA.

Alex leads a team of assistant auditors and audit analysts and will be responsible for reporting the findings of the NAA's investigations of Rail Co to a number of relevant parties, including the Minister of Transport, the board of directors of Rail Co and the Rail Co Trust Board. As part of the investigation commissioned by the Minister of Transport to be undertaken by the NAA, one of the audit analysts working on your audit team has prepared a spreadsheet supplying a variety of data following the recent passenger survey results and using other relevant performance related information.

Required:

Alex Reed has asked you to prepare a report for the Rail Co Trust Board which:

(a)   **Evaluates the implications of the findings of the passenger survey results and reviews the actual and relative performance of Rail Co over the last three years. (12 marks)**

Professional skills marks are available for demonstrating analysis skills used in reviewing the information presented in the spreadsheet.   **(2 marks)**

A few days later Alex Reed called you into his office to discuss Rail Co's governance and internal controls. During that meeting he referred to the transport report in the Beeland Herald newspaper (Exhibit 2) and handed you a copy of the minutes of the latest board meeting held by Rail Co (Exhibit 4).

Required:

Alex has asked you to draft a letter to be sent to the chairman of the Rail Co Trust Board which:

(b)   **Reviews the effectiveness of the internal controls at Rail Co using evidence from the minutes of the latest Rail Co board meeting and any other suitable source and justifies that the chief executive of Rail Co is failing in his fiduciary duties to the trustees of Rail Co.** **(8 marks)**

Professional skills marks are available for demonstrating scepticism skills in questioning the opinions and assertions made by the chief executive at the recent board meeting.

(2 marks)

(Total: 24 marks)

It is now two months after the letter was sent by the NAA to the chairperson of the Trust Board (Task 2b).

TASK 3

You are the non-executive chairperson of an ad hoc sub-committee constituted by the NCG of the Rail Co board.

As a consequence of the NAA review and the recommendations of the Rail Co Trust Board, the Minister of Transport recommended that the chief executive of Rail Co should be removed from his position. Following the termination of the chief executive's contract, the position has now been advertised both nationally and internationally and a person specification has been uploaded to the Rail Co website. In the last two weeks, two candidates have been shortlisted for final interview and a summary of their CVs is being reviewed by the nominations and corporate governance (NCG) committee of Rail Co (Exhibit 5).

Required:

Following a review of the suitability of the shortlisted candidates against the outline person specification, you have been asked by the chair of the NCG to do the following:

(a)   **Write a report to the chair of the NCG which evaluates the suitability of the shortlisted candidates for the position of chief executive of Rail Co and recommend with justification, which candidate you consider to be the most suitable for the position.**

(8 marks)

Professional skills marks are available for demonstrating commercial acumen skills in using your judgement to evaluate the relative merits of the two candidates. **(2 marks)**

(b)   **Prepare two presentation slides, with accompanying notes, to explain to the NCG, the contribution which the chief executive should be expected to make in terms of talent management, to support the necessary change programme required at Rail Co.**

(6 marks)

Professional skills marks are available for demonstrating communication skills in conveying relevant information in an appropriate tone to the NCG committee.

(2 marks)

(Total: 18 marks)

It is now three months later. A new chief executive has been appointed and is working closely with the board of directors and the Rail Co Trust Board to improve performance.

TASK 4

You are an internal auditor working for the audit and risk committee of Rail Co.

The new chief executive asked the financial controller of Rail Co to produce a spreadsheet which analyses the ticket sales and rail usage by station within the Beeland rail network and which also analyses the estimated the levels of fraud occurring across the Rail Co network.

Required:

You have been asked by the chair of the audit and risk committee to review the findings of the financial controller and present a report which requires you to do the following:

(a)   **Analyse the information presented in the spreadsheet produced by the financial controller, questioning any assumptions he may have made, and explain the implications of the findings for Rail Co.**   **(8 marks)**

Professional skills marks are available for demonstrating scepticism skills in considering the information presented in the spreadsheet and reflecting on the impact on Rail Co's revenues.   **(2 marks)**

(b)   **Recommend to the audit and risk committee, with justifications, suitable measures or safeguards which could be implemented by Rail Co to reduce the levels of fraud occurring on the network.**   **(8 marks)**

Professional skills marks are available for demonstrating commercial acumen skills in making sound recommendations for suitable measures and safeguards to reduce fraud.   **(2 marks)**

(Total: 20 marks)

TASK 5

You are a project manager working for the director of Projects and Infrastructure of Rail Co.

The director of Projects and Infrastructure is putting forward a proposal to the board of directors of Rail Co for a project to invest in an online ticket sales system. The project should be fully operational within 12 months but would need to be undertaken by an external firm of developers, as Rail Co does not possess the internal expertise. However, Rail Co would manage the project.

Required:

You have been asked by the director of Projects and Infrastructure to write a business case to the board, in which you will:

(a)   **Justify why the investment in online ticket sales could assist Rail Co in producing detailed and timely customer data to assist in customer relationship management.**   **(8 marks)**

Professional skills marks are available for demonstrating evaluation skills in assessing the impact of online ticket sales on customer relationship management.   **(2 marks)**

(b)   **Produce a project initiation document (PID) which could be used by Rail Co to assist in planning the implementation of an online ticket sales system.**   **(8 marks)**

Professional skills marks are available for demonstrating communication skills in producing a PID to be used by Rail Co.   **(2 marks)**

(Total: 20 marks)

EXHIBIT 1

Rail Co 'Getting you there, on time, in comfort'

Our mission is to provide a high quality, efficient and cost-effective rail service to all our passengers.

Our vision is to become the world leader in providing reliable, profitable and safe train passenger services in a climate which embraces new technology and diversity of ideas.

Our board

The Rail Co board is responsible for the strategic direction of Rail Co. It is responsible for supervising the operational activities of the business and providing leadership and strategic direction.

Our Chief Executive reports directly to the Minister for Transport on our leadership and long-term performance and success. The board comprises:

Henrik Kilde, non-executive chair – Appointed to the board in 2011

John Rose, Chief Executive – Appointed to the board in 2002

Helga Baum, Finance Director – Appointed to the board in 2006

Milo Strauss, Director of Projects & Infrastructure – Appointed to the board in 2012

Filip Axis, non-executive director – Appointed to the board in 2009

Felix Erikson, non-executive director – Appointed to the board in 2014

Harvey Flood, non-executive director – Appointed to the board in 2015

Salma Khan, non-executive director – Appointed to the board in 2010

Kim Lun, non-executive director – Appointed to the board in 2012

Anders Rosburg, non-executive director – Appointed to the board in 2016

Our executive committee

Operational management is delegated to members of our executive committee. The executive committee is chaired by the Chief Executive and comprises the Finance Director, the Director of Projects and Infrastructure and five other executive managers:

Lara Cook, Passenger services director – Appointed in 2004

Jasper Edberg, Asset management director – Appointed in 2007

George Fill, Director of Safety and Engineering – Appointed in 2013

Tomas Kline, Director of IT – Appointed in 2012

Brenda Suter, HR Director – Appointed in 2006

Our board committees

Our four board committees, made up of non-executive directors, assist the board with its responsibilities.

Safety, health and environment (SHE) committee

This committee monitors the integrity of the methods used to carry out SHE responsibilities. The committee evaluates whether policies and strategies are adequate and effective taking into account relevant legislation and standards.

Audit and risk committee

This committee monitors the integrity of the financial reporting and the audit process and reviews the internal control systems including risk management, regulation and compliance.

Remuneration committee

This committee is empowered under the articles of association of Rail Co to determine remuneration for directors. This responsibility reflects the business aim to provide independence of the decision-making process for remuneration and incentive schemes.

Nomination and corporate governance (NCG) committee

This committee reviews the size, structure and composition of the board and committees. The committee identifies and nominates candidates for appointment to the board and ensures that appropriate succession planning is in place.

Rail Co Trust Board

The Rail Co Trust Board is an independent statutory body, with powers vested by the Government of Beeland in its members. The Trust Board consists of ten members, all of whom are appointed by the Minister for Transport, for a fixed term of up to three years. Our board is accountable to the Rail Co Trust Board.

The Trust Board is our supreme governing body which holds us to account for delivering what we promise. It sets us a range of performance targets each year and holds the board to account for its effective and efficient use of the funds allocated to Rail Co by Government and by the fare paying passengers. The board is also accountable to the Rail Co Trust Board for our health and safety performance.

Our Chief Executive is personally accountable to the Government for Rail Co's stewardship of the public funding it receives.

EXHIBIT 2

TRANSPORT REPORT

The Beeland Herald
Beeland's most widely
read Daily newspaper

Gus Smidt, Transport Editor reports on the recently published customer survey results of Rail Co.

Is Rail Co going off the rails?

The latest annual customer survey results for Rail Co will not make comfortable reading for its Chief Executive John Rose, who predicted this time last year 'the future is bright for Rail Co'. Rail Co, the company responsible for the transport of over 50% of Beeland's commuters to their daily work destinations throughout the country, appears to be losing the support of its loyal customers. This is despite an increasing population in Beeland and significant levels of government investment in its development. Although it has invested in new trains over the last five years, commuter trains are still overcrowded. Significantly, it has failed to invest in online ticket purchasing systems and commuters are increasingly unhappy that they are only able to purchase tickets from manned ticket offices within each station. Public perception of the organisation is at an all-time low and questions will now be asked by the Minister for Transport as to why revenue growth is stagnant and why customers are increasingly unhappy with its services.

Rail Co receives an annual grant from the government of Beeland, funded by general taxation of the population, to run the business efficiently and effectively. The government also sets Rail Co a number of performance targets to meet each year. These include key performance indicators on revenue growth, cost efficiency and customer satisfaction ratings.

Despite evidence of a growth in passenger numbers (platform 'footfall') of about 15% using the railway network in the last three years,

revenue has hardly increased over the same period.

In its last two annual reports, Rail Co's directors have highlighted the risk of significant numbers of passengers travelling without tickets. It has been suggested that this could be due to the fact that Rail Co does not operate ticket barriers at many of its stations. Rail Co relies on ticket inspectors operating on train services to check tickets, but evidence suggests that this can only catch a minority of those who evade paying for tickets.

As a consequence of static sales, Rail Co has repeatedly increased its ticket prices by more than inflation in the last three years and customers have complained bitterly and many are threatening to use their cars or other forms of public transport if Rail Co does not respond effectively.

A further concern for Rail Co will be that staff turnover is at an all-time high as stated in its latest annual report, which may be due to the fact that staff wages at Rail Co have not been rising with inflation and staff are coming under increased pressure from unhappy customers.

These are, indeed, worrying developments for Rail Co, as its key stakeholders seemingly become increasingly frustrated with the lack of any meaningful response by the Chief Executive, who yesterday refused to comment on the customer survey.

However, in a statement made by the Minister of Transport yesterday, he commented that although the customer survey results for Rail Co were 'disappointing', he was confident that the situation would be addressed within the coming year. He announced that the newly appointed Chairperson of the Trust Board, the supreme governing committee responsible for the performance and governance of Rail Co, 'has the full backing of the government of Beeland to undertake a thorough and effective review, and if necessary make changes to the management and organisation of Rail Co'

EXHIBIT 3

Extract from beeland's passenger survey results for the last three years

	Percentage satisfied			Trust Board Target for 2016
	2016	2015	2014	Target growth on 2015
Overall satisfaction with your journey	87	90	92	+3%
Satisfaction with ticket buying facilities	60	64	65	+2%
Availability of staff	62	65	70	+5%
Helpfulness/attitude of staff	75	73	77	+2%
Punctuality/reliability of service	84	81	86	+5%
Value for money for price of the ticket	50	56	57	+2%

Examples of customer feedback comments:

The price of the regular ticket i buy to commute to work has increased by nearly 10% since last year. I really cannot understand why, as i do not seem to be getting more for my money.

Why is it that when I travel on business to Ayeland, I can book my train tickets online, yet, here in Beeland I can only buy a ticket at the station? This is very frustrating and occasionally, I use my car to get to work as it is more convenient than queuing for up to half an hour to buy a train ticket.

I have been a loyal customer of Rail Co for over 30 years, but I am becoming increasingly frustrated with the number of passengers who I see that are clearly boarding the train without a ticket. I pay B$45 for each ticket I buy, yet some people are travelling for free. Where are the ticket inspectors?

Competitor Performance Analysis

	ANR			Rail Co			Ceeland Rail		
	2016	2015	2014	2016	2015	2014	2016	2015	2014
Revenues (B$m)	4,420	4,212	3,990	4,100	3,998	3,880	7,542	6,983	6,650
Operating costs (B$m)	3,026	3,138	3,200	3,038	2,743	2,551	4,868	4,786	4,857
Km travelled (millions)	890	897	889	779	762	750	1,803	1,709	1,619
Percentage of trains on time	90%	85%	85%	82%	84%	87%	94%	92%	92%
Staff turnover percentage	14%	12%	15%	17%	14%	13%	8%	8%	9%
Average price per ticket (B$)	43	41	41	65	60	56	40	42	43
Average number of employees	32,890	32,788	31,987	27,455	27,190	27,365	56,367	55,798	55,105
Overall customer satisfaction	90%	88%	91%	87%	90%	92%	97%	94%	94%
Lost time injuries to staff (days)	355	361	358	481	466	459	211	232	266

Notes:

1   ANR is the state owned rail company which operates passenger services in Ayeland, a neighbouring country of Beeland. Ayeland has a population of similar size to Beeland. ANR invested in online ticket booking facilities in 2015.

2   Ceeland Rail is a state owned rail company which operates passenger train services in Ceeland. Ceeland is not a neighbouring country of Beeland but operates on the same continent. Ceeland has a larger population than Beeland but a smaller percentage of Ceeland's commuters use the rail system to travel, due to higher concentration of the population within Ceeland's towns and cities. Ceeland invested in an online ticket booking system in 2010 and over 70% of train tickets for Cee Rail are purchased online.

EXHIBIT 4

Rail Co
Board Meeting Minutes

XX/XXXX/2016

Board Members:

Present: Henrik Kilde, John Rose, Helga Baum, Milo Strauss, Filip Axis, Felix Erikson, Salma Khan, Kim Lun, Anders Rosburg, Tomas Kline, Director of IT

Apologies: None Absent: Harvey Flood

Proceedings:

- *Meeting called to order at 2:00pm by Chairman, Henrik Kilde*

Chairman's opening statement

Henrik Kilde opened the meeting with the announcement that he had been informed by the newly appointed Chairman of the Rail Co Trust Board that it had requested the National Audit Authority (NAA) to undertake a review of the operations and performance of Rail Co. He expressed his concern with this development but that the Board was expected to give its full cooperation to this investigation.

John Rose, the Chief Executive, offered his full endorsement of the Chairman's comments on supporting the NAA's investigations of Rail Co's performance. He noted that in his 14 years as Chief Executive, he has witnessed many changes and that he was confident in the current performance of Rail Co and that the NAA would not identify any problems with Rail Co.

Chief Executive's Report on customer survey results

The Chairman opened the discussion with a statement of his disappointment with the latest customer survey results and asked the Chief Executive to present an overview of the key outcomes of the latest customer survey results. The primary focus of the presentation was that Rail Co had failed to meet a number of the key performance measures set by the Trust Board for 2016. The Chief Executive did highlight that although the overall customer satisfaction target was not met, this was still at a very high level at 87%. He commented that when he took over as Chief Executive in 2002 customer satisfaction levels were at less than 65% and to have achieved such high levels of customer satisfaction is a significant achievement for Rail Co. He also highlighted that levels of punctuality had increased in the last year and this was evidence that Rail Co's investment in new trains had ensured a better service for its passengers. Rail Co's motto of 'getting you there on time, in comfort' was clearly being achieved. He stated that he believed that the target growth for punctuality set by the Trust Board for 2016 was unachievable and therefore should be ignored.

The Chairman raised his concern that customers' perception of the value for money of Rail Co's tickets had declined from last year and asked the Board to consider whether this was a reflection of increasing ticket prices. The Finance Director agreed that this was a significant concern but the Chief Executive stated that he strongly believed that the majority of customers did not understand the concept of value for money and therefore this measure was flawed.

Audit and Risk Committee Report provided by Chair, Filip Axis

Filip Axis presented a briefing to the Board on the risks of customer fraud. He noted that this has been an ongoing concern for the last few years but has not been investigated in detail. Evidence suggested that more passengers are travelling on Rail Co's network without tickets and a key factor is that approximately 40% of Rail Co's stations do not operate ticket barriers.

Mr Axis referred to a recent meeting he had held with Jasper Edberg, the Asset Management Director, in which they had discussed the installation of ticket barriers at more of Rail Co's stations to prevent customer fraud. The Finance Director was asked to present an analysis of the impact of potential fraud on Rail Co's revenues at the next Board meeting. The Chief Executive disagreed that this was a significant risk to Rail Co and that the cost of installation of ticket barriers would far outweigh the benefits. He also stated that most customer fraud was unpreventable and that this measure would merely create more customer dissatisfaction.

SHE Committee's Report provided by Chair, Kim Lun

Kim Lun outlined the key issues discussed at a meeting she recently attended with Beeland's Health and Safely Office (BHSO). She reported that the Head of the BHSO had expressed his concern with the increase in the number of injuries to staff reported by Rail Co in the last year. Kim Lun stated that she had assured the BHSO that a thorough investigation would be undertaken and that this needed to be commenced immediately. Kim Lun also noted that there had been a lack of investment in the training of staff in the last three years and that this was affecting staff morale and should be investigated by the HR Director.

The Chief Executive stated that although the HR Director was not a board member, his own opinion was that training levels were satisfactory and that there was no evidence to suggest that staff morale was low. He pointed to evidence in the customer survey report which indicated an annual growth in customer satisfaction levels in relation to staff helpfulness and attitude.

- *Other business*

    1   The IT Director made a short presentation on the use of online booking systems by other rail businesses. The presentation outlined that a number of other national train operators offered online booking facilities and evidence suggested that this had positively impacted upon revenue growth and customer satisfaction in all of these businesses. Most of the Board expressed enthusiastic interest in this potential development.

        The Chief Executive expressed his concern that investment in online booking facilities was merely a knee-jerk reaction to the current challenges to Rail Co. He suggested that improvements to training of ticket office staff would be a better investment opportunity and far less costly to Rail Co. He commented that online ticket facilities went against the traditional values of customer service focus of Rail Co.

    2   The Chairman informed the Board that the HR Director was currently in a meeting with the Head of the Beeland Rail Workers Union (BRWU) to discuss its recent demands for an above inflation rate pay increase for its workers. The Chairman expressed concern at this development, as any threat of strike action could have serious damaging consequences on the public perception of Rail Co.

        The Chief Executive stated that it was important for Rail Co to take a firm stand against any pressure from the unions for an increase in staff pay. He commented that the unions were merely taking advantage of the latest survey results to put the Board under pressure to increase levels of pay for its members. He stated that he had instructed the HR Director not to make any comment to the media on these developments. His opinion was that the media were responsible for stirring up the interest of the unions and that the media were not an important stakeholder.

- *Meeting adjourned at 4:30pm.*

- *Minutes submitted by Secretary, Joanna Vonn.*

EXHIBIT 5

Chief Executive – Rail Co
Outline person specification

Experience

1 Consistent achievement at chief executive level in an organisation of comparable size and complexity.

2 A proven track record of leading and delivery of corporate vision, strategies and objectives within a complex political environment.

3 A proven track record of successfully designing, leading and implementing cultural change.

4 Experience of building professional credibility with boards, employees, the public and the media.

Knowledge, skills and abilities

1 A comprehensive understanding of the rail industry and the political context within which it operates.

2 Well-developed leadership skills which promote a positive and motivated organisational culture.

3 An ability to develop relationships with all stakeholders which command respect, trust and confidence.

4 Financial and commercial awareness, with strong analytical and problem solving skills.

Personal qualities

1 An ability to deliver under pressure.

2 Values the contributions of others and committed to employee development.

3 A strong commitment to service excellence and continuous improvement.

4 Results focused and performance driven.

5 Leads from the front, an honest and straightforward style which gains the respect of others.

Summarised CV – Candidate A	Summarised CV – Candidate B
PROFESSIONAL EXPERIENCE	**PROFESSIONAL EXPERIENCE**
• Chief executive of JPS Express, the largest passenger train service operating company in Jayland. 2009–present • Chief executive of Beeland Oil, a multinational oil and gas company 2000–2009.	• Chief executive of BV Plc, the world's third largest engine manufacturer for the aviation industry, based in Ceeland. 2007–present • Finance director of Ceeland Rail 2004–2007
EXPERIENCE and DUTIES:	**EXPERIENCE and DUTIES:**
• Developing strategy and mission and carrying it through with confidence and vigour. • Responsible for all aspects of human performance management and development and driving enterprise human talent development. • Working on development lifecycle projects including several complex systems infrastructure investments. • Close liaison with national government regulators and rail interest groups. • Producing informative, well-organised presentations for senior management. • Regular liaison with external suppliers, the media and the public.	• Planning strategic business objectives and implementing systems to monitor on performance against key performance indicators. • Responsible for driving the growth of revenue and increased operational efficiency. • Interpreting financial data and drawing conclusions. • Identify skills gaps and providing advice on hiring strategies. • Liaising with key strategic suppliers and customers to define KPIs. • Reviewing, monitoring and authorisation of all budget expenditure. • Motivating and providing strong leadership to all departments.
KEY SKILLS and COMPETENCIES	**KEY SKILLS and COMPETENCIES**
• Ensuring that everything works to the highest possible professional standards with a focus on strong internal control. • A commitment to customer focus and driving improved performance. • A proven track record in change leadership – including the successful management and leadership of the privatisation of V Trains in 2013. • A charismatic leader with a successful track record in managing cultural change from a public sector to private sector environment. • A commitment to building and maintaining close relationships with external bodies, staff, the media, customers and the public. • An enterprising and creative thinker, with a commercial eye, exceptional financial acumen and highly effective leadership skills.	• Decisive and forward thinking, with strong vision and strategic capability. • Ability to network and liaise with stakeholders at every level, particularly customers and strategic suppliers. • Experience of project management in a highly complex engineering environment. • A proven track record of successful leadership and growth, operating within highly competitive markets. • Motivational and credible with highly effective interpersonal skills. • Highly commercial and committed to quality and innovation. • Operationally strong, financially aware and commercially astute.

EXHIBIT 6

						Initial data on stations in Region 1 - Beeland network					
Analysis of fraud - information based on 2016 analysis											
Town	Ticket barrier	Population per town	Monthly tickets sold to town	Estimated % railway users per town	Estimated monthly ticket sales per town	Variance between tickets sold v projected ticket sales	Spend per ticket sold	Estimated fraud ($) per month	Fraud % for each town (based on total population)	Estimated fraud due to poor internal control (%) (based on total population)	Preventable annual fraud ($) (based on total population)
A	y	142000	28000	21	29820	1820	59	107380	1.28%		
B	y	195000	31000	17	33150	2150	38	81700	1.10%		
C	n	110000	22000	28	30800	8800	44	387200	8.00%	6.72%	3,903,953
D	n	195000	36000	26	50700	14700	51	749700	7.54%	6.26%	7,470,856
E	y	74000	25000	35	25900	900	56	50400	1.22%		
F	y	116000	31000	28	32480	1480	52	76960	1.28%		
G	n	183000	37000	30	54900	17900	56	1002400	9.78%	8.50%	10,456,776
H	y	87000	19000	23	20010	1010	61	61610	1.16%		
I	n	144000	12000	16	23040	11040	48	529920	7.67%	6.39%	5,298,752
J	y	147000	27000	20	29400	2400	62	148800	1.63%		
		1393000	268000					3196070			
		Assumed average percentage of unpreventable fraud - Region 1							1.28%		
										Total annual preventable fraud in Region 1:	$ 27,130,338
										Extrapolate for 20 regions	$ 542,606,752

Note:
There are 20 identifiable regions within the Beeland passenger service network. For this analysis assume that all regions are of similar size and structure.

END OF QUESTION

Section 8

SPECIMEN 2 EXAM ANSWERS

2   RAIL CO

> **Note**
>
> For the Strategic Professional Examinations it is not always possible to publish suggested answers which comprehensively cover all the valid points which candidates might make. Credit will be given to candidates for points not included in the suggested answers, but which, nevertheless, are relevant to the requirements. In addition, in this integrated case study examination candidates may re-introduce points made in other questions or parts of questions as long as these are made in the specific context of the requirements of the question being answered.
>
> The suggested answers presented below inevitably give much more detail than would be expected from most candidates under examination conditions, and include most of the obvious points evidenced from the case information. The answers are therefore intended to provide a structure of the approach required from candidates, and cover the range and depth of knowledge relating to each task which might be demonstrated by the most well prepared and able candidates. They are also intended to support revision and tuition for future examinations.

TASK 1

(a)   **Briefing Paper**

FAO: Rail Co Trust Board

The agency relationship of the parties involved in Rail Co and their rights and responsibilities

Rail Co is what would be called a devolved government body operating within the public sector. In terms of strategic purpose, Rail Co exists to implement government policy in regard of passenger rail services. Therefore, its organisational objectives will largely be determined by the political leaders of Beeland. Ultimately it is the responsibility of the chief executive of Rail Co to report to the government of Beeland (through the Rail Co Trust Board) on Rail Co's stewardship of the public funding it receives.

The main parties involved in the agency relationship of Rail Co are the government, in the form of the Ministry for Transport of Beeland as the principal and the Rail Co Trust Board and the board of directors, comprising a mix of executive and non-executive officers, acting as the agents. As stated above, ultimately the chief executive of Rail Co is responsible to the government for Rail Co's management and stewardship of the public funding it receives. It is important to note that the way in which Rail Co is regulated and governed is focused on value for money rather than on the achievement of profits.

There is also a further agency relationship within Rail Co, in that the Rail Co board of directors is accountable to the Rail Co Trust Board. It is the responsibility of the Rail Co Trust Board to set a range of performance targets each year and to hold the Rail Co board to account for the effective and efficient use of the funds allocated by government and by the fare paying passengers.

A further aspect of the agency relationship in Rail Co is that the ultimate principal is the taxpayer and the customers, in that it is he or she who pays for the rail service and Rail Co exists for their benefit. It is the ultimate responsibility of the board of Rail Co to ensure that Rail Co carries out its passenger services on behalf of those who fund the activity (mainly taxpayers) and those who use and pay for the services (rail passengers). Funders (i.e. taxpayers) and customers are sometimes the same people (for instance, taxpayers who commute on Rail Co's trains) but sometimes they are not, and this could give rise to disagreements on how much is spent and on what particular provisions. Rail Co has a responsibility to all of its principals to deliver its services efficiently, effectively and offering good value for money. As is evidenced in the recent article in the Beeland Herald, many customers are not satisfied with the value for money offered by Rail Co.

It is the responsibility of the Rail Co Trust Board to ensure that the key outcomes of Rail Co are delivered by setting a range of performance targets, against which performance is measured periodically.

(b)   **The role and value of the non-executive directors on the board of Rail Co**

Not-for-profit or public sector organisations must also be directed and controlled appropriately, as the decisions and actions of a few individuals can affect many individuals, groups and organisations which have little or no influence over them. Public sector organisations, such as Rail Co, have a duty to serve the government, but must act in a way that treats stakeholders fairly.

The non-executive directors (NEDs) are not employees of the company and are not involved in its day-to-day running. The non-executive directors usually receive a flat fee for their services, and are engaged under a contract for service.

The role of NEDs is to provide a balancing influence on the board of directors and help to minimise conflicts of interest. The Higgs Report, published in 2003, summarised their role as:

*   to contribute to the strategic plan
*   to scrutinise the performance of the executive directors
*   to provide an external perspective on risk management
*   to deal with people issues, such as the future shape of the board and resolution of conflicts.

Importantly, the NEDs should have high ethical standards and act with integrity and probity. Their main role is to support the executive directors of Rail Co and monitor its conduct, demonstrating a willingness to listen, question, debate and challenge.

It is recognised as best practice that a company should have more non-executive directors than executive directors. This is the case for Rail Co, as can be seen from its structure highlighted on the Rail Co website. The NEDs of Rail Co are responsible for running the four board committees which are set up to monitor the performance of Rail Co in key areas such as health and safety and audit and risk management The NEDs are also responsible for setting and reviewing the directors' remuneration and evaluating the corporate governance structure and activities of Rail Co and ensuring that the board is adequately governed, structured and staffed. This is particularly relevant and important to a public sector company such as Rail Co, where transparency and public scrutiny are prevalent.

The chairman of Rail Co is also a non-executive director and plays a key role in the business. The chairman has the ultimate role of leading the board, whilst the chief executive leads the business. Therefore, the roles of chairman and chief executive are complementary and interlinked.

The NEDs of Rail Co can add value to the business by:

- broadening the horizons and experience of existing executive directors, particularly if they come from a wide range of both public and private sector organisations.

- facilitating the cross-fertilisation of ideas, particularly in terms of business strategy and planning.

- playing a vital part to play in appraising and commenting on Rail Co's achievement of value for money and advising on strategies to improve this.

A team of executive and non-executive directors needs to be made up of people with business acumen and hands-on experience. Non-executive directors should be able to fill the gaps in expertise not available in the executive team and provide independent and objective scrutiny to the direction of such organisations in the public interest.

TASK 2

(a) **To:** The Rail Co Trust Board

From: Audit analyst, National Audit Authority

Date: xx/xx/xxxx

A report on the customer satisfaction performance of Rail Co and the relative performance of Rail Co with its competitors over the last three years

An evaluation of the customer satisfaction survey results

	Percentage satisfied			Actual % change 2015 to 2016	Trust Board target for 2016 Target growth on 2015	Trust Board target achieved?
	2016	2015	2014			
Overall satisfaction with your journey	87	90	92	–3%	+3%	No
Satisfaction with ticket buying facilities	60	64	65	–4%	+2%	No
Availability of staff	62	65	70	–3%	+5%	No
Helpfulness/attitude of staff	75	73	77	+2%	+2%	Yes
Reliability of service	84	81	86	+3%	+5%	No
Value for money for price of the ticket	50	56	57	–6%	+2%	No

In analysing the results of the customer satisfaction survey, as indicated in the key performance measures highlighted in Appendix 3, these clearly show that overall customer satisfaction of Rail Co's services has declined in 2016. Overall satisfaction has decreased by 3% on 2015 results, and, notably, this is significantly below the target of a 3% increase for the year, as set by the Rail Co Trust Board. This is a key indicator for Rail Co as it demonstrates whether the services provided are effective in the eyes of its customers. Although 87% is still high, it does reflect a growing dissatisfaction from the point of view of the customers as a continued trend. This needs to be reversed.

Customers are also clearly not happy with the ticket purchasing facilities offered at the train stations, with a 4% decrease in satisfaction from 2015. Again, the Rail Co Trust Board target of a 2% increase on 2015 has not been met. One customer feedback comment highlights customer frustration with the lack of online facilities, 'This is very frustrating and often, I use my car instead of going by train as it is more convenient than queuing to buy a train ticket.' Other national rail operators do offer online ticket buying facilities and it would appear that its absence in Rail Co is a cause for concern, as customers are becoming increasingly unhappy with having to queue for tickets at stations.

The measure of staff helpfulness and attitude is the only performance target met by Rail Co in 2016. This is positive, as it indicates staff commitment and attitude and could be an indicator of successful staff management policies at Rail Co. The availability of staff has declined by 2% and thus clearly not achieved the target set by the Rail Co Trust Board, indicating a possible problem with adequacy of staffing levels or levels of absenteeism.

The customers' perception of the reliability of service has improved from 2015 by 3%, which is a positive outcome. This could be due to increased investment in new trains. However, if this is considered in conjunction with the results of the competitor analysis, it is evident that in fact, the punctuality of Rail Co's services is in fact decreasing year on year. These measures appear to be at odds, but it must be noted that the customers' perception of reliability could include other factors, other than trains being on time to their destination. For example, reliability could include reliability of staff on the trains or reliability of trains stopping at the correct stations.

One of the most important measures is customers' perception of value for money of the price they pay for a ticket. This has decreased significantly compared with 2015 by 6%. This is a significant negative change in customer perception and one which cannot be ignored. As stated by a customer in the annual survey, 'The price of the regular ticket I buy to commute to work has increased by nearly 10% since last year. I really can't understand why, as I do not seem to be getting more for my money.' This is important to the government because if customers do not believe that they are getting value for money and if ticket prices continue to rise, then Rail Co are in danger of losing more customers.

The above findings should also be considered in conjunction with the results of the competitor performance analysis, as discussed below.

Competitor performance analysis

	ANR			Rail Co			Ceeland Rail		
	2016	2015	2014	2016	2015	2014	2016	2015	2014
Revenue growth	4.9%	5.5%	–	2.5%	3%		8%	5%	–
Operating profit %	31.54%	25.5%	19.8%	25.9%	31.39%	34.3%	35.4%	31.5%	27%
Cost per km (B$)	3.40	3.50	3.60	3.90	3.63	3.40	2.62	2.8	3
Cost per employee (B$)	92,004	95,706	100,041	110,654	100,883	93,221	83,363	85,774	88,141
Ticket price increase p.a	4.9%	0.0%		8.3%	7.1%	–	−4.7%	−2.3%	–
Customer satisfaction improvement p.a	2%	−3%	–	−3%	−2%	–	+3%	0%	–
Injuries per staff member	1.1%	1.1%	1.1%	1.8%	1.7%	1.7%	0.4%	0.4%	0.5%

Focusing on the key findings of this analysis, it is noticeable that revenue growth is much lower for Rail Co than its two competitors. In 2016, revenue growth for both competitors was much higher than that of Rail Co. Indeed, Ceeland Rail achieved an 8% revenue increase despite a 4.7% decrease in average ticket prices, indicating that more passengers were using the network and that there may be some price elasticity of demand. Conversely, Rail Co's revenue increased by only 2.5% with an average increase in ticket price of 8.3%, indicating a significant fall in fare paying passengers on trains in 2016, but the article in the Herald newspaper indicates that there may be a 10% increase in total passengers being carried on the service making the service increasingly overcrowded and uncomfortable.

All three companies have achieved a healthy operating profit margin, but again, Rail Co is not performing as well as its competitors. Both Ceeland Rail and ANR have achieved a significant improvement since 2014 in operating profit margin, indicating an improvement in its cost control. However, Rail Co's operating profit margin has decreased by 8.4% in the same period. This should be of significant concern to the board of Rail Co as it indicates a weakness in cost control.

This point is further highlighted by considering the cost per kilometre travelled per company. Rail Co has the highest cost per kilometre, which has also risen each year since 2014. Ceeland Rail's cost per kilometre is significantly less than Rail Co and has been stable over the same period, indicating sound cost management systems. Ceeland is clearly a larger organisation than Rail Co and therefore may benefit from economies of scale, which must be taken into account, but nevertheless, both ANR and Ceeland Rail appear to be managing their costs much more efficiently than Rail Co.

Rail Co also underperforms both of its competitors in terms of trains on time and once again, it has failed to meet the target for improvement set by the Rail Co Trust Board for 2016 (an increase of 3.7% on 2015 compared to a target of +5%). Obviously, it is difficult to judge this measure without further information on distances travelled per train and train type, but it does give us an indicator of how customers are likely to perceive each company. This is indeed verified by the customer satisfaction surveys for each company, which clearly shows that the customers of the two competitors are currently far more satisfied with the services they offer. Ceeland Rail is outperforming both rivals in these two key measures.

Another important measure to consider is staff turnover, as this can be a key indicator of staff satisfaction and overall well-being of staff in the company. It is clear from the analysis that staff turnover in Beeland is high compared to the other two companies. Indeed, in 2016 it was double that of Ceeland Rail. Obviously, it is difficult to make a detailed judgement without having further information relating to staff make-up in terms of full-time and part-time staff and age and length of service. However, this measure should be a clear indicator to Beeland's management that this could be symptomatic of a high level of staff dissatisfaction compared to the competitors and the reasons must be investigated and addressed if possible. If staff are poorly trained or poorly paid, or working in an unsafe environment, then this could lead to poor motivation, which will have an overall impact on customer satisfaction and staff effectiveness. Also, staff turnover will add significant costs to Rail Co's operations.

Although this review has only considered a limited number of performance indicators, it is clear that Beeland Rail is not performing as well as its competitors and that there are a number of areas which the board must address immediately.

(b)   **The Rail Co Trust Board**
           Beeland

Xx/xx/xxxx

Dear Chairman

The following is our report on the effectiveness of internal controls of Rail Co based on the evidence I have been able to collect and analyse.

Having thoroughly reviewed the Rail Co performance data, the recent board meeting minutes of Rail Co and the transport report in the Beeland Herald, a number of internal control weaknesses can be highlighted.

First, there appears to be a serious weakness in the control of passengers accessing trains without tickets. This is referred to in the Beeland Herald transport report, where it is mentioned that this issue had already been raised in the last two annual reports. This creates a significant business risk which does not seem to have been acted upon or mitigated by the Rail Co board. It has been highlighted for over two years that Rail Co believes that significant numbers of passengers are travelling on Rail Co's network without tickets. A key internal control weakness would appear to be that approximately 40% of Rail Co's stations do not operate ticket barriers, allowing the potential for customer ticket fraud. This potentially will have seriously damaging consequences on the performance of Rail Co in that revenues are not being optimised.

Second, there appears to be a weakness in staff management and safety procedures, in that there has been an increase in the number of injuries to staff reported by Rail Co in the last year. This is evidenced in the recent performance information analysed by one of my colleagues in Exhibit 3. Although Kim Lun has assured the BHSO that a thorough investigation would be undertaken immediately, it indicates that Rail Co has potential weaknesses in safety procedures and also in staff training procedures. The performance statistics indicate that Rail Co has lower levels of training than its competitors and Kim Lun (non-executive director) has noted that there had been a lack of investment in the training of staff in the last three years, which is also a key internal control weakness and one which could seriously impede the performance of Rail Co. Staff who are not appropriately trained are more likely to have accidents and to make mistakes. Again, this will have serious repercussions on the overall performance of Rail Co and could have seriously damaging impact upon reputation if serious injuries occur.

A further internal control weakness could be seen as the lack of investment in online booking systems. Several other national train operators offer online booking facilities and evidence suggested that this had positively impacted upon revenue growth and customer satisfaction in all of these businesses (Appendix 3). Lack of focus upon IT investment and development in key strategic information systems could be seen as an internal control weakness and could hamper the long-term performance of Rail Co.

A further internal control weakness could be the current pay structure. Poorly paid staff who are dissatisfied will leave or may take strike action. HR policies on fair pay could be considered to be weak if they are not commensurate with the expected pay rate.

Throughout the board meeting, there is evidence of the chief executive's inability to react to these key internal weaknesses effectively and it would seem that in some cases, this reluctance and inactivity could have seriously damaging consequences for Rail Co. In a number of cases, there is evidence of a failure to achieve his fiduciary duty to the trustee of Rail Co.

First, his comments in relation to Rail Co's performance are inaccurate and reflect his own opinion, based on historic performance and not the actual performance in 2016. Clearly, some narrow aspects of performance have improved, but it is not in line with competitors and customer expectations in the current climate. His comment that the target for punctuality set by the Trust Board was unachievable and not relevant is highly inappropriate and shows a breach of his fiduciary duty to the trustees. It is his role as chief executive to ensure that these targets are achievable and they cannot simply be ignored. Also, his statement that customers do not understand value for money demonstrates his lack of understanding of the customers' perception of this critical measure. It is wrong for him to make such a sweeping and unjust statement and could seriously damage the reputation of Rail Co if these views were made public.

His response to the investment in ticket barriers is unfounded and demonstrates a lack of understanding of a key internal control weakness in relation to the potential level of fraud in Rail Co. He had made a significant judgement founded upon no evidence of costs outweighing the benefits and his assessment that most fraud being unpreventable is ill-judged and incorrect. Again, his lack of understanding of such an important issue is a failure of his fiduciary duty.

His comment that there is no evidence to suggest that staff morale is low is incorrect, as staff turnover is increasing, strongly indicating low morale. He pointed to evidence in the customer survey report which indicated an annual growth in customer satisfaction levels in relation to staff helpfulness and attitude but this is not linked to staff training in any way. His logic is flawed and his attitude towards staff and adequate training could be seriously damaging to Rail Co.

The CE also commented that online ticket facilities went against the traditional values of customer service focus of Rail Co. His reluctance to invest in such technology could prove to be seriously damaging to Rail Co's performance. It is clear that customers are not happy with ticket buying facilities and should this continue more will use other means of transport. To delay this decision could be damaging to Rail Co, should customers continue to choose other forms of transport to commute.

The chief executive's attitude towards the unions could be severely damaging to Rail Co, should the unions decide to take strike action. The CE commented that the unions were merely taking advantage of the latest survey results to put the board under pressure to increase levels of pay for its members. Although Rail Co must negotiate with the unions, to take an aggressive stance could be counter-productive. His comment relating to the media as an unimportant stakeholder is incorrect as adverse media reports about Rail Co are a potential reputational risk to the organisation.

In conclusion, my overall opinion is that the comments made by the chief executive demonstrate a number of serious failures and weaknesses in his fiduciary duty to the principals and trustees of Rail Co. I have grave concerns regarding his awareness of the current situation facing Rail Co and his abilities to respond effectively to the changes which will be required in the coming months.

Yours sincerely

Assistant auditor, NAA

TASK 3

(a)   **To: Chair of the Nominations Committee From: Chair of sub-committee**

Date: xx/xx/x2016

Subject: A review of the candidates for chief executive of Rail Co Introduction

The outline person specification sets out some very clear criteria for the role of CE in Rail Co, specifically the requirement for demonstration of experience at CE level in a similar organisation. Obviously an understanding of the rail industry is also an important factor to consider. Also, in a high profile public sector environment, an ability to operate successfully in a complex political environment and to manage the complex relationships with multiple stakeholders will be a key factor. Importantly, in this role of CE in Rail Co, it is clear that many changes need to be made in the near future to address its current failures and to achieve the targets and expectations of its key stakeholders and therefore the new CE should have the skills and abilities to manage and lead a dynamic change programme at Rail Co.

Candidate A

Candidate A clearly has a significant amount of experience as a CE, having worked at this level since 2000. As a CE of a multinational oil company, he will have significant experience of managing a highly complex business environment and multiple stakeholder influences, including government. Additionally, his recent CE experience is within the rail industry working for JPS Express in Jayland. Notably, he led the privatisation of JPS trains in 2013, therefore he has experience of working in the public sector environment prior to 2013. He has clear experience of working with the government and regulatory authorities, which will be a key skill in Rail Co in managing the relationship with the Trust Board and the Minister of Transport. His ability to build and maintain relationships with external bodies, staff and the media would appear to be a highly positive capability and one which is highly desirable in the current operating climate of Rail Co.

Notably, Candidate A demonstrates key skills in change leadership and human performance management. It is clear that a change programme will need to be carried out by the new CE in a number of key areas, including the improvement in the performance of human resources and key strategic project investments. Candidate A has a proven track record in change leadership and in managing complex projects and these will be key attributes. In addition, his focus upon strong internal control is a key competence required at this present time.

Candidate B

Candidate B also has a number of very positive attributes. Currently, he is not working within the rail industry, but does work for a very large aviation company which will clearly require many key leadership skills. Although he has not worked as a CE for quite as long as Candidate A, notably he has worked in the rail industry previously as a finance director for Ceeland Rail. Therefore he will have an excellent knowledge of the financial management requirements of Rail Co. His obvious skills and experience in financial management would be a hugely positive influence for Rail Co. His focus on KPIs and developing strategies for revenue growth and operational efficiency would be hugely positive for Rail Co. However, his experiences focus largely upon financial management which, although critically important to Rail Co, may be rather too narrow and not sufficiently focused upon the change leadership requirements of Rail Co. There is also limited evidence of managing stakeholder relationships in a complex environment such as Rail Co, particular the relationship with government and regulatory bodies. Also, there is little evidence of his abilities to lead change.

Recommendation

Both candidates have a wide range of skills and experience and both would bring very positive attributes to Rail Co. Overall, taking into consideration the current requirements of Rail Co and the likely changes which will need to be undertaken by the newly appointed CE in the near future, then my recommendation would be to appoint Candidate A. He has all of the relevant public sector experience, together with his experience of managing complex stakeholder relationships and his change leadership experience.

(b) **Presentation slides**

<table>
<tr><td colspan="2">

SLIDE 1

Talent	**Talent management**
• Individuals who can make a difference to organisational performance through their immediate contribution or, in the longer term, by demonstrating high future potential	• The attraction, identification, development, engagement, retention and deployment of individuals who are of particular value to an organisation
	• It is critical for Rail Co to develop, manage and retain individuals as part of a planned talent management strategy

</td></tr>
</table>

Notes:

The definition of talent emphasises that these are individuals who can make an impact on the performance of Rail Co. This is of utmost importance in the near future as Rail Co attempts to turn around its business performance.

Importantly, talent management should be seen as a key strategic management activity which sits alongside and indeed underpins the whole corporate strategy.

Many organisations consider the 'talents' of all their staff and work on ways to develop their strengths. Talent management programmes may include a range of activities such as formal and informal leadership coaching, networking events and board-level and client exposure. It can also include ensuring that all staff are adequately and effectively trained and motivated at all levels of the business

SLIDE 2 – The contribution of the chief executive in talent management	
• Important that talent management strategy is led from the top	• Driving force in attracting talent and building a high performance workplace
• Senior management team must assess the human talent needs of the change programme	

Notes:

Ensuring that the talent management strategy is closely aligned with the corporate strategy must be a priority. The CE must lead the senior management team in understanding the main priorities of the change programme in Rail Co which should then be used to develop a human talent forecast, which can help shape Rail Co's talent management strategy.

Visible senior-level support for talent management is critical, and this is best done by the CE.

The ability to attract external talent depends upon how potential applicants view Rail Co. The creation of an attractive employer brand is an important factor in recruiting external talent. Again, the CE will be a driving force in this, as the figure head and mouthpiece of the organisation he will be integral in creating the employer brand which will attract talent to Rail Co.

TASK 4

(a)

						Variance between tickets sold v			Fraud % for each	Estimated fraud due to poor	Preventable
			Monthly	Estimated %	Estimated monthly ticket	sold v projected	Spend	Estimated	town (based	internal control	annual fraud ($)
	Ticket	Population	tickets sold	railway users	sales per	ticket	per ticket	fraud ($)	on total	(%) (based on	(based on total
Town	barrier	per town	to town	per town	town	sales	sold	per month	population)	total population)	population)
A	y	142000	28000	21	29820	1820	59	107380	1.28%		
B	y	195000	31000	17	33150	2150	38	81700	1.10%		
C	n	110000	22000	28	30800	8800	44	387200	8.00%	6.72%	3,903,953
D	n	195000	36000	26	50700	14700	51	749700	7.54%	6.26%	7,470,856
E	y	74000	25000	35	25900	900	56	50400	1.22%		
F	y	116000	31000	28	32480	1480	52	76960	1.28%		
G	n	183000	37000	30	54900	17900	56	1002400	9.78%	8.50%	10,456,776
H	y	87000	19000	23	20010	1010	61	61610	1.16%		
I	n	144000	12000	16	23040	11040	48	529920	7.67%	6.39%	5,298,752
J	y	147000	27000	20	29400	2400	62	148800	1.63%		
		1393000	268000					3196070			

Initial data on stations in Region 1 - Beeland network

Analysis of fraud - information based on 2016 analysis

Assumed average percentage of unpreventable fraud - Region 1	1.28%
Total annual preventable fraud in Region 1:	$ 27,130,338
Extrapolate for 20 regions	$ 542,606,752

Note:

There are 20 identifiable regions within the Beeland passenger service network. For this analysis assume that all regions are of similar size and structure.

The spreadsheet prepared by the financial controller has identified the estimated fraud per month in Region 1, based upon the variance between actual tickets sold and estimated tickets sold per town (based on estimated percentage of railway users per town). This is then estimated as a percentage based on the total population of each town. It is notable that for each railway station which has a ticket barrier that the level of fraud is markedly lower than those stations without ticket barriers (stations C, D, G and I). Therefore, it can be assumed that ticket barriers are clearly having a direct impact on preventing fraud. The estimated railway users in the towns need further investigation. How was this calculated? Was this based on surveys or on demographic factors or both? This would have to be examined further.

The spreadsheet also calculates the percentage of unpreventable fraud at 1.28%, based upon an average of those stations which have ticket barriers (stations A, B, E, F, H, J). This presumes that there is an element of fraud occurring on Rail Co's network which cannot be prevented with the installation of ticket barriers. There will always be some degree of fraud occurring which is almost impossible to control. Again there is an assumption about preventable versus unpreventable fraud. Further information may be required to understand how this estimate was arrived at and whether this is the same at all stations and regions.

Therefore the spreadsheet takes this into account when calculating the percentage of fraud due to poor internal control (preventable fraud) at those stations without ticket barriers.

If we then use this information to calculate the total preventable fraud based upon the total population in each town, then it can be calculated that total annual preventable fraud is estimated to be nearly $B27 million in Region 1 alone. If we were to extrapolate this across 20 regions, it gives an estimated annual fraud of $B542 million. The assumption that this region is perfectly representative of other regions allowing such an extrapolation is a tenuous one. It is unlikely that the profile of towns, their demographics, and the proportion of rail users or preventable versus unpreventable fraud levels will be the same across regions. However, if these assumptions can reasonably be made, this is a significant amount and if we were to take this as a percentage of total revenue in 2016 it amounts to 12% of annual revenue. This is a staggeringly high figure and clearly a significant control problem for Rail Co. Even if the level of preventable fraud was assumed to be 50% of the calculated figure above (say $B270 million), this level of fraud is still unacceptable.

(b) The first measure which Rail Co should consider is the installation of ticket barriers at those stations with a high level of preventable fraud and which currently do not have ticket barriers. Clearly, ticket barriers are a huge deterrent to fraud, as evidence by the levels encountered at stations with barriers on the network in Region 1. Obviously, Rail Co would need to undertake a thorough cost benefit analysis on such a project but from the estimated level of preventable fraud calculated above, then it is likely that such an investment would have significant benefits for Rail Co.

A further measure would be to expand ticket offices and employ more staff at ticket offices to reduce queuing time for customers. Clearly, customers are likely to become frustrated by having to queue for tickets, particularly if they may miss their train. Expansion of ticket booths or the installation of ticket machines would provide customers with more opportunity to buy a ticket.

Another measure would be to offer customers the ability to purchase tickets whilst on the trains. This is likely to mean employing more ticket inspectors on each train. Obviously, this is likely to be costly, but Rail Co could manage this by only employing more staff on peak time trains.

Rail Co should also consider the prices it charges to customers. Some customers may be motivated to travel without a ticket due to its unaffordability. In this case, these customers will inevitably take the opportunity to travel without tickets if they can do so. This could include younger customers, such as students, for example, who cannot afford a regular high priced ticket. Rail Co should review its pricing policies and structure and consider offering a more affordable range of ticket prices to meet the needs of is customer groups, such as student concessions, off-peak travellers and frequent user discounts and passes.

Rail Co could also consider the introduction of an online train ticket booking facility. It would seem that Rail Co is indeed behind its competitors in this development and should be a serious consideration for Rail Co. Online ticket purchasing is likely to be a hugely convenient ticket buying option for its customers and is likely to encourage more customers to buy tickets in the comfort of their own home or office. Obviously, this will be a significant investment for Rail Co and a major project undertaking, but it would likely be a significant influence in reducing fraud.

Clearly, Rail Co cannot control all customer fraud and it will always encounter dishonest travellers. However, it is important to implement measures which safeguard against lost revenue which is not done with dishonest intentions.

TASK 5

(a)   **Business case for the investment in an online ticket sales system for Rail Co**
       Introduction

The following business case sets out how investment in online ticket sales could assist Rail Co in producing more timely customer data and assist in customer relationship management.

Current situation

Presently, Rail Co does not operate an online ticket sales facility for its customers. All tickets are purchased at ticket offices located at each station. Recent evidence suggests that as a result of inadequate ticket buying facilities at the stations combined with a lack of ticket barriers, there is a high level of fraud occurring in the network. Some of this fraud could be eliminated with the introduction of improved ticket buying facilities such as an online booking facility.

In addition, customers are used to being able to buy products and services online and as a modern organisation Rail Co should be considering offering customers such a facility. It has become an expectation of digital life that customers are provided with the flexibility to buy products and services from the comfort of their own home. Research also suggests that other national passenger rail service providers offer customers such a facility. Therefore, not to offer such facilities may be detrimental to Rail Co's competitive position.

Analysis of the benefits of an online ticket sales facility

The purpose of CRM is the building of relationships in order to affect customer acquisition, retention and loyalty, resulting in the development of 1:1 relationships with these customers. This 'customer focused' approach, which will involve building a strong relationship with Rail Co's customers as well as gathering, storing and sharing information about these customers across the organisation, will likely improve customer loyalty.

Electronic CRM, in the form of an online ticket sales system, would make it possible for Rail Co to have as much contact as possible with its customers through the internet. This internet support for Rail Co's customers would likely take the form of presales information, such as timetabling information, ticket purchasing services and after-sales support, such as online refunds or customer account queries. The internet would make it possible for Rail Co to have frequent contact with its customers, and so enable us to operate and maintain a detailed customer database, assisting us even further in developing better customer relationships. A further value of the internet for Rail Co could be seen in the quicker flow of information (real time sales data) and more consistent communications which can result from its use.

The effective use of CRM systems could assist in Rail Co's relationship-building activities while also contributing to the profitability of the business. Some of the goals which we should set would include retaining our existing passengers, improving customer satisfaction with the services we offer and increasing customer loyalty. Customers who receive excellent services remain loyal and a further advantage is that they provide free advertising by talking about the organisation's services.

Operational CRM includes customer-facing applications such as sales force automation, enterprise marketing automation and customer service and support. Rail Co may consider the implementation of a customer call centre, which is also a component of operational CRM. In this way, all interactions with the customer could be recorded, enabling Rail Co to gather even more data on the customer and thus track the customer.

Analytical CRM could also be used to analyse the data which has been created through operational CRM, to build a picture of the customer. Analytical CRM includes the capturing, storage, extraction, processing, interpretation and reporting of customer data stored in data warehouses. This will enable us to examine customer behavioural patterns in order to develop marketing and promotional strategies which can be tailored to specific customer groups, such as students, the elderly, daily commuters or leisure travellers.

Risk assessment

A detailed cost analysis must been undertaken to assess the financial viability of an investment in an online ticket sales system for Rail Co. Further risks should also be considered including the customer perception of such a system and also a stakeholder mapping exercise will need to be undertaken. The main risk is that customers will not use the system, either due to a reluctance to change purchasing habits or due to a lack of awareness of the facility. These risks can be overcome through adequate customer awareness strategies such as in-station advertising and national and regional TV and radio advertising.

(b) **Outline project initiation document**

Project objectives	To implement an online ticket sales system in Rail Co to enable customers to purchase tickets online as well as through ticket sales offices at train stations. The overall objective of the project is to increase customer satisfaction levels.
Anticipated benefits	<ul><li>A reduction in numbers of passengers travelling without tickets</li><li>Improved revenues and profitability</li><li>Increased levels of customer satisfaction and loyalty</li><li>Up to the minute customer data for marketing purposes</li><li>Reduced marketing costs due to online advertising</li><li>Tailored marketing approach meaning a more targeted focus on customers' needs</li></ul>
Scope	An extension of the current website to include web-based ticket booking technology and customer contact facilities. A customer database to capture customer information and booking history which can be utilised for customer relationship management and marketing purposes.
Deliverables/Outcomes	A fully operational customer ticket sales site as part of the current Rail Co website within 12 months.

Constraints	Funding – to be considered as part of an overall cost benefit analysis to be completed. Resources – the project will need to be undertaken by an external systems development provider. A tender process will need to be carried out immediately. Time – the project should be completed and the booking system fully operational with 12 months of the project start date (to be confirmed).
Key stakeholders	• Customers/fare paying passengers • Station and train staff of Rail Co • The board of directors • Rail Co Trust Board • The government of Beeland
Project team roles	Project manager (Rail Co projects and infrastructure staff) Development team (systems development supplier staff) Rail Co director of projects and infrastructure One NED
Risk assessment	Cost overruns Delays to project deadline Lack of customer usage or satisfaction with the system Systems security breaches
Cost estimates	To be undertaken
Performance measures	• Number of tickets sold online • Number of repeat purchase online • Reduction in levels of fraud • Number of customer accounts set up online • Impact on revenue growth

MARKING SCHEME

TASK 1

(a) Up to two marks for identifying and explaining the agency relationship of at least four parties involved in Rail Co. **(Up a maximum of 8 marks in total)**

(b) One mark per relevant point for assessing the role and value of the non-executive directors on Rail Co's board. The focus of the marks should be on the specific role within a public sector organisation. **(Up to a maximum of 6 in total)**

Professional skills may be additionally rewarded as in the following rubric:

How well has the candidate demonstrated professional skills as follows:	Not at all	Not so well	Quite well	Very well
(a) Communication skills in clarifying the agency relationships in Rail Co	The candidate has demonstrated poor communication skills. They have failed to present the required information in a clear, objective and unambiguous way. The answer is not communicated in an appropriate format (briefing paper) or tone (for review by the Rail Co Trust Board)	The candidate has demonstrated some basic communication skills in presenting an appropriate briefing paper format. Some relevant information is contained in the answer but some of the information is not relevant or unclear.	The candidate has demonstrated good communication skills in the presentation of the briefing paper to the Rail Co Trust Board. The candidate has presented most of the relevant issues and has done so concisely and in most cases, clearly.	The candidate has demonstrated excellent communication skills. The briefing paper was correctly structured, covered all of the relevant points needed by the Trust Board in understanding the agency relationship and was set at the correct tone.
	0	0.5	1	2
(b) Evaluation skills in assessing the role and value of the non-executive directors in a public sector environment	The candidate has failed to demonstrate any evaluation of the role of the non-executive directors. The answer is merely descriptive and contains no evidence of the use of professional judgement to evaluate the non-executives role in and value to the business.	The candidate has demonstrated some limited evaluation skills in assessing the role of non-executive directors in the business. The candidate has demonstrated limited evolution of the value of non-executive directors and there is limited focus of the public sector environment.	The candidate has demonstrated evaluation skills in assessing the role and value of the non-executive directors but the focus of the answer was not upon the public sector environment specifically.	The candidate has demonstrated sound evaluation skills in assessing the role and value of the non-executive directors and the answer is focused directly upon the public sector environment.
	0	0.5	1	2

TASK 2

(a)   One mark for each relevant calculation up to a maximum of eight marks. A further eight marks can be awarded for an evaluation of the calculations in terms of their implications for Rail Co.   **(Up to a maximum of 12 marks)**

(b)   Up to two marks for each internal control identified and evaluated up to a maximum of six marks. A further four marks for justifying, with evidence, why the CE of Rail Co should be removed.   **(Up to a maximum of 8 marks)**

Professional skills may be additionally rewarded as in the following rubric:

How well has the candidate demonstrated professional skills as follows:	Not at all	Not so well	Quite well	Very well
(a) Analysis skills in investigating and analysing the information presented in the spreadsheet	The candidate has demonstrated very limited analysis skills. The candidate has failed to select appropriate metrics or considered or analysed the information carefully. The candidate has demonstrated limited evaluation or reflection on any calculations presented.	The candidate has demonstrated some analysis skills in investigating and selecting appropriate calculations relating to Rail Co's customer survey results and its relative performance. However, there is only some evidence of reflection of the calculations presented.	The candidate has demonstrated analysis skills in selecting a reasonable range of relevant calculations on both the customer survey results and its relative performance. The candidate has made a reasonable attempt to comment and reflect on these calculations.	The candidate has demonstrated excellent analysis skills in presenting a wide range of relevant calculations on both customer survey results of Rail Co and its relative performance. The candidate has also demonstrated sound evidence of high levels reflection on and consideration of the calculations presented.
	0	0.5	1	2
(b) Scepticism skills in questioning the opinions and assertions made in the minutes to the board meeting	The candidate has failed to demonstrate any scepticism of the internal controls or of the opinions and assertions made by the chief executive. The candidate demonstrated no evidence of challenging or questioning the internal controls or the opinions of the CE. The candidate failed to clearly justify why the CE should be removed from his position.	The candidate has demonstrated some, but limited, scepticism of the internal controls and the opinions and assertions made by the chief executive. The candidate questioned some of the internal controls and challenged some of the assertions made by CE. However, the depth of the questioning was limited and the challenge to the CE's opinions was not presented in a professional manner.	The candidate has demonstrated scepticism of the internal controls or of the opinions and assertions made by the chief executive. The candidate recognised and challenged most of the internal controls. The challenge of the CE's opinions was reasonably sound. The challenge to the opinions of the CE could have been presented in a more professional manner.	The candidate has demonstrated deep scepticism of the internal controls or of the opinions and assertions made by the chief executive. The candidate strongly questioned, with evidence, the validity of the internal controls. The candidate challenged the opinions of the CE in a professional and justified manner.
	0	0.5	1	2

TASK 3

(a) Up to one mark for each relevant point which clearly evaluates each shortlisted candidate. Award up to two marks for a clearly justified recommendation.

(Up to a maximum of 8 marks in total)

(b) Up to three marks per slide and notes. Up to one mark for each relevant point made relating to the impact of talent management in the change required by Rail Co.

(Up to a maximum of 6 marks)

Professional skills may be additionally rewarded as in the following rubric:

How well has the candidate demonstrated professional skills as follows:	Not at all	Not so well	Quite well	Very well
(a) Commercial acumen skills in evaluating the relative merits of the two candidates	The candidate has demonstrated no commercial acumen in judging the relative skills and experience presented by the two candidates. The candidate has merely restated the information presented and has showed no commercial awareness of the factors affecting the successful contribution of a new CE. No use was made of the person specification	The candidate has demonstrated some commercial acumen in judging the relative skills and experience of the two candidates. The candidate has demonstrated a limited commercial awareness the factors impacting upon the successful contribution of a new CE. The candidate made limited reference to the person specification.	The candidate has demonstrated some sound commercial acumen in judging the relative skills and experience of the two candidates. This has been evaluated in some parts against the person specification. The candidate has demonstrated some good commercial awareness of the factors impacting on the successful contribution of the new CE.	The candidate has demonstrated excellent commercial acumen, using the person specification to form a clear judgement of the requirements of the role. The candidate has demonstrated strong awareness of the factors impacting on the successful contribution of the new CE and has made sound judgement on the choice of candidate.
	0	0.5	1	2
(b) Communication skills in conveying relevant information in an appropriate tone to the nominations committee	The candidate has demonstrated poor communication skills. They have failed to present the required information in a clear, objective and unambiguous way. The answer is not communicated in an appropriate format (presentation slides) or tone (for the non-executive directors of the nominations committee).	The candidate has demonstrated some basic communication skills in presenting two presentation slides. Some relevant information is contained in the answer but most of the information is not relevant or unclear and not at an appropriate tone for a non-executive.	The candidate has demonstrated good communication skills in the presentation of the two slides to the nominations committee. The candidate has presented most of the relevant issues and has done so concisely and in most cases, clearly.	The candidate has demonstrated excellent communication skills. The presentation slides and notes were correctly and effectively structured, covered all of the relevant points needed by the nominations committee to explain the contribution of talent management expected of the new CE.
	0	0.5	1	2

TASK 4

(a)   Up to one mark for each relevant point made relating to evaluating the findings of the spreadsheet identifying levels of preventable fraud in Region 1, up to a maximum of six marks. A further two marks to be awarded for an evaluation of the impact on Rail Co's revenues.   **(Up to a maximum of 8 marks in total)**

(b)   Up to three marks for each measure recommended and clearly justified.
                                                          (Up to a maximum of 8 marks)

Professional skills may be additionally rewarded as in the following rubric:

How well has the candidate demonstrated professional skills as follows:	Not at all	Not so well	Quite well	Very well
(a) Scepticism skills in considering the information presented in the spreadsheet and reflecting on the impact on revenues	The candidate has demonstrated no scepticism skills. They have failed to question the information contained in the spreadsheet nor has the candidate offered any evidence of any reflection on the implications of the results which were identifiable from spreadsheet information.	The candidate has demonstrated limited scepticism skills by questioning some of the information and calculations. However, there is limited evidence of the candidate's abilities in considering the information and reflecting upon the outcome of the calculations identified.	The candidate has demonstrated some sound scepticism skills in considering and questioning a number of the calculations in the information presented. The candidate has demonstrated some ability to reflect on the implications of the calculations undertaken.	The candidate has demonstrated excellent scepticism skills in effectively an accurately analysing the information presented in the spreadsheet. The candidate has also demonstrated a clear understanding of the implications of their calculations for Rail Co.
	0	0.5	1	2
(b) Commercial acumen skills in making sound recommend-ations for suitable measures and safeguards	The candidate has demonstrated no commercial acumen skills in that they have failed to demonstrate any awareness or judgement of the required safeguards and measures.	The candidate has demonstrated only limited commercial acumen in presenting only a very limited range of recommendations on appropriate safeguards and measures, some of which showed weak commercial judgement and understanding.	The candidate demonstrated some commercial acumen in that they recognised some of the measures and safeguards required, demonstrating some judgement and understanding.	The candidate demonstrated excellent commercial judgement, making recommendations for safeguards and measures which demonstrated strong commercial awareness and understanding.
	0	0.5	1	2

TASK 5

(a) Up to one mark for each relevant point made in relation to the impact of online ticket sales on customer relationship management for Rail Co.

(Up to a maximum of 8 marks in total)

(b) Up to one mark for each relevant and correct aspect of the PID for an online ticket sales system project for Rail Co. **(Up to a maximum of 8 marks)**

Professional skills may be additionally rewarded as in the following rubric:

How well has the candidate demonstrated professional skills as follows:	Not at all	Not so well	Quite well	Very well
(a) Evaluation skills in assessing the impact of online ticket sales on CRM	The candidate has demonstrated no evaluation skills. The candidate has demonstrated no professional judgement in considering the relevance of an online ticket sales system to Rail Co. The answer is largely theoretical and the candidate has demonstrated little evidence of an ability to take into consideration the impact of the decision on the stakeholders of Rail Co.	The candidate has demonstrated some evaluation skills in assessing the impact of an online ticket sales system for Rail Co. The candidate has used little professional judgement to evaluate the impact of the system on producing more timely customer information and in CRM. There is evidence of some limited evaluation of the impact of the decision on the stakeholders of Rail Co.	The candidate has demonstrated some sound evaluation skills in assessing the impact of an online ticket sales system for Rail Co. The candidate has made a reasonable attempt to evaluate the impact of the system on more timely customer data and improved CRM. The candidate has demonstrated a reasonable ability to assess the impact on the stakeholders of Rail Co.	The candidate has demonstrated excellent evaluation skills. They have clearly demonstrated excellent professional judgement in assessing the impact of the system on timely customer data and CRM. The candidate has also demonstrated a clear ability to assess the impact of the new system on the stakeholders of Rail Co.
	0	**0.5**	**1**	**2**
(b) Communication skills in producing a PID to be used by Rail Co	The candidate has demonstrated no communication skills. The document produced is not a useful PID document and could not be used to effectively communicate to the members of the Rail Co project in order to plan and implement the online ticket sales system.	The candidate has demonstrated limited communication skills. The PID presented would have limited use as a communication tool for the members of the Rail Co project in order to plan and implement the online ticket sales system.	The candidate has demonstrated a reasonably good level of communication skills. The PID produced has some of the required information needed to be an effective communication tool for members of the Rail Co project to plan and implement the online ticket sales system.	The candidate has demonstrated excellent communication skills. The PID produced is an excellent communication tool which could be effectively used by the members of the Rail Co project to plan and implement the online ticket sales system.
	0	**0.5**	**1**	**2**

Section 9

REAL EXAM QUESTIONS – SEPTEMBER 2018

1   COFOLD CONSTRUCTION

Cofold Construction Co (CC) is a listed construction company. Its head office is in the capital city, Lambdahasa, of the country of Omegland. Omegland has two neighbouring countries, Alphia and Betal. The countryside in both Alphia and Omegland is generally flat. In Betal, there is a large range of mountains (the Isnardi mountains) which separates its Eastern region from the rest of the country. All three countries use the same currency, the dollar ($).

The board of CC comprises 50% executive directors and 50% independent non-executive directors. The senior board members are:

Chairman	Imena Bhudia
Chief executive	Burton Vadher
Senior non-executive director	Alex Larsen

CC's core business is to provide support services, such as upgrade of electricity networks and road renewal and maintenance, in all three countries. However, it has also undertaken road construction projects of increasing size and complexity. Initially, CC carried out most of its major construction projects in Omegland, its biggest project there being a ring road around the city of Lambdahasa. CC has also started to develop a portfolio in Alphia, the biggest development there being a road between Phi City and Tautown, which was completed in 20X0.

To date, CC has not carried out any road construction projects in Betal. However, an opportunity has arisen for CC to tender for construction of a major road in Betal, which would be the biggest project which CC has undertaken to date.

The following exhibits provide information relevant to CC:

Exhibit 1:   Extracts from the most recent annual report of CC.

Exhibit 2:   Press release of the announcement of the new road in Betal.

Exhibit 3:   Forecast revenues and costs for the construction of the new road in Betal.

Exhibit 4:   Outline contents of the project initiation document (PID) and a summary of the operational issues section of the PID.

Exhibit 5:   Transcript of an emergency meeting at CC's head office.

Exhibit 6:   Report of an interview with Burton Vadher in Omegland Daily News newspaper.

The case requirements are as follows and you will be told which role you are taking in each task.

1 You are Alex Larsen, the senior non-executive director of CC.

CC has been invited to tender for the contract for the construction of the new road in Betal, as the preferred partner of Betal's government. CC's finance team has drawn up financial forecasts for the project. However, you have doubts about the contract and you want it to be discussed thoroughly at CC's next board meeting. You are particularly concerned with whether CC will be able to fulfil the criteria stated by Betal's transport minister.

Required:

Prepare a briefing paper for the board meeting, which:

(a) **Analyses the financial and non-financial issues which will affect the final decision of whether to accept the contract to build the road in Betal.**

Note: A recommendation is NOT required. **(18 marks)**

Professional skills marks are available for demonstrating analysis skills in identifying information which is relevant to the decision. **(4 marks)**

(b) **Discusses the difficulties CC may face in fulfilling the criteria stated by Desmond Otieno, the transport minister of Betal.** **(8 marks)**

Professional skills marks are available for demonstrating commercial acumen in identifying difficulties for CC arising from the criteria which Desmond Otieno has stated. **(2 marks)**

(Total: 32 marks)

2 **CC has been awarded the contract to build the road in Betal. It is now January 20X2 and planning for the project has started.**

You are Jo Issa, the project manager for the construction of the road in Betal.

You have just been appointed project manager, as the original project manager left CC suddenly one month ago. Oliver Wesonga, the junior member of the project team, began to draft the project initiation document during the time when no-one was acting as project manager. He has prepared for your review the outline contents of the project initiation document, and a summary of the section in it on the operational issues affecting the project.

Required:

Prepare a memo addressed to Oliver Wesonga which critically evaluates the outline contents and the summary of operational issues in the project initiation document which he has prepared and recommends improvements. **(14 marks)**

Professional skills marks are available for demonstrating scepticism skills in discussing shortcomings with the outline contents and summary of operational issues in the project initiation document and recommending improvements. **(4 marks)**

(Total: 18 marks)

3   It is now July 20X2, three months after CC began construction of the new road in Betal.

You are Pat Singh, a consultant employed by CC's board.

You have just left the emergency meeting regarding the incident at the construction site and are responding to the requests made by CC's chairman, Imena Bhudia, at the end of the meeting.

Required:

Prepare:

(a)   A confidential memo for Imena Bhudia, chairman of CC, which discusses the ethical and reputational concerns raised at the meeting.   **(10 marks)**

Professional skills marks are available for demonstrating scepticism skills by challenging the comments made at the emergency meeting.   **(2 marks)**

(b)   A summary for CC's board to review assessing the control weaknesses discussed at the emergency meeting, stating for each control weakness its consequence and recommendation for improvements.   **(14 marks)**

Professional skills marks are available for demonstrating evaluation skills by basing explanations of significant control weaknesses on the information provided and recommending appropriate improvements.   **(4 marks)**

(c)   A briefing paper for CC's next board meeting, advising the board of the advantages for CC of establishing a separate risk committee.   **(8 marks)**

Professional skills marks are available for demonstrating commercial acumen skills in identifying benefits that would be relevant to CC in establishing a separate risk committee.   **(2 marks)**

(Total: 40 marks)

4   It is now October 20X2, six months after CC began construction of the new road in Betal.

You are Pat Singh, a consultant employed by CC's board.

Burton Vadher, CC's chief executive, has asked you to help him to prepare for the next board meeting, which will discuss investment in big data analytics and offering long-term infrastructure management for roads in Omegland, Alphia and Betal.

Required:

Prepare TWO presentation slides, together with accompanying notes, for the chief executive to present to the board which:

–   Discusses the benefits and the costs to CC of investing in big data analytics;

–   Evaluates the possible opportunity to undertake long-term infrastructure management of roads in the three countries.   **(8 marks)**

Professional skills marks are available for demonstrating communication skills in presenting the points in the slides concisely and for supporting notes which will make the issues clear to the board.   **(2 marks)**

(Total: 10 marks)

Exhibit 1: Extracts from the most recent annual report of CC

CHIEF EXECUTIVE'S STATEMENT

CC's results have shown increased profitability and stronger cash flows. The quality and value of the newer projects have been enhanced by a more focused approach to tendering. We have avoided speculative projects and concentrated on larger projects with high margins and advantageous contract terms. We believe that these are projects which can unlock new opportunities for CC. As a result I am delighted to announce the first increase in dividends for three years.

The results reflect the successful completion of the ring route linking the main roads round Lambdahasa. The $10 billion earnings from this, CC's biggest ever construction project, have shown CC's ability to expand the scope and size of the projects which it undertakes.

CC's Stakeholder First programme, aiming to enhance our relationships with all our key stakeholders, has also delivered benefits. We look forward to the prospect of building on our strong relationship with the government of Omegland. We also continue to engage with communities affected by our work. We are mindful of the economic benefits which improved infrastructure will bring, but also want to address concerns about adverse impacts on the environment.

Looking forward, the development over the next two years of our SiteSmart initiative will improve our project management in all aspects. It will result in more effective deployment of business resources, reducing wasted time and enhancing our competitiveness by reducing project lead times. We also see the effective use of big data as an important goal. We shall be looking to upgrade our systems to take full advantage of it.

I am delighted also to report that our operations in Alphia are showing a profit for the first time in four years. The main factor depressing results in Alphia continues to be losses from the contract for the construction of the road between Phi City and Tautown. The board has reflected hard on the issues which arose on this project. We believe that the lessons we've learnt are positively influencing our systems and working practices, and this will be demonstrated on future projects.

Burton Vadher, Chief Executive

EXTRACTS FROM RISK REPORT SECTION OF ANNUAL REPORT

Board responsibilities

The board formally reviews major risks as a regular part of its agenda and has ultimate responsibility for risk management. Risk management is incorporated within operational systems and in the daily activities of CC.

Audit committee responsibilities

CC has an audit committee (the committee), comprised entirely of independent non-executive directors, in line with international governance best practice. All committee members have accountancy or finance qualifications. The committee meets every three months. It reports to the board on the significant issues considered in relation to the financial statements and on its assessment of the external audit process. The committee reviews and approves the role and mandate of internal audit, approves the annual internal audit plan and monitors and reviews the effectiveness of its work on CC's financial and accounting systems. The committee has a general responsibility for promoting sound risk management and internal control systems.

The committee is assisted in its work by a risk manager and a health and safety manager.

Specific risks

Health and safety	CC is responsible for minimising the risks of hazards and dangers to employees and others arising from its operations. The health and safety manager's principal responsibilities include maintaining health and safety documentation, organising training and accreditation for staff, reviewing health and safety reports and monitoring compliance in conjunction with internal audit.
	CC is obliged to report the $300,000 fines it paid as a result of injuries to employees arising from failures to remedy dangerous conditions on site. The health and safety manager has made recommendations for enhanced site safety procedures which will be implemented on current and future contracts.
Tendering	CC requires a stream of successful bids and projects to deliver value for shareholders. It cannot commit to too many bids, nor accept projects which offer insufficient returns for excessive risks. The board is considering specifying a minimum profit margin of 8% for most projects.
Project delivery	Any failure of projects to meet time, budget and quality requirements represents a fundamental threat to CC's business. Such failure can arise from unrealistic plans, failure to assess progress properly and lack of effective reporting. CC's SiteSmart initiative will be focused on improving project delivery.
Environment	CC's sustainability strategy is designed to deliver the environmental outcomes which society demands. CC has enhanced its programme for reducing carbon emissions. CC is focusing on reduction of energy and fuel consumption. CC also aims to minimise the disruption to communities and the natural environment caused by its activities. It consults with community representatives and other interested parties to address these issues.
Financial	Failure to maintain liquidity and meet loan repayment and covenant requirements will jeopardise CC's ability to win new contracts. CC aims to maintain a capital structure which balances equity and debt, and ensures liquidity and working capital requirements are met. The board is satisfied that undrawn bank facilities will be sufficient to meet continuing needs. The board is also confident that loans due for repayment in the next three years can be replaced by equivalent funding if required.
Business integrity and reputation	CC's board is committed to safeguarding against the risks of fraud, bribery and corruption and ensuring a commitment to honesty that avoids false claims and misleading statements. CC's code of conduct and rigorous ethics training are designed to maintain stakeholder trust in the company's integrity and avoid legal penalties and reputational damage.

Exhibit 2: Press release of the announcement of the new road in Betal dated 10 November 20X1

ANNOUNCING NEW ROAD BETWEEN GAMVILE AND LAKE ITA

A $20 billion new road scheme between Gamville and Lake Ita will transform the economy of Betal's Eastern region, cutting the average journey time through the Isnardi mountains by almost half.

Minister for Transport, Desmond Otieno, said: 'I am pleased at last to be able to confirm the scheme, which will help enhance the Eastern region's economic development. This region has been held back by the poor roads through the Isnardi mountains. Flooding during the wet season has often caused traffic delays, and sometimes the road is impassable. The new road will resolve all these problems.

We have identified a preferred partner, which we have invited to submit a detailed tender for the contract to construct the road. At the moment their identity is confidential but we hope to announce shortly who it is. I can confirm that they are from outside Betal.

Low price will be an important criterion when choosing the contractor. We shall also want the contractor to carry out the work efficiently, with its timetable being as short as possible, to ensure that disruption during construction will be kept to a minimum. The government will guarantee any debt finance that the contractor needs to fund the project.

We appreciate the concerns expressed about the impact on some villages in the mountains and the damage to the habitats of a number of species of wildlife. We shall expect our chosen contractor to limit its environmental footprint while it constructs the road. It will be required to base its construction plans on mitigating the environmental impact of the road when it opens.

When completed, we are certain that the new road will give a big boost to our country's economy and be a lasting achievement of this government.'

end

Exhibit 3: Forecast revenues and costs for the construction of the new road in Betal

It is assumed that construction will begin in May 20X2 and be completed in December 20X5

Progress payments from Betal's government are scheduled as follows:

		$m
30 April 20X3	1st interim (20%)	4,200
30 April 20X4	2nd interim (25%)	5,250
28 February 20X5	3rd interim (20%)	4,200
31 December 20X5	Final (35%)	7,350
		21,000

Projected costs

	20X2	20X3	20X4	20X5	Total
	$m	$m	$m	$m	$m
Road surfaces	1,000	1,790	1,860	1,460	6,110
Tunnels	850	1,520	1,600	970	4,940
Bridges and underpasses	380	660	690	580	2,310
Crossing and signage	110	190	210	180	690
Ground remediation and stabilisation	300	520	550	460	1,830
Drainage	230	400	410	330	1,370
Lighting	100	180	180	150	610
Fencing and safety barriers	120	210	220	200	750
Other costs	60	120	120	90	390
Total	3,150	5,590	5,840	4,420	19,000

Exhibit 4: Outline contents of the project initiation document (PID) and a summary of the operational issues section of the PID

OUTLINE CONTENTS OF PID DOCUMENT

Project aims and background

– Introduction

– Background

– Business case – benefits, costs, progress payments

– Financial budget and funding

Operational issues

– Time and cost constraints

– Risks

Personnel and responsibilities

– Project sponsor

– Project manager

SUMMARY OF OPERATIONAL ISSUES SECTION

Cost and time constraints for stages of construction

		$bn
Stage 1	Gamville–Omicon (May 20X2–April 20X3)	4.7
Stage 2	Omicon–Nuhasa (February 20X3–April 20X4)	5.5
Stage 3	Nuhasa–Zetatown (February 20X4–February 20X5)	5.2
Stage 4	Zetatown–Lake Ita (March 20X5–December 20X5)	3.6

Main risks

Risks	Risk Management
Health and Safety	– Use of health and safety manual
	– Staff training
	– On-site procedures including handling dangerous substances, removing hazards and warning of dangerous conditions, with regular monitoring by site management
	– Inspections by health and safety manager and internal audit
Supply chain	– Competitive tendering
	– Contracts showing target requirements and penalties
	– Procedures for changing terms
Environment	– Programme for disposal of waste
	– Energy conservation measures
	– Carbon emission reductions

Exhibit 5: Transcript of an emergency meeting on 20 July 20X2 at CC's head office following protests against construction of the new road in Betal

Present:		
	Burton Vadher	Chief executive
	Imena Bhudia	Chairman
	Alan Chang	Risk manager
	Pat Singh	Consultant

The meeting began at 10am. Burton opened the meeting by playing the following clip from Betal's news programme about the break-in, from earlier that morning:

> **Presenter:** Two protesters were seriously injured last night after they broke into one of the construction sites for the new road through the Isnardi mountains. The break-in is an escalation of the recent protests against the new road. Protesters have been unhappy that they have not been able to meet with Burton Vadher, CC's chief executive. Our reporter, Iris Ivezic, is outside the site. Iris, what can you tell us about the break-in and the injuries to the protesters?
>
> **Reporter:** It appears that a number of protesters created a diversion outside this entrance. Whilst the two security staff on site investigated, other protesters broke in elsewhere, close to where a break-in was attempted last week. On that occasion, the security staff spotted the protesters and prevented access. This time, however, two protesters got in. It seems that one collided with a van driven by an employee of CC. The other protester was apprehended by another CC employee, and was subsequently taken away by police.
>
> No representative from CC has made any comment about last night's events and we have not been able to speak with any of the employees involved. However, as he was led away the protester who was arrested shouted out about the protester injured by the van: 'They ran him over. The van deliberately went straight for him and ran him over.'
>
> (end of clip)

Burton:	I thought that showing the news report was the best way to brief you on what happened, although Alan has found out more since.
Alan:	I've spoken to our employees and the staff from Sholin Security, the security firm in Betal, which we use. It seems that they both went to deal with the protesters at the main entrance.
Imena:	Were there only two security staff on site?
Alan:	Yes. The contract only states that the security post should be manned at all times.
Imena:	The news report mentioned an attempted break-in last week. Were we told about it?
Alan:	The security staff said that they'd reported it to their managers, but no-one from Sholin Security appears to have contacted us.
Burton:	What more do we know about what happened once the protesters got in?
Alan:	The protester who was injured ran across an unlit service road and the van collided with him.
Imena:	Should the area have been lit better?
Alan:	Apparently lighting was one of the things picked up by Li Kurata, our health and safety manager, when he visited the site two months ago. Staff said that the lighting was going to be fixed before internal audit's visit planned for next month.
Imena:	Why isn't Li here?

Burton:	Li's been off sick for the last six weeks. We'll have to get a temporary replacement in now to fill the gap caused by Li's absence.
Imena:	Did Li submit his report on the site before he went sick?
Burton:	I did receive it but the points were generally minor. We've had so much else to discuss at board meetings recently that I haven't had a chance to report on health and safety.
Imena:	What more do we know about the protester who collided with the van?
Alan:	I haven't spoken to the van driver yet but I have spoken to the security guard who chased the protester. He didn't see the collision, only the aftermath.
Imena:	How about the protester who claimed to have seen his friend being run over?
Alan:	I'm not sure whether he would have been able to see clearly what happened as the lighting was so poor. He'd also fallen over on a patch of oil, which hadn't been mopped up. This was why the security guard was able to catch up with him.
Imena:	You told me earlier, Burton, that our lawyers have advised us not to make any statement that we are responsible and that the police and health and safety authorities will be looking at the site over the next few days.
Burton:	That's all correct. Of course we shouldn't admit to any responsibility for the injuries. I'll be flying out to Betal this afternoon. When I get out there, I'll issue a statement to the press saying that we regret the injuries, but protesters who trespass on building sites have only themselves to blame. We'll ensure the site's tidied up, lights fully on, etc. I'll also speak to the staff there and make sure they're all saying the same things. They'll get a hardship bonus because of all the stress they had last night. I'm fed up with these protesters and the way they're disrupting this contract.

Burton and Alan leave the meeting. Imena and Pat continue a private conversation.

| Imena: | I'm worried about what Burton will say and do when he's in Betal and his attitude on the issues we've discussed. Can you send me a memo before Burton goes to Betal, setting out your views? You can be as frank as you like, I shall keep the memo confidential. I'm also not happy generally with how risk has been managed and controls have been operating. I'd like you to draft me a summary of control weaknesses, and how they should be remedied. I want the board to see quickly and clearly what the problems are and what we must do. Also, other companies have separate audit and risk committees, rather than a single audit committee like CC has. Please can you prepare a briefing paper for the next board meeting, setting out the advantages for CC of having separate audit and risk committees. |

Exhibit 6: Report of an interview with Burton Vadher in Omegland Daily News newspaper – October 20X2

BIG DATA WILL HELP CC GAIN STRATEGIC ADVANTAGE

CC will be at the forefront of the construction sector in Omegland in using big data to gain strategic advantage, according to its Chief Executive, Burton Vadher: 'We must make full use of all of the information available on traffic volumes and road conditions to run our operations efficiently and seize new opportunities to enhance shareholder wealth.'

Mr Vadher wishes CC to develop big data capabilities alongside its current SiteSmart initiative. He believes that enhanced big data capabilities will help CC gain road infrastructure management contracts which are becoming available. Previously the governments of Omegland, Alphia and Betal have managed their countries' road networks themselves, only using companies like CC for specific maintenance and construction work. Now, however, the governments are looking to subcontract the management of some of their road network to private sector partners, who will plan maintenance as well as carrying it out. The private sector partners will also have ongoing responsibilities such as operating traffic control and signage systems. Their income will be in the form of fees paid by government or toll charges on road users, or a combination of both.

Mr Vadher is sure that CC will be able to provide what each government wants: 'CC will provide an integrated package of construction and support services that none of our competitors can match. We shall be the partner of choice for all three governments.'

END OF QUESTION

Section 10

REAL EXAM ANSWERS – SEPTEMBER 2018

1   COFOLD CONSTRUCTION

Tutorial note

It is not always possible to publish suggested answers which comprehensively cover all the valid points which candidates might make. Credit will be given to candidates for points not included in the suggested answers, but which, nevertheless, are relevant to the requirements.

In addition, in this integrated case study examination points made in one question may be re-introduced or fully developed in other question(s) as long as these are made in the specific context of the requirements of the part of the question being answered.

The suggested answers presented below may give much more detail than would be expected from most candidates under examination conditions; they may also have used a particular approach or model which should not be taken as the only approach or model which could have been used. Different approaches and structuring of the answers are expected and full credit will be given for relevant and appropriate solutions to the tasks given. The answers provided here are therefore intended to support revision and tuition for future examinations.

Finally, it should be noted that candidates will not get full professional skills marks in a task requirement if they have not presented their answers according to the format asked for. For example, if a task is to be completed using a report and evaluation skills are tested, even if the answer has met the specifically stated evaluation criteria, candidates will not be able to earn all the professional skills marks available if they have not used the report format.

1   (a)   **Briefing paper**

Betal road construction contract

The contract appears to be of the type which CC is aiming to win, a large project with potentially strong profits and cash flows. It offers an entry into the market in Betal at a time when it is being opened up to foreign firms. Successful completion of the contract could result in CC being given favoured status by the Betal government, enhancing its competitive position and giving it opportunities to win further major contracts in Betal.

The project is much larger than any CC has undertaken before, $20 billion compared with $10 billion for the ring route in Omegland. CC will be making a substantial commitment of resources and finance, limiting its ability to undertake other projects and diversify its portfolio. The Betal government's emphasis on its requirements to minimise time and cost bring into question the margins which CC will earn on the project and whether the contractual terms will be advantageous for CC.

The following financial and non-financial issues will have to be considered before the final decision is taken to accept the contract.

Financial issues

Directors and shareholders will clearly be concerned with the financial acceptability of the project. The forecast profit is $2 billion, offering a profit margin of 9·5% on $21 billion revenues. This is above the chief executive's target of 8%. These figures should be viewed in the light of the magnitude and the profit margins of other contracts which are currently around.

For shareholders, the contract may offer good opportunities to enhance the long-term value of CC through making an acceptable profit itself and through follow-on opportunities in Betal. However, shareholders may be worried about the possibility of losses, given the recent losses on the project in Alphia, and the reliability of CC's planning and budgeting and they may also need to be satisfied that lessons were learned from that project. CC's finance team may have been able to use what it has learnt from the project in Alphia to develop more reliable cost forecasts for this project, but this project is over mountainous terrain, where CC lacks previous experience. If, for example, the expenditure on tunnels was underestimated by more than $320 million, 6·5% of current estimated total cost, the project would not achieve the required profit margin.

Shareholders may also be concerned about the project timetable slipping, as failing to meet deadlines may jeopardise the timing and amount of revenue.

The project will tie up considerable working capital over its lifetime. Shareholder expectations may have been raised by the recent increase in dividends, and they may well be unhappy if the increase is just a one-off. Shareholders may also be worried about the liquidity of the project and the adequacy of short-term bank facilities which CC has available if required, particularly if they feel that the timetable may slip and progress payments be delayed.

Shareholders may also be concerned about the extra long-term finance required. If CC needs to make a share issue, shareholders may be worried about the outlay or the dilution of their interest if they do not subscribe. If the project is financed by extra debt, shareholders may have concerns about the extra financial risk and potential variability of earnings, and hence dividends.

CC could not also take on extra debt if it breached the requirements in the covenants laid down by current lenders. CC will be looking to refinance some current debt in the next three years. Potential lenders may be wary of prior and substantial commitments to the providers of the finance for this contract, which could make refinancing debt more problematic.

Non-financial issues

The project will also involve operations in a new country, with the probable use of local suppliers and labour, and CC having to cope with potential cultural problems. CC's previous projects have taken place in the flat countries of Omegland and Alphia, and it appears to have little experience of the mountainous terrain which the road will go through. The government believes that it will be possible to construct a road which is not significantly affected by problems with the terrain but this may be over-optimistic. It may not be possible in some areas to construct new stretches of road which give shorter journey times than the current road network.

Other resources which the project requires may be difficult to obtain. CC may have to bring in new suppliers based in Betal to reduce the risk of supply delays. It will also have to recruit manpower locally and the tight timetable may mean labour will have to be paid a premium. It will also need specialists who can oversee construction through challenging terrain. It may need to recruit them externally as it has not operated in a mountain landscape before.

CC may also currently lack the operational systems required to support a project of this size and location. The SiteSmart development is planned for the next two years, but this may cause disruption while it is happening, and perhaps be delayed, all during the contract. Arguably, it would have been better if this contract had begun in two years' time, when the SiteSmart system should be fully operational.

More generally, CC may lack the central management resources to oversee the project effectively. The audit committee and risk and health and safety managers all have significant current responsibilities and may be stretched too far to undertake the additional monitoring which the project will need.

Tutorial note

NB Note the structure of the answer i.e. using the task as a guide. This is good practice and provides the foundation for a professional approach.

(b) **Issues for CC**

The difficulties which CC will face are how Betal's government has defined its requirements, potential conflicts between different requirements, and outcomes by which the contract will be judged but CC can do little to influence.

Cost

If CC is awarded the contract, it will be at least partly because it has quoted a low price. This will limit its profit margins and may make its position very difficult if cost overruns occur, as there will be considerable government and media scrutiny. The need to keep costs down may also lead to CC's decisions on the road being influenced, for example, whether it chooses a route which will cost less to construct at particular points rather than a route which is best for traffic flow.

Timescale and disruption

Completing the road quickly may indicate that CC is being efficient. However, problems may arise if the timetable is unrealistically short. CC may have to employ extra, possibly more expensive, labour to meet deadlines, jeopardising cost control. Also taking less time may mean the period of disruption is shorter, but that does not mean that the amount of disruption will be less. There may be considerable disruption caused to nearby existing roads by construction being undertaken hurriedly. CC may also end up taking less care to minimise the disruption of natural habitats, which was been a concern noted by the minister.

Environmental footprint

CC will be judged on whether it minimises the permanent environmental impacts of the new road. However, what the government wants here is not clear. The new road will inevitably increase noise and air pollution, which CC cannot control.

Local geography may mean that the road will inevitably cause permanent disruption to some human and animal communities, as it cannot be routed anywhere else. In other places there may be a choice of routes, so CC could choose a route which minimises the negative impact on local communities and has positive impacts such as taking traffic away from the centre of villages. The introduction of road ecology measures, such as wildlife crossings, can minimise the impact on local species.

However, all of these choices and additional measures will have cost implications and possibly require more time. It is unclear how far the government would be flexible on contract terms if it meant better outcomes for the environment.

Outcomes and performance measurement

When Betal's government decides whether the quality of CC's work is good enough for CC to be paid in full, it will consider whether the roads and supporting features such as drainage and bridges have been well-constructed. These are, of course, important but they are not the outcomes which the transport minister emphasised and with which CC will therefore be associated.

Even if failure to meet the outcomes which the transport minister stated does not affect the revenue CC obtains from the contract, it may face damage to its reputation.

Some of the expectations for the new road which the press release has encouraged may be unrealistic. It is not clear, for example, how the figure of reducing journey time by almost half was estimated. Natural constraints in the Isnardi mountains may mean that it is impossible for CC to build a road which can produce that level of reduction. Both the road and CC will also be judged by how much the road alleviates traffic jams. CC may be able to do nothing about this, as traffic on existing roads switching to the new road may just transfer the problem of congestion onto the new road.

2   **To:**   Oliver Wesonga

   From: Jo Issa

   Subject: Project initiation document

   Date: XX/XX/XX

Thank you for taking responsibility for preparing the contents of the project initiation document (PID) and providing a summary of the section you have prepared on operational issues. There are a number of issues which I want to raise about what you have done, but I realise that you have not had experience of major projects like this and you should have had more help.

General comments

The contents appear to be well-organised and flow logically. The PID covers a number of significant elements.

Omissions

However, the PID also needs to include a number of other elements which are important enough to be covered under separate headings.

These include the following:

Purpose

The project background needs to define the overall purpose of the project, to build a road which is resilient and as straightforward as possible to drive. This will be what the project focuses on throughout.

Objectives

The PID should detail the financial and non-financial objectives for the project, which CC's board will use to determine whether in the end the project has achieved all its outcomes successfully. The financial objectives will be centred on achieving the forecast profit margin and keeping costs within budget. The section also needs to include the non-financial objectives of both CC and the government of Betal. Remember for CC that this project is vital in establishing the company's presence as a significant player in the construction sector in Betal. The PID also should include what the Betal government hopes to achieve by its investment – a road which is able to cope with the volume of traffic and deliver reduced journey times.

Assumptions

The detailed forecasts of benefits, costs and timings included in the detailed PID will have to be based on a number of relevant assumptions. The PID must explain what these are and the basis on which the assumptions are made. For example, the PID needs to explain assumptions about supply delivery times based on problems caused by the difficult terrain in which some of the construction will take place. The PID also needs to explain whether assumptions about completion dates are based on work being continuous or how many days will be assumed to be lost due to bad weather. Financial assumptions will also be important, particularly about cash and working capital. Certain stages of the project are due to overlap and we need to be sure that sufficient finance will be available at those times particularly.

Stakeholders

Linking in with objectives, the PID also needs to state which the most important stakeholders in the project will be, indicating their levels of influence over, and interest in, the project. Betal's government will obviously be a key stakeholder. The media and the communities along the route which may be affected will be other important stakeholders.

Constraints

The operational sector of the PID also needs to include a section on resource constraints. Manpower constraints may be significant, as CC may have to do quite a lot of recruiting in a short space of time. This will include recruiting in Betal, which may be more complicated since we have not undertaken significant projects there before, and recruitment of specialists for key project stages such as the construction of the tunnels. The PID also needs to consider whether the project will be affected by any internal constraints, such as resource demands of other current projects.

Project personnel

You have only mentioned the project sponsor and manager, although they will certainly be important members of the project team. This section should start with the overall project management structure which brings together who has authority and the lines of reporting. You also need to state who will be on the project board which will be overseeing the project, who the other members of the project team will be, and summarise their responsibilities.

Project monitoring and quality

Review and monitoring will be an integral element to provide assurance to CC's board that we are fulfilling the Betal government's requirements. The PID will need a separate section detailing the reviews which project team members and senior management will carry out, and the timetable for these reviews. There is a risk that any timetabled reviews will not pick up problems quickly enough. An important part of project management will therefore also be identifying trigger points for management to be informed immediately if, for example, construction is delayed by problems with the natural environment.

Communication

Project monitoring links in with communication, but the importance of internal and external communication warrants a separate section in the PID. Internal communication will include regular financial and progress reports, as well as one-off reports if required. External communication should link in clearly with the analysis of stakeholders, since it will be a vital part of stakeholder management. Again, it should include regular reporting as well as protocols for responding to shareholder concerns.

Operational issues

Time constraints

The time constraints section is a summary of the project milestones, which need to be supported by an extended project timetable in the body of the PID. Strictly, perhaps, the deadline details would be better included under a separate heading of deliverables. Time constraints should include important limitations in the timetable where we cannot do much, for example, not being able to do certain work during the rainy season or having to wait upon certain events to occur before particular project stages can begin.

Cost constraints

Cost constraints appear to be no more than total budgeted figures for each stage. This appears to be repeating information which would already be included in the financial budget and funding section of the report. The summarised budget should contain more detail, even though it is a summary, than a single figure for each stage. As a minimum, it needs to give a breakdown into categories of the most significant costs. The cost constraints section should include major costs which are unavoidable, for example, commitments to suppliers which we will have to make.

Risks

The risk section should link to significant risks identified in the annual report. It should include, for these risks, a summary of their likelihood, backed up with justification in the body of the PID.

The sections on health and safety and supply risks appear to be thorough, but the PID needs to say more about environmental risks. You have included measures to manage some specific important environmental risks, but CC will also need to carry out a general environmental risk assessment. You also need to say specifically what measures CC will be taking to minimise disruption to affected communities and wildlife, as Betal's transport minister has emphasised this as being important.

I appreciate that I have raised a lot of points, but I hope all my comments are helpful. Thanks again for doing this work while there was no project manager. I am very happy to discuss any aspect of this memo with you.

Jo Issa

Tutorial note

NB pay close attention to the format of the answer, clear subheadings and following the format requested

3   (a)   **Confidential memo**

        To: Imena Bhudia

        From: Pat Singh

        Date: XX/XX/XX

        Subject: Burton Vadher's comments

I am replying to your request for my views on the comments during the meeting. I appreciate that I may not be in possession of all the facts. However, I can understand why a number of the comments have caused you concern for legal, ethical and reputational reasons.

Ethical concerns

Making a statement

Our lawyers have advised against us making a statement admitting responsibility for the injuries to the protesters, and we should follow their advice. Equally, however, Burton should not rush into making a statement placing all the blame on the protesters. Not only could this be embarrassing if there is successful legal action against us, it also shows a failure to establish what happened before making a statement. Burton's desire to protect CC's staff is understandable, but this should not extend to making false or unfounded statements should staff be found guilty of misconduct at a later date.

Ethical leadership

As chief executive, Burton is responsible for taking a lead on ethical issues and establishing an ethical environment within the company. CC's annual report stresses the importance of its approach to ethics as embodied in its ethical code and its commitment to honesty which avoids false claims and misleading statements. Burton's comments and conduct appear to be short of these ideals.

Attitude to health and safety

Burton's comments appear to suggest that he is insufficiently worried about securing the safety of anyone on the site. Burton has not highlighted health and safety issues in his report at board meetings. Although he has ultimate responsibility for health and safety, he has not yet taken any steps to fill the gap left by Li Kurata's absence. His plan now to remedy problems on site seems more to do with a desire to protect CC's legal position and reputation than a concern about dangerous conditions.

Actions on site

Burton's planned actions to oversee the 'clearing up of the site' could be considered dishonest. The police and the health and safety authorities will not be getting an accurate picture of conditions on site at the time of the break-in, and Burton could be accused of tampering with evidence as a result of the actions which he intends to take.

Meetings with staff

The proposed meetings with members of staff, again, could be seen as a way of misleading the authorities by encouraging staff to make untrue statements. The proposed bonus for 'hardship' could be considered to be a bribe to make sure staff say the right things. There may also be an implied threat to any staff whose evidence is contrary to the story which Burton wants to present.

Transparency with board

Burton appears to have kept from the board a critical report which Li Kurata made about the site. Not only is this evidence of his poor attitude to health and safety, it also may raise questions about whether he is providing the board with full information, not just about health and safety issues, but other problems as well. This is clearly contrary to what is acceptable behaviour from the chief executive of CC.

Reputation concerns

Consequences of accidents

CC is already subject to media attention as a result of the protests against the new road. This is likely to worsen as a result of what happened last night. CC may suffer bad publicity if health and safety failings are found to have contributed to the accident and this may be greater because of the recent legal action taken against CC for other health and safety failings. Damage to reputation will also be greater if CC is found to have misled the authorities. The government of Betal may even seek to end the contract immediately because of misconduct. Being found guilty of dishonesty may also threaten CC's ability to win other contracts.

Attitude towards protesters

By taking this contract on, CC has inevitably associated itself with a project which is controversial and many dislike. However, Burton's failure to meet the protesters appears to be increasing the bad publicity CC is suffering, by giving a clear impression that it does not care about stakeholder concerns. This goes against what Burton has said recently in the annual report about addressing stakeholder concerns about impact upon the environment. The impression that CC has no time for the protesters will be reinforced if Burton emphasises that the accidents are their fault. Many would consider it to be poor taste for Burton to criticise strongly anyone who has been injured.

I hope these comments are helpful. I am happy to discuss them further if you have got time.

(b)   Summary of control weaknesses

	Weakness	Consequence	Recommendation
Health and safety manager	No effective oversight of health and safety due to Li Kurata's absence and no-one to whom staff and sub-contractors can communicate concerns.	Health and safety problems are not being addressed as no-one is ensuring inspections are adequate and problems are being remedied.	Appoint interim health and safety manager until Li returns from absence and ensure there is full cover when Li is absent in future.
Security presence	Inadequate number of staff on duty, demonstrating that contract specifications with Sholin Security are not detailed enough.	Security staff are unable to deal quickly and effectively with disturbances.	Discuss with Sholin Security amending contract terms to ensure adequate minimum number of staff on duty at all times.
Contact with security firm	Previous break-in was not reported to CC, demonstrating communication channels are not being used effectively.	CC was not alerted to the need to take steps such as stronger fencing and having more staff on site to prevent break-ins.	Instruct Sholin Security that all attempted security breaches should be reported directly and immediately to CC's risk manager.
Oil	Failure to clear up the oil shows failure to follow internal procedures and inadequate inspections by site management.	Increased risk of on-site accidents due to managers and staff not remedying dangerous conditions, and risk of legal penalties for failing to act.	Issue instructions to staff on all sites that health and safety instructions must be adhered to, and managers must carry out regular inspections which are evidenced.
Lighting	Failure to respond to the health and safety manager's instruction to improve lighting shows that follow-up procedures when health and safety breaches identified are inadequate.	Increased risk of on-site accidents due to personnel on site not being able to see hazards clearly, and risk of legal penalties for failing to take action.	Give site management deadlines to make improvements specified and require them to report they have done so, with follow-up health and safety visits as necessary.
Internal audit visits	Internal audit's failure to visit the site so far and the fact that the visit is scheduled rather than unannounced indicates that the programme of monitoring sites is inadequate.	Health and safety weaknesses may not be identified for some time. If staff know when the visit will be, they can make sure the site complies when the auditors are there, but are lax at other times.	Internal audit to visit sites, where health and safety risks are particularly high, more frequently and on a surprise basis.

(c)   **Briefing paper**

Advantages of establishing a separate risk committee

This paper considers the advantages of establishing a separate risk committee.

Mix of membership

The current audit committee must fulfil governance requirements and therefore consists of independent non-executive directors. A separate risk committee will not need to fulfil this requirement. It would be advantageous for it to consist of a mix of executive and non-executive directors. Executive directors can contribute knowledge of how the risks the committee is reviewing affect CC operationally. They may also have more time to commit to the risk committee's activities. Non-executive directors will be able to take a wider perspective and look at the overall risk picture CC is facing. They may also have expertise in managing specific risks such as contract management or health and safety which are important for CC.

Breadth of risks

Again, the audit committee is constrained by governance requirements to spend sufficient time on financial accounting and auditing concerns. The expertise of the committee would appear to be in the areas of accounts and audit. Collectively, the current committee may lack experience of dealing with other types of risk. A separate risk committee should have enough time to spend on other important risks and look at risks more widely, as it will not need to cover the accounting risks which the audit committee is considering. Focus on risks connected with the accounts may also mean that a lot of the audit committee's work is focused on historic issues, whereas the risk committee can have a much greater focus on dynamic risks which may have a major impact in the future.

Leadership

The audit committee has a number of responsibilities concerned with monitoring, review and auditing. They may lack the time to play a proactive role in risk leadership. In any case, it will be difficult for non-executive directors, who are not involved in day-to-day operations, to give a lead. A dedicated risk committee can feed through to the board as appropriate, to ensure that risk is considered carefully when making key strategic and operational decisions. A risk committee, in conjunction with the risk manager, can focus on ways of promoting risk awareness throughout the company.

Communication

The current system of quarterly meetings of the audit committee may handicap effective communication. The committee may be too slow to act to deal with important risks. Having a risk committee which meets more frequently should speed up communication and including executive directors will provide clear points of contact for internal communications about risk concerns. It may also simplify the risk manager's reporting lines, as the risk manager can report directly to an executive director on the risk committee.

Reassurance to shareholders

Establishment of a separate risk committee can help persuade shareholders that CC is taking risk management seriously by going beyond the requirements of governance best practice. Shareholders will welcome this reassurance, because as CC's risk report demonstrates, CC faces significant risks in areas such as health and safety and project delivery. More generally, the fact that CC is taking steps beyond the minimum requirements of governance best practice, because these are appropriate for its circumstances, shows a proactive attitude to governance and risk management which shareholders should welcome. This may be particularly important if CC suffers further adverse publicity arising from the injuries to the protester.

Conclusion

A risk committee, with membership and terms of reference tailored to CC's needs, could be a valuable part of CC's corporate governance which helps enhance performance and avoid problems.

4   **Slide 1**

Big data investment
– Available data
– Use in existing operations
– Use for infrastructure management opportunity
– Costs

Supporting notes

– **Available data**

Big data analytics can provide information about the amount of traffic and peaks and troughs in road usage. It can also provide information about the state of the roads. This includes where there are delays at any particular time, areas which may be seriously affected by bad weather, and the condition of the road surfaces and supporting features like drains and bridges.

– **Use in existing operations**

Additional data about wear on the roads should help CC to be able to forecast where and when maintenance will be required, which will be particularly useful for long-term maintenance contracts. Data about areas particularly affected by bad weather will help CC plan what work it needs to do, for example, improving drainage. Data about volume of traffic at different times or dates may help CC plan to carry out maintenance when roads are quieter.

– **Use for infrastructure management opportunity**

If CC is managing roads, big data will be helpful not only in informing CC of current conditions on the roads but also keeping road users informed. If there are problems and delays, CC should have the information to be able to deal with them as quickly and efficiently as possible and to pass information onto road users, for example, reduced speed limits and areas to avoid or alternative routes to take.

–   **Costs v benefits**

Costs will not only include set up and security costs, but also the costs of expertise to interpret the data. Any investment in big data capabilities will also need to be compatible with the current SiteSmart initiative. CC must also consider whether data about particular roads is only useful in the context of work on those roads, or whether it can be used elsewhere in the business. CC also needs to determine whether a large investment in big data will only be justified if it can gain infrastructure management contracts, because at present the number of opportunities and CC's chances of winning this type of contract are uncertain.

Alternative acceptable style for answer to first of the four points above as actual notes, representative of what is likely to be produced in an exam by a candidate:

Available data

Analytics provides data on

–   Traffic peaks and troughs

–   State of roads including delays

–   Areas affected by bad weather

–   Condition of road surfaces, bridges, drains, etc.

Slide 2

Infrastructure management opportunity
–   Service development
–   Long-term income source
–   Fees or tolls
–   Reliability of cost estimates

Supporting notes

–   **Service development**

Providing the infrastructure support would be a new service in existing locations. CC has been trying to enhance its presence in Alphia and is trying to gain a presence in Betal, so providing a new service could help it in both countries. It may help CC win construction contracts if it can also offer to provide infrastructure management of roads after they are built.

–   **Long-term income source**

Infrastructure management contracts are likely to be for a number of years and therefore provide guaranteed income for some time. They can help finance the requirements of major construction projects.

–   **Fees or tolls**

Certainty of income will depend on the mix of funding decided by the governments. Fees may be jeopardised if there is a change of government. The level of income from tolls could be much more uncertain, however. If existing roads become toll roads, traffic may use alternative routes to avoid paying the toll. If new toll roads are built, traffic may continue to use existing, free, roads.

– **Reliability of cost estimates**

CC will be committed to carrying out maintenance on the roads which it manages and the costs of maintenance should depend on the state of those roads. A much greater volume of traffic than expected may mean more maintenance is required, but there would also be greater income from tolls. The costs of operating traffic control and signage systems should be easier to predict, as these do not depend on traffic volumes, but they will depend on whether investment is required in upgraded systems which can take full advantage of the data available.

Strategic Professional – Essentials, SBL

Strategic Business Leader (SBL) September 2018 Marking Scheme

1   (a)   Up to 2 marks for an analysis of each issue which is relevant to the assessment of the opportunity.

The following are some of the issues:

Financial

–   Acceptable profit margin

–   Sensitivity of figures, uncertainties in estimates

–   Liquidity/working capital doubts

–   Extra long-term finance (government guarantee, gearing levels, covenants)

Non-financial

–   Cultural problems in new country

–   Difficult terrain, where CC lacks experience

–   More/new resources (labour, suppliers, expertise)

–   Insufficient current operating and management systems

(Up to a maximum of 18 marks)

(b)   Up to 2 marks for a discussion of each difficulty for CC of fulfilling the criteria stated by the transport minister. Difficulties may include:

–   Meeting low cost targets – affect construction choices

–   Fulfilling unrealistic timetable – increased costs and environmental disruption

–   Fulfilling environmental objectives – road inevitably cause harm, minimising impact costly and time-consuming

–   Reducing journey time – unrealistic due to natural constraints, CC cannot control use when road open

(Up to a maximum of 8 marks)

Professional skills may be additionally rewarded as in the following rubric:

How well has the candidate demonstrated professional skills as follows:	Not at all	Not so well	Quite well	Very well
1 (a) Analysis skills in identifying relevant information	The candidate has demonstrated very limited or no analysis skills. The candidate has failed to identify most of the data which is important to the decision and has failed to present the analysis in a structured way.	The candidate has demonstrated limited analysis skills. The candidate has identified some of the data which will be considered in making the decision. The answer has some structure, but the structure is not very clear. The importance of the data discussed is not clearly explained.	The candidate has presented a briefing note and has demonstrated good analysis skills. The candidate has identified most of the data which will be relevant to the decision. The candidate has structured their analysis. The structure used helps the candidate explain why the data discussed is significant.	The candidate has presented a briefing paper which has demonstrated excellent analysis skills. The candidate has identified the most important data which will be relevant to the decision. The candidate has clearly structured their analysis. The structure used helps show clearly the importance of the data being discussed.
Example	This is the type of big contract abroad which CC needs to win to maximise profits.	This is a large contract which could generate high profits. It will give CC an initial opportunity in Betal and further opportunities if the contract is successful.	The contract appears to be of the type that CC is aiming to win, a large project with good profits and cash flows. It offers an entry into the market in Betal at a good time for foreign firms. Successful completion of the contract could result in CC being chosen for further contracts by the Betal government.	The contract appears to be of the type that CC is aiming to win, a large project with potentially strong profits and cash flows. It offers an entry into the market in Betal at a time when it is being opened up to foreign firms. Successful completion of the contract could result in CC being given favoured status by the Betal government, enhancing its competitive position and giving it opportunities to win further major contracts in Betal.
	0	1	2	4

1 (b) Commercial acumen skills in identifying difficulties for CC with the criteria stated by the transport minister	The candidate has failed to demonstrate commercial acumen skills. The candidate has made no reference to the criteria stated by the transport minister, nor the implications for CC.	The candidate has shown limited commercial acumen skills. The candidate has made some reference to the criteria stated by the transport minister, but has not clearly explained why trying to fulfil the criteria will be difficult for CC.	The candidate's briefing paper has shown good commercial acumen skills. The candidate has given some explanation of the criteria stated by the transport minister and given some reasons which are relevant to CC's business why fulfilling the criteria will be difficult.	The candidate's briefing paper has shown excellent commercial acumen skills. The candidate has clearly explained the significance of the criteria stated by the transport minister and shown clearly why fulfilling all the criteria will be difficult when CC constructs the new road.
Example	CC will need to be efficient when it is constructing the road. Efficiency is one of the 3Es. It means getting the highest possible output out of inputs. It can alternatively mean achieving output, here the new road, with the minimum inputs, here the minimum amount of labour time. If CC fulfils the deadlines it has been set, it will have been efficient.	The transport minister wants CC to progress the road as quickly as possible, to be efficient, which is one of the three Es. This may be difficult because of the countryside. CC will also need to employ enough staff to get the job done on time. CC will have to decide whether it employs local staff, meaning there may be cultural problems or it gets its current staff to work more overtime, which they may not want to do, and which will be expensive.	The transport minister wants CC to progress the road quickly and this will be taken to be a sign that CC is being efficient. However, CC may not be able to be as quick as the transport minister wants. To meet deadlines, CC will need to employ more labour, which will be expensive. Taking less time may also mean that CC causes more disruption while work is taking place.	Completing the road quickly may indicate that CC is being efficient. However, problems may arise if the timetable is unrealistically short. CC may have to employ extra, possibly more expensive, labour to meet deadlines, jeopardising cost control. Also taking less time may mean the period of disruption is shorter, but that does not mean that the amount of disruption will be less.
	0	0.5	1	2

2 Up to 2 marks for discussion of each significant area omitted from the PID, up to a maximum of 10 marks. Up to 2 marks for comments on each area covered in the summary of operational issues, up to a maximum of 6 marks.

Points to include:

Omissions

- Purpose – resilient road, driven easily
- Objectives – financial and non-financial
- Assumptions – basis for financial and weather/terrain
- Stakeholders – influence/interest, government, media and communities
- Constraints – manpower, specialists, other resource demands
- Personnel – management structure and responsibilities, project board, team members
- Monitoring – regular reviews and triggers for immediate action
- Internal communication – financial and progress
- External communication

Operational issues

- Time constraints – detailed timetable and deadlines
- Cost constraints – more detail of significant costs
- Risks – community/wildlife disruption

(Up to a maximum of 14 marks in total)

Professional skills may be additionally rewarded as in the following rubric:

How well has the candidate demonstrated professional skills as follows:	Not at all	Not so well	Quite well	Very well
2 Scepticism skills in identifying shortcomings with the outline contents and summary of operational issues in the PID and recommending improvements	The candidate has demonstrated no scepticism. The candidate has failed to identify important omissions from the list of contents. The candidate has not challenged the summary of operational issues provided. The tone of the memo is not appropriate.	The candidate has demonstrated limited scepticism. The candidate has identified some of the omissions from the contents of the PID but failed to identify some important omissions. The candidate has mostly failed to identify areas missing from the summary of operational issues, or limitations of data given in the summary, or recommend improvements. The candidate has mostly failed to link the omissions or shortcomings identified with data in other exhibits. The tone of the memo is not appropriate.	The candidate has presented a memo which has demonstrated good scepticism. The candidate has identified most of the important omissions from the contents of the PID. The candidate has identified some operational areas which the summary of operational issues has not discussed and has identified shortcomings with the operational areas summarised. The candidate has provided some recommendations for improvements. The candidate has attempted to link the omissions and shortcomings identified with data in other exhibits. The tone of the memo is constructive.	The candidate has presented a memo and demonstrated excellent scepticism. The candidate has identified the major omissions in the content and the summary of operational issues, and has identified limitations with the areas which have been included. The candidate has linked the explanations of why the omissions and limitations are significant and recommendations for improvements to CC's business context and data in other exhibits. The tone of the email is constructive and the memo will be helpful for Oliver, the team member.

Example	You have included the assumed benefits, timings and costs, which is good. The project chart shows clearly what is happening and what you have assumed.	You have included the forecast benefits, costs and timings, which are all important. You will need to state what the assumptions are somewhere in this section.	The detailed forecasts of benefits, costs and timings included in the detailed PID will have to be based on assumptions. The PID will need to set out in a separate section what the assumptions are and how you have made them.	The detailed forecasts of benefits, costs and timings included in the detailed PID will have to be based on a number of relevant assumptions. The PID must explain what these are and the basis on which the assumptions are made.
	0	**1**	**2**	**4**

3   (a)   Up to 2 marks for discussion of each ethical and/or reputational issue, up to a maximum of 10 marks.

Ethical and reputational issues include:

Ethical

- Environment – ethical code and annual report statements, Burton not providing leadership

- Blaming protestors – unfounded/not true

- Lax attitude to health and safety – no replacement for H&S manager, not reporting on H&S to board

- Tampering with evidence on-site

- Pressurising staff to make untrue statements, bribery

Reputation

- Bad publicity if H&S failings found

- Threat greater – previous failings/found out for misleading authorities

- Threat greater – uncaring attitude to protestors, contradicting annual report statements

(Up to a maximum of 10 marks in total)

     (b)   Up to 3 marks for each control weakness explained, its consequences identified and recommendations for improvements made and may include the following

- No cover for H&S manager

- Inadequate security staffing

- Not reporting previous attempted break-ins

- Not clearing up oil

- Not implementing recommendation to improve lighting

- Inadequate internal audit monitoring

(Up to a maximum of 14 marks)

(c) Up to 2 marks for each relevant advantage of establishing a risk committee which is separate from the audit committee. Advantages may include:

– Include executive directors who contribute operational knowledge/time and non-executives who contribute wider/specialist risk expertise

– Focus on risks other than accounting and auditing

– Provide risk leadership, give board information required

– Meet as frequently as required

– Reassurance to shareholders/stakeholders

(Up to a maximum of 8 marks)

Professional skills may be additionally rewarded as in the following rubric:

How well has the candidate demonstrated professional skills as follows:	Not at all	Not so well	Quite well	Very well
3 (a) Scepticism skills in challenging comments	The candidate has failed to demonstrate any scepticism. The candidate has not challenged the comments made at the meeting and has therefore been unable to identify relevant ethical problems or threats to reputation.	The candidate has demonstrated limited scepticism. The candidate has challenged some of the comments made at the meeting, but has not explained clearly their ethical implications or linked the threats to reputation to information provided in the other exhibits.	The candidate has presented a memo which has demonstrated a good level of scepticism. The candidate has identified and clearly explained the ethical implications of the comments, and linked the threats to reputation to information in other exhibits.	The candidate has presented a memo and demonstrated an excellent level of scepticism. The candidate has identified, clearly explained and linked the main ethical implications to data in other exhibits, particularly the discussion of business integrity and reputation risks. The candidate has clearly explained the threats to reputation and established their significance in the context of information in the other exhibits.
Example	Protesters do not like CC anyway because the road goes through villages and wildlife habitats. Although Burton is trying to sort things out, he may fail because the protester got injured. If there are more protests, CC will have a poor reputation with government and shareholders, and the shareholders will sell their shares.	CC is already facing a lot of protests because of the road. Its reputation is likely to get worse because of the protester getting injured. CC's situation is likely to get worse if it is found to have had poor health and safety. Although Burton is trying sort things out, he may make a bad situation worse if he acts illegally and disobeys the ACCA's Code of Ethics, particularly integrity and professional conduct. This may diminish CC's reputation.	CC is already getting bad comments in the press because people are protesting against the road. Media coverage may get worse because of what happened last night. CC may suffer bad publicity if health and safety failings are found to have contributed to the accident, because health and safety is important for CC. Although Burton is trying to sort things out, he may make the situation worse if he tells lies to the authorities and then gets found out.	CC is already subject to media attention as a result of the protests against the new road. This is likely to worsen as a result of what happened last night. CC may suffer bad publicity if health and safety failings are found to have contributed to the accident and this may be greater because of the recent legal action taken against CC for other health and safety failings. Damage to reputation will also be greater if CC is found to have misled the authorities.
	0	0.5	1	2

How well has the candidate demonstrated professional skills as follows:	Not at all	Not so well	Quite well	Very well
3 (b) Evaluation skills in basing explanation of significant control weaknesses on information provided and recommending appropriate improvements	The candidate has failed to demonstrate evaluation skills. The candidate has omitted the most significant control weaknesses. The candidate has shown no professional judgement in explaining the importance and consequences of the control weaknesses identified and making recommendations to remedy them.	The candidate has demonstrated limited evaluation skills. The candidate has shown limited professional judgement in explaining the importance of the control weaknesses identified. However, the candidate has omitted some significant control weaknesses, has not explained their consequences clearly, and has not made reasonable recommendations to remedy them.	The candidate has demonstrated good evaluation skills. The candidate has shown good professional judgement in identifying most of the significant control weaknesses and explaining their importance and what their consequences are. The candidate has made some reasonable recommendations which are proportionate and may remedy the weaknesses discussed.	The candidate has demonstrated excellent evaluation skills. The candidate has shown excellent professional judgement in identifying and explaining all of the significant control weaknesses and has clearly shown the consequences of the weaknesses. The candidate has provided recommendations which are proportionate and will effectively address the weaknesses discussed.
Example	Internal audit has not visited the site yet and should do so.	Internal audit does not visit the site often enough and consequently health and safety weaknesses exist for some time. Internal audit should visit the site monthly until the health and safety weaknesses are all cleared up.	Internal audit's failure to visit the site so far indicates that the programme of monitoring sites is inadequate. Health and safety weaknesses may not be identified for some time, as staff will only try to remedy them when an audit is due. Internal audit should visit sites, where health and safety risks are particularly high, more frequently.	Internal audit's failure to visit the site so far and the fact that the visit is scheduled rather than unannounced indicates that the programme of monitoring sites is inadequate. Health and safety weaknesses may not be identified for some time. If staff know when the visit will be, they can make sure the site complies when the auditors are there, but are lax at other times. Internal audit to visit sites, where health and safety risks are particularly high, more frequently and on a surprise basis.
	0	1	2	4

How well has the candidate demonstrated professional skills as follows:	Not at all	Not so well	Quite well	Very well
3 (c) Commercial acumen skills in identifying benefits that will apply to CC in establishing a separate risk committee	The candidate has not shown commercial acumen. The candidate has not linked the benefits given to CC's circumstances.	The candidate has shown limited commercial acumen. The candidate has made some attempt to link the benefits given to CC's situation, but the candidate has not given good and clear reasons why establishing a risk committee will benefit CC.	The candidate has presented a briefing paper which has shown good commercial acumen. The candidate has explained the reasons given for establishing a separate risk committee in terms of what is advantageous for CC.	The candidate has presented a briefing paper which shows excellent commercial acumen. The candidate has strongly justified the reasons given for establishing a risk committee in terms of what is advantageous to CC and the candidate has made good use of data in the exhibits to support their arguments.
Example	CC must operate a risk committee to fulfil corporate governance requirements like Sarbanes-Oxley. Like the audit committee, the risk committee must consist of independent non-executive directors who do not have any links with CC. It is right for non-executive directors to be involved as Risk is one of the four Higgs report requirements, along with Strategy, Scrutiny and People. The risk committee of CC will be able to oversee risks, carry out risk management and employ a risk manager. They can use their different experiences when they are on the committee. It will be best if the non-executive directors on the audit committee and those on the risk committee are the same, to ensure risks are managed in CC and the same systems are used.	A risk committee will help CC fulfil the corporate governance requirements to manage risk effectively. Like other board committees, the risk committee should consist of non-executive directors, to preserve its independence from executive management. Non-executive directors will not have day-to-day responsibilities and can therefore look from the outside at the risks CC is facing, as they have knowledge of the business from an external perspective. They may have experience of risks which they can use at the risk committee. The non-executive directors who are on the risk committee may be different from those on the audit committee.	CC is required by the Sarbanes-Oxley requirements and other guidance such as the UK code to operate an audit committee consisting of independent non-executive directors. This requirement does not apply to the risk committee. It is likely to be best if the risk committee had both executive and non-executive directors. Executive directors have day-to-day knowledge of CC's operations and can look at risks regularly. Non-executive directors can look at risks 'from the outside' with a wider perspective. Non-executive directors may also know a lot about dealing with specific risks, such as contract management and health and safety which are important for CC.	The current audit committee must fulfil governance requirements and therefore consists of independent non-executive directors. A separate risk committee will not need to fulfil this requirement. It would be advantageous for it to consist of a mix of executive and non-executive directors. Executive directors can contribute knowledge of how the risks the committee is reviewing affect CC operationally. They may also have more time to commit to the risk committee's activities. Non-executive directors will be able to take a wider perspective and look at the overall risk picture CC is facing. They may also have expertise in managing specific risks such as contract management or health and safety that are important for CC.
	0	0.5	1	2

4   Up to 2 marks for each relevant item included on each slide and discussed in the supporting notes, up to a maximum of 6 marks per slide.

The following are points which may be included under investment in big data and opportunities for undertaking infrastructure management:

Big data investment

– Maximise use of available data about traffic, road conditions, weather impact

– Use data to forecast road problems and traffic usage, to determine maintenance programme

– Use data to inform road users of delays and prompt actions by CC

– Costs – set-up, security, data interpretation

– Internal systems – compatibility with SiteSmart, other uses of data

Infrastructure management

– Service development opportunity

– Enhances geographical development (Betal)

– Enhances chances of winning contracts (Alphia)

– Long-term, smooth income source

– Income uncertainties – fees and tolls

– Uncertainties over maintenance costs

(Up to a maximum of 8 marks in total)

Professional skills may be additionally rewarded as in the following rubric:

How well has the candidate demonstrated professional skills as follows:	Not at all	Not so well	Quite well	Very well
4 Communication skills in presenting concise slides and clear supporting notes	The candidate has demonstrated poor communication skills. The candidate has failed to present the information clearly in an unambiguous way. The candidate has not presented the answer in an appropriate slide and notes format, or tone for the board.	The candidate has demonstrated some basic communication skills. The candidate has presented two slides and supporting notes. However, the candidate's slides contain too many or too few points. The candidate's notes fail to explain the main points adequately for the board, and do not link clearly to the slides. The candidate's notes are not in an appropriate tone for the board.	The candidate has demonstrated good communication skills. The candidate has presented two slides and supporting notes in appropriate formats. The candidate's slides and notes are mostly concise and generally clear, and most of the supporting notes would be helpful for the board.	The candidate has demonstrated excellent communication skills. The candidate's two slides and notes are effectively and clearly structured. All of the supporting notes add value to the points made in the slides and would be helpful for the board. The candidate has used an appropriate tone for the board.
Example	The Ansoff matrix shows why we should provide this service.	Providing the infrastructure support would be a new service in existing locations, equivalent to product development in the Ansoff matrix.	Providing the infrastructure support would be a new service in existing locations equivalent to product development in the Ansoff matrix. As well as providing new services, CC may be able to gain construction contracts if it can offer infrastructure management as well once the contracts are completed.	Providing the infrastructure support would be a new service in existing locations, equivalent to product development in the Ansoff matrix. CC has been trying to enhance its presence in Alphia and is trying to gain a presence in Betal, so providing a new service could help it in both countries. It may help CC win construction contracts if it can also offer to provide infrastructure management of roads after they are built.
	0	0.5	1	2

Section 11

REAL EXAM QUESTIONS – DECEMBER 2018

1   Hi Lite

'HiLite' hotels (HiLite) is a listed hotel chain, located in the country of Deeland. Deeland has a developed economy, which has experienced strong growth in the last 15 years. Deeland also has a highly-developed tourism industry.

HiLite's competitive advantage is built on its highly competitive pricing strategy, and this has been a significant factor in its current position as the leading hotel brand in Deeland. HiLite normally attracts those travellers seeking 'no frills' accommodation, at a reasonable price and as such, is referred to as a 'budget' hotel chain. Every HiLite hotel room provides an en-suite bathroom, TV and free Wi-Fi internet access and each hotel offers a complimentary breakfast service. However, HiLite hotels do not provide additional services such as bars, restaurants or leisure facilities. Every HiLite hotel has a similar layout and design, and are mostly located at airports, city centre locations and close to major transport routes, such as Deeland's main road networks and train stations.

HiLite was founded about 40 years ago beginning with two hotels in the capital city of Deeland. Since then it has grown significantly, operating 510 hotels (approximately 46,000 rooms) by the end of the 20X7/20X8 financial year (Note: HiLite's financial year end is 30 June). It is now the largest hotel chain (in terms of number of hotels) in Deeland. Since it was founded, all of HiLite's growth has been achieved organically within Deeland, with investment being gradually made in new 'HiLite' branded hotels each year throughout Deeland. Although it is currently the leading hotel brand in Deeland (in terms of market share), HiLite faces fierce competition from several home-based and international hotel chains.

In the last 10 years, HiLite has made significant investment in web-based technology, which has resulted in over 75% of room bookings in the 20X7/20X8 financial year being completed through the HiLite website. HiLite operates with low numbers of staff in each hotel but the staff in these hotels is highly trained to provide excellent customer service. HiLite values its staff highly, and is strongly committed to staff development and retention. HiLite pays above the Deeland national minimum wage in order to encourage staff commitment and loyalty.

You are a senior business analyst working within the business analysis department of HiLite. You report to the chief business analyst, who reports directly to the finance director on a wide range of business and strategic issues.

The following exhibits should be used to undertake the tasks asked of you by the chief business analyst and the finance director:

Exhibit 1: Chief Executive's Statement: Report on Performance for year ending 30 June 20X8

Exhibit 2: Deeland Hotel Industry Report 20X8

Exhibit 3: Factsheet relating to HiLite's proposed acquisition target

Exhibit 4: Deeland Daily News article

Exhibit 5: Extract of a senior management team briefing

Exhibit 6: Board meeting minutes November 20X8

The case requirements are included in the tasks shown below:

1   The board of HiLite is currently looking to develop the HiLite business model in Veelandia, a developing country with good growth potential. However, as operating in a different country would be a new strategic direction for HiLite, the finance director has stated that before any such strategy is considered, it is important to understand the key factors in its home country of Deeland, which have driven HiLite's success.

Required:

(a)   **The chief business analyst has asked you to prepare briefing notes for the finance director, for consideration at the next board meeting, which discusses the key factors which have enabled HiLite to be successful in its home country of Deeland.**   **(16 marks)**

Professional skills marks are available for demonstrating analysis skills in investigating and considering information from a range of sources.   (3 marks)

The Board of HiLite has identified an existing chain of hotels called 'Comfi Stay', located in Veelandia, which it is considering acquiring. The chief business analyst has passed you a factsheet which he prepared containing data relating to the proposed acquisition.

Required:

(b)   **Using the factsheet referred to above and any other relevant information, prepare a report for the finance director, which evaluates the proposal to acquire the Comfi Stay hotel chain.**   **(16 marks)**

Professional skills marks are available for demonstrating evaluation skills in presenting a balanced and objective appraisal of the relevant information relating to the proposed acquisition of the Comfi Stay hotel chain.   (4 marks)

(Total: 39 marks)

2   Following a subsequent decision by the HiLite board, the proposed acquisition of the Comfi Stay hotel chain has recently been announced to the Deeland stock market and, generally, the market has reacted positively to the announcement. However, there have been some negative press reports in the Deeland Daily News about the proposed acquisition, criticising HiLite. The chief executive of HiLite is very concerned about these reports and has asked the business analysis team to consider HiLite's response.

Required:

(a)   **Prepare a draft press release responding to the criticisms assessing the social and environmental impact of HiLite's proposed investment in Veelandia, with a view to reassuring its stakeholders of HiLite's intentions to maintain its high principles and standards in acquiring the Comfi Stay hotel chain.   (10 marks)**

Professional skills marks are available for demonstrating communication skills in clarifying and conveying relevant information to HiLite's stakeholders.
(3 marks)

Although HiLite's shareholders have generally responded favourably to the proposed acquisition of the Comfi Stay hotel chain, HiLite's board is considering how it should effectively communicate with all of its key stakeholders to ensure that they understand the strategic decisions and direction of the business. The finance director has recently asked the board to consider the use of integrated reporting in assisting in this communication and in building relationships with HiLite's key stakeholders.

Required:

(b)   The finance director has asked you to provide her with briefing notes which she will use to assist her in discussions with HiLite's Board members, which assesses the role and benefits of integrated reporting in assisting effective communication and in building relationships with HiLite's key stakeholders.   **(12 marks)**

Professional skills marks are available for demonstrating evaluation skills in using appropriate professional judgement to assess how useful integrated reporting could be to the stakeholders of HiLite.   **(3 marks)**

(Total: 28 marks)

3   At the most recent board meeting of HiLite, a discussion occurred on the potential threat of disruptive technologies in the hotel industry. Following this meeting, the chief executive has requested further information for the board on this issue.

Required:

(a)   The chief business analyst has asked you to write a report for the next board meeting which discusses the potential challenges to HiLite posed by the development of the disruptive technologies which are emerging in the hotel industry, and highlight the potential application of disruptive technologies which may be considered by HiLite.   **(14 marks)**

Professional skills marks are available for demonstrating scepticism skills in probing and challenging the opinions of the board.   **(4 marks)**

At the board meeting, the finance director presented information on three risks in HiLite's current information systems environment and the board has requested further analysis of these risks.

Required:

(b)   The finance director has asked you to prepare three presentation slides (one for each risk identified) and accompanying notes for the next board meeting assessing the potential outcomes of each of the information systems risks identified by the finance director and recommend actions for each risk which HiLite should take in order to control these risks.   **(12 marks)**

Professional skills marks are available for demonstrating commercial acumen skills in demonstrating insight and understanding of the information system risks and controls.   **(3 marks)**

(Total: 33 marks)

Exhibit 1: Chief Executive Statement: Report on Performance (year ended 30 June 20X8)

Bernie Vokes, Chief Executive

In HiLite we have created Deeland's most popular hotel brand. It is the strength of our brand, along with our superb hotel staff who deliver great service every day, which underpins our success and is a key driver of our future growth. We continue to deliver a market-leading customer experience by focusing on the quality of our service, the best choice of locations and great value for money. Through our network of 510 hotels (almost 46,000 rooms), we offer customers the widest choice of locations (20% more than our nearest competitor). This means our guests are able to stay closer to their destination, which is important to both our business and leisure customers.

Another year of strong sales and profit growth

This has been another successful year for HiLite, with record levels of customer satisfaction. This has helped to achieve sales growth, leading to a rise in profits and strong returns for our shareholders. We now employ almost 11,000 people, working across our 510 hotels and Head Office. In the financial year to June 20X8, total sales grew by 9.1% on the previous year to $1,072 million. We achieved a 9.5% growth in our underlying pre-tax profit to $236 million and this growth in profit has produced a strong operating cash flow, which has supported capital investment in the business. Total hotel room occupancy remained high, as we finished the year with an average room occupancy rate of 79.5%.[1]

A continued commitment to invest

There is continuing growth of the budget hotel market as the luxury and mid-price sectors continue to decline. We offer the widest choice of locations in Deeland, the best value for money and, through investment in our sites and hotel staff, a great product in the marketplace. This year we invested over $80 million on refurbishments as well as upgrading the customers' digital experience. Our website, HILITE-Hotels.com, welcomes 80% of our customers who choose to book directly with us, giving us a significant competitive advantage.

However, the environment in which we operate is evolving. Competitor dynamics are changing, through both traditional and disruptive channels; customers are demanding more value and greater quality. Technology is developing quickly, especially digitally and, with cost structures under pressure, there is a growing need to focus on productivity and efficiency. In order to continue to be successful in the future, we will need to invest to extend our current capabilities and also build new ones.

[1] Room occupancy rate is an industry standard KPI which shows the percentage of available rooms or beds being sold for a certain period of time. The standard formula used is rooms sold/rooms available.

Key Performance Indicators (Year ended June 20X8)

Commitment to shareholders	Commitment to staff
Revenue Growth 9.1% (Target 8%)	Staff retention rate 52% (Target 55%)
Pre-tax Profit growth 9.5% (Target 9%)	6.2 training days per employee (Target 5.5 days)
Commitment to customers	**Commitment to the environment**
Customer satisfaction 91.6% (Target 90%)	2.4% reduction in CO2 emissions (Target 3%)
Customer return visits 47% (Target 45%)	Re-cycling of 85% of waste (Target 83%)

Focus for the Future

We have identified four key strategic themes to ensure the continued success of our brand.

1   Focus on growth and innovation in our core HiLite business

We must continue to develop our market-leading customer focus with further product innovation and consistent delivery of quality service and value. Innovation is vital to our future success. We must improve our digital capabilities to ensure we stay ahead in this rapidly changing environment.

2   Focus on our strengths to grow internationally

There are exciting market opportunities for establishing the HiLite brand outside Deeland. As international growth is a new area of development for HiLite, we will need to focus our resources on the best opportunities which will produce the highest returns and match our high expectations of quality, value for money and commitment to staff and sustainability.

3   Focus on supporting future growth through investment in technology and staff

To deliver long-term sustainable returns we must invest for the long term to ensure we have the skills to become more agile in digital capabilities and build efficient and sustainable infrastructure. We are committed to creating a great place to work, with a strong commitment to equality and diversity. We will continue to commit to staff development opportunities which will help them realise their potential, investing around $10 million annually in skills and development programmes. We welcome the introduction of the new Deeland National Living Wage, which we implemented six months in advance of the Government's launch date.

4   Focus on sustainability

We will continue to build on our focus and reputation of operating as a sustainable and environmentally friendly business. We are committed to continued development and investment in sustainability and environment management systems to reduce our levels of wastage, decrease our CO2 emissions and work towards becoming a carbon neutral business. Over the next three to four years we will need to upgrade our systems and infrastructure to improve our sustainable position. All of our staff will continue to be trained in environmental management and sustainability awareness and targets will continue to be set for every hotel to encourage sustainable behaviour.

Bernie Vokes

BERNIE VOKES – Chief Executive

Exhibit 2: Deeland Hotel Industry Report 20X8

20X8 – A challenging year for Deeland's Hotel Industry

by Professor R.J. STEEP, Chief Analyst of the Deeland Travel and Hospitality Institute

As 20X8 draws to a close, it looks like it will be a largely positive year for many hotels in Deeland, but that does not mean businesses can become complacent.

Tourism has continued to thrive in Deeland, despite the continued global effects of the recession, with hotels seeing an average rise in visitors by over 8% on 20X7. Deeland has a highly-developed hotel and travel industry. Both online travel agents (OTAs) and traditional high street travel companies are thriving in Deeland. Online hotel booking websites and price comparison sites are driving businesses to be more competitive and offer better and more flexible pricing options.

Continued investment

This has to a significant extent been assisted by the Deeland government's continued investment in national infrastructure, particularly the new airport recently opened in Boria, Deeland's second largest city. This generated an additional 2.5 million international visitors last year, approximately 80% of them visiting Deeland for leisure. In addition, both at national and regional level, investment has been high in road and rail network development.

This has also led to a growth in business activity in the economy, which in turn has created more opportunities and created a highly competitive environment. In 20X8, two new national branded chains of hotels have opened in the main tourist centres of Deeland. National competition remains intense and both Waterbay Leisure and ZeezeeHols Group, two of Deeland's most long-established luxury hotel chains, have both gone out of business this year. This is a stark warning for those Deeland hotels which do not remain competitive and customer-focused.

It is clear that innovation is critical to the survival of hotel businesses, and technology continues to be a key driver in the market place. Most of Deeland's hotel chains are now offering online booking facilities and as a minimum are developing online apps for multiple platforms to enable guests to communicate and manage bookings more effectively.

Impact of stakeholders

Deeland's travellers continue to be highly demanding leisure and business customers, expecting high standards but also good value for money. A recent survey of online hotel customers clearly indicated that 70% would shop around for the best deal in the best location. The hotel and travel industry was hit hard in many countries by the recession and a number of hotel and travel companies went out of business. However, those which survived did so by focusing on customer needs and operating efficiently.

The government also continues to value the hotel and travel industry. Nearly half of the universities in Deeland offer travel and tourism qualifications which are highly regarded throughout the region. The government has recently announced further investment and tax breaks for employers offering job creation schemes in a wide range of industries, including travel and tourism.

Challenges in the hotel industry for 20X9 and beyond

Customers want an outstanding, personalised experience

If the hotel industry in Deeland wants to deliver an outstanding, individualised customer experience, it must understand customers' needs. This will be a challenge because customers' needs are continually evolving and they are increasingly demanding personalised communications (via multiple electronic platforms), excellence in delivery as well as a demand for value for money.

Recruiting and retaining the right people

Many of Deeland's hotels are finding it increasingly difficult to recruit and retain individuals with the right blend of interpersonal and technical skills. Developing and implementing an effective recruitment strategy and retaining skilled employees are difficult. Recent research shows that the hotel sector has some of the highest staff turnover rates of any industry (average staff turnover rate per hotel in 20X8 is likely to be as high as 60% per annum).

Changing competitive dynamics

There is little doubt that the competitive landscape is changing. One evident trend is increasing consolidation, especially among hotels. Much of the merger and acquisition activity stems from companies' objectives to gain market share and vertically integrate their product offerings (i.e. businesses operating in the budget segment want to buy into the mid-range or luxury hotel segment and vice-versa).

The nature of competition itself is also changing. New business models are emerging to meet the evolving consumer needs, as mentioned earlier, posing significant challenges to traditional hospitality businesses. For instance, the world's largest accommodation provider, 'Rent-a-Room', does not own a single hotel room or any of the lodgings it advertises. Instead it operates as an online marketplace, enabling travellers to lease or rent short-term lodging including holiday rentals, homestays, or hotel rooms.

So, for many of Deeland's hotel operators these are exciting but challenging times and those who survive will be those that keep up with the pace of change in the industry.

Exhibit 3: Factsheet relating to HiLite's proposed acquisition target prepared by Chief Business Analyst of HiLite

Comfi Stay Hotel Chain

KEY BUSINESS/INDUSTRY DATA

- Comfi Stay is a family-run business, which has lacked investment in the last 10 years.

- All 20 hotels in the chain have been in operation for over 18 years and are located in main coastal resorts of Veelandia. These are in premium locations but with out-dated facilities.

- Mid-range hotels, some with additional leisure facilities such as gyms and pools. Not classed as budget hotels.

- Veelandia is 5,000 miles from Deeland. It has a developing economy, but low wage rates and there is some evidence of poor employment practices in the country. Some evidence of use of under-age labour (minors) in the hotel industry has been found.

- Veelandia has a thriving tourism industry.

KEY INVESTMENT DATA: (based on a 6-year investment plan)

NOTE: All figures used have been converted into Deeland's home currency ($)

	Year						
	0	**1**	**2**	**3**	**4**	**5**	**6**
Revenues		48,180,00	48,180,00	53,961,600	53,961,600	53,961,600	53,961,600
Initial investment	80,000,000						
Refurbishment	10,000,000	5,000,000					
Environmental investment		1,000,000	1,000,000	1,000,000	1,000,000	1,000,000	1,000,000
Training costs		3,000,000	1,500,000	1,500,000	1,500,000	1,500,000	1,500,000
Operating costs		21,681,000	21,681,000	24,282,720	24,282,720	24,282,720	24,282,720
Total costs	90,000,000	30,681,000	24,181,000	26,782,720	26,782,720	26,782,720	26,782,720
Cash flow	90,000,000	17,499,000	23,999,000	27,178,880	27,178,880	27,178,880	27,178,880
Discount factor 12%	1.00	0.89	0.80	0.71	0.64	0.57	0.51
Present value	90,000,000	15,624,107	19,131,856	19,345,390	17,272,670	15,422,026	13,769,666
Net present value	**10,565,715**						

Additional Information:

- It is expected that some of Deeland's hotel managers would need to relocate to Veelandia (for approximately 3–12 months, on a temporary basis) to assist in training and staff development in the first year of operations and will be required to carry out on-going mentoring activities for the next two years.

- Finance for this investment would be available through a combination of equity and debt finance.

Exhibit 4: Newspaper article following the recent announcement of HiLite to acquire the Comfi Stay Hotels chain in Veelandia

---

Deeland Daily News

Has HiLite hit a low?

Business Briefing: Hotel News

Senior Business Reporter, A.J Talling questions the motivations of HiLite's latest business venture.

HiLite hotels recently announced it was making an approach to buy the struggling Comfi Stay hotel chain in Veelandia. Comfi Stay's owners, the DeWalt family, announced their intention to sell the business three months ago, having seen revenues decline steadily in the last three years. Its Chief Executive and founder Anders DeWalt admitted in an interview last month that the family has failed to recognise and keep up with the investment demands of a modern hotel, but was confident that a new owner could revitalise the business. But is its potential acquisition by HiLite a positive move for the Deeland-based budget hotel business?

Reading its recently published Chief Executive's Statement, HiLite is a business which clearly prides itself on the value it places on its staff and maintaining strong employment rights. However, staff in Comfi Stay hotels are currently paid well below the rate of pay earned by their equivalent staff in Deeland. They also work longer hours per week with few employment rights, such as holiday or sick pay. Most of Comfi Stay's staff are women, who are offered few opportunities for training or staff development. In addition, Comfi Stay's policy of only employing men as hotel managers and senior staff in its hotels would seem to be in stark contrast to the strong focus on equality within HiLite's employment practices.

Staff pay and conditions may not be the only concern for HiLite. Comfi Stay was fined by the government of Veelandia less than two years ago for polluting the local waterway in its main coastal tourist town, with an outflow of untreated effluent. The cause was outdated waste and toilet facilities which it said would be addressed, but limited recent investment in the Comfi Stay hotel chain suggests otherwise. HiLite will have to invest significant sums of money to make the hotel chain a viable and sustainable part of its business, if it wishes to adhere to its high expectations for environmental sustainability.

Although Veelandia has a thriving tourist economy, which has in fact grown since the global economic recession, it is a country of limited environmental awareness. National recycling levels are 50% less than other countries in the region and its reported CO_2 emissions are the worst in the region.

So why is the Comfi Stay hotel chain of interest to HiLite? Seemingly, foreign companies like HiLite wish to exploit this low wage economy, where a poorly educated population is happy to be in employment at whatever the rate of pay and where profits can be maximised by exploiting locals and tourists alike, with scant regard for the impact on its people or its environment. For an organisation like HiLite, this must be a questionable, and some may suggest, an unethical direction of development for HiLite to follow.

Exhibit 5: Extracts of HiLite senior management team briefing after an article was published in the Deeland newspaper following the announcement of the proposed acquisition of the Comfi Stay Hotel chain.

Attendants:

Bernie Vokes – Chief Executive

Jay Brown – Sales and Marketing Director

Tomas Myer – Operations Director

Elizabeth Fox – Finance Director

Jay Brown:	I think we need to consider how we communicate such major strategic decisions, such as our proposed investment in Comfi Stay hotels, more effectively to our wider stakeholders.
Tomas Myer:	I'm not sure there is any need for this. We don't want to over react to the recent article in the Daily News. Let's be realistic. Our shareholders are only interested in the bottom line. So, as long as the Comfi Stay hotels make them a profit, they won't care much about anything else. Our hotel customers, likewise, are really only interested in their own personal experience for the duration of their stay in one of our hotels. And do our hotel staff really care about more than how much they get paid and when their next day off is?
Bernie Vokes:	I disagree with you Tomas. We must consider all of our stakeholders and how we should communicate our activities to them. Both shareholders and customers are changing in their attitudes and expectations of us. Not only in the products and services we offer, but also in how we communicate with them.
Jay Brown:	Yes, I agree Bernie. In particular, we should seriously consider how we report our social and environmental activities to our stakeholders. I believe it could be a strategic advantage for us to do so.
Tomas Myer:	Strategic advantage? How? I just don't see what information would interest our stakeholders, other than we are profitable and our prices are the most competitive in the market! We are a budget hotel and our strategic advantage is based on our price, not on communication of useless information to our stakeholders.
Elizabeth Fox:	Actually Tomas, we have a wide range of stakeholders, who are interested in a wide range of aspects of our business. Effective communication with them is critically important to us and them. My own opinion is that introducing integrated reporting would offer us the best solution in communicating and building relationships with our stakeholders.
Tomas Myer:	But surely, the press statement that we are going to release in response to the accusations in the *Deeland Daily News* is satisfactory for all our stakeholders, isn't it?
Bernie Vokes:	Not all of our stakeholders will see our press statement or have any idea about our proposed acquisition.
Tomas Myer:	So why bother telling them what they don't need to know?
Bernie Vokes:	OK everyone. I think we need some further consideration of this. Elizabeth, could you ask one of the business analysis team to provide us with some more information on the importance of communication with our key stakeholders and the role that integrated reporting could play in assisting this communication?

Exhibit 6: Board meeting minutes – November 20X8

Board members:

Present: Chairman, Chief Executive, Finance Director, Operations Director, Sales and Marketing Director

Proceedings:

Meeting called to order at 2:00 p.m by Mr L Crane, Chairman

Opening statement

The Chairman opened the meeting, stating that the meeting had been scheduled to discuss the challenges faced by HiLite in managing and developing its information systems. He noted that he personally found the rapid development in information technologies difficult to keep pace with, but was confident that HiLite would develop appropriate responses to these developments.

Agenda item 1: Disruptive technologies

The first agenda item was introduced by Jay Brown, the Sales and Marketing Director.

Miss Brown expressed her concern that the 'hotel' concept is under threat, as there have never been more alternatives for customers to staying in a traditional hotel. In particular, she explained the emergence of 'Rent-a-Room'. She had emailed the handout below to the board in advance to help their understanding of a new threat.

Explanation of Rent-a-Room

'Rent-a-Room' is a totally online marketplace which offers 'flexible hospitality', enabling guests to quickly and conveniently book short-term room lodgings with third party 'hosts'. These include apartment rentals, homestays, hostels and hotel rooms.

Rent-a-Room receives a percentage service fee from both the guests and the hosts for every booking made. It has over 2 million accommodation listings in 60,000 towns and cities across the world.

Notably, it doesn't own any of the lodgings it advertises.

Many of the hosts listed with Rent-a-Room offer high speed internet and Wi-Fi facilities plus extras such as web-movies and the prices charged are often far lower than our hotel room prices.

Mr Tomas Myer, HiLite's Operations Director stated his belief that the Rent-a-Room concept is a limited threat to HiLite's established business model. His opinion was that 'It's just people sleeping on the floor of a friend's house and raiding their fridge in the morning. It's hardly what we offer. Customers want far more than that.' He also expressed his belief that this would be a short-lived phenomenon: 'The threat from Rent-a-Room is clearly more of an 'if' rather than a 'when'. I think we should not over react and just let this blow over.'

Mrs Elizabeth Fox, HiLite's Finance Director, commented that technology was likely to be a key disruptive influence on the future of the hotel industry. She explained that modern travellers and primarily the 'millennials' (those people born approximately 20–40 years ago) are looking for value for money, flexibility and the ability to manage their whole stay, from booking through to flexible check-out, all via their smartphones. She also noted that smartphone apps are now being developed to enable smartphones to be used as an alternative to a key for door entry systems to hotel rooms.

Other technological developments in the hotel industry were discussed, including the emergence of online travel agencies (OTAs) and hotel comparison and booking sites, and the development of personalised technologies, such as smartphone apps which provide guests with personalised services such as customised local offers from business partners, including booking facilities at local restaurants and cheap tickets for local attractions. Elizabeth Fox concluded the discussion with the statement that 'Hotels can no longer simply rent rooms – we need to give the traveller more reasons to book with us directly.'

The Chief Executive, Bernie Vokes, summarised by stating that HiLite could not ignore disruptive technologies and that before any decision is made on how to react to these, HiLite must assess the extent of this strategic threat, before identifying relevant responses.

Agenda item 2: Information systems risks and controls

The Finance Director opened the discussion on information systems risks and controls with the statement that, although HiLite has invested significant amounts of money in its website in the last few years, it has not developed a clear information systems strategy. Also, she expressed her concern that control and management of the risks to its IT/IS environment have not been adequately addressed.

The Chairman commented that HiLite has not experienced any breaches of its information systems and that therefore, 'we must be doing something right'. The Finance Director presented to the Board what she considered to be the three key information systems risk considerations in the slide (Appendix 1) below. The Finance Director recommended that these risks should be prioritised and that HiLite must take appropriate action to control these risks.

The Finance Director presented Appendix 1 to the Board.

ACTIONS TO BE ADDRESSED BEFORE THE NEXT BOARD MEETING:

1   Identify the challenges posed by disruptive technologies and recommend applications for disruptive technologies by HiLite.

2   Identify appropriate actions to control HiLite's information systems environment.

3   Investigate the possibility of recruiting an IT Director.

Meeting was concluded at 3.30pm.

APPENDIX 1:

INFORMATION SYSTEMS RISKS : KEY CONSIDERATIONS

RISK	CAUSES OF RISK
1. Lack of focus on IT/ IS Strategy	Weak focus on IT/ IS strategy and weak strategic leadership of our IT/IS development. Limited support for IT/ IS strategy at Board level.
2. Cyber and data security breaches	Failure to update our information systems in line with latest cyber security threats. Lack of appropriate internal physical and access controls
3. Business continuity threat	Insufficient planning for business continuity. Lack of awareness at Board level of the importance of critical information systems.

Section 12

REAL EXAM ANSWERS – DECEMBER 2018

1 HILITE

> **Note**
>
> It is not always possible to publish suggested answers which comprehensively cover all the valid points which candidates might make. Credit will be given to candidates for points not included in the suggested answers, but which, nevertheless, are relevant to the requirements.
>
> In addition, in this integrated case study examination points made in one question may be re-introduced or fully developed in other question(s) as long as these are made in the specific context of the requirements of the part of the question being answered.
>
> The suggested answers presented below may give much more detail than would be expected from most candidates under examination conditions; they may also have used a particular approach or model which should not be taken as the only approach or model which could have been used. Different approaches and structuring of the answers are expected and full credit will be given for relevant and appropriate solutions to the tasks given. The answers provided here are therefore intended to support revision and tuition for future examinations.
>
> Finally, it should be noted that candidates will not get full professional skills marks in a task requirement if they have not presented their answers according to the format asked for. For example, if a task is to be completed using a report and evaluation skills are tested, even if the answer has met the specifically stated evaluation criteria, candidates will not be able to earn all the professional skills marks available if they have not used the report format.

1 (a) Briefing notes: Factors enabling HiLite's success in Deeland

If we are to consider developing the HiLite brand within another country, a useful starting point would be to understand the key factors which have made HiLite so successful in Deeland, and then assess the availability of these same factors and conditions in other countries. This would allow us to evaluate the viability of such a strategy and assess our ability to achieve sustainable competitive advantage overseas. Below are key factors present in Deeland which have helped HiLite to be successful.

Factor conditions

We should start by assessing the factor conditions, which include the physical resources, human resources, knowledge and infrastructure present within Deeland, which HiLite is able to access. Deeland has some advantages in regard of its factor conditions, as it has a well-developed infrastructure, based on sound local and national investment policies in air, road and rail travel. A new airport has recently been constructed in Deeland's second largest city, generating an additional 2.5 million overseas passengers to Deeland last year. This is likely to have a significant impact on tourism and the number of visitors to Deeland and therefore will obviously assist in supporting the hotel industry and, of course, our own business.

As a business, we have exploited the transport infrastructure which Deeland offers, locating our hotels on major road networks and near to rail stations. National and regional level investment in such infrastructure has been a great advantage to our business.

Also, Deeland's education system is another endowment to HiLite's service supply. The education system supports the travel and tourism industry with many of Deeland's universities offering highly regarded travel and tourism qualifications, which in turn leads to the availability of highly skilled human resources within the hotel and tourism industries. However, we must be aware that although the education system supports the provision of labour in the industry, we appear to have a problem in recruiting and retaining skilled staff and this is something we must work on in the future.

Therefore, Deeland has positive factor conditions in both infrastructure and human resources which have had a positive effect on the success of our business.

Demand conditions

When an organisation is located in a country where the home market demand is strong and where home-based customers are sophisticated and require high standards of innovation and/or quality, this can assist it in achieving sustainable competitive advantage.

In the case of Deeland, it is evident from the recently published 20X8 Hotel Industry Report, that travellers in Deeland continue to be highly demanding customers, who expect high standards but also value for money. It is noted in the report that a recent survey of online hotel customers clearly indicated that 70% would shop around for the best deal in the best location. This indicates that our customers are sophisticated and this must drive us to respond to their needs.

Therefore, focusing on our customers' needs and our particular focus on value for money, as highlighted in the Chief Executive's Report on Performance, has helped HiLite to offer services which are in line with customer demands. This has allowed us to maintain and strengthen our competitive advantage, whilst other organisations, such as Waterbay Leisure and EzeeHols Group, two of Deeland's most long established luxury hotel chains, have both gone out of business this year. It is evident that they have not responded effectively to the needs of its home-based customers.

Related and supporting industries

The success of an industry can also be influenced by other industries/organisations which support it and supply it. In the case of HiLite, our location in Deeland provides us with an advantage due to the highly developed hotel and tourism industries within the country. Travel companies both online and on the high street are thriving in Deeland, which clearly will support and enhance the business opportunities of HiLite.

Online hotel booking websites and price comparison sites are also a key factor in driving the success of hotel businesses. In particular, the price comparison websites, comparing our prices with our closest competitors drives our business to be more competitive and to offer better and more flexible pricing options for customers. Only those hotels which can respond to this and are adaptable and flexible to customer pricing demands will survive and remain competitive. This is a potential reason why the two luxury hotel chains mentioned in the previous section have gone out of business this year.

In addition, growth in the business activity in the overall economy of Deeland, will also support the development of more business travel in the country which is another factor in supporting the growth and development of our business traveller provision and opportunities in Deeland.

Firm strategy, structure and rivalry

Success can be influenced by the way an organisation is created, organised and managed. Evidence suggests, from the comments made in the recent Chief Executive's Report on Performance for 20X7/20X8 that in Deeland there is continuing growth of the budget hotel market, as the luxury and mid-price sectors continue to decline. This is an obvious advantage for HiLite, as we are the leading budget brand hotel chain in Deeland. Therefore, we are perfectly placed to exploit the overall market conditions in the economy. Our brand is a key strength and we must ensure we maintain this strong brand image and customer loyalty to the brand.

Our brand itself is the focus of our overall strategy, which is one of value for money and overall operating efficiency in order to ensure the best price for our customers. As stated above, we have highly demanding business and leisure customers in Deeland who are looking for value for money and best price and are prepared to shop around for this. Therefore, our strategy of a value for money approach, as highlighted in the Chief Executive's Report on Performance 20X7/20X8, should assist in building upon this demand from customers and provide us with sustainable competitive advantage.

Competitive rivalry is also a key consideration, with growth in business activity in the economy driving more opportunities and creating a highly competitive environment. As can be seen in the Hotel Industry Report for 20X8, two new national branded chains of hotels have opened during this year in the main tourist centres of Deeland and national competition remains intense. This rivalry is a key factor in encouraging us to innovate and be flexible to our customer demands, in particular to respond to key trends in the industry, such as technological developments and in particular, the threat of disruptive technologies. The two luxury chains of hotels which have recently gone out of business in Deeland may indeed point to the fact that the intensity of rivalry in the industry is affecting the luxury end of the market more adversely than the more flexible budget hotels. This supports our overall strategic position as a budget hotel operator.

Government support

It is clear that the Deeland government is supportive of the travel and hotel industry in a number of ways. As already mentioned, investment in infrastructure at both a regional and national level is a major influence on attracting travellers to Deeland, in particular the investment in the new airport, as previously highlighted. Additionally, support in the education sector to develop skilled and well-trained staff for the travel and tourism industry is also a key factor in ensuring a high level of supply of talented and well-educated staff for our hotels.

A further factor highlighted in the Hotel Industry Report 20X8 is that the government of Deeland has recently announced investment and tax breaks for employers offering job creation schemes in a wide range of industries, including travel and tourism. Again, this points to a high level of government support to encourage a thriving business economy, including the tourism and hotel industry. HiLite could take advantage of such tax breaks.

Tutorial note

NB Please note the way the answer has used the format of Porters Diamond to structure the answer. Whilst this is perfectly acceptable, it is not critical to use a model to gain good marks in SBL.

(b)

Tutorial note

Under exam conditions, candidates would not be expected to replicate the financial table presented in Exhibit 3 within the body of the report which they have been asked to present to the finance director. It has been included in the answer below for the purpose of demonstrating how a professionally presented report should have been provided to the finance director in a real-life situation.

To: The Chief business analyst

From: Senior business analyst

Date: xx/12/20X8

An evaluation of the proposed acquisition of the Comfi Stay hotel chain

Introduction

The following report presents an evaluation of the proposal to acquire the Comfi Stay hotel chain located in Veelandia. The report will consider the financial viability of the proposal and also consider a range of other criteria upon which to base the final decision and will evaluate the implications of this proposal for HiLite.

Financial considerations

Table 1: Financial evaluation of the proposal (Note all figures have been converted to the $)

	Year						
	0	1	2	3	4	5	6
Revenues		48,180,00	48,180,00	53,961,600	53,961,600	53,961,600	53,961,600
Initial investment	80,000,000						
Refurbishment	10,000,000	5,000,000					
Environmental investment		1,000,000	1,000,000	1,000,000	1,000,000	1,000,000	1,000,000
Training costs		3,000,000	1,500,000	1,500,000	1,500,000	1,500,000	1,500,000
Operating costs		21,681,000	21,681,000	24,282,720	24,282,720	24,282,720	24,282,720
Total costs	90,000,000	30,681,000	24,181,000	26,782,720	26,782,720	26,782,720	26,782,720
Cash flow	90,000,000	17,499,000	23,999,000	27,178,880	27,178,880	27,178,880	27,178,880
Discount factor 12%	1.00	0.89	0.80	0.71	0.64	0.57	0.51
Present value	90,000,000	15,624,107	19,131,856	19,345,390	17,272,670	15,422,026	13,769,666
Net present value	10,565,715						

From the net present value calculation of the proposed acquisition of the Comfi Stay hotel chain (Table 1), it would appear tobe financially viable, returning an NPV of nearly $10.6 million. This equates to a return on the initial investment of 13.2%. Discounted payback occurs at approximately five years and three months.

However, it would be necessary to assess the viability and reliability of the data contained in the above NPV to assess how realistic the revenue predictions are, based upon predicted customer numbers and revenue per room calculations. Economic conditions may be difficult to predict in a country such as Veelandia and we would need to take a cautious approach in any forecast revenue results. Likewise, although our initial investment and refurbishment costs may be relatively straightforward to assess, long-term costs in training and operations need to be carefully considered, particularly in the light of the lack of investment which has been carried out in these hotels previously.

We should also consider foreign currency risk exposure, in relation to the stability of the Veelandia currency. We have never operated any hotels overseas and this brings with it a number of challenges for our business in terms of translation and transaction risks. We have carried out our NPV calculation in our own currency ($), but we must consider the potential impact of the Veelandia currency fluctuations in particular on our forecasted revenues and operating costs.

Before making any decision based upon these financial results, I would like to see possibly a range of NPV calculations based upon best and worst-case scenarios. In addition, before proceeding with the acquisition of the Comfi Stay hotel chain, we should also consider a range of other issues which are set out below:

Strategic fit of the proposed acquisition

We should assess whether the proposed acquisition of Comfi Stay is in line with our strategic position; that is, does it have a strategic fit with the rest of our business? We should also consider the cultural fit with our existing operations, particularly as the Comfi Stay hotel chain is located in a different country, 5,000 miles away.

As the Comfi Stay hotel chain is within our current sphere of business operations as a hotel, it would be considered to have a strategic fit. However, the strength of that strategic fit may be questionable, based on the fact that it is a mid-range hotel chain offering additional facilities such as gyms and pool facilities. Our current HiLite hotels located in Deeland do not offer such additional facilities and we would need to carefully consider how to integrate Comfi Stay's hotels into the HiLite brand, which is based upon a 'budget' offering. Therefore, strategic fit may not be as clear-cut as we may think.

However, it is evident from the recent Hotel Industry Report for 20X8, that consolidation in the marketplace is becoming common, and hotels operating within different sectors of the market are consolidating through acquisition. Therefore, it would seem that this option could be suitable, based upon recent acquisition activity in the market. Also, our chief executive has suggested in his Report on Performance for 20X7/20X8 that HiLite is considering the strategic direction of developing the HiLite brand overseas and therefore this would exploit this potential opportunity for us.

Another consideration is the cultural fit of the Comfi Stay hotel chain. As Veelandia is located over 5,000 miles away from Deeland and the fact that the hotels are not budget hotels, there may be cultural differences to consider. The fact that it is a family-run business may also mean that it has a family-based culture which may be difficult to change and integrate into our current operations and style of management.

National culture is also clearly different in Veelandia and may be challenging for HiLite. Poor employment practices and evidence of use of under-age labour in the hotel industry in Veelandia must be thoroughly investigated and we must make sure that our own cultural behaviours are transferred to replace ones which are clearly not suitable for our own operations. This must be a priority for HiLite, as our own reputation could be damaged by association with the Comfi Stay hotel chain if we do not address these issues. However, we will also be sensitive to cultural differences and only make changes where necessary.

Acceptability of the acquisition

When considering the acceptability of the proposed acquisition of the Comfi Stay hotel chain, we need to evaluate whether it is consistent with our current objectives in terms of risk and return, and importantly whether it will be acceptable to our stakeholders.

When considering the calculations of net present value, it would be prudent to test the sensitivity of some of our assumptions to evaluate the overall impact of and potential sensitivity of these factors on the final outcome. For example, a failure to achieve the expected occupancy levels from year 3 onwards could reduce the final NPV significantly, as expected revenues would be significantly reduced. Any combination of variable changes needs to be tested, to assess our sensitivity to potential changes in the underlying assumptions made and the risks which these changes may pose. We must also verify the accuracy of our assumptions.

We also need to consider acceptability of the proposed acquisition to our stakeholders. Our own staff based in Deeland may be largely indifferent to the decision, but those hotel managers who may be requested to re-locate may potentially be reluctant (or conversely may indeed be enthusiastic at the proposal). We must ensure that this is communicated effectively to these hotel managers in good time, should the decision to acquire Comfi Stay be made. Staff in Veelandia will likely react positively to this investment, if it means that employment will continue and there is likely to be a high possibility of improved employment rights and an improvement in working conditions and opportunities for training.

Our shareholders are likely to be favourable towards the strategy if it creates a positive return on shareholder wealth. The chief executive has clearly stated in his Report on Performance that this is a proposed strategy and therefore shareholders will be accepting of this business development opportunity, as long as it impacts favourably on the profits of the business. However, we must be mindful of the impact of this decision on our shareholders if they believe this decision may impact adversely on our reputation, as this could indeed impact adversely on shareholder wealth. Effective and regular communication with our shareholders must be carried out.

Customers in Veelandia may not favour this direction for Comfi Stay hotels if it means an increase in prices. However, hotel refurbishments and updates should increase the quality of the hotel offering, which have clearly become outdated due to lack of investment. This improvement to the quality of the Comfi Stay hotels should satisfy potential customers.

We also need to consider how the wider community and the media will react to this decision. There is a risk that it will be seen as unfavourable by the wider public, as Veelandia does not operate to the standards of Deeland and may be seen as being unethical to operate in a low wage economy. We must make it clear to these stakeholders that it is our intention to operate at the highest ethical standards within Veelandia, should the acquisition be successful. For example, we should follow strict guidelines on offering a fair wage to employees and not allowing under-age workers.

Assessment of resource requirement of the proposed acquisition

We must also consider whether we have the resources we need to carry out the acquisition of the Comfi Stay hotel chain. It would appear that we have the necessary funds available to undertake the strategy, through a combination of debt and equity. We are a highly profitable business and shareholders will be expecting us to continue the growth in profit which we have achieved in recent years. Therefore, shareholders should be supportive of such an investment through equity and debt finance.

We also need to consider our core competences and our strategic capabilities required to undertake this acquisition. We have never undertaken an acquisition strategy before, therefore we must assess our own management skills and capabilities to undertake this strategy successfully. Without the necessary expertise, we could make a number of errors in the process of acquisition, resulting in its failure. We may need to consider hiring external consultants to assist with the acquisition process.

We must also assess our skills and competences to operate and manage these hotels in Veeladia. We have highly skilled staff who can be used to train and work with the Comfi Stay hotel staff to ensure that we manage the transition carefully and successfully. However, it is likely that local staff will not have the same level of training, commitment and loyalty which will need to be developed if the venture is to succeed. This may be a large barrier to overcome. However, the planned investment in training local staff is significant and therefore this should go a long way to ensuring that the proposed acquisition is successful. However, on-going management and monitoring of local staff and management will be critical.

Concluding comments

There are a number of positive factors to suggest that the acquisition of Comfi Stay hotel chain is a viable strategy for HiLite. However, the board of directors should prioritise which aspects of the decision criteria are most important to the success of the venture before making a final decision.

2   (a)   PRESS RELEASE

Tutorial note

NB it is worthy of note that the purpose of a press statement is to inform, communicate and persuade the reader.

For immediate release

HiLite's proposed acquisition of the Comfi Stay hotel chain, Veelandia

HiLite Hotels, Deeland's most popular and largest budget hotel chain, has recently announced its intention to acquire the family-run 'Comfi Stay' chain of hotels, located in Veelandia. Since the announcement, there have been some concerns raised that the acquisition of the Comfi Stay hotel chain goes against the high principles and standards which HiLite strives to attain.

HiLite wishes to make clear the following points in response to these concerns:

1   Employees' rights

Although the Comfi Stay hotel chain is located in a low wage economy, it would be HiLite's intention to ensure that its staff located in Veelandia are not exploited in any way, and if it is found that child labour is being used or staff are working excessive hours, then this practice will immediately be ceased on acquisition. HiLite values its hotel staff highly and is committed to ensuring that it is a great place to work, and this commitment will also be given to its hotel staff in Veelandia.

It is not unethical for HiLite to pay staff in Veelandia below the rates which its staff in Deeland are paid, particularly if the wage rates are favourable when benchmarked within the local economy, for similar employees in the hotel sector. This is common business practice across many industries operating in multiple locations. However, as stated above, it is not the intention of HiLite to exploit staff located in Veelandia.

HiLite invests around $10 million annually in skills and development programmes for its staff in Deeland, and has implemented the new Deeland National Living Wage six months in advance of the government's launch date. Therefore, rates of pay will be reviewed for all staff and will be commensurate with the role undertaken and the expected and fair wage rate in Veelandia. We will provide training opportunities for all staff and will also offer employment contracts which will give employees security of employment.

2 Employment opportunities

HiLite's intention is to provide employment and development opportunities for the staff employed in all of its hotels. Over the next six years, HiLite intends to invest $10 million in training and staff development in Veelandia to ensure staff there are as highly skilled as those operating in Deeland.

In line with our diversity and equality policies, HiLite will immediately cease the policy of only employing male hotel managers and will implement a policy of selection for senior roles based upon experience and suitability for the role and not based upon gender, age or ethnicity. Obviously, HiLite will need to ensure cultural sensitivity in all of its employment activities but will ensure that its own employment policies, in terms of equality and diversity, are adhered to, wherever it is located throughout the world.

3 Environmental investment

In terms of the environmental impact of the decision to acquire the Comfi Stay hotel chain, HiLite intends to invest $6 million over the next six years in environmental investment in the Comfi Stay hotels. This should go some way towards prevention of further incidents of pollution which have recently occurred in some of its hotels.

In addition, a thorough investigation of environmental practices and policies of the whole business and at individual hotel sites would need to be carried out to assess any further investment, training or policies which need to be implemented throughout the Comfi Stay hotel chain. It will be expected that all of Comfi Stay hotels will operate to the same environmental and sustainable standards as all HiLite hotels, once the environmental investments are fully operational.

Targets will be set and monitored by HiLite for all of the Comfi Stay hotels in terms of recycling, CO_2 emissions and levels of wastage, in line with those operated throughout the rest of the business and training will be given to all staff in environmental management activities. These targets will need to be set to reflect the local resources available to each hotel to undertake environmental management activities such as the existence of local re-cycling depots.

4 Long-term approach

It would also be HiLite's long-term intention to work with the government of Veelandia and the travel and tourism industry in the country to try to work together on improving the environmental awareness in the whole industry.

HiLite intends to take a pro-active approach to managing the social and environmental impact of its activities in Veelandia. Experienced hotel managers from HiLite will be seconded to Comfi Stay hotels to ensure a smooth transition and to assist in the training of local staff to run and manage the operations effectively. Although the Comfi Stay hotels are located 5,000 miles away from the main operations of the business, they will be expected to adhere to the corporate guidelines and standards set by HiLite.

It is the intention of the management of HiLite to invest in re-vitalising the Comfi Stay hotel chain to develop long-term employment opportunities for staff and to provide a great location for international travellers to visit.

For any further information please contact our Sales and Marketing Department.

(b) **For the attention of the Finance Director**

Notes on the role and benefits of integrated reporting to stakeholders

Aims of integrated reporting in effective communication

If we are to implement an integrated reporting approach, we should do so with the aim to improve the quality of information we provide to our stakeholders and to promote a more efficient approach to our corporate reporting activities which consolidates and draws upon different communication strands and methodologies. This should enable us to present a more efficient, cohesive approach to stakeholder communication.

Role of integrated reporting

HiLite's integrated report should be designed to benefit all of our stakeholders who are interested in how we create value over time, including our hotel staff, the hotel customers, local communities where our hotels are located, suppliers and, of course, our investors. Importantly, our ability to create value is linked directly to the value we create for those stakeholders.

The primary role of an integrated report is to improve the quality of information available to our stakeholders, by communicating broader and more relevant information which can assist them in effective decision making, in particular for our investors (however, investors form only a part of this system). Research indicates that investors want broader information which goes beyond pure financial data, similar to the needs of our wider stakeholder groups mentioned above.

The benefits of integrated reporting

The benefits to stakeholders of using a broader information set are numerous and have been highlighted in several studies which have surveyed stakeholder attitudes to such information. The benefits include (amongst others): an improved relationship between HiLite and our investors, a greater insight for our hotel customers and our hotel staff into our organisation's business model and the benefits we can offer them, strategy and long-term outlook, as well as a greater understanding of our use and dependence on different resources and 'capitals' and our access to and effect on them.

HiLite's investors in particular would benefit from such information which informs investment decision-making. Using a broader set of information can also benefit them by providing a greater understanding of the drivers of our performance and value creation. With this information, they can be more confident of our long-term outlook and our ability to create value over time.

Benefits recognised at the company level could also impact on our stakeholders. For example, studies suggest that companies who adopt an integrated reporting approach outperform those which do not and have more long-term investors. This will clearly benefit all of our stakeholders, including our hotel staff and our customers.

Building relationships with our stakeholders

By providing information which stakeholders need, value and find useful will help us build long-term relationships with these stakeholders. Information which stakeholders would value includes an overall explanation of our business model, how we generate our business and a well-articulated strategy and a clear understanding of our anticipated future opportunities/direction and risks. Stakeholders could then use this information in many ways, including to help manage investment risk, evaluate the hotel industry dynamics and the regulatory environment and to assess HiLite's long-term prospects and stability.

This will be useful for our investors, but would also be important to our staff who are looking for employment stability and future employment prospects. Our local communities will also wish to see our commitment to the local economy in to the future. As a hotel business, we can stimulate local economies by bringing in tourists to the area to spend money in the local economies in which we operate.

Integrated reporting could help us to focus on aspects which materially affect our long-term ability to create value. Through communication to our stakeholders and transparency, the application of integrated reporting allows us to 'tell our own story', preventing analysts and external observers (such as the recent newspaper article) from making assumptions on our behalf.

Although institutional investors are largely interested in the financial performance and quantitative key performance indicators of HiLite, assessing other performance indicators is also likely to play a pivotal role in an investment decision-making process, including wider information for instance, environmental, social and governance issues, which will help investors to assess investment risks more fully.

Reporting on broader areas of value creation is likely to be important to a wide range of stakeholders also, offering an insight into business strategy, performance, governance and prospects, encouraging improved relationships with customers, employees, suppliers and local communities. Stakeholders are able to use integrated reporting information in the following ways:

- Economic analysis: to understand trends and externalities in the hotel industry which could affect the economic outlook and value creation of HiLite.

- Industry analysis: to understand factors driving competitiveness in the hotel industry and the potential for sustained value creation in an industry.

- Company strategy: to understand management quality and corporate strategy and evaluate our ability to respond to emerging trends in the hotel industry, such as disruptive technologies and consolidation of the industry.

3   (a)   To: the Board of Hilite

From: **Senior business analyst**

Date: **XX/12/20X8**

The impact of disruptive technologies on HiLite

Tutorial note

NB Remember when preparing the answers for tasks in SBL it is important to use the format requested.

Introduction

The following report will evaluate the potential strategic impact on HiLite of the disruptive technologies which are emerging in the hotel industry, and will consider the range of technologies emerging in the industry and the likely impact they could have on HiLite. The report will also highlight a number of potential applications of disruptive technologies which HiLite may consider implementing.

The emergence of disruptive technologies

A disruptive technology is a new emerging technology which unexpectedly displaces an established one with the outcome of 're-shaping' that industry, or indeed, creating a new one. Today's hotel customer is looking for a more unique and personal experience, valuing variety, choice and individuality, which disruptive technologies are attempting to address. So, what can we do to protect ourselves against disruptive technologies, and attract guests to stay in one of our HiLite hotels? The answer would seem to be to offer a more personal, individual unique service and experience, matching customers' budgets and spending patterns. The use of disruptive technologies may help us move some way towards achieving this, or if we choose to ignore this development, may in fact be a considerable competitive threat to our future. The comments made by the sales and marketing director, that the concept of a hotel is under threat, may be considered to be somewhat pessimistic, but her overall assessment of the growth and emergence of disruptive technologies must be taken seriously by the board. It is unlikely to be an issue which will simply 'blow over', as suggested by one of the board members.

The challenges posed by disruptive technologies

As discussions at the recent board meeting highlighted, there have never been more alternatives to staying in a 'traditional' hotel, such as ours. Online accommodation providers, such as 'Rent-a-Room' and perhaps more importantly, access to such a wide range of alternative accommodation provision options through the internet, has never been easier or more convenient for customers.

Disruptive technologies such as 'Rent-a-Room' are a real threat to HiLite and the comments made by the operations director at the recent board meeting should be challenged. The belief that the threat is an 'if' rather than a 'when' is indeed incorrect and likely to be dangerous to our long-term existence, as clearly Rent-a-Room is already a present and growing threat to us. There is clearly no 'if' as to the emergence of disruptive technologies and therefore this is a threat we must address. We simply cannot wait for it to go away. This is evidenced by the Hotel Industry Report for 20X8 which points to the changing competitive dynamics as one of the main challenges for the hotel industry for 2019 and beyond.

Flexibility

The hosts advertising with Rent-a-Room have the flexibility to be able to offer a wide range of services, such as individually tailored breakfast requirements, local on-site knowledge to offer up to the minute recommendations for highlights of the city, or providing introductions to local contacts which can get customers the best up to the minute offers. This provides guests with a far more customer-focused and individualised service than a 'homogeneous' service provider like HiLite could ever hope to successfully or economically provide.

In addition, the majority of hosts in this online 'space-sharing' environment, are likely to have high speed internet and web-movies for their own use, so those benefits can automatically be included in the price to guests, which is often considerably less than a hotel room, due to the significantly lower overheads incurred by host providers. Therefore, these alternative hosts are not only challenging us on product offering, but more importantly, on price. As we are a low-price focus business, our whole basis of competitive advantage is being challenged by disruptive technologies.

Wider choice of product offerings

The comments made by the finance director at the recent board meeting demonstrate a clear and realistic understanding of the challenges faced by HiLite from disruptive technologies. We must not be complacent and think that our customers will be satisfied with what we offer and will not be tempted by the offerings of disruptive technologies. We must be aware that disruptive technologies such as Rent-a-Room can create some novel product offerings and as the number of these offerings grow and the choice becomes wider, the more the traditional mainstream hotel user will be tempted to try out these offerings.

Personalisation

For a homogeneous product offering such as ours, we are likely to face significant challenges in being able to personalise our customer experiences. For Rent-a-Room hosts, personalisation of customer experience is significantly easier, as they are only dealing with one customer at a time, making the process straightforward. However, HiLite manages 46,000 hotel rooms across 510 hotels, meaning that personalisation of customer offerings is not only likely to be logistically difficult but also very expensive. Our hotels run with low levels of staff, albeit staff who are highly trained in customer services, but offering such high levels of personalisation will be a significant challenge.

Smartphone technology

Disruptive technologies do not only take the form of alternative product offerings such as Rent-a-Room. The use of smartphone applications in a range of ways from customisation through to door entry technology is a major development in the industry and one which we must consider. Although it is evident that customers are demanding greater flexibility, we would be faced with considerable obstacles if we changed the customer check-in process, to enable greater customer flexibility through smartphone technology. New software would need to be installed to manage the secure interface with customer smartphone apps with our hotel property management system, bringing with this the risk of data corruption and external systems access threats. The cost would also be significant.

There is also the problem of universal access for all of our customers, as many may not use smartphone technology. Implementing new door entry technology will also be expensive with the need for multiple entry and access systems including smartphone access and key card access. Managing multiple access methods adds unnecessary operational complexity for us which is likely to be a major barrier.

Potential for application of disruptive technologies by HiLite

However, we could consider some less expensive adaptations of disruptive technologies. There are opportunities for personalisation in the form of smartphone apps capable of providing information to guests throughout their stay in a destination, giving us the opportunity to enhance the guests' experience – such as local weather reports, local events and ticket offerings and also restaurant, theatre or other visitor attraction booking facilities through third party channels close to our hotels. We could also offer advance booking facilities to local gyms or sporting events which are taking place nearby. Overall, we should look into the possibility of offering an online and mobile interactive concierge facility for our guests which provides the facility to book rooms, extra services and personal experiences unique to them, on the move. This could be a starting point for HiLite to move into a more personalised service which moves us some way towards addressing the threats of the disruptive technologies in the hotel industry. However, much more work and evaluation of this threat must be done on an on-going basis. It can no longer be ignored.

Conclusion

Disruptive technologies present significant challenges to our business. As stated, we can no longer simply offer hotel rooms to our guests – we need to become a relevant focal point for destination experiences and tailor our offerings to more individual customer needs. This will be a significant challenge to us and one which we simply cannot ignore.

(b)

Risk 1: Lack of focus on IT/IS strategy

Outcomes

- HiLite's business strategy is not supported by IT/IS strategy, leading to failure

- Business opportunities missed due to poor IT/IS strategy

- Wasted resources due to lack of strategic leadership and direction

Recommended actions

- Employ an IT director

- Align the business strategy with the IT/IS strategy

Notes:

Outcomes

A fundamental starting point of a well-managed and controlled information system is the development of an information system strategy. A major risk to the long-term success of our business is our lack of strategic focus on information systems and its importance to achieving our overall business strategy. If our business strategy is not supported and integrated with our information systems strategy, then it is likely that our overall business objectives will not be successfully achieved. For example, our strategic focus of 'growth through innovation' as defined in our Chief Executive's Statement, would be jeopardised if this innovation was not considered alongside the appropriate technologies which can support and drive such innovation.

Without adequate focus on the strategic importance of information systems then it is likely that business opportunities such as innovation in product and service delivery could be missed which may harm our competitive advantage and result in our competitors moving ahead of us. Likely also to waste resources on ineffective systems which do not add value to our business.

Recommended actions

A contributory factor towards this lack of focus on the importance of an information systems strategy is the fact that we do not have an IT director who can lead our information systems development needs. For a business of our size and the nature of the dynamic technological developments occurring, an IT director would seem to be essential. We should therefore consider the employment of an IT director who would then provide a strategic focus and direction for our information systems to ensure that the information system strategy is supported and it enhances the overall business strategy.

As stated above, it is likely that business opportunities could be missed as a result of a poor focus on IT/IS strategy. Therefore, a key recommendation is that we must ensure that any strategy we consider in the future must be aligned to our IT/IS strategy. We should consider how our IT/IS capabilities and activities can enhance or potentially inhibit our strategic direction and how we must develop out IT/IS capabilities to support our strategic direction.

Risk 2: Cyber and data security breaches

Outcomes

- Loss of key organisational and customer data

- Severe business interruption leading to loss of business

- Damage to reputation and financial cost due to compensation and legal claims

Recommended actions

- Invest in the latest cyber security systems and controls

- Implement and upgrade information systems physical and access control environment

---

Notes:

Outcomes

Cyber and data security breaches are a significant threat to modern businesses, including HiLite. As an organisation, we could be vulnerable to the threat of external hacking of our key organisational data. A considerable threat could also be that of virus infection which could corrupt, or in the worst-case scenario, delete or disable our critical operating systems. The consequences of such threats are that our business would suffer severe interruption, particularly our online booking facility for customers which would be unable to function, leading to loss of business and dissatisfied customers.

Similarly, internal physical and access control weakness in our information systems environment could lead to system failure or corruption of data. Allowing unauthorised or untrained staff access to our information systems could result in data breaches and incorrect processing of bookings or transactions. Correcting these errors will be costly and time consuming. Consequently, any breaches to the security of our information is likely to be highly damaging to our reputation and also may result in costly compensation claims from customers who have been affected by any such breaches.

Recommended actions

We must make sure that we operate the latest industry standard firewalls and virus protection software and procedures. Regular testing of our security systems should be carried out and back-ups of all our data undertaken regularly and stored separately.

Access to our systems internally should be given to only authorised and trained staff. Authority of systems usage should be set and authorisation controls such as passwords and user ID systems should be used at all times. The system should produce regular reports on systems access and usage which should be monitored by IT staff and any exceptions should be reported.

Risk 3: Business continuity threat

Outcomes

- Unable to operate effectively due to no disaster recovery plan

- Loss of business/damage to reputation

- Cease to operate

Recommended actions

- Implement a disaster recovery plan

- Strategic level focus on role of IT/IS in overall business activities

---

Notes:

Outcomes

There is a lack of awareness at board level of the importance of our critical information systems on the continuity of our operations and the need to ensure that we have plans in place to ensure business continuity, should a disaster event take place. With insufficient planning and risk assessment it is likely that HiLite will not be ready for a business-critical event.

This may result in the business being unable to operate for a period of time, within which we will lose customers, and revenue will be severely affected. Our reputation is also likely to be damaged if our disaster recovery plans are ineffective or inadequate.

In the worst-case scenario, the business may not be recoverable and we could go out of business.

Recommended actions

The board must implement a disaster recovery plan to encompass a range of potential threats to our information systems including terrorist attacks, cyber-attacks, fire, flood or any other potential critical systems threat. We need to assess which disasters may occur and assess their level of threat to the business and ensure we have sufficient arrangements to manage such an event.

This reiterates a point made in a previous slide that the focus of information systems should be at the strategic/board level of the organisation. Our information systems should be seen not only as critically important business assets but also as key drivers of our business strategy and therefore it is important that we have a strategic focus and direction for our information systems.

Strategic Professional – Essentials, SBL

Strategic Business Leader (SBL) December 2018 Marking Scheme

1   (a)   Up to 2 marks for each relevant point made in discussing the factors which have enabled HiLite to be successful in its own country.

To including following points:

- Well-developed infrastructure
- New airport – significant impact on tourism
- Locating hotels on major road networks and near to rail stations
- National and regional level investment
- Education system which supports travel and tourism industry
- Highly skilled human resources in the hotel and tourism industries
- Travellers in Deeland highly demanding
- Customers are sophisticated
- Offering services in line with customer demands
- Maintain and strengthen competitive advantage
- Competitors gone out of business
- Highly developed hotel and tourism industries within Deeland
- Travel companies thriving
- Hotel booking websites and price comparison sites – driving the success of hotel businesses
- Flexible pricing options
- Growth in the activity in the overall economy
- Continuing growth of the budget market
- HiLite – perfectly placed to exploit overall market conditions
- Brand is focus of its overall strategy
- Value for money approach in building sustainable competitive advantage
- National competition remains intense
- Intensity of rivalry affecting luxury end of the market more adversely
- Supportive of travel and hotel industry
- Investment in infrastructure
- Support in education sector
- Tax breaks

(Up a maximum of 16 marks in total)

Professional skills may be additionally rewarded as in the following rubric:

How well has the candidate demonstrated professional skills as follows:	Not at all	Not so well	Quite well	Very well
1 (a) Analysis skills in identifying relevant information	The candidate has demonstrated no analysis skills. They have failed to effectively use and consider the appropriate and relevant data sources presented in the exhibits (particularly Exhibit 1 and 2). There is very little evidence of the candidate investigating the relevant information provided.	The candidate has demonstrated some basic analysis skills, by presenting some evidence of investigating a limited set of relevant data sources presented in the exhibits. There is some relevant analysis contained in the answer but most of the answer is merely restatement of the information provided, rather than clear demonstration of analysis.	The candidate has demonstrated some good analysis skills. The candidate has investigated and used most of the appropriate and relevant information contained in the exhibits and, in most cases, has attempted to demonstrate investigation and analysis rather than mere restatement of the information.	The candidate has demonstrated excellent analysis skills. The candidate has also demonstrated an ability to investigate and analyse a wide range of appropriate information from the exhibits and the candidate has presented a sound and well-considered analysis and investigation of the most relevant information presented to them.
Example	The candidate has provided little structure to their answer, presenting a poorly considered and limited number of points, which may include reference to Deeland's infrastructure, customers and/or competitors but there is no logical or clear analytical approach taken.	The candidate has recognised that Deeland has a well-developed infrastructure and has described these, including the new airport, but these have merely been stated and not analysed in terms of their impact on supporting the development of HiLite's growth.	The candidate has correctly considered strong home demand as identified from the Hotel Industry Report and has recognised the potential threat that customers are prepared to shop around. However, the candidate has not then considered the information from the Chief Executive's Report relating to offering value for money in order to ensure that customers remain loyal, demonstrating less well developed analytical skills than an answer assessed as 'very well'.	When considering the strong home demand, the candidate has assimilated information from both the Hotel Industry Report (relating to the highly demanding customers of Deeland and their indication that they are prepared to shop around), with the Chief Executive's Report indicating HiLite's focus on value for money to address these customers' demands. The candidate has recognised the clear link between these two pieces of information and has also considered that other organisations have not responded as successfully as HiLite. This demonstrated strong analytical skills.
	0	1	2	3

(b) Up to 2 marks for each relevant point for evaluating the proposal to acquire the Comfi Stay hotel chain.

Points to include:

- Positive NPV – so likely to be acceptable
- Return on initial investment of 13.2%
- Discounted payback of approximately five years
- Need to assess viability and reliability of the data
- Economic conditions may be difficult to predict
- Foreign currency risk exposure
- Undertake sensitivity analysis

Strategic fit

- Within current sphere of business operations as a hotel
- Consider how to integrate Comfi Stay's hotels into a budget brand
- Consolidation in the marketplace is becoming common
- Considering overseas development fits with this proposed strategic direction
- Cultural fit needs consideration
- Family-run business
- National culture different
- Reputation issues must be considered

Acceptability

- Consistency with current objectives
- Test sensitivity of assumptions in the NPV
- Staff based in Deeland may be indifferent to the decision
- Hotel managers requested to re-locate may be reluctant
- Staff reaction
- Shareholders' reaction
- Customers' reaction
- Wider community and the media views

Resources requirement

- Availability of funds
- Shareholders supportive of an investment
- Consideration of core competencies and capabilities
- On-going management and monitoring of local staff critical
- Local staff may not have skills and competencies

(Up a maximum of 16 marks in total)

Professional skills may be additionally rewarded as in the following rubric:

How well has the candidate demonstrated professional skills as follows:	Not at all	Not so well	Quite well	Very well
1 (b) Evaluation skills in presenting a balanced and objective appraisal of the relevant information relating to the acquisition of the Comfi Stay hotel chain	The candidate has failed to demonstrate any suitable evaluation skills. The answer is merely descriptive and repetitive of the information provided in the fact sheet and contains no evidence of the use of professional judgement to evaluate/appraise the acquisition proposal objectively.	The candidate has demonstrated limited evaluation skills in appraising only some of the relevant information related to the acquisition of the Comfi Stay hotel chain. There was some judgement shown but this was weak, as the answer was not well balanced (For example, there was NO financial analysis at all or the candidate presented ONLY financial analysis).	The candidate has presented a report and demonstrated good evaluation skills in providing an objective and well balanced appraisal and a good range of the financial and evidence of professional non-financial information related to the acquisition of the Comfi Stay hotel chain. The candidate demonstrated sound evidence of professional judgement in providing a largely balanced objective evaluation of the relevant sources of information.	The candidate has presented a report and demonstrated excellent evaluation skills in objectively appraising most/all of the relevant financial and non-financial information related to the acquisition of the Comfi Stay hotel chain. The candidate demonstrated excellent judgement in assessing a wide range of facts and evidence from various sources to and present a well-balanced and objective report, which was highly suitable for evaluation of the Comfi Stay acquisition.
Example	The candidate has only described the results of the NPV calculation, with little or no other appraisal of any other information presented to them.	The candidate has appraised the results of the NPV, including a discussion of the return on investment and payback but has provided no other appraisal of the non-financial information, therefore the answer has not considered all potential relevant information and is therefore not balanced.	The candidate has considered both the financial and non-financial information but has not used all of the relevant information available, such as the lack of evaluation of the strategic fit, based on the location of Comfi Stay and the differences in its operations and culture. Also, the candidate has considered some of the stakeholders but not all of the most relevant ones. Therefore, the answer is not adequately balanced or objective for all potential stakeholders.	The candidate has objectively considered the NPV data and recognised the need to assess the viability and reliability of the data contained in it and they have also considered the need to evaluate the sensitivity of the data. This shows clear objectivity. They have also clearly assessed strategic fit in terms of operational and cultural factors and have presented a sound evaluation of a range of stakeholders and the acceptability of the investment to these, including staff, customers and shareholders. Therefore, the answer is well balanced.
	0	1	2	3

2   **(a)**   Up to 2 marks for each relevant point made, in relation to assessing the social and environmental impact of the proposed investment in Veelandia and considering how this reassures the stakeholders of HiLite.

Points to include:

1   Employees' rights (SOCIAL)

- Intention to ensure staff in Veelandia are not exploited

- Stop child labour or excessive working hours

- Values all staff highly

- Not unethical to pay staff below rates in Deeland

- Invests in skills and development programmes

- Implemented Deeland National Living Wage six months in advance

- Fair wage rate in Veelandia

- Training opportunities for all staff

- Offer security of employment

2   Employment opportunities (SOCIAL)

- HiLite intends to invest $10 million in training and staff development in Veelandia

- Follow diversity and equality policies

- Selection for senior roles on experience

- Cultural sensitivity in employment activities

3   Environmental investment (ENVIRONMENTAL)

- Investing in environmental systems

- Investigation of environmental practices and policies to be carried out

- Comfi Stay hotels to operate the same environmental and sustainable standards as HiLite hotels

- Targets set and monitored in recycling, CO_2 emissions and wastage

- Training given to staff in environmental management activities

4   Long-term approach (SOCIAL and ENVIRONMENTAL)

- Work with the government of Veelandia and travel and tourism industry to improve environmental awareness

- Pro-active approach to managing social and environmental impact

- Hotel managers from HiLite seconded to Comfi Stay hotels

- Comfi Stay hotels expected to adhere to corporate guidelines and standards set by HiLite

- Develop long-term employment opportunities and provide a great location for international travellers

(Up to a maximum of 10 marks)

Professional skills may be additionally rewarded as in the following rubric:

How well has the candidate demonstrated professional skills as follows:	Not at all	Not so well	Quite well	Very well
2 (a) Communication skills in clarifying and conveying relevant information to HiLite's stakeholders	The candidate has demonstrated poor communication skills. Presentation format is weak/ inappropriate and the information presented is not relevant to reassure the stakeholders of HiLite's social and environmental intentions. This communication would not be appropriate for HiLite's stakeholders. There is no evidence of counter arguing the points made in the News article.	The candidate has demonstrated limited communication skills in attempting to present the answer in a valid format. The communication may be appropriate for only some of HiLite's stakeholders and overall, it lacks clarity. Much of the content does not appropriately convey the most relevant information to HiLite's stakeholders of its social and environmental intentions of the acquisition.	The candidate has demonstrated reasonably good communication skills in presenting a press release which is well laid out and in which some of the content would be relevant, convincing and reassuring to several of HiLite's stakeholders. The press release would likely be appropriate to persuade some of its stakeholders of its social and environmental intentions of the acquisition.	The candidate has demonstrated excellent communication skills. The press release is well presented, clear and concise and would be understandable and reassuring for most/all of its stakeholders. The press release would be appropriate to persuade most/all of its stakeholders of its social and environmental intentions of the acquisition. The press release is clear and communicates the most relevant points very effectively.

Example	The candidate's answer is totally theoretical and makes no reference to the specific social and environmental activities proposed by HiLite.	There is little evidence that the format is appropriate for a press release. The answer is brief and covers only a very limited range of social and/or environmental factors such as the more obvious ones in the information, such as child labour and HiLite's investment in training. The answer will not be sufficient in terms of depth and coverage to convince its wide range of stakeholders of its commitment to employment opportunities, diversity and environmental commitment.	The press release is set out in an appropriate and well-structured format, but the answer has addressed only some of the stakeholders' concerns. Therefore, the answer focuses on the social concerns in relation to HiLite's commitment to staff, the value it places on them, its commitment to diversity and equality, and its intention to commit to investment in staff development (most of which is from the CE's Report on Performance). However, the answer does not consider the environmental considerations and the stakeholders who would be interested in this information.	The press release will be well set out and include key headings such as 'employees rights' and 'environmental investment'. In terms of content, the answer will reaffirm to all of its interested stakeholders the intended focus on employment opportunities, for example, including reference to HiLite's commitment to staff, the value it places on them, its commitment to diversity and equality, and its intention to commit to investment in staff development (most of which is from the CE's Report on Performance). This will be written in a way to reassure a wide range of stakeholders (including employees, shareholders, the public and customers) of HiLite's social intentions. The answer will also be further developed in the same way to address the environmental concerns of its key stakeholders (Including investment in environmental management systems to address government concerns).
	0	1	2	3

(b) Up to 2 marks for each relevant point made in relation to assessing the role and benefit of integrated reporting in assisting effective communication and building relationships with key stakeholders.

Points to include:

Role of integrated reporting in communication/building relationships

- Designed to benefit all stakeholders

- Primary role to improve quality of information available to stakeholders

- Communicating broader and more relevant information to assist decision-making

- Information which goes beyond pure financial data

- Providing information which stakeholders need, value and find useful will help build long-term relationships

- Stakeholders use information in many ways – manage investment risk/ evaluate hotel industry dynamics/assess regulatory environment/assess term prospects and stability

- Important to staff looking for employment stability/employment prospects

- Local communities want to see commitment to local economy in the future

- Allows us to 'tell our own story', preventing analysts and external observers from making assumptions

- Investors largely interested in quantitative KPIs but other indicators important in decision-making process (environmental, social and governance issues)

- IR offers insight into business strategy, performance, governance and prospects, encouraging improved relationships with stakeholders

Benefits of integrated reporting

- Improved relationship between HiLite and investors

- Greater insight for customers and staff into organisation's business model and benefits offered to them

- Strategy and long-term outlook

- Greater understanding of use and dependence on resources and 'capitals'

- Investors benefit from information which informs decision-making

- Using broader set of information can benefit them by providing a greater understanding of value creation

- More confident in long-term outlook

(Up to a maximum of 12 marks)

Professional skills may be additionally rewarded as in the following rubric:

How well has the candidate demonstrated professional skills as follows:	Not at all	Not so well	Quite well	Very well
2 (b) Evaluation skills in using appropriate professional judgement to assess how useful Integrated Reporting could be to HiLite	The candidate has failed to demonstrate any evaluation skills. The candidate has failed to evaluate the usefulness to HiLite of integrated reporting in communications and relationships with its key stakeholders. There is no evidence of the candidate using sound professional judgement and the answer is purely descriptive and theoretical. .	The candidate has demonstrated some, but limited, evaluation skills. There is some limited evidence of the candidate applying some professional judgement in assessing the usefulness of integrated reporting in communicating and building relationships with HiLite's key stakeholders, but this has not been developed effectively throughout the whole answer.	The candidate has demonstrated reasonable evaluation skills. They have used some sound professional judgement in evaluating and assessing the usefulness to HiLite of integrated reporting in communicating and/or building relationships with key stakeholders. However, the answer lacks full development in terms of a full and complete assessment of the usefulness of <IR> to HiLite.	The candidate has presented briefing notes and demonstrated excellent evaluation skills. The candidate has demonstrated excellent professional judgement in assessing a wide range of factors to assist them in fully considering the usefulness to HiLite of integrated reporting in communicating and building relationships with its key stakeholders. The answer is well developed, objective and takes into account most/ all of the potential implications of the decision to implement <IR>.
Example	The answer will describe integrated reporting and the inclusion of the six categories of 'Capital' but does not demonstrate any application of this to HiLite and the relevance to it and its stakeholders.	The candidate has attempted some application of the benefits of <IR> to HiLite, but the examples of application are brief and limited. There is some reference to HiLite's shareholders use of <IR> to make better investment decisions but little more than this.	The candidate has considered the benefits and impact of <IR> for a number of stakeholders, including shareholders and staff and there is evidence of some professional judgement in identifying these as key stakeholders of HiLite (i.e. shareholders will be able to make better informed long-term investment decisions). However, other important stakeholders have not been considered or the depth of consideration is not strong.	The candidate has clearly considered the benefits and impact of <IR> for a wide range of its stakeholders including its hotel staff, hotel customers, shareholders and the local communities, and has clearly identified the importance to these stakeholders of the type and quality of information <IR> would provide. Examples of considerations would be the improved relationship with its shareholders by giving them information to manage their investments, a better understanding of the value of business for its customers and a better relationship with its staff through a more open and long-term approach for them to consider their future employment prospects. Importantly, evaluation skills have been demonstrated by recognition of a range of benefits to key stakeholders and HiLite itself.
	0	1	2	3

3 (a) Up to 2 marks for each relevant point related to the challenges of the disruptive technologies which are emerging in the hotel industry.

Disruptive technologies – Definition/explanation points

- New emerging technology which unexpectedly displaces an established one

- Hotel customer looking for a more unique personal experience

- Offer more personal, individual unique service and experience, matching customers' budgets and spending patterns

- Growth of disruptive technologies must be taken seriously

- Unlikely to be an issue which will 'blow over'

Challenges posed

- Re-shaping the industry

- Online accommodation providers – convenient for customers

- Comments made by the OD should be challenged

- Changing competitive dynamics

- Rent-a-Room hosts have flexibility to offer a wide range of services

- More customer-focused and individualised service than a 'homogenous' service provider like HiLite

- Price considerably less

- Competitive advantage being challenged

- Comments made by FD more realistic

- Must not be complacent

- Likely to face significant challenges in personalising customer experiences

- Considerable obstacles to customer check-in process, to enable greater customer flexibility through smartphone technology

- New software to manage secure interface between customer smartphone apps and hotel property management systems

- Risk of data corruption and external systems access threats

- Problem of universal access – many may not use smartphone technology

- New door entry technology expensive

Up to 2 marks for each relevant recommendation for the potential application of disruptive technologies by HiLite.

Application of disruptive technologies

Points to include:

- Consider less expensive adaptations of disruptive technologies

- Smartphone apps providing information to guests throughout their stay

- Local weather reports, local events, ticket offerings and restaurant, theatre or visitor attraction booking facilities

- Advance booking facilities to local attractions or sporting events

- Online and mobile interactive concierge facility for guests – facility to book rooms, extra services and personal experiences unique to them

- A starting point to move into a more personalised service

(Up to a maximum of 14 marks in total)

Professional skills may be additionally rewarded as in the following rubric:

How well has the candidate demonstrated professional skills as follows:	Not at all	Not so well	Quite well	Very well
3 (a) Scepticism skills in probing and challenging the opinions of the Board, in a professional and courteous manner	The candidate has demonstrated no scepticism skills. They have failed to question the opinions of the board members and have failed to challenge information presented in the exhibits relating to the potential impact on HiLite of disruptive technologies in the hotel industry.	The candidate has demonstrated some, but limited, scepticism skills. There is some evidence of questioning the opinions and assertions made by some of the board members in relation to their opinions on disruptive technology, but this was limited and the challenge was not presented in the most appropriate or professional manner/style.	The candidate has demonstrated a reasonable level of scepticism skills. The candidate has questioned and correctly challenged a number of the assertions made by board members in relation to their opinions on disruptive technology, but could have presented more evidence to support their challenge to these assertions.	The candidate has presented a report and demonstrated excellent scepticism skills. The candidate has strongly but appropriately questioned and challenged the assertions made by board members in relation to their opinions on disruptive technology, and has presented suitable and well-argued evidence to support their challenge to these opinions. The response was appropriate and courteous for a report at this level.

Example	The answer makes no reference at all to the comments made by the operations director or those made by the finance director, therefore there is no evidence of demonstrating scepticism in countering these comments.	The answer is phrased in a manner which would be considered inappropriate in response to a board level discussion. Also, the candidate has identified the comment made by the operations director as being incorrect but has not presented a reasonable or justified challenge to his comments nor used any evidence in the exhibits to counter the comments made.	The answer clearly commits to challenging and explaining this challenge to the operations director's opinions at the recent board meeting. However, the candidate has presented only limited evidence from the exhibits to support their challenge to the threat of Rent-a-Room and therefore has not demonstrated strong professionalism (for example, they have recognised information from comments made at the board meeting but could also have used other evidence in other exhibits). In addition, the answer could have been phrased in a more professional and courteous tone.	The answer is presented in a courteous manner, in that it does not state that the operations director is 'wrong', rather, that his views should be challenged and re-considered. Also, the answer clearly commits to challenging and indeed explaining this challenge to the operations director's opinion with reference to the evidence presented by the finance director and from the Industry Report. The candidate has also presented sound evidence to support their challenge by using the evidence relating to the threat of Rent-a-Room from the exhibits, demonstrating sound professionalism.
	0	**1**	**2**	**3**

(b) Up to 2 marks for each relevant point made, in assessing the potential outcomes of each of the information systems risks identified by the finance director.

Up to 2 marks for each justified recommended action which HiLite should take in order to control these risks?

Risk 1: Lack of focus on IT/IS strategy

Outcomes

- Risk to long-term success of business – if business strategy not supported/ integrated with information systems strategy

- Business opportunities could be missed – harming competitive advantage

- Waste resources on ineffective systems

Recommended actions

- Employment of an IT director

- Ensure that any strategy considered must be aligned to IT/IS strategy

Risk 2: Cyber and data security breaches

Outcomes

- Vulnerable to threat of external hacking of key organisational data
- Threat of virus infection
- Online booking facility unable to function
- Internal physical and access control weakness
- Unauthorised or untrained staff access
- Damaging to reputation and costly compensation

Recommended actions

- Operate latest industry standard firewalls and virus protection software
- Regular testing of security systems
- Back-ups of all data undertaken regularly and stored separately
- Access to systems given to only authorised and trained staff
- Authorisation controls such as passwords and user ID systems
- Regular reports on systems access and usage

Risk 3: Business continuity threat

Outcomes

- May not be ready for a business-critical event
- Lose customers, and revenue
- Reputation damaged if disaster recovery plans are ineffective/inadequate
- Worst-case scenario – could go out of business

Recommended actions

- Implement a disaster recovery plan
- Assess level of threat to the business and ensure sufficient arrangements to manage such events

Up to 4 marks maximum per slide presented (3 slides × 4 marks each)

(Up to a maximum of 12 marks in total)

Professional skills may be additionally rewarded as in the following rubric:

How well has the candidate demonstrated professional skills as follows:	Not at all	Not so well	Quite well	Very well
3 (b) Commercial acumen skills in in demonstrating insight and understanding of the information systems risks and controls	The candidate has demonstrated no commercial acumen skills and has demonstrated poor judgement of the outcomes of the information systems risks identified by the finance director. They have failed to demonstrate any insight in arriving at appropriate and relevant solutions for HiLite to address these information systems risks.	The candidate has demonstrated limited commercial acumen skills and has demonstrated limited judgement of the outcomes of the information systems risks identified by the finance director. There is evidence of some, but limited, insight and acumen as they have presented only a very limited range of relevant actions to address these information systems risks.	The candidate has presented slides with clear notes and demonstrated reasonably good commercial acumen skills. The candidate has demonstrated evidence of sound judgement in identifying some of the outcomes of the information systems risks identified by the finance director. The candidate has demonstrated some commercial acumen in recommending a reasonable number of relevant actions to address these risks.	The candidate has presented slides with clear notes and demonstrated excellent commercial acumen skills. There is evidence of well-developed and strong commercial judgement of the potential outcomes of the information systems risks identified by the finance director. Also, the range of actions to address these risks demonstrates excellent insight and commercial acumen.
Example	The answer in relation to Risk 1 is merely descriptive and there is no reference to the commercial impact of a lack of IT/IS strategy on the achievement of overall business objectives. There are no recommendations presented.	For Risk 1, the candidate has recognised the link between IT/IS strategy and overall business strategy but this is merely theoretical and not considered in terms of the IT/IS needs of HiLite. Also, the answer has provided few, if any potential relevant recommended actions and, for example, for Risk 1 has not recognised the importance of strategic leadership, i.e. an IT director, demonstrating weak commercial acumen.	For Risk 1, there is evidence of commercial acumen through recognising the link between having an IT/IS strategy and the achievement of overall business strategy and this is applied directly to HiLite's business strategies. However, recommended actions are limited and not sufficient to address the risks (for example, the candidate has not recognised the relevance of employing an IT director and/or ensuring that the IT/IS and business strategy are developed together). Therefore, the candidate's demonstration of commercial acumen is not fully developed.	For Risk 1, the candidate has clearly recognised the commercial impact of a sound information strategy upon the successful achievement of HiLite's overall business strategy and the potential for business opportunities to be missed and has consequently recommended and justified sound commercial solutions to these potential risks, including the relevance of employing an IT director. The answer focuses directly and correctly on how this strategic risk could affect the long-term survival of the business. Overall, application of how these three strategic risks can impact on the commercial viability of HiLite and how they should be addressed is clearly the focus of the answer demonstrating strong commercial acumen.
	0	1	2	3

Section 13

REAL EXAM QUESTIONS – MARCH/JUNE 2019

1   SMARTWEAR

SmartWear is a long established clothing retailer in Noria, a highly-developed northern European country, which is currently in the middle of a deep economic recession. The country is also experiencing political uncertainty because of its coalition government, who many influential commentators believe will not last for its full term of office. These two factors have contributed to record high levels of unemployment, low business confidence and a steady decline in the standard of living of the general population. The company also operates in two other countries on the European continent, Southland and Centrum.

SmartWear has enjoyed long-term business success mainly due to the fact that it has carefully positioned itself towards the lower end of the clothing retail sector. It sources its products directly from suppliers in low-cost economies, and it has been able to target a mass market with consistently low prices. This has meant that during the recent economic downturn in Noria it has been able to profit from the growing number of price-sensitive consumers, who have switched from the more high-end of the clothing retail market to budget retailers like SmartWear – who are the market leader in this high volume market.

SmartWear's long term strategy has always been based on a low cost – low price business model, which is described through its mission statement and strategic goals. However, following a prolonged period of expansion and growth, including successfully penetrating several other European markets, the company is for the first time experiencing a marked downturn in both its operational and financial performance. This appears to be in part due to economic pressure and the growing intensity of competition in all of its markets, both at home and abroad.

At a recent board meeting to discuss the latest set of disappointing financial results, it was proposed that an external consultant be appointed to investigate the deteriorating performance of SmartWear and propose the best way forward for the company.

You are the external consultant engaged by SmartWear, and you have gathered the following information to help you with your assignment:

Exhibit 1: Briefing notes prepared by the business development department for the consultant.

Exhibit 2: Transcript of a recent SmartWear Board meeting discussion.

Exhibit 3: An article from the Noria Herald dated 21 February 20X9.

Exhibit 4: Comparative macroeconomic data for Noria, Southland and Centrum.

Exhibit 5: Executive Summary of the SmartWear Internal Audit Report on Supply Chain Management.

Exhibit 6: Customer Database Management System (CDMS) Financial Investment Appraisal.

The case requirements are included in the tasks below:

1   It is apparent that the downturn in SmartWear's performance can be in part attributed to external factors beyond the company's direct control. A recent national newspaper article further confirms that the economic situation in Noria has made trading conditions tough for business. Therefore, a good understanding of those external environmental factors negatively affecting the SmartWear business model is essential so that action can be taken to remedy the current situation and improve the future prospects for the company and its investors.

The board of SmartWear wants to fully understand how the general environment is impacting on the company, as this will directly influence its ability to enable the business to succeed and prosper. The board has asked you to brief the board on this issue for their next board meeting.

Required:

Prepare a briefing paper to be presented at the next board meeting, which:

(a)   **Analyses the environment in which SmartWear operates and consider how this might impact its business model, mission and strategic goals.   (10 marks)**

(b)   **Assesses the major risks presented by SmartWear's current business model, and suggests appropriate mitigating actions to manage these risks.**

(10 marks)

Professional skills marks are available for evaluation skills by assessing the identified risks at SmartWear objectively. **(4 marks)**

(Total: 24 marks)

2   The board is becoming aware that Noria may not be the suitable country that it was 15 years ago for a business like SmartWear to operate successfully in. The financial performance of SmartWear in Southland is significantly better than that being achieved in the more established homeland of Noria, or in its other European markets like Centrum, so the board has asked you to help them understand why this is the case.

To help with this task, you have gathered summarised information on the country of Southland, where SmartWear opened its first retail outlet six years ago, together with comparative data for Noria and the neighbouring country of Centrum. The company now has over 30 retail outlets in all major towns and cities across the country of Southland, where the economy is booming, and Southland generates the most of SmartWear's revenue as a national market after Noria.

Required:

Prepare a report for the board, in which you:

(a)   **Analyse the company's strategic position in the Southland market to determine why SmartWear appears to be performing so well in this particular country compared to Noria.**   **(8 marks)**

Professional skills marks are available for demonstrating analysis skills in determining SmartWear's strategic position in the Southland market. **(2 marks)**

The board agreed that a radical response to the current situation was required to reassure investors and the stock market by showing them that the SmartWear board remained in control of the business, and was willing to take essential action when necessary. The board decided that the company needed to rationalise its operations by closing the 20 worst performing retail outlets in Noria, and withdrawing entirely from the neighbouring country of Centrum, where SmartWear's 15 retail outlets were all suffering heavy losses and showing absolutely no sign of recovery.

(b)   **Evaluate the strategic and ethical implications to SmartWear of the planned shop closures in Noria and the withdrawal from Centrum.**   **(12 marks)**

Professional skills marks are available for applying scepticism skills to the underlying issues and problems which may arise from this strategic decision.

(2 marks)

(Total: 24 marks)

3   The executive summary of an internal audit report on SmartWear's supply chain management has been given to you by the chair of the audit committee. The report identified a number of significant issues in areas such as an appraisal of existing suppliers' performance and internal reporting provisions.

On behalf of the board of directors, the chair of the audit committee has asked you to provide the buying and merchandising director with an objective appraisal of the supply chain management arrangements at SmartWear to effectively address the various issues raised in the report.

Required:

Draft a memo to the buying and merchandising director, which evaluates the effectiveness of internal control systems at the company, particularly on the procurement side, and recommends control improvements to rectify the identified areas of concern.   (12 marks)

Professional skills marks are available for commercial acumen skills when recommending solutions to those issues highlighted in the internal audit report.
(4 marks)

(Total: 16 marks)

4   Recently commissioned market research has concluded that SmartWear appears to have no clear understanding of the profile of its customer mix, and as a result operates quite unsophisticated and ineffective marketing campaigns. Recent financial results indicate that SmartWear is finding it hard to both retain and get repeat business from existing customers, and the company is clearly losing market share to both established competition and newer e-retailers.

The sales and marketing director has been considering the development and implementation of a sophisticated customer database management system (CDMS), incorporating a customer loyalty scheme, to replace the existing very basic customer database. The marketing department has undertaken a financial appraisal of this proposal to supplement the market research findings, and this indicates that it is financially viable in net present value (NPV) terms. You have advised the sales and marketing Director that for the board to agree to the proposal, a clearly stated business case and more reliable evaluation of the financial viability of the project will be needed. She agreed and asked you to help her in this regard.

Required:

Write a report on behalf of the sales and marketing director, for presentation to the board which achieves both of the following:

(a)   **Describes the benefits of introducing a customer database management system, including the loyalty scheme, for SmartWear.**   **(6 marks)**

Professional skills marks are available for commercial acumen skills by demonstrating awareness of business and wider external factors impacting on the decision to implement the CDMS.   **(2 marks)**

(b)   **Evaluates the marketing department's NPV analysis that supports the CDMS investment, questioning any underlying assumptions made.**   **(10 marks)**

Professional skills marks are available for displaying scepticism about the cash flow forecast used to support the proposal.   **(2 marks)**

(Total: 20 marks)

5　Severe criticism was forwarded to the chairman of SmartWear from an influential institutional shareholder about what it perceived as the short-sighted and narrow focus of the board on the low cost – low price business model. However, the board considers this criticism to be unjustified, since its focus has always been on the wider and longer-term strategic interests of SmartWear that has enabled it to achieve sustainable business growth.

The board believes the most probable reason for the criticism is a lack of understanding by certain investors of the SmartWear business rationale and the company's integrated thinking. To further improve the effectiveness of communication with investors, and the wider stakeholder community, the board of SmartWear decided to adopt its own version of the integrated reporting <IR> framework. The board unanimously agreed that the best results would be achieved when the company takes a more holistic view of its operations and performance, and so you are tasked to brief the board on how to make this message clearer to investors.

You have been asked by the CFO to help him make the case and persuade the board and his own finance team that integrated thinking and the Integrated Reporting <IR> framework should be adopted at SmartWear.

Required:

(a)　**Prepare one slide [with appropriate notes] for a brief presentation to be given by the CFO at the next board meeting which describes the benefits of integrated thinking within SmartWear to all stakeholders.** **(6 marks)**

(b)　**Prepare a briefing paper for the CFO to allow him to address the wider finance team to explain how corporate reporting using the <IR> framework provides more relevant information for SmartWear's shareholders about the creation of sustainable long-term value.** **(6 marks)**

Professional skills marks are available for demonstrating appropriate communication skills to the different audiences. **(4 marks)**

(Total: 16 marks)

Exhibit 1: Briefing notes prepared by the business development department for the consultant

> **SmartWear Mission Statement:** Our mission is to make the widest range of good quality fashion, which is responsibly sourced, available to everyone at affordable prices.
>
> To achieve the mission, the Board has agreed the following strategic goals:
>
> 1   Continued investment in all of our core markets that continue to offer significant growth opportunities to satisfy the needs and demands for low cost products and services of all our customers.
>
> 2   Develop strong, long-term relationships with our key suppliers based on mutual respect and serving each other's interests.
>
> 3   Function with the highest ethical standards of social responsibility, expecting the same from all business partners.
>
> 4   Maintain a successful and viable company that delivers healthy financial returns to our investors.
>
> 5   Be a responsible custodian and user of natural resources which are managed in a sustainable way.

> **Governance arrangements**
>
> SmartWear has a balanced board of directors, most of whom have been with the company for more than a decade and whose responsibilities cover all of its core business functions. The five Non-Executive Directors [NEDs] ensure that the board and the company remain fully compliant with the Noria Code of Corporate Governance; a listing requirement for all companies on the Noria Stock Exchange.
>
> The NEDs, being part of the unitary board, discharge their duties and responsibilities through a number of sub-committees [e.g. the audit committee] with expressed authority to challenge and scrutinise the executive members of the board.

> **Business development**
>
> Since it was listed on the Noria Stock Exchange five years ago, SmartWear has enjoyed meteoric success. At that time, it had only 40 retail outlets in Noria, but since then through careful and planned investment, the company has achieved sustained growth and become a substantial multi-national business with over 100 outlets in Noria and a similar total number of stores in several other European countries.
>
> Industry analysts have remarked that SmartWear has never exploited e-commerce opportunities, when there have been several new entrants into the market in the past few years who only sell online. The convenience and quality of service that these e-retailers provide has proven to be very appealing to many of SmartWear's traditional customers, who have shifted their shopping patterns and loyalty. The absence of detailed customer data has prevented SmartWear from mitigating the risks presented to its market share from e-commerce.

Exhibit 2: Transcript of a recent SmartWear board meeting discussion which took place before the external consultant was appointed

Chairman	The next item on the agenda is a review of our recent financial performance, which I know is of real concern to us all, particularly with the poor economic conditions we currently face in Noria, and the weak performance of our operations in Centrum.
	This is despite a somewhat optimistic recent newspaper article report suggesting that things in Noria may improve next year. So, I have asked the Finance Director to present us the facts so that we can decide on the best way to move the business going forward.
Finance director	Thank you, Mr Chairman. It is true that our current financial statements do not present the company in a particularly strong position. However it is not all bad news. The profit levels have fallen primarily because our sales revenue has dropped significantly over the last year. However, we have managed to maintain tight cost control over our suppliers so our gross profit margins are still holding well. Unfortunately, we are victims of our success in recent years, which means that we now have significant infrastructure costs and overheads to carry because we are much larger business than we were previously.
NED, stood and got the attention of the finance director	I'm sorry to interrupt you, but I have something important to add at this point as it may alter what you say next. One of our larger institutional investors contacted me, because we have other mutual business interests, stating in very clear terms that they were dissatisfied with the level of returns they are currently getting on their investment in SmartWear. They have seen a significant fall in share price value and are concerned about whether there would be any proposed annual dividend. I would just like to provide them with assurances that these rumours are wrong, and that they can expect our share price to rise again in the near future.
Finance director	Thank you for bringing this matter to our attention, as I too have had difficult conversations with a number of investors over the past few weeks. I suspect that it might be from some of my discussions that they are worried about a suspension of the dividend. However, I'm afraid it is true, and it was going to be one of the proposals I was to table later at this board meeting. With the current state of company finances it would be negligent of me as finance director to recommend a dividend this year and deplete our cash reserves further.
	Also, in accordance with Noria Stock Exchange listing rules, the company has to issue a profit warning when forecast earnings levels fall significantly below analysts' expectations, which I regret they now do. This is likely to result in a further downward adjustment in our share price, at least in the short term.

NED interrupted again	This institutional investor further suggested to me that the strategic direction of the company is completely wrong, and that SmartWear has become out of touch with its core customers. He suggested that this is the main reason why the company has been losing sales to competition, and unless the board make radical changes the situation may get far worse.
	I'm afraid that simply informing our investors that things are as bad as they thought will not reassure them about the board's ability to turn around the business. The absence of detailed and accurate information about customers, and the lack of technology to systematically capture and analyse such information, is putting SmartWear at a competitive disadvantage.
	Therefore, I propose that we engage the services of an external consultant to investigate what is currently wrong with SmartWear, and to report back with proposals on how the business can return to success. A fresh pair of eyes is always useful when a critical and objective appraisal of a difficult situation – like this – is required.

Exhibit 3: An article from the Noria Herald dated 21 February 20X9

Noria Herald

More doom and gloom on the horizon

Having already suffered more than three years of economic misery there is still no end in sight for the poor people of Noria. A recent report issued by the Finance Ministry has forecast negative economic growth, which in reality means further decline for Noria during the whole of this year and possibly beyond. Price inflation has been running at nearly 7% for over a year, which is high for the Noria economy, but with a stagnating economy the central bank will be reluctant to raise interest rates. So, with more than 8% of the adult population currently unemployed and an austerity programme imposed by government because of reduced taxation revenue – the prospects in Noria still look pretty bad!

The big question must be – are there any signs of economic recovery, which a reporter from the Noria Herald asked the Finance Minister at a press briefing yesterday. To which his reply was: 'So, if we are able to successfully survive the 20X9 period without any more important businesses going into liquidation or further heavy job losses, then it seems that an economic recovery may start as early as next year ... that is our expectation, but we have to wait and see.'

Exhibit 4: Comparative macroeconomic data

	Noria	Southland	Centrum
Population	• 10,400,000 • Working age population 6,550,000 • Growth rate +0.2% per annum • 38% under 30 years	• 5,780,000 • Working age population 3,450,000 • Growth rate +0.8% per annum • 43% under 30 years	• 3,250,000 • Working age population 1,860,000 • Growth rate +1.4% per annum • 52% under 30 years
Unemployment rate	• 8.8% current year • 9.1% last year	• 6.2% current year • 5% last year	• 12.0% current year • 10.5% last year
Average annual earnings	$48,500	$51,700	$38,500
Central bank interest rate	• 1.50% • Unchanged over 18 months	• 2.50% • Increased by 1.0% over 18 months	• 6.00% • Increased by 2.5% over 12 months
Inflation rate	2.2% [stable]	1.4% [stable]	3.8% [rising]
Consumer debt as a percentage of Gross Domestic Product	• 88% [and falling very slowly]	• 67.5% [and falling slowly]	• 115% [and rising]
Political and economic system	• Democratically elected coalition government • Free market economy • Developed capital markets	• Democratically elected government • Free market economy • Developed capital markets	• Democratically elected government • Emerging economy • Developed capital markets
Dominant business sectors	• Financial services • Retail • Defence technology • Tourism	• Financial services • Retail • Shipping and transportation • Technology development	• Agriculture • Steel production • Mining • Tourism

Exhibit 5: Executive summary of the SmartWear internal audit report on supply chain management

Introduction

This report analyses the effectiveness of the supply arrangements between SmartWear and its core suppliers, all of whom are based in countries in South East Asia. The report itself was requested by the audit committee when information about alleged poor working practices among some suppliers was brought to its attention. However, the scope of this internal audit extended beyond this narrow social responsibility issue into broader operational and financial management aspects of the SmartWear supply chain.

Supply chain management is particularly important to SmartWear because as a retailer a very significant proportion of direct costs relate to inventory purchases, which in turn directly impacts on corporate profitability and investor returns.

1   Appraisal of existing suppliers' performance

Most suppliers have been working with SmartWear for more than five years, and there have been no reported instances when purchase orders have not been completed on time or in full. This has led to a rather complacent attitude from the buying department who do not see the point in 'fixing something that isn't broken'. As a result, if no quality problems arise the buyers rarely contact the suppliers, which led to a culture of carelessness. Supply contracts are awarded for a period of between three and five years, with prices charged indexed to inflation. This means that prices rise annually by only a few percentage points, which is then built into the SmartWear budgeting process. No effort is made by the buying department during a contract period to compare what prices the company is paying to its suppliers compared with the industry average or competition.

The allegations that have been made about poor working conditions in some supplier factories have gone unchallenged, and even possibly unnoticed by the buying team. If the suppliers had been more effectively monitored, then the buying department would have identified a clear contravention of the general terms and conditions contained within all SmartWear supply contracts. These standard terms are a reflection of SmartWear's own corporate social responsibility commitments. However, as the buying department operates as a cost centre, the buyers' primary motivation is always to keep costs down rather than monitor the ethical practices of the suppliers.

2   Reporting weaknesses

There is an expectation that any serious breach of supplier performance or unacceptable behaviour would be reported to senior management, so that an appropriate and measured response could be made. However, the word serious is rather subjective and it is entirely up to the buying department whether or not to escalate any matter. Consequently, if a serious issue is not raised then the buying and merchandising director would not be aware of any problem, and so he would not bring it to the attention the board. The absence of formalised regular reporting means that supply chain issues are only ever considered by the board of SmartWear when an exceptional event occurs, and this has not been the case over the past two years. Therefore, the board has been working on the assumption that supply chain management in the company is operating efficiently and effectively, when this audit has shown this not be the case. This represents a serious internal control weakness which needs to be rectified.

Exhibit 6: Customer database management system [CDMS] financial investment appraisal

(All figures $ millions)	Note	0	1	2	3	4	5
Investment in CDMS technology	1	(38.0)					
Operating costs			(2.0)	(2.0)	(2.0)	(2.0)	(2.0)
Additional contribution	2		22.0	22.0	22.0	22.0	22.0
Interest payable on loan	3		(3.0)	(3.0)	(3.0)	(3.0)	(3.0)
Net cash flow		(38.0)	17.0	17.0	17.0	17.0	17.0
Corporation Tax at 30%			(5.1)	(5.1)	(5.1)	(5.1)	(5.1)
Post tax net cash flow		(38.0)	11.9	11.9	11.9	11.9	11.9
Discount factor at 10%	4	1.000	0.909	0.826	0.751	0.683	0.621
Present value of net cash flows		(38.0)	10.8	9.8	8.9	8.1	7.4
Net Present Value 7.0		7.0					

Notes

1   Total investment comprises:

  –   Initial capital outlay.

  –   Sales tax on the purchase price recoverable through the Noria tax authorities.

  –   Installation and system testing costs.

  –   Staff training on the CDMS.

  –   Five-year maintenance and support contract with the supplier.

2   It is estimated that the CDMS will directly generate additional contribution from new and retained customers.

3   A new $38 million loan will be taken out to finance the project, with interest payable at 8% per annum.

4   The SmartWear weighted average cost of capital of 10% is used as the project discount factor.

Section 14

REAL EXAM ANSWERS – MARCH/JUNE 2019

1   **SMARTWEAR**

Strategic Professional – Essentials, SBL   **March/June 2019 Sample Answers**

> **Note**
>
> It is not always possible to publish suggested answers which comprehensively cover all the valid points which candidates might make. Credit will be given to candidates for points not included in the suggested answers, but which, nevertheless, are relevant to the requirements.
>
> In addition, in this integrated case study examination points made in one question may be re-introduced or fully developed in other question(s) as long as these are made in the specific context of the requirements of the part of the question being answered.
>
> The suggested answers presented below may give much more detail than would be expected from most candidates under examination conditions; they may also have used a particular approach or model which should not be taken as the only approach or model which could have been used. Different approaches and structuring of the answers are expected and full credit will be given for relevant and appropriate solutions to the tasks given. The answers provided here are therefore intended to support revision and tuition for future examinations.
>
> Finally, it should be noted that candidates will not get full professional skills marks in a task requirement if they have not presented their answers according to the format asked for. For example, if a task is to be completed using a report and evaluation skills are tested, even if the answer has met the specifically stated evaluation criteria, candidates will not be able to earn all the professional skills marks available if they have not used the report format.

1   (a)   **Briefing paper: Environmental analysis**

Introduction

The operating environment that SmartWear has been experiencing has been very challenging and could explain in part the reasons for the recent downturn in its business fortunes. Although competition will undoubtedly have a significant part to play, all businesses will have been exposed to the same general environmental conditions. So, gaining a better understanding of the environment will help the board to decide how best to successfully adapt the current operations of SmartWear, and take advantage of opportunities emerging from the external environment.

Political issues

The precarious situation of the coalition government in Noria has created a sense of uncertainty within the business community. Without confidence in political continuity, investors are less inclined to risk their money. This will make it more difficult for companies, like SmartWear, to raise the necessary finance to grow the business further, or even sustain its current position. The high levels of growth which had been previously achieved no longer appear to be achievable, so the SmartWear board may need to reconsider the company's strategic goals and focus on consolidating the company's position in the market during this difficult and uncertain political period.

Economic factors

The current record high levels of unemployment, high price inflation and a resultant deep recession does not help the retail sector in Noria. However, it is reasonable to assume that with less disposable income, consumers would be more inclined to purchase their clothing needs from value retailers like SmartWear. Indeed, the company has benefited from this economically-driven behavioural shift.

Should an economic recovery start next year, as suggested by the Finance Minister, then this would improve business prospects for all retailers in Noria. With rising employment and lower inflation, consumers may decide to return to more upmarket clothing retailers and away from low-end companies like SmartWear. The board should consider its international portfolio of businesses in order to manage the risk associated with diverse national economies, since currently inflation and unemployment in Southland is much lower than in Noria. Therefore, any planned strategic expansion should be in international markets rather than domestically.

Social developments

The demand from consumers for cheaper clothing has required these items to be sourced from low cost economies. There has become an expectation that clothing will remain low priced, which limits how companies like SmartWear can compete. This could increase the number of new entrants into the low end of the market and suggests that only those companies who are able to sustain high volume sales will succeed in the long run. The board needs to bear all of this in mind when it is considering its growth plans and deciding how best to satisfy consumer demands going forward.

Technological influences

The growth of e-commerce in the general retail sector has completely altered the competitive dynamic. Once developed, any online platform can be extended to include a variety of products, therefore new clothing e-retailers can emerge from previously non-competing businesses who have simply broadened their product offering. The resultant increased supply of clothing goods to the market with potentially contracting demand will put downward pressure on prices, squeezing the margins of all companies including SmartWear. The board is advised to consider the opportunities presented to SmartWear from developing and operating its own e-commerce platform, as this could allow for substantial revenue growth without the need to establish a costly network of retail outlets and would allow a rationalisation of the portfolio of physical retail outlets, to release funds and reduce operating costs.

Tutorial note

NB Please note the way the answer has used the format of PESTEL to structure the answer. Whilst this is perfectly acceptable, it is not critical to use a model to gain good marks in SBL.

(b)   **Major risks arising from the SmartWear business model**

Operational risk

There is a high dependency on overseas suppliers to continually provide SmartWear with the necessary clothing items to sell in its European retail outlets. These manufacturers are based a considerable distance from the core sales markets, which can make the supply lead time very long and reduces the company's ability to respond to changing customer demands. This could lead to the added risk that if goods are over-ordered from the manufacturers then any surplus over demand may need to be sold at a discount, thereby reducing profitability.

To reduce the company's exposure to these operational risks, SmartWear needs to focus on the skills of the professional buyers who work closely with the marketing and sales teams to accurately predict the continuous demand levels for all clothing items. This should ensure that there is neither a 'stock-out' where any goods demanded are unavailable to customers, nor excessive inventory held. An effective inventory management system would provide information on levels of stock held in each retail outlet so that these could be internally re-distributed to meet volatile sales demands, rather than requiring new products to be ordered.

Strategic risk

The company currently pursues a cost leadership strategy which enables it to competitively price its products in its target markets; which has proved successful to date. However, cost leadership means that SmartWear must be the lowest cost supplier to the market, which is only possible if it can maintain high volume activities to absorb its cost base. However, with the growing emergence of e-retailers in the market, who do not need to employ sales staff or operate costly retail outlets, it threatens the fundamental cost effectiveness of the current SmartWear business model.

To mitigate these risks the board needs to rethink its whole strategic approach. It would not seem feasible for SmartWear to devise a strategy to differentiate its business, as this would cause brand confusion to its core customer base and require significant investment. Therefore, the emphasis should be on cost control, with any avoidable costs extracted from the business model. At the same time the company could continue to invest in those overseas markets which are more receptive to the current business model. This would result in further scale economies, particularly if non-core business functions are centralised rather than duplicated.

Foreign exchange risk

SmartWear currently operates in Noria and two other European countries, with their own currency. Also, the manufacturers of all SmartWear products are based in Asia and will expect payment in their functional currencies. Therefore, the current business model exposes the company to volatility in the relative movement of exchange rates which could potentially result in higher costs, consume excess cash and reduce corporate profitability. As a listed company in Noria, SmartWear will have to prepare its financial statements in the Norian currency. This requires the value of assets and liabilities held in each operating country to be translated to the Norian currency, again possibly negatively impacting on declared profit. As inflation in Noria is rising in comparison with the countries in which it obtains its supplies, there will be an upward pressure on direct costs. If foreign exchange risk is not managed effectively, any negative effect on reported performance could signal a reduction in SmartWear's share price to the stock market and this would not be well received by investors.

To reduce the possible damaging consequences of foreign exchange movements on SmartWear's business operations and reported performance, the board should ensure that it has effective treasury management. This will ensure that any transaction exposure, deemed too risky for the company, is hedged using appropriate financial instruments. To minimise any losses on translation of assets and liabilities from overseas operations matching could be employed, with SmartWear ensuring that liabilities are matched as closely as possible with assets for all of the different foreign currencies it deals in.

Competition risk

Competition is normally the greatest risk to any commercial organisation, since there is a limited amount of market available for all to compete in. The SmartWear business model has successfully positioned itself at the low end of its target market, where it has become the market leader. However, during the economic recession in Noria, it is likely that many established competitors will also seek to gain more of the lucrative budget-conscious end of the clothing market. This is directly targeting SmartWear's dominant position, which has already resulted in an erosion in its market share. The risk is that unless action is taken by the board, the situation will worsen and SmartWear will cease to be market leader.

To limit the potential damaging effect of competition, SmartWear need to engage more closely with its customers. By anticipating and satisfying the changing demands from its core markets, the company can stay ahead of competition by successfully adjusting its marketing mix. Although there is no guarantee of customer loyalty, such a proactive approach will make the company more aware of the risks presented by competition and deal with them more effectively.

Market risk

This relates to the risk of changing conditions in the marketplace, such as the increasing tendency of consumers to shop online. This particular aspect of market risk presents significant challenges to traditional retail businesses like SmartWear, where failure to successfully adapt could make the current business model obsolete over a relatively short period of time.

To reduce the market risk, SmartWear needs to adapt and embrace the growing online shopping public as this could result in substantial revenue growth, which is core to achieving its strategic goals. The board needs to commission market research and evaluate the option to develop and manage its own online sales platform.

Tutorial note

NB Please note the answer has addressed the major risks facing the current business model of Smartwear. These would include those risks challenging the future success of the business and will be drawn from the scenario and supporting exhibits.

2   (a)   Report

To: The Board From: Consultant

Ref: Southland market

Introduction

This report provides an analysis of SmartWear's strategic position in the Southland market, with a particular emphasis on why this specific country appears to be a suitable location for a clothing retailer, and discusses the implications of withdrawing from the market in Centrum.

Factor conditions

The basic and advanced factors describe the country's resources and how it chooses to invest in itself, which can often be relevant to the competitiveness of particular industries. The factors vary in nature and range from availability of human resources, levels of education and knowledge to infrastructure, liquidity on stock markets and available natural resources.

Although Southland does not have a particularly large population, around 60% are of working age and over 90% of these are in employment. This group will comprise the potential market for all clothing retailers, such as SmartWear, who could further refine and target the under 30-year-old age group. It is also clear that the country has extensive transportation links between its population centres, which is of critical importance for SmartWear in allowing goods to be moved to market cheaply and quickly.

Domestic demand conditions

Domestic demand conditions in any country can be a major source of competitive advantage for that country. It is not only the size of the market which is important, but also the relative sophistication of domestic customers. The configuration of a market often shapes how competitors interpret and respond to customers' demands, which in turn encourages companies to be innovative and enhance their competitive positions and meet the high standards required for service delivery.

The existence of a vibrant and competitive domestic retail industry in Southland is suggested because retailing is one of the country's dominant business sectors. Consequently, it is likely to have the positive characteristics which should make it an attractive proposition for SmartWear to operate its business model in.

Related and supporting industries

The success of any market depends both on the presence of suppliers and related support industries within the country. Therefore, apart from access to available sources of direct supply, a network of related and supporting organisations is equally important if a company is to succeed in a particular country. In the retail sector, where the companies only sell what others make, it is vital that there are reliable transport and distribution systems to continuously supply the retail outlets with goods for its shelves. Also, there needs to be well developed marketing media accessible to effectively promote the business offerings to a wide consumer audience.

Southland, being a developed European country with good transport links and concentrations of population in major cities, is very likely to have the right infrastructure to support a vibrant retail industry. The developed capital markets provide companies with a source of finance which is necessary to promote their business in a free market economy. Therefore, it seems to be an ideal location for SmartWear to further grow its business successfully.

Firm, strategy, structure and rivalry

This aspect is concerned with how businesses are organised and managed, and the culture they adopt to achieve corporate success. These can vary considerably between countries, with cultural aspects in particular significantly influencing how competition develops.

In Southland, where SmartWear now operates 30 retail outlets since it opened its first store six years ago, it is delivering significantly better financial performance than at home. This suggests that the SmartWear business model suits the retail environment and culture in Southland, so it is a suitable country to further grow the business.

(b) The decision to close the 20 worst performing retail outlets in Noria and withdraw and close all 15 stores in the country of Centrum, presents a number of strategic implications for SmartWear.

1   These closures represent a reduction of between 15% and 20% of current business operations. Although this does not necessarily equate to a similar reduction in revenue, and may improve overall reported profit, it will give the impression to the market that the business is contracting. As such it might be more difficult for the company to raise finance from new investors, particularly if the stock market reflects the perceived downsizing with a commensurate fall in share price.

2   The financial resources which would be released from the sale of any redundant property, as well as savings in running costs, could be reassigned to more lucrative and profitable areas of the business. Alternatively, these funds could be used to invest and grow the business in countries more conducive to the SmartWear business model, such a Southland.

3   The decision to close so many retail outlets at one time for purely financial reasons may prove very unsettling and disconcerting to employees not directly affected by the planned closures. In any service company like SmartWear, where they are heavily reliant on the performance of their employees, it is essential that staff remain closely engaged in the business at all times. Therefore, the board will need to be set aside sufficient resources for a change management programme which not only covers the planned closures but also manages the remaining business, and communicates the rationale behind the decision to all key stakeholders. It might also be necessary for a public relations exercise to be conducted to preserve the company's reputation in the wider market place.

4   Withdrawing entirely from a country may have considerable implications on the company, both financially and legally. There will undoubtedly be statutory redundancy payments due, and these may be significant depending on the number of staff employed and their length of service. There may be a prescribed redundancy procedure to follow to ensure that the company is fully compliant with local employment law. There could also be residual taxation issues which need to be addressed before the SmartWear can repatriate its invested funds and completely withdraw from Centrum.

The ethical issues arising from the decision to both reduce activity in Noria close operations entirely in Centrum should be carefully considered as it is pragmatic, in a purely business sense.

1   SmartWear is currently incurring heavy losses, which can be attributed to the underperforming operations in Noria and Centrum and there are no reliable signs of recovery or turnaround. Consequently, the decision is in the best interests of the investors in SmartWear, to whom the board has a fiduciary duty. It would be unethical to continue to operate knowing that it is destroying business value and potentially harming other areas of the business.

2   The fairness of the decision depends on whose perspective is being considered. Those employees who are to be made redundant may consider that they have been treated unfairly by SmartWear, however, if objective criteria have been fairly and consistently applied when taking the decision, then the company cannot be accused of acting unethically. The fact that all affected retail outlets are to close means that all staff are to be made redundant, so in legal terms no employees are being unfairly dismissed.

3   There appears to be no legal reasons why the company cannot reduce its operations in Noria, withdraw from Centrum and make staff redundant. So, provided that SmartWear has strictly adhered to relevant employment legislation there is no legal impediment to taking this decision. The decision may ultimately preserve far more jobs elsewhere throughout the company over the long run. Therefore, on balance the decision is the ethically right course of action for the company if it will help it to prosper and remain a going concern.

4   The social footprint which would be left following SmartWear's withdrawal from Centrum may have residual damaging consequences for that country's economy. With rising unemployment, it is quite probable that the redundant staff will find it very difficult to obtain alternative employment.

Conclusion

Viewing all of the national influencing factors holistically, it is apparent that Southland offers a good business environment for a clothing retailer like SmartWear. Results over the first six years that SmartWear has been operating in this country illustrate that the market is well established and a good strategic fit for the SmartWear's business model. If the board is considering further growth opportunities then developing the Southland market further appears a suitable option to pursue.

The decision to reduce capacity in Noria and withdraw completely from Centrum seems, on balance, to be ethically acceptable. The consequences to those losing their jobs may seem harsh, but the outcome may ultimately deliver the greatest good to SmartWear, its investors and its many stakeholders.

Tutorial note

NB Please note the way the answer has used the format of Porters Diamond to structure the answer. Whilst this is perfectly acceptable, it is not critical to use a model to gain good marks in SBL.

3   Memo

To: Buying and merchandising director From: Consultant

Ref: Supply chain management issues

Introduction

The recent internal audit report on the supply chain management arrangements at SmartWear highlighted a number of issues which require your immediate attention. There were three areas which clearly indicate internal control weaknesses with the procurement processes at SmartWear that illustrate operational inefficiencies and have negative impacts on the company's financial performance.

(i)   Cost controls

As already stated, the buying of clothing from overseas suppliers comprises a significant proportion of the SmartWear cost structure. However, as the business is positioned at the low-price end of the market, the only way that margins can be sustained is through very effective cost control.

The internal audit report claims that a 'culture of carelessness' has developed among SmartWear buyers who do not engage closely with the clothing suppliers. The result is that the cost of individual supply contracts is not periodically reviewed or compared against industry averages, and only renegotiated when they come up for renewal after several years. This means that SmartWear could be incurring avoidable increases in its cost base, and a resultant erosion of gross margins. This is particularly damaging during the periods of economic difficulty when other structural costs are rising due to higher inflation, but the company is unable to raise its own selling prices to compensate without damaging its competitive position.

(ii)   Corporate social responsibility issues

Supply contract terms and conditions stipulate minimum standards for the treatment of a supplier's workforce. However, recent reports have clearly indicated that some SmartWear suppliers have been in breach of this contract term, but the buying team has not challenged these manufacturers' practices. This could be because the buying department is under pressure to maintain low costs, so they do not wish to impose additional costs on the suppliers who may attempt to pass these on to SmartWear.

A stated strategic goal of the company in its mission statement is to function at the highest standards of social responsibility, and to expect the same from its suppliers. It is therefore wholly unacceptable to knowingly permit such unethical practices to continue for financial expediency. This has been compounded because the issue was not reported to the board and now this association may damage the reputation of SmartWear with consumers and investors.

(iii)   Poor reporting around supplier relationships

Key to any control system is regular and accurate reporting on performance so that any problems or serious issues can be identified and rectified without unnecessary delay. At SmartWear only those issues which are considered to be of a serious nature are brought to the attention of the board and senior management. However, the basis upon which the term 'serious' is defined is open to wide interpretation. The result is that low level staff are deciding which matters need to be escalated, and this in turn could lead to cover ups or business failures going unaddressed.

Procurement is a core function of the SmartWear business, since it accounts for a significant proportion of direct cost and so influences the company's profitability. The board, being accountable to the shareholders, must ensure that it safeguards corporate assets and maximises shareholder returns. However, in the absence of reliable and complete information the board is currently unable to discharge its duties effectively; this leaves the company's investors exposed to avoidable lower returns.

Recommended control improvements

Each of the procurement control weaknesses evaluated require an appropriate and immediate response from the board. The following recommendations are proposed for your further consideration:

(i)   Cost controls

The buyers need to be tasked to be more proactive in their management of the supply contracts to ensure that the company is getting best value for money. Contract periods could be shortened to allow for any potential cost savings to be realised more frequently. The careful monitoring of the quality of the products manufactured and the efficient delivery of orders placed should ensure that the suppliers aim to continuously meet the terms of their contracts with SmartWear.

The buyers require carefully drafted job descriptions, setting out the expectations and competences needed to fulfil this important role at SmartWear. Management should then set individual objectives and targets, with performance-based rewards, to motivate the buying team to deliver results which will ultimately improve corporate performance.

(ii)   Corporate social responsibility issues

Those suppliers who are in clear breach of their supply contract need to be formally advised that they must immediately bring the working conditions at their factories up to the minimum acceptable standard, or the contract will be cancelled. However, their remedial actions will need to be independently validated and that this might best be achieved through SmartWear auditors making periodic unannounced spot checks at supplier factories.

A concerted public relations effort will need to be made to reassure the buying public and investors that SmartWear has taken the necessary action to deal with the issue. This will require the drafting of a clearly worded statement communicated on the most appropriate media.

It is also important to stress to the buying department that although prudent financial management of the supply chain is key to business success, any unethical behaviour presents a major risk to the company.

(iii)   Poor reporting around supplier relationships

Standardised procurement reports should be produced and submitted to senior management on a frequent basis. These reports must provide an update on all current supply contracts, and remove any subjectivity by defining the reporting parameters. This control will ensure that the procurement team do not become complacent and manage the supply chain effectively and in the best interests of the company. Through these reports the board will be fully aware of this important aspect of the SmartWear business model, and so can take appropriate action to optimise operational and financial performance.

4   Report

Tutorial note

NB Remember when preparing the answers for tasks in SBL it is important to use the format requested.

To: Board

From: Sales and marketing director

Ref: Benefits of a customer database system

Introduction

The evaluation of any major business investment must consider a wide range of strategic and operational factors, and it seems apparent from the current performance of SmartWear that the company is not effectively engaging with its customer base. The development of a customer relationship management [CDMS] system, which includes a customer loyalty programme, would help to attract new business, improve customer retention and yield more sales.

(a) There are a number of benefits arising from the development of a customer database system (CDMS) for SmartWear, these include:

The primary purpose of a CDMS system is to help a business engage more effectively with its customer base, by helping everyone in the company better understand the needs of the and requirements of the customers. Without a thorough appreciation of each relationship, it will be difficult for SmartWear to exceed customer expectations and gain sustainable competitive advantage. The CDMS provides users with ready access to relevant data using a single common and controlled interface, wherever they work in the company including overseas operations. CDMS empowers users to deliver a more responsive service to customers, which ultimately contributes towards their increased retention through the associated loyalty scheme.

Through a better alignment of customers and core business processes, a CDMS system can help the company attain greater market share and grow more efficiently in its target markets.

The centralisation of customer and business process data offers the opportunity to convert these into meaningful decisions and profitable actions. Big data which accumulates in the CDMS system is not in itself a solution, but the basis for developing new insights which can be used to develop the business further. Having access to all customer and related business data in one database allows for timely and well-informed decisions to be taken which can enable the company to be more responsive to its core markets. A CDMS system will help SmartWear use this understanding of the marketplace and then to successfully target further growth.

CDMS technology allows all staff to get their work done anywhere and at any time, by providing a set of tools to improve customer relationships and the associated business process which matter. If the staff are unable to access customer data, they are unable to engage with customers, therefore by accessing the CDMS data remotely, it allows them to work at any location – so increasing their productivity.

Controlling access to sensitive customer information is critically important and is required by data protection legislation. This can be achieved by securely storing the CDMS database at one location in the cloud, which offers significantly greater protection compared to storing customer data locally in spreadsheets or on multiple systems. Through high level security and automatic back-up, this data can be protected from unexpected and unforeseen events. CDMS security profiles and settings enforce controls so that both teams and individual users have appropriate permissions to access records consistent with their role.

(b) It is essential that the investment is also acceptable in financial terms by delivering enhanced returns to shareholders. The financial appraisal illustrates that the new system will deliver a net present value [NPV] of $7 million during the first five years of its operation, and this yields an 18·4% return on the initial cash outlay. However, this NPV computation is based on a number of underlying assumptions which are questionable in terms of their accuracy and relevance.

1   Contribution, being the excess revenue generated after variable costs have been deducted is also constant at $22 million throughout the five-year period. The estimated amount is questionable because it would be highly unlikely that such a large benefit could be gained in the first year. It is also unlikely that it would be a constant amount over the whole period, as it should reflect the company's forecast sales profile, which should be assumed to rise each year, as this is fundamental to the justification of the CDMS investment. This amount will also be impacted by inflationary pressure, and for both these reasons these benefits should be forecast to rise annually from a lower initial figure over the five-year period under consideration.

2   The total investment figure of $38 million includes the cost of a five-year maintenance and support contract. It is more likely that the agreement is to pay a maintenance charge each year rather than the whole amount at the start of the five-year period, therefore this cost should have been spread evenly over the duration of the contract period by allocating 20% of the total contract sum to each of the five periods. The terms of the agreement need to be reviewed so that this can be clarified.

3   It is known that during periods of economic recession inflation can run quite high. Despite this the costs of operating the CDMS is set at a constant level of $2 million each year. This is quite unrealistic and unless all prices and costs are expressed in money terms rather than real terms, the marginal effects must be accurately reflected in the cash flows.

4   The 8% interest payable on the loan should not be included as a separate cash flow item since it is part of the financing decision and is included within the discount factor. This means that using the current weighted average cost of capital is not truly reflective of the financial risk associated with the investment. However, if interest costs are included in the cash outflows, the equity cost of capital, not the weighted average cost of capital, should be used in the computation. However, the equity cost of capital, which would be at a higher rate, due to the financial risk it incorporates, is not available in the case information.

5   Corporation tax is correctly charged [or refunded] against net cash flows. However, the tax rules regarding this type of investment need to be considered as it might be possible to claim allowances. These have not been considered or included in the NPV computation, but could be a significant financial incentive for SmartWear. Any allowances claimed would increase the post-tax next cash flows and improve the resultant NPV.

6   It is probable that there would need to be an injection of additional working capital to operate the CDMS post-implementation, and this is a relevant cash flow. However, as this is viewed as a five-year project, the additional working capital invested would be returned to SmartWear at the end of time period 5.

Conclusion

By developing a CDMS strategy SmartWear should be able to significantly increase the revenue generated from all of its markets, thereby turning around those currently poorly performing areas. Using the data collected, more effective and targeted marketing campaigns can be conducted, helping the company to promote its products to new customers. This will generate a new revenue stream and help to deliver the stated strategic goal to grow in all core markets.

After applying the adjustments to the NPV computation suggested above, the board needs to compare the costs and benefits of the new CDMS system against the current arrangements. Clearly there are risks associated with any business decision. However, it is apparent that the risk of doing nothing seems far greater. The opinion of the institutional investor, discussed at the recent board meeting, suggesting that SmartWear was becoming too remote from its core markets, provides some justification for changing the current system.

5   Note that a typical candidate may only make 5–6 bullet points, but this answer includes a comprehensive range of points, some of which a well prepared candidate might have made.

(a)   **Board presentation on integrated thinking**

Slide 1

Benefits of Integrated Thinking
1   Holistic and strategic perspective
2   Long v short term outlook
3   Improved corporate reputation
4   Better corporate governance
5   Increased employee engagement
6   Enhanced stakeholder management
7   Transparent and effective communication
8   Effective risk management
9   Increased connectivity

Notes:

1   By taking a holistic or integrated approach, the board of SmartWear is provided with a full range of inter-related factors which allows it to focus on creating sustainable business value from a strategic perspective. The strategic focus and future provides great insight into the interdependency between strategy, the business model and value creation. To help the board turn around the business and create value, it should adopt integrated thinking as this will enable the alignment of the low cost-low price business model to the changing market opportunities and enable the company to improve performance sustainably.

2   The board needs to devise and implement a successful strategy which focuses attention on key business issues which drive performance and value creation in the long term so that it can turn around business fortunes. Integrated thinking utilises a broader information base than traditional business decision-making, which tends to focus on relatively short-term financial outcomes. The board's decision on whether or not to implement the proposed CDMS must be based on a range of integrated issues, and not simply the appraised financial outcome.

3   Joined up thinking which results in better performance can be used to promote and market the business more widely. This will strengthen the corporate image and reputation of SmartWear and could allow it to capture even greater market share, as well as consolidating its dominant position in the market place. There is a direct correlation between brand value, good reputation and business value; so the shareholders will ultimately benefit for this approach.

4   Integrated thinking can lead to improvements in the governance arrangements in SmartWear by enhancing accountability over a broad base of business capitals as well as encouraging a greater understanding of their interdependencies. The resultant better corporate governance should offer greater assurance to shareholders that the board is acting in their best interests through the careful stewardship of all business assets.

5   At SmartWear, employees can make a very valuable contribution to the operational effectiveness of the company. The knowledge and capabilities of employees must be developed and utilised to best effect, and this can best be achieved through integrated thinking. This management approach actively encourages employee engagement in all aspect of business activity such as better engagement with customers via CDMS and empowers individuals to contribute to the delivery of higher levels of performance.

6   Successful stakeholder management is vital for any successful business, as it enables the company to respond to the demands of its key stakeholders quickly and effectively. Integrated thinking contributes to good relationships with key stakeholders as it considers how and to what extent the company understands, takes into account, and responds to their legitimate needs and interests.

7   Integrated thinking requires the continuous transfer of information throughout the company, and so by default improves the lines and nature of internal communication. This more transparent approach will improve inter-departmental cooperation and enhance the efficiency and effectiveness of business operations. This should reduce avoidable and unnecessary costs being incurred and improve SmartWear's financial performance.

8   Many investors struggle to understand how managing the relevant risk factors contributes to value creation over time into investment decisions, because the information which is often presented is insufficiently strategic, comparable and sector specific. As a result, there is the risk that capital is not being directed efficiently towards retail models at SmartWear which create rather than destroy value.

9   Two of the biggest challenges faced by any company are breaking down organisational silos and changing existing data capture processes. Integrated thinking will challenge these entrenched behaviours allowing for improved connectivity of people and information, thereby giving the board a holistic view of the interrelated and dependent factors which affect SmartWear's ability to create value over time.

(b)   Briefing paper for CFO

Tutorial note

NB *Remember when preparing the answers for tasks in SBL it is important to use the format requested.*

Introduction

The integrated reporting <IR> framework is a more informative model of external reporting to stakeholders, as it gives them a broader and richer picture of the organisation and how value can be created in the longer term and in a more sustainable way. It therefore gives them a better basis for decision-making and whether to buy, hold or sell their investments.

I will now brief you on why shareholders will find this a more useful model. Essentially it is because the <IR> framework of external reporting focuses on a wider range of sources of value creation than the traditional reporting model which concentrates mostly on financial information. It is based on the concept that there are a wider range of capitals which the organisation has control or influence over and how maintenance and development of these capitals over the short and longer term can affect and create value in other capitals, including financial capital.

The primary purpose of <IR> is to improve the quality of information available to providers of financial capital, including investors, by communicating broader and more relevant information which can assist then in their investment decisions. The SmartWear board has decided that an effective way to promote integrated thinking throughout the company is to implement a version of the <IR> framework. This will encourage more holistic thinking about the suitability of various strategic approaches which both grasp business opportunities and mitigate business risks, while building greater investor and stakeholder confidence in the company. Indeed, by improving internal management processes, <IR> can also lead to greater trust and credibility with customers – and this is key to SmartWear's future success.

The <IR> framework comprises six different reporting components or capitals as they are referred to. When considered in an integrative manner these capitals will provide a more complete appraisal of SmartWear's performance to investors, and other users of corporate information, and allow the board to make more informed strategic decisions.

Financial capital refers the pool of funds which are available to SmartWear, including both debt and equity finance. The focus here is on sourcing necessary funds, rather than their application in the business. However, investors will want to know how financial capital has been deployed in the past, and what the future plans based around a holistic and well-rounded strategy might be. With more integrated thinking and management <IR> provides far greater clarity on core business issues and performance, which can be very reassuring to investors.

Intellectual capital is fundamental to future earning potential, linking investment, innovation, knowledge management and managing external relationships to the delivery of competitive advantage. The careful management of supplier networks and understanding the changing market conditions, through the new CDMS system, will demonstrate a good use of intellectual capital in SmartWear. Effective development of intellectual capital leads to innovation and investment in resources which can have a longer term and more sustainable benefit for financial capital.

Human capital consists of the capabilities, knowledge, skills and experience of the company's employees and management. This is particularly important to a service organisation like SmartWear, as retailers are reliant on their staff to generate business value. Understanding the importance of human capital in SmartWear should focus management attention on developing talent and realising the financial benefits of investing in our human resources.

Social and relationship capital at SmartWear relates specifically to the strength and efficacy of supply chain relationships and customer loyalty. It is only by building such relationships that a retail company can operate as a successful business. The proposed changes to improve supply chain management arrangements alongside the development of the new CDMS system will enhance social and relationship capital in SmartWear. Building social capital internally and externally leads to more motivated and productive workforce and engaged, loyal and profitable customers.

Natural capital refers to any inventory of natural resources or environmental assets which could provide a flow of useful goods or services, both now and in the future. The promotion of a strong social and environmental responsibility ethos in the SmartWear will strengthen its reputation among consumer and the investment communities, such as adopting a responsible purchasing policy of sourcing local products, where possible, and using suppliers which have a more responsible attitude to product packaging and environmental management. A better reputation in these areas will make the company more attractive to invest in and do business with leading to an increase in financial capital over the longer term, regardless of the short-term costs of following such policies.

Strategic Professional – Essentials, SBL

Strategic Business Leader (SBL)   **March/June 2019 Sample Marking Scheme**

1   **(a)**   Up to 2 marks for each well-developed aspect of general environmental analysis such as the suitable use of PEST, or PESTLE, SWOT.

(Up to a maximum of 10 marks)

  (b)   Up to 2 marks for each major risk facing SmartWear assessed, including the following:

  –   Operational risk

  –   Strategic risk

  –   Foreign exchange risk

  –   Competition risk

  –   Market risk

(Up to a maximum of 6 marks)

Up to 2 marks for each relevant mitigation to an assessed major risk facing SmartWear, such as those listed above. (Up to a maximum of 6 marks)

(Up to a maximum of 10 marks in total)

Professional skills may be additionally rewarded as in the following rubric:

How well has the candidate demonstrated professional skills as follows:	Not at all	Not at all	Not at all	Not at all
1 Professional skills marks are available for evaluation skills by appraising and assessing the identified risks at SmartWear objectively before relevant solutions are suggested.	The candidate has failed to demonstrate evaluation skills. The candidate has omitted significant areas of risk from the answer, and has shown no professional judgement in explaining how to mitigate those risks that were assessed.	The candidate has demonstrated some limited evaluation skills. The candidate has attempted to assess some risks facing SmartWear and suggested some relevant mitigating actions. However, the candidate has omitted some of the most significant risks and failed to clearly explain their consequences to SmartWear. Also the candidate did not make reasonable or sensible recommendations to mitigate the risk assessed.	The candidate has demonstrated good evaluation skills. The candidate clearly attempted to assess some of the most significant risks facing SmartWear at this time and suggested some appropriate actions to mitigate their damaging consequences. However, more care and attention should have been applied to assess and control those risks that specifically related to the SmartWear business model. The answer has been presented in a briefing paper format.	The candidate has demonstrated excellent evaluation skills. The candidate assessed the most significant risks facing SmartWear and its business model. The candidate recommended mitigation actions that are both proportionate and will effectively address the major risks assessed. The answer has been presented in a briefing paper format.
	0	1	2	3

2   (a)   Up to 2 marks for the analysis of each aspect of SmartWear's performance in the country of Southland using the information provided:

– Factor conditions

– Domestic demand conditions

– Related and supporting industries

– Firm strategy and competitive rivalry

(Up to a maximum of 8 marks)

(b)   Up to 2 marks for each strategic and or ethical implication arising from the decision:

– Perceptions of divestment as a strategy

– Increased profitability due to cost savings

– Financial resources released for more productive activities

– Effect on employees and social footprint from unemployment

– Legal and regulatory issues

– Maximum of 8 marks for strategic issues

– Maximum of 8 marks for ethical issues

(Up to a maximum of 12 marks)

Professional skills may be additionally rewarded as in the following rubric:

How well has the candidate demonstrated professional skills as follows:	Not at all	Not at all	Not at all	Not at all
2 (a) Professional skills marks are available analysis skills by the careful consideration of information and findings, and reflecting on how they can be used to understand SmartWear's strategic position in the Southland market.	The candidate demonstrated poor or no analysis skills. The candidate failed to identify or use the data required to analyse SmartWear's strategic position in the Southland market. Those analytical points that were made were not supported by the evidence provided in the case study.	The candidate demonstrated limited analysis skills. The candidate has identified some of the data provided in order to analyse SmartWear's strategic position in the Southland market. However, the structure of the answer was not very clear or easy to follow.	The candidate demonstrated good analysis skills. The candidate has presented a report which has identified most of the data necessary to analyse SmartWear's strategic position in the Southland market. The candidate attempted to structure the analysis in a coherent and logical way, which made it fairly easy for members of the SmartWear board to follow.	The candidate demonstrated excellent analysis skills. The candidate has presented a report which has identified and used the most important and relevant data to analyse SmartWear's strategic position in the Southland market. The candidate provided an answer that was structured and presented in a way that made it user-friendly for the SmartWear board.
	0	0-5	1	2

How well has the candidate demonstrated professional skills as follows:	Not at all	Not at all	Not at all	Not at all
2 (b) Professional skills marks are available for applying scepticism by probing deeply into the underlying issues and problems that may arise from this strategic decision, beyond what is immediately apparent.	The candidate has failed to demonstrate any real scepticism. The candidate merely identified a number of strategic and/or ethical issues without into how they related to – or arose from – the decision taken.	The candidate has demonstrated some limited scepticism. The candidate attempted to probe into some of the strategic and/or ethical implications of the closure decision taken by the SmartWear board. However, the tone of the answer fell short of the level of scepticism expected.	The candidate demonstrated a good level of scepticism. The candidate has identified and clearly explained most of the strategic issues and ethical concerns that may arise from the closure decision taken by the SmartWear board. The answer provided offered reasonable balance and depth of discussion.	The candidate demonstrated an excellent level of scepticism. The candidate has identified and clearly explained the main strategic issues and ethical concerns that are likely from the closure decision taken by the SmartWear board. The answer focused directly on the implications to SmartWear as a business, and the positive and negative impacts the decision will have on its stakeholders.
	0	0-5	1	2

3   Up to 2 marks for the evaluation of the internal control at SmartWear in each area identified in the internal audit report. [Max 2 marks per issue]

The candidate may deal with the issues and the recommendations together:

–   Cost control issues

–   Corporate and social responsibility issues

–   Reporting and supplier relationship issues

(Up to a maximum of 6 marks in total)

Up to 2 marks per recommended improvement to each of the areas of control weakness identified, such as within those headings listed above. [Max 2 marks per recommendation]

(Up to a maximum of 6 marks)

Professional skills may be additionally rewarded as in the following rubric:

How well has the candidate demonstrated professional skills as follows:	Not at all	Not at all	Not at all	Not at all
3 Professional skills marks are available for commercial acumen by using professional judgement when recommending solutions to those issues highlighted in the internal audit report.	The candidate has not demonstrated commercial acumen. The candidate made no attempt to link the internal control issues in the audit report to the associated improvements.	The candidate has demonstrated limited commercial acumen. The candidate made some attempt to evaluate the issues and recommend improvements but did not extract these from the report. Then answer lacked a coherent and logical structure.	The candidate has demonstrated good commercial acumen. The candidate mainly used the information contained in the report to evaluate the internal control problems and recommended control improvements. The answer was a memo but could have been structured and presented more clearly for the benefit of the buying and merchandising director.	The candidate has demonstrated excellent commercial acumen skills. The candidate correctly used the information contained in the report to evaluate the internal control problems and provided sensible recommended control improvements. The answer was a memo which was structured logically and targeted at the needs of the buying and merchandising director.
	0	1	2	4

4 **(a)** Up 2 marks for benefit of a customer database management system:

- – Engaging more effectively with customers to create loyalty
- – Harnessing the benefits of big data for analysis and decision-making
- – More flexible ways of working
- – Data security

(Up to a maximum of 6 marks in total)

(b) Up 2 marks for each developed point about any errors, assumptions or omissions identified in the CDMS investment appraisal:

- – Inherent unreliability of cash flow forecasting
- – Optimistic assumption of early year benefits
- – Assumption of constantly accruing benefits
- – Assumption that maintenance and support would be paid for in one year
- – Assumptions around constancy of the CDMS operating costs
- – Including finance costs when discounting by WACC
- – Impact of capital allowances on cash flows

(Up to a maximum of 10 marks in total)

Professional skills may be additionally rewarded as in the following rubric:

How well has the candidate demonstrated professional skills as follows:	Not at all	Not at all	Not at all	Not at all
4 (a) Commercial acumen by demonstrating the benefits of introducing a CDMS system at SmartWear.	The candidate has not shown commercial acumen. The candidate has not made any attempt to link the benefits of introducing a CDMS to the current situation at SmartWear.	The candidate has shown limited commercial acumen. The candidate made some attempt to link the benefits of introducing a CDMS to the situation at SmartWear. However, the candidate has not tailored the response specifically to the needs of the sales and marketing director.	The candidate has shown good commercial acumen. The candidate has explained the benefits of introducing a CDMS to the situation at SmartWear and made a concerted effort to address the needs of the sales and marketing director. The answer is in report format.	The candidate has shown excellent commercial acumen. The candidate has strongly described the benefits of introducing a CDMS to the situation at SmartWear, with respect to the current position that they find themselves in. The candidate clearly considered the issues from the perspective of the sales and marketing director. The answer is in report format.
	0	0-5	1	2

How well has the candidate demonstrated professional skills as follows:	Not at all	Not at all	Not at all	Not at all
4 (b) Scepticism skills by questioning the facts presented, as sufficient evidence to support the NPV computation.	The candidate demonstrated no scepticism. The candidate has failed to identify important omissions from the NPV computation contents. The candidate has not challenged the underlying assumptions.	The candidate demonstrated limited scepticism. The candidate has identified some of the omissions and errors from the NPV computation. The candidate made a limited attempt to challenge some of the wrong underlying assumptions but was not overly convincing.	The candidate demonstrated good scepticism. The candidate's report has identified most of the important omissions and errors from the NPV computation and explained them fairly clearly in the answer. The candidate challenged most of the wrong underlying assumptions.	The candidate demonstrated excellent scepticism. The candidate's report identified all of major omissions and errors from the NPV computation. The candidate challenged the main incorrect underlying assumptions coherently, logically and convincingly.
	0	0-5	1	2

5   (a)   One mark per bullet point and accompanying explanatory note for the slide about how integrated thinking contributes to the creation of long-term value at SmartWear:

   –   Holistic perspective

   –   Consideration of short and long term

   –   Adding value

   –   Sustainable growth

   –   Improved reputation and governance

   –   Connectivity

(Up to a maximum of 6 marks)

   (b)   Up to 2 marks for fully explaining each aspect of <IR> integrated reporting to the finance team and how each would lead to creating long term shareholder value for SmartWear investors.

   –   Financial capital

   –   Intellectual capital

   –   Human capital

   –   Social capital

   –   Natural capital

(Up to a maximum of 6 marks)

Professional skills may be additionally rewarded as in the following rubric:

How well has the candidate demonstrated professional skills as follows:	Not at all	Not at all	Not at all	Not at all
5 Communication skills and the ability to persuade investors using compelling and logical arguments about integrated thinking. Persuade using compelling and logical arguments demonstrating the ability to counter argue when appropriate.	The candidate demonstrated poor communication skills, and failed to present the information clearly in an unambiguous way. The candidate did not communicate effectively to the audience.	The candidate demonstrated some basic communication skills. However, the candidate's statement did not adopt an appropriate tone for communication to the audience.	The candidate demonstrated good communication skills. The candidate has presented the answer in a suitable format for the audience, both with the slides and briefing paper. The tone and style adopted is appropriate for effective communication to board.	The candidate demonstrated excellent communication skills. The candidate provided slides and notes that communicated the main facts about integrated thinking to the board. The notes were structured in a way that was both informative to the audience and would have been convincing to shareholders about the merit of adopting <IR>.
	0	0-5	1	2

Section 15

REAL EXAM QUESTIONS – SEPTEMBER/DECEMBER 2019

1 OVERVIEW

Dulce Co (Dulce) is a listed company which manufactures and sells high quality chocolate and confectionery (other sweets). It was founded over 100 years ago by the Reece family in Northland, initially operating from one shop in a small town. Over the years, Dulce has grown steadily and has been very successful, becoming a household name in Northland and the surrounding countries. Its reputation and success have been built on the high-quality products it manufactures and sells. It offers products across a wide price range, optimising its appeal and affordability to potential customers. Dulce's products include a wide variety of boxed chocolates, confectionery (other sweets such as candies, ice-cream and toffee), and novelty occasion and seasonal items (such as chocolate teddy bears). Dulce's products are often bought as gifts on special occasions and for seasonal events and celebrations.

Dulce manufactures all of its products in its single factory in Northland and the products are then sold through a variety of sales channels. This comprises Dulce's own high street shops located in Northland, the Dulce website and a number of retail partners, including several of the main supermarkets, department stores and gift shops in Northland. At present, Dulce sells all of its products through retail partners under its 'own label'. That is, all of Dulce's products sold by its retail partners bear Dulce's name and branding.

Dulce is listed on the Northland stock market and adheres fully to the government's corporate governance guidelines in terms of board and committee structure and operations. Dulce operates two divisions: retail and operations. The retail division is responsible for Dulce's shops and online sales. The operations division is responsible for managing suppliers and the production process.

Although Dulce remains one of the most trusted and recognisable brands in Northland, it has faced challenges in recent years. These challenges have largely been driven by changes in customer tastes and buying habits, increased competition from online retailers, fluctuating raw material prices and the economic recession impacting on customers' disposable incomes. Although Dulce has remained profitable, growth has stagnated in the last three years and the board of directors is currently undertaking a strategic review, focusing on how it can develop and grow the business and on how it can improve business performance. The board is also in the process of reviewing its risk management activities with a view to ensuring that these risks do not impede the achievement of its strategic aims.

You are a senior business manager reporting directly to the finance director of Dulce and you work on a wide range of strategic level projects and activities. You are often asked by the finance director and other board members to report to them on a variety of strategic level issues and you are currently working for the board on the current strategic review process.

The following exhibits provide information relevant to Dulce:

Exhibit 1: Extracts from Dulce's annual report 20X8, highlighting Dulce's mission, strategic aims, products and ethical sourcing standards.

Exhibit 2: A slide deck presented by the sales director outlining Dulce's proposed sales development strategies.

Exhibit 3: A data sheet presenting information relating to proposed orders from Excelsior department store and BB supermarket.

Exhibit 4: An email containing Dulce's current risk register.

Exhibit 5: A newspaper article relating to child-labour practices in the supply chain of the chocolate manufacturing industry.

Exhibit 6: Summary of a brainstorming meeting outlining key business activities and operations of Dulce.

The case requirements are included in the tasks shown below:

1   You have recently attended a meeting with the finance director and the sales director, where it was discussed how Dulce should develop and grow the business. The sales director is about to make a presentation to the rest of the board on a number of sales development strategies which he proposes will assist Dulce in achieving its stated strategic aim of developing its product range and its markets.

Required:

(a)   **The sales director has asked you to provide a set of notes to accompany the presentation he has prepared for the board, which discuss how the sales development strategies he has proposed will assist Dulce in achieving its strategic aim.**

     Note: Slides are not required.   **(16 marks)**

     Professional skills marks are available for demonstrating commercial acumen skills in showing clear awareness of the organisational and wider external factors which could contribute to the achievement of Dulce's strategic aim.   **(4 marks)**

At the same meeting, the sales director advised the finance director that Dulce is currently considering manufacturing a range of three new luxury hand-made chocolate products (A, B and C) for two retail partners, Excelsior department store and BB supermarkets. However, due to a current shortage of skilled labour in hand-made production techniques, Dulce would currently be unable to supply both of the retail partners' orders in full. Therefore, Dulce must decide which order should be prioritised and be completed in full and which could be partially completed, in order to optimise the use of the skilled labour available.

Following this meeting, the finance director requested one of the finance team to compile a data sheet for you, relating to both potential orders, and she has asked you for a full evaluation of the two orders so that a final decision can be made.

Required:

(b)   **Prepare a report for the finance director which:**

     (i)   **Evaluates the financial and non-financial implications of Dulce prioritising one order over the other; and**   **(12 marks)**

     (ii)   **Recommends, with justification, which order should be prioritised.**   **(4 marks)**

     Professional skills marks are available for demonstrating communication skills in using compelling and logical arguments and clarifying the information presented to convey relevant information to the finance director.   **(4 marks)**

                                   (Total: 40 marks)

2 The audit and risk committee is currently carrying out an annual strategic review of Dulce's risk management activities. As part of this review, the chairman of the audit and risk committee has asked you to assist him in considering how the risks included in the current risk register could have an impact on the achievement of Dulce's strategic aims.

Required:

(a) **Compile a table for the chairman of the audit and risk committee which:**

   (i) **Analyses how the risks identified in the current risk register could have an impact on the achievement of Dulce's strategic aims; and**

   (ii) **Recommends mitigating activities for each of these risks.**   **(16 marks)**

   Professional skills marks are available for demonstrating analysis skills in considering the risks identified by Dulce.   **(4 marks)**

The audit and risk committee is also aware of discussions from a senior leadership team meeting regarding the use of child-labour on cocoa farms supplying the chocolate manufacturing industry. At this meeting, which you also attended, there was a discussion regarding Dulce's response to the findings of a recent news article. The operations director stated that no response is needed, as most customers are unaware of the issue, and the use of child-labour is common amongst most cocoa farmers and is an accepted practice. However, the human resource director insisted that this risk must be removed at all costs and that Dulce must stop using all cocoa farmers who use child-labour immediately and look for new cocoa farmers. The finance director suggested that Dulce should continue to use its cocoa farmers but that it must control and monitor them more effectively to maintain ethical standards.

Required:

(b) **You have been asked by the chairman of the audit and risk committee to prepare three presentation slides, with accompanying notes, for presentation at the next board meeting, which:**

   (i) **Identify how each risk response suggested by the three directors would be categorised using an appropriate risk management framework**   **(4 marks)**

   (ii) **Evaluate the appropriateness of the risk responses of the operations director and the human resource director; and**   **(6 marks)**

   (iii) **Consider the suggestions of the finance director, including recommendations for TWO control activities which should be implemented to assist in managing this risk.**   **(6 marks)**

   Professional skills marks are available for demonstrating scepticism skills in challenging the opinions of the board made in relation to the risk responses to the use of child-labour in Dulce's supply chain.   **(4 marks)**

                                                                    (Total: 40 marks)

3   You recently attended a brainstorming meeting with some of the directors of Dulce. At this meeting the participants brainstormed the key processes and activities Dulce should focus on to achieve performance excellence, with the aim of increasing customer retention and loyalty. Following this meeting, the finance director has asked you to consider the brainstorming meeting summary in order for the directors to evaluate how Dulce is achieving performance excellence.

Required:

Present a set of briefing notes for the finance director which evaluate the extent to which the criteria for achieving performance excellence are being met by Dulce, using the findings of the brainstorming meeting.   **(16 marks)**

Professional skills marks are available for demonstrating evaluation skills in using professional judgement to appraise objectively the findings and opinions of the directors.

(4 marks)

(Total: 20 marks)

Exhibit 1: Extracts from Dulce's annual report 20X8

DULCE

Make every day special

Who we are

We are Northland's most famous confectionery maker, providing our customers with quality chocolate and confectionery for over 100 years.

Mission

Our mission is to be Northland's best loved confectionery brand, bringing our customers together to make every day special.

Our strategic aims

1   We aim to develop our product range and our markets, by focusing on offering customers the products they demand in the locations they are demanded.

2   We aim to focus on performance excellence in our leadership, operations, supplier management, customer engagement and staff development to build and maintain strong customer relationships.

What we make

Boxed chocolates	Chocolate figures	Chocolate bars
Chocolate bags	Chocolate truffles	Candies
Ice cream	Toffee	Fudge

What we believe

Ethical sourcing

– We buy most of our cocoa from two of the world's most respected cocoa suppliers, which are expected to ethically source all of our cocoa supplies.

– Over 200 different raw materials go into our chocolates, many of which are sourced by our suppliers from cocoa farmers in the countries of Geeland and Rodia. We demand the highest levels of ethical, social and environmental standards from our suppliers.

– Our suppliers regularly visit and audit all of the largest cocoa farms each year.

– It is also important to us that all of the farmers who supply our cocoa suppliers are treated fairly and paid appropriately and in line with local wage standards.

– We like to build long-lasting relationships with suppliers which are open and honest. We buy key cocoa supplies with forward contracts to reduce, as much as possible, the uncertainty in the cocoa buying process and work with suppliers to choose the optimal time and quantity for purchases.

– We support international initiatives to improve livelihoods of cocoa farmers and promote responsible labour practices. Our cocoa suppliers employ thousands of people both directly and indirectly in processing cocoa and monitoring and auditing the cocoa farms they work with.

– We invest in international initiatives which provide farm workers with basic healthcare services and educational opportunities.

Exhibit 2: Proposed sales development strategies

DULCE

SALES DEVELOPMENT STRATEGIES

A presentation by the sales director

Slide 1

DULCE SHOPS

– 165 high street shops – our main sales channel in Northland (despite declining annual sales for last three years)

– Require investment in refurbishment and staff training to improve customer experience

– Close 20 shops next year to focus on most profitable locations

Slide 2

DULCE WEBSITE

– Used to sell our whole range of products (to individuals and corporate clients)

– Possibility to develop other gift ideas (such as flowers, greeting cards, gifts and food hampers)

– Role in international sales growth

– Forecast growth in international website sales in the next five years

Slide 3

RETAIL PARTNERS

– Strong growth in sale of Dulce's boxed chocolate ranges to supermarkets in the last two years

– Aim to sell a wider range of our products to retail partners in the next two years

– Aim to sell to a wider range of retail partners in the next two years (more gift shops and department stores)

Slide 4

Exhibit 3: Data sheet on proposed orders

DATA SHEET: NEW LUXURY HAND-MADE CHOCOLATE RANGE

General information

– Proposal to manufacture and sell three new luxury hand-made chocolate products (Boxes A, B and C).

– Production constrained by skilled labour availability for hand-made products.

Excelsior order

– Excelsior is a high-class department store, located in the capital city of Northland.

– Dulce has not worked with Excelsior before.

– Reputation for selling high quality, exclusive products.

– Dulce's new products (A, B and C) would be sold as Excelsior's 'own label' chocolates.

– Order is initially for a three-month period only.

– Considering purchasing other luxury hand-made products from Dulce if these products are successful.

BB supermarkets order

– BB is Northland's second largest supermarket chain.

– Dulce has been supplying BB with its normal range of Dulce branded chocolates for over five years.

– The proposal is for BB to order the same three products (A, B and C) as above, but to sell them in BB supermarkets under Dulce's manufacturing brand label.

– Sales would initially be for three months and only offered in 10% of its supermarkets. However, BB is confident that sales would be rolled out to the remaining of its supermarkets across Northland after the three-month trial period.

Forecast demand per product per month

Available skilled labour hours per month = 30,000			
	Box A	Box B	Box C
Contribution per box ($)	8	9	6
Labour hours per box (Hr)	2	3	3
Contribution per labour hour ($)	4	3	2
Proposed order of each box per month:			
Excelsior	2,000	2,000	2,000
BB supermarkets	3,000	3,000	3,000

Exhibit 4: Dulce's current risk register

To: **Senior business manager**

From: **Chair of risk and audit committee**

Subject: **CONFIDENTIAL: Dulce risk register**

Please find attached the current risk register compiled by the audit and risk committee, which we are in the process of reviewing. I have forwarded it for your consideration and assistance.

 ATTACHMENT: Dulce risk register

Risk item	Risk manager	Description	Rating
Competitive marketplace	CEO	– The global confectionery market has many strong players. Our competitive position depends on our continued ability to offer products which strongly appeal to consumers and which are readily available in the places they are demanded.	HIGH
Key input prices are driven by commodity markets	Operations director	– Adverse changes in certain commodity prices (particularly cocoa supplies) could affect our liquidity and profitability.	MEDIUM
Our products must have the highest integrity	Manufacturing director	– Product contamination (for example, uncleanliness or impurities in the materials or production process) could be harmful to customers. – Unethical sourcing of materials could severely damage our reputation.	HIGH
We depend on the skills, enthusiasm and wellbeing of our staff	The board	– Poor staff management or lack of skills in our whole team could result in the loss of the competitive advantage derived from our highly skilled staff or the loss of staff to competitors. – We rely heavily on the loyalty and commitment of our staff.	MEDIUM

Exhibit 5: Newspaper article about child-labour

CHILD-LABOUR PRACTICES LEAVE A BAD TASTE FOR NORTHLAND CHOCOLATE MANUFACTURERS

NORTHLAND BUSINESS TIMES
A report by retail editor Lee Bale

The countries of Geeland and Rodia supply more than 70% of the world's cocoa. The cocoa they grow and harvest is sold to 90% of global chocolate companies, including those based in Northland. However, in recent years, several organisations and journalists have exposed the widespread use of child-labour on cocoa farms in both Geeland and Rodia.

The realities of child-labour

Cocoa is a commodity crop grown primarily for export. As the chocolate industry has grown over the last 20 years, so has the demand for cheap cocoa. However, on average, cocoa farmers in Geeland and Rodia earn less than $2 per day, an income significantly below the poverty line. As a result, they often resort to the use of child-labour to keep prices competitive.

The children of Geeland and Rodia are surrounded by intense poverty, and most begin working at a young age to help support their families and many offer vital sources of income for the poorest families. Children are mostly used to climb the cocoa trees to cut bean pods using a machete. These large, heavy, dangerous knives are the standard tools for children on the cocoa farms, which violates international labour laws relating to eliminating the worst forms of child-labour. In addition, over 40% of child-labourers in Geeland and 60% in Rodia working on cocoa farms do not attend school.

Is child-labour free chocolate possible?

Despite their role in contributing to child-labour, the chocolate industry has not taken significant steps to remedy the problem. Within this billion dollar industry, chocolate companies have the power to end the use of child-labour by paying cocoa farmers a living wage for their product. The chocolate industry is also being called upon to develop and financially support programmes to educate children working on cocoa farms. However, to date, the industry has seemingly achieved limited success in removing child-labour and a lack of transparency is characteristic of the chocolate industry as it consistently fails to act.

The truth is that consumers today have no sure way of knowing if the chocolate they are buying involves the use of child-labour. Despite the fact that last month a Northland journalist investigating farms in Rodia (where Northland chocolate companies buy cocoa) filmed illegal child-labour practices, a recent public survey in Northland highlighted that less than 5% of customers were aware of child-labour practices in the chocolate manufacturing industry.

Clearly, Northland chocolate manufacturers have a long way to go to address these unethical activities and until they do, the ethical standards of these manufacturers must be called into question.

Exhibit 6: Summary of brainstorming meeting

MEETING NOTE: During the meeting, the directors used the Baldridge model as a framework to assess Dulce's approach to performance excellence

Section 16

REAL EXAM ANSWERS – SEPT/DEC 2019

Strategic Professional – Essentials, SBL **Sept/Dec 2019 Sample Answers**

In the Strategic Professional Examinations it is not always possible to publish suggested answers which comprehensively cover all the valid points which candidates might make. Credit will be given to candidates for points not included in the suggested answers, but which, nevertheless, are relevant to the requirements. In addition, in this integrated case study examination candidates may re-introduce points made in other questions or parts of questions as long as these are made in the specific context of the requirements of the question being answered.

The suggested answers presented below inevitably give much more detail than would be expected from most candidates under examination conditions, and include most of the obvious points evidenced from the case information. The answers are therefore intended to provide a structure of the approach required from candidates, and cover the range and depth of knowledge relating to each task which might be demonstrated by the most well prepared and able candidates. They are also intended to support revision and tuition for future examinations.

1   (a)   **Slide notes (to accompany the sales director's slide presentation)**

DULCE SHOPS

1   As the shops are our primary sales channel, they should play a key role in the growth and development of Dulce and should help us to achieve our strategic aim. A sales development strategy based on our current shops would be considered as market penetration, where we aim to increase the share of our existing market using our existing product range.

2   However, this is likely to require us to improve relationships with customers in our shops. Annual sales in our shops have decreased for the last three years, so we clearly need to focus on customer service to make sure customers return to our shops, to make repeat purchases throughout the year. This could be helped by investment in refurbishment to encourage customers into our shops.

3   This could be helped by more investment in staff training and in selecting the best performing shops in the prime locations. Investment needs to be made in improving our customer experience, which will help us to engage better with customers and provide them with a wide range of high quality products within a high-quality environment.

4   The closure of 20 of our shops (12%) may be an effective way of improving our image with customers. However, we must only close those shops which are not profitable or which do not support our brand.

5 These strategies should help us achieve our strategic aim, providing that we ensure the products demanded are available to customers. Shops are also possibly the best place to assist in achieving our strategic aim, as shops offer our customers actual experience of our brand and it is where we can build and develop strong customer relationships.

DULCE WEBSITE

1 Our website provides us with the ideal sales environment to offer new products. However, we need to be careful that these new products do not impact on our confectionery sales nor the high-quality image we strive to achieve. This could help to achieve our strategic aim only if these new products are actually demanded by the customers. However, we need to undertake further research to understand the extent to which customers are interested in buying these products through the Dulce website.

2 Our website provides us with the opportunity to develop our market, as it is a medium to sell our whole range of existing products to a wider range of customers, such as corporate and international customers. There is a large potential for international sales growth using the Dulce website, helping us to achieve our strategic aim. However, this will be very dependent on us developing the suitable infrastructure to support international sales growth.

3 However, we must manage our website sales channel very carefully, to ensure that it supports the Dulce brand image and that sufficient resources are deployed to ensure that it operates effectively.

4 International website sales, which we are predicting will grow strongly in the coming years, will also help us to develop our market, through targeting a wide range of overseas customers.

RETAIL PARTNERS

1 We should consolidate our position with our current retail partners, through careful management of our relationship with our supermarket customers in particular. We have achieved strong growth in supermarket sales of our 'own label' chocolate ranges in the last two years and consolidation will maintain strong working relationships with the supermarkets, some of which are large organisations.

2 Retail partners also give us an opportunity to penetrate the market, by selling more of our own label products to current retailers over the next few years. This will assist in achieving our strategic aim. We should also aim to sell to a wider range of retail partners (gift-shops and department stores) which would also help achieve our strategic aim.

3 Producing a luxury hand-made chocolate range is also a potential product development strategy and should help to achieve our strategic aim in providing a wide range of Dulce products where they are demanded.

4 The production of luxury hand-made products to new retail partners would help us to diversify and should assist in the achievement of our strategic aim. It could be an exciting development for Dulce but is likely to require some investment in staff training and appropriate equipment.

(b) (i) To: **Finance director**

From: **Senior business manager**

Date: **1 September 20X8**

An evaluation of the financial and strategic implications of prioritising the order for Excelsior department store compared with prioritising the BB order

Introduction

The following report will compare and contrast the prioritisation of the two potential orders for our proposed new luxury hand-made chocolate range. The report will also recommend which order should be prioritised to provide maximum benefit for Dulce.

An evaluation of the option to prioritise the order with Excelsior

Financial

The calculations presented below take into account the fact that we have a limiting factor in our skilled labour hours and it is this factor which will limit our ability to manufacture both orders in full. We should focus on maximising the contribution from the limited skilled labour hours available.

Labour hours per unit	2	3	3
	A	B	C
	$	$	$
Contribution per unit	8	9	6
Contribution per labour hour	4	3	2
Production order	1st	2nd	3rd
Total labour hours available per month			**30,000**

1 Prioritise order for Excelsior

Production for Excelsior	A	B	C	
Units	2,000	2,000	2,000	**Total hours used**
Hours	4,000	6,000	6,000	**16,000**
Labour hours remaining to produce BB order =		14,000		

Production for BB	1st	2nd	3rd	
	A	B	C	
Units	3,000	2,666	0	
Hours	6,000	7,998	0	**13,998**
				29,998

Contribution per month from prioritising the Excelsior order:

	A	B	C	Total
Contribution	$	$	$	$
Excelsior	16,000	18,000	12,000	46,000
BB	24,000	23,994		47,994
Total	40,000	41,994	12,000	93,994

Non-financial considerations:

If we prioritise the order with Excelsior we will achieve our strategic aim of developing our products in a location where they are demanded, by selling a newly developed hand-made product to a new customer.

However, a concern of this proposed order is that it amounts to a relatively small production run: 6,000 boxes per month for three months only. These hand-made chocolates will be very labour intensive, requiring nearly 16,000 labour hours each month. In addition, we will need to take into account additional costs such as training and supervision which will also need to be factored in to our decision. However, we do not know that Excelsior will place any further orders, but one of our proposed strategic development opportunities (as proposed by the sales director) is to produce a wider range of products to sell to other retailers, and therefore it remains a possible opportunity. This new product line could prove to be highly lucrative if Excelsior places future orders.

A further consideration is that these products will be sold under Excelsior's own brand name and not Dulce's. However, it would be a great opportunity for us to work with Excelsior and develop a new market, but it would not assist in developing our own reputation in manufacturing a luxury brand.

A further consideration is that undertaking a contract with Excelsior may have a negative impact on our long-term relationship with BB supermarkets. We must not allow a potential contract with Excelsior to adversely affect this, as we sell our own label products through BB's supermarkets. If we prioritise the Excelsior order, then BB will not receive its full order of Box B and would not receive any Box Cs.

An evaluation of the option to prioritise the order with BB supermarkets

Financial

From the analysis given below, prioritising this order will give us a lower contribution than prioritising the Excelsior order. This is because if Dulce prioritises BB's requirements, based on ranking the contribution per hour of labour available, prioritising the BB order would mean that Dulce will be able to produce and sell 1,000 fewer units of B and has to make 1,000 more units of C. As each unit of B makes $3 more contribution than C, prioritising this order will yield $(1,000 \times 6 - 1,000 \times 9)$ or $-\$3,000$ contribution, compared with prioritising the Excelsior order. However, non-financial factors must be considered (as discussed below) before making a final decision.

2 **Prioritise order for BB**

Production for BB	A	B	C	
Units	3,000	3,000	3,000	
Hours	6,000	9,000	9,000	**Total hours used**
				24,000

Labour hours remaining to produce Excelsior order = 6,000

Production for Excelsior	1st	2nd	3rd	
	A	B	C	
Units	2,000	666	0	
Hours	4,000	1,998	0	**5,998**
				29,998

Contribution from prioritising the BB order:

	A	B	C	Total
Contribution	$	$	$	$
BB	24,000	27,000	18,000	69,000
Excelsior	16,000	5,994	–	21,994
Total	40,000	32,994	18,000	90,994

Non-financial considerations:

We must carefully manage our relationship with BB as the second largest supermarket chain in Northland. We have a strong and established relationship which we could build upon by selling this new luxury range. The main advantage of prioritising the order with BB is that it would be an excellent opportunity for us to use our proprietary brand name to enter the luxury chocolate market, which we cannot exploit with the Excelsior order.

BB forecasts it could sell these products in more of its supermarkets after the initial three months trial and therefore presents us with an opportunity to develop these products into the longer term, thus achieving our strategic aim. However, future sales would be dependent on improving our availability of skilled labour, which will need further investment if we are to be able to commit to future orders with BB. It is likely to require a significant number of dedicated staff and more supervision. Investment in training and equipment will also be necessary. Further analysis and discussions with BB would need to be undertaken regarding the long-term viability of the contract, but if acceptable, then this investment would be considered appropriate.

(ii) Recommendation

Based on both the financial and non-financial considerations, despite the lower contribution earned by the BB order, it is recommended that we prioritise our order with BB. We have a long-standing business relationship with BB and they have offered us the potential to sell Dulce's branded luxury chocolates. In purely financial terms, this option is not as preferable as the Excelsior order but the risks of working with Excelsior are much higher, as a new retail partner with no absolute guarantee of future orders beyond three months. In addition, the loss of Dulce's 'brand' association with these new products is not acceptable and would not contribute to the achievement of our strategic aims.

ACCA marking guide	Marks
(a) Award up to 1 mark for each relevant point explained in relation to the proposed sales development strategies (up to a maximum of 6 marks for each sales development category). Up to a maximum of 16 marks. **Key points** **DULCE SHOPS** – Market penetration – increase share of the existing market using existing products. – Primary sales channel to increase the penetration of products. – Focus on creating better relationship with customers – customer service. – Investment in refurbishment to encourage customers into shops. – Investment in staff training and best location. – Investment in improving customer experience, to engage better with customers and provide them with a wide range of high quality products. – Closure of 20 shops (12%) an effective way of improving the customer perception. – BUT – only close under-performing shops or those which do not enhance image. – Help us achieve strategic aim, providing that products which customers demand are provided in the shops. – Shops are possibly the best place to achieve strategic aim – customers experience for themselves the brand. **DULCE WEBSITE** – Ideal sales environment to offer new products ideas. – Means of achieving product and market development. – New products should not detract from confectionery sales – not impact on the quality image of Dulce. – Could help achieve strategic aim if new products are demanded by the customers. – Undertake research to establish whether customers are interested in new products through website. – Website provides opportunity to develop the market, sell whole range of existing products to a wider range of customers (corporate clients and international customers). – Large potential for international sales growth but dependent on developing suitable infrastructure to support international sales growth. – Must manage website carefully, to ensure it complements overall brand image. – International website sales allows us to develop our market reach further – allows opportunity to sell products to customers who are not able to purchase them elsewhere.	

RETAIL PARTNERS
- Consolidation strategy with current retail partners – management of relationship with our supermarket customers.
- Strong growth in supermarket sales of 'own label' chocolate ranges in the last two years – consolidation will maintain strong working relationships.
- Opportunity for market penetration – sell more ranges of own label products to current retail partners over the next two years.
- Counteract the fall in sales which may arise from the closure of shops.
- Assist in achieving strategic aim.
- Producing a luxury hand-made chocolate range is also a potential product development strategy.
- Complement sales of other chocolates currently sold by retail partners. This should help to achieve our strategic aim.
- Luxury hand-made products sold as own label products – diversification strategy.
- Open up a new market but will require investment in staff development.

Professional skills

16
—
4
—
20
—

(b) **(i)** 1 mark for each correct calculation (up to a maximum of 8 marks). For each evaluation, award up to 4 marks for relevant supporting calculations.
1 mark for each non-financial issue identified, relevant to prioritising Excelsior order (up to a maximum of 4 marks).
1 mark for each non-financial issue identified, relevant to prioritising BB order (up to a maximum of 4 marks). Up to a maximum of 12 marks in total.

(ii) Up to 2 marks for each point made and justified in relation to an overall recommendation (up to a maximum of 4 marks).

Key points
Prioritising the Excelsior order
Non-financial considerations:
- Achieve strategic aim of developing both products and markets, by selling hand-made product to a new customer.
- However, products sold under Excelsior's own brand name.
- Opportunity to develop a new market opportunity but will not assist in developing own reputation.
- Could prove to be highly lucrative in the future but further orders not yet agreed.
- Proposed order is very short term at only three months (only 6,000 boxes per month).
- Very labour and cost intensive – require 16,000 hours of labour per month for this order.
- Risk there may be no long-term benefit in relation to Excelsior. However, proposed strategic development opportunities are to produce a wider range of products through production of chocolates for other retailers, and therefore it is a possible opportunity.
- May have negative implications on relationship with BB Supermarkets.
- Have a long-term relationship with BB, an established customer.
- Must be careful not to allow a contract with Excelsior to damage this relationship.
- If this order optimised, BB will not receive its full order.
- If Dulce undertakes Excelsior order, it must maintain a strong relationship with BB.

Prioritising the BB Supermarkets order

Non-financial considerations:

- BB is second largest supermarket chain in Northland and an established relationship with Dulce which we could build upon through selling this new luxury product.
- The biggest advantage of prioritising the order with BB – great opportunity to enter luxury hand-made chocolate market with own label.
- Excellent opportunity to develop product range in the longer term and improve our brand image, achieving our strategic aim.
- Future sales dependent on improving availability of skilled labour – need investment.
- Likely to require significant number of staff and, in addition, more supervision and investment in training and equipment.

Recommendation

- Despite lower contribution earned by the BB order, it is recommended that order with BB is prioritised.
- A long-standing relationship with BB and presents Dulce with potential to sell own brand luxury chocolates.
- In purely financial terms, not as preferable as the Excelsior order but risks of working with Excelsior are much higher.
- Excelsior – new retail partner. No real guarantee of future orders beyond three months.
- Loss of own brand association with this new product is not acceptable and would not contribute to the achievement of our strategic aims.

	16
Professional skills	4
	20
Total	40

Professional skills may be additionally rewarded as in the following rubric for 1(a):

How well has the candidate demonstrated professional skills as follows:	Not at all	Not so well	Quite well	Very well
Commercial acumen skills in showing clear awareness of the organisational and wider external factors which could contribute to the achievement of Dulce's strategic aim.	The candidate has not demonstrated commercial acumen. The candidate has failed to link their discussion of Dulce's sales development strategies to the achievement of its strategic aim. The candidate has failed to demonstrate any awareness of either the organisational factors or the wider external factors in Dulce's achievement of its strategic aims.	The candidate has demonstrated limited commercial acumen. Some attempt has been made to link the sales development strategies to the strategic aim. Some of the discussion of the product and market strategies demonstrated commercial awareness but the candidate has failed to appreciate a number of the organisational and external factors affecting the achievement of its strategic aims.	The candidate has demonstrated good commercial acumen. Most of the discussion recognises the link between the sales development strategies and its strategic aim. The candidate's answer has demonstrated good commercial awareness in recognising some of the external and organisational factors affecting the achievement of its strategic aims, for example, customer demand for its new products.	The candidate has demonstrated excellent commercial acumen. All of the candidate's discussion within all of the sales development strategies considered recognises the link between the product and market circumstances of Dulce with its strategic aim. The candidate's answer has demonstrated a very high level of judgement and commercial awareness of a wide range of external and organisational factors impacting on the achievement of Dulce's strategic aims.
	0	1	2	4

Professional skills may be additionally rewarded as in the following rubric for 1(b):

How well has the candidate demonstrated professional skills as follows:	Not at all	Not so well	Quite well	Very well
Communication skills in using compelling and logical arguments and clarifying the information presented to convey relevant information to the finance director.	The candidate has demonstrated poor skills in presenting a logical argument for either the Excelsior order or the BB order. The style and presentation of the candidate's argument would not be suitable for presentation to the finance director. There was no overall recommendation made, demonstrating poor communication skills.	The candidate has demonstrated some basic communication skills. The candidate has used an appropriate report format but the tone of the answer is not appropriate for presentation to the finance director. The candidate has demonstrated some evidence of presenting a logical argument in favour of either the Excelsior or BB order in parts of the report but most of it is not clear or logically presented.	The candidate has demonstrated good communication skills. The candidate has presented most of the relevant information required by the finance director. The arguments are mostly presented in a logical way and the candidate has used most of the relevant information needed to support their argument. The candidate has used an appropriate tone for the finance director.	The candidate has demonstrated excellent communication skills. The candidate has presented a clear, balanced and logical report, showing clearly the arguments for either optimising the Excelsior order and the BB order. The candidate has used an appropriate tone for the finance director and has presented a compelling and logical recommendation.
	0	1	2	4

2   (a)   **(i) and (ii) Briefing table**

Risk	Risk assessment	Proposed mitigating activities
Competitive marketplace	Failure to anticipate/react to changes in consumer trends or a failure to invest in our business growth and development in relation to our competitors is likely to reduce demand for our products, resulting in loss of competitive advantage, reduced market share and reduced sales.	Dulce must continue to focus on identifying and developing new product ideas. For example, our proposal to develop luxury hand-made chocolate products is offering our customers a greater range of products to maintain our competitive position.
	Failure to invest in maintaining our competitive position may harm the image of our brand, as our competitive position depends on our continued ability to offer products which appeal to customers and which are readily available in the places they are demanded by customers.	Developing our staff skills in hand-made chocolate products will help us build on performance excellence which should assist in building effective customer relationships and maintenance of our competitive position and brand image.
	If we are not able to satisfy customer needs effectively and/or react to what our competitors are doing, this will threaten our sustainability in the market place as our competitors may respond more effectively than ourselves. There is likely to be a high risk to the achievement of our strategic aims of growing and developing our products/ markets and developing and maintaining strong customer relationships.	Our multi-channel sales network is a means by which we aim to satisfy consumers' needs, whilst also mitigating the overall risk to the business from a downturn in any specific sales channel.
		Working with new retail partners widens our opportunities to increase our sales network and remain competitive in our operational activities.

Key input prices are driven by commodity markets	Significant adverse changes in certain commodity prices (particularly cocoa supplies) could affect Dulce's profitability and therefore on our ability to offer a wide range of products due to a reduction in our investment in product development. High commodity prices may result in us having to reduce our range of products which would impact on our ability to meet our strategic aim of developing the widest range of products for our customers. This may impact on us achieving our strategic aim of maintaining and developing customer relationships, as we may lose customers if we reduce our product range.	Dulce must continue to buy its key inputs forward and work with suppliers to choose the optimal time and quantity for purchases of cocoa supplies. This policy provides a stable cost base for us to make optimum trading and pricing decisions. By hedging, it may mean that, on occasion, we pay more for our key ingredients than the prevailing market rate, but this will protect the consumer from potentially widely fluctuating prices and protects us from potential losses and the loss of trust of our customers.
Our products must have the highest integrity	Product contamination, caused by unclean production processes or defective raw materials, or unethical sourcing of materials could severely damage our reputation. If our integrity is called into question by our customers, then this would severely impact on our ability to develop and maintain customer relationships, as it would challenge the effectiveness of our leadership, operations and supplier management. It would also impact on our ability to develop new markets, as it would be far more difficult to attract new customers if they question our systems and the quality and integrity of our products.	We must ensure that we maintain rigorous security systems throughout our supply chain to guard against poor quality/defective supplies. In the unlikely event that these policies and systems fail, we must implement a robust process for product recall and consumer communication, in addition to comprehensive insurance cover. Being open and honest with our customers will be critical in order to maintain strong customer relationships and trust in our product, therefore regular communication is vital. We must maintain strong relationships with suppliers to ensure that ethical sourcing from cocoa farms is being adhered to. This may mean that we will need to take more control of the supplier audit process ourselves. We need to audit all cocoa farms at least once per year.

Risk

We depend on the skills, enthusiasm and wellbeing of our people

Poor staff management or lack of skills in our whole team could result in the loss of our competitive advantage or the loss of staff to competitors. Any loss of staff will inevitably result in the loss of skills from our business, which will impact on our ability to achieve performance excellence and thus achieve our aim to develop and maintain strong customer relationships.

Without adequately motivated and skilled staff, we are also unlikely to develop the products our customers demand and thus will not achieve our other strategic aim of product development.

We rely heavily on the loyalty and commitment of our staff at all levels of the business and any loss of key staff, particularly in our leadership team, will inevitably impact on our competitive position and our ability to deliver performance excellence.

Management must continually evaluate the balance of skills, knowledge and experience within the team when considering the role and capabilities required for a particular position.

Staff must be kept informed of internal and external developments through regular communications.

Strong staff appraisal systems and a focus on staff development will help to create loyalty and commitment of our staff.

Regular training and skills development should build on performance excellence, help us to be innovative in product development and maintain the loyalty and commitment of staff.

Strong recruitment processes, formalised succession planning and on-going individual training and development plans will mitigate the risk of the loss of key staff.

(b)   (i)

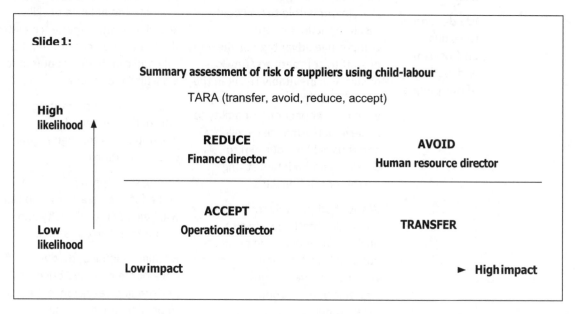

Slide 1:

Summary assessment of risk of suppliers using child-labour

TARA (transfer, avoid, reduce, accept)

A common framework for evaluating response to risk is to use the TARA approach. This considers risk in relation to how likely is the risk of occurring, and the extent of its impact on us, should it occur.

The human resource director's recommendation fits with the high impact/high likelihood approach. The impact is high, particularly on our reputation and on the lives of those being exploited and the likelihood is also high. It is stated in the article that this is a widespread practice in the industry and therefore it is highly likely that some of the cocoa farmers who supply us do use child-labour. Therefore, the risk response advocated by the human resource director is to AVOID this risk, by finding alternative cocoa suppliers.

The operations director's recommendation fits with low impact/low likelihood approach, in that he believes that the impact of this risk is low as most customers are unaware of child-labour practices. Therefore, the risk response his argument most closely follows is to ACCEPT this risk and take no action.

The finance director's recommendation fits with the low impact/high likelihood approach, in that the risk is likely to be of low impact in the context of the industry-wide use of child-labour by cocoa farmers and the lack of awareness of its customers, but the likelihood is high, given the high number of cocoa farmers we use in Geeland and Rodia. Therefore, the risk response would be to REDUCE this risk, through improved control activities.

(ii)

> **Slide 2:**
>
> **Consideration of risk responses**
>
> **HR DIRECTOR**
>
> **AVOID**
> – Unlikely high impact
> – Impractical
> – High costs
> – Will not address the issue
>
> **OPERATIONS DIRECTOR**
>
> **ACCEPT**

Notes:

HR director

AVOID

To avoid the issue of child-labour is not the most suitable solution for Dulce. The newspaper article indicates the scale of the issue in the whole industry and, therefore, identifying and using cocoa farmers who do not use child-labour may be impractical, taking into account the large number of cocoa supplies we need. There are advantages, in that it may attract a new range of customers who only buy products from guaranteed ethical sources but it is unlikely that these gains will off-set the cost of sourcing new cocoa farmers and the potential loss of customers due to likely price increases of our products.

The impact of this issue is not considered to be high, as most customers are not aware of these labour practices and are unlikely to change their buying behaviour if they did. As chocolate is a low value product for consumers, this issue is unlikely to be a major factor in the purchasing decision of most customers.

Overall, it would be better to remain working with these cocoa farmers to put in place controls to ensure child-labour practices are monitored and assistance is given to provide education and support to both farmers and the children working on these farms. Therefore, the suggestion by the human resource director may not be the best solution to the risk.

Operations director

ACCEPT

Although the use of child-labour in cocoa farming is common practice, that does not mean that we should merely accept it and not attempt to improve the situation.

Although the risk of child-labour which would be used by our cocoa farmers is likely to be of low impact on our overall business, from the evidence in the news article, it is likely to be of high likelihood and therefore the assertion by the operations director may not be justified. Evidence suggested in the article indicates that the majority of the cocoa farms located in the two cocoa growing countries do use child-labour. Therefore, it would seem highly likely that some, if not a significant number of the cocoa farmers supplying our key suppliers, do use child-labour.

Obviously, doing nothing will cost nothing and it means no change in what we do. However, it goes directly against our stated beliefs as an organisation, as evidenced in the ethical sourcing statement of our annual report. We also run the risk that ethical consumers in Northland will seek alternative chocolate suppliers. Our strategic aim is to develop and maintain strong customer relationships and this approach would likely go against this aim.

We have clearly stated in our beliefs that we promote responsible labour practices. This must include the use of child-labour, therefore to merely accept this and not attempt to address this use with positive actions to assist cocoa farmers and the children they employ would be against our ethical beliefs.

(iii)

Slide 3:

FINANCE DIRECTOR

REDUCE

- Unlikely to be eliminated but can:
  - Reduce child-labour
  - Invest
- Improve reputation
- Increase costs

CONTROL ACTIONS:

1 Annual audit
2 Review payment rates
3 Investment

Notes:

This is likely to be the most realistic option, given that the impact of the risk for our business is probably quite low, but the likelihood of the use of child-labour by cocoa farmers is high. We should consider how we can reduce the levels of child-labour used by cocoa farmers and try to work with these farmers to improve the working and living conditions of child-labourers. As an organisation which believes strongly in its ethical stance, we must take positive action where possible by paying fair prices and providing a premium to invest in local communities.

Importantly, this should have positive benefits for the farmers and the people they employ. For us as a business, it should improve our reputation in the industry and thereby attract more customers. However, we will also have to consider the costs involved, as if we decide to increase our rate of pay to cocoa farmers to reduce the need for child-labour, then this may impact on our customers, through pricing, and our overall profitability.

Control actions:

1 Undertake regular audits. We must play a more active role in the audit process of the cocoa farmers to ensure that we are satisfied with the labour practices being used. We must also cease using any supplies from cocoa farmers who do not adhere to the standards which we set.

2   We should regularly review the rates we pay for our cocoa supplies to ensure that this is fair and is not forcing the exploitation of child-labour. We must monitor industry standards and national wage rates in the countries where our cocoa farmers are located and ensure that we set a fair rate above the poverty line.

3   We should invest in and support international initiatives for training of farm owners and workers in the issues around using child-labour.

Note: Only TWO control activities are required and only two will attract marks.

ACCA marking guide		
		Marks
(a) (i) Award up to 2 marks for each relevant point made and discussed in relation to the impact of each risk identified in the risk register on the achievement of the strategic aims (up to a maximum of 4 marks for each risk category identified). Up to a maximum of 8 marks in total.		
(ii) Award up to 2 marks for each mitigating activity identified and justified. Up to a maximum of 8 marks in total.		

Competitive marketplace
Risks
–   Failure to anticipate/react to consumer trends/failure to invest in business growth and development likely to reduce demand
–   Resulting in loss of competitive advantage, reduced market share and reduced sales.
–   Failure to invest in maintaining competitive position may harm Dulce brand.
–   Competitive position depends on continued ability to offer products which appeal to customers and are available in places demanded.
–   If not able to satisfy customer needs and/or react to competitors, this will threaten sustainability in the market place.
–   High risk to the achievement of strategic aims.

Mitigating activities
–   Focus on identifying and developing new product ideas.
–   Develop staff skills in hand-made chocolate products to build on performance excellence – assist in building customer relationships and maintaining competitive position and brand image.
–   Invest in multi-channel sales network to satisfy consumers' needs, whilst mitigating the risk to the business from a downturn in any specific sales channel.
–   Work with new retail partners and opening Dulce cafés widens opportunities to increase our sales network.

Key input prices are driven by commodity markets
Risks
–   Adverse changes in commodity prices (particularly cocoa supplies) affects profitability and ability to offer a wide range of products.
–   High commodity prices may result in reducing range of products.
–   Impact on ability to meet our strategic aim of developing wide range of products.
–   Impact on achieving strategic aim of maintaining and developing customer relationships – may lose customers if we reduce our product range

Mitigating activities
- Continue to buy key inputs by forward contracts.
- Work with suppliers to choose optimal time/quantity for purchases of cocoa supplies.
- This policy provides a stable cost base.
- By hedging, may pay more for key ingredients than prevailing market rate, but will protect consumer from widely fluctuating prices and protects Dulce from potential losses.

Our products must have the highest integrity
Risks
- Product contamination could severely damage our reputation.
- If integrity is called into question – severely impact on ability to develop and maintain customer relationships.
- Challenge the effectiveness of our leadership, operations and supplier management.
- Impact on ability to develop new markets – difficult to attract new customers if question systems, quality and integrity of products.

Mitigating activities
- Maintain rigorous security systems throughout supply chain.
- If these fail, must implement a robust process for product recall and consumer communication and comprehensive insurance cover.
- Open and honest with customers to maintain strong customer relationships and trust – regular communication is vital.
- Maintain strong relationships with suppliers to ensure ethical sourcing from cocoa farms is being adhered to.
- May need to take more control of the supplier audit process ourselves.
- Audit all cocoa farms at least once per year.

We depend on the skills, enthusiasm and wellbeing of our people
Risks
- Poor staff management/lack of skills – result in loss of competitive advantage or loss of staff to competitors.
- Loss of staff will result in loss of skills from our business – impact on ability to achieve performance excellence.
- Without motivated and skilled staff – unlikely to develop products customers demand.
- Rely heavily on loyalty and commitment of staff – any loss of key staff impact on competitive position and ability to deliver performance excellence.

Mitigating activities
- Evaluate balance of skills, knowledge and experience within the team when considering the role and capabilities for a position.
- Keep staff informed of internal and external developments through regular communications.
- Strong staff appraisal systems and a focus on staff development.
- Regular training and skills development should build on performance excellence.
- Strong recruitment processes, formalised succession planning and on-going individual training and development plans.

	16
Professional skills	4
	20

(b)   (i)   1 mark for each correct application of the risk responses within the TARA framework (up to 3 marks). 1 mark for using the TARA framework (up to a maximum of 4 marks).

         (ii)   Award up to 2 marks for each point discussed in relation to consideration of the HR director's response (up to a maximum of 4 marks).

              Award up to 2 marks for each point discussed in relation to consideration of the operations director's response (up to a maximum of 4 marks).

         (iii)   Award up to 2 marks for each point discussed in relation to consideration of the finance director's response (up to a maximum of 4 marks).

              Up to 2 marks for each control activity recommended (up to a maximum of 4 marks).

              Up to a maximum of 16 marks in total for 2b.

         (i)
- Use of the TARA approach.
- HR director response fits with the AVOID approach.
- Impact is high, particularly on reputation and lives of those being exploited.
- Likelihood is high. Widespread practice in the industry.
- OD's recommendation fits with ACCEPT approach.
- He believes impact is low as most customers are unaware of child-labour practices.
- Therefore – take no action.
- FD's approach fits with REDUCE approach.
- Low impact in the context of the industry-wide use of child-labour by cocoa farmers and the lack of awareness of its customers.
- Likelihood high, given high number of cocoa farmers used in Geeland and Rodia.

                                                      4

         (ii)
- To avoid issue is not the most suitable solution for Dulce.
- Identifying and using cocoa farmers who do not use child-labour impractical.
- May attract new range of ethical customers but unlikely these gains will off-set cost of sourcing new cocoa farmers.
- Impact not considered high, as most customers are not aware of these labour practices and unlikely to change their buying behaviour.
- Unlikely to be a major factor in the purchasing decision of most customers.
- Better to work with cocoa farmers to put in place controls to monitor and assist.
- Although the use of child-labour in cocoa farming is common practice, does not mean that we should merely accept it and not attempt to improve the situation.
- Child-labour likely to be low impact on overall business, but is high likelihood and therefore assertion by OD may not be justified.
- Likely that some, if not a significant number, of cocoa farmers supplying key suppliers do use child-labour.
- Doing nothing will cost nothing.
- Directly against our stated beliefs as an organisation, as evidenced in the ethical sourcing statement of our annual report.
- Strategic aim is to develop and maintain strong customer relationships – this approach likely go against this aim.

                                                      6

(iii)
- Most realistic option, given impact is probably quite low, but likelihood is high.
- Need to consider how to reduce levels of child-labour used by cocoa farmers/try to work with farmers to improve conditions of child-labourers.
- Must take positive action by paying fair prices and providing a premium to invest in local communities.
- Should have positive benefits for the farmers and the people they employ.
- Should improve Dulce's reputation in the industry and attract more customers.
- Consider the costs involved – increasing our rate of pay to cocoa farmers may impact on our customers, through pricing, and our overall profitability.

Control actions:
- Undertake regular audits. Play active role in audit process of the cocoa farmers to ensure that we are satisfied with practices being used.
- Cease using supplies from cocoa farmers who do not adhere to the standards set.
- Regularly review rates we pay for cocoa supplies to ensure that this is fair and not forcing the exploitation of child-labour.
- Monitor industry standards and national wage rates in the countries where our cocoa farmers are located and set a fair rate above poverty line.
- We should invest in and support international initiatives for training of farm owners and workers in the issues around using child-labour.

6

Professional skills — 4

Total — 20

Professional skills may be additionally rewarded as in the following rubric for 2(a):

How well has the candidate demonstrated professional skills as follows:	Not at all	Not so well	Quite well	Very well
Analysis skills in considering the risks identified by Dulce.	The candidate has demonstrated poor or no analysis skills. The candidate has made points which are not supported by the available evidence and has not investigated how these risks link to the achievement of the strategic aims. The candidate has not used a suitable format to answer the question.	The candidate has demonstrated limited analysis skills. Some of the candidate's points arise from evidence identified from the case but the consideration of the impact on the strategic aims is often missing or unclear. The candidate has presented the answer in a reasonably clear format but has not investigated all of the risks adequately for the intended audience.	The candidate has demonstrated good analysis skills. Most of the candidate's points are based on evidence identified from the scenario and the candidate has made a reasonable attempt to consider the impact of the risks on the strategic aims. The candidate has presented the answer in a clear format and most of the risks are investigated adequately for the intended audience.	The candidate has demonstrated excellent analysis skills. All of the candidate's points are based on evidence identified from the scenario and throughout the answer there is a clear consideration of the impact on the strategic aims. The candidate has presented the answer in a logical structure and it is entirely suitable for its intended audience.
	0	1	2	4

Professional skills may be additionally rewarded as in the following rubric for 2(b):

How well has the candidate demonstrated professional skills as follows:	Not at all	Not so well	Quite well	Very well
Scepticism skills in challenging the opinions of the board made in relation to the risk responses to the use of child-labour in Dulce's supply chain.	The candidate has failed to challenge the opinions presented by the board members to assess how realistic their proposed risk responses are for Dulce.	The candidate has made a weak attempt at challenging the opinions presented by the board members and by doing so did not adequately probe and question the opinions of the directors or the information presented in the sources given in the scenario.	The candidate has made a good attempt at challenging most of the opinions of the board members. They have also made some attempt to probe the sources of information presented in the scenario but this was not presented in the most professional manner.	The candidate has made an excellent attempt at challenging the opinions presented by all of the board members identified in the question. They have probed and questioned all of the key sources of information in the scenario and have used this to justify, in a professional manner, their challenge to the opinions presented.
	0	1	2	4

3 BRIEFING NOTES

The criteria used to assess performance

The term 'performance excellence' refers to an integrated approach to organisational performance management which results in:

- delivery of increasing value to customers and stakeholders

- improvement of overall organisational effectiveness

- organisational and personal learning

The Baldrige framework used by the directors during the brainstorming meeting is a holistic approach which sees the organisation as a group of linked processes with each criterion linked to the others.

Evaluation of Dulce's processes

1 Leadership

This area considers our senior leaders' responsibilities, with the aim of creating an organisation which is successful now and in the future. Senior leaders play a central role in communicating and setting values and directions for all stakeholders and creating an organisational focus on action.

We identified in the brainstorming session that Dulce has a strong leadership team but we also need to assess how our senior team leads the organisation and develops plans for the future. An example to support our effective leadership is that the board regularly reviews our mission and aims, which is a key process of effective leadership.

A further key question to ask in relation to our leadership processes is how is Dulce governed and how do we manage our relationships with the wider society? Although in the brainstorming session we identified that we have 'strong governance procedures', in that we follow our government's corporate governance guidelines, we need to analyse this further to understand whether our current governance processes are effective and how effectively we interact with the wider society.

We clearly have processes in place to engage effectively with our customers but we also need to consider other processes which may allow us to engage with all stakeholders, in particular our investors and suppliers. More effective interaction with the wider community may bring positive attention in the wider society and present us with more opportunities to attract new customers.

2 Strategy

This category considers how we develop strategic objectives and action plans, implement them, change them if circumstances require, and measure progress. This category stresses that our organisation's long-term organisational success and competitive environment are key strategic issues which need to be integral parts of overall planning.

This area was not considered as part of our brainstorming session and therefore is an area which requires attention. While we clearly review our vision and mission and undertake strategic planning, how we execute these plans effectively needs to be considered. Given the nature of our market place, as identified in the risk register, our market demands us to be agile and prepared for unexpected change, including volatile economic conditions or changing customer tastes which could impact on our marketplace.

3   Customers

This category requires us to consider how we engage customers for long-term marketplace success, and stresses customer engagement as an important outcome of an overall learning and performance excellence strategy. For Dulce, the voice of the customer will provide meaningful information not only on our customers' views but also on their behaviours and on how these contribute to our current and future success in the industry. Therefore, we need to ask how do we obtain information from customers and how do we engage with customers and build long-term relationships with them?

In the recent brainstorming session, we identified a number of processes which we carry out in relation to our customers, including sending out regular email and promotional offers to customers in order to stimulate interest and loyalty which should assist us in understanding their views and maintain a relationship with customers. Customer surveys are a useful way of engaging with customers to assess and respond to their needs. We also identified training our staff in customer engagement which is likely to be an important process in developing and maintaining customer loyalty and retention and building relationships with our customers.

4   Measurement, analysis and knowledge management

This category is the main point within the criteria for all key information on effectively measuring, analysing, and improving performance and managing organisational knowledge to drive improvement, innovation, and organisational competitiveness. Key to this use of data and information are their quality and availability.

In our brainstorming session, we identified our performance measurement activities relating to key financial, shareholder and customer performance measurement. Importantly, we must consider how useful this information is to us and how we can use it to drive improvement and innovation. We also identified our use of big data analytics which should be a key driver in analysing and understanding key performance information and using this for our competitive advantage (particularly in relation to customer activity and preferences).

5   Workforce

This category addresses key workforce practices. This includes those directed toward creating and maintaining a high-performance environment and those directed toward engaging our staff to enable them and the organisation to adapt to change and succeed.

One of the key questions to evaluate our staff processes is how do we build an effective and supportive workplace? From the brainstorming session, we identified the process of undertaking regular staff training and skills updates, which should help our staff to remain loyal and motivated, which in turn should impact on the quality and innovation of our products.

A second question to consider is how do we engage with staff to achieve a high-performance work environment? From the brainstorming session, we identified the use of annual appraisals and staff surveys which should assist in making staff feel engaged. However, we would need to assess this further by asking staff how far they believe that these performance appraisal and staff surveys assist in their overall engagement in the business. Staff surveys will only assist in achieving performance excellence if staff feel engaged and committed to the process and believe that their opinions are valued and acted on by senior leadership.

Engaged and committed staff throughout our business, from senior management to shop assistants, will drive product innovation and customer engagement and loyalty, assisting in us achieving our strategic aims.

6 Operations

This category asks how do we focus on our organisation's work, product design and delivery, innovation, and operational effectiveness to achieve organisational success now and in the future. Key questions we must ask are how do we design, manage and improve our key products and work processes and how do we ensure effective management of our operations?

From our brainstorming session, we identified the investment we have made in the latest production processes, which should improve our operational effectiveness. Also, investment in e-commerce should assist us in developing and delivering our operations overseas and to new customers. We also identified our regular re-design of products which is a key criterion in our ability to be innovative, in order to continue to satisfy customer needs and build long-term relationships.

7 Results

This category provides a systems focus which encompasses all results necessary to sustain our organisation: our key processes and product results, our customer-focused results, our workforce results, our leadership and governance system results, and our overall financial and market performance. This is not something which we considered in our brainstorming session.

Therefore, we must now capture and measure the 'real-time' information (measures of progress) for evaluating, improving, and innovating processes and products, in alignment with our overall organisational strategy. Using all of the information we have gathered from understanding the importance of the processes we carry out in the previous six areas, we need to now focus on monitoring the outcomes of our operational performance which can then help us to predict our future performance and drive performance excellence throughout our business.

ACCA marking guide	Marks
Up to 2 marks for each point from the brainstorming summary discussed and applied correctly to the Baldrige framework (up to a maximum of 16 marks). If the candidate has NOT used the Baldrige model but has adequately discussed performance excellence in Dulce, using the brainstorming information, then award up to the maximum marks available. However, answers must be centred on performance excellence. Up to a maximum of 16 marks. **Leadership** – Considers senior leaders' responsibilities – senior leaders play central role in communicating/setting values, direction and creating organisational focus on action. – Dulce has strong leadership team but need to assess how senior team leads organisation and develops plans for the future. – Board regularly reviews mission and aims, which is key process of effective leadership. – Brainstorming session identified 'strong governance procedures', but must analyse this further to understand effectiveness of governance processes. – Need to consider processes to engage with all stakeholders, in particular our investors and suppliers. – More effective interaction with the wider community.	

Strategy
- Considers how to develop strategic objectives and action plans, implement them, change them and measure progress.
- Stresses that organisation's long-term organisational success and competitive environment are key strategic issues and integral parts of overall planning.
- This area was not considered in brainstorming session and therefore an area which requires attention.
- How we execute our plans effectively needs to be considered.
- Market demands for Dulce to be agile and prepared for unexpected change, including volatile economic conditions or changing customer tastes.

Customers
- Consider how to engage customers for long-term marketplace success.
- Customer engagement as an important outcome of an overall learning and performance excellence strategy.
- How do we obtain information from customers and how do we engage with customers and build long-term relationships with them?
- In the brainstorming session, identified a number of processes in relation to customers, including regular email and promotional offers.
- Customer surveys useful in engaging with customers to assess/respond to needs.
- Training staff in customer engagement – developing/maintaining customer loyalty and retention and building relationships.

Measurement, analysis and knowledge management
- Measuring, analysing, and improving performance and managing organisational knowledge to drive improvement, innovation, and organisational competitiveness.
- Key to this use of data and information are their quality and availability.
- In brainstorming session, identified performance measurement activities relating to key financial, shareholder and customer performance measurement.
- Consider how useful this information is how to use it to drive improvement and innovation.
- Big data analytics a key driver in analysing and understanding key performance information.

Workforce
- Considers key workforce practices.
- Creating and maintaining high-performance environment directed toward engaging staff.
- How do we build an effective and supportive workplace?
- From brainstorming session, Dulce undertake regular staff training and skills updates.
- How do we engage with staff to achieve a high-performance work environment?
- From the brainstorming session, identified use of annual appraisals and staff surveys to assist staff engagement.
- Need to assess this by asking staff how far they believe these assist in overall engagement.
- Only assist if staff feel engaged and committed to the process and believe opinions are valued and acted on.
- Engaged and committed staff throughout business drive product innovation and customer engagement and loyalty.

Operations
- Considers how we focus on our organisation's work, product design and delivery, innovation, and operational effectiveness to achieve organisational success
- How do we design, manage and improve key products and work processes?
- How do we ensure effective management of our operations?
- From brainstorming session identified investment made in the latest production processes, which should improve our operational effectiveness.
- Investment in e-commerce should assist in developing and delivering operations overseas and to new customers.
- Regular re-design of products key criterion in ability to be innovative, in order to continue to satisfy customer needs and build long-term relationships.

Results
- Considers a systems-focus which encompasses all results necessary to sustain organisation.
- Key processes and product results, customer-focused results, workforce results, leadership and governance system results, and overall financial and market performance
- Not considered in our brainstorming session.
- Must now capture and measure 'real-time' information (measures of progress) for evaluating, improving, and innovating processes and products.
- Need to focus on monitoring the outcomes of operational performance which can help to predict future performance and drive performance excellence.

	—
	16
	—
Professional skills	4
	—
Total	**20**
	—

How well has the candidate demonstrated professional skills as follows:	Not at all	Not so well	Quite well	Very well
Evaluation skills in using professional judgement to appraise objectively the findings and opinions of the directors.	The candidate has failed to demonstrate evaluation skills. The candidate has not effectively appraised the information presented and has merely listed information already given or has presented a purely theoretical answer with no evaluation demonstrated. The candidate has demonstrated poor professional judgement by failing to use an appropriate framework to structure their answer.	The candidate has demonstrated weak evaluation skills. The candidate has shown limited professional judgement in appraising the information provided but has used an appropriate framework. However, the candidate has not used the framework appropriately to evaluate the findings of the board members in the most effective way. They have demonstrated weak judgement of the findings of the board members in relation to performance excellence.	The candidate has demonstrated good evaluation skills. The candidate has shown good professional judgement in selecting and applying a suitable framework to evaluate the findings of the board members. The candidate has made some reasonable assertions in their appraisal of the findings and has demonstrated in a number of areas effective judgement of the findings of the board members in relation to performance excellence.	The candidate has demonstrated excellent evaluation skills. The candidate has shown excellent professional judgement in selecting and applying effectively a suitable framework to evaluate the findings of the board members. The candidate has made sound and very well justified assertions and has demonstrated clear and objective judgement of the findings of the board members in relation to performance excellence.
	0	**1**	**2**	**4**

Section 17

REAL EXAM QUESTIONS – MARCH 2020

1   OVERVIEW

Techthere4U Co (TT4U) is a firm of information technology consultants founded 20 years ago. Initially offering advice on computer efficiency and security, the company has expanded to offer a range of services, including technology support and data hosting. It currently employs 75 staff members which have grown from six since its establishment.

TT4U has based its success in the past on its good knowledge of clients' businesses and its ability to match the solutions it provides with business requirements. TT4U has had a diverse client base, operating in a wide variety of industry sectors.

The four consultants who initially founded the company remain on the board in key executive roles. The board is constituted as follows:

Board role	Comments
Chairman and non-executive director	Appointed two years ago, partner in a large law firm
Chief executive officer (CEO)	Original founder
Services director (SD)	Original founder, leads TT4U's team for smaller businesses
Marketing director (MD)	Original founder, leads TT4U's team for larger businesses
Information technology director (ITD)	Original founder, leads TT4U's public sector team
Finance director (FD)	Appointed four years ago
Non-executive director	Appointed two years ago, former partner of a large accountancy firm

Below board level, operational staff are allocated to one of the three teams serving particular types of client. Teams are led by the relevant founder-director for that team.

Two years ago, the company achieved a listing on its national stock exchange for smaller companies. TT4U is compliant with the corporate governance code enforced by this stock exchange. The founder-directors continue to own a majority of shares, but the company now also has external shareholders. Some of these external shareholders have indicated that they would like to see the company achieve a full listing on the main national stock exchange within three years.

TT4U's CEO believes that TT4U needs to undergo an internal transformation in order to be able to retain current clients and deliver the expansion required to obtain a full listing. She believes that the company's current structures are now insufficient to respond quickly enough to changes in the external environment and meet clients' evolving demands.

TT4U's board has decided to engage an external consultancy firm, Stubfield, to help in evaluating various strategic options and advising on decisions. You are the leader of the team from Stubfield, responsible for producing sections of a report and various other documents.

The following exhibits provide information relevant to the case study.

Exhibit 1: Transcript of directors' meeting about issues to be discussed with Stubfield consultants.

Exhibit 2: Summary of Mieobed client approach devised by Business Tomorrow magazine.

Exhibit 3: Blog on IT consultancy sector on Business Tomorrow magazine website.

Exhibit 4: Extract of results of client survey.

Exhibit 5: Discussion of threatening letter about TT4U's largest client, Rex Investments.

Exhibit 6: Appraisal of cloud services investment prepared by the recently appointed assistant to the finance director.

The case requirements are included in the tasks below:

1 TT4U's chief executive officer is concerned about the possibility that major contracts will not be won or renewed and would like your views on what the main risks are for TT4U.

   Required:

   (a) **Prepare briefing notes for the board which analyse the main risks which threaten TT4U being awarded new contracts and retaining current contracts.** **(8 marks)**

   Professional skills marks are available for demonstrating analysis skills in establishing the risks relating to TT4U. **(2 marks)**

   At the recent directors' meeting, the information technology director proposed that TT4U should develop new services in relation to the Internet-of-things. The services director proposed that TT4U should focus on winning more government sector work. The chief executive officer wants your report to include consideration of these two strategic options.

   Required:

   (b) **Prepare a section of your report which evaluates the two strategic options proposed by the directors.** **(12 marks)**

   Professional skills marks are available for demonstrating evaluation skills in using professional judgement to objectively appraise the two strategic options proposed by the directors. **(4 marks)**

   TT4U's chief executive officer would like to have an independent external view on what was discussed at the meeting about the threatening letter. In particular, she doubts the views of the marketing director that TT4U can simply rely on its data controls. She is also uncertain whether TT4U should disclose nothing to Rex Investments, as the marketing director suggested.

   Required:

   (c) **Prepare a confidential email for the chief executive officer which:**

   - **advises on the actions which TT4U can take to ensure that the controls on the confidentiality of data operate effectively; and**

   - **discusses the risks and ethical issues relating to communicating the threat to the client, Rex Investments.** **(12 marks)**

   Professional skills marks are available for demonstrating scepticism skills in challenging the views of the marketing director. **(3 marks)**

(Total: 41 marks)

2   The assistant to the finance director has prepared a summary of the investment appraisal of the planned development of TT4U's cloud-based services. The chief executive officer has given you a summary of the analysis which has been prepared, as she is unsure whether it is satisfactory. She also wants you to brief the board on how the new services should be e-marketed.

Required:

(a)   **Prepare a section of your report which critically evaluates the investment appraisal produced by the finance director's assistant.** **(8 marks)**

Professional skills marks are available for demonstrating scepticism skills in questioning the investment appraisal prepared by the finance director's assistant. **(2 marks)**

(b)   **Prepare briefing notes for the next board meeting which recommend how e-marketing can be used to attract and retain clients for TT4U's new cloud-based services.** **(10 marks)**

Professional skills marks are available for demonstrating commercial acumen skills by showing awareness of effective methods for e-marketing the new cloud-based services. **(3 marks)**

(Total: 23 marks)

3   The chief executive officer believes that TT4U's current structure will have to change if TT4U is to introduce the new Mieobed approach to client relationships successfully. The chief executive officer knows that she must take ownership of the transformation. She feels, however, that she needs guidance on the transformation process and how she should lead this process, including communicating the need for change to employees.

Required:

(a)   **Prepare an email for the chief executive officer which advises her on the responsibilities and activities involved in preparing for and implementing the transformation of TT4U effectively.** **(10 marks)**

(b)   **Prepare a letter to all employees, which will be signed by the chief executive officer, explaining:**

–   **the benefits of implementing the new Mieobed approach for TT4U and its employees; and**

–   **the main changes to team structures and behaviours below board level which the new Mieobed approach will require.** **(10 marks)**

Professional skills marks are available for demonstrating communication skills in persuading employees of the benefits of TT4U adopting the new approach in its working practices. **(3 marks)**

The chairman wants the board to be briefed on aspects of corporate governance which need to change if the new Mieobed approach to client relationships is to be introduced successfully.

Required:

(a) Prepare briefing notes which advise the board on the changes required to:

– the membership of the board; and

– the information supplied to the board

to reflect TT4U's developing business needs and to make TT4U more responsive to its clients' needs. **(10 marks)**

Professional skills marks are available for demonstrating commercial acumen skills in identifying changes to the membership of the board and information supplied which are realistic for TT4U and will generate better relationships with clients. **(3 marks)**

(Total: 36 marks)

Exhibit 1: Transcript of directors' meeting about issues to be discussed with Stubfield consultants

Chief executive officer (CEO)	I've called this meeting to discuss the areas that we want Stubfield consultants to consider. I know that some of you feel that Stubfield will be looking at areas of our business where we shouldn't need advice and that they may exceed their remit.
	Nevertheless, some of our investors have communicated the view that we need external advice about our business. They feel that we're too reliant on existing business from our long-term clients. We should be providing more new services and winning new clients.
	We've advanced discussions on developing our new cloud-based services. This will enable us to extend the cloud-based services we provide. You'll recall these include provision of private clouds for specific clients and cloud integration services, enabling clients to connect their data and applications and give them more flexible access to their data resources. We have available an appraisal of our planned investment.
Finance director (FD)	As you're aware, I've been on sick leave so didn't prepare the appraisal myself. Johan, who recently joined the department to assist me, carried out the appraisal. I haven't reviewed the appraisal in detail yet. However, I see at a glance that the payback period is just outside the three-year limit that we set.
Marketing director (MD)	I had hoped to come today with some proposals for marketing the cloud-based services. However, I've been spending a lot of time dealing with Rex Investments, which, as you know, is a very difficult client. I think our launch of these services must make a big impact as a means of attracting the new business we need for expansion.
CEO	As you remember, I asked for suggestions from yourselves about areas where we can expand further. I've received two proposals, one relating to the Internet-of-things and the other to government sector work.

IT director (ITD)	We need to look beyond cloud-based services and expand in an area where we can show we can provide fresh solutions. I'd be very excited about us developing more expertise and services relating to the Internet-of-things. There is massive potential for extending internet connectivity beyond standard devices to everyday objects, such as household appliances, and making the most of the data they can generate. There are so many possible sectors – health, construction, transport, agriculture – where there are opportunities that we can explore.
Services director (SD)	I think we should focus on winning more government sector work. A lot more is available now and we already have some work on which we can build. We have the size and range of services to be looking at winning much larger contracts. I believe we are in a position to become a trusted partner for government. The government sector is less demanding of innovation than the private sector. It is therefore a lower risk option for us, as we can secure the contracts by strong service performance without the risks attached to market leadership in new services.
CEO	Now I would like us to consider the issues raised by the recent client survey. I very much regret that we haven't carried out a survey like this for some years. For me, it highlights the need to transform our business to bring our clients much closer to us.
	I intend that we should move forward by adopting the Mieobed approach to engaging with client stakeholders in our sector, which Business Tomorrow magazine devised. The approach is based on building open and sharing relationships with clients that help them create new sources of value for their business.
SD	I assume you'll be considering how staff should be persuaded to buy into the transformation before the new approach is implemented.
CEO	I shall, and I shall also be looking at how we operate as a board. Three directors currently combine board responsibilities with operational line management of teams. This is a model which we've had since we started, but it may not be appropriate any more. I also want to look at the way TT4U is structured as a whole. I think we ought to be much more of a matrix organisation, which should result in better communication and mutual learning.
SD	I certainly agree internal communication could be improved. I know staff are told not to sit at the same desks each day, but to sit at different desks next to different people. However, we all know the three teams sit in the same areas each day, separate from each other. We have our intranet, but the lack of contributions from staff on it is embarrassing.

MD	I think we need to go much further than having one-off client surveys. We need to be considering the current state of relationships with clients as an agenda item at every board meeting. We have to develop key performance indicators beyond clients gained and lost each period, so that we have a better idea of how we are performing in the areas that most affect client satisfaction.
	We must also consider how we are perceived in relation to our competitors. Although we do have a regular report on competitors' new product offerings, that doesn't tell us how satisfied our clients are with our services in comparison with the services our competitors offer.
CEO	Thank you for your contributions. I shall ask Stubfield for their views on the risks that we face and the strategic options that we've discussed, as well as how we can introduce the Mieobed approach successfully.

Exhibit 2: Summary of Mieobed client approach devised by *Business Tomorrow* magazine

M	ission-driven	Driving strategy and attracting client stakeholders by a strong mission
I	nteractive	Participation of client stakeholders enhancing our organisation and theirs
E	mpowering	Enabling client stakeholders to realise personal and organisational potential
O	pen	Building on the knowledge and experience of client stakeholders by sharing and collaborating
B	oundaryless	Taking client stakeholders on a journey beyond existing boundaries, to transform their operations and unlock value in new areas
E	thical	Founding client stakeholder relationships on responsiveness, fairness, honesty, responsibility and transparency
D	ata-focused	Maintaining tight security of client stakeholder data whilst enhancing its accessibility

Exhibit 3: Blog on IT consultancy sector on Business Tomorrow magazine website

Business Tomorrow

Not just services, but service By Abby Urquhart

How can IT consultants stand out?

IT consultants are struggling to come to terms with what their clients take for granted. The days when they can sell themselves on the basis of being practical business advisers rather than IT experts are long over. Consultants need not bother tendering for work unless they can combine strong client and business sector knowledge with awareness of the latest applications.

Is leading innovation in cloud-based services the way forward?

Anyone who is marketing themselves as having distinctive capabilities in helping clients set up on the cloud has clearly been left well behind. Clients are now expecting the full package of cloud maximisation services.

Is the Internet-of-things an area firms can develop?

The Internet-of-things, extending connectivity and networks to traditionally non-internet connected objects such as cars and household lights, has been the next big development for some time. However, a number of sectors have clear needs for enhanced communication and monitoring. The medical sector has been eager for applications which enable remote health monitoring and notifications if emergencies arise. The building sector has been keen to develop devices which oversee electronic systems within homes and offices to detect fire risk or wasteful energy usage.

Involvement though remains risky. Development is driven more by technology than its usefulness for business transformation. There are also the security and surveillance concerns, the dislike of being watched by inanimate objects.

Is client service still important?

Business Tomorrow's recent survey suggests that client service remains a problem for many consultants. Our survey shows that the consultants who are responsive, who use business approaches of client participation and mutual development like Business Tomorrow's Mieobed approach, are making the largest profits.

What business is available for firms providing top-class service?

Lots of work. There are more longer-term government sector contracts available than ever before. These contracts won't be won or retained if firms don't meet government's ever-stricter service requirements. Ultimately firms cannot take for granted any of their clients' continued business. Many firms have seen long-term relationships with clients end recently. The loyal client, previously prepared to put up with less than excellent service, no longer exists.

👍 Like 85   👎 Dislike 9

Comments (2)

Ken Yardley: Firms I've dealt with often don't seem to get the basics of communication right. They don't answer their phones. They don't respond to emails within 24 hours. They don't listen to what I'm asking or telling them.

Xin Chan: The reason why Internet-of-things hasn't developed as quickly as expected is that many applications don't survive the pilot stage, since many businesses' systems are not able to cope.

Exhibit 4: Extract of results of client survey

TT4U		%	Comments
Service provision flexibility	Excellent	17	'Service provision was exceptionally good when they first started advising us. But now we just seem to be getting the basic service.'
	Good	56	
	Average	16	
	Poor	11	
Innovation	Excellent	9	'TT4U seems good at, and comfortable with, providing the same services that it has always provided. If I wanted new services, I'd certainly go elsewhere.'
	Good	57	
	Average	22	
	Poor	12	
Information provision	Excellent	20	'For an IT consultancy, its website is really poor – it lacks detailed information about services, difficult to navigate.'
	Good	53	
	Average	20	'Its website does look old-fashioned and hasn't changed much for ages. It's noticeable that other consultants' websites are interactive and appear to evolve in response to what users want.'
	Poor	7	
			'They don't make enough use of messaging and social media.'
			'How much you're told about what they're doing seems to depend on the staff involved.'
Staff			
Knowledge	Excellent	41	'They appear to know our business well and how to make best use of the technologies we have.'
	Good	38	
	Average	15	'I've marked them down because they don't appear to know about their own services. I've asked staff on various occasions about other services I know TT4U provides and they have had to ring round the office for an answer.'
	Poor	6	
Responsiveness	Excellent	20	'Emails are never answered the same day.'
	Good	30	'They often answer the question they wished you'd asked rather than the question you did ask.'
	Average	28	
	Poor	22	'You know you can always talk to the services director when you need to. I like how he's always kept in touch with us.'

Proactiveness	Excellent	16	'We call them, they never call us.'
	Good	47	'I would have liked them to have told us that we needed to invest in new systems before our old systems became too slow and unreliable.'
	Average	22	
	Poor	15	'Some staff members really make you feel you're working with them as a team. It's not consistent across the whole company, sadly.'

Exhibit 5: Discussion of threatening letter about TT4U's largest client, Rex Investments

IT director (ITD)	We've had an anonymous threat to reveal confidential data on Rex Investments unless we pay $20,000.
Marketing director (MD)	Surely we've received threats like this before and nothing has come of them?
ITD	We have, but this is a much more specific threat. It is quite detailed about the data. We do hold the data and it is confidential.
MD	We must have all the necessary controls in place – anti-virus software, passwords, etc.
ITD	I'm confident that the controls we need are there.
MD	Then we don't need to pursue this further. Whoever's making the threats didn't get the information from us. We're computer consultants. Of course we have complete and fully-functioning controls. The one thing I'd say is that we shouldn't tell Rex Investments about this. As you know, they are our largest client. Relations with them are difficult enough at the present. If we tell them, it shows we don't believe our own systems are secure. It will give them a very good reason to terminate our contract.
Chief executive officer (CEO)	I nevertheless believe that this could be a serious risk for us. I don't think we can just say that we have controls. We need to have strong assurance they are operating as they should be. If our controls haven't been working, we have to try to detect who's accessed the information. I'll ask Stubfield for views on these issues.

Exhibit 6: Appraisal of cloud services investment prepared by recently appointed assistant to the finance director

Net present value calculation

Year		0	1	2	3	4
	Note	$000	$000	$000	$000	$000
Sales	1		8,000	10,250	13,250	15,500
Contribution	2		4,400	5,638	7,288	8,525
Marketing costs	3		(600)	(769)	(994)	(994)
Other fixed costs			(900)	(900)	(900)	(900)
Pre-tax cash flows		0	2,900	3,969	5,394	6,631
Taxation paid	4		(725)	(992)	(1,349)	(1,658)
Post-tax cash flows			2,175	2,977	4,045	4,973
Investment		(10,000)				
Terminal value	5					1,500
Cash flows		(10,000)	2,175	2,977	4,045	6,473
Discount factor	6	1.000	0.943	0.890	0.840	0.792
Discounted cash flows		(10,000)	2,051	2,650	3,398	5,127
Net present value years 1–4		3,226				
Net present value years 5–10	7	23,632				

Notes:

1 Sales are based on expected increases in markets, clients served and prices.

2 Contribution is assumed to be 55% of revenue each year in line with current margins.

3 Marketing costs are assumed to increase in line with sales up to year 3.

4 Tax rate is 25% of pre-tax cash flows.

5 Terminal value represents assumed realisable value if services are no longer viable after four years.

6 Discount factor of 6% is after-tax interest rate on current long-term loans, as this project is to be financed by a long-term loan.

7 Year 5–10 figure is post-tax discounted cash flow for year 4 multiplied by six.

Payback calculation

Year	0	1	2	3	4
	$000	$000	$000	$000	$000
Cash flow	(10,000)	2,175	2,977	4,045	6,473
Cumulative	(10,000)	(7,825)	(4,848)	(803)	5,670

Payback = 3 years + (803/(803 + 5,670)) × 12 months = 3 years 1 month

Comments:

1   Project shows a positive present value after four years and a much greater present value if the services can be offered in their current form beyond four years.

2   The payback period is slightly greater than the target set by the directors, which suggests the project should be rejected.

3   Nevertheless, sensitivity analysis should be carried out to determine the probability of loss and hence whether the project should be undertaken in its current form.

REAL EXAM ANSWERS – MARCH 2020

1 (a) Briefing notes on risks to contracts

These notes deal with the main risks which may affect Techthere4U Co (TT4U) winning and retaining contracts.

Strategic

The fundamental strategic risk is failure to fulfil clients' evolving demands, resulting ultimately in loss of contracts and decline in revenues. Aspects of this risk include lack of awareness of what clients want. There may also be a lack of resources to respond to client demands for new services or better provision of existing services. There is possibly a lack of high-level awareness of recent developments, as there have been no recent appointees from the IT industry to the board.

The risk is also related to competitor actions, of competitors providing new services first or having a business model which provides better awareness of client demands and standards of client care. TT4U has traditionally not differentiated itself from competitors by offering new services first, but early development of new services may be a critical factor in winning new work. The results of the survey suggest that some clients believe that there is a lack of commitment to innovation.

Operational

In the client survey, responsiveness to clients, internal knowledge, communication and flexibility are all criticised. Methods of communication with clients seem old-fashioned and the website is criticised for being poorly designed. If operations are poor, these may be hygiene factors which influence clients' contract renewal decisions.

An important selling point of cloud-based services which TT4U plans to offer is flexibility and ease of use. If the cloud is difficult to access in many places or there are frequent interruptions of service, TT4U will not be providing perhaps the most important deliverable.

Key person

Key person risk particularly applies to the founder executive directors, given their central place in TT4U throughout its history and the contacts they have built up. The departure of any of them could be seen as indicating that TT4U is undergoing a period of instability. Other staff may have particular close relations with some clients or expertise which may adversely impact TT4U if it was lost, particularly if they joined competitors.

Competition

TT4U may be less visible than other firms. Competitors may be attracting more business by better use of online tools such as search optimisation or better generation of publicity about the services which they are offering. The comments in the survey suggest that clients find TT4U's website poor and believe the company is not making enough use of other media.

Data

All the data management services provided by TT4U, not just those on the cloud, generate risks of loss to their clients. These include the risks of loss or corruption of data, whether due to accident or deliberate action by hackers. There is also the risk of confidential data being accessed by unauthorised users, and publicised or used for illicit advantage.

Reputation

Bad publicity about the services TT4U offers or the public loss of important clients can affect reputation. It may be particularly serious if TT4U is associated with a major problem, for example, a leakage of confidential data. Reputation risk can also relate to criticisms that TT4U is generally not providing a good service. The article highlights important features of service and the client survey indicates TT4U has problems in some of these areas. If these problems are publicised online by users, this can erode confidence in what TT4U offers.

(b) **Extract from report on the two proposed strategic options**

Introduction

This section considers the two proposed strategic options put forward by the services and information technology directors.

Internet-of-things development

Advantages of strategy

Developing services in relation to the Internet-of-things has been highlighted by the recent article as a potential means of rapid growth through market development, fulfilling the desire of investors for the company to expand. Finding a niche and being able to innovate in it could enhance TT4U's wider reputation.

Some of the problems in relation to Internet-of-things development appear to be an over-concentration on technology rather than business requirements. Matching business needs with available business technology has been a core competence for TT4U in the past. Adoption of the Mieobed approach with its focus on enhanced understanding of clients' requirements to help them transform their business would seem compatible with this new development.

Concerns with strategy

However, commitment to particular markets may be risky for TT4U. It has traditionally had a diversified client base, and commitment to particular sectors may require significant investment without necessarily guaranteeing success. If, for example, TT4U wants to provide data hosting services in connection with the data generated by the Internet-of-things, it may need enhanced capacity to process and store the data. If TT4U is to be an early mover, there may be problems with the reliability of the technology.

Whatever the sector chosen, TT4U may need to recruit staff with previous experience in work connected with the Internet-of-things. This may be costly, but may bring to TT4U valuable new expertise at a time when TT4U is looking generally to develop staff expertise by sharing knowledge and experience.

There could be problems with selling services to existing clients. The technology may be of limited application to TT4U's current client base. They may lack the system capabilities to develop effectively and problems could damage TT4U's standing with them.

Risks relating to security and also privacy have also been highlighted. Depending on which services TT4U offers, it may be more vulnerable to security breaches and also breaches of privacy regulations than for other services. These may result in legal penalties and significant threats to reputation.

Government sector development

Advantages of strategy

The policy of seeking more contracts in the government sector represents a form of market development if contracts are to be obtained from more bodies. Seeking more contracts systematically would represent a more coherent strategy in this area as contracts won previously appear to have been on a one-off basis. Winning more contracts can lead to 'success breeding success' with the target of becoming a preferred supplier to the government sector.

Many opportunities appear likely to become available soon in the government sector. Having been successful at fulfilling smaller contracts for this sector, TT4U seems well-placed to seek larger contracts as it expands.

The contracts available will represent a cash stream which should be guaranteed for a number of years. This can be set off against shorter-term private sector work which may be more vulnerable to economic downturn. Some of the contracts will be high profile, so winning them can provide good publicity for TT4U.

Concerns with strategy

Possible issues with the work include profitability. Whatever the exact priorities, government sector work will be concerned with the 3Es – economy, efficiency and effectiveness. Because of the desire to meet economy targets, the margins available on the work may be lower than on commercial contracts. Serving the government sector effectively may also require investment in staff who possess knowledge of the sector being served, for example, education.

As noted above, public sector work is high profile. If there are major problems with contracts and these are publicised and blamed on TT4U, the company's reputation could suffer seriously.

The argument that needing to provide innovative services will be less of an issue in the government sector may have some substance. However, one of the key aspects of the Mieobed approach is encouraging clients to unlock value (for themselves and TT4U) in new fields of business development. The public sector may offer limited opportunities for that approach.

Operating the Mieobed stakeholder approach may be more complex in the government sector because of the different stakeholders with differing objectives. The priorities of the government officials with whom TT4U deals may change if there is a change of government and new conditions may be imposed.

Governments may use a number of strict indicators relating to value for money which TT4U has to fulfil. It may mean a greater demand for resources and opportunity costs in taking staff away from other work. Fulfilling government requirements will mean that TT4U has to address quickly some of the service issues identified in the client survey.

Conclusion

If the proposals are not mutually exclusive, TT4U may consider investing in both of them. They represent different types of development, so improving diversification, and have different risk-return profiles. Investing in the Internet-of-things is high risk but could generate high earnings. Investment in public sector work could provide steady cash flows to help fund investment in other areas.

(c)   **Email**

To: **Chief executive**

From: **Consultant**

Date: **1 March 20X0**

Subject: **Response to threat to reveal information**

Dear CEO

You asked me as someone outside the company to give my views on the controls which are significant in relation to threats to data and also the comments made by the directors about the threat to reveal confidential information.

Control issues

You rightly believe that TT4U cannot just say it has complete confidence in its controls and not give the issue further consideration. TT4U has a fiduciary duty to take sufficient care to ensure confidential data remains secret. In addition, clients are very sensitive about the growing threat of cybercrime, indeed TT4U advises them on how to combat it. If it became public that TT4U had been the victim of cybercrime through poor data protection practices, the loss of credibility for TT4U would potentially represent a big risk to income from existing and new services.

I have no reason to doubt what the director says about the procedures already being in place. Given that TT4U is advising clients on implementation of these procedures, it would be worrying if TT4U did not have them in place itself. However, you are right that there is a distinction between having the controls in place and the controls operating effectively. It is possible that lack of care or complacency may undermine the operation of important controls.

Even though TT4U has a system of access controls in place, this may be undermined by staff being careless with their password security. More regular changing of passwords may reduce this threat. TT4U should also review who has access to which parts of the system and restrict permissions for staff so that they have the minimum of access rights which they require to carry out their work. Access rights to the system must also be immediately terminated as soon as someone leaves TT4U.

Regular reminders to staff can help reduce complacency. This may particularly apply to having effective procedures to protect laptops taken away from the office. These should have the same level of protection as devices kept in-house, including having anti-hacking protection as well as anti-virus software. They must be updated at the same time as in-house computers. Staff should also be told to avoid poor data security practices, for example, forbidding them to copy sensitive data onto memory sticks.

As regards detection of someone obtaining information illicitly, you should start by looking at past and present staff who were able to access this data and considering whether there are any unusual or suspicious factors in relation to them. I assume the system logs failed attempts to log on, and this must be regularly reviewed in case any patterns appear to be emerging. You need also to ensure you understand what represents 'normal' use of the system, which acts as a yardstick to use to detect unusual patterns of use, for example, copying of large amounts of data.

Threat to reveal confidential information

Even if you have complete confidence in the control system, the threat cannot be brushed off, as the person contacting you has clearly illicitly obtained specific information and may be threatening other companies. You should consider contacting the authorities as they may be able to link the threats in with other cases. The authorities may insist on the client being informed. You should not pay the sum demanded, as this is unethical and could lead to further threats.

There is a risk that Rex Investments' confidence in TT4U may be undermined if it is told about this threat. I appreciate concerns have been raised about client relations and it is quite possible that the client will ask for additional assurance on the controls which you operate.

However, the risks relating to not telling Rex Investments are greater. Disclosure of the information from other sources may permanently damage the relationship and may provide Rex Investments with a reason to terminate the contract. Bad publicity relating to this disclosure may mean other clients do not wish to use the data services you provide. It is likely to threaten the success of the investment in the cloud-based services. More fundamentally, one aspect of the Mieobed approach which you are planning to introduce is data security.

Following the ethical principles of honesty and transparency would also suggest informing the client of a threat to its data. Again, I refer to Mieobed, which is underpinned by the process of open communication with clients. Failing to tell the client about this threat would suggest that TT4U is not taking the Mieobed approach seriously.

Lastly, it is possible that the person making the threats did not obtain the information from your systems but from Rex Investments. A further ethical reason for informing Rex Investments is that it may help in detecting who is making the threat and perhaps also highlight to the client shortcomings in their own procedures for keeping information confidential.

Please contact me if you want to discuss these issues further.

Regards

Stubfield

ACCA marking guide		Marks
(a)	Up to 2 marks for each risk discussed.	
	Risks can include:	
	– Strategic	
	– Operational	
	– Key person	
	– Marketing	
	– Access problems	
	– Data threats	
	– Reputation	
	(Up to a maximum of 8 marks in total)	
		8
	Professional skills	2
(b)	Up to 2 marks per relevant point.	
	Up to 7 marks for discussion of each of the two options, within that up to 4 marks for discussion of advantages of pursuing the strategy and up to 4 marks for discussion of concerns with the strategy.	
	Internet-of-things	
	Advantages can include:	
	– Easy means of expanding the company	
	– Enhancing reputation for innovation	
	Concerns can include:	
	– Over-commitment	
	– Need for expert staff	
	– Problems with client systems	
	– Data and security risks	

Government sector

Advantages can include:

- Coherent approach to area where one-off success has been achieved
- Availability of opportunities
- Guaranteed cash stream

Concerns can include:

- Low profit margins
- Compatibility with other strategies
- Reputation risk
- Requirements of different stakeholders
- Government targets

(Up to a maximum of 12 marks in total)

———

12

———

Professional skills

4

———

(c) Up to 4 marks for prevention controls, can include:

- Passwords
- Limitation of access
- Procedures for mobile devices
- Configurations used

Up to 3 marks for detection controls, can include:

- Review of staff who have left
- Review failed attempts to log on
- Review for unusual activity

Up to 3 marks for risk issues relating to communicating with the client, can include:

- Weakening client's trust
- Client reaction if information is disclosed
- Reputation risk if made public

Up to 3 marks for ethical issues relating to communicating with the client, can include:

- Complying with authority's demands
- Honesty/transparency
- Compatibility with policy (Mieobed)
- Help detection

(Up to a maximum of 12 marks in total)

———

12

———

Professional skills

3

———

Total

41

———

Professional skills may be additionally rewarded as in the following rubric:

How well has the candidate demonstrated professional skills as follows:	Not at all	Not so well	Quite well	Very well
1 (a) Analysis skills in establishing the risks relating to TT4U. (Briefing notes)	The candidate has provided a generic list of risks which are not linked to the information given in the exhibits.	Some of the risks discussed by the candidate are supported by information in the exhibits. However, the significance of most of the risks in relation to TT4U's winning and retaining contracts is not clearly shown.	Most of the risks discussed are linked to data in the exhibits and the answer shows how they may affect TT4U's winning and retaining contracts. The answer is in the correct format.	The answer is constructed round riskswhich will be important for TT4U winning and retaining contracts. The significance of these risks is clearly explained and is supported by data taken from the exhibits. The answer is in the correct format.
	0	0.66	1.33	2
1 (b) Evaluation skills in using professional judgement to appraise objectively the two strategic options proposed by the directors. (Report section)	The candidate has only discussed one of the options. The candidate has discussed both options but not considered both the advantages and concerns. The discussion is not related to TT4U's positioning or organisational implications.	The candidate has discussed both options and made some attempt to discuss advantages and concerns. However, the discussion lacks focus on TT4U's competitive position and there is little discussion of the organisational implications for TT4U.	The candidate has provided a reasonably balanced discussion of both options. The discussion makes reference to the wider implications for TT4U's positioning and the organisational developments which will be needed. The answer is in the correct format.	The candidate has provided a well-balanced discussion of both options. The discussion shows both options clearly in the wider organisational and competitive context. The answer is in the correct format.
	0	1.33	2.66	4

How well has the candidate demonstrated professional skills as follows:	Not at all	Not so well	Quite well	Very well
1 (c) Scepticism in challenging the views of the marketing director. (Confidential email)	The candidate has only discussed risk or ethical issues. Discussion is purely in general or theoretical terms with no relation to TT4U's circumstances.	The candidate has discussed risk and ethical issues. The candidate has failed to consider both the risks of disclosure and non-disclosure. The discussion of ethics is mostly theoretical, with limited relation to TT4U's circumstances.	The candidate has discussed risk and ethical issues. The answer shows awareness of both risks of disclosure and non-disclosure. The discussion on ethics shows how broad ethical principles can be applied to TT4U's circumstances. The answer is in the correct format.	The candidate has discussed risk and ethical issues. The answer gives a clear explanation of the risks of disclosure and non-disclosure. The discussion on ethics is based round TT4U's situation, using general ethical principles as appropriate to support the analysis. The answer is in the correct format.
	0	**1**	**2**	**3**

2 (a) Extract from report on summary of investment appraisal of new cloud-based services

Introduction

This section examines the issues connected with the summary which has been prepared and recommends improvements and areas where further detail is required.

Net present value calculation

Sales

Having a single sales revenue figure, even if this is a summary, is quite inadequate and the comment about the drivers of sale increases is unhelpful. There is no justification for the varying % of sales increases; splitting the figure down by the services offered, at a minimum distinguishing the revenue from the provision of private cloud services from cloud integration services, will give a better picture of how increasing the services offered may lead to revenue increases over time. The assumption about increased client base needs to be linked to how new services are to be marketed, and how much the focus will be on winning new clients as opposed to selling additional services to current clients. TT4U is operating in a very competitive market for cloud services, so any assumptions about being able to increase prices are doubtful.

Contribution

If different services are provided, contribution may vary on them. A figure chosen may do as a broad estimate, if it is the sort of margin which TT4U has been generating recently. However, there is no detail about variable costs. These may change over time as the service offered becomes more mature and the cost per client of providing each service falls.

Other costs

The marketing costs will depend on when new services are introduced. If they are introduced gradually over the three-year period, the estimates may be reasonable. However, if most of the services are being introduced soon, marketing is likely to peak in year 1. The fixed costs figure appears to be a general estimate. No justification is given as to why the figure is unchanged over time. In addition, the figure is sufficiently large to need breaking down into different elements and clarifying the assumptions for each element.

Tax and working capital

Using the current tax rate is a reasonable assumption if it is not expected to change much in the next few years. However, the figure does not take account of any allowances which may be available on the investment expenditure. It would also be likely that the investment would require some working capital and this needs to be brought into the calculation.

Investment

If services are likely to be developed over the next few years, then a single immediate figure for investment at the start will not be realistic. The realisable value given at year 4 lacks justification. It is difficult to see what would be realised and whether it would have any value, given the fast-changing nature of the industry.

If the net present value figure is extended to year 10, the realisable value should be excluded from the calculation as the investment is not finishing at year 4. Taking the post-tax cash flow at year 4 and using a multiple of 6 as the basis for years 5–10 has not been justified. The figure used should be discounted at the relevant discount factor for each year, not the discount factor for year 4. It is ultimately, however, questionable whether the investment should be extended to 10 years, as this seems a long period for an investment in fast-changing IT.

Discount rate

The discount rate used is incorrect. The weighted average cost of capital should be used if business and financial risk remain at the same levels. This is likely to be higher than the cost of debt, since equity has a higher cost than debt, meaning the net present value will be smaller. If either risk changes significantly, a project-specific cost of capital should be used.

Payback period calculation

The approach taken to calculate the payback period is correct, although the figures may not be reliable due to the concerns raised above. Net present value is theoretically the best method to determine whether an investment should be undertaken. However, payback can be used as an initial indication if directors are uncertain about the timeframe over which the investment will be profitable and want to ensure it is recouped quickly. The investment is only marginally outside the payback period and the uncertainties connected with the figures suggest the investment should not necessarily be rejected because it fails to meet the payback criterion.

Sensitivity analysis

The summary is incorrect in saying that sensitivity analysis will show the probability of making a loss. It will just show the amount by which figures need to change for the investment to make a loss. Sensitivity analysis also treats individual figures as independent variables, whereas there may be connections between them (for example, between revenue and marketing expenditure) or the same factors may affect more than one variable (for example, competitor response affecting income from more than one service). Scenario analysis, showing results under different optimistic/pessimistic outcomes, is likely to be more valuable.

Conclusion

The project's failure to meet the payback target period should not by itself lead to the project being rejected. The decision should be primarily based on a revised NPV calculation using the correct cost of capital and re-considering the assumptions. If the revised NPV calculation shows a positive present value for years 1–4 only, the board should consider accepting the project.

(b)   Briefing notes for board meeting

E-marketing cloud-computing services

The purpose of these notes is to discuss ways in which e-marketing can be used to promote the new services. The notes will be a combination of new ideas and methods which TT4U is already using, but should review and may need to enhance. The notes also show how the methods should be used within a framework of attracting and retaining clients.

(i)   Attracting clients

Reaching potential clients

TT4U may look at whether its search engine positioning needs to be improved. Possibly the launch of new services is the time to make use or more use of methods such as banner advertising. TT4U needs to consider the branding messages the advertising will promote, possibly separately branding the new services from TT4U's existing business.

Interesting potential clients

TT4U should look to make the most of methods such as tweeting or Facebook pages to promote interest in its new services. Social media postings could cover concerns clients have, for example, about the lack of connectivity between data holdings, which TT4U's new services will address. Social media can also promote TT4U's expertise by providing opinions or guidance from a director or employee.

The information about the new services on TT4U's website needs to indicate clearly the ways TT4U's services will provide maximisation of value for clients and the unique selling points which TT4U's services have. It needs to show clearly that it is addressing what is of interest to potential clients by, for example, providing answers to frequently asked questions about cloud services. Infrastructure issues should be regarded as a priority, as the ability to search the site easily can help keep users interested and prompt them to revisit the website.

TT4U then needs to make sure it makes maximum use of the data it has about website visitors to develop its website continuously. The pattern of clicks will help establish what particularly interests different visitors. Questionnaires about what visitors are interested in can be used to see how to develop content further, for example, in greater emphasis on data management and hosting.

Gaining potential clients

Turning users into clients needs to be focused on using the data about what they are interested in to attract them to the services offered. A personalised approach focused on opt-in emails and text messages, tailored to what is of interest to clients, is core. These messages need to encourage two-way communication. Not only will that interest clients more, but it will highlight the proactive and collaborative attitudes which the new business approach will be promoting.

TT4U can also use media releases to target particular groups, for example, clients using certain cloud services. Whilst these are less tailored, they can be used to create interest. They can be followed up by tailored communications to individual clients subsequently.

(ii)   **Retaining clients**

The same emphasis on personalised communication needs to be used for current clients. The focus needs to be on continuous dialogue. More regular client surveys, focusing on what they are likely to be most concerned about, need to be undertaken. TT4U must remember this personalised approach is not just about what is delivered but how it is delivered – how proactive TT4U is with its clients.

TT4U's website should also help develop relationships with clients by getting them to register or perhaps subscribe to particular content. The website could provide a chat or messaging option.

As well as TT4U's website, other methods which could be developed include newsgroups and business blogs. Newsgroups would keep clients interested by highlighting new developments with the cloud which are linked to the services which TT4U provides.

Providing services which can only be accessed by clients, for example, extranets, can also help generate loyalty. Again it is important that these are tailored to what is important to clients and generate responses from TT4U.

TT4U needs to consider how proactive staff are in dealing with client concerns, how quickly they respond when clients contact them and also how easy it seems to be for them to answer client queries. A business offering IT expertise needs to ensure that the knowledge and awareness which all its staff have is clear to clients. TT4U should also emphasise the existing knowledge it has of existing clients' systems as a selling point for helping them develop effective cloud computing service offerings.

	ACCA marking guide	
		Marks
(a)	Up to 2 marks for discussion of revenue	
	Up to 2 marks for discussion of contribution	
	Up to 2 marks for discussing payback	
	Up to 1 mark each for discussing other points such as marketing, fixed costs, tax, working capital, investment, terminal value, the discount factor and sensitivity analysis	
	(Up to a maximum of 8 marks in total)	
		8
	Professional skills	2
(b)	1 mark for each method recommended. These can include:	
	Attracting clients	
	– Search engine positioning	
	– Banner advertising	
	– Social media	
	– FAQs/other things of interest	
	– Ease of access	
	– Review evidence of what interests clients and adopt website	
	– Opt-in emails and text messages	
	– Media releases	
	Retaining clients	
	– Client surveys	
	– Development of relationship – registration/subscription	
	– Newsgroups and business blogs	
	– Extranets	
	– Staff responsiveness to queries	
	(Up to a maximum of 10 marks in total)	
		10
	Professional skills	3
Total		23

Professional skills may be additionally rewarded as in the following rubric:

How well has the candidate demonstrated professional skills as follows:	Not at all	Not so well	Quite well	Very well
2 (a) Scepticism in questioning the investment appraisal prepared by the finance director's assistant. (Report section)	The candidate has just stated that some of the figures are unrealistic and has not questioned in detail the assumptions made. The candidate has only considered the net present value calculation.	The candidate has questioned the assumptions behind some of the figures but the questions raised about the assumptions are not always clear. The candidate has said little about the payback period or the comments.	The candidate has questioned the assumptions behind most of the significant figures in the net present value calculation and has also commented on the other elements in analysis. Most of the questions raised are reasonable. The answer is in the correct format.	The candidate has questioned the assumptions behind all of the significant figures in the net present value and the significant elements of the rest of the analysis. The questions raised are linked to TT4U's situation as appropriate. The answer is in the correct format.
	0	**0.66**	**1.33**	**2**
2 (b) Commercial acumen by showing awareness of effective methods for the new cloud-based services. (Briefing notes)	The candidate has listed methods without any attempt to link them to TT4U's circumstances or what is being promoted.	e-marketing The candidate has made an attempt to link some of the methods discussed to the cloud services being promoted but the answer is not well-related to TT4U's circumstances and does not indicate an overall approach to marketing.	The candidate has linked most of the methods to the cloud services being promoted and to what TT4U is trying to achieve and the answer has attempted to follow an overall framework for marketing. The answer is in the correct format.	The methods suggested are clearly shown to be relevant to promoting cloud-based services and to TT4U's objectives. The methods suggested are described within a clear framework for attracting and retaining clients. The answer is in the correct format.
	0	**1**	**2**	**3**

3 **(a)** **Email**

To: **Chief executive**

From: **Consultant**

Date: **1 March 20X0**

Subject: **Transforming TT4U**

Dear CEO

You asked me for my thoughts on the transformation process and how you should lead it, including communicating the need for transformation positively. Attached is the draft letter to employees for your approval which you asked me to prepare. Obviously please contact me if you would like to discuss comments and amendments.

Your responsibilities and the board's responsibilities

You are quite right in supposing that you have to lead the transformation, as the successful implementation of the Mieobed approach could be vital for TT4U's long-term success. You will need to promote the Mieobed approach as a coherent whole and sell it to staff.

However, senior management at TT4U has always operated, and been seen as operating, as a team. Your first task will therefore be to convince the rest of the board of the need for transformation, so that they become as enthusiastic about it as you are. Successful implementation will depend on their convincing staff to embrace the transformation. Before presenting the approach to staff, you need to make a clear and detailed presentation to the other directors at the next board meeting, showing how adopting the Mieobed approach will fulfil TT4U's needs and emphasising the need for all the board to provide leadership.

Preparing for transformation

Explaining the Mieobed approach will not be enough by itself. Some staff may see the way it promotes improvements, but others may have more difficulty seeing how it applies or will be sceptical about it. You will therefore need to explain what is driving the transformation and the adoption of the Mieobed approach, and create the motivation for transformation.

When introducing the Mieobed approach, you need to do it in the context of both the culture of TT4U and the practical aspects of the business. You will need to communicate changes in culture, including changes in assumptions about how communication takes place and how clients are viewed. You will also need to show how internal changes, particularly changes in organisation structure, will mean a need to change behaviour towards other members of staff.

Practical aspects of the business which you need to consider include how organisational structure changes will follow through into changes in jobs and responsibilities, and also changes in processes and rewards. These are discussed further in the attached letter. To decrease staff's uncertainties, you will need to oversee the drafting of an operational plan covering these areas.

The letter also mentions staff enhancing their skills. This is an important selling point to staff as well as an important success factor in the transformation. You will need to consider the training staff will need and draw up a training programme, maybe with the assistance of an external experienced trainer.

Lastly, the transformation may require changes in TT4U's information systems and flows of information to the board. You and the IT director will need to consider the information needs of the board, including those highlighted by the marketing director, and draw up a plan so that TT4U's systems can provide the information required.

Implementing transformation

There should be a structured process for transformation in place. Given that participation is a core element of Mieobed, adopting a consultative process through meetings and praising and rewarding good suggestions will reinforce the messages you want to put across and is most likely to motivate staff.

Participation by staff should also be part of the transformation process itself. Ideally, staff should themselves have significant involvement in creating new behaviours and working routines. However, if it appears that the transformation process is slower or not transformational in the way you wish it to be, you may need to intervene and provide direction so that the transformation programme is consistent with your future strategy.

The attached letter emphasises the need for staff to get used to working with different people in different teams. To underline the importance of this, staff should be involved in team-building exercises, in teams with other staff whom they do not work with normally. This could be combined with staff involvement in creating new routines, with teams' contributions being enhanced by having staff with a range of perspectives arising from the different work experiences they have had.

Once transformation has happened, the final stage is ensuring staff are behaving in new ways and setting new standards. You will need to obtain evidence, from senior management keeping an eye on what is happening and human resource information such as appraisal meeting feedback, that changes have been embedded throughout the organisation and staff are not going back to old ways of working. The new behaviours expected can be reinforced by changing the mission, objectives and key performance indicators of TT4U.

Communication

The approach is based around open communication and you will undermine your own message if you are seen as not communicating clearly and completely throughout the transformation process. You have to take a position of being prepared to give full explanations and follow up queries when resolved. This may involve releasing news (particularly any bad news) earlier than you would feel comfortable with, but this will be necessary to promote staff confidence in the transformations and the message you will be delivering.

Please contact me with any issues you want to discuss further.

Regards

Stubfield

(b)   **Letter**

TT4U Head Office

1 March 20X0

Dear colleagues

I am writing to tell you about how we, the directors, plan to transform TT4U's business approach. A key element which we plan to introduce is participation. We will therefore need your help to make it a success.

We have decided to change our business approach because of demands for enhanced client service levels in our sector. I know we have always tried to connect with our clients and our client survey showed that some clients greatly appreciate our work. However, the survey has also shown that we need to improve in certain areas. We must therefore make this our top priority.

We are going to draw our clients closer to us by open communication and demonstrating complete empathy with their needs. We also need to understand how we can tailor our services so we can take them on a journey. We must see them as stakeholders in our work, with what we do determined by what they need and how their operations can be improved.

Benefits for our company

By knowing what is driving their business, we can develop what we offer to our clients, so that they obtain more services and

generate more revenue for us. If they have a close relationship with us, it is less appealing for them to change suppliers.

We also learn by talking to clients, and developing services in conjunction with them. What we develop for one client, we can adapt for others. What we learn from clients can enhance the contribution of our most important asset – you, our staff.

Benefits for you

I am so excited to be introducing this new approach because of the value which it will provide for you. We shall be giving you the training you need to develop knowledge of all our services and your personal skills. You will also be developing your capabilities by undertaking a wider variety of stimulating work, connecting with clients so that you understand what they require, and also working with, and learning from, different colleagues on different jobs. You will be given enhanced responsibility for maintaining dialogue with clients. Helpful suggestions will be rewarded as will outstanding client service.

How your work will change

I am sure you are asking what this will mean in your day-to-day work. The structure that we are used to, of three departments, will be loosened. You will be working with different teams to service different clients or on developing particular services. Teams will contain a mixture of expertise so that we can learn from each other.

This team structure will also help enable more communication. We all have a part to play in this. When you are in the office, do not sit in the same place with the same people every day but sit with, and talk to, different colleagues. Do not just read the intranet, but make use of it. Participate in discussion forums. Pass on to your manager and colleagues ideas you have had and insights you have gained from clients.

Finally, make our clients and our stakeholders the centre of your world. It goes without saying that clients should be responded to quickly however they contact us. Make sure you respond fully to their concerns. However, if we are to take clients on a value-enhancing journey, we need to do more than react, we need to be proactive. We all have a role to play with individual clients in making suggestions to them, using our knowledge and experience and awareness of their needs to help their organisation fulfil its full potential.

This is a start of a conversation between us. We will be talking together much more about this in the weeks and months to come. I look forward to discussing it with you.

Yours sincerely

Chief executive officer

(c) **Briefing notes on board membership and information flow**

The changes suggested to board composition and information flow reflect the need for development in TT4U's governance as it is growing and seeking to be more responsive to its clients' needs.

Executive team

The current executive team has combined operational management responsibilities with taking on board roles part time up to now. However, TT4U is now large enough to warrant full-time commitment to board roles and perhaps greater delegation to a management team immediately below board level. There is a case for the following roles being full time:

- Operations director – an additional role to the CEO and services director, to oversee and co-ordinate the new, more complex structure.

- Marketing director – concentrating on the effective marketing of new services and leading the winning of business from new clients.

- Human resources director – TT4U's size, the importance of key staff to the business and the forthcoming changes in structure with impacts on staff development and motivation all suggest a separate board role for human resources. Most likely an external specialist should be recruited.

Non-executive directors

The non-executive directors recruited so far help ensure TT4U complies with legal and regulatory requirements. TT4U will probably have to recruit more non-executives when it becomes fully listed. If the right non-executive directors are recruited now, they could make a strong contribution to the business at an important time for its development.

The board should consider carefully what knowledge and experience new non-executive directors should ideally have, but directors with the following backgrounds would appear to be particularly valuable:

- Experience and knowledge of the IT sector, who have worked for businesses which 'do things differently' from TT4U and businesses with a strong record of innovation in the sector.

- Experience in client service who can view this aspect of what TT4U offers critically.

Information supplied to board

The board needs to be supplied with sufficient and timely information about developments in the wider environment relating to client service. It is not enough just to know what competitors are offering. More information is needed on how services are provided and how competitors are measuring the strength of their client service. The board should also be supplied with available external information about how TT4U is ranked for client service compared with its competitors.

Findings derived from e-marketing initiatives should be summarised for every board meeting, including interest shown on the website and response to website surveys. Action taken in response to previous findings should be summarised.

The board should obtain and discuss summaries of relationships with current clients. Client feedback should be sought on a continuing basis, and not just one-off surveys, if TT4U is to show itself to be serious about the Mieobed approach. The board should be particularly concerned with feedback from larger clients and clients whose contracts are coming up for renewal.

The board should also be informed immediately if there are signs of serious problems with client relationships. These can be major complaints from clients or events such as major system outages which can trigger problems with clients.

The summaries should be supported by summaries of key performance indicators which focus on client service. These include response times to client communications, meetings with clients and additional services sold to clients. Although it is more difficult to measure, there should be indicators of TT4U's flexibility in responding to client requirements. Dialogue with clients may provide the best indicators of this.

ACCA marking guide		Marks
(a) Up to 2 marks per relevant suggestion. Max 4 marks for suggestions relating to chief executive officer and board's responsibilities, can include: – CEO leading transformation – CEO persuading rest of board – Board must take a leadership role Max 8 marks for general issues relating to the transformation process, can include: – Explaining drive for change and creating motivation – Detailed planning – operational, training, information provision – Participation by staff – Need for direction – Team building – New behaviours embedded – Full and complete communication (Up to a maximum of 10 marks in total)		—— 10 ——

(b)   Up to 2 marks per relevant suggestion.

Max 4 marks for benefits to TT4U, can include:
- Clients want more services
- Clients tied into TT4U
- Services developed for one client sold to others

Max 4 marks for benefits to employees, can include:
- Training in services offered and personal skills
- On-the-job development
- Greater responsibility
- Rewards for suggestions/good client service

Max 5 marks for changes in structures and behaviours, can include:
- Flexible teams
- Greater communication
- Responsiveness to clients
- Proactivity with clients

(Up to a maximum of 10 marks in total)

      10

Professional skills

      3

(c)   Up to 2 marks per relevant suggestion.

Max 6 marks for suggestions relating to membership of board, can include:
- Operations director
- Marketing director
- HR director
- NEDs

Max 6 marks for suggestions relating to information supplied, can include:
- Measures of competitor client service and comparison with TT4U
- E-marketing/website feedback
- Feedback from current clients
- Problems with client relationships
- Client service KPIs

(Up to a maximum of 10 marks in total)

      10

Professional skills

      3

Total   **36**

Professional skills may be additionally rewarded as in the following rubric:

How well has the candidate demonstrated professional skills as follows:	Not at all	Not so well	Quite well	Very well
3 (b) Communication skills in persuading employees of the benefits of TT4U adopting the new approach in its working practices, using the appropriate format. (Letter)	The candidate has not made any attempt to use persuasive language in communicating the changes to employees. The tone of the answer is a factual list of benefits.	The candidate has made some attempt to use persuasive language but has not maintained a persuasive tone throughout the letter, or much of what is said is unlikely to appeal to employees.	The candidate has used persuasive language throughout the letter and most of what is said should appeal to employees. The answer is a letter addressed to employees.	The candidate shows a clear purpose throughout the letter of persuading employees. The arguments used are convincing and related to objectives in the Mieobed approach. The answer is a letter addressed to employees.
	0	**1**	**2**	**3**
3 (c) Commercial acumen in identifying changes to the membership of the board and information supplied which are realistic for TT4U and will generate better relationships with clients. (Briefing notes)	The candidate has just quoted from corporate governance best practice without relating the changes to TT4U's circumstances. The information the candidate suggests should be supplied would not help the board assess relations with clients.	The candidate has made some suggestions of board changes and information flows which relate to TT4U's circumstances. However, some of the recommendations are not realistic or would not help TT4U improve relationships with clients.	The candidate has justified most of their recommendations by reference to TT4U's circumstances and the recommendations appear to be realistic for TT4U. The answer is in the correct format.	The candidate has related all their recommendations to TT4U's circumstances. All the recommendations appear to be realistic and beneficial for TT4U's relationships with its clients. The answer is in the correct format.
	0	**1**	**2**	**3**

In the Strategic Professional Examinations it is not always possible to publish suggested answers which comprehensively cover all the valid points which candidates might make. Credit will be given to candidates for points not included in the suggested answers, but which, nevertheless, are relevant to the requirements. In addition, in this integrated case study examination candidates may re-introduce points made in other questions or parts of questions as long as these are made in the specific context of the requirements of the question being answered.

The suggested answers presented below inevitably give much more detail than would be expected from most candidates under examination conditions, and include most of the obvious points evidenced from the case information. The answers are therefore intended to provide a structure of the approach required from candidates, and cover the range and depth of knowledge relating to each task which might be demonstrated by the most well prepared and able candidates. They are also intended to support revision and tuition for future examinations.

Section 19

REAL EXAM QUESTIONS – SEPTEMBER/DECEMBER 2020

1 OVERVIEW

The Bloom Conservation Organisation (BCO) is a not-for-profit charitable organisation set up to protect endangered wildlife around the world. It was founded 50 years ago by Dana Bloom, a wealthy entrepreneur with a passion for wildlife protection. She set up the BCO wildlife park in her home country of Geeland and, since it was founded, the wildlife park has provided intensive hands-on management of some of the world's most threatened animals. In the wildlife park, animals breed and increase in number while the keepers and wildlife experts study them to learn more about what they need to thrive in the wild again, before releasing them. The BCO also operates 20 'in the field' animal protection programmes (that is, animal welfare and management activities occurring in the animals' natural habitats) in 15 countries worldwide. The BCO employs teams of locally-based wildlife experts and volunteers to manage and protect some of the most endangered animals in the world.

Much of the BCO's income comes from donations from the public and from corporate donors. The BCO also generates income from legacies, which are donations left when people die. Geeland, as with many other developed economies around the world, has suffered from an economic recession for several years and many charitable organisations have struggled to survive in such difficult economic times. However, the BCO has managed to maintain its position as a world-leading charity in wildlife protection by implementing programmes of cost cutting, rationalisation, and more targeted and active promotion of its activities.

The BCO has a board of trustees which oversees the management of the charity, which is undertaken on a day-to-day basis by the management board. Dana Bloom, who is now over 80 years old, has very recently stepped down from her role as chairperson and a new chairperson, Rani Jeffels, has just been appointed. Rani Jeffels has a strong commercial background, having previously been a chief executive of several of Geeland's leading corporations.

You work as a senior finance manager of the BCO.

It is currently September 20X1.

The following exhibits provide information relevant to the case study.

Exhibit 1   Extracts from the BCO's annual report – the extracts highlight the BCO's mission, vision, aim, and objectives and its main activities in the latest financial year ending 30 April 20X1.

Exhibit 2   'About us' page of the BCO website – the website page sets out the leadership structure and governance of the charity.

Exhibit 3   BCO's financial activities and KPIs – a summary of the income and expenditure of the BCO for the last two financial years (20X0 and 20X1), including a summary of its KPIs.

Exhibit 4   Charity sector research report – a recent research article detailing the main threats and opportunities facing the charity sector.

Exhibit 5   The BCO's risk register – the latest risk register, identifying the key risks and mitigating activities identified by the risk committee.

Exhibit 6   Article on charity leadership – a news article on the recent bad publicity surrounding leadership issues in the charity sector.

The case requirements are included in the tasks shown below:

1   The new chairperson, Rani Jeffels, has recently commenced his new role with the BCO and wants to find out as much as possible about the organisation. He has called a meeting with the management board and has asked for each board member to make a short presentation to assist him in better understanding the BCO. The chief finance officer (CFO) has been asked to present on the BCO's governance principles and activities, and its financial and non-financial performance in the latest financial year. The CFO has asked you to assist him in preparing for his presentation.

Required:

Prepare a briefing note for the CFO which:

(a)   **Explains:**

(i)   **The specific nature of the principal-agent relationship of the BCO as a charitable organisation;**

(ii)   **The advantages for the BCO of having a two-tier board structure; and**

(iii)   **How the BCO's mission and strategic objectives meet its key stakeholder needs.**   **(12 marks)**

Professional skills marks are available for demonstrating *commercial acumen* skills in demonstrating understanding of organisational issues relevant to the BCO. **(2 marks)**

(b)   **Analyses the financial and non-financial performance of the BCO in the latest financial year, 20X1, providing reasons for and implications of the results.**

(13 marks)

Professional skills marks are available for demonstrating analysis skills in considering the relevant information and evidence relating to the BCO's financial and non-financial performance.   **(3 marks)**

(Total: 30 marks)

2   In its recently published annual report, the BCO set out three strategic objectives for the next five years. The new chairperson is keen to understand in more detail how the BCO's external environment will impact on these strategic objectives and has asked the CFO to provide him with this information. The CFO has asked for your assistance in preparing his report.

Required:

(a)   Prepare a report for the CFO which evaluates the extent to which the external environment could impact on the BCO's strategic objectives. **(15 marks)**

Professional skills marks are available for demonstrating evaluation skills in objectively appraising the facts, opinions and findings relating to the BCO's external environment. **(4 marks)**

In addition to the recent investment made in updating the members' database management system, the chief executive officer highlighted in the annual report that the BCO is looking for further opportunities to invest in e-business technologies. The CFO has been asked to make a presentation to the board of trustees and he has asked for your assistance in preparing his presentation.

Required:

(a)   Prepare three presentation slides (with accompanying notes) which recommend, with clear justifications, three applications of information technology that the BCO could use to enhance its e-business capabilities. **(15 marks)**

Professional skills marks are available for demonstrating communication skills in using compelling arguments to persuade the board of trustees of the potential of e-business technologies for the BCO. **(4 marks)**

(Total: 38 marks)

3   The chairperson has asked to meet with the chief executive officer (CEO) to discuss the BCO's current risk management approach. The chairperson has concerns that the current risk register does not adequately evaluate the seriousness of the risks identified and that some relevant risks are not covered at all. He is also concerned that the risk mitigating activities are inadequate, in the light of recent changes and events in the external environment.

The CEO disagrees and thinks that the risk register and its risk mitigating activities are sufficient, and that the chairperson is overreacting to the BCO's latest financial results and the industry research report. She has asked for your assistance on this matter.

Required:

Prepare a confidential report which evaluates the BCO's current risk register and the adequacy of each of the risk mitigating activities, clearly highlighting whether the chairperson's concerns are justified. **(15 marks)**

Professional skills marks are available for demonstrating scepticism skills in questioning appropriately the opinions expressed by the chairperson and the CEO. **(4 marks)**

(Total: 19 marks)

4   Soon after you completed your report on the BCO's risk register and risk mitigating activities, you attended a meeting with the CEO and the chief finance officer. At the meeting the CEO raised her concerns that the board of trustees does not have a sufficient mix of skills and diversity and that the management board had, in the recent past, not undertaken sufficient professional development. She has requested a meeting with the chairperson to discuss this issue further. The CEO has asked for your assistance in preparing for this meeting.

Required:

Prepare a briefing paper for the CEO which explains:

(i)   The importance for the BCO's board of trustees to have a sufficient mix of skills and diversity; and

(ii)   The importance of continuing professional development for the BCO's management board members to ensure that the BCO meets its obligations to its stakeholders.

(10 marks)

Professional skills marks are available for demonstrating commercial acumen skills in showing awareness of organisational and wider external factors affecting the work of the BCO's board of trustees and management board.   **(3 marks)**

(Total: 13 marks)

Exhibit 1: Extracts from the BCO's annual report highlighting the BCO's mission, vision, aim and objectives and its main activities in the latest financial year ending 30 April 20X1.

Our mission

Protecting and conserving our wildlife for future generations. Our vision

A safer, healthier world where people respect and support our wildlife.

Our aim

To support and increase the number of healthy and thriving wildlife communities across the world and encourage everyone to be more involved in the natural environment they live in.

Our strategic objectives

We have set out three clear strategic objectives for the next five years. These are:

–   Ensure that 100 threatened species are protected and returned to their natural habitat.

–   Invest in 100 wildlife habitat projects across the world, through providing training and education for local staff, volunteers and communities.

–   Ensure one million people are better connected with nature, through education and awareness of the natural world they live in.

Review of 20X1

Our financial position continues to be challenging. Operating a world-class wildlife park and global animal protection programmes is costly, hence our need for a range of income streams. This year, we reluctantly raised the price of admission to the wildlife park for the first time in five years. This decision was taken with a view to using the increased revenue to invest in better long-term facilities and experience for our visitors. Our wildlife park facilities continue to be popular, resulting in increased revenues from our on-site shop and café.

Income from legacies was down on 20X0, a continuing trend on the past few years, highlighting the volatile nature of reliance on legacy income. We sold one of our properties in the last year and two more will be sold next year to fund the extension of the visitor centre, which we hope will contribute to our objective of connecting people with nature. We were also successful in securing over $2 million in grant-funded donations over the next few years. This is a significant source of income for the BCO and we are grateful to those organisations which have awarded these grants.

A huge amount of work over the year went into updating our members database management system, which will be in place in 20X2 and allow us to communicate more effectively with members and permit online fee payments. Further investment in information technology is a key to our growth in the coming years, in our drive to streamline our business and to educate and communicate more effectively with our stakeholders. We will be launching a re-designed website in 20X2 and are looking for new opportunities to use e-business technologies more effectively in areas such as online education, digital marketing and social media.

It is with great sadness that we said goodbye to Dana Bloom last month. Our founder had been a tireless supporter of the BCO and her work, imagination, vision and determination has played a vital role in making the BCO the world-leading charity that it is today. She has been inspirational in creating a world where many endangered animals have been given a chance to thrive. We wish Dana a very happy and peaceful retirement.

Exhibit 2: 'About us' page of the BCO website, which sets out the leadership structure and governance of the charity.

BCO's leadership

Our two-tier board consists of the board of trustees and the management board.

Board of trustees

The governance of the BCO is vested in our board of trustees, which has overall control of the charity and is responsible for monitoring its strategic direction and ensuring it is in line with our mission and objectives. It is also responsible for monitoring the risks to which the charity is exposed, through the risk committee.

Board of trustee members

Chairperson – Rani Jeffels (61 years old) – Rani joined the board in August of this year. He has a masters' degree in economics and joins the BCO having had a successful and varied career in industry, where he held numerous senior managerial positions, including chief executive of Springvale Foods Plc.

Dr Boris Tilley (68 years old) – Dr Tilley has been a trustee of the BCO for 12 years. He has had a lifelong passion for animal protection, having worked for many overseas animal charities throughout his career. He has a doctorate in literature.

Mavis Reece-Boyd (73 years old) – Mrs Reece-Boyd has been a trustee of the BCO for 11 years and is a lifelong friend of Dana Bloom and a keen supporter of animal protection. She has a degree in fine art.

Sir Henry Ryde (75 years old) – Sir Henry has been a trustee of the BCO for 14 years and has a strong commercial background, having worked in the financial services industry before retiring and taking up his position with the BCO.

Dr Hardeep Khan (48 years old) – Dr Khan has a masters' degree in animal protection science and has worked in many of the most important animal protection sites across the world. He joined the board three years ago.

Stella Bond (58 years old) – Mrs Bond has been a trustee of the BCO for eight years and has commercial experience in retail sales.

Management board

Our highly experienced and dedicated management board is responsible for the day-to-day business of the BCO. It's main duties are to develop and propose strategies to achieve our mission and objectives and to measure and report on the BCO's performance. It takes responsibility for the management and delivery of our activities.

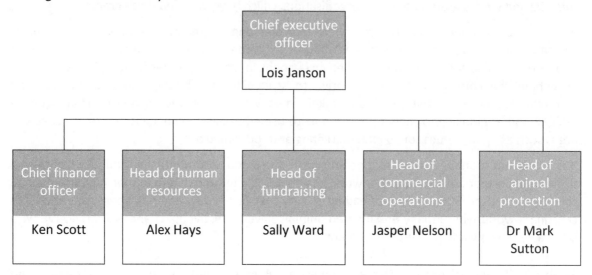

Exhibit 3: A summary of the income and expenditure of the BCO for the last two financial years (20X0 and 20X1), including a summary of its KPIs.

Summary of Financial Activities:

Year ended 30 April	20X1	20X0
Income	$000	$000
Wildlife park admissions	3,103	3,005
Membership fees:		
– Individual	1,973	1,923
– Corporate	210	90
Education programmes	2,023	2,155
Wildlife park shop and café	5,675	4,923
Donations, grants and legacies	7,283	8,625
Other – sale of property	525	–
Total Income	**20,792**	**20,721**
Expenditure		
Charitable Activities		
Animal support costs: Wildlife park (staff/animal food/medical/facilities)	10,063	9,220
Animal support costs: In the field (staff/facilities/transport/medical)	4,265	4,000
Staff training	1,000	1,110
Commercial Activities		
Costs of operating wildlife park shop and café	3,533	4,163
Costs of other commercial income	1,695	1,570
Total Expenditure	**20,556**	**20,063**
Net Income	**236**	**658**

	20X1	20X0
Number of paid staff employed (wildlife park and in the field)	344	351
Number of volunteers (wildlife park and in the field)	180	154
Key Performance Indicators		
Wildlife park visitor numbers	258,583	263,595
Income per visitor from café and shop	$21.95	$18.68
Average training days per staff member	4.8	5.1
Cost per staff training day	$606	$620
Number of external education training programmes run	145	151
Number of animals returned to natural habitats	1,680	1,595

Exhibit 4: A recent charity sector research article detailing the main threats and opportunities facing the charity sector.

Why charities must change

THE GLOBAL CHARITIES INSTITUTE FOR RESEARCH

By Professor Aksel Parish

A number of events and changes have happened in the last couple of years which have given the managers of many charities some cause for concern.

Since the global recession over a decade ago, many countries are still feeling its effects and governments globally have been financially under pressure. This has impacted on the wider population, whose income has also been over-stretched.

Linked to this is the general financial position of charities. Many charities have for too long been over-reliant on a small number of funding options. If a funding source ends, the impact on a charity can be immediate and devastating. Many publicly-funded grant awarding bodies and corporate supporters of charities have reluctantly had to reduce their support for charities both financially and in terms of volunteering, as they have seen their own incomes reduced by the financial crisis.

However, public expectations of the work done by charities are still high, which places increased demands on all charities, and many have found themselves at risk of being unable to meet expectations. For example, many global nature and animal protection charities have seen demand for their support and protection increase dramatically, as habitats around the world are being increasingly destroyed by human activities. However, year-on-year these charities struggle to maintain stable funding levels.

Some of the decrease in charitable funding has been caused by 'donor fatigue', as people have become over-exposed to charitable requests and therefore stop donating. Some charities have been accused of 'hard-selling' their services, by bombarding donors with requests by post, email and on the streets. Charities have no doubt become more aggressive in trying to win donor support, resulting in some local authorities banning street donations to stop aggressive donor collection tactics. This also impacts badly on the general reputation and perception of the sector. More legislation is expected in the coming years to stop the use of 'hard-sell' marketing tactics used by some charities.

A younger generation of donors has also been brought up in a time of austerity and is less likely to donate to charitable causes. Some charities have recognised the younger generation as a potential source of donations and have used new forms of technology, such as social media platforms and mobile technologies, to effectively communicate and interact with a potential new source of supporter. However, some charities have been slow to protect and nurture the customers and donors they already have, missing the opportunity to build better relationships with them to encourage retention through the use of e-marketing and communication strategies. A failure to innovate or update organisational systems to match the needs of the society we live in may be a major downfall for many charitable organisations.

Exhibit 5: The BCO's latest risk register, identifying the key risks and mitigating activities identified by the risk committee.

Potential risk	Potential impact	Risk mitigating activities
Fund-raising pressures	– Insufficient income to cover expenditure – Reputational risks of campaigns or methods used to raise funds	– Implement appropriate cost budgeting procedures – Monitor the adequacy of financial returns achieved (benchmarking comparisons) – Report fund-raising activities to stakeholders in annual report
Loss of key staff	– Experience or skills lost – Operational impact on key animal protection projects	– Succession planning – Agree notice periods and handovers – Review recruitment processes and policies
Increased competition in the sector	– Loss of income – Reduced public profile	– Monitor methods of service delivery – Monitor public awareness and profile
Operating in dangerous locations around the world	– Staff/volunteers injured or killed carrying out their responsibilities	– Monitor and review activities in recognised dangerous locations and procedures to remove staff at short notice – Closely work with local security and safety services – Regular training

The risk committee is chaired by the BCO's chairperson and has two other board of trustee members. The committee meets once a year to review the risk register and the activities being undertaken by the BCO to monitor and manage risks.

Exhibit 6: A news article on the recent bad publicity surrounding leadership issues in the charity sector.

The Geeland Times

Are charity leaders out of touch?

Charities under increasing pressure to improve sector.

By Grace Kline, Charities Analyst

Research for the Geeland Charity Commission has found that people are increasingly concerned about how charities spend their money and how they are managed and led.

The main reason given for trusting charities less, cited by over one-third of people questioned, was negative media coverage. Stories to have hit the headlines since the last survey include the collapse of two major health charities amid allegations of financial mismanagement, and the general perception that some charities are run more like clubs for old school friends, with boards of trustees being out of touch and unskilled for the modern world in which they operate.

Some of the major problems of charities in recent times have been poor strategic direction, driven largely by charities being led and managed by boards which seem to lack awareness of the changing world they now operate in. Many charities seemingly lack direction, strategy and forward planning, with issues being addressed piecemeal with limited strategic reference. Some of the blame for this

has been laid firmly at the door of the trustees, those people tasked with setting the charity's strategic direction. In a modern world, where charities are facing similar commercial pressures to profit making organisations, the question is whether charities can be run effectively by trustees with no commercial background and with limited understanding of strategy formulation.

In a presentation to Geeland's charity leaders this week, the Charity Commission's chairman, Lief Morten, said that the decline of the charity sector was 'a wake-up call for everyone who runs a charity'. He said 'Poor fundraising practices, poor management and weak, out of touch leadership have all combined to reduce public confidence in the charity sector.'

Morten said: 'The public wants to see charities account better for how they spend their money and that charities are making a positive difference to their causes. However, the damage done to the sector by these examples of bad practice must be balanced by the vast amount of energy, commitment and hard work put in by most charities.'

REAL EXAM ANSWERS – SEPT/DEC 2020

Strategic Professional – Essentials, SBL   **Sept/Dec 2020 Sample Answers**

In the Strategic Professional Examinations it is not always possible to publish suggested answers which comprehensively cover all the valid points which candidates might make. Credit will be given to candidates for points not included in the suggested answers, but which, nevertheless, are relevant to the requirements. In addition, in this integrated case study examination candidates may re-introduce points made in other questions or parts of questions as long as these are made in the specific context of the requirements of the question being answered.

The suggested answers presented below inevitably give much more detail than would be expected from most candidates under examination conditions, and include most of the obvious points evidenced from the case information. The answers are therefore intended to provide a structure of the approach required from candidates, and cover the range and depth of knowledge relating to each task which might be demonstrated by the most well prepared and able candidates. They are also intended to support revision and tuition for future examinations.

1   (a)   Briefing Note Section 1

(i)   The principal-agent relationship of the BCO

Fiduciary relationship

The BCO's board of trustees, acting as the principal, is responsible for good governance, but they rely on many different people to be able to govern well: staff, volunteers and importantly, the management board. In a principal-agent relationship, the principal engages the agent to perform a service on their behalf which involves delegation of some decision-making authority to the agent. The relationship creates a fiduciary relationship between the board of trustees and the management board, which means the management board, acting on behalf of the trustees, must carry out the assigned tasks with the principal's best interests (and therefore those of the BCO's diverse stakeholders) as a priority.

Represent stakeholders

The board of trustees, as the principal, represents the interests of the BCO's stakeholders, which will include not only those stakeholders and organisations which have contributed or donated funds to the charity but also the people and animals living in the wildlife communities we operate in, our staff, our wildlife park visitors and the wider community. The management board, as the agent, undertakes responsibilities assigned by the board of trustees. The management board therefore has an obligation to undertake their responsibilities assigned with a certain level of skill and care, using the particular skills and expertise each member has been employed for.

Reward

As agents, the management board is financially rewarded to discharge responsibilities delegated to it, without conflicting with the interests of the stakeholders which the board of trustees represent. The board of trustees is not financially rewarded for their role, as it effectively acts on behalf of the stakeholders of the BCO.

(ii)   The advantages of a two-tier board structure

   –   One advantage of this governance arrangement is that there is a clear and distinct separation of duties between the monitoring function of the board of trustees and those being monitored (the management board).

   –   Additionally, the supervisory role of the board of trustees acts as an effective safeguard against management inefficiency and against fraud or irregular activities. All of this helps to maintain the trust of the stakeholders, in particular those donating funds to the BCO, who will seek reassurance that their funds are being used appropriately by the BCO.

   –   A further advantage is that the board of trustees, in its supervisory role, will consider the needs of all of our stakeholders, including staff and the wider community to ensure that their interests are also taken into account and the actions of the management board do not affect them adversely.

   –   The two-tier system also encourages transparency within the charity, between the two board levels and between the board of trustees and the stakeholders they represent. This transparency is particularly important in the charitable sector whereby the charity must be accountable for the diverse range of funds it receives.

(iii)   How our mission and objectives meet stakeholder needs

   –   For most profit-seeking organisations, the mission and objectives are largely driven by the needs of the principal; that is the owners or shareholders. In particular, the objectives will be mainly focused on ensuring that the principals' returns are maximised. However, as already discussed, our principals are acting on behalf of a wide range of stakeholders and therefore our mission and objectives will have a different focus.

   –   Our mission is firmly focused on protecting and conserving the world's wildlife for the future. This meets the needs of a wide range of stakeholders, including the wildlife itself and the people who live and work within the communities in which they live. In addition, the wider community will also benefit from a world in which wildlife can thrive and live safely in its natural habitat.

   –   The first objective of protecting and returning the 100 threatened species to their natural habitats meets the needs of the threatened species themselves and the communities which they come from. Therefore, this objective meets our stakeholder needs.

- The second objective of investment in 100 wildlife habitat projects across the world through training and education for local staff and communities also meets the needs of our stakeholders, including staff and local people, who require the specific knowledge and skills to ensure that habitat projects are successfully run and managed and that donors' funds are used effectively.

- The third objective to ensure 1 million people are better connected with nature meets the needs of our wider communities and population to understand and appreciate the natural world they live in. If the wider population appreciate and understand the natural world better, this will impact directly on the wildlife species the BCO is ultimately set up to protect.

(b) **Briefing Note Section 2**

Financial performance evaluation

The BCO maintained more or less a steady state from 20X0 to 20X1, based on levels of income and expenditure, although our surplus decreased by $422,000. Income from charitable activities increased by 5% in the year, much of which was as a result of admissions to the wildlife park. However, visitor numbers to the wildlife park were down by nearly 2% (258,583, compared to 263,595 in the financial year 20X0), meaning that the increase in revenue from wildlife park admissions came from the increased price we charged this year to visitors to enter the wildlife park. This is a concern, as visitors to the wildlife park are a key source of income. If visitors continue to fall, then this could have a knock-on impact on income from other sources, such as individual membership and income from the wildlife shop and café, if less visitors use our facilities.

However, despite the fall in visitor numbers the income from the wildlife park shop and café increased by 15%, from $4,923,000 to $5,675,000. This is encouraging and demonstrates that our shop and café are popular and a potential source for future revenue growth. This suggests that our shops and cafés are operating effectively.

Corporate membership income has grown significantly (133%) from $90,000 to $210,000 but is still a very small proportion of our income (1%) and we must look to grow this, through further work with corporate partners. Individual membership grew only slightly which we need to improve on. However, this could be looked at positively, considering that visitor numbers to the wildlife park dropped in the year and therefore our conversion rate of converting visitors to members has in fact improved. Therefore, our on-site membership marketing activities appear to be operating effectively but we still need to do more to convert visitors to members and attract more visitors overall.

Two areas of concern in relation to our revenue from commercial activities are from education and training programmes and donations and legacies. Income from running education and training programmes was 6% lower than last year. This, combined with the KPI showing that we ran fewer external education and training programmes in 20X1 compared to 20X0 (145 v 151) is concerning, when considering our long-term objective of increasing our commitment to educating and training our stakeholders. This clearly does not meet this objective. This is something we must focus on in the coming years if we are to ensure that our strategic objectives are met.

Donations, grants and legacies income reduced by nearly 16% (from $8,625,000 to $7,283,000). This is particularly concerning, as these are our primary sources of income. However, we could perceive this as a positive direction, as our total income in fact increased in 20X1, despite this decrease in this primary revenue source, meaning we are improving in other revenue sources. In 20X0 donations, grants and legacies were 42% of total income, whereas in 20X1 it was 35% of total income. This indicates that we have reduced our reliance on this income source and increased other sources to compensate, although we should note that some of this has come from the sale of property assets which is not a recurring or sustainable source of commercial income. This means we must not be complacent, as the donations, grants and legacies will continue to be important to source of income in the future and therefore we must try to maintain our active work in seeking these sources of income and looking for ways to support that donor income with sustainable commercial initiatives.

Expenditure has increased in the year by nearly 2.5%, which, although not overly concerning, must be something we monitor closely. We spent significantly more on animal support costs, which increased in the year by 8%. This is something that we must investigate further. This rise may be due to inflationary pressure on the underlying costs of resources (veterinary costs, animal feed and staff pay rises) or it could suggest we are being inefficient in our cost management procedures and are not controlling these costs effectively and making the best use of our resources. We have an obligation to obtain the optimum value for money for our stakeholders and we must manage our funds appropriately.

Costs of commercial operations reduced by 15% which is very positive. This may be due to fewer properties to manage (we sold a property in 20X1) or it could be because we have managed our shop and cafe more efficiently. We may be able to learn lessons from our cost management processes in our commercial operations and transfer these to our management of animal welfare costs.

Non-financial performance evaluation (key performance indicators)

The overall number of staff we employed decreased but we were able to attract more volunteers to work for the BCO. Although this should be seen as a positive factor, in that we are clearly attracting external support for our activities, we must be careful that we do not use volunteers to replace the skills and expertise of employed staff, some of whom will be trained experts. Obviously, we will need to monitor whether it is skilled animal welfare staff who are being replaced by volunteers, or more unskilled temporary staff in non-animal related areas (such as visitor centre staff). Loss of expert staff and a net reduction in human capital may impact detrimentally on our effectiveness.

As mentioned above, visitor numbers to the wildlife park are down but on average each visitor actually spent more money when they visited ($3.27). This is a positive factor and we should look to investigate how we can encourage visitors to spend more in the wildlife park, by increasing and continually improving the facilities and attractions we have on site and also investigate more fully where customers spend the most.

Training days were down on 20X0 as too were external training programmes run. These outcomes do not fit with our objectives of increasing education and training and we must address these if we are to achieve our stated strategic objectives.

Our programmes to re-introduce animals to the wild continue to be successful as more animals were returned to their natural habitats in 20X1 compared to 20X0. This should be a key focus of our performance measurement, as ultimately, this is the reason for our existence. All of our activities are carried out with this as our main objective.

ACCA marking guide	
	Marks

(a) Award 1 mark for each relevant point made in relation to the three specific areas covered.
Award up to a maximum of 4 marks for each requirement section.
Up to a maximum of 12 marks

Key Points

(i) **The principal agent relationship of the BCO**
– Fiduciary relationship
– Principal responsible for good governance
– Agent tasks assigned by principal
– Management board financially rewarded
– The board of trustees not financially rewarded

(ii) **The advantages of a two-tier board structure**
– Board of trustees – monitor activities of the management board
– Clear separation of duties
– Maintain trust of stakeholders
– Encourages transparency

(iii) **How our mission and objectives are driven by stakeholder needs**
– Principals acting on behalf of a wide range of stakeholders
– BCO mission – driven by needs of these stakeholders
– First objective – needs of threatened species and communities
– Second objective – needs of staff/locals
– Third objective – needs of wider communities

(b) Up to 2 marks for each relevant point related to the financial and non-financial performance of the BCO, (1 mark for identification of a relevant issue – 1 additional mark for clearly discussing the reasons for and/or implications of each relevant issue).
1 mark for each relevant calculation up to a maximum of 4 (no marks for merely repeating numbers already presented in the exhibit).
Up to a maximum of 13 marks

Key points

Financial

– Charitable activities income – driven by increased admission prices
– Visitor numbers down – concern
– Increase income from increased entry price
– If visitors drop – lose income from shop and café
– Income from shop and café increased – positive
– Corporate membership grown significantly – but small proportion of income
– Individual membership grew slightly – positive
– Income from education and training programmes decreased – impact on SO's
– Fewer external training programmes – does not meet SO's
– Donations, grants and legacies reduced – primary sources of income
– Reduced reliance on this income source – positive
– Animal support and welfare costs increased – cost control
– Inefficient cost management procedures
– Costs of commercial operations reduced – possible efficiently

Non-financial performance (KPIs) – Staff employed decrease – impact on delivery of programmes – Attracted more volunteers – but not use volunteers to replace skills and expertise – Are skilled animal welfare staff being replaced by volunteers? – Visitor number down – but each visitor spent more – Training days per staff lower – impact on programme delivery – External training programmes reduced – impact on SO's – Re-wilding programmes successful – ultimate objective	
Total	30

Professional skills may be additionally rewarded as in the following rubric for 1 (a):

How well has the candidate demonstrated professional skills as follows:	Not at all	Not so well	Quite well	Very well
Commercial acumen skills in demonstrating an understanding of the organisational issues relevant to the BCO	The candidate has demonstrated no commercial acumen. The candidate has failed to demonstrate an understanding of how the structure and relationships within the BCO are driven by its organisational context and its objectives. The answer was purely theoretical.	The candidate has demonstrated limited commercial acumen. Some commercial awareness was demonstrated in understanding of the BCO's organisational context and activities as a charity, but the candidate has failed to consider a number of the most relevant factors.	The candidate has demonstrated good commercial acumen. Most of the discussion demonstrated good commercial awareness in recognising how the BCO's objectives and organisational context, impact on its activities and management structure. The candidate covered a good range of relevant commercially sound points.	The candidate has demonstrated excellent commercial acumen. The answer demonstrated a very high level of judgement and commercial awareness of how BCO's objectives and the impact on the BCO's board structure and activities of its organisational context. The candidate's answer was very well applied.
Briefing Note			The format of the briefing notes is appropriate and suitable for · presentation to the chief finance officer.	The format of the briefing notes is appropriate and suitable for presentation to the chief finance officer.
	0	0.5	1	2

Professional skills may be additionally rewarded as in the following rubric for 1 (b):

How well has the candidate demonstrated professional skills as follows:	Not at all	Not so well	Quite well	Very well
Analysis skills in considering the information relating to the BCO's financial and non-financial performance.	The candidate has demonstrated poor or no analysis skills. The candidate has merely restated the information presented in the exhibit, with no consideration of the implications of this information to the BCO.	The candidate has demonstrated limited analysis skills. Some of the answer demonstrated some analytical skills but there was insufficient analysis and understanding of the relevance and impact of the key aspects of the results.	The candidate has demonstrated good analysis skills. Most of the answer was based on evidence identified from the scenario information and the candidate has made a reasonable attempt to analyse a range of key financial and non-financial issues and demonstrated reasoning and understanding.	The candidate demonstrated excellent analysis skills. All of the candidate's analysis is based on evidence identified from the scenario and there is a clear and logical analysis of the most relevant financial and non-financial factors and has presented clear and logical reasoning.
Briefing Note			The candidate has presented the answer in a briefing note format and most of the analysis is adequate for the intended audience.	The candidate has presented the answer in a briefing note format and the analysis is highly relevant for the intended audience.
	0	1	2	3

2 (a) To: **Chief finance officer**

From: **Senior finance manager**

Date: **XX/XX/20X1**

Subject: **The impact of the external environment on the BCO's strategic objectives**

Introduction

When setting our strategic objectives, a key element of this process is to evaluate the external environment and its impact on those objectives. Importantly, we must continually assess our external environment to monitor its continued impact on our strategies and to identify how we should respond to these external events to ensure we maintain our strategic direction. Achievement of our strategic objectives will be affected by the current global economic climate and the pressure this places on individuals and corporations, on whom we rely for donations and for support.

Political environmental impact

As noted in a recent charity industry research article, many governments around the world have been financially overstretched by the global recession. This has had severe consequences for ourselves and the whole charity sector, as increases in austerity measures have impacted negatively on the business community and on the wider population. At the same time, demands placed on charities like ourselves have in fact increased as a result of the political and economic climate.

The recent charity sector report also noted that publicly-funded grant awarding bodies have reduced support for charities both financially and in the number of volunteers, evidence again of changing political priorities that we are vulnerable to as an organisation. However, this aspect of the political environment has not had such a significant effect on the BCO in the last year, as we were still able to secure $2 million of publicly funded grants in 20X1, evidence of effective management of this aspect of our external environment.

Economic environmental impact

All of our strategic objectives will require significant financial resources, in particular our wildlife protection activities, both within the wildlife park and in the overseas locations where we operate our programmes. In the next five years our primary objective is to protect 100 species and return them back to the wild. This will be expensive and therefore we will need to balance this with the financial resources we have available.

A large proportion of our donations come from legacies which, from our annual report, have been decreasing in recent years. This is a major concern for its impact on our ability to achieve our strategic objectives, without reducing the funding we put into these projects or reducing the number of projects we invest in. It is likely that as donors face periods of economic uncertainty, then donations to charities will likely decrease, threatening the achievement of our strategic objectives.

Compounding this is the fact that the demands placed on charities like ours are in fact increasing as a result of the current economic and political environment. As the recent research report highlighted, many global nature and animal protection charities have seen demand for their support and protection increase, as animal habitats are being destroyed by human activities, largely caused by changing economic priorities and policies. Our strategic objectives of returning 100 species to the wild and investing in 100 projects will be threatened if such economic pressures increase over the next five years.

Also, as evidenced in our recent financial results, our operational costs are also increasing, possibly as a result of inflationary pressures caused by the current economic environment. We have a duty to our stakeholders to operate economically, but this is going to be challenged and ultimately may impact on the quality of our programmes, if costs continue to rise.

Social environmental impact

Evidence from the recent charity sector report suggests that some of the decrease in charitable funding has been caused by 'donor fatigue', whereby people have become over exposed to charitable requests and therefore, have reduced or stopped donating. As competition amongst charities increases for the limited charitable donations available, it is inevitable that society will be put under pressure and may in fact turn away from charitable funding. This would be a severe risk to all of our strategic objectives, as without these donations, and the continued awareness and support from society, we simply cannot function. This is both from a financial point of view and from our staffing and volunteering perspective. Pressurised fund-raising tactics employed by some charities, such as bombarding donors with donor requests by post, email and on the streets has clearly had a negative effect on donation levels across the whole sector and we must identify strategies to minimise this impact.

Understanding the changing demographics is also an important aspect of our environmental analysis. As the research report suggested, the younger generation of donors have been brought up in a time of austerity and therefore less likely to donate spare money to charitable causes. This age group however is more accessible, through changing technology, which we could and should exploit.

Technological environmental impact

Technology could be viewed as a positive or negative influence on our strategic objectives. The internet and its global reach has allowed our message to be spread globally through the use of our website, which we intend to re-launch next year. Improved communication about all of the work and activities we undertake could have a significant positive impact on our ability to generate donations from further afield than Geeland.

However, the technological environment has advanced beyond the application of an informational website, allowing for the opportunity to build better relationships with stakeholders through the use of such technological applications of online marketing, online education and training, online donations and a wide range of interactive social media applications. A failure to innovate or update systems to match the needs of society we now operate in may be a major downside to us.

Ecological environmental impact

Fundamentally, the BCO was set up to meet a demand to protect the ecological environment, and our key external drivers have, and always will be, primarily to meet ecological needs. As the recent research report suggest, many global nature and animal protection charities have seen demand for their support and protection increase dramatically, as habitats around the world are being increasingly destroyed by man-made activities, yet year-on-year these organisations struggle to maintain stable funding levels. Therefore, the changing and growing ecological demands placed on us will present us with both opportunities and challenges in the future. It is likely that, with increasingly limited resources, we are going to have to prioritise the work we do and the areas we invest in, which may compromise the achievement of our first two strategic objectives.

Legal environmental impact

Charities have no doubt become more aggressive in trying to win donor support and some local authorities have banned street donations in their local towns to stop aggressive donor collection behaviour. This also impacts badly on the general reputation and perception of the sector. Also, more legislation is expected to reduce the use of 'hard-sell' marketing tactics used by some charities. Even if we are not involved in such tactics ourselves, this legislation will affect us and this may impact on our ability to raise funds in certain areas, such as on-street collections or postal adverts. With pressures already facing us on reduced income streams, this additional legislation could impact further on our income, thus impacting on achievement of our strategic objectives.

Summary

The current external environment is creating significant pressures on ourselves and the charity sector as a whole and these pressures will affect our ability to raise sufficient funds and awareness of our activities to achieve our strategic objectives, but there are some significant opportunities associated with some of these factors. It will be critical for us to therefore constantly monitor these external factors to assess how we can address and manage their effects on our strategic objectives, particularly in their impact on our ability to raise funds.

(b)

Slide 1:

Social Media Presence

Features:
- Two-way communication
- Highly interactive
- Multi-media – text, videos, audio

Benefits:
- Global 24/7 communication
- Reach wide demographic
- Inexpensive form of communication and marketing
- Build emotional connection proactively

Notes

Social media is a critical component of many modern organisations' e-business strategy and is an increasingly effective strategy for charities to adopt to interact with supporters globally. Social media will allow us to enter into two-way communication and engage with a vast number of supporters one-to-one.

Social media platforms are especially relevant if we want to engage with a younger generation of supporters. Comment boards, forums, likes and tweets give us the opportunity to engage proactively with those who are interested in and support the BCO's work. This opens up lines of communication for those who want to make direct contact with us, which are currently not available.

The biggest advantage is that social media has a global reach and is inexpensive. Social media can therefore be an effective way for us to build global support, boost donations, share success stories, encourage people to sign up to campaigns or to volunteer and to demonstrate the impact of our animal protection work around the world.

Importantly, social media gives the BCO the chance to make emotional connections. Use of images, videos and human reactions are what will really bring the work of our charity to life. Potential volunteers are more likely to get involved if they can picture the animals and habitats we are trying to help. Donations will be more forthcoming if people can directly see and experience the work we do.

Social media encourages our supporter to interact through 'likes', 'comments', and writing blogs or uploading photos and videos to personalise involvement with us. Using social media could help us create our own BCO online community.

Slide 2:

On-line education and training delivery

Features:
- Web-based training modules
- Use mobile technologies – laptops and smartphones
- Electronic resource library
- Continuous availability

Benefits:
- Cost savings in physical delivery
- Globally accessible training on demand
- Savings in time and resources
- Source of income

Notes

One of our strategic objectives for the next five years is to provide training and education for staff, volunteers and communities, and a further strategic objective of delivering online education and awareness programmes to connect people to the natural world. Both of these objectives will be costly in terms of time and money and without online delivery may in fact be impossible to realistically achieve.

Using our website, we can offer web-based training and education programmes to our staff and volunteers anywhere in the world, accessible through a range of mobile devices and at any time of day or night. Online delivery allows global access, meaning we can offer training and education programmes globally without having to spend money on sending training staff and physical training documents and manuals. This will be a huge cost saving for us.

On-demand access also offers total flexibility, making it more likely that users will make use of our resources at a time that suits them. This means they are not having to use vital work time to attend physically delivered courses.

Similarly, online education and awareness delivery allows us to more easily spread our vision and activities globally to as many people as possible in a cost-effective manner.

We could also offer our online courses to external customers who are willing to pay for them and the materials we use. This could be an alternative form of income for us, selling our expertise globally.

Slide 3:

Digital marketing

Features:
– User friendly website and mobile applications
– Search Engine Optimisation
– Analytics to tailor marketing messages

Benefits:
– Marketing tailored to the individual
– Reduces costs of traditional direct marketing activities
– Updated instantly
– Attract volunteers/staff

Notes

Marketing is often seen as an activity reserved for commercial organisations, undertaken to secure additional awareness and ultimately, increased sales of its products and services. However, marketing is equally important to a charitable organisation such as the BCO. Digital marketing is more cost effective and should assists in reaching a wider audience for our marketing message.

The first element of e-marketing for us, is an effective and well-designed website, something which we are planning on undertaking next year. This needs to be located easily through effective Search Engine Optimisation (SEO), and ensuring our website remains easy to use, accessible and importantly, easy to find.

The potential development of mobile applications is another source of digital marketing. Apps are convenient and accessible on the go for many people, particularly the younger generation, and could be a beneficial method of marketing.

Application of digital marketing is particularly useful as it allows us to tailor messages to individuals and groups who show an interest in what we do. Again, this is a major positive in creating a strong marketing message to potential donors and customers. It is also a positive way of accessing potential volunteers and attracting interest of potential staff in a cost-efficient way.

ACCA marking guide		Marks
(a)	1 mark for each relevant point made (do not penalise candidates if they have not used a PESTEL approach to structure their answer). If PESTEL is used then award a maximum of 4 marks for each category. Up to a maximum of 15 marks	
	Political environment impact	
	– Governments financially overstretched	
	– Increases in personal and business taxation rates	
	– Impact on wider population and business community	
	– Strategic objectives require significant financial resources	
	Economic environment impact	
	– Donations and legacies decreasing – global recession impact	
	– Concern for ability to achieve strategic objectives	
	– Economic changes globally impacting demand charities like BCO	
	– Strategic objectives threatened if revenues decrease	
	– Serious harm to our reputation and ultimately in our ability to survive	

Social environment impact
–   'Donor fatigue' – over exposed to charitable requests
–   Society under pressure
–   Severe risk to strategic objectives
–   Engage younger generation
–   Austerity – less prone to donate

Technological environment impact
–   Prospective positive and negative influence
–   Internet allows globally reach
–   Positive impact on ability to generate donations
–   Opportunity to build better relationships with donors
–   Use online marketing, electronically delivered training and online donations
–   Failure to innovate – major consequences

Ecological environment impact
–   Key external driver
–   Many similar charities seen demand increase dramatically
–   However – struggle to maintain stable funding levels for such organisations
–   Threat to survival

Legal environmental impact
–   Local authorities banned street donations
–   Impacts badly on general reputation/perception of sector
–   Need to retain strong legal support
–   Cost of regulation (health and safety increasing costs)

(b)   For each slide, award 1 mark for each relevant and applied point made within the accompanying notes.

Up to a maximum of 5 marks for the notes on each per slide.

Maximum of 15 marks

Key points

Slide 1

Social media
–   Build supporters, boost donations, share success stories
–   Engage with a younger generation of supporters
–   Two-way communication – interactive
–   Global reach – cost effective
–   Make emotional connections
–   Use of images, videos, comments
–   Encourages supporter to interact – create online community

Slide 2

Online delivery of training and education
–   **Strategic objectives – invest in providing training and education**
–   Costly – time and money without online delivery
–   Deliver anywhere in the world
–   Use of mobile devices – any time of day or night
–   Global access – without physical costs
–   Huge cost saving and source of funds
–   Allows BCO to share knowledge cost effectively

Slide 3

Digital marketing
–   Cost effective – assists in reaching a wider audience
–   Need well-designed website
–   Requires effective Search Engine Optimisation (SEO) – easy to find
–   Technology extended for non-members online donations
–   Includes mobile applications, another source of e-marketing
–   Apps convenient and accessible
–   Tailor messages to individuals and groups
–   Access potential volunteers and attracting interest of potential staff

Total	38

Professional skills may be additionally rewarded as in the following rubric for 2 (a):

How well has the candidate demonstrated professional skills as follows:	Not at all	Not so well	Quite well	Very well
Evaluation skills in objectively appraising the facts, opinions and findings relating to the BCO's external environment.	The candidate has failed to demonstrate any evaluation skills. The candidate has not appraised the information presented and has merely re-stated information already presented. The candidate has shown poor professional judgement in failing to appraise the appropriate information in a useful and objective way.	The candidate has demonstrated weak evaluation skills. The candidate has shown limited professional judgement in appraising the information provided but has used an appropriate framework to structure the answer. However, the candidate has not adequately evaluated the information in an objective or useful way.	The candidate has demonstrated good evaluation skills. The candidate has shown good professional judgement in selecting and applying a suitable framework to evaluate the information and has made some reasonable assertions. They have demonstrated a reasonable appraisal of the information presented.	The candidate has demonstrated excellent evaluation skills. The candidate has shown excellent professional judgement in evaluating the most relevant external environmental factors impacting on the strategic objectives. The candidate has made very well justified assertions about the external environment and has demonstrated clear and objective judgement.
Report Format			The answer is presented in a suitable report format.	The answer is presented in a suitable report format.
	0	1.33	2.66	4

Professional skills may be additionally rewarded as in the following rubric for 2 (b):

How well has the candidate demonstrated professional skills as follows:	Not at all	Not so well	Quite well	Very well
Communication skills in using compelling and logical arguments to persuade the Board of trustees of the potential of e-business technologies for the BCO.	The candidate demonstrated no or poor communication skills. The candidate has failed to present a logical argument for e-business technologies. The style, tone and presentation of the slides and notes would not be suitable for presentation to the Board of trustees.	The candidate demonstrated some basic communication skills. They have demonstrated some evidence of presenting relevant arguments for e-business technologies but some of it is not clear or insufficient to communicate effectively to the Board of trustees.	The candidate demonstrated good communication skills. They have presented a good range of logical and clear arguments for application of e-business technologies. However, some key points were missing and/or the arguments were not fully developed.	The candidate demonstrated excellent communication skills. They have presented a clear, balanced and logical presentation, giving clear and logical arguments for the application of e-business technologies. The answer is logical, clear and persuasive.
Slide Presentation			The candidate has presented the answer in a suitable presentation slide and note format.	The candidate has presented the answer in a suitable presentation slide and note format.
	0	**1.33**	**2.66**	**4**

3 To: **Chief executive officer**

From: **Senior finance manager**

Date: **XX/XX/20X1**

Confidential: **Evaluation of BCO's risk register and risk mitigating activities**

Introduction

The following report will consider the BCO's current risk register, as presented in our latest annual report and assess whether the risk mitigating activities are adequate, particularly taking into consideration the current environment and challenges facing the charity sector, as outlined in the recent research report.

BCO's risk register and risk mitigating activities

Risks identified

The current risk register identifies four potential risks for the coming year which are all relevant and important risks facing the BCO at this point in time and all are correctly identified as key risks to our organisation. I will consider the adequacy of the risk mitigating activities of each in turn below.

1   **Fund-raising**

The risk register identifies that we may not be able to raise the required level of funding to cover our costs. From an analysis of our latest annual report it is clear that the BCO's income is just managing to cover its expenditure and in fact, had we not sold a property in the year, then the BCO would have been in deficit. Therefore, this is a genuine and significant risk for the forthcoming years. As the charity sector has clearly come under scrutiny and much criticism recently, we will face significant challenges in the coming years to increase our income, without undertaking more promotion and awareness programmes, which inevitably will cost money. We will have to balance this drive for increased income with ensuring our activities remain ethical and do not harm our reputation.

Adequacy of risk mitigating activities

Implementing appropriate cost budgeting procedures is clearly an important aspect of managing our expenditure, but it does not actually address how to increase income streams. Therefore, this risk management activity has limited scope to improve our fundraising risk. All it does is manage the costs we incur.

Similarly, benchmarking our financial returns is a relatively reactive approach to mitigating our risks and will not assist us in achieving increased income streams. Stewardship reporting for stakeholders in our annual report is a key aspect of transparency and communication with our stakeholders, but again, it will not directly assist in overcoming the risks of our ability to raise sufficient funds.

Overall, I consider that the chairperson has a valid point in regard to whether our risk mitigating activities relating to fund raising are adequate and that he is not over-reacting. Our current risk mitigating activities are only likely to give us increased information on potential reasons of our fund-raising levels and costs and not how to address/improve them.

2   **Loss of key staff and employment issues**

This is a significant risk to the BCO, as our staff are a key asset in the delivery of our animal protection activities. We invest significant sums in training staff and it could be a huge financial and potentially reputational loss when staff leave. If we lose that expertise, which we have to then either buy in or re-train we run the risk of not attaining the high standards of operation we set for ourselves. Therefore, this is a key and therefore justifiable risk to focus on as an organisation.

Adequacy of risk mitigating activities

Currently, our risk management activities include succession planning, agreement of notice periods and review of recruitment processes and policies. These would seem to be suitable risk management activities to assist in reducing and eliminating some of the risks associated with the loss of staff. Succession planning is a critical aspect of ensuring staff continuity and successful handover of responsibilities when staff leave the organisation. This should ensure that we have a definite plan in place to ensure that remaining staff are ready and prepared to take on new roles and responsibilities when required. Also, this should assist in motivating remaining staff. Review of recruitment policies and processes is also a critical aspect in ensuring that we employ staff with the correct skills and attitudes, therefore hopefully resulting in lower staff turnover. However, a key aspect of mitigation which is not considered is training programmes, which would be an effective way of motivating staff to remain committed to the organisation and thus reduce the levels of staff turnover. This may be a reason why the chairperson believes that our risk mitigating activities are insufficient. Therefore, it is recommended that our risk register should also include activities to improve retention.

Overall, our risks management activities relating to this risk are reasonably sufficient and the chairperson may be over critical of our risk management activities for this risk category. However, we must also include the implementation of appropriate and regular training programmes and skills updates for staff to enhance motivation and therefore improve retention.

3   Competition

Competition in the charity sector is a key risk for the BCO, as evidenced in the recent sector research report, as a result of several external environmental factors. This competition inevitably means that we face a significant risk of reduced income and subsequently, a potential loss of public awareness and profile, should potential donors and supporters choose to support alternative causes. Therefore, the Risk committee is correct to include this within our risk register.

Adequacy of risk mitigating activities

Our current risk register suggests that we should manage this risk using methods such as monitoring of service delivery and monitoring public awareness and profile. I would suggest that the chairperson may be correct in his concerns with risk management of the risk from competition, as these activities are likely to be inadequate to effectively manage such a serious threat to our position. Monitoring of public profile and service delivery are useful starting points to assess our situation in the competitive environment and they may indeed assist us in identifying areas for improvement. However, they are not sufficiently proactive to ensure we do stay ahead of our competitor and therefore the chairperson is correct in his concerns relating to the activities we undertake to mitigate this risk. We should be considering activities such as ensuring and managing key stakeholder awareness and customer/donor generation/retention strategies. Therefore, I believe that the chairperson is not over reacting to the consequences of this risk and is correct in his assessment in the adequacy of our risk management activity.

4   Operating in dangerous locations around the world

Because we operate our animal protection activities across the world it is inevitable that some activities will take place in dangerous locations and therefore this is a significant risk and must be considered as part of our risk register. One issue that is not considered however, which I believe should be, is the potential litigation which may occur as a result of injury or death to any of our staff or volunteers. Therefore, the chairperson is correct in his assessment of the adequacy of our assessment of this risk and is not over reacting to the recent challenges in the sector.

Adequacy of risk mitigating activities

Activities such as monitor and review activities in recognised dangerous locations and procedures to remove staff and volunteers at short notice are key risk management activities but we must also ensure that these are carried out regularly and tested regularly. A close relationship with security and safety services is also a key risk management activity and is evidence of a proactive risk management approach. Therefore, I would in fact agree with the chief executive in this case and conclude that the BCO appears to have adequate risk management activities in this particular risk category.

Other issues to consider and concluding comments

A more general observation to make is that the BCO has a functioning risk committee, chaired by the chairperson and with two other board of trustee members, which meets once per year. In the past this may have been sufficient, at a time when the charity sector was more stable and predictable than the current environment. However, in recent times the environment has changed significantly, and it could be argued that in the light of the current rapidly changing external environment and the increasing threats this causes, the Risk committee should in fact meet more than once per year. This would reassure key stakeholders of our commitment to managing risks effectively. Therefore, in this respect, the chairperson may have a relevant cause for concern in the overall functioning of the Risk committee.

Although the risk register contains four key areas of risk facing the BCO, the chairperson is also correct in challenging the adequacy of this register, in terms of whether it covers all of the risks currently facing the BCO. The recent sector research report makes it quite clear that there are a wide range of threats and challenges currently occurring in the charity sector and many are not addressed in our current risks register. For example, there is a significant risk from the changing demographics and how we reach these in order to stay relevant as a charity. Additionally, our lack of use of technology and the potential threats this brings must be considered as a key risk. Risks such as rising operating costs, possible litigation and continued recession should also be considered.

Therefore, although our risk register has several positive attributes, the risk mitigating activities need to be reviewed and we must also update our risk register to include the current external challenges faced. Therefore, I would disagree in several cases that our risk analysis and our risk mitigation activities are sufficient and the chairperson is justified in his concerns of the adequacy of our risk management activities.

ACCA marking guide	
	Marks
Up to 2 marks for a discussion of the general issues relating to BCO's risk management activities.	
1 mark for each relevant point made relating to the BCO's risk register and the associated risk mitigating activities.	
Up to a maximum of 4 marks for each risk category from the risk register discussed.	
Up to a total of 15 marks	
Key points	
General issues	
Environment changing significantly – should meet more than twice per year.	
Reassure key stakeholders of our commitment to managing risks effectively.	
Chairperson may have a relevant cause for concern in functioning of Risk committee.	
Risks identified	
1 *Fund-raising*	
– Significant risk	
– Significant challenges in coming years	
– Balance drive for increased income with ethical behaviour	
Adequacy of risks mitigating activities	
– Budgeting important – but not address need to increase income streams	
– Limited scope to reduce fundraising risk	
– Benchmarking – reactive approach to risk management	
– Not assist in achieving increased income streams	
– Stewardship reporting – not directly assist overcoming risks	
– Overall, Chairperson has valid point in regard to adequacy of risk management activities	

2 *Loss of key staff and employment issues*
- Significant risk – staff key asset
- Invest significant sums in training staff
- Lose that expertise – risk of not attaining high standards of operation
- Justifiable risk to focus on

Adequacy of risk mitigating activities
- Succession planning – ensuring staff continuity and handover
- Ensure plan in place so staff prepared to take on new roles
- Motivate remaining staff
- Review recruitment policies – critical in ensuring staff have correct skills
- Risks management activities sufficient and appropriate
- Training and retention not included – significant omission

3 *Competition*
- Key risk – recent sector research report
- Reduced income & loss of public awareness and profile
- Correct to include this in risk register

Adequacy of risk mitigating activities
- Monitoring of service delivery and public awareness – inadequate to manage serious threat
- Useful starting point
- Not sufficiently proactive
- Chairperson correct in concerns relating to the management of this risk

4 *Operating in dangerous locations around the world*
- Significant risk
- Need to include potential litigation – injury or death to staff or volunteers

Adequacy of risk mitigating activities
- Monitor/review activities in dangerous locations/procedures to remove staff – key risk management activities
- Also ensure these tested regularly
- Close relationship with security and safety services – key risk management activity
- Evidence a proactive risk management approach
- Adequate risk management activities in this risk area

Other issues to consider and concluding comments
- Chairperson's concerns justified
- Significant risk from changing demographics
- Lack of use of technology and potential threats this brings considered as key risk

Total   19

Professional skills may be additionally rewarded as in the following rubric:

How well has the candidate demonstrated professional skills as follows:	Not at all	Not so well	Quite well	Very well
Scepticism skills in questioning appropriately the opinions expressed by the chairperson and the chief executive officer	The candidate has failed to challenge the opinions raised by the chairperson and the CEO relating to risks in the BCO's register and the adequacy of its current risk management activities. The answer is descriptive and there is no evidence of questioning the opinions in an appropriate way.	The candidate has made a limited attempt at challenging the opinions of the chairperson and the CEO in relation to the risk register and the adequacy of the current risk management activities. There is some evidence of evaluating the risk management activities but this is limited.	The candidate has made a reasonably good attempt at challenging the opinions of the chairperson and the CEO in relation the contents of the risk register and the adequacy of the current risk management activities. There is evidence of a number of challenges made to the comments made in an appropriate way.	The candidate has made an excellent attempt at challenging the opinions of the chairperson and the CEO in relation the contents of the risk register and the adequacy of the current risk management activities. There is excellent evidence of the candidate recognising and challenging most of the relevant issues in BCO's risk report in an appropriate way.
Report Format			The answer is presented in a correct report format.	The answer is presented in a correct report format.
	0	1.33	2.66	4

4   FAO: Chief executive officer

Briefing Notes

A recent news report highlighted the apparent weaknesses in some organisations in the charity sector and the potential implications this may have, in terms of poor strategic direction and loss of funding.

(i)   Board of trustees' skills and diversity

Currently, our Board of trustees does appear to lack diversity. This is evidenced in the following analysis of a board of trustee members:

1   Five of our six trustees are over the age of 55 and only two are women. A lack of diversity in age range of our trustees could mean that, although vastly experienced in their own areas of expertise, our trustees may lack the knowledge and awareness of the changing world we now operate in, particularly in terms of technology and the changing needs and lifestyles of our customers.

2   In addition, it would seem that only Rani Jeffels, our chairperson has recent commercial experience. Two other trustees do have some commercial background but it is questionable whether this is sufficiently recent to assist in the modern environment we operate in. As discussed in a recent news article, in a modern world where charities face similar commercial pressures to profit making organisation, we need to consider whether the BCO can be run effectively by trustees with such limited commercial background and with a potentially limited understanding of strategic management.

3   Three out of six of our trustees have been members of the board for over 10 years. Again, although vastly experienced and knowledgeable of our operations, there is also an argument that the board of trustees now requires new ideas and that our trustees could be out of touch and unskilled for the modern world in which we operate and the modern charitable environment.

These factors above should be a cause for concern for the BCO – as our trustees do not represent the wide spectrum of the BCO's stakeholders. Our board of trustees is a fundamental aspect of the success or failure of our organisation, as it is its responsibility to set out our strategic direction. If they do not have the up to date skills and mix of experience and diversity to do this successfully then we are at risk of losing our strategic direction.

(ii)   Continuing development for management board members

1   Continuing professional development for our management board should assist members to think together from a more strategic perspective and should help to build a strong management team. Often a board has little time in board meetings to get to know each other, as everyone is focussed on the job at hand and on their own areas of responsibility. Taking time out for board development allows board members to interact in a less structured environment, helping to build a more cohesive team.

2   Also, importantly our management board has legal duties to use reasonable care, skill and diligence. Keeping the management board members informed and up to date in their areas of expertise and in general legal and regulatory knowledge ensures that they can effectively discharge this duty. The management board must be conversant with changes in regulation, legislation and the operating environment the BCO operates in if it is to manage its strategic direction effectively.

3   The culture of the BCO will largely be driven by the tone set by our management board, which permeates throughout the organisation. By investing in management board development, we can set out a clear signal to the rest of the BCO that it values continual learning. This will encourage our staff and volunteers to want to continuously learn and develop, creating a learning organisation environment, critical in these challenging competitive times we face.

4   Continuing professional development should help to motivate and retain good board members. They will value an organisation which invests in them, which leads to increased motivation, loyalty and retention helping to contribute positively to the achievement of our strategic objectives.

5   As an organisation we are facing increasing challenges from our environment and we need to be innovative in the ways we operate and raise funds. Continuing professional development will assist management board members to be more innovative in their thinking as, people who have been trained well in how to do their jobs are more likely to be more confident and innovative. This in turn should helpfully assist in offering the BCO greater competitive advantage in the form of both improved processes, and also an increased likelihood of new products or services to meet our ever-changing environmental demands.

ACCA marking guide	Marks

1 mark for each relevant point made and applied to BCO.
 Up to a total of 6 marks per section
 Up to a maximum of 10 marks
 (i)   Board of trustees with a sufficient mix of skills and diversity
    – Five 55+ & only two women
    – May lack knowledge/awareness of changing world
    – Particularly in technology and needs and lifestyles of customers
    – Only new Chairperson has recent commercial experience
    – Two others have commercial background – sufficiently recent?
    – Charities facing similar commercial pressures to profit making organisation
    – Limited understanding of strategic management
    – Three trustees – on board for over 10 years
    – Not represent wide spectrum of stakeholders
    – Risk of losing strategic direction
 (ii)   Continuing development for management board members
    – Build a strong management team
    – Interact to build more cohesive team
    – Up to date in areas of expertise and legal and regulatory knowledge
    – Culture driven by tone from management board
    – Set out a clear signal it values continual learning
    – Encourage staff and volunteers
    – Creating a learning organisation environment
    – Motivate and retain good board members
    – Encourages innovative
    – Increase confident	

Total	13

Professional skills may be additionally rewarded as in the following rubric:

How well has the candidate demonstrated professional skills as follows:	Not at all	Not so well	Quite well	Very well
Commercial acumen skills in showing awareness of organisational and wider external factors affecting the work of the BCO's board of trustees and management board.	The candidate has not demonstrated commercial acumen. They have failed to link their discussion of the activities of the board of trustees and the management board to the external environment which affects them. The answer is largely descriptive, with little reference to the needs of the BCO's stakeholders.	The candidate has demonstrated limited commercial acumen. Some attempt has been made to consider relevant skills, diversity and CPD relating to the BCO, but this has not been linked adequately to the needs of the external environment and the BCO's stakeholders.	The candidate has demonstrated good commercial acumen. A reasonable amount of the answer is linked directly to the required skills, diversity and CPD requirements of the BCO, and there has been some attempt to consider the impact and needs of the external environment and the BCO's stakeholders.	The candidate has demonstrated excellent commercial acumen. Most of the answer is linked directly to the required skills, diversity and CPD requirements of the BCO, and the candidate has clearly and correctly considered the impact and needs of the external environment and the BCO's stakeholders.
Briefing Notes			The answer is presented in the correct briefing note format.	The answer is presented in the correct briefing note format.
	0	1	2	3